DUBLIN SLUMS, 1800-1925

DUBLIN SLUMS, 1800-1925
A Study in Urban Geography

JACINTA PRUNTY

IRISH ACADEMIC PRESS

First published in [1999] in Ireland by
IRISH ACADEMIC PRESS
Northumberland House
44, Northumberland Road
Ballsbridge, Dublin 4

and in the United States of America by
IRISH ACADEMIC PRESS
c/o ISBS, 5804 N.E. Hassalo Street,
Portland, Oregon 97213-3644

Website: http://www.iap.ie

Copyright © 1998 Jacinta Prunty

British Library cataloguing in publication data:
A catalogue record for this title
is available from the British Library.

ISBN: 0-7165-2538-0 (cloth)
ISBN: 0-7165-2690-5 (paper)

Library of Congress cataloguing in publication data:
A catalogue record for this title
is available from the Library of Congress.

All rights reserved. No part of this publication may be reproduced, stored in or introduced into a retrieval system, or transmitted, in any form or by any means (electronic, mechanical, photocopying, recording or otherwise), without the prior written permission of both the copyright owner and publisher of this book.

Printed in Ireland
by ColourBooks Ltd

For my parents, Agnes and Joe Prunty

CONTENTS

Foreword by Emmet Larkin ix
List of maps, tables and plates xi
Abbreviations xiv
Acknowledgements xv

1
1. Dublin Slum Matters 1800-1925: An Overview

17
2. The Slums Exposed, Dublin 1800-1854

62
3. A Matter of Life and Death: Public Health 1800-1900

109
4. To Grasp the Housing Nettle, Early Initiatives, 1876-1900

153
5. Health and Housing: Policy Shifts, 1900-1925

195
6. Idle Vagrants and Sturdy Beggars: the State's Response

234
7. Church Charities Respond: Women and Children, 1850-1900

274
8. A Classic Slum: Dublin North City

336
9. Conclusion

348
Appendix: Dublin Street Names, 1850's

351
Bibliography

359
Index

FOREWORD

This is a very impressive, if a very sad, story. Impressive because of the importance of the subject and the great professional care with which it is handled. Sad because it is also the story of a deadly urban disease that was allowed to run its course. The pathology of this disease, in its particular manifestation in Dublin between 1800 and 1925, is as gripping as it is frightening. While the causes, processes, development, and consequences of this urban cancer are all clinically described and authoritatively diagnosed in their horrific detail, the great themes of urban history and geography are also laid bare for the consideration of the concerned reader, who cannot but wonder at the end of the story how the human race has ever managed to get anything done, let alone survive.

Of all the urban slumdoms produced in the western world in the nineteenth century, Dublin was apparently unique in that its slums were not a product of the industrial revolution. Dublin, in fact, suffered more from the problems of de-industrialization than industrialization between 1800 and 1850. Dublin had always had, of course, its slums but in the late eighteenth and early nineteenth centuries they were largely confined to the mews, back alleys, courts and lanes, and though in close proximity to the town houses of the aristocracy and gentry and the homes of the professional and merchant classes, they remained a thing apart. The great change came with the sharp economic downturn consequent on the great fall in prices for agricultural products in 1815, when the gracious Georgian mansions of the Dublin elite gradually became the tenements of the poor and the working classes. This process was greatly accelerated by the increase in population in Dublin from about 175,000 in 1813 to some 250,000 in 1850, or by 43 percent. The influx was mainly from the poverty-stricken countryside as Dublin literally became another pool of Bethesda. The elites aggravated the problem by fleeing the inner city to the unincorporated suburbs, thus further reducing the economic base on which the rebuilding of the social infrastructure depended.

The effective result was that for more than a hundred years virtually nothing was done about providing affordable housing for the poor and the working classes of Dublin. By 1914, for example, nearly 26,000 families, or 35 percent of the population of the inner city still lived in 5,000 tenements, while more than 20,000 of those families lived in one room, and another 5,000 had only two rooms and a great many of these families took in lodgers to help pay the rent. Indeed, the ultimate act of charity must have taken place when one of these slum dwellers offered to loan her lodger to a neighbor in order to tide the latter over a difficult period. In any case, it was from these foul and crowded tenements that for a century oozed all the fearful concomitants of Dublin slum life. Infant mortality, contagious diseases, widespread prostitution, endemic drunkenness, pitiful wages, exorbitant rents, high unemployment, child neglect and gross criminality all rolled on in a seemingly interminable vicious cycle. While considerable efforts were made between 1800 and 1925 to ameliorate these social horrors through private charity and limited state assistance to the "deserving poor", these palliatives proved to be ineffective over the long run because they dealt with effects rather than causes.

The root cause of these dreadful social conditions was poverty and only massive government interference in the form of a comprehensive welfare state could solve that problem in the long run. In Ireland, and particularly Dublin in the nineteenth century, however, the economic system could not bear the costs of a comprehensive welfare state, and hence the resort to pragmatic *ad hoc*, and piece-meal efforts to deal with the immediate effects rather than the basic cause. The Dublin slums, therefore, were not the cause of all these fearful social conditions, but rather their *locus*, and it is as a *locus* that the how rather than the why of the Dublin slums is explained. The inability to deal with the basic cause of poverty for more than a century, however, resulted in the creation of a "culture of poverty," which, when the economic system was finally able to bear the costs of a comprehensive welfare system, had basically changed the terms of the givens. What had been created by this "culture of poverty," for which the Dublin slums had provided the space, was a mind-set rooted in a way of life that had been institutionalized over a very long period of time. In effect, a long-term material deprivation had produced the social conditions that resulted in a crippling of the will of the poor to do more than survive. The ultimate lesson perhaps to be learned from this thoughtful, original, and compassionate study of the human condition, is that the psychological scars of the "culture of poverty" are much more intractable than even the problem of poverty itself, and a mind-set that took more than a century to crystallize in the Dublin slums will not be dissipated in a generation.

The University of Chicago   Emmet Larkin
June, 1997

LIST OF MAPS, PLATES AND TABLES

END PAPERS:
City of Dublin surveyed by M. Thomas Campbell, under the directions of Major Taylor, 1811
Housing Map, central city, showing decayed housing areas (shaded), third class tenements (black), and tenements condemned as dangerous (X), Dublin Civic Survey 1925

FIGURES		PAGE
1.1	Dublin city and townships, *Thom's Almanac and Official Street Directory*, 1898	15
2.1	St Luke's Parish, *Exact Survey of the City and Suburbs of Dublin*, John Rocque 1756, sheets 3, 4	23
2.2	St Catherine's Church and Cork Street, location of House of Recovery (1802), *Exact Survey of the City and Suburbs of Dublin*, John Rocque 1756, sheet 4	24
2.3	Barrack Street, north city, *Exact Survey of the City and Suburbs of Dublin*, John Rocque 1756, sheet 1	32
2.4	Classification of major Dublin streets, William Wilde, 1851	43
2.5	Average annual mortality according to locality, Dublin 1851	46
2.6	Distribution of housing valued at under £10, Dublin 1854	50-1
2.7	Low-value housing and industrial activity, south western sector, Dublin 1854	56
2.8	South western sector, *City of Dublin surveyed by M. Thomas Campbell, under the directions of Major Taylor, 1811*	57
2.9	Socio-economic patterns in Dublin City, 1850-54	60
3.1	Sanitary arrangements approved by British municipal authorities: (a) Corporation of Bradford, (b) Corporation of Rochdale	89
3.2	Sanitary arrangements approved by British municipal authorities: (a) City of Manchester, (b) Corporation of Edinburgh, (c) Corporation of Rochdale	90
3.3	Registered slaughter houses, Dublin 1879	92
3.4	Sketch plan re nuisance occasioned by dairy yard adjoining Mercer's Hospital, Dublin, 22 July 1875	95
3.5	Municipal improvements, Dublin Corporation 1879-1884	98
3.6	Proposed Cork Hill building and general improvement scheme, by Thomas Drew C.E., 1882	100
3.7	Disinfecting depot and laundry, Marrowbone Lane, 1899	104
3.8	Typhoid fever Dublin 1882-1893	105
3.9	Infectious diseases, Dublin 1894	107
4.1	Dr Mapother's unhealthy areas, Dublin 1876	119
4.2	Ormond Market c.1854	122
4.3	Dublin Corporation Ormond Market housing scheme, 1914	123
4.4(a)	The Dublin Improvement Scheme, 1877 Ground Plan of Area No. 1, Coombe	124
4.4(b)	Coombe Scheme, Dublin Artisans' Dwellings Company, 1879	124
4.5	Plunket Street and Patrick Street, 1837	130
4.6	Dublin Artisans' Dwellings Company scheme Plunket Street (Thomas Davis Street) and Iveagh Trust buildings, Patrick Street, 1939	131
4.7	Houses condemned and closed by Dublin Corporation 1879-1882	136
4.8	Percentage tenement housing, Dublin 1850	148
4.9	Percentage tenement housing, Dublin 1900	149
5.1	Dublin city dispensary districts (prior to the 1900 extension of the city boundaries) and principal areas of poverty, Edgar Flinn, 1906	158
5.2	Derelict sites, dangerous buildings, and insanitary areas, Dublin 1914	172
5.3	Artisans' dwellings completed / planned (municipal and private companies), Dublin 1914	173

5.4 City of Dublin: New Town Plan, Central Improvements, *Dublin of the Future: The New Town Plan*, Abercrombie, Kelly and Kelly (Liverpool, 1922)	186
5.5 Wood Quay ward: relative density of population and death rates, *Dublin Civic Survey*, hygiene map, 1925	189
5.6 Inns Quay ward: relative density of population and death rates, *Dublin Civic Survey*, hygiene map, 1925	190
5.7 Central city, showing decayed housing areas (shaded), third class tenements (black), and tenements condemned as dangerous (X), *Dublin Civic Survey*, housing map, 1925	192
6.1 Places of birth, Dublin 1881	199
6.2 South Dublin Union workhouse, c.1854	220
6.3 North west institutional sector, Dublin c.1854	222
7.1 Religious denominations, Dublin 1861	236
7.2 Roman Catholic parishes, 1800-1900	238
7.3 St Brigid's Nurses, 1868-1875	245
7.4 Selected Ragged / Poor Schools, Dublin 1850-1900	249
7.5 Asylums for women, Dublin 1851-1883	268
8.1 Case study area, Dublin north city	275
8.2 Gardiner Street - Mountjoy Square, *City of Dublin surveyed by M. Thomas Campbell, under the directions of Major Taylor, 1811*	277
8.3 Tenement Dwellings, 1850, St Mary's and St Michan's Parishes, Dublin	290-1
8.4 Ladies' Association of Charity 1851-1856, St Mary's and St Michan's Parishes, Dublin	294-5
8.5 Gloucester Street - Mountjoy Square, Griffith's Valuation, 1854	296
8.6 Tenement Dwellings 1900, St Mary's and St Michan's Parishes, Dublin	308-9
8.7 Ladies' Association of Charity 1895-1900, St Mary's and St Michan's Parishes, Dublin	312-13
8.8 Church Street c.1854	317
8.9 Corporation of Dublin Beresford and Church Street Housing Scheme 1914 (Amended Plan)	322
8.10 Coles Lane c.1854	326
8.11 Moore Street Market, *Insurance Plan of Dublin, sheet 3, April 1926*, Charles E. Goad	327
8.12 North City survey: schemes in contemplation by the housing committee, Dublin Corporation, 1918	329
8.13 Mountjoy ward: relative density of population and death rates, *Dublin Civic Survey*, hygiene map, 1925	334

APPENDIX
Dublin street names, 1850's	348

TABLES
2.1 Population of Dublin in 1798, as divided into its nineteen Parishes and two Deaneries, Whitelaw, 1805, p. 14	21
2.2 Population table III, Parish of St. Luke, 1798, Whitelaw 1805	22
2.3 Number of families which occupy each class of house accommodation, City of Dublin 1841, 1851	42
2.4 Classification of major Dublin streets, William Wilde, 1851	44
3.1 Annual mortality, Dublin, Belfast, London, Edinburgh, Glasgow, 1866-1909	73
3.2 Annual mortality, selected urban sanitary districts, Ireland 1873-1912	75
3.3 Annual mortality, Dublin city and suburbs 1866-1911	76

3.4 Return of sanitary operations carried out in the year 1883, Dublin Corporation 79
4.1 House accommodation of families, Dublin city 1841-1911 111
4.2 Tenement houses: rateable values and rents, 1879 126
5.1 Births and Deaths, and Rate of Mortality in London, Edinburgh, Glasgow, Dublin and Certain Indian and Foreign Cities, May 1906 154
5.2 Deaths from TB and other 'general' diseases, Dublin 1896-1911 160
5.3 Returns by Dublin Corporation Sanitary Staff, 1913 174
5.4 Number of tenements of one room, of two rooms, of three rooms, of four rooms per 1,000 total tenements in principal cities of the United Kingdom 174
5.5 Corporation of Dublin: summarised history of each housing scheme, presented to the Local Government Housing Inquiry, 1913 175
6.1 Estimated numbers requiring poor relief, Dublin 1836-1837 213
7.1 Irish Church Missions Schools and Homes, Dublin 1849-1900 248
8.1 Relief distributed by the Ladies' Association of Charity of St Vincent de Paul, Metropolitan Branch, 1851 300

PLATES

2.1 Ward's Hill, New Row, Irish Architectural Archive C2/658 52
2.2 North and south docks, view of Dublin city published 1846, TCD 53
2.3 Church Street, view of Dublin city published 1846, TCD 54
2.4 Royal Barracks, view of Dublin city published 1846, TCD 55
2.5 Forbes' Cottages, off Marrowbone Lane, Grand Canal Harbour, RSAI 37 58
4.1 Fade Street, c 1879, copy of photo by Millard & Robinson, Irish Architectural Archive C4/666 113
4.2 Newmarket Street, 2 closets for 70 people 1913, RSAI 85 114
4.3 Brady's Cottages, 16 Francis Street, 1913, RSAI 18 116
4.4 Henrietta Buildings, Henrietta Place, 1913, RSAI 62 117
5.1 'The last hour of the Night', by Harry Clarke, *Dublin of the Future: The New Town Plan*, Abercrombie, Kelly & Kelly, Liverpool, 1922 184
7.1 'The Night School', ICM 1862 251
7.2 'The Scripture Reader', ICM 1862 251
8.1 Gardiner Street Middle 1980, Geoffrey White, Irish Architectural Archive 7/25v1 280
8.2 Gardiner Street Lower 1950s, T. Affleck, Greaves, Irish Architectural Archive 7/24v4 280
8.3 Church Street 1861, Irish Architectural Archive 35/27v1 319
8.4 Ward's Cottages, Church Street 1913, RSAI 57 319
8.5 Tickell's Court, 18 Beresford Street 1913, RSAI 58 321
8.6 Angle Court, Beresford Street 1913, RSAI 60 321
8.7 Church Street housing scheme: bird's eye view from NE, 1918 323
8.8 Riddell's Row, Moore Street 1913, RSAI 86 324

ABBREVIATIONS

ARDP	Association for the Relief of Distressed Protestants
DADC	Dublin Artisans' Dwellings Company
DDA	Dublin Diocesan Archive, Clonliffe College
GA	Holy Faith Archive, Glasnevin, Dublin
HC	House of Commons papers
HTPAI	Housing and Town Planning Association of Ireland
ICM	Irish Church Missions
NDU	North Dublin Union
NLI	National Library of Ireland
OS	Ordnance Survey of Ireland
RCBL	Representative Church Body Library, Rathgar
RCPI	Royal College of Physicians of Ireland
RPDCD	Reports and Printed Documents of the Corporation of Dublin
SBO	St Brigid's Orphanage
SDU	South Dublin Union
Soc. Stat. Inq. Soc. Ire. Jn.	
	Journal of the Social and Statistical Inquiry Society of Ireland
TB	Tubercular disease, including phthisis
UCD	University College Dublin
WNHAI	Women's National Health Association of Ireland

ACKNOWLEDGEMENTS

My thanks to Professor Anngret Simms, Department of Geography, UCD, who directed the PhD research upon which this book is based, and whose wise guidance and warm support throughout helped bring it to completion.

A wide variety of persons and institutions have also assisted in its production. This research was first undertaken at the request of Sr. Rosemary Duffy, general leader of the Holy Faith Sisters, and the general leadership team, at the time, Srs. Constance Loughran, Miriam Anne Lucas, Mairéad Holton and Carmel Campbell. Sr. Rosemary and her colleagues gave every support and encouragement throughout, and Srs. Laurentina Kennedy, Martina Traynor and Josephine Dowling, as part of the Aylward House community, made the facilities of the Generalate available to me. Their support was backed up at regional level by the kind interest of Sr. Frances Barrett, Sr. Barbara Perry, Sr. Irene Dunne and the regional team.

Colleagues and postgraduate friends in the Department of Geography, UCD, were always most helpful. Professor Anne Buttimer, head of department, made valuable suggestions at the early stages of this research and was most interested and supportive throughout. Dr Joe Brady gave unstinting assistance with computer matters; his patience and kindness are much appreciated. Dr Arnold Horner helped substantially, lending me very valuable maps and reports, and introducing me to the resources of the departmental map library. Mr Stephen Hannon, cartographer, was unfailingly generous with his expertise and time, from the first cartographic discussions through to the final reprographing. His colleague, Ms Sheila McMorrow (now TCD) also provided valuable assistance. Drs William Nolan and Kevin Whelan showed great interest throughout, lending me material, directing me to sources and literature, and their interest and suggestions were always appreciated. Geraldine Grenham, Jean Molloy and Frances Scally, departmental secretaries, have provided moral support and practical back-up in many ways.

I received the help and advice of many academic friends in UCD over the years, notably Dr Margaret MacCurtain, Professor Mary Daly, Dr T. P. O'Neill and Dr Howard Clarke (History), and Professor Helen Burke (Sociology). I am grateful to Dr Raymond Gillespie and Ms Mary Cullen (History, Maynooth) and the Irish Association for Research into Women's History, and to Professor Jim Walsh, Professor Patrick Duffy and colleagues in the Geography Department, Maynooth for their interest and support. During a study period in England Professor Hugh Clout and Dr Richard Dennis of University College London were most welcoming, Dr Maria Luddy (Education, Warwick) directed me to useful material, while Professor Peter Clark of the Centre for Urban History, Leicester University, was also most helpful, especially through the study opportunities afforded by the EUROCIT urban history project and the Tempus/Erasmus programme. Active encouragment to move from thesis into publication form was provided by Professor Emmet Larkin (History, Chicago) and Professor Richard Lawton (Geography, Liverpool), while Mr Michael Adams, now of Four Courts Press, was primarily responsible for making this possible. Ms Linda Longmore, his successor in Irish Academic Press, took charge of the final typescript; I am indebted to her for her patience and professionalism.

Over the course of this research I have lived in the Coombe, New Ross, Tallaght and St Mary's Road, Ballsbridge, and I extend my thanks to each of the sisters who have supported me in innumerable ways. The thesis and final book were both submitted from the Coombe, and a special word of appreciation to Srs. Rosaleen Cunniffe, Cathleen Flynn, Hilda Murphy, Jane Forde and all who shared very practically in the final production stages. Sr Benignus McDonagh made available the records of St Brigid's Orphanage, provided photocopying facilities, and helped in numerous other ways; Srs. Pauline Clarke and Bernadette Grace assisted in the slow task of extracting information from the orphan registers. The Glasnevin community was always most welcoming on my many visits; special thanks to Sr. Assisi Tattan (archivist 1981–91) and Sr. Theodore Bugler (present archivist). Siobhán Fitzpatrick SRN helped with medical details. Srs. Euphrasia Bergin and Barbara Perry gave me the initial encouragement to undertake post-graduate research, and their continued interest and support are much appreciated.

For access to Irish Church Missions material I am indebted to Mr. B. E. Sloan, Croydon, and to Rev. Bridcott, Bachelors Walk, who made me most welcome. Mr David Sheehy, Dublin Diocesan Archive, Clonliffe, was unfailingly helpful and generous in locating material, as were Ms Mary Clark of the Dublin Corporation Archive, City Hall, Ms Siobhán de hOir and Ms Orna Somerville, Royal Society of Antiquaries in Ireland, Ms Anne Healy of Kevin Street Library, and Ms Máire Kennedy and Ms Thecla Carleton of the Gilbert Library, Pearse Street. Thanks are also due to the staff of the National Library (Sr. Frances Lowe and colleagues), Official Publications and Special Collections of the Main Library, UCD (Mr Tony Eklof, Ms Norma Jessop) the Architecture Library, UCD (Ms Julia Barret) the National Archives (Ms Rena Lohan), the Irish Architectural Archive (Ms Anne Sinnott), the Church Representative Body Library (Mr Raymond Refaussé), and Fingal County Council archive (Ms Tina Hynes). Mr Richard Haworth, Freeman Library, TCD, Ms Mary O'Doherty,

Mercer's Library (RCSI), and Ms Barbara Ní Floinn, Department of Irish Folklore UCD located important material on my behalf, as did Mr Robert Mills, Royal College of Physicians in Ireland. For access to the records of the Gloucester Street asylum I extend my thanks to Sr Lucy Bruton and the Sisters of Our Lady of Charity of Refuge. Mr Jim Cooke, Ringsend Technical School, kindly alerted me to Dickens material relating to Dublin. I am indebted to Mr Seamus Rogers, Commissioner of Valuation, for permission to utilise maps from the General Valuation Office, Ely Place, and to Mr Pat Scanlon for his practical help in locating maps. Ms Aislinn Collins assisted with figure 4.4. Permission to reproduce photographs was granted by the Irish Architectural Archive and the Royal Society of Antiquaries of Ireland, while the Ordnance Survey (Phoenix Park) allowed the reproduction of figures 1.1, 4.5, 4.6. Mr David Jennings (Archaeology, UCD) prepared several of the plates for publication.

Postgraduate geography friends have helped throughout with their interest, companionship and practical help. Ms Martina O'Donnell and Drs Edel Sheridan (Göttingen), Hélène Bradley (Chichester), Ruth McManus (Dundalk), and Ríonach Ní Néill all provided essential support, and will welcome this publication knowing its gestation. Other postgraduate support came from Margaret Preston (History, Boston) who generously placed source material including transcripts of Poor Law manuscript records, at my disposal, and Dr Mary Ann Lyons (History, Maynooth), who was ever ready to listen and understand. Other friends who have been particularly encouraging are Monica Delaney CHF, Mary O'Byrne, Anna Byrne DC, and Lorraine Quinn. My former school teachers in geography and history, Sr Anne Marie Stacey CHF and Ms Anne Clare MA, must be thanked for the fascination with one's immediate neighbourhood and the excitement of travelling into the past which they sowed in me and indeed in many others who benefited from their commitment and enthusiasm.

My family have been most understanding and supportive throughout. Michael and Catherine Prunty located useful source material, Kieran Prunty has done many deliveries and collections in connection with this study, while Edel Fitzgerald looked after me very well during my stay in London. To my parents and to each of my brothers and sisters and their families I extend my thanks.

Financial assistance towards the publication of this book has been received from the Sisters of the Holy Faith, Glasnevin; Agnes and Joe Prunty; the EUROCIT urban history project; the UCD Women Graduates Association; and from Professor Anne Buttimer, UCD. To each I extend my appreciation, and also to the Department of Geography, UCD which met the considerable expense, over an extended period of time, involved in the preparation of the maps and figures.

DUBLIN SLUM MATTERS 1800-1925:
AN OVERVIEW

INTRODUCTION

Underpinning the social unrest and political upheaval which marked Dublin city c.1800 was yet another virulent outbreak of contagious disease, just one of many recurring outbreaks of typhoid and other contagions which had little regard for class distinctions. The vast throngs of poor became more and more threatening to the better off, particularly when as beggars and costermongers and possible carriers of disease, they invaded the public urban spaces of the streets and parks.

On investigation all aspects of poverty were found to be inter-connected: high mortality, poor sanitary provision, overcrowded and substandard housing, 'immorality, vagrancy and casual work, drunkenness and the dispiritedness due to unemployment, criminality and the mixing of all sorts in the 'rookeries' of the back streets; illiteracy, prostitution, irreligion, the disintegration of the family unit, and indeed the degeneration of the 'urban' race. The spiralling nature of poverty, where children born into such circumstances were unable to escape, was especially worrying.

The slum question in Dublin 1800–1925 revolved around a number of key issues: contagious disease, poor sanitation, tenement accommodation, overcrowding and moral degradation, vagrancy and homelessness, and the policing, control and relief of the poor by both state and charity organisations. Such is the extent of intertwining and overlap that no angle of the slum story can be examined without reference to other aspects, with repetition, circling and backtracking more characteristic than linear progress. Criticism of public health structures in the early nineteenth century, for example, was overtaken by the question of controlling the vagrant and vagabond, carriers of disease within and beyond the slums, with the matter of municipal reform topping the agenda again at midcentury. Enthusiasm for slum clearance and new construction in the 1870s was rapidly superseded by uneven enforcement of new sanitary legislation, while at the opening of the twentieth century the question of contagious disease, this time pulmonary tuberculosis, once more dominated public discussion. The approach taken in this study is to combine three principal strands: the question of contagious disease and public health (Chapters 2, 3 and 5), sanitation and the housing challenge (Chapters 4 and 5), and vagrancy and poor relief, especially as it applied to women and children (Chapters 6 and 7). Both city-wide and local (Chapter 8) scales of analysis are employed, and a wide range of sources, created by both statutory/official bodies and by charities, are utilised. As a study in urban geography maps are central to this analysis, while the overlapping nature of the story requires constant cross-referencing between maps and text; appendix A (location map) may be of assistance.

The Concept of 'the Slum'

The concept of the 'slum' developed over time, from early rather vague associations with a shady otherworld to more exact associations with occupancy rates and standards of sanitary provision. The earliest recorded definition is found in Vaux's *Vocabulary of the Flash Language* (1812), where 'slum' is entered as a synonym for 'a racket', any particular branch of depredation practised by thieves, and a 'lodging slum' defined as 'the practice of hiring ready furnished lodgings and stripping them of the plate, linen and other valuables'.[1] While initially associated with the activities and slang of thieves, 'sharpers' and cheats, the term 'slums' was in use in England by the 1840s in reference to areas of bad housing.[2] Dictionary entries from the 1870s define 'slums' as dirty, muddy back streets, and conjecture a possible German etymology, from *schlamm*, mire, as in the Bavarian *schlumpen*, to be dirty.[3] By the end of the century the term was widely utilised to describe 'a squalid street or neighbourhood, a rookery, usually in the plural', while concern with such spatial concentrations of poverty had led to its adaptation as a verb, 'to explore poor quarters out of curiosity or charity'.[4] H.J. Dyos, writing in relation to the London slums, warns that the term was applied with varying force throughout the nineteenth century, and with different emphasis at any one time by different social classes; 'it was being used in effect for a whole range of social and political purposes, and the very districts which were liable to be labelled with it were approaching that condition at different speeds and for various reasons'.[5] Contemporary definitions point to the enduring place of slum studies in urban geography:

An area of overcrowded and dilapidated, usually old housing, occupied by people who can afford only the cheapest dwellings available in the urban area, generally in or close to the inner city. The term usually implies both a poverty-ridden population, an unhealthy environment, and a district rife with crime and vice; is also often associated with concentrations of people in certain ethnic groups.[6]

[1] James Hardy Vaux, 'Vocabulary of the Flash Language' (1812) in *The Memoirs of James Hardy Vaux*, first edn. 1819; facsimile edn. Noel McLachlann ed., (London, 1964).
[2] H.J. Dyos, 'The Slums of Victorian London', *Victorian Studies* XI, (1) 1967, p. 8.
[3] Walter W. Skeat, *An Etymological Dictionary of the English Language* (Oxford University Press, first edn. 1879–82, impression 1963); Albert Barrère, Charles G. Leland, *A Dictionary of Slang, Jargon and Cant* (London, 1897).
[4] John S. Farmer, W.E. Henley, *A Dictionary of Slang and Colloquial English* (London, 1912).
[5] Dyos, 'The Slums of Victorian London' (1967) p. 9.
[6] R.J. Johnston et al, (eds), *Dictionary of Human Geography*, third edition (Oxford, 1994).

In Dublin the emotive term 'slums' was slow to gain widespread usage until the later nineteenth century, with generalised reference to the 'ancient parts of this city', and labels such as 'purlieus' and 'fever nests' more widely used. However, in 1898 the *Daily Nation* ran a series of perceptive articles in which the conditions of 'slum life' endured by 'the enormous slum population' were dramatically exposed, the intrepid newspaper reporter or 'commissioner' accompanying Sir Charles Cameron, chief medical officer, and the secretary of the Public Health Department of the Corporation, on a fact-finding tour of tenement dwellings in varying states of maintenance, a 'round of slumming' that left the journalist more depressed than hopeful.[7] Cowan's *Report on Dublin Housing* (1918) uses the term freely throughout, opening with the rhetorical question, 'Do the slums make the slum people or do the slum people make the slums?'.[8] Environmental determinism, in his view, prevails for the average person, and just because some certain heroic individuals rise above their appalling surroundings and secure 'comparative comfort and happiness' against all the odds, does not negate that central reality. In fact, 'such heroism should be uncalled for in any civilised country'. Considering the appalling conditions under which an estimated 27,000 Dublin families then dwelt, Cowan maintained 'the wonder is not that the slum dwellers are what they are, but that they are not unspeakably worse'.[9] The term 'slum' was most stridently adopted in the 1936 *Irish Press* 'Slum Dublin' and 'National Slum Survey' campaigns, with calls for the citizenry to move into the 'front line trenches' in the war against the 'slum monster'.[10]

The nineteenth century concept of the slum is directly related to urbanisation; while conditions in rural areas could indeed be appalling, it was held that the close confinement which city living required in itself promoted poor health, both moral and physical. Even where food, shelter, clothing, exercise and other necessities were in good supply, the 'insalubrity of the air' ensured that higher mortality would be found among city workers than among agricultural workers who were similarly circumstanced.[11] While this could be most strikingly illustrated in the case of heavily industrialised cities such as Manchester and Birmingham, the same was held to be true for Ireland in general, with comparisons drawn between the immunity of 'the average agricultural labourer in Mayo' who lives largely out of doors, keeps his door open, and regards his house merely as a shelter, compared with the 'ordinary average denizen of a town' who yields easily to bronchitis or consumption.[12] Against such a backdrop, there was a strong

---

[7] P.C. Cowan, *Report on Dublin Housing*, (Dublin, 1918) p. 4.
[8] *Daily Nation*, 'Dublin's Plague Spots' 'The Slum Evil', 'Our Northside Slums', 1–5 September 1898.
[9] Ibid., p. 5.
[10] *Irish Press*, 2 October 1936.
[11] Anthony Wohl, *The Eternal Slum, Housing and Social Policy in Victorian London* (London, 1977), pp. 6–7
[12] *Third Report of HM Commissioners for Inquiring into the Housing of the Working Classes (Ireland, 1885)*, c–4547-I, Evidence of Thomas Grimshaw (registrar general) qs. 23,178–23, 179 (hereafter *Housing Inquiry 1885*).

movement in favour of placing destitute and orphan children from the city slums in the care of rural families (Chapter 7), to the benefit of their physical and moral health. The garden suburbs movement of the late nineteenth and early twentieth century, as taken up in Dublin, was similarly dismissive of city living, pinning its hopes on a bright and airy future in a suburban idyll, with any reform of the city slums merely ameliorative or emergency action pending removal of all such residents to suburban bliss (Chapter 5).

Slum Measurement

Changes in the concept of the 'slum', and in the particular concern which was uppermost at any one time, parallel changes in the larger 'question of the poor'. Of increasing nineteenth century concern in both instances was the challenge of measurement. At what point can a person be classed as poor, or their living conditions a slum? Poverty is both relative and variable: relative because the awareness of poverty is governed by the pattern of needs and values which exist in a given society, and variable because many factors continually influence living standards.[13] Increasing Victorian middle class 'respectability', for example, made multiple occupancy of rooms a scandal, particularly the indiscriminate mixing of adults and teenagers of both sexes. Engineering advances, with the Vartry water scheme (1863–68) and the Main Drainage scheme (1892–1906) made the universal provision of adequate water and sewage facilities a possible, if ambitious, goal. The definition of 'slums' therefore is continually open to revision, for it rests on social values and judgements as to what constitutes an unacceptable and intolerable degree of hardship, and these vary both historically and geographically.

'Absolute' slum measurements rest on defining a minimal level of physical need, thus establishing a 'slum line' below which a residence is classed as unfit for human occupation. Determining what constitutes a 'minimal level' in nineteenth century sociology and human geography relied much on human perception, but also involved the evolution of 'scientific' measures of absolute physical needs, such as comparing mortality statistics on both geographical and class bases, or quantifying in cubic feet the amount of living space per person, or the numbers of persons per privy.[14] Typical is the distinction between house class and accommodation class in the Irish census from 1841, where slum accommodation can range from families occupying a single room in a (formerly) high-status house, down to families in sole possession of an insanitary hovel (Chapter 4).

'Relative' slum measurements class conditions as unacceptable in relation to others in society, thus 'the poor' are defined as 'those in society whose incomes and opportunities are so far removed from the rest of society that they cannot

---

[13] W.P. Blockmans and W. Prevenier, 'Poverty in Flanders and Brabant for the Fourteenth to the Mid-Sixteenth Century: Sources and Problems' in *Acta Historiae Neerlandicae*, vol. X (1978), p. 21.

[14] For example see *Housing Inquiry 1885*, qs. 22,125–22,127; 22,170–22,236.

attain a standard of living which is deemed acceptable in society'.[15] By 1918, for example, recently completed municipal housing schemes (Fairbrothers Fields and the McCaffrey estate) are praised as showing a great advance on schemes completed four years earlier (Church Street and Ormond Market) 'which are already out of date in accordance with good standards, inasmuch as the houses are too small'.[16] Steadily rising living standards elsewhere ensured that condemnation was extended from one-family occupancy of a single room to cases where two-room occupancy or situations where the sexes could not be separated was classed as slum living. The constant reformulation of acceptable standards of living, both minimal and relative, was paralleled in the fields of public health and mortality.

The obsession with measurement and classification ran through the allied debate on the suppression of vagrancy and the relief of the poor, with constant efforts to divide the 'deserving' from the 'non-deserving' poor, that the former might be treated with some humanity and the latter punished as their sloth deserves. The Mendicity Association made a very simple two-way division: those who were unable to work at any employment due to infancy, age or infirmity, and all other mendicants whose 'rooted habits of idleness, vagrancy and vice' could only be reformed by hard labour.[17] More sophisticated analyses were required in the case of classifying children, with St Brigid's schools challenging the public view of slum children, running half-naked about the streets, as 'corrupt and almost irreclaimable'; St Brigid's classed such children 'as naturally intelligent, quick and amenable to discipline', requiring only care and instruction to become Christian men and women and an asset to society.[18] While distinguishing between 'steady' children of 'good, though poor, parents', and those of the 'wild' and 'criminal classes', hope was held out for all, if only sufficient attention be paid from an early age.[19]

The Statistical Revolution

An essential backdrop to all nineteenth century slum campaigning was the development of the science of statistics, described in 1814 as 'a term lately invented' to denote 'that department of science which has been defined "the knowledge of the present state of a country with a view to its future improvement."'[20] In its theory and methods the new branch of learning provided the basis for

---

[15] Lorraine Joyce and A. McCashin, *Poverty and Social Policy*, the Irish National Report presented to the Commission of the European Community, (Dublin, 1981), p. 8.
[16] Cowan, *Report on Dublin Housing* (1918) p. 3.
[17] *Report of the Association for the Suppression of Mendicity in Dublin for the Year 1818* (Dublin, 1818), p. 5.
[18] *St Brigid's Orphanage, Twenty Eighth Annual Report*, 1885, pp. 12–13 (hereafter *SBO*).
[19] *SBO Thirty First Annual Report*, 1888, pp. 19–22.
[20] William Shaw Mason, *A Statistical Account or Parochial Survey of Ireland* (Dublin, 1814), pp. vii–viii.

modern political economy, sociology and town planning, promoting the mass accumulation of facts and figures on an unprecedented scale. The expansion of data collection and analysis that characterised the nineteenth century is epitomised by the research of Charles Booth, whose voluminous survey attempted to 'enumerate the masses of the people of London in classes according to degrees of poverty or comfort, and to indicate the conditions of life of each class',[21] and then present these results cartographically. From the outset he hoped that this careful stating of the facts would be 'of use in helping social reformers to find remedies for the evils which exist,' or 'prevent the adoption of false remedies.' He despised the approach of 'agitators' and 'sensational writers' who confound 'starving millions' with the working classes and those in distress.[22] Put simply, 'a better stating of the problems involved' was the first step to dispelling the 'helplessness' which pervaded all, based on the home truth that "We are a long way towards understanding anything under our consideration, when we have properly laid it open, even without comment".[23]

The generation of the data on which such forward planning could be based was very similar throughout the British Isles: innumerable Royal Commissions of Inquiry and lesser investigating committees, while various new bodies such as, in Ireland, the Commissioners for National Education (1831), Poor Law Commissioners and local boards of poor law guardians (from 1838), and the Local Government Board (1872) all contributed to the ever-mounting volumes of print. Municipal government expanded greatly in numbers employed and in responsibilities, with the establishment of separate committees to deal with issues such as public health, markets and housing, each generating their own minutes, inquiries, reports and proposals. 'Resting not on visionary theory but on the sure basis of investigation and of experiment'[24] church charities, philanthropic associations and professional bodies assembled their own databanks in the promotion of their aims, which generally also required interaction with a multiplicity of agencies. The *Dublin Statistical Society*, founded 1847, (from 1861 the *Statistical and Social Inquiry Society of Ireland*) contributed to the international debate on the multifaceted 'slum question' through its coverage of sanitary affairs, the housing of the labouring classes, and the boarding out of pauper children.[25] And all the time individuals and groups provided commentaries on the facts and analyses provided by other bodies.

---

[21] Charles Booth, *Life and Labour: Third Series, Religious Influences* (London, 1902), vol. 1, p. 3.
[22] Booth, *Life and Labour: Poverty*, (1889), vol. 1, p. 155.
[23] Ibid., p. 7.
[24] Mason, *A Statistical Account* (1814), p. viii.
[25] It co-operated with the *Economic and Statistical Section of the British Association*, with the *Charity Organisation Society* of London, and with the *State Charities Aid Association of New York*; 'What the Statistical and Social Inquiry Society of Ireland has effected, 1847–1880', appendix to *Report for 1881 of the Statistical and Social Inquiry Society of Ireland*, pp. 146–153.

The registration of births and deaths from 1864 (with accurate death rates from 1879) provided data which allowed reliable statistical tables on Irish mortality to be compiled for the first time.[26] Comparisons were drawn between death rates in Dublin and various other Irish and British urban centres, and annual progress (or regression) in lowering the death rate could now be charted. A sophisticated census (from 1841) provided a mass of information on each household in the country, while the General Valuation of Ireland, (Dublin: 1852–1854) and the new and revised Ordnance Survey large scale town plans made it possible to map various phenomena with great facility. The correlation of disease with professional classes or occupations, the calculation of indices of overcrowding, and the mapping of 'insanitary' or 'unhealthy' areas proposed for redevelopment, are examples of the practical employment of such data which was of great consequence to the poor.[27]

From the time of Whitelaw's pioneering efforts at ascertaining the exact population of the city of Dublin (1805, see Table 2.1), the move to gather quantifiable reliable and up-to-date and data gathered momentum; by 1925 a wealth of statistical information, with continuous additions and amendments, on innumerable matters relating to the Dublin slums, had been generated.

However, the amount of resources invested in assembling information through the laborious interviewing of witnesses, verbatim recording, and painstaking surveying, left little space or energy for critical analysis. A recurrent theme in nineteenth century social studies is the gap between monumental tomes and practical efforts. The questions of poverty, disease, slum housing and poor relief were susceptible to an infinite amount of painstaking research, but the translation into effective action was invariably fraught with innumerable complications. The story of the Dublin slums is that of a succession of authorities repeatedly identifying in graphic detail the very same 'black spots', with the very same processes in train, and once more passionately urging the case for reform, so that certain areas which were notorious at the end of the eighteenth century, reappear in every successive report, and are not tackled until well over a hundred years later.

Political Philosophy

Diametrically opposed schools of thought on the causes, and appropriate responses, to the destitution which fed slum conditions competed for attention in

---

[26] From 1879 figures for interment in the cemeteries within the Metropolitan Registration District were available to the Corporation's health officials, as well as the official registration figures for deaths. *Reports and Printed Documents of the Corporation of Dublin*, vol. 1 (1879) p. 266 (hereafter *RPDCD*).

[27] See annual reports of the Medical Officer of Health, and of the Sanitary Committee, and Housing Committee, *RPDCD* 1876–1918; for indices of overcrowding see also Charles Eason, 'The Tenement Houses of Dublin: Their Condition and Regulation,' *Stat. Soc. Inq. Soc. Ire. Jn.*, 10, (79), (1899), pp. 383–388.

the nineteenth century on an international basis. The prevailing economic policy of *laissez faire* defended the rights of free trade and opposed all government interference in the 'natural' economic order:

> The people can help themselves. Only they can put restrictions on the increase of their numbers, and keep population on a level with capital. Their fate is given into their own hands, they are responsible for their own conditions; the rich are no more responsible for their condition than they are responsible for the condition of the rich, and if they cannot help themselves, all experience demonstrates that the rich cannot help them.[28]

The contrary argument was given with ever increasing force and conviction, upholding that while 'all legislation is to some extent an interference with the liberty of the subject' still it is 'that interference which a mother exercises for the welfare of her offspring, which the doctor wields for the recovery of the patient'.[29]

It was against this background of competing ideologies that the extension of state powers in nineteenth century Ireland has to be set. The part played in municipal and national life by the formal agencies of government at the opening of the century was very small, and the creation of a reliable and tolerably efficient civil service took time.[30] The fear that the extension of state aid might erode individual self-reliance and self-respect underpinned every discussion, and the thought of massive central taxation was a concept still unfamiliar. The refusal of the English administration to allow outdoor food stations during the 1840s famine, under the aegis of the local poor law guardians, until February 1847, at which stage thousands had died of starvation and disease,[31] was the most appalling example of adhering closely to *laissez faire*. Within the cities, in advance of the extension of the franchise, there was little political capital to be made by housing the voteless, and aggravating those rate-payers and business and property interests upon whom the city finances depended. However, state aid and control increased inexorably throughout the nineteenth century: through the national schools (1831), the Poor Law Union workhouses (1838), the General Valuation of Ireland (1830–1860), decennial censuses from 1841, Public Health Acts 1848 and 1870s, culminating in what would have been unimaginable in 1800: the housing of the poorest in state-subsidised accommodation, and the general acceptance of such loss-making activity.[32]

---

[28] *The Economist*, 22 December 1849.
[29] Thomas Beames, *The Rookeries of London: Past Present and Prospective* (London, 1852), p. 140.
[30] R.M. Hartwell, *The Long Debate on Poverty: Eight Essays on Industrialisation and the Condition of England* (London, 1972) p. 92.
[31] see Virginia Crossman, *Local Government in Nineteenth Century Ireland* (Belfast, 1994), p. 48.
[32] For a review of increasing state control and its relation to charity societies see Kathleen Woodroofe, 'In the Midst of Victorian Plenty,' *From Charity to Social Work in England and the United States* (London, 1962; 1974 edn.), pp. 3–24.

The Churches and the Urban Poor

The major Christian churches played an important role in the direct relief of the urban poor, but were also central to the more general formulation of attitudes towards the city's poor and policies intended to reform or at least mitigate the worst excesses of their lot. The encyclical of Leo XIII *Rerum Novarum* (1891) was the first lengthy exposition by the Roman Catholic church on the rights of labour, the role of the state *vis à vis* the poor, bound in justice to 'duly and solicitously provide for the welfare and comfort of the working people'.[33] The message of *Rerum Novarum*, composed in response to the 'spirit of revolutionary change' which was sweeping industrialised Europe,[34] was solidly gospel based; more homely but no less valid articulations of the gospel challenge were being presented on an almost weekly basis throughout the preceding decades by church activists of the different denominations, who regularly prefaced their appeals with a verse from scripture:

He that receiveth one such little child in my name, receiveth me. Mt.18.5 (St Vincent's Orphanage, North William Street, Dublin, 1857)

Rescue the Poor and deliver the Needy from the hand of the Sinner. Ps. 81:4 (House of Protection for Distressed Young Women of Unblemished Character, Ash Street, Dublin, 1851)

Go out quickly to the streets and lanes of the city and bring in the poor and maimed and blind and lame. Lk. 14:21 (Dublin City Mission, 1862)

He that hath pity upon the Poor lendeth unto the Lord and that which he hath given will he pay him again. Prov. 19:17 (Elliot Home for Waifs and Strays, Dublin, 1872)

Patrick Corish dates the origins of general Roman Catholic institutions from 1771 when Teresa Mullaly, who was responsible for bringing Nano Nagle's Presentation sisters from Cork, opened an illegal girls' orphanage in Mary's Lane, Dublin. This was followed by a number of small-scale charities caring for orphans and widows especially, and managed by lay Catholics.[35] The emergence of native religious orders, their association with urban centres, and the steady increase in their numbers and the scale and variety of their ministries has been tracked by Caitríona Clear.[36] In the case of Dublin the Sisters of Charity (from 1815, founded by Mary Aikenhead), the Loreto Sisters (from 1822, Frances Ball) and the Sisters of Mercy (from 1831, Catherine McAuley) were all founded within the diocese during the episcopate of Dr Daniel Murray (coadjutor 1809, succeeded 1823, died 1852), and each made the service of the city's poorest a priority from the outset. Under the authoritative leadership of Paul Cullen, archbishop of Dublin 1852–79, (cardinal from 1866), the defence of Catholic rights and the care of the poor went hand in hand, and became highly charged political issues. Cullen called on his fellow bishops:

---

[33] Pope Leo XIII, *Rerum Novarum*, reprinted in William Gibbons (ed.), *Seven Great Encyclicals* (New York, 1963), section 27, p. 16.
[34] Ibid., section 1, p. 1.
[35] Patrick Corish, *The Irish Catholic Experience: An Historical Survey* (Dublin, 1985), p. 168.
[36] Caitriona Clear, *Nuns in Ninteeneth Century Ireland* (Dublin, 1987), pp. 36–44.

to succour your perishing brethren, to treat them with all possible kindness and compassion [lest] you fail in one of the most obvious and essential duties of the episcopal charge. On the day which [the Church] placed the pastoral staff in our hands she made mercy to the poor one of the subjects of that solemn examination to which she subjected us.[37]

Joseph Lee claims that 'no Irish figure of his generation championed so insistently the rights of the urban poor as this son of a prosperous farmer' and that 'the plight of the poor was one of the most insistent themes of his pastorals and private writings'.[38] Cullen has also been credited with 'rehabilitating a people emerging from centuries of oppression, intimidation and deprivation'.[39] The boom in church building and the spread of new convents and associated institutional buildings are only the more obvious manifestations of the important role of the Catholic church in Dublin and indeed in Ireland under Cullen. Emmet Larkin has credited him with 'spearheading the consolidation of the devotional revolution', wherein the attention of a more numerous but also better conducted and educated clergy was directed to the pastoral care of a long-neglected people, committed to increasing participation in the sacraments but bolstering this prime pastoral concern with a range of devotional exercises such as Eucharistic adoration, the rosary, sodalities, novenas, processions and retreats.[40] Catholics in general responded readily and indeed wholeheartedly to the lead given by their church; the genuine concern for their material and social improvement as well as for their spiritual and moral welfare which the clergy and church bodies displayed were undoubtedly among the reasons for the increase in church practice among Dublin's most downtrodden residents. On the Protestant side the very active involvement of Cullen's counterpart Archbishop Whately in chairing poor inquiries and as a member of the Board of Commissioners for National Education, as well as his close association with the Irish Church Missions which targeted the city slums for converts, are some of the better-known aspects of his genuine interest in the welfare of the city's poorest.[41]

The numerous Protestant and Catholic church-connected charitable enterprises varied considerably in scale, resources and relative importance. Despite some very important denominational and class differences, there is more to unite than separate them. Both were keenly interested in the question of relieving the poor, and could be very imaginative in their approach. There was a certain conservatism evident on both sides, with the maintenance of class distinctions, such as providing education for those of 'respectable' backgrounds apart from that provided for the 'labouring classes'. The upholding of social and political stability was important. The attitude of the Association for the Relief of Distressed Protestants (ARDP) typifies that of very many of the institutions which were to operate in Dublin's poorest areas:

[37] Rough notes for addresses to synod of bishops, 1861, DDA: 333/5 no. 171.
[38] Joseph Lee, *The Modernisation of Irish Society, 1848–1918* (Dublin, 1973), p. 45.
[39] Dermod McCarthy, *St Mary's Pro-Cathedral, Dublin* (Dublin, 1988), p. 17.
[40] Emmet Larkin, *The Historical Dimensions of Irish Catholicism* (Washington, 1984), pp. 77–78.
[41] See Chapter 7.

It has pleased God, in the inscrutable paths of his Providence, and in his wise and righteous government of the world, that as there are distinctions in rank and station, position and occupation, there should also be variety in the circumstances of the different classes of mankind. And accordingly, from the earliest records of the human race, it will be found that a certain proportion of the poor and needy have been consigned a condition of dependence upon the sympathy and assistance of those who may have the larger share of this world's goods at their command. This state of things, and the solemn obligation necessarily arising from it, is recognized by One who "spake as never man spake" when he said "the poor ye have with you always, and whensoever ye will, ye may do them good".[42]

The ARDP regarded its Protestant poor as a potentially stabilising influence in an increasingly turbulent society.[43] The Irish Church Mission credited their Coombe schools with exercising a 'holier, gentler influence' and 'transforming lawless ruffians into loyal quiet citizens',[44] while in Townsend Street, 'formerly a nest of everything vile and ungodly' the presence of the mission headquarters, it was claimed, had 'civilized' the area.[45] Similarly support for Catholic institutions was advertised as promoting social order, keeping the very poor from 'gnawing in their despair the very bonds of society'.[46]

The efforts of one denomination were used as a spur to the other to match them in generosity, so that the poor in fact did benefit. The new Catholic Asylum for Blind Females in the Portobello Hotel was regarded as 'magnificent' by their Protestant counterpart, the Molyneux Asylum; however underlying this admiration is the widespread fear of losing one's own co-religionists to competing institutions, a fear which was usefully exploited by all sides for fundraising purposes:

While we cannot but admire the zeal of that party [the Roman Catholic hierarchy], we should endeavour, with God's help, to emulate it, and advert the dangers which such a movement threatens to the cause of genuine Christianity. The Blind are physically the most helpless of our race, and the most open to imposition by pretended friends; and the danger is fearfully increased when to their natural helplessness are added the claims and temptations of deep poverty.[47]

Both Catholic and Protestant charities generally divided the poor on a 'deserving' and 'non-deserving' basis, and claimed to afford relief 'as may tend not to encourage a system of beggary and dependence, but to lift out of poverty and raise to self-supporting and honest industry'.[48] The assistance offered by both was very similar: varied outdoor relief, controlled by a committee which

---

[42] *Thirty Second Annual Report of the Association for the Relief of Distressed Protestants*, (hereafter ARDP), 24 Feb. 1869, p. 1.
[43] Kenneth Milne, *Protestant Aid 1836–1986: A History of the Association for the Relief of Distressed Protestants* (Dublin, 1989), p. 4.
[44] Alexander Dallas, *The Story of the Irish Church Missions, continued to 1869* (London, 1875), p. 179.
[45] *'Them Also,' the Story of the Dublin Mission* (London, 1866), p. 41.
[46] *SBO Fifth Annual Report 1861*, p. 11.
[47] Fundrasing leaflet for new Molyneux Church and Blind Asylum, 1860, DDA: 333/5 no. 177.
[48] *Thirtieth Annual Report of the ARDP*, 1867, p. 1.

organised visitation and inspection of the circumstances of each applicant; orphanages (both indoor and outdoor); Sunday and day schools; female 'penitentiaries' and refuges for girls 'at risk'; asylums for widow, the blind, deaf and dumb, and mentally handicapped. One important common feature was the way charities set up to tackle one aspect of poverty very soon become aware of acute needs in other areas, so that several institutions offered more than one form of assistance. The poor and 'ragged' schools for example, generally provided some at least of the children attending with a daily breakfast, occasional clothing, and assistance to their families, as funds and the level of organisation permitted. Where charities confined themselves to one particular concern they usually had an informal if not official link with other charities controlled by the same denomination, and thus could have particular cases dealt with by a more appropriate agency. And common to all denominations was the important role played by women in tackling poverty: in the orphanages and schools, the asylums, homes and penitentiaries, in home visitation and sick poor nursing and in the essential fundraising, women did practically all the planning and work.[49]

Urban Slums: The International Debate

Concern with the urban slum was not a peculiarly Dublin phenonomen; similar questions vexed cities in the US, Britain, Australia, continental Europe and elsewhere. Booth gives the rationale behind his comprehensive social geography survey of London (1886–1903):

It is likely enough that wherever poverty exists, it is accompanied more or less by the same circumstances, but each town and each country may have its own particular difficulties or faults, and so may serve to point a warning while it seeks an escape or cure. The swollen aggregation and congestion of London, the overcrowding on the banks of the Tyne, the one-roomed life of Glasgow, the ruined houses, rags and dirt of Dublin, the teeming tenements of New York or the 'double-decker' block dwellings of Chicago, may be each in their own way supreme, but we are nowhere very far removed from any of these conditions, and have much to learn from any investigation so conducted as to add to the common stock of knowledge.[50]

Alan Mayne in his work on nineteenth century Sydney asserts that the representational field from which the slumland characterizations were drawn was common to city people throughout the English-speaking world. His reading of sensational newspaper slum stories of the 1880s as 'a sequence of contrived performances' has direct applicability to the telling of the Dublin slum story.[51]

The 'slum annals' produced in Dublin in the period 1800–1850 most closely parallel the British experience, which is not surprising considering the close links many of the Dublin surveyors had with British cities at the time. Dr Speer,

---

[49] See Margaret Preston, 'Mothers' Meetings and Ladies' Teas: Lay Women and Philanthropy in Dublin: 1860–1880', unpublished MA (history) thesis (UCD, 1991).
[50] Charles Booth, *Life and Labour: Notes on Social Influences and Conclusion* (London, 1902), vol. 9 (final volume), part 1, p. 30.
[51] Alan Mayne, 'Representing the Slum', *Urban History Year Book* (Leicester, 1990), p. 67.

the officer attached to the Dublin Dispensary in the early 1820s, in his 'Inquiry into the Causes and Character of the Diseases of the Lower Orders in Dublin', (1822) compared the slum situation in Dublin with what he had already witnessed in dispensary practice in London.[52] There are many points of contact between Dublin and British slum discussions: the 'otherness' of the slums, despite their close proximity to 'the brightest prosperity';[53] the increasing sophistication of data collection and the 'professionalization' of social services; the reluctance of central authority to tackle the problem in an era of *laissez faire*; and the fear of revolutionary discontent. Throughout the British Isles the appropriate role of the poor law system, and the questions of outdoor relief, vagrancy, the needs of destitute children, and women, were important aspects of the debate. Charity, and the ideological, religious and practical debates that attended it, were of great importance in all cities.[54] Favourable and unfavourable comparisons were drawn between the slum housing of Dublin and other cities.[55] In the face of very apparent and widespread need, the search for controlling mechanisms by which charitable and public assistance could be limited to the 'deserving' and 'helpless' poor was part of an urgent international debate, with the merits of poor law systems in Edinburgh, Bath, Hamburg, Munich, Amsterdam, Paris, New York and elsewhere scrutinised and compared with the system proposed for or prevailing in Dublin.[56]

Within a British Empire context the Dublin slums were considered 'mission territory', with so many souls so surely lost to popery. There were many connections with 'mission work' elsewhere. One of the most famous of London reformers was the Dublin-born Dr Thomas Barnardo who began his mission to poor children in the ragged schools of the Liberties,[57] while the London-based Irish Church Missions Society had to struggle to keep good agents working in Dublin when better salaries were on offer from 'the city missions of London and the great towns of Scotland'.[58] Within Dublin, aggressive Protestant missionary activity targeting the city slums (see Chapters 7, 8) was vehemently

[52] T.C. Speer, 'Medical Report containing an Inquiry into the Causes and Character of the Diseases of the Lower Orders in Dublin', *Dublin Hospital Reports*, vol. lll, 1822, pp. 161–200.
[53] Thomas Jordan, 'The Present State of the Dwellings of the Poor, chiefly in Dublin' in *Journal of the Dublin Statistical Society*, vol. 2, (1857), p. 13.
[54] Gareth Stedman Jones, *Outcast London* (London, 1971) p. 240.
[55] London efforts seen as superior to Dublin, see: Jordan, *op.cit.*, pp. 12–19; Dublin efforts defended, see 'The Tenement Houses of London and Dublin Compared,' in *RPDCD* 136 (3), (1894), pp. 85–89.
[56] *Observations on the House of Industry, Dublin and on the Plans of the Association for Suppressing Mendicity in that City* (Dublin, 1818), p. 8. *Report of a Committee Appointed by the Society for the Prevention of Pauperism in the City of New York on the Expediency of Erecting an Institution for the Reformation of Juvenile Delinquents* (New York, 1823); *Arguments in Proof of the Necessity and Practicability of Suppressing Street Begging in the City of Dublin; illustrated by some Important Facts respecting other Institutions which have been Established in Other Places for the Purpose* (Dublin, 1817).
[57] Donal Ford, *Dr. Barnardo* (London, 1958, reprint 1966), pp. 16–19.
[58] Minutes of the Irish Church Missions, 27 October 1864, no. 4027.

opposed by Catholic charity workers, with none more active than Margaret Aylward and Fr John Gowan of St Brigid's Orphanage and Poor Schools:

> Why do not these ladies and gentlemen spend their money at home, and rescue the many infants that are every year put to death by their own unnatural parents in England? Why do they not look to their own great Babylon, where thousands of children and youths are kennelled in dens not fit for wild beasts, growing up without God, immersed in physical squalor, with the instincts of beasts of prey, and in fact menacing at no distant day to wreak a terrible revenge on society. These Pharisees send many thousands of pounds sterling to Ireland every year to seduce our children from the ancient faith, while all that misery, destitution and crime stagnates and putrefies at their own doors.[59]

Demographic Change and Boundary Restrictions

The demographic stagnation and constrained boundaries of Dublin city was a matter of incessant complaint throughout the nineteenth century. In 1800 Dublin was easily the second largest city in the British Isles and among the ten largest in Europe. By 1850 she was merely fifth in the UK rankings and by the end of the century was to suffer the ultimate indignity of being overtaken by 'upstart' Belfast as Ireland's largest city.[60] Between 1850–1914 Belfast's population increased from 100,000 to 400,000; Dublin only managed to creep up from 250,000 to 300,000 in the same period.[61] While most cities in the neighbouring isle were experiencing substantial increases in population, and finding along with the increased pressure on accommodation increases in rateable valuation and hence income, they generally managed to extend their municipal boundaries to provide land for building and also to include suburban properties in their rates. Dublin experienced the opposite fate: slow population growth, decaying building fabric, low rateable valuation, outmigration of the wealthiest who succeeded in keeping themselves aloof from the city's troubles, and loss of status in both a British Isles and European context.

The migration of the better-off to the suburbs, particularly to Rathmines, was an important factor in Dublin poverty patterns, as important symbolically as it was in practical terms. Figure 1.1 illustrates the extent of the urban area in 1898 where growth in the municipal area, circled by the canals, was well outstripped by developments in the independent townships, especially Pembroke and Rathmines/Rathgar. The withdrawal of the old Protestant ascendancy to virtual 'self-government' in these southern townships represented spatially their withdrawal from involvement in municipal politics, and the takeover of the Corporation by middle class Catholic nationalists. The poor were abandoned to the city's beneficence, and the city denied the contribution, both financially and morally, which it could be expected that the wealthiest would make. Despite what was called 'the physical absurdity of dividing that which was, in the main, one

---

[59] *SBO Eighteenth Annual Report* 1875, p. 9.
[60] Mary E. Daly, *Dublin: The Deposed Capital, A Social and Economic History 1860–1914* (Cork, 1985), p. 2.
[61] Joseph Lee, *The Modernisation of Irish Society 1848–1918* (Dublin, 1973; 1983 reprint), p. 9.

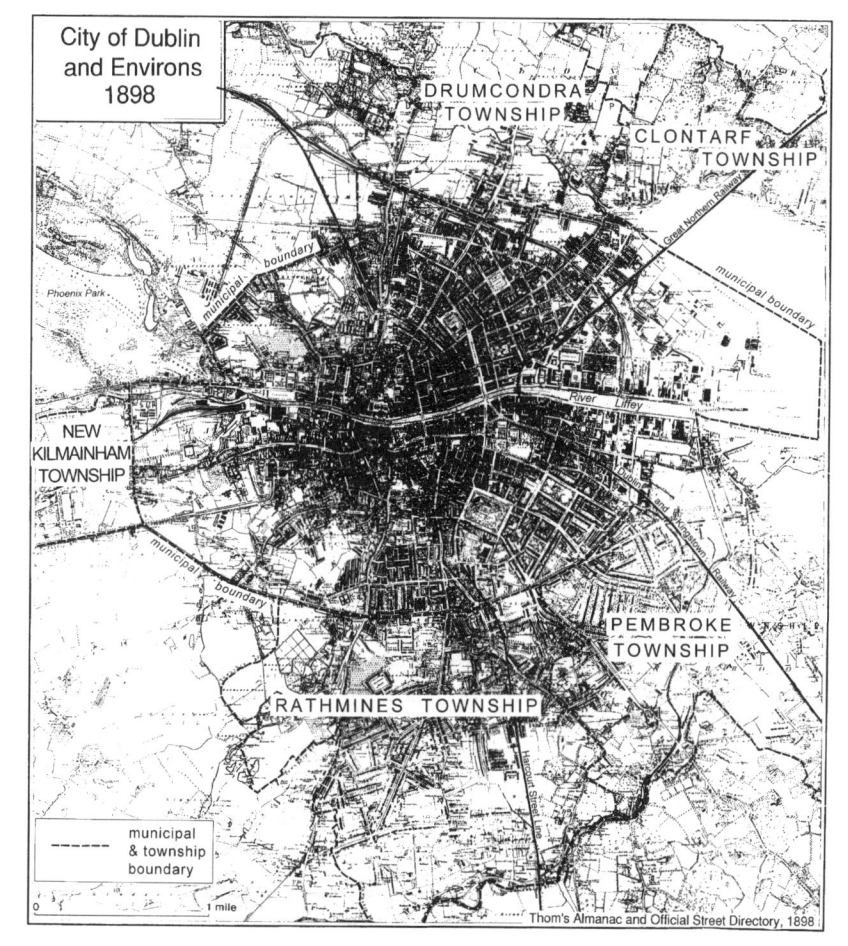

Figure 1.1 Dublin city and townships, *Thom's Almanac and Official Street Directory, 1898*

and the same city' along a 'purely arbitrary line, as it depends on the accident of the existence of the two canals and the Circular Road' the townships successfully fought off all nineteenth century efforts to absorb them into the city.[62] The north side north and Kilmainham townships were annexed in 1900, the southern townships maintaining their aloofness until 1930.

Phases in the Dublin Slum Story

The relentless exposure of slum conditions which characterised the early stages of the slum debate in Dublin (1798–1850s), was concerned mostly with infec-

---

[62] Charles Dawson, 'Greater Dublin: Extension of Municipal Boundaries', *Stat. Soc. Inq. Soc. Ire. Jn.*, 10, 78, (1898), pp. 341–349.

tious disease (Chapter 1). Reports on the sanitary nightmare which was Dublin city were valuable in raising public awareness of the nature and extent of poverty, and allow recurring themes to be identified. The slum surveys also lay the basis for the construction of a slum geography: areas which feature repeatedly in early surveys (such as Whitelaw 1798/1802, Willis 1845) are examined in conjunction with street classification schemes (from the censuses of 1841 and 1851), and areas of low value housing (based on Griffith's Valuation of 1854, all Chapter 2). While the areas of public health (Chapter 3, 5), housing (Chapter 4,5) and poor relief (Chapter 6,7) overlap considerably, it is possible to follow through developments under each heading, with some key dates marking distinct phases: the Dublin Improvement Act 1849, which remodelled the Corporation substantially, and enlarged its powers and responsibilities, while the Public Health Act of 1875 (extended to Ireland in 1878) has been described as a 'boundary stone' in the British Isles slum reform movement, dividing the first phase, based on sanitary legislation, from the concerns with housing reform which were to dominate the later decades of the nineteenth century and continue into the twentieth century.[63] While tracing developments in public health 1848–1900 (Chapter 3), followed by early housing initiatives 1876–1900 (Chapter 4), both strands are again treated together (Chapter 5) when policy shifts which marked the first two decades of the twentieth century are examined. The questions of vagrancy, mendicancy and poor relief are examined under two headings: the state's response, featuring the House of Industry and later poor law workhouse (Chapter 6), and the response of church charities, especially with regard to the care of children and women in need (Chapter 7). These issues are explored on scales varying from city-wide to the local street or court, while the final study (Chapter 8) examines the dynamic nature of slum creation and efforts at relief and reform in the case of the north city parishes of St Mary's and St Michan's. The concluding chapter (chapter 9) draws together the main threads of what is a complex story.

---

[63] Harry Barnes, *The Slum: Its Story and Solution* (Hempstead, 1934), p. 11.

THE SLUMS EXPOSED:
DUBLIN 1800-1854

For these painful, and often disgusting details, I should, perhaps, apologize to the reader: but he will have the candour to reflect, that my sole and anxious object is, to have evils of such serious magnitude alleviated, or, if possible, removed; that, to be removed, they must first be known; and that, to persons of elevated rank and station, who alone possess influence sufficient for a work so truly humane, faithful description is the only means by which they can learn the existence of such evils.[1]

INTRODUCTION

The first half of the nineteenth century was marked by a steady succession of published surveys and commentaries exposing the horrors of the 'other world' of the Dublin slums. The spread of infectious disease was bound up with the geography of poverty, the dread of infection providing the single most potent reason for efforts to eradicate 'fever nests' and 'plague spots', which threatened the rich of Dublin as well as the poor, so that 'all classes therefore are directly interested in rendering the homes of the people cleanly, commodious and healthful'.[2] Clergymen, medical doctors, sanitary officers, journalists, elected representatives, philanthropic activists both men and women, and commissioners officially appointed to inquire into the condition of the Dublin poor, undertook at various intervals to present their discoveries and convictions to a largely disinterested public.

The context within which each survey or commentary was created was particular to itself. The slums became a focus of interest at times of civil unrest, as in the aftermath of the 1798 rebellion; whenever contagious fever threatened to overspill to the better streets and houses; when the importunities of vagrants and

---

[1] James Whitelaw, *An Essay on the Population of Dublin, being the Result of an Actual Survey taken in 1798 with Great Care and Precision, to which is added the General Return of the District Committee in 1804, with a Comparative Statement of the Two Surveys, also Several Observations on the Present State of the Poorer Parts of the City of Dublin* (Dublin, 1805), facsimile reprint in Richard Wall (ed.), *Slum Conditions in London and Dublin* (Farnborough, Hants, 1974), (hereafter *Survey*).

[2] Charles A. Cameron and Edward D. Mapother, 'Report on the Means for the Prevention of Disease in Dublin', *Reports and Printed Documents of the Corporation of Dublin*, vol. 1 (1879), p. 344 (hereafter *RPDCD*).

beggars could no longer be tolerated; when the publication of reliable census returns and mortality statistics provided irrefutable evidence of appalling numbers of infant deaths among segments of the population.

Despite the differences in the immediate circumstances leading to each report, they have much in common. Each in turn was directed 'to those whose sympathy with the wretched or whose avocations in life, prompt them to devise schemes for the appalling sufferings of the poor'.[3] Their success in stirring the social conscience of the better-off and those in power cannot be quantified, but judging from the endless repetition of identical complaints there was a considerable time-lapse between the initial survey and the action so urgently advocated. Most of the early surveys were associated with or sponsored by public hospitals: the Cork Street and Hardwicke fever hospitals, while the Willis survey, though a private undertaking, also originated from an institution, this time the North Dublin Union workhouse.

The methodology employed in each case involved substantial field surveying by the author himself, with or without assistants; indeed it was on the testimony that nothing was included excepting only those circumstances 'as have occurred under my own immediate notice' that the authority of these reports rested.[4] While aiming at a comprehensive treatment of the prevailing general situation, individual cases, 'typical' of the mass, were always included as eyewitness accounts to excite pity, outrage and, hopefully, to precipitate action. Most were innovative and meticulous in their data collection, presentation and analysis: parish population tables with houses inhabited and waste (Whitelaw 1805), average occupancy per room (Cheyne 1818), measures of life expectancy (Willis 1845), tables of mortality (Wilde 1841), well in advance of what might be termed the 'official' statistical tables of the census and Registrar General's office. From the outset there was an effort to distinguish between levels and causes of poverty, to try and go beyond an undifferentiated mass of poverty.

The style of writing employed aimed at being persuasive yet reasoned, appealing not alone to the reader's common humanity but to his/her sense of logic, emphasising in each case how ignoring the problems increased costs to society, whether through the burden of hospital, prison and workhouse rates, or through the loss of earning powers. Each introduced the reader to the topic as if writing about a foreign land, requesting that disbelief be suspended as this 'exploration' commences, a voyage to 'another world' where the 'natives' were depicted as 'denizens' and 'poor creatures', despite the proximity of the slums to the wealthy districts. In every case also the initial concern – generally the control of contagious disease – very rapidly extends beyond the question of isolating the diseased, into the realms of domestic and public sanitation, control of mendicancy, the

---

[3] Thomas Willis, *Facts Connected with the Social and Sanitary Condition of the Working Classes in the City of Dublin* (Dublin, 1845), (hereafter *Social and Sanitary Condition*).

[4] T.A. Murray, *The Situation of the Poor in the Metropolis as Contributing to the Progress of Contagious Diseases*, prepared 'by the Desire, and at the Expence of the Society for Bettering the Condition of the Poor', (Dublin, 1801), p. i, (hereafter *Situation of the Poor*).

landlord / tenant relationship, and legislation governing all such areas. And while the circumstances of each family or household may be meticulously observed and recorded, it is always as recorded by the outsider; the voices of the poorer residents themselves are rarely if ever heard. It is typically the perspective of the educated and professional gentleman, with a clerical or medical background, with a genuine concern for his fellow citizens, whose voice is most clearly heard.

Of the reports which were published between 1800 and the 1850s, three phases may be identified: the first covers surveys undertaken in response to fever outbreaks in 1798, 1801–02, and 1817–18, including those connected with the establishment of the Cork Street *House of Recovery* or Fever Hospital. The second phase focuses on the utter inadequacy of 'private' or voluntary efforts to control fever outbreaks or relieve those in need, based on the experience of the 1831–32 cholera epidemic, as reported by Francis White (1833).[5] In the same year *The Royal Commission of Inquiry into the Conditions of the Poorer Classes in Ireland* was established to report on the best means for relieving destitution; it interpreted its brief more widely to include establishing the reasons for such destitution, with special reports on vagrancy and mendicancy in Dublin, and Dublin charities.[6] The third phase revolves around the first reliable census, 1841, and the special reports accompanying it and the 1851 census on the city of Dublin, prepared by William Wilde. Reports by Thomas Willis (1845) and Thomas Jordan (1857) combine primary research with information gleaned from the census.[7]

In the construction of a slum geography covering the entire municipal area more generalised sources prove invaluable. The exact identification of individual premises is made possible by the publication of the barony of Dublin section of the General Valuation of Ireland (popularly known as Griffith's Valuation) in 1854. Created in conjunction with the five-foot sheets of the Ordnance Survey, this central government initiative allows all residences of low rateable value to be mapped with a high degree of accuracy. The commercial street directories enter premises let in tenements, which further assists the construction of a geography of poverty, while the classification of individual streets by William Wilde (1841, 1851) is invaluable in monitoring the process of downgrading which affected certain north city residential streets. The surveys and reports expose the horrors of the slum situation; the valuation, directory and other material allow the exact mapping of slum areas within the context of the dominant social and economic patterns in the city at midcentury.

---

[5] Francis White, *Report and Observations on the State of the Poor of Dublin* (Dublin, 1833), (hereafter *Report on the State of the Poor*).

[6] *First, Second and Third Reports of the Commissioners for Inquiring into the Conditions of the Poorer Classes in Ireland* (London, 1835–36); Helen Burke, *The People and the Poor Law in Nineteenth Century Ireland* (Dublin, 1987), p. 19.

[7] Willis, *Social and Sanitary Condition* (1845); Thomas Jordan, 'The Present State of the Dwellings of the Poor, chiefly in Dublin', *Journal of the Dublin Statistical Society*, vol. 2 (1857), pp. 12–19, (hereafter 'Dwellings of the Poor').

i) Fever Reports, 1801–1819
James Whitelaw *Survey* 1805

Whitelaw's *An Essay on the Population of Dublin being the Result of An Actual Survey taken in 1798 . . . also, Several Observations on the Present State of the Poorer Parts of the City of Dublin, 1805* introduces many of the most intractable aspects of the nineteenth century Dublin poverty situation, and focuses especially on the geography of poverty. Whitelaw was the Anglican vicar of St Catherine's, a parish embracing a large portion of 'what we may emphatically call, the region of filth and misery'.[8] Accomplished in several fields of knowledge, he has been described as an eminent geographer; his *System of Geography* and map of the entire canal system of Ireland were to be unsurpassed for some time.[9] His Dublin survey was conducted over five months and involved his 'careful supervision' for at least another two years.[10] A large-scale and reliable town plan showing 'narrow back courts and lanes off the principal streets' was essential to Whitelaw's purpose; this was provided by Rocque's four-sheet *Exact Survey of the City and Suburbs of Dublin 1756* which Whitelaw 'generally found minutely exact' (Figures 2.1, 2.2).[11] Armed with his map extracts and notebook, 'undeterred by the dread of infectious diseases, undismayed by degrees of filth, stench and darkness inconceivable by those who have not experienced them', Whitelaw personally surveyed every residence in the very poorest areas, and with a team of able assistants, who were closely supervised, systematically examined every other part of the city.[12] His initial survey was undertaken in the 'burning months of the summer of 1798'; widespread fear of being suspected of disaffection, overtaken by rumours that the survey would result in measures to relieve the poor, ensured very full co-operation with what was a government-sanctioned but privately-funded survey.[13]

The first objective was to provide 'an accurate, well-arranged census of a considerable capital', which could be readily updated.[14] Whitelaw produced a composite population table which was divided on the basis of sex and class (upper and middle classes, their servants, and lower class), and the number of houses (inhabited and waste), with the average population per house in each of the nineteen parishes and two deaneries in Dublin (see Table 2.1). His 1798 total for the city was 172,091, with an average number of 11.17 individuals per house, and a gender balance of 56 females: 44 males. Population tables for each of the individual parishes/deaneries were also appended; in Table 2.2, the Parish of St Luke, for example (see Figure 2.1), the gender balance and average household number for each street and court can be deduced, with densities as high as 27

---

[8] Whitelaw *Survey* (1805), p. 65.
[9] Richard Wall, introduction to *Slum Conditions in London and Dublin* (Farnborough, Hants, 1974).
[10] Ibid.
[11] Ibid., p. 52.
[12] Ibid., pp. 4–6.
[13] Ibid., pp. 4–5.

The Slums Exposed: Dublin 1800–1854

Population of Dublin in 1798, as divided into its nineteen Parishes and two Deaneries.

INDEX to Tables.	NAMES OF PARISHES, &c.	UPPER AND MIDDLE CLASSES. Males.	Females.	Total.	SERVANTS OF DITTO. Males.	Females.	Total.	LOWER CLASS. Males.	Females.	Total.	TOTAL Males.	TOTAL Females.	GRAND TOTAL.	NO. OF HOUSES. Inhabited.	Waste.	Average to a House.
I.	Parish of St. James,	342	367	709	97	201	298	2432	2665	5097	2871	3233	6104	538	32	11.34
II.	St. Catharine,	991	846	1837	378	660	1038	7608	9693	17301	8977	11199	20176	1481	140	13.62
III.	St. Luke,	150	148	298	32	75	107	2846	3990	6836	3028	4213	7241	454	41	15.95
IV.	St. Nicholas without the Walls.	347	347	694	50	169	219	4861	6532	11393	5258	7048	12306	950	55	12.95
V.	St. Nicholas within the Walls.	163	153	316	45	92	137	306	362	668	514	607	1121	107	10	10.48
VI.	St. Audeon,	585	513	1098	156	302	458	1612	2023	3685	2353	2838	5191	415	53	12.5
VII.	St. Michael,	124	108	232	10	50	60	1064	1243	2307	1198	1401	2599	163	20	15.94
VIII.	St. John,	316	333	649	46	118	164	1577	1752	3329	1939	2203	4142	295	31	14.08
IX.	St. Werburgh,	609	551	1160	98	253	351	941	1177	2118	1648	1981	3629	305	33	11.9
X.	Deanery of Christ-church,	25	10	35	3	4	7	80	111	191	108	125	233	23	2	10.1
XI.	St. Patrick,	76	64	140	14	30	44	832	1065	1897	922	1159	2081	162	11	12.84
XII.	Parish of St. Bridget, or St. Bride,	1287	1445	2732	195	580	775	2054	2448	4502	3536	4473	8009	744	27	10.76
XIII.	St. Peter,	2283	3017	5300	1217	2048	3265	3390	4108	7498	6890	9173	16063	1512	116	10.61
XIV.	St. Anne,	1486	1737	3223	715	1286	2001	870	1134	2004	3071	4157	7228	711	36	10.17
XV.	St. Andrew,	1489	1373	2862	289	661	950	1738	2132	3870	3516	4166	7682	709	63	10.83
XVI.	St. Mark,	599	684	1283	121	354	475	3127	3797	6924	3847	4845	8692	646	61	13.45
	Total Population on the South side of the River Liffey.	10872	11695	22567	3466	6883	10349	35338	44282	79570	49676	62821	112497	9215	731	12.2
XVII.	Parish of St. Paul,	781	1002	1783	186	444	630	3321	4170	7491	4288	5616	9904	1050	116	9.43
XVIII.	St. Michan,	1312	1409	2721	374	772	1146	6375	7850	14225	8061	10031	18092	1520	141	12.56
XIX.	St. Mary,	2452	3014	5466	979	1771	2750	3859	4579	8438	7290	9364	16654	1590	43	10.47
XX.	St. Thomas,	1316	1624	2940	650	1087	1737	1787	2098	3885	3753	4809	8562	892	82	9.6
XXI.	St. George,	817	1011	1828	766	997	1703	688	877	1565	2211	2885	5096	587	89	8.68
	Total Population on the North side of the River Liffey,	6678	8060	14738	2895	5071	7966	16030	19574	35604	25603	32705	58308	5639	471	
	Spring-garden, a suburb beyond the Circular-road, omitted in the Parishes of St. Thomas and St. George; taken from the return of the Conservators, in 1804,												1286	345	0	
	TOTAL Population North of the Liffey,												59594	5984	471	
	TOTAL Population of Dublin in 1798,												172091	15199	1202	

Table 2.1 Population of Dublin in 1798, as divided into its nineteen Parishes and two Deaneries, Whitelaw 1805, p. 14.

persons per house in Ardee Street and a significant excess of females over males in most streets and courts. However, the detailed survey sheets, which included house numbers, state of repair, class divisions, names and occupations of proprietors, and reference to tenement status, survive for only two streets, The Poddle and York Street, and so preclude the compilation of a comprehensive social geography of the city.[15] It is the accompanying *Essay*, which was intended to bring the general results before the public, which is most valuable, as it identifies some elements of the slum situation which are of even greater importance fifty years later.

The 'ancient parts of this city' were noted for their narrow streets, numerous lanes and alleys, and crowded houses with very tiny back-yards, most of them occupied 'by working manufacturers, by petty shopkeepers, the labouring poor, and beggars, crowded together to a degree distressing to humanity'. This confusion of industrial, residential and institutional land uses is evident in the classification created by Rocque, where 'warehouses, stables &c.' densely pack the spaces behind the rows of dwelling houses (Figures 2.1, 2.2). The rent for a single room

---
[14] Ibid., p. 3.
[15] As 'its bulk (two folio volumes) renders its publication inexpedient', Whitelaw had it lodged in Dublin Castle, from whence it was transferred to the Public Records Office, and destroyed, with so much else, in the fire of 1922.

No. III.

Parish of Saint Luke.

NAMES OF STREETS, &c.	POPULATION.			HOUSES.	
	Males.	Females.	TOTAL.	Inhabited.	Waste.
Coomb, S. side entire,	525	614	1139	73	8
Cain's-alley,	56	72	128	6	0
Green's-alley,	8	16	24	4	0
Daniel's-alley,	56	120	176	11	0
Three-nun-alley,	23	32	55	5	0
Stillas's-court,	58	74	132	7	0
Poddle, S. side, from No. 13 to No. 17,	40	58	98	8	0
New-market,	432	614	1046	62	6
Ardee-street, or Crooked-staff,	151	177	328	12	2
Ardee-row, or Mutton-lane,	95	167	262	16	1
Atkinson's-alley,	18	29	47	4	0
Brabazon's-street, or Truck-street,	122	160	282	18	3
Brabazon's-row, or Cuckold's-row,	75	94	169	13	5
Hunt's-alley,	31	58	89	5	0
Fordam's-alley,	328	570	898	53	1
Skinner's-alley,	322	491	813	52	1
New-row-on-the-Poddle,	359	453	812	52	7
Ward's-hill,	28	24	52	6	2
Mill-street,	139	206	345	25	4
Warren's-mount,	25	15	40	3	0
Mill-lane,	19	42	61	4	1
Sweeny's-lane,	54	64	118	6	0
Black-pitts, W. side,	64	63	127	9	0
TOTAL	3028	4213	7241	454	41

Table 2.2 Population table III, Parish of St. Luke, 1798, Whitelaw 1805.

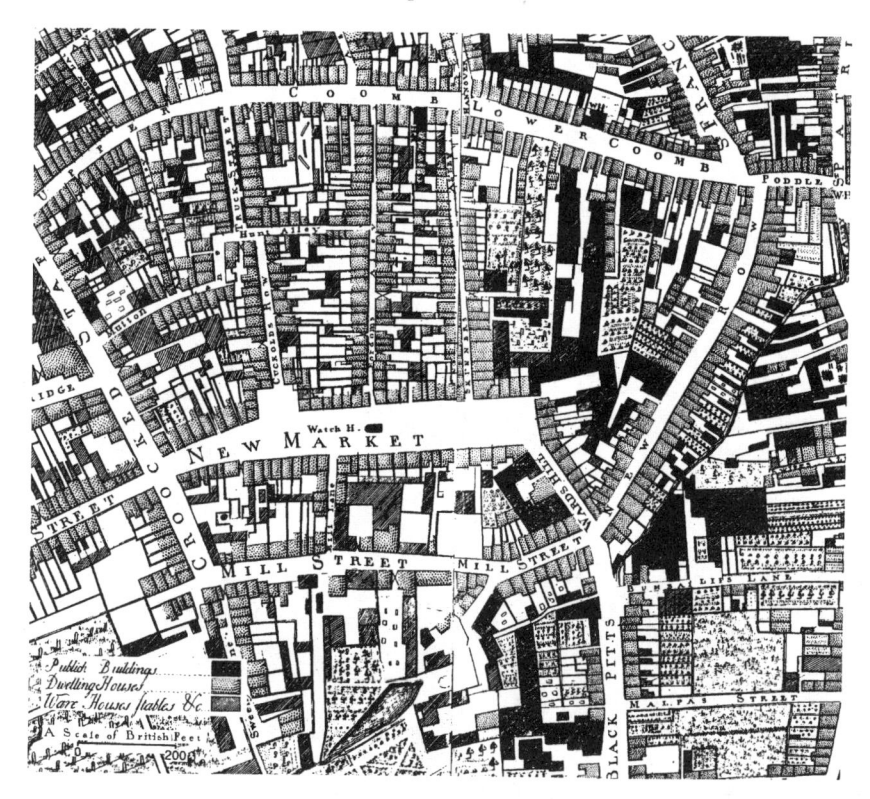

Figure 2.1 St Luke's Parish, *Exact Survey of the City and Suburbs of Dublin*, John Rocque 1756, sheets 3, 4

'in one of these truly wretched habitations' was from one to two shillings per week, 'and, to lighten this rent, two, three and even four families become joint tenants'. During his early-morning surveying Whitelaw 'frequently surprised from ten to sixteen persons, of all ages and sexes, in a room, not fifteen feet square, stretched on a wad of filthy straw, swarming with vermin, and without any covering, save the wretched rags that constituted their wearing apparel'. It was under such circumstances that he 'frequently found from thirty to fifty individuals in a house'.[16]

The tenement system, which was to be the single most unfortunate element of the Dublin housing crisis, was well established in the poorest areas by the beginning of the nineteenth century; so too was the steady outmigration of the better off to the new suburbs, leaving the medieval core to decay, and the burden of its poor to be carried by those who remained. Very little rebuilding or improvements were undertaken in the older parts of the city between the time of this survey and the later nineteenth century, as later commentators repeatedly testify.

[16] Whitelaw, *Survey* (1805), p. 50.

Figure 2.2 St Catherine's Church and Cork Street, location of House of Recovery (1802), *Exact Survey of the City and Suburbs of Dublin*, John Rocque 1756, sheet 4

The most immediate consequence of the colonisation by several families of the houses built originally for one was the disgraceful state of the sanitary accommodation, described by Whitelaw 'in painful and often disgusting details'.[17] The biggest difficulties lay in the enclosed nature of the yards, too many persons reliant on too few privies, and the lack of enforceable regulations: 'The stench of filth in an open street, may be dissipated by an unobstructed current of air; but that arising from human excrement, in narrow yards enclosed by lofty buildings, must operate with unchecked malignity'.[18]

Distinct but inter-related areas of concern were to occupy local administration and philanthropic persons such as Whitelaw throughout the nineteenth century. Accumulations of dung from city centre dairy yards and the regulation of dairy business,[19] the closing of private dung yards and the role of the state in 'scavenging',[20] the licensing and later state provision of slaughter houses,[21] the overcrowding of burial yards, where 'in order to make room for others, bodies have been taken up in an absolute state of putrefaction, to the great and very dangerous annoyance of the vicinity' all important public health matters. So were too are the questions 'why brothels, soap manufactories, slaughter houses, glass-houses, lime kilns, &c. are permitted to exist in the midst of a crowded population', the profusion of 'dram-shops, the most alarming of all nuisances' and the distribution of houses of 'ill fame'.[22]

Cork Street 'House of Recovery' or Fever Hospital, 1801

A report on the *Situation of the Poor in the Metropolis as Contributing to the Progress of Contagious Diseases* was published in 1801, prepared by T.A. Murray 'by the Desire, and at the Expence of the Society for Bettering the Condition of the Poor'. In that year the fever epidemic raging since 1798 throughout Ireland had reached its peak, its virulence increased by crop failure so that 'the price of bread and potatoes, both of bad quality, together with that of every necessity of life, was raised beyond all precedent'.[23] In Dublin the only provision for fever patients was the Hardwicke Hospital, attached to the House of Industry (see chapter 6); at least 2,000 persons 'of the lowest rank' died of fever here in 1800–01, 'a proof of the distress of the poor of Dublin which needs no comment'.[24]

The 1801 report on the *Situation of the Poor* was commissioned to generate support for the establishment of a specialised fever hospital or House of Recovery,

---

[17] Ibid., p. 64.
[18] John Norwood, 'On the Working of the Sanitary Laws in Dublin, with Suggestions for their Amendment', *Soc. Stat. Inq. Soc. Ire. Jn.*, 6, (43), (1873), p. 239; also *RPDCD*, vol. 3 (1879) pp. 230–242; Whitelaw, *Survey*, (1805), p. 55.
[19] Whitelaw, *Survey* (1805) p. 60; Norwood (1873), p. 235; *RPDCD*, vol. 3, (1879), pp. 793–794.
[20] Norwood (1873,) p. 239; *RPDCD*, vol. 3, (1879), p. 799.
[21] Norwood (1873), p. 236; *RPDCD*, vol. 3, (1879), pp. 792–793.
[22] Whitelaw, *Survey* (1805), pp. 61–62, 64.
[23] Murray, *Situation of the Poor*, (1801), pp. 16–17.
[24] Ibid., p. 18.

modelled on an institution recently opened in Manchester. This was founded on the premise that the condition of the homes of the poorest was such that fever could only effectually be contained by the rapid removal of afflicted persons and 'contacts' to an isolated hospital.[25] The site chosen for the House of Recovery in Cork Street, the Liberties, fulfilled the requirements ideally: 'in an airy situation, detached from other buildings, in the neighbourhood of a populous district of the town and large enough to accommodate as many patients as the funds of the House shall, at its opening, be deemed adequate to support'.[26] Figure 2.2 illustrates this situation: on the southwestern limit of the densely built-up area, from whence persons could be rapidly and safely removed 'in a sedan chair, provided with a moveable lining', at the expense of the institution.[27]

To illustrate the necessity of establishing what would undoubtedly be a major public expense, Murray expounded on the miasmic theory of disease and its relation to the living conditions prevailing in the city slums, the 'system of domestic economy' of the poorest families, and the utter inadequacy of measures currently in force.[28]

The theory of contagion had not yet gained popular acceptance, although there was an increasing body of evidence to demonstrate that the incidence of fever could be traced from one family member or household or contact to another. The miasmic theory focusing on the role of the atmosphere in spreading disease, was favoured. Murray defined 'infectious' disease as 'that which occasion the sick person to taint the atmosphere around him, so that it becomes capable of exciting in others, who are exposed to it, a similar disease'. Where the exhalation or 'noxious effluvia' was deposited on 'various substances, especially wood, cotton, or woollen cloths' it could 'stagnate' and similarly serve to taint the atmosphere at some future date.[29] Claims that the proposed fever hospital would simply concentrate contagion and 'infect the whole surrounding atmosphere and endanger the safety of all the neighbourhood', not to mention hastening the dispatch of all directly connected with it, were refuted on the grounds that the contagious atmosphere would be 'rendered perfectly innoxious by being *diluted* in a sufficiently large quantity of pure air'.[30] The virulence of any outbreak of fever therefore depended on 'the quantity of infectious effluvia with which the air is impregnated', along with whatever impurity may already be 'stagnant' in the air, and the 'degree of weakness in the bodies, or depression in the minds' of residents already exposed to the vitiated atmosphere.[31]

Not alone did close and dirty living conditions provide ideal means for the spread of disease, but it was further claimed that in the slums could be found the

[25] Ibid., p. 4.
[26] Ibid., p. 11.
[27] Ibid., p. 12.
[28] Ibid., p. i.
[29] Ibid., p. 2.
[30] Ibid., p. ii.
[31] Ibid., p. 2.

very origins of contagious fevers, as such require, 'for their first production, nothing more than the effluvia of the living body, become putrid by stagnation, and may of course arise in any ill ventilated or crowded place'.[32]

Murray claimed that an exploration of 'the recesses of poverty and disease in the metropolis' would reveal how ideally situated were these dwellings for the spread of infection: 'on all sides closely surrounded by buildings and in their whole appearance indicating filth and dirt' their 'interior arrangements' very obviously 'wholly incompatible with cleanliness and with comfort'.[33] His attention was specially drawn to the air of the tenement rooms, where despite the foulness the windows 'cannot be opened without admitting air apparently more noxious, certainly not less offensive, than that already contained in the room'. Even where there might be some advantage to be gained by opening the windows he found 'the sashes have frequently been rendered by age or accident immovable, wood or paper has been substituted for broken panes of glass, and every crevice is so carefully stuffed by woollen rags or some other filthy substance, that as a means of admitting fresh air the windows are often totally useless'.[34]

While the lot of the poorest of the Liberties was pitiful at the best of times, sickness proved calamitous: 'improvident for the future while their labour enabled them to procure the means of subsistence; perhaps in their most fortunate days earning too little to admit of any savings, every evil is now doubled'. There was no remedy but to dispose of some article from their already small stock of clothes or furniture, 'to enable them to meet the exigency of the moment'.[35]

Once generated, disease spread uncontrollably from room to room and from floor to floor through well-meaning visitors, 'sentiments of humanity and affection prevailing over those of timid precaution' at least initially. Even distant houses of the rich could be infected, as disease was carried back from the tenements through visiting servant friends and relations. The constant turnover of lodgers in a typical house and the pressure for accommodation ensured a 'succession of fresh subjects for its attack'.[36]

Modern medical research shows how the generalised eighteenth and nineteenth century term 'fever' in fact covers two distinct infections with similar epidemiologies: typhus fever and relapsing fever, both caused by micro-organisms transmitted by the human body louse, a parasite which thrives in close and dirty living conditions. Dysentery, which regularly accompanies or follows fever and famine conditions, is caused by the dysentery bacillus and spread by flies, by direct contract or by pollution of the water by faeces infected with the bacillus. Poor nutritional status renders persons particularly susceptible to dysentery, again a situation too often found in the Dublin slums.[37]

---

[32] Ibid., pp. 5–6.
[33] Ibid., p. 3.
[33] Ibid., p. 4.
[35] Ibid., p. 5.
[36] Ibid., p. 7.
[37] Laurence M. Geary, 'Famine, Fever and the Bloody Flux', in Cathal Poirtéir (ed.), *The Great Irish Famine* (Cork, 1995), pp. 75–77.

Observations on the Circumstances which tend to generate and propagate Contagion in the Liberties on the South Side of the City of Dublin and on the means of removing them, 1802

Setting up the Cork Street Fever Hospital was an admirable project, and most generously supported by bankers, brewers, businessmen, the guilds and many titled members of Dublin society, as is evidenced from the list of donors and subscribers. However, investigations into the fever question which had initially led to proposals for this new hospital very quickly 'unavoidably compelled' the trustees into much more provocative considerations.[38] Questions of the gross inadequacy of current legislation, balancing 'private exertion' and 'public interference', reforming legislation in favour of the tenant over the landlord, and administrative inefficiency, were among the issues the trustees raised.[39] Anticipating criticisms that they were 'intruding into matters which are out of our proper sphere' the trustees upheld that there was an 'inseparable and necessary connexion' between the living conditions of the citizens and the internal operations of the House of Recovery, 'in order to give complete efficacy to the whole system of measures to be adopted in order to abate contagion'. The trustees therefore regarded the institution as holding a dual mandate: to relieve those suffering from fever, and 'to counteract the progress of infection, and to eradicate as far as possible the causes of it'.[40]

The trustees directed their energies towards publicising and resolving the single issue which they understood to be at the heart of the fever question: the accumulation of filth in the backyards. The houses in the Liberties 'are in general unprovided with necessaries or those necessaries are so choked up and obstructed as not to serve for any purpose of cleanliness'. The result was that the filth of the house was suffered to accumulate for several years, 'and those immense heaps of putrid sordes (*sic*) piled up in close and confined backyards, surrounded with high walls, that interrupt the free circulation of air, cannot fail to generate and propagate contagion'.[41] Ruinous houses, and the abandoned lower stories of some houses, acted as common receptacles for all manner of filth.[42]

The landlords of these wretched houses, 'not residing in general in the neighbourhood of them' took no interest either in removing the nuisances, or 'assisting or encouraging their tenants in any disposition or effort of their own towards cleanliness'. The onus therefore fell totally on the poorest of tenants, for whom 'the only means at present in their power' was 'the expence and trouble of looking for and paying a dirtman who is to provide a carman from the country to

---

[38] Trustees of the House of Recovery or Fever Hospital in Cork-Street, *Observations on the Circumstances which tend to generate and propagate Contagion in the Liberties on the South Side of the City of Dublin and on the means of removing them* (Dublin, 1802), pp. 11, 24 (hereafter Cork Street Trustees).
[39] Ibid., p. 34.
[40] Ibid., pp. 24–25.
[41] Ibid., p. 4.
[42] Ibid., pp. 6, 7.

carry away the filth'.[43] And this step, if taken, was in breach of the law, which expressly forbade any person 'to empty any boghouse or begin to take away any night soil from any house' excepting between the hours of 11pm and 6am and then the mode of conveyance could only be 'in a cart or car floored and enclosed by a boarded framework'. Country carts were not so ideally constructed, nor would their drivers be in the city after dark.[44]

The 'habitual residence in the midst of filth and nastiness', it was claimed, undermined not alone the physical but also the moral health of the citizens, brutalizing them until decency 'is blunted and sometimes even extinguished among them'. The downhill slide could be tracked: 'long habituated to the effluvia of the dunghills within a few feet of their dwellings, they become reconciled to it within doors', and allow filth to accumulate in their stairs, passages, and even bedrooms. Their sensitivities thus coarsened, the 'pernicious influence' extended to their 'dress and their persons'.[45] The House of Recovery aimed to counteract this by gradually inculcating a sense of the value and importance of cleanliness 'by practical illustrations of the benefits resulting from it'. Hence the 'set of rules to be observed by the inhabitants of those houses from which the Patients are removed and rewards for a punctual compliance with them'.[46] But the best exertions of the House of Recovery personnel were of little worth 'while the back yards of the houses continue choaked up with heaps of putrid filth, and until some means are devised for the regular and periodic removal of it'.[47]

The law as it stood facilitated the collection of the 'external filth' of the routeways or free thoroughfares 'by a scavenger who contracts for the purpose with the Grand Jury of the Manor Court of St Thomas Donore'. While the performance of this duty left much to be desired, the 'comparatively free circulation of air in the open streets' was welcomed. The neglected areas were 'the gutters or channels that adjoin the flag or pathways', noteworthy for their 'stagnant putrescency', but which could be easily remedied by opening communications with the main sewers. Also in need of immediate attention were the 'dunghills, slaughtering houses, and stagnant pools of the Liberties' which the trustees considered might all be proceeded against as nuisances, under the common or statute law as it stood, the principal difficulty being that the sentence would fall on the occupier rather than, more fairly, upon the landlord.[48]

The 1802 Cork Street hospital report on contagion also included a lengthy critique of the parliamentary act *For the Improvement of the City of Dublin and the environs thereof, by the better paving, lighting and cleansing the same*' 1789 under which the Commissioners for Paving were created.[49] The powers of the Paving

[43] Ibid., pp. 21–22, p. 5.
[44] Ibid., pp. 17, 22.
[45] Ibid., p. 6.
[46] Ibid., p. 25.
[47] Ibid., p. 27.
[48] Ibid., pp. 4, 7, 11.
[49] 29 George lll c.61.

Board included responsibility for ensuring the proper paving, cleansing, and lighting of the streets, the erection of fountains and conduits for the use of the poor and the public, the erection of common sewers and drains, cesspools, and for preventing and removing 'nuisances, encroachments and annoyances' within the city, and to levy rates for these purposes, including intervening wherever a private sewer, drain or cesspool, 'shall become choaked up and ruinous' (*sic*) so as to 'affect or injure pavement or become offensive to the inhabitants' carrying out the necessary works, and charging the parties responsible.[50] Under this act inspectors of nuisances were to be made constables. Further restrictions were imposed under a supplementary act of 1790 which imposed on owners and occupiers the duty of covering 'with such quantities of lime or earth as shall be sufficient to prevent any stench or annoyance' any filth from slaughter houses, shambles, or privies which might be laid for the purposes of manure on any land within the city boundary.[51]

The powers vested in the Paving Commissioners were accepted as 'highly useful and salutary', but had proved worthless to date in the fever dens of the Liberties; this was the legislation under which the city was to labour until the Dublin Improvement Act, 1849. The utter neglect of the back yards was due to the primary responsibility of the Paving Board for transport matters and 'the safety and accommodation of passengers', so that 'nuisances, &c. *as connected with public roads*' were the principal concern. The penal provisions concerning the removal of filth by country carts, and the impossibility of holding a landlord accountable for the provision of 'dirt holes &c', where multiple tenancy was the norm, were used to illustrate the irrelevancy of the statutes. Nor were the regulations governing the spreading of manure of any account, for these related 'to accumulations of filth, *voluntarily* made for some *particular purpose*,' and so could not be applied to 'dunghills &c. &c. *in back yards that are accumulated of necessity*'.[52]

An immediate and massive clean-up of all current accumulations of back-yard filth in the Liberties was called for by the trustees as a first step in the battle against fever. The Grand Canal 'affords a ready channel for sending it to a considerable distance in the country', where it would be welcomed, being 'all useful and profitable manure'.[53] Landlords might be prevailed upon to assist, 'the attention of farmers in the country might be excited by public advertisement', the proprietors of carts used in cleansing other parts of the city might be induced to co-operate, 'all these means might be brought into action at once' and a major clean-up of the Liberties effected. All that was necessary was public support for the project, and the superintendence of competent persons who were armed with the necessary powers.

[50] Cork Street Trustees (1802), pp. 16, 15, 18.
[51] 30 George lll c.56, 61; Cork Street Trustees (1802), p. 19.
[52] Cork Street Trustees (1802), pp. 21, 22.
[53] Ibid., p. 28.

To prevent new accumulations of filth the trustees proposed the construction of sewers 'to connect with the great public sewer that runs thro' the Coombe'.[54] Once the means had been provided 'for keeping up a regular system of cleanliness' the trustees proposed working on the morals and habits of the residents, insisting on the strict exercise of legal powers 'punishing the offensive neglect of cleanliness', and rewarding those who 'shall distinguish themselves by superior attention to this point, as well in their persons as in their habitations'.[55] Legislative reform was cautiously advocated, the trustees keenly aware that any proposal 'directly compelling' owners to build 'necessaries' at the rear of their premises would be regarded as an outrageous infringement on landlord rights; the diplomatic stance adopted was that, perhaps, some law whereby fines were imposed both on landlords and occupiers might be considered salutary.[56]

J. Cheyne, Hardwicke Fever Hospital, 1818

Dr Cheyne of the Hardwicke Fever Hospital was anxious to impress upon the public that the fever of 1818 did not arrive unexpectedly, but that 'the diffusion of the epidemic depended more upon its predisposing causes than upon any peculiar activity of its contagious principle'. In fact, he could authenticate that even in the healthiest year of the preceding ten years, 'there was a sufficient stock of contagion in this city to infect its inhabitants'; all that was required for the fever to extend itself more or less widely, was for certain conditions to be fulfilled, 'at the head of which are unquestionably an insufficiency of wholesome food and despondency'.[57] In the most recent outbreak those who succumbed had 'during a season of unparalleled distress, been scantily fed and clothed' and had 'laboured under great depression of mind'; they had also had contact or 'close approximation' for days or weeks with persons affected with fever.[58] Cheyne was speaking with considerable authority: the Hardwicke Fever Hospital operated as 'the chief receptacle of the aged, when labouring under diseases of a mixed nature assuming the form of fever'; although attached to the House of Industry (Chapter 6), such patients were admitted from the entire city and environs.[59]

To 'throw some light upon the causes of the uncommon prevalence of fever in Dublin' the hospital authorities directed two medical inspectors, Dr Peebles and Mr McDowell, to undertake a special inspection of Barrack Street and Church Street, the two streets which had provided the hospital with the greatest numbers of patients during the four month period, September–December 1818

---

[54] Ibid., p. 29.
[55] Ibid., p. 31.
[56] Ibid., p. 32.
[57] J. Cheyne, *Medical Report of the Hardwicke Fever Hospital for the year ending on the 31st March 1818 including a brief account of an epidemic fever in Dublin* (Dublin, 1818), p. 50, (hereafter *Hardwicke Fever Hospital*).
[58] Ibid., p. 4.
[59] Ibid., p. 88.

32   *Dublin Slums*

(see Figure 2.3, also Chapter 8). In the case of Barrack Street the inspectors reported on its very low-lying position, on the north bank of the Liffey: 'the river at high-water is nearly on a level with the cellars', while at its eastern extremity were found yards for cattle and slaughter houses. The houses were very crowded: '52 houses contain in 390 apartments 1318 persons, of which number 32 adults are unemployed, the greater number of whom are in a state of extreme indigence'.[60] The several public houses were much frequented, and many of the cellars were used as 'public eating rooms'. The recent decrease in the numbers of soldiers barracked in the city had had serious economic repercussions, as 'soldiers and their followers' had previously afforded 'means of subsistence to many roomkeepers, who are now in great distress'. The virulence of the fever among the local prostitutes contrasted with the relative freedom from fever among the soldiers; this was accounted for by the difference in 'predisposing

Figure 2.3 Barrack Street, north city, *Exact Survey of the City and Suburbs of Dublin*, John Rocque 1756, sheet 1

[60] Ibid., p. 47.

causes' among them, for as one medical officer noted, 'the pay of the soldier is ample, he is well clothed, well fed, well lodged, and well looked after, and all his wants in health as well as in sickness are provided for'. Not so the 'women of the town'.[61] Barrack Street produced 111 cases of fever over three months, but this number was partly due to an influx of country people: 'Many of the inhabitants of Dunboyne, Maynooth and Swords, (all stations for labourers from Roscommon, Mayo, Leitrim, Sligo, Cavan and Monaghan) who laboured under fever in the month of September [1817], when they understood the nature of their illness, had themselves conveyed into Dublin' in the hope of being admitted to hospital, and by taking a night's lodging in Barrack Street or Church Street enabled the disease to get a firm footing.[62]

The survey of Barrack Street and Church Street found that conditions there were ideal for the spread of disease: wherever there were communities of the poor which had 'little connexion with the higher ranks of society' and were destitute of employment, and consequently 'ill supplied with food, clothing and fuel', and furthermore 'were so dispirited as to be indifferent to the danger of infection' the disease spread 'with celerity, and pertinaciously maintained its influence'.[63] Further outbreaks of fever could be guaranteed.

Considerable energy and intelligence had been expended on the slum question as a result of the succession of epidemics between 1798 and 1819. Obnoxious smells of all sorts, whether from the filthy bodies or bedding, or from the massed breaths in overcrowded rooms, or the overpowering stench of nearby dungheaps in dairy yards and animal entrails in slaughter houses, or the accumulation of several years of human and animal excrement in enclosed yards, were regarded as the source of disease. Despite the flaws in the miasmic theory, it provided a useful point of departure. The *rickettsia*, the parasites which cause typhus, are easily spread through the invisible means of louse excrement which dries to a fine dust; the crowded and filthy conditions which favour lice infestation are generally malodorous as well. Most of the factors which allowed such dangerous situations to exist were identified; workable and sometimes ingenious solutions offered; and good public health, economic and social reasons forwarded for their adoption. It was clear that it was necessary to go beyond the limited thoroughfare approach, literally to move into the back yards and even into the private dwellings of the people, under the heading of the 'public good'. The legislation was faulty, but simple practical measures were even more urgently required: provision of receptacles for filth, and their collection, without which imposing fines on these very poor people 'would be as inoperative as it would be unjust'.[64] Private exertion could achieve little without public help.

---

[61] Ibid., p. 51.
[62] *First Report from the Select Committee on the State of Disease and Condition of the Labouring Poor, in Ireland*, 1819, appendix p. 78.
[63] Cheyne, *Hardwicke Fever Hospital* (1818), p. 49.
[64] Cork Street Trustees (1802), p. 23.

The Diseases of the Lower Orders in Dublin, T.C. Speer, 1822

Alternative perspectives on the circumstances of the slums were provided by the physician to the Dublin Dispensary, Dr T.C. Speer, in his *Inquiry into the Causes and Character of the Diseases of the Lower Orders in Dublin*, 1822.[65] Widening the discussion beyond that of epidemic disease to the larger reality that amongst the crowded poor 'seem to exist the true cradle and depôt of general disease', he laid most emphasis on social and moral factors, while not discounting the role of the environment.[66] He himself was of Dublin birth but had spent most of his professional life in England, and sought to compare the condition of the Dublin poor with what he knew of the poor in British cities. To lend weight to his report he claimed that dispensary practice 'is perhaps the most complete introduction to the diseases and indeed to the distresses, habits and character of the lower orders of a city', a place where 'sorrows and sufferings' which 'shame will hide from the public eye' are unveiled.[67]

The climate, situation, soil and water, though 'marked with certain peculiarities' were inadequate to explain 'that vast and complicated mass of disease which [the poor of Dublin] present'.[68] Poverty was described as the chief cause of disease, with diet as 'the chief genus', both in terms of quantity and quality. Potatoes, 'always a favourite, and always easily obtained', formed 'the great barrier to the ravages of hunger, and indeed constitutes almost the only one'.[69] Tea was the other mainstay: 'it seems, indeed, the general panacea, always affording comfort, calmness and consolation; constituting not only the leading article of breakfast and supper, but often of dinner, and over its placid inspirations their happiest hours seem to be passed'.[70] Whiskey was regarded as 'a cure for all complaints, and all weathers'; taken in small quantities but on an empty stomach, 'in its intoxicating draughts their misery is forgotten'.[71] The only other addition to their diet was salt, and salt fish, usually herrings, favoured for its cheapness and 'stimulating and sapid quality'. In his expansive condemnation of this general diet Speer made no distinctions between what was morally, socially and medically good, so that the 'general indulgence in weak, watery, enervating liquids' namely tea, along with the ingrained 'habits of indolence', their preference for '*stimulating* or flavourous, rather than *nourishing* food', in the case of salt fish, their love of whiskey, and their 'carelessness and want of nourishing solids' excepting only potatoes, all tended to a multitude of illnesses, including diseased stomach and liver, 'cutaneous affections', 'wasting, emaciations, depraved habits,

---

[65] T.C. Speer, 'Medical Report containing an Inquiry into the Causes and Character of the Diseases of the Lower Orders in Dublin', *Dublin Hospital Reports*, vol. III (1822), pp. 161–200, (hereafter *Diseases of the Lower Orders*).
[66] Ibid., p. 163.
[67] Ibid., pp. 166–167.
[68] Ibid., pp. 165–166.
[69] Ibid., p. 180.
[70] Ibid., p. 183.
[71] Ibid., pp. 182–183.

and that long and melancholy list of nervous derangements connected with worn out constitutions'.[72] To further aggravate the effects of such a poor diet, Speer criticised the 'conduct of their meals' where 'little or no attention is paid to system or regularity; the periods between each are mostly accidental; fasting seems a daily exercise with them; they are quite accustomed to it'.[73]

The diet and habits of the Dublin poor were such that one would expect a decrease in population, 'and that the successions of a puny and debilitated offspring' would have contributed to its decline' but in the oldest and narrowest parts of the city 'houses are crowded with people and rooms with children, and the proportion of births to deaths appears to be increasing every year'.[74] Submission to Providence, he claimed, dominated the issue of procreation: 'Potatoes were always cheap, and women always prolific, and they seem to have a general maxim, that what God created God will provide for'.[75] This extended to a general attachment to 'the doctrine of fatalism' whereby 'they believe that their own exertions are of very little use, and that whatever happens is from an inevitable destiny' to which 'they bow submissively, and with it they are perfectly satisfied'. 'Indolent, prodigal and careless, they look not to the wants of the morrow; and if they can satisfy the common cravings of nature they appear contented'.[76]

The resilience of the hard-pressed Irish, and of the Dublin poor in particular, was presented as the lighter side of the national character, whereby the 'principle of *thinking* being so subordinate to that of *feeling*, and their principle of *feeling* being subject to such rapid changes and vicissitudes' leads to 'that freedom, lightness, and carelessness which makes them happy even in their miseries, because unmindful of them'. Their zest for life was remarkable, 'universally good natured, careless, warm in heart, hospitable, grateful', they all 'know each other and help and love each other and chat and gossip about their neighbours' affairs, much more than they *think* about their own'. However it was this very character which militated against improvement in their condition: they were too sociable to better their own individual situation, for it was maintained that *comfort* always requires a healthy selfishness.[77]

Speer confirmed the findings of earlier investigators concerning the filth of the narrow and crowded streets, and like others both before and after him had been 'obliged to wade through masses of filth enough to sicken the stoutest and strongest – masses which have remained undisturbed for months, perhaps for years, and thus generating the most putrid effluvia'.[78] Indoors the atmosphere was similarly vitiated, 'ventilation and circulation of air are completely suppressed; windows generally hermetically sealed down, crowds of beings exchanging the

[72] Ibid., pp. 181, 185.
[73] Ibid., p. 189.
[74] Ibid., p. 190.
[75] Ibid., p. 193.
[76] Ibid., pp. 195–196.
[77] Ibid., pp. 194–6.
[78] Ibid., p. 198.

exhalations of each others lungs, and thus diffusing contagion in every shape and direction'.[79]

Speer's particular contribution however was in the portrayal of a 'subculture' among the slum dwellers, where the standards of nutrition, cleanliness, tidiness, thrift, and self-interest promoted by the middle classes found little currency. 'Dirt and sloth' were compounded together so that to tackle the slum problem would require the reformation of both morals and manners.[80] While there was lots of sympathy for the plight of the poorest attending his dispensary, where 'we find poverty and disease mutual cause and effect', this articulation of the slum problem, which in effect heaped blame on the slum dwellers for the circumstances of their lives, and separated them from mainstream society, was to be an important strand in the debate.[81]

ii) Fever Reports 1830s
Cholera Epidemic and the Relief of the Poor
Mansion House Committee, Dublin 1833

An outbreak of Asiatic cholera in 1832–33 led to widespread alarm and distress, and generated a new spate of slum inquires. The provision of more hospital accommodation was one area of tension. On 27 March 1832 the Lord Lieutenant ordered that the Richmond General Penitentiary be reserved for cholera patients, but the House of Industry 'dreading the effects of any communication' between the two sought isolation measures. (see Chapter 6, Figure 6.3).[82] The House of Industry refused all requests to admit cholera patients into the general part of the institution, 'the dread of infection amongst the poor being so great' that the physicians feared some patients, still ill, would leave the establishment, and 'spread disease and panic thro' the city'.[83] But the hospital's problems were simple in comparison with the city-wide distress, which was further compounded by the failure of the public to contribute voluntarily to its relief on anything like the scale the crisis demanded. 'Melancholy accounts' overwhelmed the Mansion House Committee, the central office from which most of the funds raised were disbursed through the officers of health of the individual parishes. Under such pressure the Mansion House Committee directed four of its members to undertake a 'personal inspection into the state of the poor' on its behalf.[84] The

---

[79] Ibid., p. 193.
[80] Ibid., p. 196.
[81] Ibid., p. 167.
[82] Proceedings of the Corporation instituted for the relief of the poor and the punishing Vagabonds and Sturdy Beggars in the county of the City of Dublin, (hereafter House of Industry Proceedings), 27 March 1832; 9 August 1832.
[83] House of Industry Proceedings, 22 July 1833.
[84] White, *Report on the State of the Poor* (1833); Committee (Dublin, 1833); the committee members were: Sir William de Bathe (baronet); Rev Mr. Flanagan, (PP St Nicholas Without); Beresford Burston Smyth (barrister); Francis White (secretary).

resulting survey provides some of the most distressing pictures of life in the Dublin slums.[85]

The main body of the report consists of about fourteen case studies; each has exact address, number of inmates, occupations, recent history of contagion, and a description of the state of the dwelling, including sanitary provision. The report opens with a description of what the officers encountered in the Liberties. Typical was Hamilton's Court off Skinner's Alley (see Figure 2.1), which consisted of 'three compartments of narrow houses containing 182 inmates, principally mendicant lodgers, in abject misery and want'; the houses faced onto an open sewer without any outlet 'choked up with stagnant and putrefactive matter' and rendering the locality 'pestilential'.[86] The 172 inmates of the 'two front, four back' houses in Hassett's Gateway 'heretofore industriously employed in the woollen, cotton and silk line,' were all reduced to the lowest levels of destitution 'from the decline of those branches of trade in which they were engaged'.[87] The situation of Rowley's Court, off Hamilton's Row in the Liberties[88] was pitiful in the extreme:

The front and back houses contain between fifty and sixty abandoned females, who are in the extremest state of penury, filth and moral and physical degradation: no words can give any adequate description of their condition, or of the horror with which they are regarded by the neighbourhood, and by the Officers of Health, who will not even enter the premises. In one of those wretched abodes I saw three women lying on dung with scarcely a covering, and four more of them sitting opposite to an open hearth without fire, eating some broken potatoes off the earthen floor.[89]

It was claimed that 'other parts of the Liberty are similarly circumstanced, in consequence of their unemployed population, and by an influx of poor from various parts of the city and county who crowd into these districts where they can obtain cheap lodgings.[90]

In the vicinity of King Street, north of the Liffey (Figure 2.3), similar cases awaited the inspectors, with countless foul ashpits, 'dirt holes' and privies, many with no private sewer. A maze of dwellings was found behind several of the main houses, with access only through the hall door or a narrow winding entry arched over, to courts and inner courts, including ruinous houses greatly overcrowded.[91] Added to this were the dark wet cellars into which every kind of filth drained, and although the most unhealthy of dwellings were occupied by hundreds of families.

---

[85] Ibid., p. 12.
[86] Ibid., p. 12.
[87] Ibid., p. 13.
[88] This court was, according to White, in the parish of of St. Luke and St. Nicholas Without (Figure 2.1); there was a court of the same name off Denzille Street, a location which would also suit the facts recounted.
[89] White, *Report on the State of the Poor* (1833), p. 13.
[90] Ibid., p. 14.
[91] Ibid., p. 15.

But the distribution of a 'dense, pauper population', where inevitably 'disease is engendered and most frequently assumes a malignant character', was not at all confined to the oldest and most decayed parts of the city. To the amazement of the inspectors they found 'even in the immediate neighbourhood of some of the most respectable parts of the city' extremes of wretchedness which even the Liberties could not surpass. In Sycamore Alley, off Dame Street, were found 235 'miserable inhabitants' divided between six houses; in one house there had been 26 cases of cholera; in six houses 100 cases. In Leinster Lane and courts off Merrion Street and Clare Street were found families 'equally wretched with those already described', such as in Lacy's Lane where the situation of the residents, mostly female, was described as 'nothing but one scene of filth, misery and want' despite being '*in the vicinity of one of our best squares, within the wealthiest parish in the Metropolis*' (*sic*).[92]

The widespread poverty problem was exacerbated by the rapacity of some landlords, who 'exact their rent with great severity, compelling the inmates to pawn their clothing to satisfy the weekly demands', but themselves making no effort to repair the premises, or keep the ashpits or sewers in a proper state.[93]

The gentlemen investigating on behalf of the Mansion House Committee concluded that the 'periodical visitations of sickness' that Dublin, in common with the rest of Ireland, experienced were no longer matter for wonderment; the extent and nature of the poverty problem ensured that the situation could not be otherwise.[94]

Poor Inquiry (Ireland) 1833

In his role as member of the *Commission of Inquiry into the Poorer Classes in Ireland*, which among other aims sought to assess the extent and causes of begging in Dublin, Francis White again contributed to publicising the condition of the city slums.[95] Along with Frederick Solly Flood he sought out 'some of the most wretched parts of the city where they were informed that beggars, and the very poorest classes, resided' to judge for themselves what the average gains from mendicancy might be. Although expecting scenes of distress they were stunned by what they found. Women greatly outnumbered men in the catalogue of distress: by eleven to one among those reliant on the pittance supplied by the Mendicity Institution (see Chapter 6) totally dominating begging in the city, and found in the most unthinkable slum conditions.[96] Typical was the case of Fordham's Alley, between the Coombe and Newmarket in the Liberties (see Figure 2.1). Here 'in regular succession' they inspected most of the houses

[92] Ibid., p. 20.
[93] Ibid., p. 19.
[94] Ibid., p. 21.
[95] *Poor Inquiry (Ireland)*, 1836, Appendix (C), part II, 'Report on the City of Dublin', p. 27* [evidence collected 1833].
[96] Ibid.

between the hours of 7–9am. Outwardly the houses appeared 'ruinous, and falling rapidly to decay'. Inside 'a complete staircase was not to be found, and in attempting to gain the upper rooms, amid the filth and darkness which prevailed, the greatest care was necessary to clamber up by the help of logs of wood, which formed a substitute for the usual means of ascending'. In one first-floor room, about 9 feet by 12, 'the *light struggled* for admittance through a hole in the wall where once had been a window' (*sic*), the rest of the opening was stuffed with scraps of wood and paper providing 'little or no protection from the inclemency of the weather'. Gradually the commissioners distinguished the occupants: in the farthest corner stretched on a litter a mother of about sixty years, and her two daughters, 'their emaciated forms bore testimony to the assertion that they had scarcely tasted food for three days'. Another corner held 'a woman too ill to move', with her two daughters, who relied on the Mendicity for their daily food, and a weekly allowance of 2*s* 6*d*. On yet another 'little heap of straw' lay an old woman, 'whose tattered garments and squalid appearance at once betokened her mendicant profession', while 'two other equally wretched objects' were also present. The 'mistress of the room' had risen to prepare breakfast for seven of the occupants from three potatoes and a pennyworth of bread. This landlady, an occasional servant, 'being out of work was not less an object of commiseration that her lodgers', had resorted to subletting the room at 3*d* per lodger per week, however, she was then in arrears of 1*s* 6*d* which she found impossible to make up. The furnishing in 'this abode of misery' was listed: an old table, two shelves, an earthenware pan, a tea-pot, and a basin which contained the potatoes. In another room the commissioners found 'a poor forlorn creature, who declared she had not a friend upon earth'. A charwoman, who had 'met with an accident from being run against by a car' her damaged leg 'presented a frightful oedimatous swelling' and she lay on 'some straw worn to dust' until 'death should release her from her sufferings'. And as the two gentlemen who conducted this enquiry stressed: 'Such was the condition of almost every inhabitant of a street, which a witness who had passed in it the whole of his life, remembered to have resounded from one end to the other with the glad sounds of industry, but where now out of 700 inhabitants, not six families maintained themselves by their own labour, and in which the Assistant Commissioners did not, after a long personal investigation, discover one blanket'.[97] This bleak picture was not confined to the few streets surveyed, but assuredly could be found among hundreds of other houses 'whose outward appearance was not better than those of Fordham's-alley'.[98]

Thomas Willis, *Facts connected with the social and sanitary conditions of the working classes in the city of Dublin*, 1845

An incisive and highly critical report by Thomas Willis, guardian of the North Dublin Union, was yet another effort to drag the slum question into the public

[97] Ibid., pp. 27*–28*.
[98] Ibid., p. 28*.

domain. He undertook an investigation into whether the high mortality within the workhouse was any worse than that prevailing in the district immediately outside (see Chapter 3). Reporting directly before the cataclysm of the great famine (February 1843), Willis wrote passionately of the scandal that in a country so blessed by nature in its soil and climate, and part of the most powerful and wealthy empire yet assembled, the great mass of the people should be sunk 'in the lowest depths of misery and consequent degradation', apparently '"without the pale" of protection and civilization,' in a state 'altogether barbarous'. Those in Dublin were not any worse off than the people of the provinces, but 'all alike are sunk into that state of abject misery for which there is no parallel in any country in Europe'.[99]

The realities of life within the single-roomed tenement were spelled out by Willis, in relation to his area of special study, the parish of St Michan's (see Figure 8.1, Chapter 8):

Within this space the food of these wretched beings, such as it is, must be prepared; within this space they must eat and drink; men, women and children must strip, dress, sleep. In cases of illness the calls of nature must be relieved; and when death releases one of the inmates, the corpse must of necessity remain for days within the room.[100]

Addressing his findings to 'those who take an interest in the well-being of their fellows' in the hope that 'the benevolent of every shade of politics', who 'in the intervals of party strife, might assemble to devise means for alleviating at least some portion of the accumulated misery of our poor brethren', Willis could see no possibility of reform unless the political will was there.[101] The scandal was now too well known.

(iii) Census of Ireland, Reports and Surveys 1841–1854
William Wilde, *Special Sanitary Report upon the City of Dublin*, 1841/1851

The publication of the first highly detailed and reliable all-Ireland census in 1841 ushered in a new era in social investigation. The availability of basic information, such as demographic size and structure, occupation, place of birth, class of accommodation and levels of literacy, provided social surveyors and philanthropists with a mountain of statistics from which they could quarry as suited the purpose in hand. From the outset the Irish census commissioners went well beyond enumeration and classification alone. Resourceful and energetic contributors such as surgeon William Wilde investigated how the census data could be utilised in conjunction with other facts (such as mortality statistics) to describe the state of Ireland on a sound scientific basis. The housing situation throughout the island was to receive particular attention, while the slum conditions and high

---

[99] Willis, *Social and Sanitary Condition* (1845), pp. 16–17, 21.
[100] Ibid., p. 45.
[101] Ibid., p. v.

death rates of Dublin had earned such notoriety by 1841 that a *Special Sanitary Report on the City of Dublin* was commissioned.

House Classification

The census commissioners expressed the opinion that a census ought to be a 'social survey not a bare enumeration', but were constrained from making 'searching and minute' inquiries by the fear of non-cooperation among the people, who were unlikely to appreciate how personal information would be rendered anonymous when amassed and averaged out. However, the directive to make a return of houses was interpreted broadly to include details on the quality of accommodation each family was provided with, the commissioners hoping thus 'to throw some useful light upon the general condition of the community, as there can be no more obvious indication of the advances and condition of the people than improvement in the quality of their residence'.[102] In practice the census administrators used the following criteria in assessing the value or condition of a house: extent (measured by number of rooms), quality (measured by number of windows), solidity (shown by the material of its walls and roofs). The fourth or lowest class comprised one-roomed, thatched, mud cabins without windows. Slightly better, but still lowly were third class houses, mud cabins with two to four rooms and windows. The typical second class house in an urban context was 'in a small street', having from five to nine rooms and windows, while 'first class houses were all those of a superior description'.[103]

Multiple occupancy made that classification insufficient in itself, as a family which had sole possession of a fourth class hovel was possibly no worse off than a family sharing a single room with perhaps two other families and lodgers, in what was technically a 'first class' house. This limitation was overcome by considering not alone the house quality, but the number of other families with which this house was shared. Thus where more than five families occupied a first class house, each family was judged to have fourth class accommodation. Similarly, third class accommodation was entered where a first class house was occupied by four or five families, where a second class house was occupied by two or three families, or where a third class house was occupied by one family.[104] Table 2.3 summarises the classes of house accommodation recorded for Dublin city in the censuses of 1841 and 1851.

Street Classification

The classification of house accommodation was taken up by the surgeon William Wilde in his *Special Sanitary Report on the City of Dublin*, appended to the

---

[102] *Report of the Census Commissioners, Ireland* (1841), p. vi.
[103] Ibid., p. xiv.
[104] Ibid., xvi.

In houses of the	City of Dublin civic district								Total			
	Number of families occupying											
	1st. class acc.		2nd. class acc.		3rd. class acc.		4th. class acc.		Families		Houses	
	1841	1851	1841	1851	1841	1851	1841	1851	1841	1851	1841	1851
1st. class	5605	5604	4559	4609	4962	6131	12050	16104	27176	32448	10171	10827
2nd. class			3853	4736	6093	6742	10151	11341	20097	22819	8289	9693
3rd. class					1242	1457	815	545	2057	2002	1494	1680
4th. class							181	49	181	49	155	44
Total	5605	5604	8412	9345	12297	14330	23197	28039	49511	57318	20109	22244
%	11.3	9.8	17.0	16.3	24.8	25.0	46.9	48.9	100	100		

Source: Census of Ireland, Table of house accommodation 1841 (table V, p.26) 1851 (table V, p.21)

Table 2.3 Number of families which occupy each class of house accommodation, City of Dublin 1841, 1851.

census of 1841 and revised and extended for publication with the census of 1851. Regarding the division into wards as too crude a basis on which to distinguish the better-off areas from the slums, Wilde created his own street classification, the 1851 version of which is mapped as Figure 2.4 (Table 2.4) This street scheme was based on 'their wealth, character, more or less healthy position, and the occupations of their population'.[105]

'First class private streets' included all the squares, principal private streets, and residences of the 'highest classes of society', but excluded associated lanes, mews, passages &c.. The highest concentration of solidly top class residences was to be found in the south eastern quarter, centred around St Stephen's Green, Merrion Square and Leeson Street, while the north eastern sector included individual streets and squares of similarly high status, such as Henrietta Street, Eccles Street and Mountjoy Square. 'Second class private streets' were likewise occupied by 'the upper ranks of society' but inferior as respects locality and houses, many in 'less healthy' locations, and some with shops intermixed, such as York Street, Dominick Street Lower and Gloucester Street. Most of the second class residential streets (Figure 2.4) are situated close to those of the first class,

[105] William Wilde, 'Special Sanitary Report on the City of Dublin', *Census of Ireland 1841*, pp. lxviii.

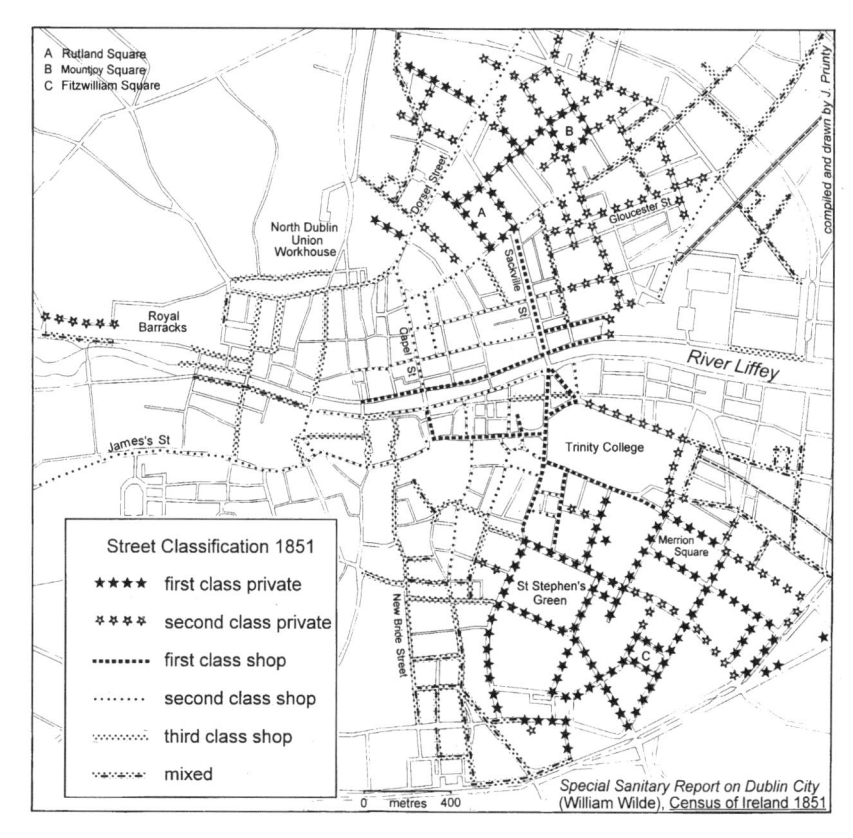

Figure 2.4 Classification of major Dublin streets, William Wilde, 1851

again dominating both the north east and south east sectors. However, a steady shift in favour of the south eastern quarter can be traced from the changes in status between 1841 and 1851 (Table 2.4, streets entered in italics). In 1841 both the north city and the south city could each claim 19 first class residential streets. By 1851 there were 11 first class residential streets on the north side, as others such as Gardiner Street and Gloucester Street Upper and Lower, had been downgraded to second class residential. The south city total moved up to 25 first class residential streets, with the addition of new developments such as Earlsfort Terrace, Harcourt Terrace, Wilton Square and Wilton Terrace.

The highest ranking retail streets link together the south and north city high-status residential areas: from Grafton Street, Dawson Street and Dame Street through to Bachelor's Walk, Eden Quay and Abbey Street Lower, with Sackville Street providing the principal north city focus (Figure 2.4). The division between 'private' and 'shop' streets was not always clear; among some of the 'first class shop streets' private residences were to be found, as in Dawson Street, Lower Baggot Street and Sackville Street. The distinction between residential

Dublin Slums

1st Class Private Streets		2nd Class Private Streets		1st Class Shop Streets	
South.	North.	South.	North.	South.	North.
Adelaide-road.	Cavendish-row.	Baggot-street Lower (part of).	*Belvedere-place.*	Baggot-street Lower (part of).	*Abbey-street Lower.*
Castle-yard, Upper and Lower.	Denmark-street Great Eccles "	Brunswick-st. Great (part of).	Beresford " Blackhall-street.	Clare "	Bachelor's-walk. Eden-quay.
Earlsfort-terrace.	Gardiner's-place.	*Harcourt-place.*	Blessington "	College-green.	Ormond " Lower.
Ely-place.	Gardiner's-row.	Harrington-street.	Buckingham " Up.	*College-street.*	Ormond " Upper.
Fitzwilliam-place, Sth.	George's-street Great.	Holles "	Charles " Gt.	Dame "	Sackville-street Lr.
Fitzwilliam-square.	Granby-row.	Merrion " Lr.	Cumberland " Nth. Lower.	Dawson "	Sackville " Up.
Fitzwilliam-street Lr.	Henrietta-street.	Molesworth "	Cumberland " Nth. Upper.	D'Olier "	
Fitzwilliam " Up.	Mountjoy-square.	Mount " Lr.	Dominick " Lr.	Essex-bridge.	
Harcourt "	Rutland "	Pembroke " Lr.	*Fitzgibbon "*	Foster-place.	
Harcourt terrace.	Temple-street Upper.	Peter-place.	*Frederick "*	Grafton-street.	
Hatch-street.		Warrington-place.	*Gardiner "*	Leinster "	
Herbert-place.		Westland-row.	*Gloucester " Up. and Lower.*	Morrion-row.	
Herbert-street.		York-street.	Grenville "	Nassau-street.	
Hume "			Hardwicke-place.	Parliament "	
Kildare-place.			Hardwicke-street.	Westmoreland "	
Kildare-street.			Margaret-place.		
Lesson " Lr.			Montpelier-hill.		
Merrion-square.			Nelson-street.		
Merrion-street Upper.			Richmond-place.		
Mount " Cres.			Richmond-street.		
Mount " Upper.			Russell-place.		
Pembroke " Upper.			Russell-street.		
Stephen's-green.			Rutland " Upper.		
Trinity College.			Sherrand " Lower.		
Wilton-square and terrace.			Sherrand " Upper.		
			Synnott place.		
			Talbot-street.		

1st Class Shop Streets		2nd Class Shop Streets		Mixed Streets	
South.	North.	South.	North.	South.	North.
Anglesea-street.	*Abbey-street Middle.*	Bride-street.	Barrack-street	Bishop-street	*Bayview.*
Anne "	Abbey " Upper.	*Bridgefoot-street.*	Brunswick " North.	*Brunswick " Great (part of).*	*Berkeley-street Lr.*
Aston's-quay.	Amiens "	*Cook "*	Church "	Camden " Lower.	*Berkeley " Up.*
Aungier-street.	Arran-quay.	Cuffe "	Ellis's-quay.	Canden " Upper.	Blackhall-place.
Bridge " Lower.	Bolton-street.	Fishamble "	Hay-market.	*Charlemont-mall.*	*Brighton-cottages.*
Bridge " Upper.	Britain " Great.	Fleet "	King-street.	*Charlemont-place.*	*Charleville-mall.*
Castle "	*Capel "*	Johnston's place.	Moore "	Charlemont-street	*Cobourg-place.*
Christ Church-place.	Dorset " Lower.	Kevin-street Cross.	North-wall.	*Charlotte "*	Dominick-street Up.
Church-lane.	Dorset " Upper.	Kevin " Lower.	Pembroke-quay.	Cumberland " Sth.	*Edward-terrace.*
Cork-hill.	*Drumcondra-road (part of).*	Kevin " Upper.	Queen-street.	Denzille "	*Flood's-buildings.*
Corn-market.	Earl-street.	King " South.	Smithfield.	Digges "	*George's-place.*
Crampton-quay.	*Henry "*	Mercer "	Tighe-street.	Erne " Lr.	Granby-row Upper.
Duke-street.	*Inns-quay.*	*New-row West.*		Erne " Up.	*Hackett's-buildings.*
Essex-quay.	Mary's-abbey.	Redmond's-hill.		Frederick "	Marlborough-street.
Eustace-street.	*Mary-street.*	Stephen-street Lower.		French "	Mecklenburgh " Up.
George's " Great.	Pill-lane.	Stephen " Upper.		Grand Canal "	*Mountjoy " Lr.*
Hawkins's "	Stafford-street.	Werburgh "		*Grantham "*	*Mountjoy " Mid.*
High "		Wexford "		Gratton "	*Newcomen-place.*
James's-gate.		Winetavern "		*Hamilton-row.*	*Newcomen-terrace.*
James's-street.		Wood-quay.		*Harcourt-road.*	*North-strand.*
Merchants'-quay.				*Heytesbury-street.*	*Oriel-street Lower.*
Mount brown.				*Heytesbury-terrace.*	*Oriel " Upper.*
Palace-street.				*Lennox-street.*	*Palmerston-place.*
St. Andrew "				Lincoln-place.	Parkgate-street.
Suffolk "				Peter-street.	*Portland "*
Thomas "				*Pleasant "*	*Preston "*
Trinity "				Queen's-sqaure.	Rutland " Lr.
Wellington-quay.				Richmond-street.	*Sackville-gardens.*
Wicklow-street.				Ship " Gt.	*Serville-place.*
William "				*Synge "*	Summer-hill.
				Usher's island.	Summer-hill Lower.
				Usher's-quay.	*Summer-hill parade.*
				Wentworth place.	*Summer-street.*
					Waterloo-buildings.
					Waterloo-terrace.

Key
italics not classed in 1841
italics changed class since 1841

Table 2.4 Classification of major Dublin streets, William Wilde, 1851.

and commercial streets became even less definite as the status dropped. 'Second class shop streets' were inferior to the class above, but 'generally in the vicinity', such as South Great George's Street and William Street (south side) and Henry Street and Abbey Street (north side). Two of the oldest city thoroughfares, stretching to the north (Bolton Street / Dorset Street) and to the west (Thomas Street / James Street) were also classed as second class shop streets, each with a long tradition of grocers, bakers, victuallers, vintners, innkeepers and provision dealers of all sorts. The 'third class shop streets' were 'generally inhabited by the lowest class of traders, huxters, and are also the residences of artizans'. In figure 2.4 a clear pattern westwards can be traced, including the area west of Stephen's Green (South King Street, Mercer Street, Bride Street), behind the more valuable quayside premises (Fishamble Street, Bridgefoot Street), and around Smithfield market and the nearby barracks area (North King Street, Queen Street, Barrack Street) all classed as 'third class shop streets'. The final division, headed 'mixed streets' included 'small shops and the private residences of the middling classes', such as Bishop Street, Camden Street, Charlemont Street (south city) and Marlborough Street, Berkeley Street and Mountjoy Street Upper (north side). There was a large expanse of the city excluded in the above classification (Table 2.4, Figure 2.4); these 'small streets, lanes and alleys' not otherwise classified, were considered on the basis of the ward to which they belonged.[106] The exclusion of the entire south western Liberties quarter is itself testimony to the difficulty inherent in classifying individual streets in this long-established industrial quarter with its dense population, mixed landuses and complex morphology (see Figures 2.1, 2.2).

Average Annual Mortality

The distinct social geography which Wilde identified through his street classification, he then used to analyse the average annual mortality rate for the city, to disturbing effect (Figure 2.5). Allowing for the limitations of the mortality statistics prior to compulsory registration, and the inbuilt distortion where large numbers of persons died in city hospitals and workhouses, enormous discrepancies were still established beyond question: percentage mortality for first class private streets was .75% for south city first class private streets, and .82% for the same class north of the Liffey; third class shop streets returned mortality rates of 2.01% and 2.14% south and north respectively. The minor streets and lanes of Wood Quay returned a rate of 2.16%, and Royal Exchange 2.38%. This translated into averages of 1 death per 132.8 persons on the south and 1 death per 122 persons on the north city first class streets, while in Inns Quay ward, for example, the rate was 1 death per 40.5 persons. But even these figures did not fully represent the extent to which life was 'disposable' in the poorer areas. In

---

[106] William Wilde, 'Special Sanitary Report on the City of Dublin', *Census of Ireland 1851*, pp. 479–480.

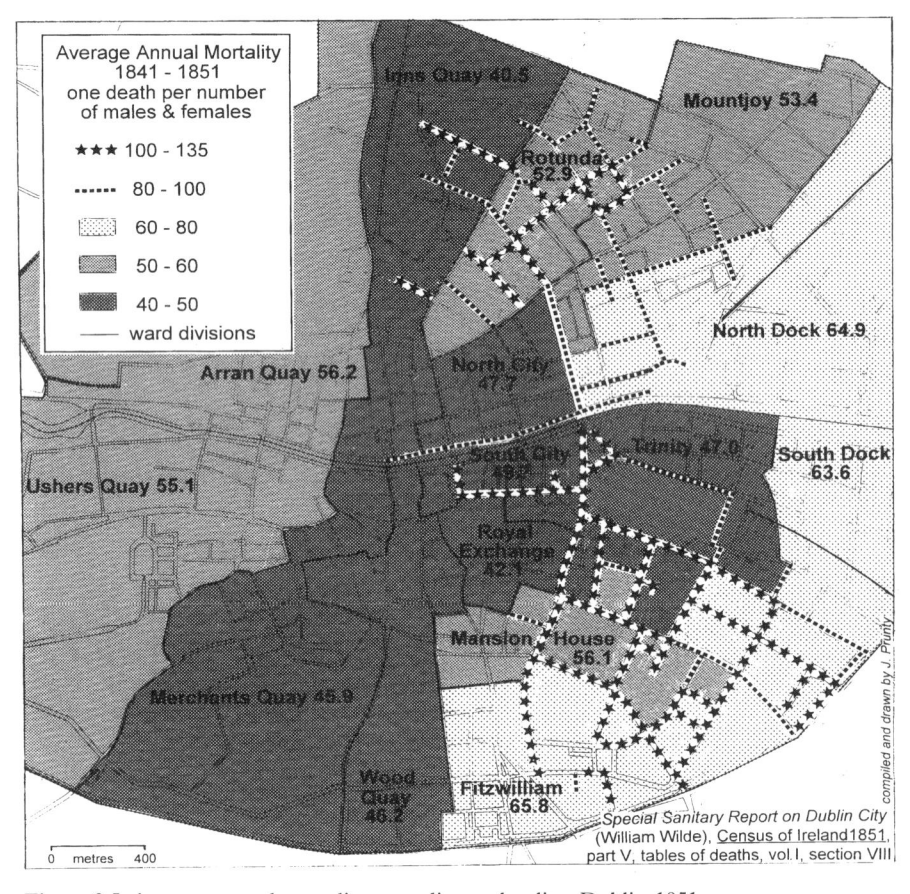

Figure 2.5 Average annual mortality according to locality, Dublin 1851

the well-to-do streets the average age of death was 30–35 years; in the third class shop streets and the back alleys of the inner city wards, the average age at death was 5–10 years, with South City ward and Trinity ward returning the scandalous range of 1–5 years. The massive loss of infant life in the slums could be illustrated in the case of South City ward: among a total baptised population of 1,076, at least 222 were dead before their first birthday, a further 327 before their fifth birthday, and another 113 before the age of ten, ie: 62% of all children born had died within the first ten years of life. The comparable figure for an average first class residential street, north or south, was 30%. And the slum figures were undoubtedly understated, as far more of 'the poor labouring under disease' were removed to public or charitable hospitals where they died, and thus were not included in these statistics, while the wealthy generally died on their own premises. Wilde upheld that not alone were the 'results of locality' essential influences in determining the geography of death, but that slum areas suffered across the entire range of zymotic or infectious diseases.

Wilde followed this geographical analysis of mortality with an attempt to correlate profession or calling with life expectancy, and to measure the influence of locality in hastening or delaying death. Higher figures were returned for clergymen and medical doctors than their respectable addresses would lead one to expect, but this was a result of their unusual exposure to infectious disease; legal practitioners had the greatest longevity of all, many living to 'extreme old age'. Second class shopkeepers were peculiarly hit by infectious disease, while dressmakers as a group were also particularly vulnerable. The great mass of persons classed as 'third class families' undertaking a wide range of trades but united by their common habitation in the most unhealthy locations, were by far the most susceptible to disease and to death in childbirth, their average age at death being 1–5 years.[107]

Wilde's novel efforts to link mortality with the social geography of the city faced some stiff and very public opposition, such as that of John Aldridge, medical doctor.[108] In the absence of a proper register of deaths, Aldridge dismissed Wilde's calculations as mere probabilities, and the huge discrepancy in deaths between first and third class streets he regarded as utterly contrived, as he claimed due regard had not been taken of the numbers of wealthy persons who leave their city residence to die in the country or in other lands, nor of the number of servants and governesses of the first class streets who however die in hospitals or poor lodgings. While firstly doubting whether 'the unhealthiness of the city, in comparison with that of the country, is due to structural defects that are capable of being amended'[109] Aldridge then grudgingly admits that matters such as sewers and water supply *'have* great influence in shortening the term of human existence'. However, even after this admission, he claimed that 'the true rates of mortality' between the wealthy and poor streets 'are nearer equal', as disease spreads into the streets of the wealthy, affecting many a 'stout barrister' or 'aristocratic girl'.[110] Undue notice had been taken, he claimed, of the sanitary and living arrangements of the 'poor and ragged and ill fed inhabitant of the cellar or garret'.[111] Aldridge condemned as amateurish contemporary investigations into the condition of the Dublin poor, the 'unaided and desultory inquiries of philanthropic individuals' such as that undertaken by Wilde. While Aldridge's criticisms are very poorly founded – most of those who published inquiries into the state of the poor had impeccable professional credentials, as clergymen, medical officers and doctors – nevertheless he represents one strain of opinion, namely that the whole question of the slums had been overstated, in any case what mattered were the lives of the wealthy, useful rate-paying members of society, the public were tiring of the constant call on their emotions, their conscience

---

[107] Wilde 'Special Sanitary Report' (1851), pp. 479–502.
[108] John Aldridge, *Review of the Sanitary Condition of Dublin*, (Dublin, 1847); first printed in the *Dublin Quarterly Journal of Medical Science*, May 1847.
[109] Ibid., pp. 13, 16.
[110] Ibid., p. 17.
[111] Ibid., p. 16.

and their purse, and really the solution should be resigned to the anonymous hands of government, whose 'duty and prerogative' it is to protect the health of the nation.[112]

iv) Mapping Social Areas, Dublin 1850–1854
Griffith's Valuation, Dublin 1854: houses valued under £10

The General Valuation of Ireland, directed by Richard Griffith, was a country-wide undertaking, by which all land and buildings were to be valued for the purpose of assessing local rates, using the administrative framework of the poor law unions and electoral divisions, and published in full (1838–c.1862). In the case of Dublin city, information was published in 1854 on the basis of the 15 wards which together formed the municipal area, extending to the Royal Canal on the north side and the Grand Canal to the south. The valuation was based on a detailed survey of the city, recording the names of occupiers as well as immediate lessors, with each entry exactly located on the accompanying five feet Ordnance Survey sheets. It was intended to be revised at intervals; however no subsequent full-scale revision took place, and we are reliant on the field books of the valuers and the hand-written revisions entered on the valuation maps for all subsequent changes.[113] As an invaluable source for reconstructing past geographies, they have been exploited by John Martin, who first mapped each of the city wards separately, street by street, and from this produced an overall map of social areas of the city.[114] Sample extracts from the valuation maps feature later in this study: Ormond Market (Figure 4.2), the south and north Dublin union workhouses (Figures 6.2, 6.3), and Church Street and Cole's Lane (Figures 8.8, 8.10).

Figure 2.6 maps the distribution of all low value housing, according to Griffith's Valuation of 1854. The £10 value has been selected as a cut-off point on the basis of the Corporation franchise, ie: to elect members to Dublin Corporation, one had to be the occupier of premises in the borough rated £10 or upwards, and also have three years' continuous residence in the city. That led to a very small pool of voters, calculated in 1885 as less than 2% of the city's residents.[115]

While this identifies all premises the occupants of which were excluded from active involvement in civic life, it cannot be considered the only key to areas of low status housing. The practice of subdivision led to persons having third or fourth class accommodation in houses of the first or second class, as identified in the census (Wilde, 1841, 1851 see Table 2.3). The case of houses valued over

---

[112] Ibid.
[113] For a typical call for revaluation see Charles Dawson, 'The Valuation of the City of Dublin,' *Soc. Stat. Inq. Soc. Ire. Jn.*, 10, 77, (1897), pp. 320–325.
[114] John H. Martin, *Aspects of the Social Geography of Dublin City in the Mid Nineteenth Century*, unpublished MA thesis in Geography (UCD, 1973).
[115] *Third Report of HM Commissioners for Inquiring into the Housing of the Working Classes*, Minutes of Evidence &c., Ireland, 1885, C–4547–I, qs. 21,768–21,770; 21,942–21,950.

£10 but in tenements, which become an increasingly significant element of the housing market in the second half of the century, will be dealt with in Chapters 4 and 8. Figure 2.6 also excludes some very poor single-room accommodation which was to be found in lowly commercial streets such as Francis Street, where shoemakers, curled-hair manufacturers, new-milk dairy men and rag-and-bone dealers had their businesses. As many such premises were valued at over the £10 limit, and their commercial standing masked whatever tenement accommodation was also present, they cannot be fairly represented either in maps of low-value housing or of tenement distribution. Figure 2.6 therefore cannot be regarded as a definitive slum map, but as a useful guide to the lowest quality housing, and the closest such construction possible in the absence of household census data for this period.

Dublin City, 1854

The most striking aspect of the city's housing pattern (Figure 2.6) was the widespread distribution of low-value residences. There was practically no part of the built-up area which did not include some low-value housing. However, distinct patterns can be discerned. On the south side the greatest concentrations of housing valued under £10 were found in the oldest parts of the city. In the medieval core, around the Castle, Christ Church Cathedral, Cook Street, Back Lane, and behind Fishamble Street were significant clusters of poor housing, while the transitional area between St Stephen's Green and the Liberties proper had significant pockets of poor housing behind the principal thoroughfares. The Liberties, the extensive south-city area west of the medieval core, and the focus of Whitelaw's survey, had the greatest concentration of housing valued under £10 in the entire city. Here decayed eighteenth century housing such as that in Ward's Hill, New Row (Plate 2.1) was common. The density of housing was remarkable, with literally every square foot of land behind the main thoroughfares commandeered. In Coles Alley off Tripoli, for example, 27 houses valued between £2 and £5 10s were packed tightly together, along with sheds and yards (Figure 2.2). Along important arteries such as James's Street and the Coombe, tenements were intermixed with lowly commercial premises.

Figure 2.6 reveals an extensive network of poor courts and alleys off Townsend Street, creating an enclave of slum housing in the wedge between the river and the northern boundary of Trinity College, as in the much larger 'East End' sector in London. A similarly poor area was to be found on the north bank of the Liffey. A view of Dublin in 1846 (Plate 2.2), gives an impression of the local morphology of these dockside slum areas.

On the north side between Sheriff Street and Mayor Street West the General Valuation lists at least 34 courts and laneways, each with its own complement of poor cottage dwellings, average valuation £2 15s. This irregular configuration of cottages and small houses hidden behind the quayside warehouses, competes for space with vitriol and 'old vinegar' works, coal yards, dairy yards, pig yards, cattle

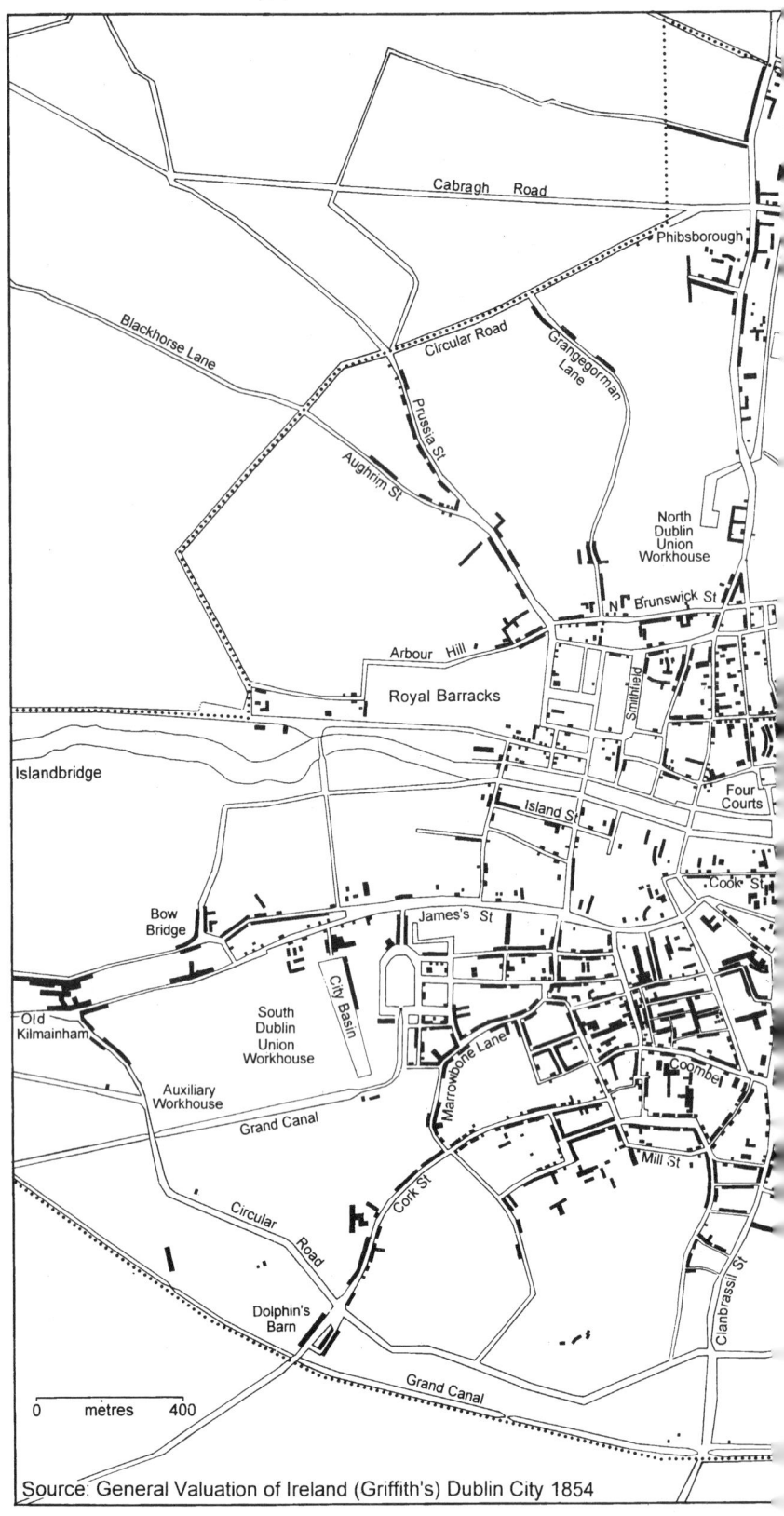

Figure 2.6 Distribution of housing valued at under £10, Dublin 1854

Source: General Valuation of Ireland (Griffith's) Dublin City 1854

House Valuation 1854

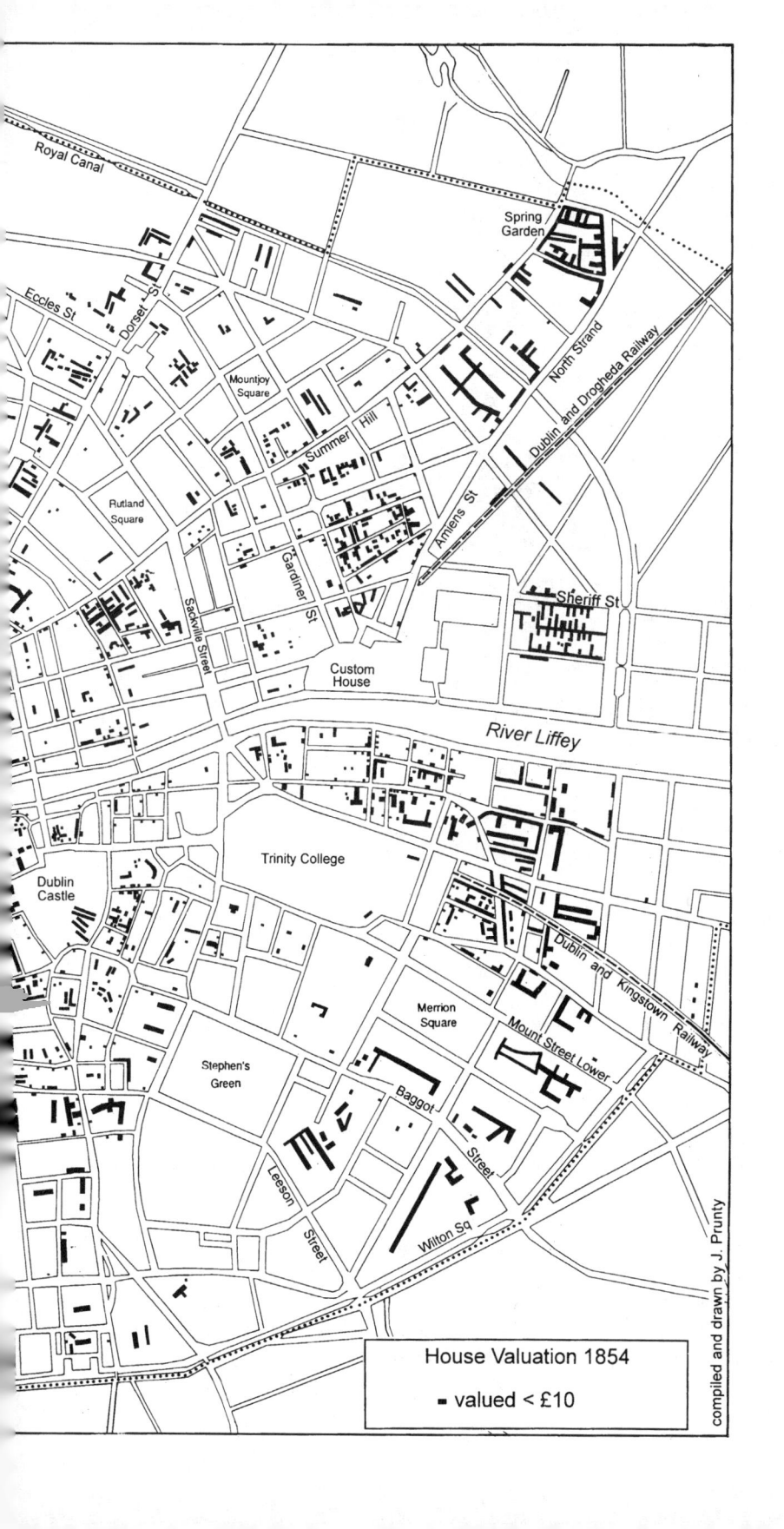

■ valued < £10

compiled and drawn by J. Prunty

Plate 2.1 Ward's Hill, New Row, Irish Architectural Archive

sheds, a railway carriage factory, and open land described as 'waste' or 'building ground'. Insignificant housing straggles out towards the north east, in association with the railway and the canal, along Amiens Street into the North Strand, and tracing the line of the Ballybough Road (aptly, the road to *Baile Bocht*, the settlement of the poor, the 'Irishtown' of the 'English' city). This low-lying area to the north east of Mountjoy Square (and the associated high-status housing of the Gardiner estate) included Spring Garden and Taaffe's Village, which was appropriately titled 'mud village' on the Campbell/Taylor map of 1811.

On the south dock the intermixing of obnoxious land uses with residences of low value behind City Quay is also evident in Figure 2.6. The railway lines and stations on both sides of the city (1834 Dublin–Kingstown; 1844 Dublin–Drogheda, Plate 2.2), reinforced rather than created this distinct social geography, further isolating the mixed docks working-class housing areas and ensuring their continued environmental unattractiveness. In the vicinity of Westland Row station on the south side were innumerable small pockets of poor housing: along Sandwith Street, Hanover Street East, Cumberland Street South and Boyne Street and the lanes and courts associated with them. A complex courtyard formation characterised this area, with much infilling hidden behind terraces of three and four storey houses. The parish priest of St Andrew's, Westland Row, (the church which adjoins the Dublin and Kingstown railway station visible in

Plate 2.2 North and south docks, view of Dublin city published 1846, TCD

Plate 2.3 Church Street, view of Dublin city published 1846, TCD

Plate 2.2, southside), spoke of such enclaves of squalid poverty within this, 'the richest parish in the city', with two, three, sometimes more families in one small room, 'the bed, straw or shavings, sometimes neither; the clothing the rags they have on them during the day'. Such scenes could be witnessed any day in 'Bass Place in the rere of Merrion Square, Leeson Place in the rere of Stephen's Green. All the lanes off Townsend Street, Temple Bar, the streets between Townsend Street and the Quays, the lanes off the Quays'.[116]

Other north city concentrations of low-value housing (as discussed in Chapter 8) focused around the axes of Gloucester, Mecklenburgh and Montgomery Streets, in the lanes and alleyways to the north of Dorset Street, and to the west of Sackville Mall around the old clothes markets of Moore Street and Coles Lane (Figure 2.6). There was also an extensive poor area around the old Ormond Market, with its fish, fruit, vegetable, potato and egg markets; low value housing continues north/northwestwards from Ormond Market until halted by the

[116] Canon Gregory Lynch to Dr. Cullen, 23 May 1861, DDA: file 1, 340/1 no. 78.

institutional sector dominated by the North Dublin Union workhouse and associated hospitals, Grangegorman/Richmond prison and lunatic asylum, and the Royal Canal harbour, subsequently the Broadstone railway station. Plate 2.3, which shows this area to the rear of the Four Courts and crossed by Church Street, illustrates the extent to which these institutions dominate the geography of the north western part of the city. The Royal Barracks further to the west (Plate 2.4, now the National Museum at Collins Barracks) continues this type of domination, its sheer scale and its unsavoury associations (see Chapter 8) very effectively discouraging high-class residential development in this district. It is not surprising that the routeways which border these institutions are lined with low value houses or cabins, such as along Blackhorse Lane, Grangegorman Lane, Stoneybatter, Phibsborough, and Aughrim and Prussia streets.

South Western Sector, Dublin 1854

The pattern of low-value housing in the south-western sector is best explained by reference to the industrial heritage of the area, as depicted in Figure 2.7. The framework for development in this locality was provided by a series of ancient routeways, and a network of fast-flowing streams and man-made watercourses, a pattern which underwent substantial revision at various intervals, such as in the

Plate 2.4 Royal Barracks, view of Dublin city published 1846, TCD

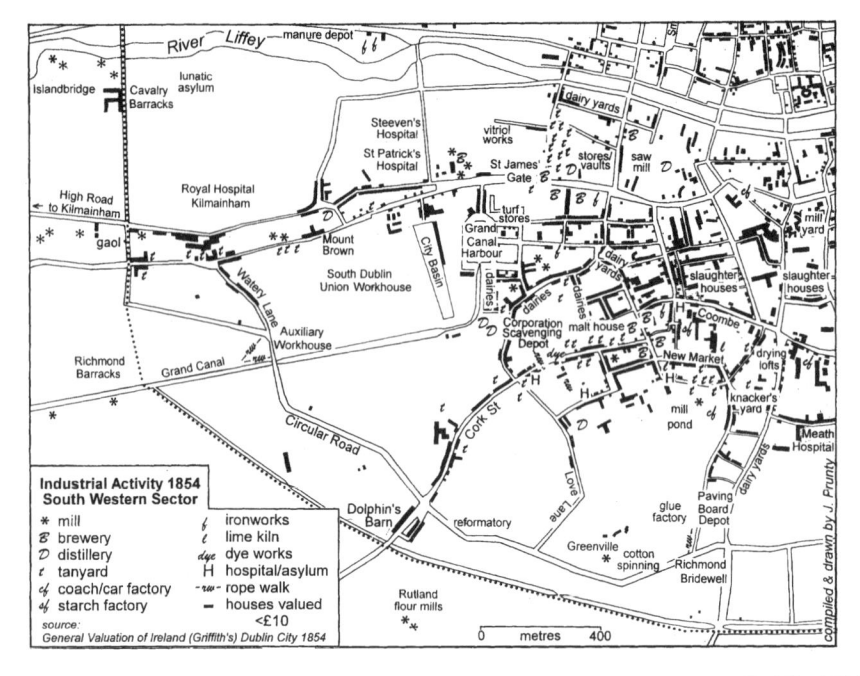

Figure 2.7 Low-value housing and industrial activity, south western sector, Dublin 1854

1750s when the Grand Canal reached the city, and the canal harbour near James' Street was constructed. The steep changes in gradient which provided these rivers with their motive power is evident in Figure 2.8, where hachuring highlights the Poddle valley along the Coombe (*cúm*, a hollow) and alongside New Row; the steep fall into the Liffey north of the axis marked by James' Street–Thomas Street–Cornmarket–High Street; and the relative height of New Market, overlooking Mill Street and the nearby mill pond. Figure 2.7 maps the local landuses, as recalled in Griffith's valuation, against the backdrop of low value housing for 1854.

The south western sector is dominated by activities for which considerable water supplies are a pre-requisite: breweries and distilleries; mills for corn and flour but also for wool, cotton and oil (with a large number of mills unspecified); paper mills, saw mills, and timber works; tanning and associated drying lofts; foundrys and ironworks; dyehouses. Tanning was dominated by small operators, but there were some larger businesses, such as Hays Brothers in New Row. There were also considerable concerns for the manufacture of ropes, cars and coaches, starch, vitriol (sulphuric acid/sulphates), glue and lime. At least two knackers' yards can be identified, one entirely circled by housing (Fumbally's Lane/Malpas Street) and the other, in Mill Street, in near-similar circumstances. Floor-cloth making is recorded for 32 Chancery Lane. Brickmaking appears to be extinct by 1854, but is recalled in the name Brickfield Lane.

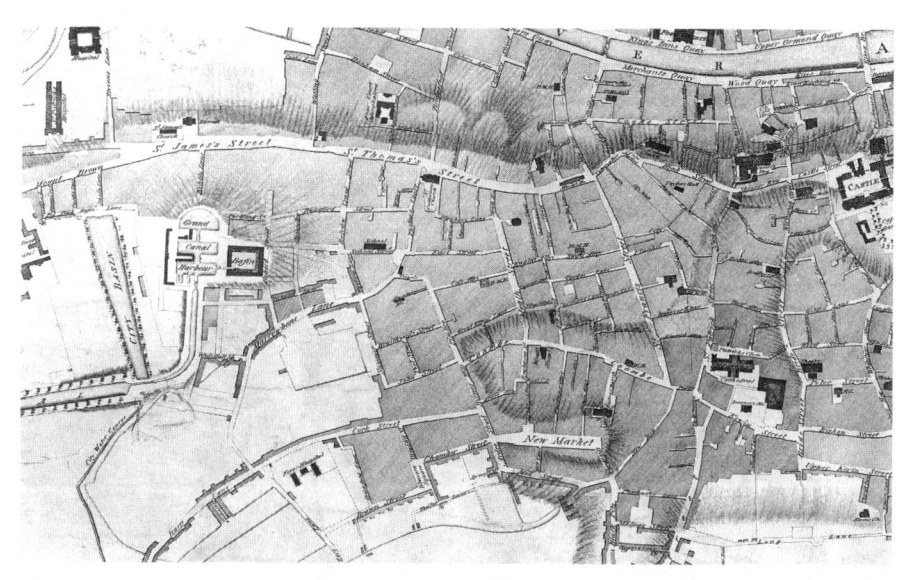

Figure 2.8 South western sector, City of Dublin 1811, Campbell/Taylor

The other dominant landuse in this sector is institutional: military barracks and military hospitals, other hospitals and asylums, the South Dublin Union workhouse and its auxiliary, a reformatory and bridewell, and extensive depots for municipal purposes, such as the scavenging yard in Marrowbone Lane, the paving board depot off New Row, and a manure yard near Islandbridge.

It was not possible in Figure 2.7 to map a range of other widely dispersed and significant landuses as they are simply too numerous: workshops, stores, stabling, forges, bakeries, vaults and yards. In Cutpurse Lane, directly south of Cornmarket among tightly packed courtyards and alleys, there was an establishment which boasted 21 two-horse stables and lofts. The canal company and other operators maintained turf stores, sheds and yards adjoining the canal harbour, while the larger breweries and distilleries also had very extensive storage areas. Plate 2.5, showing Forbes Cottages, Grand Canal Harbour, typifies the way slum housing was to be found in the midst of industries of the most objectionable sort. Only major concentrations of slaughter houses and dairy yards are indicated in Figure 2.7; these are also to be found dispersed throughout the built-up area.

The Liberties textile industry, dating largely from the Huguenot influx of the late seventeenth century, had contributed to speculative investment in high-density working class residential development, accounting for the extensive spread of housing valued under £10 in this sector (Figure 2.6). It also explains the incongruous mixing of densely packed gabled houses and large mansions interspersed with mills and yards.[117] The decline of the textile industry, lamented by commentators in the 1830s especially, can be noted by reference to

---

[117] Niall McCullough, *Dublin: An Urban History* (Dublin, 1989), p. 58.

Plate 2.5 Forbes' Cottages, off Marrowbone Lane, Grand Canal Harbour, RSAI 37

the fate of individual premises during the later nineteenth century. The 'tenter fields', where cloth was spread on hooks for drying (as illustrated in the Rocque extract, Figure 2.2), were to be superseded in part by the large stove tenter house of Mr Pleasants (erected 1815), a premises which after a brief period as an auxiliary workhouse was to become St Joseph's Night Asylum for Women and Children (1860, Chapter 7). Weavers' Hall on the Coombe (Figures 2.1, 2.8, marked WH), houses a very poorly-funded ragged school in the 1850s. Poole Street, Weavers' Square and New Row (Plate 2.1, Figure 2.2) with their characteristic 'Dutch Billies', gable-ended houses with lofty, well-lit upper rooms for weaving, are reduced to tenement status, along with other homes which once housed well-to-do manufacturing families. Wandering into the Coombe on a Dublin visit in 1853 Charles Dickens described it as a 'long, straggling estuary between houses (I cannot call it a street) turning from the bottom of Francis Street to Ardee Street and Pimlico and possessing vomitoria seemingly innumerable, in the shape of lanes, back streets, courts and blind alleys', with an 'almost indescribable aspect of dirt and confusion, semi-continental picturesqueness, shabbiness – less the shabby of dirt than that of untidiness – over-population, and frowsiness generally, perfectly original and peculiarly its own'.[118]

[118] Quoted in Jim Cooke, 'Charles Dickens, a Dublin Chronicler', *Dublin Historical Record*, 1989, pp. 97–98.

The complex but stubbornly downward shifts in the fortunes of the textile industry can be traced by reference to maps, valuation and other records;[119] similarly the rising star of brewing and distilling can be charted, as both land and premises throughout the south western sector were steadily bought up by the larger concerns. By 1854 the expansion of Guinness's Brewery, St James' Gate, was well underway; nearby the distillery of Henry Roe and Sons, and Power's Distillery (both James' Street) occupied large sites, while between Marrowbone Lane and Grand Canal Harbour was the distillery of Jameson and Robertson. Smaller but still important operations were found nearer Newmarket: Watkin's Brewery and Hely's Brewery (on either side of Ardee Street), and Busby's Distillery (New Row). The most obvious transformation was along Watling Street, which in 1854 was the site of innumerable tanyards and skinning establishments along with a small Roman Catholic chapel; by the early 1900s it had been largely overtaken by Guinness's.

West of the built-up area (Figure 2.7) there were significant but little-discussed areas of low value housing in conjunction with 'obnoxious' and industrial land-uses. At Islandbridge, between the cavalry barracks and a lunatic asylum (to which certain residents of the House of Industry were removed when their former home became the North Dublin Union workhouse, see Chapter 6), there was a cluster of low-value housing in conjunction with woollen and flour mills and an associated mill race, along the banks of the Liffey. At Kilmainham, where the Cammock (or Camac) River is thoroughly exploited for power, and literally in the dark shadow of the gaol, were several flour and other unspecified mills, in association with low-value housing. Where Old Kilmainham intersects with Watery Lane several tanyards alongside houses of the lowest description (valued c.£1 10s); were found, while a similar concentration characterised nearby Mount Brown.

The Social Geography of Mid Nineteenth Century Dublin

By combining the information gleaned from Griffith's Valuation (1854) and the commercial and street directories (*Shaw's* 1850, *Thom's* 1851, 1854) on house valuations, tenement status and extent of the business district, along with the information provided by Wilde in the censuses of 1841 and 1851, a generalised picture of the dominant social and economic patterns in the city at midcentury can be created, (Figure 2.9), following on the model created by Martin (1988).[120] The patterns of affluence and decay were profoundly influenced not only by the

---

[119] see Jacinta Prunty, 'The Textile Industry in Nineteenth Century Dublin: Its Geography, Structure and Demise', in Herman Diederiks and Marjan Balkestein (eds) *Occupational Titles and Their Classification: the Case of the Textile Trade in Past Times* (Göttingen, 1995) pp. 193–216.

[120] John H. Martin, 'The Social Geography of Mid Nineteenth Century Dublin City' in William J. Smyth and Kevin Whelan, (eds.), *Common Ground: Essays on the Historical Geography of Ireland* (Cork, 1988), p. 182.

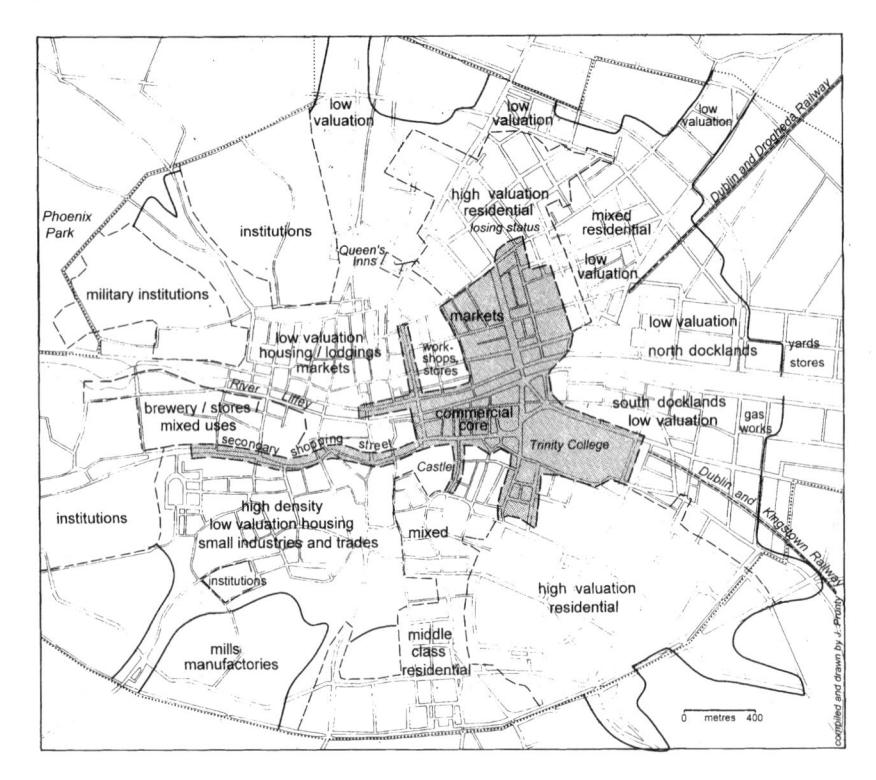

Figure 2.9 Socio-economic patterns in Dublin City, 1850–54

enduring fabric of streets and buildings from the previous era, but also by deep-rooted historical processes which, in some cases, stretched back for hundreds of years.[121] The early industrial centre of the Liberties, the blocking of westward expansion by the Phoenix Park and institutional land uses, the gradual and irreversible relocation of the centres of commerce and fashion to the east, led the centre of wealth to focus by the mid-nineteenth century on the fine northside Georgian squares of Mountjoy and Rutland, joined by elegant Sackville Mall to their southside counterparts, St Stephen's Green, Merrion and Fitzwilliam Squares. The broad segregation of the wealthiest from the poorest is the pattern most readily apparent on a city-wide scale. The high value sectors (houses valued £50+) are to the north and north-east of Carlisle Bridge, along Sackville Street, including the commercial heartland around College Green, and the residential squares of the south and south east, Dublin's 'Belgravia'.

Within the overall social geography of Dublin however, the slums cannot be regarded as discrete areas, but as part of every sector of the city: dominating the medieval core and the north city markets area, the low-lying North Strand area,

[121] Ibid., p. 173.

and the docklands on either side of the river, but in the stable lanes of the well-to-do residential squares and streets, and in courts and laneways behind the principal commercial streets. The north east sector (Chapter 8), was at midcentury poised precariously between aristocracy and slumdom; however, the nature of the free property market is such that once downward decline is in place it is only a matter of tracking its speed. In the case of the once-glorious Gardiner estate the fall was to be rapid, despite efforts along small stretches to halt its pace.

Conclusion

By mid-century the horrendous conditions of living in the Dublin slums had been authoritatively investigated and well publicised. A geography of disease and of premature death had been established, although it must be noted that coverage was uneven, the medieval core and north city markets area receiving most of the attention because of their notoriety, while 'newer' but equally miserable slums along the north and south docks, to the North Strand and on the western fringes went relatively unvisited. As early as 1818 one commentator summed up the slum geography as the two core areas of the medieval city and low-lying north city markets, with 'less prominent masses of wretchedness scattered over the other quarters of the city'.[122]

While the central concern in the early stages of the slum debate in nineteenth century Dublin was the generalised question of infectious disease, the later debate was to separate into three identifiable but still interlinked strands of research: the challenge of public health protection and sanitary reform; the housing problem; the question of relief of the poor, and the relative roles of state and voluntary bodies. It was also to move beyond the tight municipal boundary to envy the healthy suburbs beyond, and in time, to see in the urban fringe hopes for resolving the Dublin slum problem.

---

[122] *Observations on the House of Industry, Dublin and on the Plans of the Association for Suppressing Mendicity in that City* (Dublin, 1818), p. 24.

～3～

A MATTER OF LIFE AND DEATH: PUBLIC HEALTH, 1800-1900

Disease, generated in these abodes of rags, and toil, and misery, not infrequently stalks within the threshold of the wealthy and the proud, and when it does, its attacks are often accompanied with a virulence that sets all human aid at nought.[1]

INTRODUCTION

The sanitary disaster which was early nineteenth century Dublin was tackled spasmodically, each development a delayed reaction to yet another outbreak of contagious disease. The panic generated by these recurrent epidemics focused attention on the 'nests' of fever which were the city slums, resulting in some very perceptive and constructive reports (Chapter 2) but in the nature of crisis management, the earliest efforts merely exposed the utter inadequacy of the structures in place.

For most of the century urban life by definition was held to be less healthy than rural or suburban alternatives, and there was plenty of evidence to substantiate this claim. T. C. Speer, dispensary doctor in Dublin in 1818, claimed that while all large cities were susceptible to disease, contagion was not solely to blame. City life led to 'peculiarities of habit, occupation and character' which, when compared with the more 'natural' way of life associated with 'agriculture and rural affairs' could not but have 'distinct and decided effects on our physical frame' and 'powerful and peculiar influences' in the production of disease.[2] But whatever role city lifestyles might play in predisposing persons to disease, there was no disputing the fact that once generated, disease spread more rapidly among a poor urban population than among their country cousins: '*Contagion*, taken in the wide and general sense of the term, constitutes the grand connecting and assimilating principle of *city disease*'.[3]

---

[1] Thomas Willis, *Facts Associated with the Social and Sanitary Conditions of the Working Classes in the City of Dublin* (Dublin, 1845), p. 51, (hereafter *Social and Sanitary Conditions*)

[2] T.C. Speer, 'Medical Report containing an Inquiry into the Causes and Character of the Diseases of the Lower Orders in Dublin', *Dublin Hospital Reports*, vol III (1822), pp. 162–163.

[3] Ibid., p. 162, (hereafter *Diseases of the Lower Orders*).

As with every angle of the slum 'problem', the question of public health is impossible to disentangle from the allied areas of housing and subsistence, with so many paths leading to the one discouraging conclusion: that to effectively remedy one set of evils requires concurrent advances on other fronts. Municipal structures within which these issues could be vigorously addressed were central to any progress, and city administration was grossly underdeveloped in early nineteenth century Dublin.

The key public health questions were reformulated by successive individuals and institutions, each from their own perspective and with their own favoured remedies, but with a remarkable amount of convergence. Advances on one front, while long-urged and very welcome, often served merely to expose gross inadequacies in other areas, so that progress over time was not at all a simple matter. 'To avert epidemics, or mitigate their effects' was regarded as the principal public health concern in the early nineteenth century.[4] From this perspective the issues of isolation of fever cases, sewage disposal, water supply, and the scavenging of roads and lanes came to dominate the discussion. Advances in the collection and classification of statistics, and in the new 'sanatory science' (*sic*), also advanced the cause of 'public health', as the data upon which opinions were offered became more sophisticated and authoritative, and what might be regarded as minimally acceptable standards of life expectancy, health care and home accommodation were formulated. There was a perceptible movement, both literal and figurative, from public places into private domains, as under the banner of the 'common good' concern shifted from public highways into back lanes and courts. The back-yard and internal sanitary arrangements of individual houses, and even the dimensions, furniture arrangements and ventilation of bedrooms became the subject of close official scrutiny. By the end of the century the question of public health had extended to encompass issues such as the provision of public wash houses and bath houses, water closets and urinals, parks, markets and slaughter houses, as well as road widening schemes, while a considerable number of full-time staff was employed by the Corporation, especially in the core areas of public and domestic 'scavenging'. Contagious disease was still the primary concern, but the fever crises of the first half of the century had given way to more intractable long-term killers such as pulmonary tuberculosis.

Emergency Provisions, 1800–1850

The establishment of the Dublin fever hospitals in the first two decades of the nineteenth century could be considered the opening salvo in the public health campaign. The Cork Street Fever Hospital or *House of Recovery* (see Chapter 2) was very clear in its founding ambition to tackle the appalling home conditions of its patients or prospective patients as an integral part of its contribution towards

[4] Ibid., p. 162.

reducing the incidence of fever.[5] However, the hospital authorities appear to have attempted, or at least achieved, little outside the walls of the institution. The very principle of removing infectious cases to hospital was a mode of 'containing' disease that was in itself of questionable value. Writing in 1845 Willis criticised such a short-sighted approach, which succeeded in removing 'some portion of the contagion with the individual' but only to spread it into other channels, or concentrate it within the 'pestilential walls' of a hospital, 'without at all diminishing the productive causes of contagion'. Willis upheld that if a fraction of the energy and resources devoted to the charitable hospital care of the sick could be redirected into means for 'extinguishing the contagion itself', all would benefit immeasurably, from the poorest to the heaviest-burdened rate-payer.[6]

Whatever their limitations, however, the fever hospitals were central to all practical efforts made to research and contain infectious disease in the city in the period 1800–1818. The House of Industry hospitals, as major recipients of state money, were the principal state instrument in efforts to control the spread of typhus, relapsing fever and associated dysentery. Typical was the order given on 9 September 1817, when Mr Peel (Chief Secretary of State) directed the governors of the House of Industry, already caring for large numbers of fever patients in the associated Hardwicke Fever Hospital, to 'extend your inquiries into all those parts of the city wherein fever may have shown itself or where, from the neglect of cleanliness and density of the population, its appearance may be apprehended'. They were 'to undertake, at the public charge, the whitewashing of their houses, or the removal of filth from their doors, or to adopt any other measure of this nature calculated to discourage the introduction, or to check the progress of fever'.[7] The government established four soup kitchens under the management of the House of Industry, 'for the purpose of supplying nutritious soup to all, at the rate of 1/2d for the quart'.[8] They undertook to separate the infected from the healthy, while over two years at least 20,000 suits of clothes 'underwent the operation of washing, stoving, and exposure to the air' and 200 'extern paupers' of the House of Industry were employed in cleansing courts and back yards, while collections of 'putrefying animal and vegetable substances' were arranged.[9]

A hard-hitting report of 1833 (see Chapter 2), commissioned by the Mansion House Relief Committee established 'during a time of unexampled suffering

---

[5] Trustees of the House of Recovery or Fever Hospital in Cork-Street, *Observations on the Circumstances which tend to generate and propagate Contagion in the Liberties on the South Side of the City of Dublin and on the means of removing them* (Dublin, 1802), (hereafter Cork Street Trustees).

[6] Willis, *Social and Sanitary Conditions* (1845), pp. 55–56.

[7] F. Barker, J. Cheyne, *An Account of the Rise, Progress and Decline of the Fever lately Epidemical in Ireland, Together with Communications from Physicians in the Provinces and Various Official Documents*, vol. I (Dublin, 1821), (hereafter *Account of the Fever*).

[8] Ibid., p. 17

[9] Ibid., p. 123

frightfully aggravated by a desolating disease' exposed the utter inadequacy of leaving the sanitary affairs of the city to parish vestries.[10] As things stood, sanitary matters were in effect ignored until there was yet another outbreak of fatal fever, 'the alarm spreads amongst the community, and it is only then that the provisions of the act which relates to Boards and Officers of Health are brought to bear'.[11] Under legislation passed in 1818 and 1819, the creation of parochial health boards was provided for, 'and the powers of such Boards, for the prevention of contagion as well as for the cure of disease were defined'.[12] Officers of health were to be appointed annually, 'to act without salary and to exercise powers of cleansing streets, and removing nuisances and of fumigating the houses, clothing and bedding of the poorer inhabitants as also to the prevention of vagrancy, to guard against the communication of contagion by strolling beggars'. While the civic-minded parishioners who were appointed 'evinced the most laudable zeal to relieve the wants of the distressed poor, and to carry into effect the necessary measures for the prevention of disease', the funds at their command were derisory, so that they were 'in most instances disheartened by the embarrassing circumstances which surrounded them'. The parish vestries were unable to raise sufficient voluntary funds, 'and the levying of a sufficient sum by assessment had been found to be utterly impracticable'.[13]

During the 1832–33 cholera epidemic the Mansion House Committee led a dramatic sweep of the city slums, with the assistance of the parish officers of health, the Commissioners for Paving, and the Magistrates of Police, and unnamed others, so that 'the City was put into an admirable state of cleanliness, the apartments of the poor inhabitants white-washed and purified, and hitherto unknown comforts were administered to these distressed creatures'. Such emergency measures could do little lasting good; the minimum requirement was the annual election of parochial officers of health, who would be obliged to enforce 'the wise provisions' of existing legislation, regardless of whether or not there was an outbreak of fever. Only through a 'well-regulated system of this kind' would the link between filth and fever be broken, and the 'extent and virulence of epidemic diseases' be lessened.[14] To render the city fever-free required more than the generosity of a few unpaid parish officers and the intermittent subscriptions begged and bullied from the hardpressed public. A more equitable and effective scheme was long overdue.

The infant mortality in the North Dublin Union workhouse was so alarmingly high in the early 1840s that it had been dubbed 'Infant Slaughter House'.[15] On

---

[10] Francis White, *Report and Observations on the State of the Poor of Dublin* (Dublin, 1833), pp. 30–31, (hereafter *Report on the State of the Poor*).
[11] Ibid., p. 26.
[12] 58 George lll cap. 49 and 59 George lll cap. 41; White, *Report on the State of the Poor* (1833), p. 25.
[13] Ibid., p. 28.
[14] Ibid., pp. 24, 26.
[15] Ibid., p. 8.

his election as guardian by the rate-payers of the Linen House Ward, Thomas Willis undertook to examine these allegations for himself. The first step was to determine what was the comparative infant mortality among children of the same class and age outside the workhouse, an inquiry which led to the shocking conclusion that 'the deaths among the workhouse children 'were not greater than the same class furnished outside the workhouse, and not more than might have been expected from the state of destitution and wretchedness in which the mothers of the infants were sunk when seeking admission'.[16] While it exonerated the workhouse from blame, Willis explained that the project 'imperceptibly led far beyond my intended limits' to produce mortality tables based on over 3,000 families 'indiscriminately taken from house to house, and from cellar to garret, principally in the poorer streets of St. Michan's parish', including all premises 'save some few that were occupied by parties so apparently respectable as to forbid any inquiries of this nature'.[17]

The infant mortality among the 12,280 children (excluding all still-births and unbaptised infants) was between 32% and 36% for infants under two years 'but in some wretched localities, even above 50%, and if the most destitute were selected, the mortality would be much greater' such figures, Willis claimed, were 'without parallel, unless in some of the manufacturing towns in England'.[18] By the age of five more than half of the age cohort had died, and by the time that group reached twenty-one years, more than two thirds had died.[19]

What was most disturbing was that these premature deaths could not be explained away by inherited defects from sickly or older mothers: more than half the mothers were not themselves Dublin born, 'they were married young, and are very generally healthy; there is no curvature of spine among them – no malformation, their bodies are as nature formed them – perfect'. In fact everything pointed to the likelihood of their offspring being hardy infants: 'having never submitted to the destructive pressure of stays, their labours are natural; their love of offspring is boundless, and having no employment the maternal duties are never deputed to others'. While these mothers 'cannot boast of much mental culture' they were nevertheless full of 'moral virtue', having been spared what Willis considered the 'demoralizing contagion of the workshop or the factory'.[20] It was the Dublin slum environment in itself that undermined the constitution, and brought huge numbers of infants to a premature grave.

The sporadic and desultory manner in which street cleansing was carried on in the first half of the century was criticised by Willis, who reported that while other countries were subject to occasional epidemics, in Ireland every visitation of disease degenerated into 'contagious fever, a plague at our very doors', quite

[16] Ibid., p. 9.
[17] Ibid., p. 10.
[18] Ibid., pp. 10, 14.
[19] Ibid., p. 13.
[20] Ibid., p. 14.

simply because 'no care has ever been continuously extended to the comforts of the poor'.[21] He summed up the situation as it stood in 1845:

> Occasionally, as when the fearful ravages of cholera spread terror and alarm among the comfortable classes, or when the extent and malignity of epidemic fever so crowd the hospitals that the dependants of the wealthy can find no place within these establishments, active, but only temporary, efforts have been made to produce greater cleanliness in the localities occupied by the poor. Boards of health have then been formed; parochial officers, inspectors, and visitants nominated, who day after day, during the continuance of the alarm, visited the back courts and streets, caused the yards to be cleaned, the cess-pools emptied, &c.: but a few weeks and all were again as before the terror had arisen – the boards were dissolved, and the wretched localities of the poor relapsed into their wonted filth.[22]

Thus stood the situation on the brink of the great famine.

Municipal Restructuring, 1841–1851

The structure of local administration in early nineteenth century Dublin was complex beyond comprehension; at least, that was the considered opinion of contributors to the 1840s debate on municipal reform.[23] In 1843 there were sixteen distinct tax regimes in operation, each collected by a separate collector, so that 'scarcely a week passes without the visit of some Tax Collector or another', which was both harassing and costly.[24] Payment of the Poor Law rate entitled householders valued over £10 to vote in municipal elections; however, most of the other taxes had little to do with enfranchisement.[25] Each operated its own list, with so much overlapping and multiplication that they were 'unnecessary for any good purpose and creative only of confusion and useless expense', serving only 'to confound what is already too confused, to mystify and perplex what should be simple'.[26]

Highlighted as most glaringly unjust, as well as inefficient, was Minister's Money, a tax which was rated parochially according to the amount due to the Protestant clergyman for his support. However, there was no regard taken of the size of the parish, its population, the ability of the residents to pay, or indeed their religious adherence. Hence the smaller the parish, the higher had to be the valuation on each holding so that the aggregate amount could be raised; those parishes within the medieval city walls were the worst affected. This injustice was exacerbated by using the valuation calculated for Minister's Money as the

---

[21] Ibid., p. 47.
[22] Ibid.
[23] See *Statement as to Local Taxation of the City of Dublin and Suggested Amendments to the Municipal Act, 3rd and 4th Victoria. cap 108, 109*, 10 January 1843, (hereafter *Statement as to Local Taxation, Dublin*, 1843).
[24] The sixteen taxes were: Poor Law rate; Parish cess; Minister's Money; Grand Jury cess; paving & lighting tax and watering tax; Wide Street tax; pipe water tax; police tax; Stephen's Green tax; Poddle tax; cholera tax; Mountjoy Square tax; tax for payment on debt on St. George's Church; Quay Wall tax; Merrion Square tax; borough rate list. *Statement as to Local Taxation, Dublin*, 1843, p. 18
[25] Ibid.
[26] Ibid., pp. 5, 19

basis for the paving and lighting tax. Thus where the paving and lighting tax was 'chargeable at the rate of 4s 6d on the shilling of Minister's Money', householders in St Audeon's paid £12.13s to the Paving Commissioners, the wealthiest household in Fitzwilliam Square paid £6.16s; in all £54 in taxes was required of the city centre household, and just over £27 from the household in the Square.[27] And to further burden the poorest areas, only residents were taxed; house property owners, such as those in the Liberties 'where large sums are raised from the wretched inmates of rooms, garrets and cellars for rents' were exempt if they chose not to reside on the premises with their lodgers.[28] Wherever arrears mounted up there was a periodic re-assessment on the 'solvent resident householders' of the parish in which the monies were owed. In summary, 'the poor who live in those parts of the City which have been and are fast falling to decay, are ground down and oppressed with double the amount of Local Taxation payable by the affluent residents of our Squares'.[29] The system provided every possible incentive for the better-off to continue abandoning the oldest and poorest parts of the city, hastening the decline of these areas into slums.

Not alone was the system of raising local taxes inefficient and unjust, but the way in which these funds were spent was also open to sharp criticism, as there was little possibility of cost-saving co-operation. The Paving Board, consisting of three paid commissioners appointed by the Lord Lieutenant, was established in 1807 (to replace the commission of 1783/4 which was suspended on 'charges of irregularities, well founded') and had responsibility for the lighting, paving, cleansing, and sewering of the city.[30] The Wide Streets Commissioners had been created in 1757 for the purpose of both widening existing streets and creating new streets; the splendid thoroughfares of Dame Street, Nassau Street, Westmoreland and D'Olier Streets, are all testimony to the extensive powers and zeal of this eighteenth century body. The Grand Jury, the Commissioners of Paving and Lighting, and the Commissioners of Wide Streets each raised their taxes and spent their funds without reference to the other authorities.

In the debate which preceded the Dublin Improvement Act (1849) there was a call that all municipal improvements 'should be made conducive and subservient to a large and comprehensive plan of sanatory (sic) reform, and especially to everything which would improve the comforts, the habits and the health of the humbler classes of our fellow citizens'.[31] This noble ideal was not acted on, as was the case with so many previous excellent suggestions, but by transferring the powers of the Wide Streets Commissioners and the Paving Commissioners to the reformed Corporation, an essential first step was taken towards creating a single authority with comprehensive responsibilities. If given the necessary resources and legislative powers, this new body was poised to effect change.

[27] Ibid., p. 7.
[28] Ibid., p. 10.
[29] Ibid., p. 8.
[30] Charles Cameron, *Municipal Public Health Administration in Dublin* (Dublin, 1914), p. 99.
[31] *Statement as to Local Taxation, Dublin*, 1843, p. 8.

The Sanitary Campaign: First Manoeuvres, 1849–1874

The newly reformed Corporation was not initially noted for its sanitary exertions. The Dublin Metropolitan Police, instituted in 1838 and empowered to act as inspectors of nuisances, were called to fulfil that duty from 1848. However, it was claimed that 'theoretically the ordinary police are supposed to prevent people from throwing slops, and so on, into the streets, but practically they do not do so' and as the police were not under metropolitan control there was little that could be done about it.[32] The one policeman recruited specifically and paid for by the Corporation (from 1851) as an 'inspector of nuisances' also had 'duties of a totally opposite character to perform'.[33] His city-wide one-man public health operations included enforcing the removal of swine from dwellings, and from yards where kept offensively, and ordering the construction, repair and cleansing of out-offices and closets; while in theory he could bring legal proceedings to close insanitary houses, in practice the lengthy appeals which ensued meant the occupiers would be long decimated by typhus before a final decision was reached.[34] The City Health Preservation Committee was unsuccessful in securing any government money towards the cost of implementing the existing sanitary laws, and the Court of Queen's Bench upheld that the borough fund could not be used to carry out the provisions of the Nuisances Removal and Diseases Prevention Act. The cost of abating nuisances was to be recovered from the guilty parties, a requirement which rendered the act useless.[35]

The Corporation came under pressure from all sides to effect some improvements; the Lord Lieutenant, following on a report of the Police Commissioners showing the insanitary conditions under which the poor lived, remarked that 'the scenes of wretchedness and immorality which the enquiry disclosed imperatively called for the most prompt and energetic interference of the Council'.[36] Thomas Antisell, a prominent surgeon, condemned the 'ignorance and incompetence of the Paving and Watering Boards', under whose management 'Dublin is notoriously the worst sewered, lighted, cleansed and watered city in the empire, and about the highest taxed'.[37] The practice of emptying the sewers into the river Liffey had, he claimed, made it 'a hotbed of contagion', and as if not satisfied with that, 'to ensure certain disease, this filthy river water must be brought to our doors in the water-carts' for washing the streets.[38] Both 'public health and public economy' demanded sweeping changes in the city administration; such

---

[32] *Third Report of HM Commissioners for Inquiring into the Housing of the Working Classes (Ireland), 1885*, Evidence of Dr Cameron, qs 22,355–22,364, (hereafter *Housing Inquiry 1885*).
[33] *Housing Inquiry 1885*, qs. 22,090–22,091.
[34] Charles Cameron, *Appendix A(4)*, *Housing Inquiry 1885*, p. 107.
[35] Cameron, *Municipal Public Health Administration* (1914), p. 20.
[36] Ibid., p. 21.
[37] Thomas Antisell, *Suggestions towards the Improvement of the Sanatory Condition of the Metropolis* (Dublin, 1847), p. 5, (hereafter *Suggestions*).
[38] Ibid., pp. 8, 17.

important questions as gas, lighting, water, sewering and scavenging should not be left to the 'jealousies' of private companies, but under one public and efficient board.[39]

In 1851 the first Corporation 'inspector of nuisances', a policeman, was formally appointed; the first 'sanitary returns' listing the number of complaints and the action taken on each was prepared; by 1859 the entire sanitary staff numbered three officers but aided by the police, and action was largely confined to the 'abatement of nuisances'; no houses were closed, although efforts were made to close the worst of the cellars, and modest efforts made to improve street scavenging. By-laws for the regulation of lodging-houses were made in August 1851, but success was limited to the listing of the lodging houses and a little white-washing. The inspection of slaughter houses was also instigated, public urinals constructed from 1856, and a public analyst, Dr Cameron, appointed in 1862 to implement the Adulteration of Foods Act 1860. Dublin led the United Kingdom in this regard, as the only city where these new provisions were actively put in force, with a line of successful prosecutions against confectioners, bakers, butchers, grocers and milk suppliers for marketing dangerous or substandard produce.[40] One observer writing in 1857 considered the improvements which had been so recently rendered in the wilderness of filthy lanes, alleys, and courts as 'little green spots on which the mind can rest', but emphasised that there still remained 'much at which humanity shudders'.[41]

June 1864 saw the appointment of Dr Edward Mapother as the first medical officer of health to Dublin Corporation, a promising move as Mapother committed himself to campaign on the 'pressing necessity for immediate legislation' in the sanitary domain. With the support of the Poor Law Commissioners for Ireland, and several other local authorities as well as Dublin Corporation, the Sanitary Act, 1866 received the royal assent on 7 August 1866, at the height of yet another epidemic, this time of cholera. It was put into effect within the month, as orders and notices regarding the control of the disease were urgently framed, and its provisions rapidly submitted 'to the trying ordeal of judicial decision'.[42]

The Sanitary Act 1866 embodied the provisions of the English Sanitary Statutes 1855, and extended them to Ireland. While 1866 is widely regarded as marking the birth of effective sanitary legislation in Dublin, in practice the act was 'a chaotic jumble of sanitary statutes', a 'complicated code' of inconsistent and confused sections, hastily constructed from an amalgam of subsidiary acts,

[39] Ibid., pp. 9, 26.
[40] Cameron, *Municipal Public Health Administration* (1914), pp. 20–25.
[41] Thomas Jordan, 'The Present State of the Dwellings of the Poor, chiefly in Dublin', *Journal of the Dublin Statistical Society*, vol. 2 (1857), pp. 17–18. (hereafter 'Dwellings of the Poor').
[42] John Norwood, 'On the Working of the Sanitary Laws in Dublin, with Suggestions for their Amendment', *Soc. Stat. Inq. Soc. Ire. Jn.*, vol. VI part XLIII (1873), pp. 230–242, (hereafter *Sanitary Laws*).

and proved of limited usefulness.[43] However, on the organisational front it led to a new body with a specific brief, the *Public Health Committee*, formed from 'Committee Number 2' whose responsibilities ranged from pipe water, markets and weigh houses to sanitary matters.[44] It was claimed that before 1866 'literally nothing' was done 'in the way of inspecting the dwellings of the working classes'.[45] However, blame for inaction must be widely spread, one reviewer in 1873 claiming that 'impatience of taxation by rate-payers without, and opposition from false economists within their body' had led to much good being left undone.[46] The 1866 act did so little to increase the effective powers of the public health authority that the period 1849–1874 can be treated as one.

The one outstanding success during this period was the 'wholesome and abundant' supply of the 'purest soft water' provided for the city by the Vartry water scheme, 1863–1868. It replaced the unsatisfactory and insufficient water supply provided by the canals and associated city reservoirs (at Blessington Street Basin on the north side, and at James's Street Basin and Portobello Harbour on the south side, 1773–74). The Vartry scheme was welcomed by all commentators. 'No city in the kingdom is better supplied with this chiefest necessity of life', and credit was heaped on all involved in the construction of the splendid engineering works. 13.5 million gallons was available to the city and surrounding districts each day, an amount far in excess of demand, and while the cost at £550,000 was ahead of the estimate, nevertheless it was held that 'few cities have obtained so fine a supply, delivered at high pressure, on such moderate terms'.[47] A statute was raised in Sackville Street in honour of its leading figure, Sir John Gray M.D. in 1879. However, even this achievement had its shadow side. The infrastructure to distribute the water within the poorer districts was very limited, so that ten years after its arrival complaints were made that many residents were reliant for drinking water on water 'taken from the cistern intended to supply the water closet' resulting in typhoid.[48] In the poorer quarters fountains were advocated, and 'if some contrivance could be adopted whereby they would not, by waste of water, render the adjacent pavement sloppy, so much the better'.[49]

Mortality Statistics

Central to the public health campaign was accurate information on disease and mortality. In reflecting on the epidemic of 1817–1818, the medical officers of the House of Industry regretted that their statistics were so inaccurate, as 'in many

---

[43] Ibid., p. 230
[44] Cameron, *Municipal Public Health Administration* (1914), p. 32
[45] *Housing Inquiry 1885*, qs. 22,080
[46] Norwood, *Sanitary Laws* (1873), p. 232.
[47] Ibid.
[48] Charles Cameron, Edward Mapother, 'Report on the Means for the Prevention of Disease in Dublin', *RPDCD*, vol. 1, (1879), pp 345–346, (hereafter *Prevention of Disease*).
[49] Ibid., p. 346.

towns the extent of the population is imperfectly known', while the hospital registers failed to take account of readmissions, relapses, and the different types of fever with which a person might be admitted.[50] The 'protracted and sifting inquiry' held by the guardians of the North Dublin Union in the 1840s into the rate of infant mortality in their workhouse exposed how even the most basic demographic facts were impossible to ascertain. Willis, an accomplished statistician himself, strongly advocated a 'well-regulated system for registration of births, baptisms, marriages and deaths', in the absence of which we are 'continually liable to be misled by vague opinions as to the duration of life'.[51] In his own efforts at determining whether or not the mortality among workhouse children was in excess of what might be found among children of the same class and age out-of doors, he was obliged to undertake primary data collection, based on an infant population of above 12,000 in the parish of St Michan's. In compiling the tables of mortality he found inaccuracies in the ages returned, but was satisfied with the cruder measure of percentage dead among baptised infants: 'the fact of being alive or dead is not likely to be misstated'.[52]

The publication of the census returns of 1841, with its 'immense mass of information crowding in on us on every page' was warmly welcomed by Willis and others for whom the abject poverty of the large majority was a matter of genuine concern. Described as 'one of the very few useful works on Ireland, undertaken and carried out with a true straight-forward spirit' it was the first authoritative and universal collection of census data, and provided a basis from which advances could be measured over ten-year intervals.[53] The tables on house accommodation, for example, provided a country-wide context into which the Dublin slum situation could be placed. Willis noted that 81.46% of the entire population had only 3rd and 4th class accommodation, and of these 52.12% had only a mud hovel/single room; within Dublin the census testified that almost half of all families had 'the wretched and pestiferous accommodation of a single room' (see Table 2.3).[54]

The implementation of compulsory registration of births, deaths and marriages in 1879 was the single most important step in the public health campaign to date. If previous records are to be believed, up to then substantially more persons were buried than died in Dublin! There was an immediate increase in 1879 of 10% deaths over the number registered in the preceding year, and it was claimed that from then on very few deaths escaped being officially recorded.[55] Variations in Dublin's geography of death could be followed from 1877 when the annual overall mortality figure was broken down into three north city, four south city, and four

[50] Barker and Cheyne, *Account of the Fever* (1821), p. 81.
[51] Willis, *Social and Sanitary Conditions* (1845), pp. 20–21.
[52] Ibid., p. 38.
[53] Ibid., p. 23.
[54] Ibid., pp. 30–31.
[55] 'Report of the Public Health Committee, Breviate for August 1879', *RPDCD*, vol. 3 no. 183, (1879), p. 152.

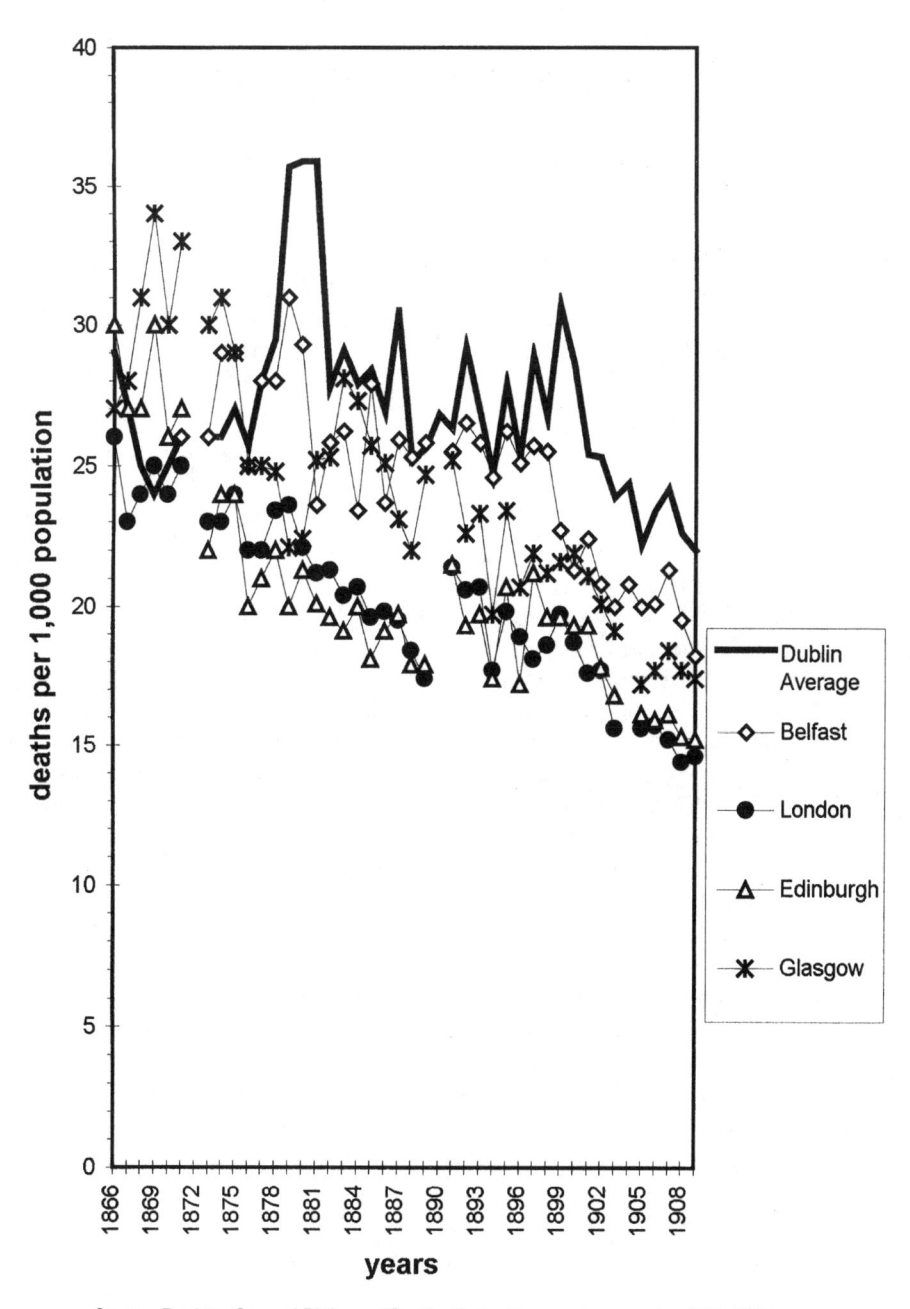

A Matter of Life and Death: Public Health, 1800–1900 73

Source: Register General Births and Deaths (Ireland), annual summaries 1866-1909

Table 3.1 Annual mortality, Dublin, Belfast, London, Edinburgh, Glasgow, 1866–1909.

suburban districts (see Chapter 5, Figure 5.1 for city divisions). Numbers of persons per acre in each district were included in analyses from 1881, while links between occupation, social geography and disease, pioneered in Wilde's census reports for 1841 and 1851 (Chapter 2, Figure 2.5) were explored in the annual summaries for Dublin from 1880. The headings under which causes of death were entered were expanded and refined, while accompanying age/sex data and meteorological information allow a range of correlation possibilities to be explored.

Such detailed and reliable statistics made it possible to formulate slum problems in numerical terms, and to track progress towards specified targets. The most important goal was towards an 'acceptable' or normal rate of mortality, with the standard set by the Registrar General of England in 1857 adopted by the authors of the *Manual of Public Health for Ireland* (1875):

> 17 in 1,000 [deaths] is supplied as a standard by experience. Here we stand upon the actual. Any deaths in a people exceeding 17 in 1,000 annually are unnatural deaths. If the people were shot, drowned, burnt, poisoned by strychnine, their deaths would not be more unnatural than the deaths wrought clandestinely by disease in excess of the quota of natural deaths; that is, in excess of seventeen deaths in 1,000 living.[56]

A league table of death rates, which includes Irish and British urban centres (Tables 3.1, 3.2), cities in other parts of the British Empire, and major European and world cities (see Chapter 5, Table 5.1), places Dublin's problem of excessive mortality in a larger context. In 1879 the rate of mortality in Dublin was 35.7 per 1,000, massively higher than London (23.6), Glasgow (22.4) or Edinburgh (21.3), (Table 3.1). While her British neighbours had still some distance to cover to reach the recommended figure of 17:1,000, each continued to make progress at a rate which left Dublin still stubbornly well behind by 1909, when the death rate was 22:1,000. Within Ireland (Table 3.2) Dublin still maintained a significant lead over other urban centres from 1873–1912, with Belfast the most serious contender for that unhappy distinction. Within the Dublin Registration District (Table 3.3), the relative healthiness of the suburbs compared to the centre city persists throughout. Substantial swings in the death rate for Dublin are accounted for by varied but virulent outbreaks of contagious disease, such as measles, influenza, whooping cough and 'diarrhoeal diseases' (mostly diarrhoea and dysentery but also 'simple cholera' and 'choleraic diarrhoea'). However, such outbreaks merely overlie a very high more general death rate, with pulmonary tuberculosis (pthisis) and 'diseases of the respiratory system' together accounting for the greatest number of deaths (see Chapter 5). The vulnerability of the Dublin slum population to periodic visitations of contagious disease was paralleled in other Irish urban sanitary districts (Table 3.2) where hard-won gains could be similarly rendered invisible as outbreaks such as measles swept through poorly housed and underfed populations. The compilation of reliable mortality statistics

---

[56] Quoted in Thomas W. Grimshaw, J. Emerson Reynolds, Robert O'B. Furlong, John William Moore, *A Manual of Public Health for Ireland* (Dublin, 1875), p. 116, (hereafter *Manual*).

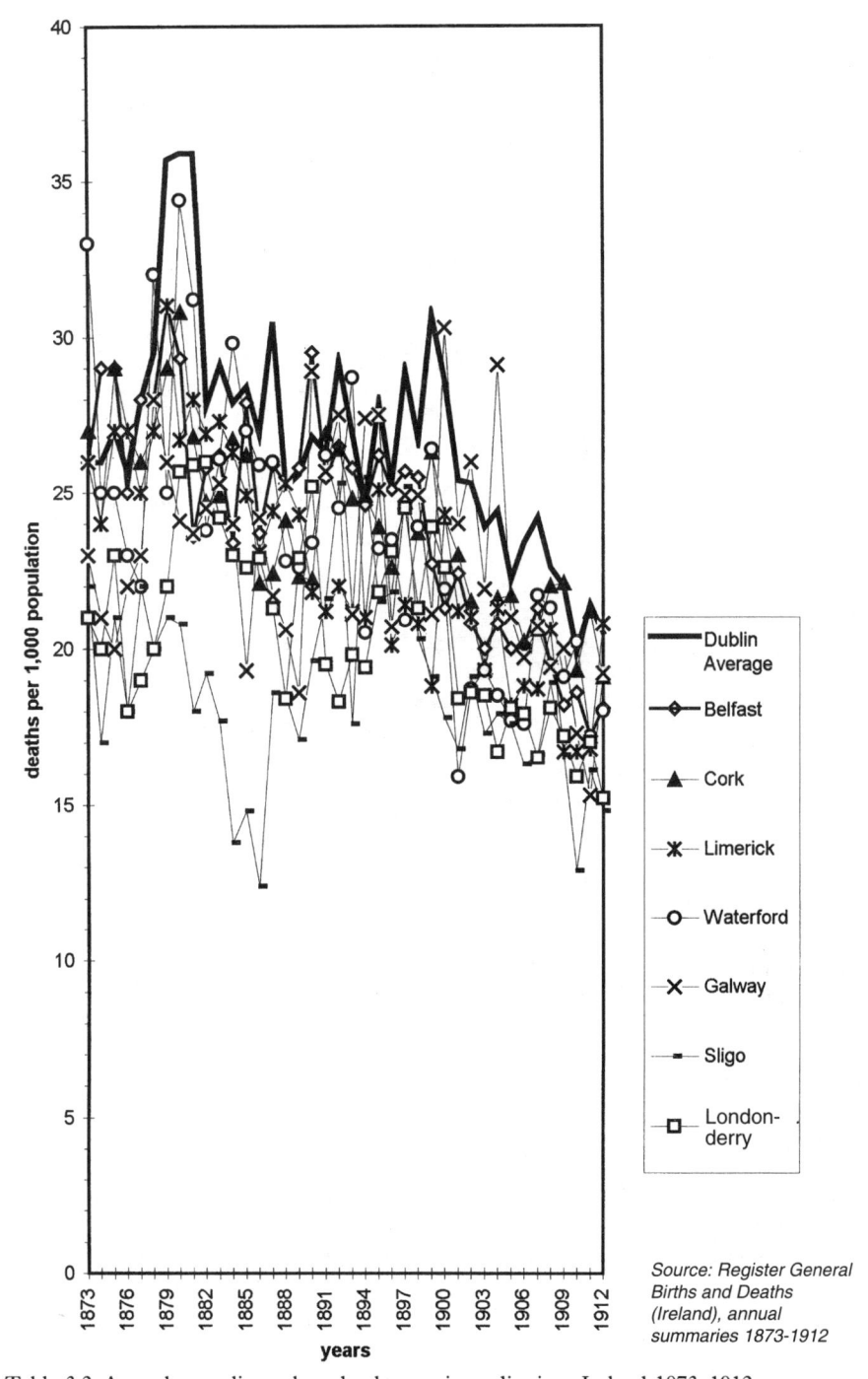

A Matter of Life and Death: Public Health, 1800–1900

Table 3.2 Annual mortality, selected urban sanitary districts, Ireland 1873–1912.

Source: Register General Births and Deaths (Ireland), annual summaries 1873-1912

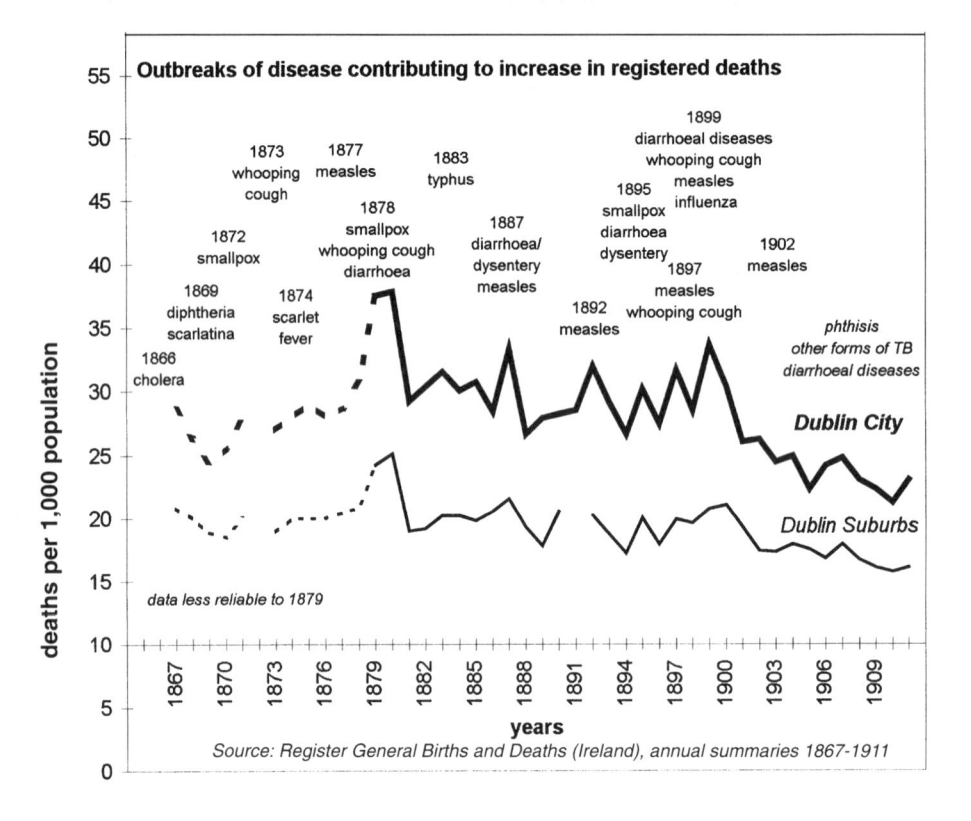

Table 3.3 Annual mortality, Dublin city and suburbs 1866–1911.

through the development of the Register General's office, enabled life chances within and between urban centres to be compared, while the appendixed notes from individual officers' weekly reports provide valuable local detail. From 1879 on they progressively undermined whatever grounds might be offered for pleading ignorance of the slum situation.

The Sanitary Campaign: Gaining Ground, 1874–1899

The Public Health (Ireland) Act, 1874 marks the beginning of a more professional approach to eradicating the urban 'fever nests', although it was the provisions of the more comprehensive 1878 public health legislation which were to prove more useful. Under the Public Health (Ireland) Act 1874,[57] staffing arrangements were formalised and expanded, and efforts were made to ensure country-wide coverage:

---

[57] 37 & 38 Victoria, c. 13, 1874.

every dispensary medical officer became *ex officio* a medical officer of health. In Dublin these numbered fifteen, 'each was to receive the magnificent salary of £10 per annum', a salary fixed by the Corporation but paid by the Poor Law Boards of Guardians. Under a 'sealed order of the Local Government Board' dated 21 October 1874 the Corporation was directed to create three new posts: consulting sanitary officer, and medical officer of health, first filled by Dr Edward Mapother and Dr Charles Cameron respectively, both at a salary of £300 per annum; and the post of executive sanitary officer, to which Mr James Boyle was appointed, at £200 per annum.[58] Henceforth the inspectors of nuisances were to be known as sanitary sub-officers. Under this Act the Local Government Board for Ireland was constituted the supreme public health authority for Ireland, with the privilege of sending its officials to the meetings of the sanitary authorities and their committees. The appointment and dismissal of staff at local level was subject to its approval, and it could also direct that sanitary posts were filled.[59] In practice it acted as a watch-dog, putting pressure on local sanitary authorities to put new and existing legislation into effect. In the case of Dublin its most public contributions were at the *Royal Sanitary Commission* 1879/80, the report it requested on the excessive mortality in Dublin city in 1900, and the housing inquiry, launched at its insistence in 1913.[60]

The increasing professionalism of the approach to public health was marked by the publication of the first *Manual of Public Health for Ireland* (1875), the authors of which included Dr Thomas Grimshaw, one of the foremost experts on the state of the Dublin slums. Of more importance on the ground was the shift towards increasing the number, range and status of 'sanitary staff'. Before 1866 only one 'inspector of nuisances' was employed. By 1873 the Corporation had a sanitary staff of 24: a medical officer of health, a public analyst, a secretary, 15 police officers acting as sanitary inspectors, a clerk, three inspectors of food and two disinfectors, a considerably more enlightened level of staffing at the time than many other towns and cities. Twelve years later the staff numbered 36, excluding stablemen, whitewashers and labourers, the main increase being in the arrival of 12 civilian sanitary inspectors, while the services of 9 police officers were also maintained. During the 'apprehended visitation of cholera' in 1884 an additional 16 officers were employed and retained for six months.[61] Police were preferred for the role of inspectors, 'inasmuch as their uniform more or less suggested authority, and the people submitted to their suggestions and paid more attention to them'; civilian officers were also clad in a special uniform to give them extra standing in their difficult work.[62]

---

[58] Cameron, *Municipal Public Health Administration* (1914), p. 37.
[59] Ibid., p. 38.
[60] *Report of the Departmental Committee appointed by the Local Government Board for Ireland to inquire into the Housing Conditions of the Working Classes in Dublin* (Dublin, 1914).
[61] Charles Cameron, *Appendix A(4), Housing Inquiry 1885*, p. 107.
[62] Evidence of Alderman Meagher, *Housing Inquiry 1885*, qs 22,158–22,163.

The Public Health Act of 1878 'enlarged the powers of the Sanitary Authorities', and there were some changes at the top, with a further new post: Medical Superintendent Officer of Health. Edward Mapother was elected, but resigned soon after; Charles Cameron succeeded him, from 21 August 1879, and headed the Public Health Committee of the Corporation.[63] With the adoption of the new legislation in 1879, there was widespread optimism that the authorities were on the brink of moving towards a resolution of the enormous health problems facing the city. In the report for 1879 Cameron detailed the task ahead, repeating the concerns of the previous years, but now confident advances would soon be made. Progress, or lack of it, on the agenda thus outlined may be tracked by reference to the subsequent quarterly breviates and annual reports of the *Public Health Committee*. Outspoken commentary and criticism were provided by the *Dublin Sanitary Association*, and the *Statistical and Social Inquiry Society of Ireland*, among other interested groups and individuals. Public lectures, publications, leaflets, court cases, newspaper articles and advertisements all contributed to lively and informed debate among the middle and professional classes; among the poor the unannounced raids by health officials and inspectors, wielding notebooks and tape measures (to ascertain cubic capacity), and the field visits of engineers and innumerable sub-committee members, brought the changes in legislation close to home. The promotion of public health, inextricably bound up with the slum question in Dublin, was a topic from which no citizen living within the municipal boundary could now remain aloof.

While a multitude of overlapping concerns about the slums crowd the period 1879–1899, a number of key issues can be identified: at what might be termed the 'household level' the recurring concerns were domestic scavenging, the relative merits of privies *vs.* water closets, house disinfection, and the legal obstacles to the inspection of tenement houses and yards. At the district and city level the questions of public scavenging and 'places not in charge of the Corporation', main drainage, the regulation of bakeries, dairy yards and slaughter houses, the provision of public markets, baths and wash-houses, and road widening and allied 'municipal improvements' dominated the agenda. Periodic outbreaks of contagious disease, such as increases in typhoid (enteric fever) in the late 1870s and 1880s, created some alarm, uneasy reminders that the fever panic of the first half of the century could not yet be considered history. Table 3.4 lists the sanitary exertions of Dr Cameron and his staff in 1883, and provides a useful summary of the diverse responsibilities which had been assumed or forced on the Corporation as the local sanitary authority by that time.

Domestic Scavenging

The major concern under the respectable heading of 'domestic scavenging' was the toilet question. To what extent should, and could, the health authority inter-

---

[63] Cameron, *Mimicipal Public Health Administration* (1914), p. 39.

RETURN OF SANITARY OPERATIONS CARRIED OUT IN THE YEAR 1883

Sewers and House Drains constructed on demand of Sanitary Authority	537
Do. repaired and cleansed	2263
Water-closets constructed	970
Privies constructed	42
Ashpits constructed	313
Ashpits rebuilt and altered according to specification supplied by Public Health Committee	15
Privies and Water-closets cleansed	637
Dwellings repaired	6457
Privies and Water-closets repaired	2490
Dwellings cleansed	8531
Dwellings condemned and closed, being unfit for human habitation	271
Rooms in other Houses closed, being unfit for human habitation	128
Dwellings reported to the City Engineer as being dangerous	56
Cellar Dwellings condemned and closed	41
Yards and External Premises cleansed	2225
Lanes and Alleys cleansed by private parties	396
Accumulations of Manure removed	944
Swine removed from Dwellings	32
Other Animals removed from Dwellings	28
Swine removed from Yards where kept offensively	306
Miscellaneous Nuisances abated	1269
Inspections of Tenement Houses	49976
Do. Tenement Rooms	204743
Do. Nightly Lodging Houses	2176
Do. Bakeries	1588
Do. Slaughter Houses	2640
Do. Dairy Yards	2909
Certificates of Destitution to entitle to Gratuitous Interment	501
Water-taps supplied to Tenement Houses	265
Sanitary Defects discovered	33978
Do. remedied	33748
Infected Dwellings inspected and cleansed	1073
Do. chemically disinfected	1073
Reports received from Medical Sanitary Officers	561
Patients removed by Hospital Cabs	160
Removals for Disinfection by Vans	2062
Disinfecting Chamber used by Persons	1081
Number of Articles Disinfected	11153
Infected Mattresses and Beds burned, their owners compensated	1117
Detections of Unsound Food	202
Convictions for selling Adulterated Food	39
Do. Refusing to sell Food to Inspectors	4
Do. for Breaches of Explosives Act	5
Do. for Nuisances from Smoke	1
Do. for Breaches of Building Laws	4
Do. Nightly Lodging-keepers, for Breaches of By-laws	2
Do. of Dairy Yard Owners, for Filthy Premises	4
* Do. for Establishing noxious Trades Workshops without due Notice	2
Do. for Ordinary Sanitary Offences	3135
Notices served	13750
Summonses served	3211
Total Number of Convictions	3196
Cases Dismissed	15

* Mr. D. Toler, Food Inspector, prosecuted two manufacturers of sausages whose premises were in a very filthy condition. They were fined £1 and 5s. respectively.

Source: Public Health Report for 1883, DCRPD, 1984, vol II, no. 70, pp 68-69

Table 3.4 Return of sanitary operations carried out in the year 1883, Dublin Corporation.

vene in the sanitary arrangements of individual private houses, even where these were sublet to a unreasonable degree, with toilet accommodation designed for a single family now shared by anything up to 100 persons? And in many the original minimal arrangements were in place, with little maintenance, for the preceding century or more. Few of these 'sanitary conveniences' were either sanitary or convenient, particularly for the women members of the household, while allowing human faeces to stay in close contact with residents guaranteed that infectious disease, such as dysentery, would follow. In 1879 the situation occupied the attention of both the city engineer, who was required to report to a *Royal Commission of Enquiry into the Sewerage and Drainage System of Dublin*, on how far a proper system of domestic scavenging would lessen the need for a system of main drainage, and the medical superintendent officer of health, who was called to account for the excessive mortality in the city.

Neither gentleman relied on delicate allusions or generalities. The facts were plain. In 1879 there were an estimated 7,800 water closets in Dublin, according to Parke Neville, the city engineer. While this number was daily increasing, there were still over 17,200 houses which relied solely on the outdoor dry closet or privy system. By a conservative estimate the toilet situation in at least 12,000 of these houses, mostly tenements, required 'immediate attention', and the efforts of the sanitary authorities to date were derisory: 'it is useless to think of repairing privies &c by cleaning them out and treating them to a little whitewash once a-year or so, while they are allowed to get filled to overflowing with filth of all kinds, until they cannot be entered, and then the yard is made use of instead, and the whole back premises gets saturated with urine, excreta and the slops and garbage from the house'. He could cite innumerable examples, such as the yard behind one crowded tenement house where the stones were swimming 'in black, putrescent matter, which on being disturbed gave out horrid stenches'.[64] Charles Cameron, chief medical officer, could testify to equally disgusting situations. In Maguinness's Court he found 'an ashpit containing certainly not less than a ton-weight of semi-fluid filth, exhaling the most disgusting odour'. The residents in the back rooms of the houses in Townsend Street which overlooked this cesspool testified to the stench and the injury to health.[65] Throughout the poorer areas the yards were generally of clay, and thus often damp, which was a danger to the children who were too often unshod, and the entrances to them so difficult that 'the tenants prefer the more convenient access to the street, and empty their slops into the street during the absence of the police'.[66] Even more revolting was the situation where there was no yard at all, and the privy was to be found in

---

[64] Parke Neville, 'Report of the City Engineer to lay all necessary evidence before the Royal Commission of Enquiry into the Sewerage and Drainage System of Dublin, and their Effects on the Sanitary Condition of the City', *RPDCD*, no. 184, (1879), p. 181, (hereafter *Sewerage and Drainage Inquiry*).

[65] Charles Cameron 'Report for the Month ended 3 September 1879', *RPDCD*, vol. 3 (1879), p. 154.

[66] Evidence of Dr Cameron, *Housing Inquiry 1885*, qs. 22,058.

'some such objectionable situation, as the area or kitchen', ie: the small space below ground-level fronting the cellar kitchen, with no possibility of removing effete matter.[67] Cameron found many of the ashpits in lanes and courts were much too large and 'in free communication with each other', so that the ashpit was a 'mere cesspool, containing a semi-liquid putrefying mass'. Maguinness's Court, Townsend Street was full of 'certainly not less than a ton-weight of semi-fluid filth, exhaling the most disgusting odour' so that residents of rooms overlooking this cesspool could never open their windows. The response of the health authority in this case was to demand that the nuisance 'be considerably reduced in size, and provided with a cover'.[68]

According to the city engineer it would be fruitless to introduce daily domestic scavenging unless there was first a blitz on the outdated privies and ashpits. 'Any really effective system must be accompanied with the removal and rebuilding of them all. Nothing short of this, I maintain, will remove the present evil'.[69] The accumulated filth of decades needed first to be removed, 'the old cesspool under seat of privies and the ashpit should be cleaned out thoroughly, as well as all the area of yard adjoining that may be saturated with filth, and then the space filled in with good, dry, builder's rubbish or some such material'. It was necessary that in each a new privy, with flagged bottom should be constructed, with a proper receptacle to be collected by the night-soil men 'every second day, if not every day'. Such drastic measures had proven essential in a 'midden town' such as Manchester; other places including Liverpool, Glasgow, and Edinburgh had to make similar investment of municipal funds.[70] If domestic scavenging was to be effective in Dublin following on the complete overhaul of yards and privies, 'the present system and mode of working must be entirely altered, and a new and effective staff employed'.[71]

There was no way the crisis could be tackled except at public expense, and in a professional, organised manner. Despite strong arguments that 'it was opposed to all principles of political economy to clean tenements and yards', the Public Health Committee, under the chairmanship of Mr Gray, persuaded the Corporation to undertake the activity on a limited basis, on the grounds that such a move was essential to the protection of public health.[72] In 1883 the Corporation claimed credit for the cleansing of over 2,000 yards and 'external premises', along with forcing the construction, repair and cleansing, and reconstruction of hundreds of sewers, house drains, privies, water closets and ashpits (Table 3.4). By 1885 it was claimed that there was not a solitary objection to the Corporation's initiative, despite the cost of £3,000 per annum to the city's rate-payers.[73] In 1898

[67] Ibid.
[68] 'Report of the Public Health Committee', *RPDCD*, vol. 3, no. 170 (1879), p. 154.
[69] Neville, *Sewerage and Drainage Inquiry* (1879), p. 180.
[70] Ibid., p. 181.
[71] Ibid., p. 183.
[72] *Housing Inquiry 1885*, qs. 22,072–22,080.
[73] Evidence of Dr Cameron, *Housing Inquiry 1885*, qs. 22,241–22,244.

Dr Cameron brought a *Daily Nation* journalist to see the improvement wrought by the Corporation, and referring to the introduction of 'the proper class of closets and the concreting of the yards' of selected houses, asked, 'What more can the Corporation do than they have done, shutting up offensive ashpits and cellars? And now, does it not remain for the tenants themselves to keep their places clean?'[74]

The question of whether water closets should be promoted in place of the dry privies had serious ramifications; in 1879 the sewers were grossly inadequate to the task in hand, and the Liffey was the sole destination, with disastrous results.[75] By 1885 the Corporation was using a loan of £1,000 to enforce the erection of water-closets, in tenement houses 'the owners of which were unable or unwilling to do the work themselves'.[76]

The Dublin Sanitary Association disagreed with the enthusiasm of Dr Cameron and the Corporation's Public Health Committee for the new-fangled water-closet system. Frederic Pim, honorary secretary, brought evidence before the Housing Inquiry of 1885 testifying to the filth of individual water closets which was as bad as anything that the old privy system could offer: numbers 36 and 37 in James's Street had two water closets completely choked up to the level of the seat as there had been no water supply for some time, while in numbers 33 and 34 South King Street, the water was flowing perpetually but uselessly, the water closets choked and full. It was held that this system was too vulnerable for widespread adoption in the Dublin tenements, for 'the filthy habits of one single inmate may render decent cleanliness impossible', through throwing something unsuitable down the toilet. And as with the privies, the number of water closets was utterly inadequate to the population. Their location – as in the case of 33 and 34 South King Street, in a cramped yard beside a large ashpit, and bounded by the wall of a slaughter house – was often totally unsuitable.[77]

The sanitary habits of the occupants of the lowest class of tenements were attacked with such vigour that on a pilot basis, the 'pail system of depositing excreta' was recommended, a system which it was claimed was rapidly extending in England.[78] Those reared in the country but settled in Dublin were accused of 'throwing out the offal of the houses upon the pavement. They seem to think they are still in the country, and contributing to their manure heaps'; the police were regarded as the only persons who could effectually deal with such nuisances.[79]

The Inspection of Tenement Houses and Yards: Legal Obstacles

While the public health authority could decide on what were sanitary nuisances

---

[74] *Daily Nation*, 3 September 1898.
[75] Neville, *Sewerage and Drainage Inquiry* (1879), pp. 185–186.
[76] *Housing Inquiry 1885*, qs. 22,128.
[77] Evidence of Frederic William Pim, *Housing Inquiry 1885*, qs, 22,609–22,637.
[78] 'Report of the Public Health Committee', *RPDCD*, vol. 3, no. 170 (1879), p. 154.
[79] Cameron & Mapother, *Prevention of Disease* (1879), p. 352

or structural deficiencies, file complaints, issue orders and even pressurise the local authority to introduce limited domestic scavenging, the questions of legal title and definition always returned. Who could be called to account, and forced to make good the defect? And should the matter come under the heading of housing reform or sanitary improvement?

Under the first serious attempt at slum housing reform, the Artisans' and Labourers' Dwellings Act 1868 (Torrens Act)[80] the local authority, on the report of their medical officer of health that premises were 'in a state injurious to health, or unfit for human habitation' could order the owner to execute the necessary structural improvements according to prepared specifications; in default the Corporation could carry out the necessary work and obtain a court order demanding payment from the owner. Such a provision, 'most useful in intention and just in principle' was utterly unworkable in the case of the Dublin tenements. Both the officer of health and the engineer had to prepare reports, then both reports had to be served on the owner, a sitting of the authority to hear objections had to be held, then the plans had to be prepared, then a second sitting to hear objections to these, and at each stage there was the possibility of appeals to Quarter Session and then to the Queen's Bench, and pending final appeal no work could be done. The term 'owner' was complicated beyond belief in the case of the Dublin tenements; where there were several owners of a single house they often held 'fractional undivided shares in common, some of these persons living far away, some minors, or married women, or otherwise under disability, some persons of most limited means'.[81] Where there were several owners the right of carrying out the work had to be offered to each in turn; the owner ordered to execute the work had the option of demolishing the premises, but was not to prejudice the operation of existing leases in the covenant! Wherever the ownership could be ascertained, the person had some means, and the premises was of sufficient value that the outlay might be recouped, it appeared likely, on paper at least, that the work would eventually be done. The Dublin system of immediate lessors, 'little removed socially from their lodgers, letting in tenements at the last possible shilling and at the least possible outlay' rendered any such hopes futile. The 1879 amendment to the Artizans' and Labourers' Dwellings Act[82] brought some slight improvements, but gave the owner the alternative power of compulsory purchase in every case. Wherever an owner was compelled to make improvements he/she could require the local authority to purchase the premises, 'and the lands thus acquired may be applied to any sanitary purpose, or to a highway, street or public place'.[83]

It was the later public health legislation which was to prove more useful.

[80] 31 & 32 Victoria, c.131, sections 6–9, 14, 22
[81] F. R. Falkiner, 'Report on Homes of the Poor', *Soc. Stat. Inq. Soc. Ire. Jn.* vol. Vlll, part LIX, (1882), p. 267, (hereafter 'Homes of the Poor').
[82] 42 & 43 Victoria, c.64 (The Artizans' and Labourers' Dwellings Act 1864, Amendment Act 1879).
[83] Falkiner , 'Homes of the Poor' (1882), pp. 266–267.

Under the Public Health (Ireland) Act 1878, which consolidated and amended all previous sanitary legislation, the Corporation as sanitary authority was granted 'large compulsory powers of enforcing structural improvements in the city houses'. Now its remit extended to insufficient sewerage, whitewashing and cleansing, defective water supply, abatement of nuisances, etc.. Wherever the owner or occupier failed to comply with the demands of the sanitary inspector, the Corporation was entitled to undertake the necessary work itself and either recover the expenses in court or levy a 'private improvement rate' on the occupier, which with 5% interest was to be paid over a period not exceeding thirty years. Thereupon the difficulties resembled those of the inoperative Torrens Act (1868): the definition of 'owner' and the intricacies of recovering the costs in the Dublin tenement situation. Only in the case of abatement of nuisances could the Corporation obtain a preliminary judicial inquiry or order; wherever else it took the initiative it was 'at the risk of recovering it from a doubtful defendant, doubtfully solvent often, or by an exceptional rate leviable upon doubtful property'.[84]

Genuine efforts to improve the structural arrangements of tenement houses were, it was claimed, impracticable 'owing to the habits of the inmates, and the certain destruction which awaited improved appliances'.[85] At the Royal Commission Inquiry of 1879 some property owners testified that the 'more worthless tenants frequently, on falling into arrear, wilfully dilapidate or permit dilapidation whilst under notice of eviction, whilst they cannot be dispossessed even by summary order in less than an average of six weeks'; those victimised in such a situation were the 'more well conducted tenants' who had to meet increased rents.[86] Strict punitive measures were recommended, especially the power of summary eviction on the order of a divisional justice, and the Corporation was urged to enforce the registration of tenement houses, a power available under the Public Health Act of 1878, but initially avoided by the Corporation.[87]

Public Scavenging and 'Places not in Charge of the Corporation'

Concern with the internal sanitary arrangements of the tenement houses and their yards occupied the attentions of the medical officers and city engineer, but it was the filth of public streets and open places that drew most of the complaints from the ordinary rate-payers. During 1879 the state of the laneways was under discussion; much 'organic filth' was deposited 'after the scavengers had visited the lanes, and usually about breakfast time' where it would then remain for two or three days. But however objectionable the lane and street rubbish might be, from a sanitary point of view it was held that it would be preferable 'to allow the mud in the wide streets to remain, and to speedily

---

[84] Ibid., p. 238.
[85] Ibid., p. 269.
[86] Ibid., p. 269.
[87] Ibid., p. 270.
[88] 'Report of the Public Health Committee', *RPDCD*, vol. 3, no. 170 (1879), p. 154.

remove from the narrow courts the refuse which is daily deposited therein'.[88] Wet streets were considered dangerous, emitting noxious fumes, so the 'thorough and frequent cleansing of the footpaths and streets' would speed up the process of drying out after rain, and so diminish 'the actual amount of damp in the streets'. However, the material with which the streets were laid was an important factor in determining how successful any scavenging would be; the widespread macadamized street pavement was condemned as damp, and a pavement of 'smooth stones, between the intervals of which greenstone, or whin gravel and asphalte, should be placed, so as to form with the stones a tolerably impervious pavement, though wherever possible the ideal, asphalte, should be laid'.[89] The costs of the public health campaign were ever-escalating.

Little progress had been made by 1884, when the newly-appointed Superintendent of Cleansing, James Young, held that there was no city or town 'similar in extent, population, or importance to Dublin' in the United Kingdom in which the public thoroughfares were so abused, serving as 'receptacles for house, fish, vegetable and other shop refuse, and every kind of filth'. Part of the difficulty in resolving this problem was the division of responsibility; ironically, the increased professionalism with which the public health issue was being treated had led to a replication of agencies, reminiscent of the pre-1849 municipal situation. The Dublin Metropolitan Police had the duty of preventing the abuse of the streets, the Public Health Committee was supposed to compel house owners to provide proper receptacles for house-refuse, while the Cleansing Committee undertook the regular scavenging of the streets and lanes. Each of these three authorities operated within a separate administrative division. To ensure 'combined action and a satisfactory result' the superintendent of scavenging in 1884 tabulated 354 streets and lanes regularly abused, the sanitary, police and cleansing divisions to which each belonged, how often per week each was scavenged, and the type of refuse deposited there, such as stable manure, house refuse and fish.[90]

The problem was always that of the back lanes. Not alone were they used as open toilets by some residents or passers-by, 'they also serve as depots in which, night after night, cartloads of rubbish or refuse are deposited by persons who take advantage of the darkness or the temporary absence of the police to effect their purpose'. Vegetable refuse, warehouses' and stores' refuse, builders' refuse, stable manure, and the waste of fish markets and slaughter houses were among the cartloads of rubbish surreptitiously dumped to be removed at the expense of the rate-payers through the Cleansing Committee.[91]

Successful street scavenging created another problem for the authorities: where to locate large depots for receiving street manure and mud. Stanley Street off Grangegorman Lane to the north, and Marrowbone Lane and Wood Quay to

---

[89] Cameron & Mapother (1879), pp. 342–343.
[90] James Young, 'Report of the Superintendent of Cleansing on the Condition of the Back Streets and Lanes of the City, caused by the Deposit of Refuse upon them', *RPDCD*, vol. 1, no. 30 (1884), pp. 203–207.
[91] Ibid., pp. 203–207.

the south, were the earliest locations, both adjoining densely populated poor districts. The move in 1879 was to relocate such depots outside the city, but pending that at least to separate the 'mere mud' from the 'objectionable refuse', the latter to be carted out of the city 'to some open place, not near a habitation'.[92] The masses of waste vegetable matter in summer, the 'large quantity of the stalks and outer leaves of cabbages, which are to be met with in the vegetable markets and in the steamboat quays', was considered the chief cause 'of the nuisance which is observable at the Corporation depot, Stanley Street'.[93] Ideally, two new, large depots were needed, one north, one south of the city, fronting the canals as was the case in Birmingham; from here the manure could be sold to contractors, who could transport it by boat into the country, and also carry rubbish to some waste land for deposit. The alternative under consideration was to dump street scavenge at sea. Parke Neville, city engineer, held that such rubbish could be carried by tram and deposited at Annesley Bridge, and the strand being reclaimed at Ringsend.[94] However necessary such initiatives might be in the context of the city slums, they were not always appreciated by the neighbouring sanitary authorities. The Guardians of the North Dublin Union lodged formal objections with the Public Health Committee of the Corporation in August 1880 against a manure depot on the southern bank of the Royal Canal near Lower Dorset Street; the deposit of decayed vegetables and other nuisances was 'calculated to create an epidemic in a very populous neighbourhood quite convenient to St Francis Xavier's Schools, Mountjoy Prison and the Whitworth Hospitals'.[95] Whatever choices were made, criticism from some source was inevitable.

The Main Drainage Epic

Efforts to 'cleanse' the city slums and the larger municipal area, and to bring down the death rate, came back again and again to the question of 'main drainage': not alone were visible accumulations of filth offensive, but the inhalation of sewer gas was held responsible for typhoid fever, sore throats, and diarrhoea, a matter of great concern as the Liffey banks 'are swarmed by an overworked and badly fed people'.[96] In 1853 Parke Neville, city engineer, prepared a general plan for the improvement of the sewerage of the city. In his plans he was 'bound by the levels &c. of the large old sewers and rivers which formed the outlets for the drainage of the city into the Liffey'; he improved these 'low-level tide-locked sewers' as best he could by 'putting egg-shaped or semicircular invert bottoms into them, and by bringing them to regular gradients to prevent stagnant water lying in them'.[97] Further progress was to be very slow, as the scale of the

[92] Cameron & Mapother, *Prevention of Disease* (1879), p. 347.
[93] Ibid.
[94] Neville, *Sewerage and Drainage Inquiry* (1879), pp. 184–185.
[95] Minutes of the North Dublin Union, Resolution, 10 August 1880.
[96] Antisell, *Suggestions* (1847), p. 6.
[97] 'Report of Parke Neville, City Engineer, for the years 1882 and 1883', *RPDCD* vol. 2, no. 108 (1884), p. 475, (hereafter Parke Neville, City Engineer, 1884).

solution was formidable: a system of main drainage, which would place unspeakable pressure on municipal finances, at a moment when so many more visible crises intruded themselves on the attention of the councillors.

A main drainage scheme was legislated for in 1870; its abandonment led to the inquiry of 1879 into the best means now to be adopted regarding the drainage and sewerage of the city. In the intervening period the townships of Rathmines and Pembroke (see Figure 1.1) had disengaged themselves from the scheme and were constructing their own main drainage works, distancing themselves in the most blatant way from any inclusion in the municipality. The revised estimate for the city's downgraded plans of 1879 was £350,000,[98] a level of funding which was all the more difficult to raise now that the wealthy townships had opted out.

Critical attention was directed spasmodically at the city engineer's office. Complaints in 1884 that the pipe sewers this department had directed to be laid for short lengths of streets, lanes and alleys from 25–150 yards long were too small and should have been of brick construction were vehemently refuted, and the blame placed on those who abused the sewers, especially the residents of the poorer parts of the city who 'make use of the gullies and ventilating grates for depositing the refuse of their dwellings' leading to frequent stoppages, and the street scavengers who, when unsupervised, found this a tempting way of 'easily and quickly disposing of the mud'.[99] The city engineer was adamant that the blame for the high death rate should not be laid at his sewers: 'from above thirty years personal observation' he could state categorically that the high mortality 'arises from the filthy, overcrowded and impoverished condition of the habitations of the poor'.[100] And for that claim there was overwhelming evidence.

The main drainage campaign was tied in to the privy *vs.* water closet debate. The substitution of water closets for privies in the better-off establishments in the city was proceeding apace regardless of the destination of the water-born sewage, i.e., the river Liffey. One line of argument held that the evils arising from the discharge of sewage into the Liffey were outweighed by the evils produced by the storage of sewage for any length of time in the city; 'continuous discharge' was of the essence. However, the tidal movements of the Liffey caused the mouths of the drains to be sealed up so that the dangerous gases frequently 'regurgitate into the houses and produce disease'. And aside from the main sewers which led into the Liffey, the sewers connecting individual houses, 'even in the best quarters' were found 'as a rule to be very defective'.[101]

In 1879 the city engineer estimated that there were about 7,800 water closets in the city, with the number constantly increasing; the existing sewers had to cope with this effluent along with street refuse washed in by rainwater, and the contents of 'all urinals, slop closets, including domestic scullery troughs &c.'. The only way the Liffey could be restored to its former (relatively) healthy state

---

[98] Neville, *Sewerage and Drainage Inquiry* (1879), p. 186.
[99] Parke Neville, City Engineer (1884), pp. 474–475.
[100] Ibid., p. 475.
[101] Cameron & Mapother, *Prevention of Disease* (1879), p. 345.

was by preventing the sewage going into it in the first place.[102] The various means adopted by comparable British cities to deal with the challenge of house-scavenging and sewage disposal were worth exploring, and to that end Parke Neville was despatched on a fact-finding mission which included Birmingham, Bradford, Manchester, Leeds, Liverpool, Glasgow and Edinburgh. In Bradford the authorities were trying unsuccessfully to reform the old midden system by introducing an improved design (Figure 3.1a). Neville was more impressed with the systems adopted in Rochdale (Figure 3.1b), Manchester (Figure 3.2a) and Edinburgh (Figure 3.2b), which first eliminated the old cess pools by clearing them out, filling them in with dry builders' rubble, and then constructing single or multiple privies on a cement floor, the contents to be carried away by cart, at municipal expense, at least every second day. A box or tube for ashes was to be part of each unit, ready for the scavenger to cover the sewage as it was thrown into the cart; responsibility for ensuring a ready supply of ashes ready was to rest on the householders. In Rochdale a superior type of collecting van had been developed (Figure 3.2c). The construction of 'cleansing passages', and the paving or cementing of surrounding yards were also required of this system, so that it was not a cheap option, nor did it remove the urgency of reviving the main drainage project, for the Liffey would continue to be used as an open sewer by the multiplying water-closets and other contributors.

The debate over privies *vs* water-closets and the diversion of sewage away from the Liffey continued; in 1885 Dr Cameron upheld that the water closet system was ideal for Dublin on the basis that any system which gets rid of the excreta of the human population was to be promoted, 'and I am utterly opposed to the storing of human excreta within a few feet of human habitations'. On that basis, he considered the 'mischief' done to the river Liffey from the water-borne sewage as 'extremely small compared with the mischief done by storing excrement in the yards of small houses', refusing to accept that the Liffey in itself was the cause of the high death-rate in Dublin. He preferred the 'expeditious and cleanly method' of the water-closet system over the pail system as operated in Birmingham, Rochdale and Manchester, where the pails were removed every day in carts and brought to the manure works (Figures 3.1, 3.2). That said, Cameron insisted that water closets, as with dry privies, should be in the yard, not the house (unless there were servants to take care of it), where if it does get into a bad condition it would do less damage than when in the house itself.[103] Funds to commence work on the long-debated main drainage scheme were raised in 1892, and in September 1906 the scheme was in operation, relieving the lower reaches of the Liffey, at least officially, from the task of carrying sewage for the first time since the city's foundation.

---

[102] Neville, *Sewerage and Drainage Inquiry* (1879), p. 186.
[103] Evidence of Dr Cameron, *Housing Inquiry 1885*, qs 22,243–22,253.

A Matter of Life and Death: Public Health, 1800–1900   89

a) BRADFORD CORPORATION

Approved Plan of Privies and Ashpit.

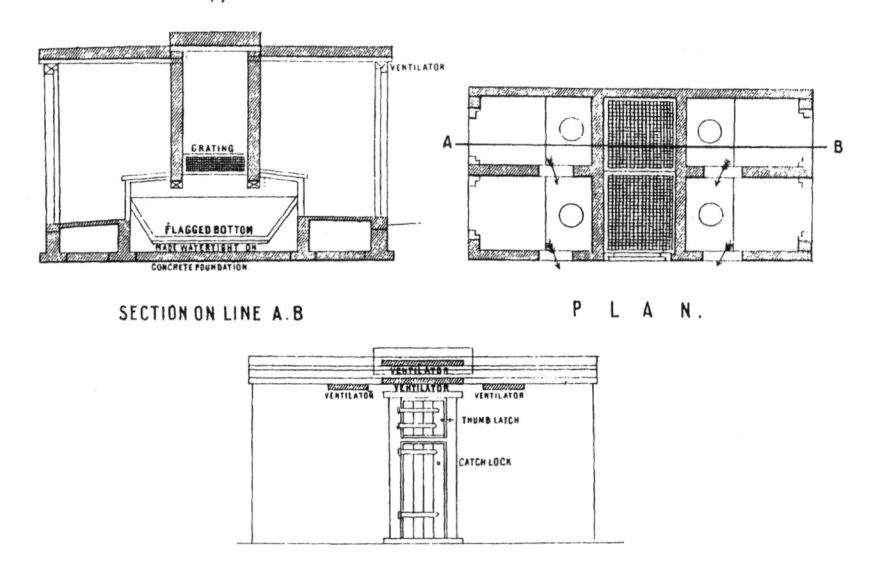

SECTION ON LINE A.B   P L A N.

ELEVATION.

b) ROCHDALE CORPORATION

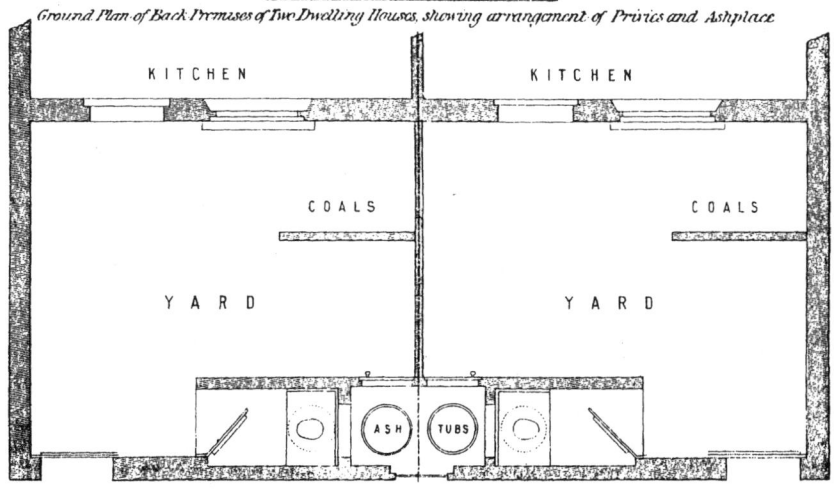

Ground Plan of Back Premises of Two Dwelling Houses, showing arrangement of Privies and Ashplace

Source: Report of the City Engineer, *RPDCD*, III (184) 1879, pp 164-167

Figure 3.1 Sanitary arrangements approved by British municipal authorities: (a) Corporation of Bradford, (b) Corporation of Rochdale.

90   *Dublin Slums*

a) CITY OF MANCHESTER

Detail Drawing attached to Specification of Privies

b) EDINBURGH CORPORATION

Dry Earth Closet in Burnet's Close, Edinburgh

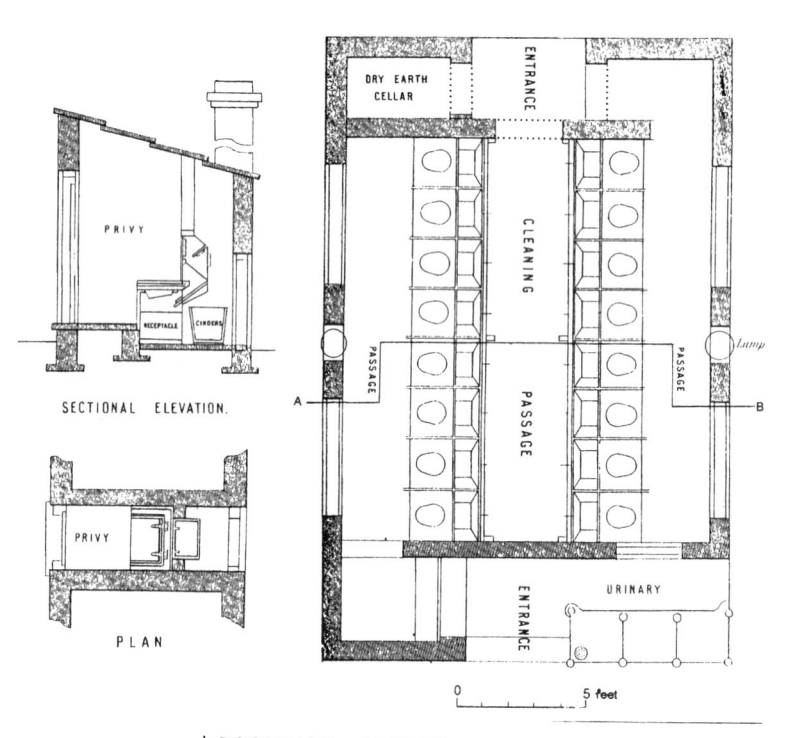

c) ROCHDALE CORPORATION

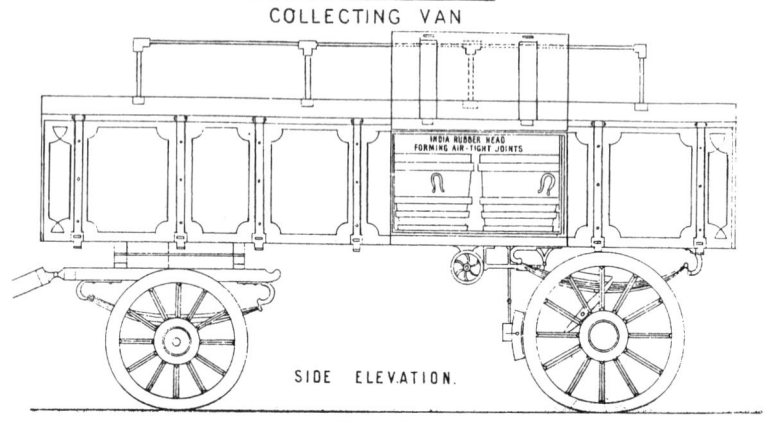

Report of the City Engineer, *RPDCD*, III (184) 1879, pp 164-167

Figure 3.2 Sanitary arrangements approved by British municipal authorities: (a) City of Manchester, (b) Corporation of Edinburgh, (c) Corporation of Rochdale.

Regulation of Slaughter Houses and Dairy Yards

City centre slaughter houses and dairy yards were recognised as 'public nuisances' from at least the end of the eighteenth century. The Cork Street Trustees condemned dairies 'as they are generally kept, a most offensive nuisance', as well as slaughter houses, and the operation of 'unwholesome trades'.[104] Whitelaw (1805) experienced the nastiness of city-centre slaughter houses in a memorable manner when he attempted to record the population of a ruinous house in Joseph's Lane, near Castle Market; his progress was interrupted 'by an inundation of putrid blood, alive with maggots, which had, from an adjacent slaughter yard, burst the back-door, and filled the hall to the depth of several inches', a scene to which the locals seemed inured, as they waded through the filth to reach the staircase.[105] Despite such disgusting scenes and smells, the regulation of both dairy yards and slaughter houses was one of the more vexatious issues in the public health debate. They were an intrinsic part of the slum districts: the distribution of the 99 slaughter-houses registered with Dublin Corporation in 1879 (Figure 3.3) points to their concentration in the most congested parts of the city. On the south side the most noteworthy concentrations were around Patrick Street and the aptly-named Bull Alley and directly north of the Coombe, around Garden Lane/Spitalfields/Carman's Hall. There were slaughter houses along Thomas Street, leading west, and along Lower Camden Street, leading south. Both the south docks district (the lanes off Townsend Street) and the transition area around Chatham Street were also represented. North of the Liffey there were two major concentrations: between Moore Street and Coles Lane (Sampson's Lane, Market Place, see Chapter 8), and around Ormond Market (including Beef Row and Walker's Alley). Close to the Royal Barracks (see Figure 2.3, Plate 2.4) there were also several licensed slaughter houses. However, the most noteworthy aspect of the distribution is its dispersed pattern: on the south side practically all of the low-value residential areas (see Figure 2.6) are represented, with only the south eastern Fitzwilliam/Pembroke estate sector managing to avoid such obnoxious activities through restrictive clauses in their leases. In the north eastern residential Gardiner district, with the breakdown of tight estate management, several slaughter houses could be found, as well as in the older markets districts.

The regulation of slaughter houses was a task of enormous dimensions. The licensing system did more to protect the owner and operator of a slaughter house than further the cause of public health. All owners possessing licences granted before the municipal restructuring in 1849 could not be made to surrender them 'unless under the authority of an Act of Parliament'; under the Public Health Act 1878 the Corporation had power to impose stringent regulations on their operation, but once these were complied with had no further powers.[106] The by-laws passed in 1882 allowed for the licensing, registering and inspection of

---

[104] Cork Street Trustees (1802), p. 8.
[105] Whitelaw, *Survey* (1805), p. 53.
[106] Cameron & Mapother, *Prevention of Disease* (1879), p. 348.

92   *Dublin Slums*

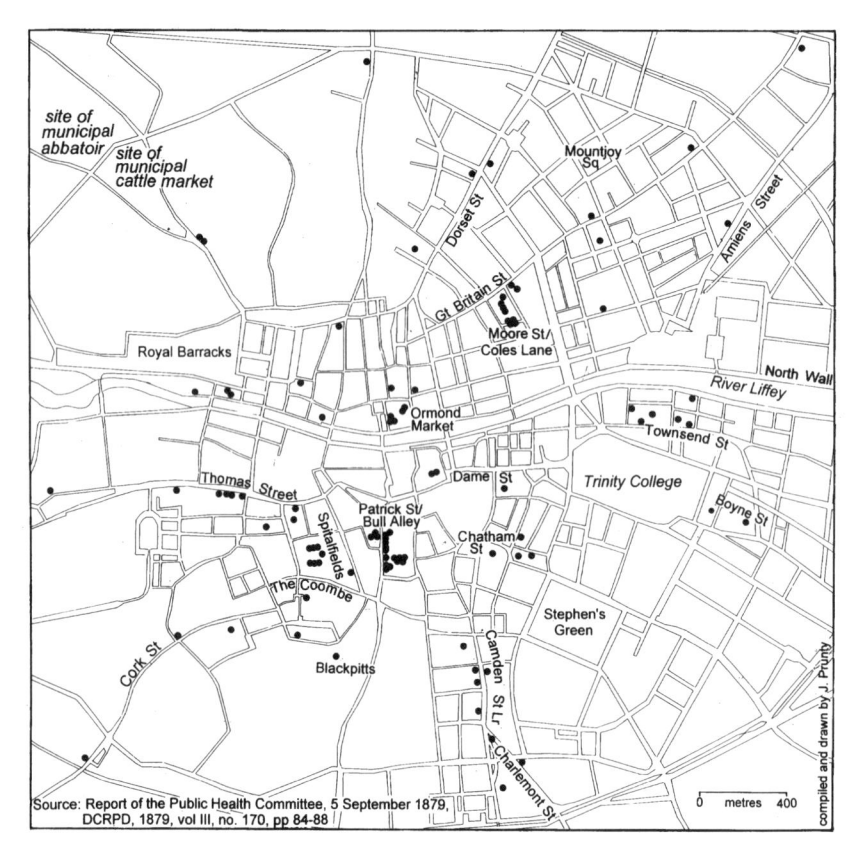

Figure 3.3 Registered slaughter houses, Dublin 1879

slaughter houses, 'for preventing cruelty therein; for keeping the same in a cleanly and healthy state; for removing filth at least once in every twenty-four hours, and requiring a sufficient supply of water'.[107] The Corporation could of course purchase the licences, but at inflated prices, the bargaining power lying with the licensee. In 1893 a special officer to inspect the city slaughter houses was appointed, and the policy of removing such unsuitable land uses from the city centre pursued with new earnestness. Within six years the number of slaughter houses was reduced from 72 to 63; a further nine were purchased by the philanthropic Iveagh Trust, to be levelled as part of the Bull Alley scheme of block dwellings and the adjoining St Patrick's Park (see Figures 4.5, 4.6). The medical officer for health repeatedly urged that 'all the most objectionable ones should be abolished, even if the cost were considerable'.[108]

---

[107] *The Dublin Civic Survey Report* (Liverpool, 1925), p. 53.
[108] Charles Cameron, *Report of Public Health Committee for 1899* (Dublin, 1900), p. 956.

The most positive way forward was the provision of excellent public abattoirs, ideally one on either side of the Liffey, promoted in 1879 as 'one of the most important sanitary improvements that could be effected in Dublin'. Here the 'animals intended for human food could be slaughtered with the least amount of suffering, and their carcasses dressed in a cleanly matter'. It would also greatly facilitate the detection of diseased meat.[109] Private operators could only be coaxed to relocate, the general hope being that 'those holding licenses would soon see that it would be to their advantage to use the public abattoirs, with the convenient appliances with which they would be provided'.[110]

The apathy or hostility of private slaughter house owners towards the proposed model abattoir was only one of the difficulties the Corporation faced. The Guardians of the North Dublin Union (NDU) were the sanitary authority (under the Public Health (Ireland) Act 1878) for the district beyond the North Circular Road, and objected 'strongly and earnestly' to the proposal. Public slaughter houses would depreciate the values of local property, in an area 'which is now and has been for sometime rapidly improving'. It would be uncomfortably close to the Protestant Female Orphan House and two Catholic churches, and would 'cause and be the resort of a class of persons notorious for unruly and improper conduct'. The NDU Guardians could see no reason why any of a number of sites within the city boundary, such as in the vicinity of the North Wall, could not be utilised instead.[111] The Local Government Board supported the Corporation's proposal, the city boundary was extended to include the contentious site, and a model abattoir opened in 1882 (Figure 3.3). However, many of the slaughter house operators that it was hoped to attract failed to relocate, and in some respects the Corporation had only itself to blame. The Public Health Committee compromised their own medical officers' campaign against city slaughter houses. In 1906 the committee supported the application of the owner of a disused swine slaughter house at no. 3 Carman's Hall, adjoining Spitalfields, a most densely populated and insanitary district, to recommence operations there, on the basis that 'it would conduce more to the welfare of the Country to slaughter all the pigs possible at home, and export the meat'.[112] Rather than develop to cover all aspects of the city's slaughter needs, the new city abattoir was to operate alongside over 50 private, poorly inspected slaughter yards in traditional locations (Figure 3.3, see also Chapter 8, Figure 8.11).[113] By 1925 this municipal asset was condemned as utterly inadequate under every possible heading.[114]

---

[109] Cameron & Mapother, *Prevention of Disease* (1879), pp. 347–348.
[110] Ibid., p. 348.
[111] Minutes of the North Dublin Union, Resolution, 29 November 1879.
[112] 'Report of the Public Health Committee in re renewal of the licence of an old slaughter house at No. 3 Carman's Hall', *RPDCD*, vol. 2, no. 145 (1906), pp. 503–504.
[113] *Dublin Civic Survey*, 1925, p. 53.
[114] Ibid., pp. xix, 53.

While the keeping of cows was less of a health risk than the slaughtering of animals, the massive number of city dairy yards, and the state in which many were kept, rendered such a distinction unimportant. The addresses of dairy yards, the owners of which were prosecuted for their filth and squalor, are evidence of how dairy yards were an intrinsic part of the local geography of slum areas. As with slaughter houses, recorded objections date back to the surveys of the early nineteenth century (Chapter 2).

The difficulties surrounding their regulation are exposed in the complaint made by Mercer's Hospital in 1875 to the Local Government Board, against 'the nuisance and injury caused to the patients' by the condition of an adjoining dairy yard, the property of Andrew Moore (Figure 3.4).[115] On inspection the secretary of the Public Health Committee of the Corporation found 70 cows, 4 pigs and 4 horses, 'all kept in a fairly cleanly condition', the yard paved, sewered and kept in a 'cleanly state', excepting a manure heap 'amounting to about 30 loads'. The Corporation was utterly powerless to move against the large number of animals kept once the yard was in a 'cleanly' state; it could only act against accumulations of manure. In this case the inspector's order that the manure heap be removed forthwith was repeatedly ignored, court proceedings were required, and eventually a magistrate's order obtained and grudgingly complied with. This included a requirement that future accumulations of manure be at point B (Figure 3.4). The nonsense of such limited powers was outlined by the officer, who could supply any number of examples of dairy yards kept in a worse state and in more threatening locations. In the dairy yard adjoining Mercer's Hospital few of the cows had more than 240 cubic feet space each; in the dairy yards adjoining the former House of Industry hospitals in the north city (Chapter 6, Figure 6.3) an average of 470 head of cattle were kept during the winter, with about 230 cubic feet of space per beast, insufficient to allow two adjacent animals to lie down at the same time. In London the minimum cubic space per animal was fixed by law at 600 feet.[116]

It was only when an outbreak of typhoid in the respectable Pembroke township was traced definitively to a city centre dairy yard in 1879 that sufficient energy was generated to tackle the scandal. Their regulation required constant vigilance, as of their nature it was 'almost impossible to prevent them, more especially when situated in densely crowded districts, becoming a nuisance'. By the end of 1899 there were 531 dairies and milk shops, and 227 cowsheds registered within the city and under the inspection of the Sanitary Department.[117] However, the consensus of all, bar the dairy owners, was that cows should be kept 'in yards on the outer ring of the city, and not in its central and more densely populated portions'.[118] But how far out from the built-up area? There was little advantage

---

[115] James Boyle, letter to the Public Health Committee, 'Public Health Report', *RPDCD*, no. 36 (1875), pp. 8–11.
[116] Ibid., p. 10.
[117] Charles Cameron, *Report of Public Health Committee for 1899* (Dublin, 1900), pp. 957–959.

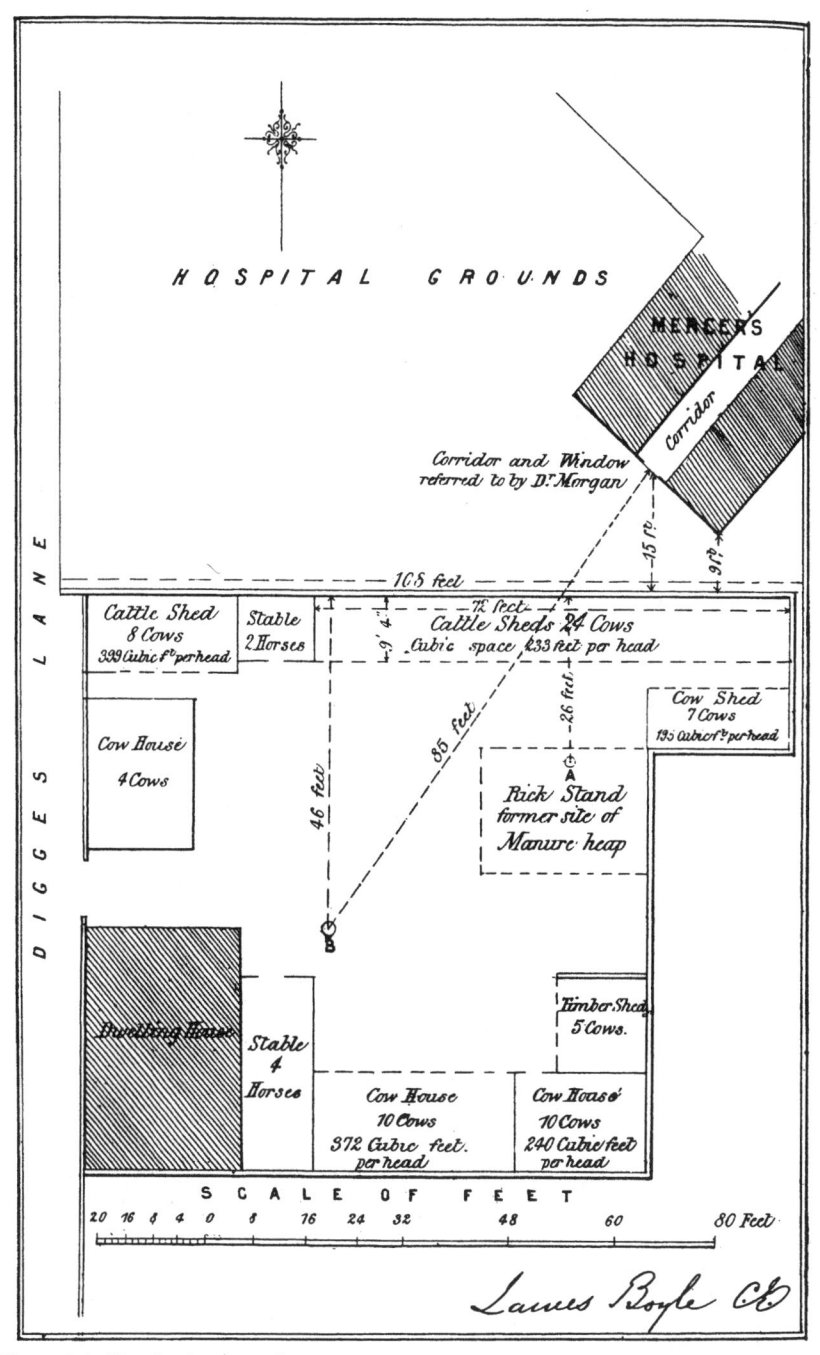

Figure 3.4 Sketch plan re nuisance occasioned by dairy yard adjoining Mercer's Hospital, Dublin, 22 July 1875, Report of Public Health Committee, *RPDCD*, I (36) 1875, p. 11

in the city's sanitary officers advocating dairy-yards beyond their jurisdiction, and there was plenty of evidence to show that an unregulated country dairy could be every bit as unwholesome and dangerous as a city cowshed. In 1899 vendors of milk whose supply was sourced outside the municipal boundary were obliged to register with the Corporation, and some whose premises were unsatisfactory were prevented from trading. Where disease was noted, the milk, butter and eggs found on the premises could be destroyed immediately by the inspecting officers.[119] But in the meantime, cows continued to be kept in substantial numbers in downtown Dublin.

Markets

The control of wholesale markets was an important municipal responsibility, as the Lord Mayor of Dublin was constituted 'sole Clerk of the Markets within the City' (*sic*) under 'ancient charters' and more relevantly, under the Dublin Improvement Act 1849. This act also empowered him to reform the city markets, a task which was not faced until the 1880s when land in the neighbourhood of Smithfield was offered to the city engineer's department as a site for wholesale markets.

The need for wholesale markets, properly regulated, with financial benefits accruing to the Corporation, was long argued. A *Royal Commission on Fairs and Markets in Ireland* 1852–1853 reported that the very necessary reform of the Dublin markets was beyond the ability of the Lord Mayor, an officer of one year's standing, in the face of 'vested interest and established usages', 'and when unofficial persons attempt any improvement, the crippled finances and cloud of compensations to be afforded scare away all change'.[120] In 1875 proposals were presented by Francis Morgan, law and land agent, to Committee Number 2 (the markets committee), proposing sites for new markets in potatoes, fruit and vegetables, and fish, along with significant improvements in the layout and operation of the hay and straw market (Smithfield) and the pig market (Hay Market, see Figure 2.3).[121] The 'disgusting state' in which fish was sold by 'filthy and drunken women sitting obstructively on the footways and pavement in Pill Lane and Patrick Street' was, it was claimed, 'a living reproach to corporate administration' 24 years after the powers to reform such situations had been placed in the hands of the city administration.[122] And it was a no-win situation: in 1878 and 1879 the police magistrate refused to levy fines on dealers in fish standing in Pill Lane as there was no designated market in which they could sell

---

[118] Cameron & Mapother, *Prevention of Disease* (1879), p. 348.
[119] Charles Cameron, *Report of Public Health Committee for 1899* (Dublin, 1900), pp. 957–959.
[120] *Report of Royal Commission to Inquire into the Fairs and Markets in Ireland*, vol. 41 (1852–1853), p. 31, quoted in 'Report of Markets Committee', *RPDCD*, vol. 2 (1886), p. 304.
[121] Francis Morgan, 'Report of Markets Committee', *RPDCD*, no. 19 (1875), pp. 3–11.
[122] Ibid., p. 5.

their wares.[123] The vegetable markets brought their own particular problems, at least some of which did not require any major municipal intervention to alleviate. The carriage of untrimmed vegetables into the city led to hundreds of tons of decaying vegetable matter, so that an exasperated Dr Cameron, having heard yet again the reasons favouring this practice, exclaimed, 'surely if in other towns, cabbages are deprived of their stalks and some of their outer leaves before being exposed for sale, the same practice might be adopted in Dublin!' The question of who really controlled the markets constantly recurred: 'salutary regulations' could be made if the wholesale vegetable markets were in the possession of the Corporation, but pending that development there was little that could be done by the markets committee, despite its best intentions.[124]

The Corporation's plans to reform the fish, vegetable and general markets of the north city, was a long running saga that was to culminate in 1894 in the erection of the magnificent covered north city markets, on the site between Mary's Lane and Old Pill Lane (realigned and widened). On the south side a long-standing slum area to the west of Stephen's Green 'occupied by slaughter houses, stables, and 119 tenement houses' between South Great George's Street and Fade Street (see Figure 2.6 and Plate 4.1) was redeveloped by the South City Markets company. This company was formed to erect a public market and widen streets in connection with it, under the provisions of a special act with compulsory powers.[125] The Gothic red brick and terra-cotta building, with a glass-roofed market in the interior, was erected 1878–81. The company's main role in the slum story was to effect comprehensive redevelopment of a mixed residential district solely for commercial purposes, in the hope that its location on the edge of the retail and financial core of the city (near Dame Street) would ensure success.

Municipal Improvements, 1884

In 1877 the Corporation promoted an Improvement Bill which failed to become law; however, the objects of this bill are a good indication of the changing agenda of the public health movement, as it pushes for structural transformation rather than simple regulation. The Corporation sought extensive powers to create new streets and to widen and improve existing streets; fourteen such schemes were detailed, none of which were undertaken until after 1880. It was also concerned with the creation of new thoroughfares by owners of ground, who 'lay out streets through their property, throw some rubbish on the intended carriageways and paths, let the ground by the foot frontage', on which small dwelling-houses were rapidly erected and immediately occupied; these streets were then abandoned by

---

[123] *Report on Fairs and Markets* (1852–1853) . . . in 'Report of Markets Committee', *RPDCD*, vol. 2 (1886), p. 307.
[124] Charles Cameron, 'Report of the Public Health Committe in re Daily Removal of House Refuse', *RPDCD*, vol. 2, no. 38, (1886), p. 404.
[125] Evidence of Alderman Valentine Dillon, *Housing Inquiry 1885*, qs. 23,048–23,083.

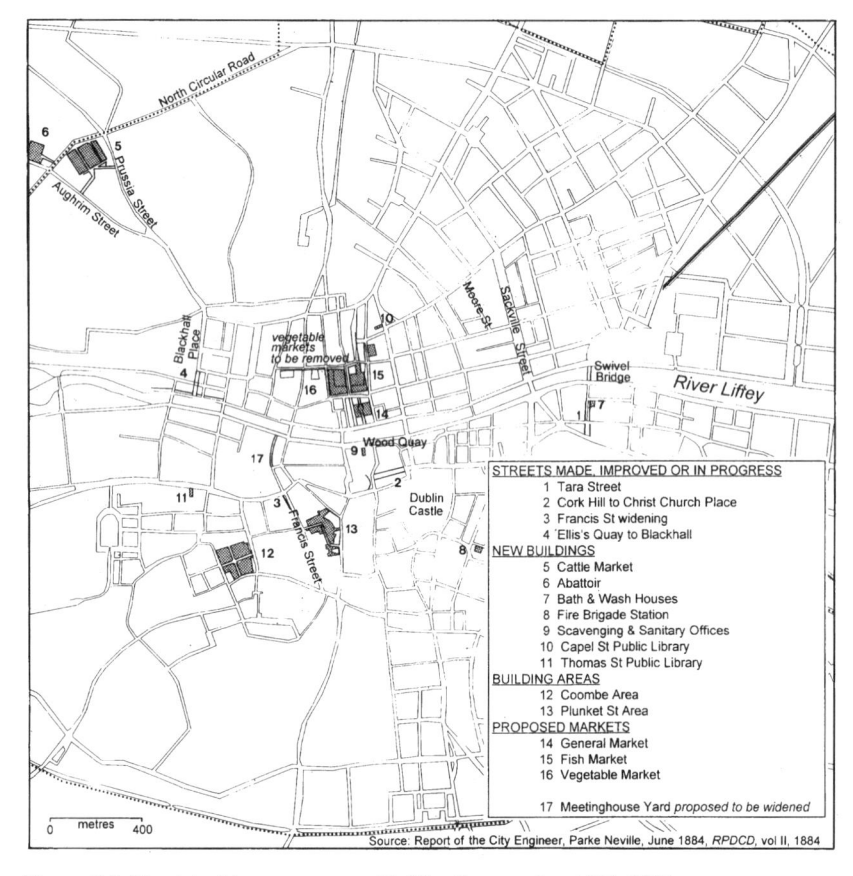

Figure 3.5 Municipal improvements, Dublin Corporation 1879–1884.

the landlords, 'hoping to force the Corporation to take it off their hands'.[126] A listing of such abandoned streets for 1868 includes much of the Sheriff Street district in the north docks, built without reference to water or sewerage, where the appalling environmental conditions prevalent in the older parts of the city were being reproduced in 'new' slums.[127]

In 1884 the annual report of the city engineer included a map showing the municipal improvements completed, in progress, or planned. This map (Figure 3.5) serves to illustrate the increasing range of the Corporation's activities, and what the engineering department at least regarded as the way forward. Excluding only the fire brigade station in Chatham Street, the other features, sixteen in all, were in direct response to some aspect of the slum question.

[126] Parke Neville, *Report to the Right Hon. The Lord Mayor, Aldermen and Burgesses of the City of Dublin on the General State of the Public Works of the City under their Control* (Dublin, 1878), pp. 31–32.
[127] Ibid., p. 33.

Of the individual buildings with which the Corporation can be credited, the cattle market and abattoir at Aughrim Street were at the time its greatest boast. The proposed north city markets, so long in planning, are here represented, although the Ormond Market site was to be developed for housing rather than a 'general market' as here indicated. Calls to establish public baths 'in which a cold bath could be procured for a penny, and a hot one for two pence, the boon would be a valuable one to the poorer citizens' had been answered by the erection of baths at Tara Street (1885), but were not followed up by a north city establishment, despite petitions on behalf of that district.[128] The Iveagh Trust baths and wash houses (completed 1906) were to supplement the Tara Street provision very valuably. Other socially useful 'reforms' in or adjoining slum areas were the fine new public libraries, as in Thomas Street, Great Brunswick Street (Pearse Street) and Capel Street.

The 1884 map (Figure 3.5) includes the Coombe and Plunkett Street housing schemes, undertaken by the Dublin Artisans' Dwellings Company on land cleared and serviced by the Corporation, and marks its first tentative steps towards direct involvement in the housing market (Chapter 4). However it was the Corporation's achievements in the field of public and domestic scavenging, and the enforced closure of insanitary dwellings, that was its principal though modest contribution to improving housing conditions up to this date (Table 3.4).

The schemes involving totally new roads were those at Tara Street, which required the building of the Swivel Bridge to link it to Beresford Place; the short new road which opened up 'a fine line of thoroughfare from the quays northwards' leading via Blackhall Place and Manor Street to the Metropolitan Cattle Market and the new abattoir; and the creation of Lord Edward Street, opening up the vista from the City Hall on Cork Hill to Christchurch Cathedral.[129] The clearance of 'a lot of miserable tenement buildings (mostly unoccupied)' along Meetinghouse Lane facilitated the creation of a 'handsome and convenient new street', now St Augustine Street, linking Usher's Quay to Thomas Street. The north end of Francis Street was to be widened to double its width, 'a long projected and much wanted improvement'.[130] The Tara Street project was applauded in 1885 for opening up air space through a very unhealthy area, while similar hopes were held out for the planned Cork Hill project.[131]

The proposed Cork Hill building and general improvement scheme proposed by Thomas Drew in 1881–82 (Figure 3.6) was a hugely ambitious undertaking, intended not alone to rectify one of the longest-lamented bottle-necks in the city traffic flow, the impossibly sharp turn at Cork Hill and the steep ascent up Castle Street to Christ Church Place, but also to remodel the entire traffic circulation and built fabric of this medieval quarter. His plan included four entirely new

---

[128] Cameron & Mapother, *Prevention of Disease* (1879), p. 352.
[129] Parke Neville, 'Annual Report of the City Engineer', *RPDCD*, 1884, p. 461.
[130] Ibid.
[131] *Housing Inquiry 1885*, qs 21,888–21,891.

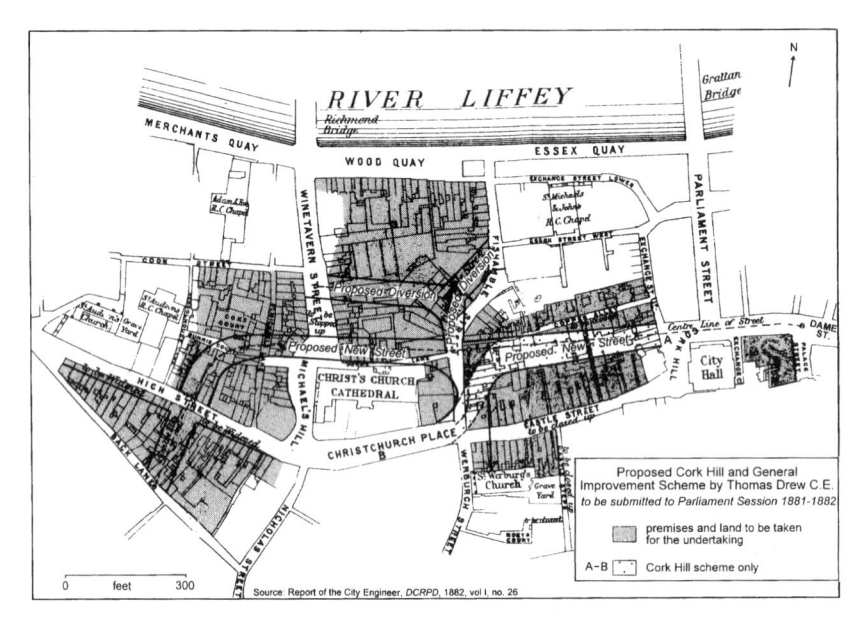

Figure 3.6 Proposed Cork Hill building and general improvement scheme, by Thomas Drew C.E., 1882.

streets, the widening of others (Fishamble Street, High Street), the closure of Castle Street, Copper Alley, part of Winetavern Street and numerous smaller lanes and courts, and the sacrifice of over 100 premises, including some very poor slum fabric. It is not surprising that Drew's ambitions (Figure 3.6) were shelved in favour of a much more modest scheme, as advertised in Figure 3.5 (1884) but not completed until 1892. The political will, municipal organisation, financial resources and sheer boldness of vision which a city-centre scheme such as Drew proposed were well beyond the bounds of possibility in late nineteenth century Dublin.

The more modest plan, a single new street from Cork Hill to Christ Church Place (Figure 3.6), was to prove sufficiently daunting. The Corporation overstretched itself by interpreting its street widening powers under the 1878 Act 'in a wide sense so as to enable them to take a tract of land at each side of the street in order that they might themselves appropriate the profits of the improvement'. However, the Local Government Board, as the regulatory body over the local sanitary authorities, interpreted the Act in a narrower sense, and only gave power to take sufficient land for the street itself. The Corporation was left with narrow strips of ground of absolutely no use to any person except the owner of the land behind them, and was not able to diminish the expense of the scheme by selling the frontages as it had hoped.[132]

[132] *Housing Inquiry 1885*, qs. 21,956–21,961.

Public Parks

While the interests of the sanitary authorities penetrated the interior arrangements of individual residences, it was claimed in 1881 that 'no improvement of the house interiors or enforcement of the sanitary laws will prove an effectual remedy for the low social condition of the poorer population without a simultaneous effort to improve the out-door life'. To that end the opening up of St Stephen's Green to the public in 1877, thanks to the munificence of Lord Ardilaun of the Guinness family, was applauded. 'A few strict magisterial decisions' had succeeded in sorting out 'the rough conduct which characterized the early months' and all was now approaching a very civilized standard, and 'even the least educated are learning to respect what is intended for their advantage'.[133] But while St Stephen's Green and the Phoenix Park were wonderful municipal assets, they were 'quite unavailable for the daily life of many thousands of children in the city lanes and alleys'. What was recommended was a large number of small areas dispersed throughout the city, which with little outlay could be transformed into recreation grounds for children; there were innumerable open spaces, or areas covered by ruins perfectly suited, some of which were owned by the Corporation. There were also several old graveyards, now closed, which 'with due sanctions against desecration, planted with shrubs and flowers and furnished with seats' would prove ideal.[134] By 1900 some advances had been made, with Queen's Square (1888), Blessington Street Basin (1891), Hill Street open space (1895) and St Michan's Park (1898) all under the care of the Corporation and available to the citizenry.[135]

Contagious Disease

The epidemics of contagious disease which marked the early decades of the nineteenth century had greatly decreased in virulence by the end of the century (see Table 3.3), but in no way was it a matter for complacency. In the area of primary vaccination against smallpox Dublin could hold its head high, for it was claimed that 'as a rule' it was 'better carried out in Dublin than in many other places'. However, the disease had not entirely disappeared, and re-vaccination was considered desirable at adult stage.[136] In cases such as scarlatina the removal of patients to hospital had to be followed by adequate isolation of all contacts, and the thorough disinfection of the dwelling, furnishings and especially clothing and bedding, an enormous challenge when the level of resources and popular knowledge of health matters is considered.

Dublin was well provided with fever hospitals from the early decades of the nineteenth century; in fact the number of fever wards attached to so many of the

---

[133] *RPDCD* vol. 2, reports nos. 7, 27, 51 (1876); vol. 3 no. 131 (1877); see also St Stephen's Green (Dublin) Act 1877, 40 & 41 Vict, c. cxxxiv.
[134] Falkiner, 'Homes of the Poor' (1882), p. 270.
[135] 'Report on Public Health for 1900', *RPDCD* vol. 3 (1901), p. 407.
[136] Cameron & Mapother, *Prevention of Disease* (1879), p. 349.

general hospitals of the city was criticized in the 1870s, as 'serving to scatter contagion around the city rather than minimizing the foci of contagion'.[137] Hospitals had been repeatedly criticised for the 'mischievous results arising from congregating the sick within their walls', and certainly the high death rate from 'adventitious diseases', i.e., those contracted on admission to the hospital, gave good grounds for worry.[138] The 1878 public health act was a blunt instrument in this regard, allowing only for the compulsory removal from tenements to 'hospital sheds' if judged necessary for medical treatment.[139] What was badly needed for the next stage was a place of recovery where 'strict separation of the convalescents from the different zymotics will be insisted upon'.[140] Efforts of the Corporation in the early 1870s to build a convalescent hospital met with trenchant opposition: 'the very mention of the establishment – the convalescent hospital – was sufficient to alarm a neighbourhood'.[141] Doubts as to whether the Corporation could legally establish a convalescent home outside the borough boundary were expressed, and the law as to the fund from which the cost should be defrayed was so uncertain that despite the purchase of a six acre field the matter was left in abeyance in 1873.[142]

Within the tenements, the disinfection procedures also brought their own difficulties. Among the hospital records on multiple admissions from single houses and relapses, statements such as 'readmitted to hospital, in consequence of sleeping in their infected bedding' underlined the uselessness of even the best hospital care if the home environment was neglected.[143] Compensation was allowed to poor persons whose infected clothing and bedding was burned under the Public Health Act (1878). The public health committee employed a 'chief disinfector' who was responsible for supervising the limewashing operation. While the job was underway, the hapless residents were put out in the halls or the stairs, banned from sheltering in a neighbour's room lest they spread contagion. Along with the hardship involved, such an unsatisfactory state of affairs 'tends to unduly hasten the purifying operations, which require to be carefully and deliberately carried out'. Dr Cameron's brilliant resolution of the problem was to request his public health committee to supply alternate temporary shelter for such exigencies.[144] In this matter the sanitary officials had overstepped themselves. Not a single person would agree to enter the 'small wooden house, mounted on wheels', 'drawn by horses and provided with everything that they could want' which Dr Cameron had designed for their reception while their premises were being disinfected; 'they preferred lying out on the stairs', saying their neighbours

---

[137] Ibid., pp. 350–351.
[138] Willis, *Social and Sanitary Conditions* (1845), p. 56.
[139] Cameron & Mapother (1879), pp. 350–351.
[140] Ibid.
[141] Norwood, *Sanitary Laws* (1873), p. 236.
[142] Ibid., pp. 236–237.
[143] Willis, *Social and Sanitary Conditions* (1845), p. 53.
[144] Cameron & Mapother, *Prevention of Disease* (1879), p. 350.

would laugh at them if they entered it. Repeated personal intervention by Dr Cameron was to no avail; regardless of who tried to persuade them, this was one public health innovation which was going nowhere, and the contraption was ultimately converted to an office at the disinfecting chamber.[145]

The proudest boast of the public health committee was the development of a purpose-built disinfecting depot and laundry at Marrowbone Lane (Figure 3.7) in 1899. This state-of-the-art facility ensured that once disinfected, clothing could no longer come in contact with either persons or clothing awaiting this treatment, but left the depot by an entirely separate route. It was built as a self-sufficient unit complete with its own furnaces, autoclaves, disinfecting chambers, baths, and stables. Such organisation and investment is evidence of the increasing professionalism which characterised the public health movement by the end of the century. Table 3.4 is a reminder of the scale of such operations, as undertaken in 1883.

Explaining Typhoid, 1882–1893

In the last decades of the nineteenth century the prevalence of enteric fever (typhoid) despite the provision of the excellent Vartry water supply and improvements in the alleged causes, such as filthy dairy yards, was a matter of continuing disquiet.[146] Concern with the subsoil as a reservoir of disease was voiced in 1879, with the promotion of asphalte as a house foundation, to prevent 'the ascent into the interior of houses of underground foul air, and of damp – both fertile causes of disease'. While most houses had 'loose and pervious foundations' those in lowlying districts and supplied with an underground storey were most at risk.[147] Cellar dwellings inhabited by the very poorest, such as that beneath 31 City Quay which was 'noisome and very wet', were typically associated with typhoid.[148] However the fever appeared to have little regard for class distinctions, despite increasing geographical distance between the poorest and richest in late nineteenth century Dublin.

In an effort to account for its spread the Dublin Sanitary Association commissioned a report in 1894 which confirmed that the death rate from this cause was higher in Dublin than in any other town in the United Kingdom, excepting Belfast.[149] It was not confined to the city, but was also prevalent in the suburbs. As part of its investigation, all incidence of the fever within the city boundary was mapped for 1882–1893 (Figure 3.8).[150]

[145] Ibid.; Evidence of Dr Cameron, *Housing Inquiry 1885*, qs 22,409–22,410.
[146] 'Report of the Public Health Committee', *RPDCD*, vol. 3, no. 136 (1894), pp. 31–33.
[147] Cameron & Mapother, *Prevention of Disease* (1879), p. 343.
[148] Charles Cameron, 'Report of the Public Health Committee, Breviate for September 1879, Cellar Dwellings,' *RPDCD*, (1879), p. 931.
[149] Main findings summarised in 'Report of the Public Health Committee', *RPDCD*, vol. 3, no. 136 (1894), pp. 29–37.
[150] 'Report of the Public Health Committee', *RPDCD*, vol. 3, no. 93 (1888); see also *Dublin Corporation Plans and Maps*, Pl/6.

Figure 3.7 Disinfecting depot and laundry, Marrowbone Lane, Dublin 1899

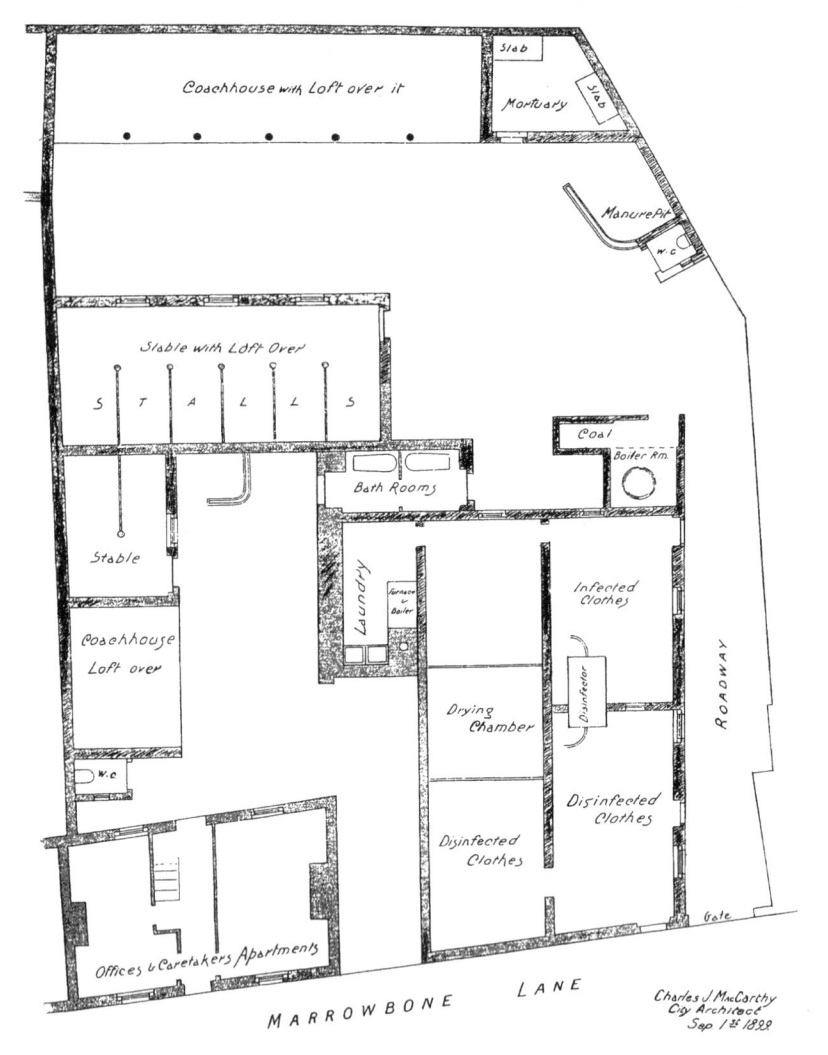

Typhoid cases were widely distributed (Figure 3.8), with high status areas such as Merrion Square, Stephen's Green, Baggot Street and Mount Street all reporting incidences. However, it was clearly more prevalent among the densely inhabited poorer areas. The 'general idea' that typhoid fever affects the upper classes more than the lower classes was thus disproved. Dr Cameron's statistical table for 1892–93 showed that among the 'professional and independent class'

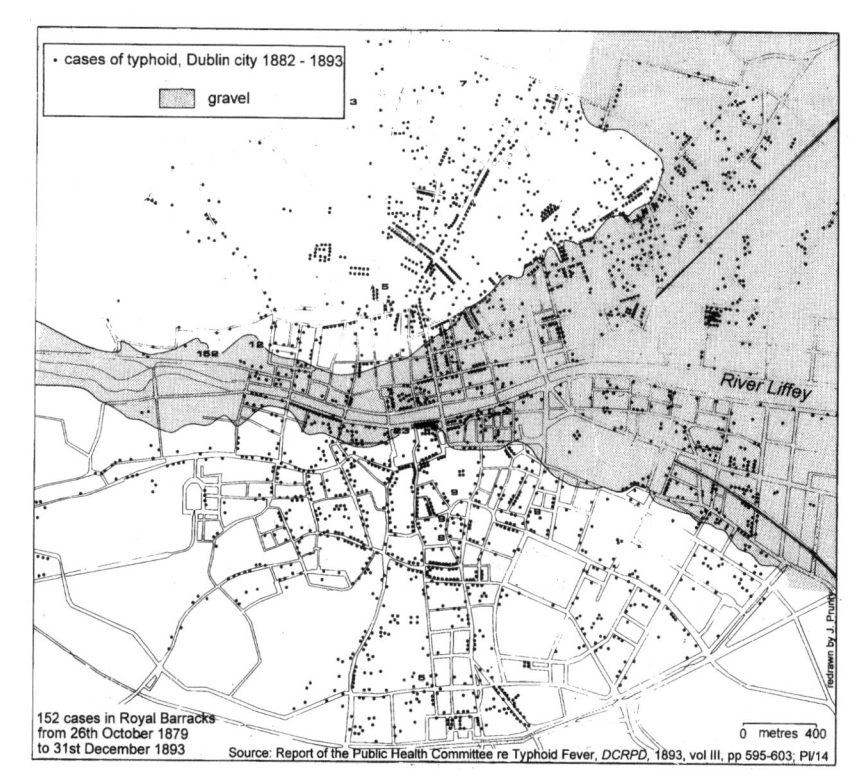

Figure 3.8 Typhoid fever Dublin 1882–1893.

deaths from typhoid averaged 25.7 per 100,000 population; the corresponding figure for 'hawkers, porters, labourers, &c.' was 57.5 per 100,000. However, the highest figure of all was among the 'middle class' averaging 71.1 per 100,000.[151] The most recent theory, which the committee adopted (and which modern medical theory confirms), was that the typhoid bacilli flourish best in diluted sewage, and so the water-carriage system of sewage disposal greatly facilitated its spread. Faulty drainage in middle class areas, where water closets were being rapidly but inefficiently connected to the main sewers, was the likeliest cause of this high mortality.

Causal connections between the local geology and the spread of the disease were sought. If the disease was aerobian and water borne it would thrive in the gravels where the water table was proven to fluctuate more and so is more aerated. The gravel bed of the Liffey, indicated in Figure 3.8, should therefore account for the greatest concentration of typhoid. The connections were not conclusive, for the low-lying areas, such as Gloucester/Mecklenburgh street, North Strand and Sheriff Street on the north side, and Townsend Street, and Cook

---

[151] 'Report of the Public Health Committee', *RPDCD*, vol. 3, no. 136 (1894), p. 28.

Street on the south side, were also areas of poor sanitary accommodation and general deprivation (see Figures 2.6, 2.9). As typhoid was at least as prevalent on the surrounding clays, the Sanitary Committee blamed the large quantity of dilute sewage in the subsoil, and advocated a massively expensive drainage programme as the only effective remedy.

Notifiable Infectious Diseases, 1893

Continuing concern with the geography of disease resulted in the publication of alphabetical lists of all Dublin streets where cases of infectious diseases occurred; the list for 1893 (appendixed to the public health report of 1894), is mapped as Figure 3.9.[152] As a record of morbidity rather than mortality it is an important illustration of how far public health has advanced by the end of the century: moving from the geography of death to the geography of disease is eminently hopeful. In the street lists of infectious disease, house numbers were suppressed, so that the distribution in Figure 3.9 must be regarded as approximate, especially along rather long stretches, such as Great Britain Street (39 cases). Allowing for such limitations, the pattern which emerges cannot fail to startle by its distinctness.

The single greatest concentration of disease was within the densely crowded Ormond Market area (see Figure 4.2) where 64 cases were reported, a district which features in every discussion of insanitary housing and general deprivation. Practically as bad were nearby North Anne Street, Stafford Street, and Jervis Street with high incidences also recorded for Capel Street, Church Street, and North King Street, although being longer streets the relative concentration is not as high as it initially appears. The other areas of greatest morbidity on the north side were in the vicinity of Gloucester Street, Mecklenburgh Street, and Lower Gardiner Street, the North Strand, Seville Place, and the Sheriff Street docks area (see Figure 2.6, also Chapter 8).

To the south of the river the small warren of alleys bounded by Thomas Street, the Coombe, Francis Street and Meath Street, including West Park Street, was the least healthy place to live (see Figure 2.7). The entire Liberties area had a high rate of infectious disease, extending to Bride Street and Aungier Street, while Temple Bar, Cornmarket, Fishamble Street and High Street were all areas of high morbidity. The Plunket Street scheme, centred on John Dillon Street (see Figure 4.6) reported 23 cases in all, while the artisans' dwellings scheme in the Coombe (see Figure 4.4) reported only 12 cases, figures which were considerably below the average in the immediate locality.

[152] The notifiable diseases included: typhoid fever, measles, erysipelas, choleraic diarrhoea, diarrhoea, dysentery, scarlatina, cholera infantum, cholera nostros, puerperal fever, croup, smallpox, typhus fever, diphtheria. There were also many cases of 'undefined fever'. Whooping cough was a notifiable disease in 1893 and so appears in this list; however, as the 'uselessness' of reporting this disease is noted, and it was removed from subsequent lists, it is omitted in both mapping and discussion.

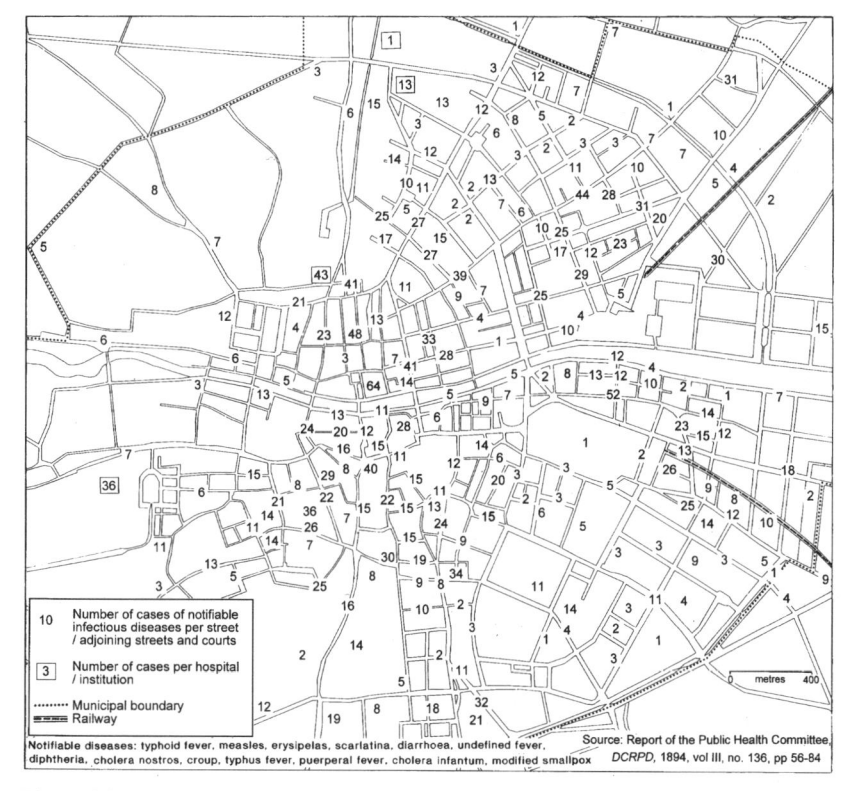

A Matter of Life and Death: Public Health, 1800–1900

Figure 3.9 Infectious diseases, Dublin 1894.

The Townsend Street area, extending to Grattan Street, and Grand Canal Street, wedged between the railway and the top class residential Merrion Square (which returned 3 occurrences of infectious disease between 95 residences) was also noted for poor health standards (see Figure 2.6, Plate 2.2). Townsend Street alone reported 52 cases. The numerous poor houses both on and to the rear of Poolbeg Street, Grattan Street, Erne Street and Cumberland Street South all returned high figures.

One other area noted for a high incidence of disease was the Charlemont Street area, to the south west of Stephen's Green, and on the road to Ranelagh. This area featured in the register of slaughter houses in 1879 (Figure 3.3), and included some low value housing in courts and alleys (Figure 2.6) but otherwise received little attention in slum inquiries. Tenement housing in Camden Street Lower and associated courts (Camden Row, Camden Court) returned 21 cases of infectious disease; Charlemont Street returned 32 cases, Charlotte Street 11 cases, and South Richmond Street 7 cases, providing cause for concern. The chances of contracting any one of a range of potentially fatal diseases may have been highest in certain notorious slum districts but other areas could not be considered entirely safe.

Residents of even the high class south-eastern sector had good cause to concern themselves with infectious disease, which was barely contained on the margins. Residents of the poorest areas were too long acquainted with the dangers.

Conclusion

As the nineteenth century closed, there was clearly a lot of unfinished business if the high rate of mortality in the Dublin slums was to be brought down, and indeed if the whole notion of 'fever nests' was ever to be consigned to the past. Warnings to 'all sections of our citizens' to face up to the 'slum evil' in our midst, 'or else punishment neither light nor pleasant will follow as a consequence of their apathy and neglect', continued to be made.[153] The prevalence and spread of highly contagious disease had first precipitated action under the banner of public health; inquiries into the vital matters of diet, water supply and sanitation led inexorably to the consideration of housing questions, and both led full circle back to the sheer destitution of the majority of the city's population, how they survived from day to day, and how they managed when crisis struck. Little could be solved in isolation, yet intervention had to be made at certain points, or nothing whatsoever would improve. It was, quite literally, a matter of life and death.

---

[153] *Daily Nation*, 5 September 1898.

~4~

TO GRASP THE HOUSING NETTLE:
EARLY INITIATIVES, 1876-1900

One of the most obvious tests of the condition of the working classes is the state of their dwellings. It is generally allowed that the dwelling or the house accommodation is closely connected with the improvement or elevation of the occupier.[1]

INTRODUCTION TO THE TENEMENT ISSUE

The investigations into the prevalence of infectious disease in Dublin undertaken in the early decades of the nineteenth century (Chapter 2), by courageous individuals such as Revd. James Whitelaw and the promoters of the Cork Street Fever Hospital, laid the foundations for slow but hopeful progress in public health matters. The advances in 'sanitary science' and associated administrative structures (Chapter 3) from 1850 on laid the foundations for the regular and rapid removal of human and other waste, and brought an abundant supply of fresh, clean water within reach of most citizens, contributing in no small way to ending epidemic outbreaks of some of the most feared contagions such as typhoid and cholera. With the notable exception of pulmonary tuberculosis, controls were in place to minimise the spread of most of the other recognised zymotic diseases.

But while the slums debate was initially most concerned with the accumulations of filth in congested districts creating 'nests of fever', there was from the outset an inextricable concern with the larger housing question. As early as the Willis survey of 1845 the provision of 'residences fit for human beings' was presented as the primary area of reform. From this core the moral and social improvement of the poorest classes could be pursued.[2] Willis raised questions about recent investment in hospitals, dispensaries and workhouses, which could be counterproductive, preventing 'the attention which should otherwise necessarily be paid to the comforts, and particularly the state of the dwellings of the poor', lulling the public into a false sense of security, while the root causes lay

[1] Thomas Jordan, 'The present state of the Dwellings of the Poor, chiefly in Dublin,' *Journal of the Dublin Statistical Society*, January 1857, p. 12, (hereafter 'Dwellings of the Poor').

[2] Thomas Willis, *Facts Connected with the Social and Sanitary Conditions of the Working Classes in the City of Dublin*, Dublin, 1845, p. 32, (hereafter *Social and Sanitary Conditions*).

festering.[3] In 1857 Thomas Jordan, in an address to the Dublin Statistical Society similarly focused on the state of the dwellings of the poor, a scandal which extended beyond health or sanitary considerations. It was fruitless to speak of morals and religion when 'the wretchedness by which he is surrounded certainly does not open the poor man's mind to charity and love' nor can he entertain 'just views of Providence' when surrounded by 'squalor and destitution'.[4]

These horrors were tackled through enforcing sanitary regulations, facilitating and initiating slum clearance schemes, and – very hesitantly – through direct involvement in house construction and the control of tenancies. Private and philanthropic companies pioneered the erection of improved housing for workers, often on sites cleared and serviced by the municipality; municipal schemes were a later and most urgent development. However, the route taken to tackle slum housing was always circuitous, with several efforts at back-tracking, periods when the pace slowed down to a near halt, when inspired plans lay mouldering on shelves and legal obstacles halted movement on all fronts, and when the energy which should have been expended in the direction of the housing crisis was redirected to other, and often lesser, struggles.

In the Dublin slums constant reassessments of the situation were most discouraging, as each report and inquiry revealed the entrenched nature and enormous scale of the outstanding problems, set against a worsening economic and fiscal situation. Dublin was falling well behind the rate of progress recorded in British cities, as far as mortality rates were concerned (see Table 3.1). Under the heading of housing quality, the numbers of families in third and fourth class accommodation, as defined by the census (see Chapter 2, Table 2.3) was also to be disgracefully high. Table 4.1 charts the variations from 1841–1901. The greatest number in fourth class accommodation was recorded at the post-famine census of 1851, peaking at 28,039 families or 49% of the total number of families recorded for the city. However, the intercensal reductions which followed were painfully small, with the first fall minimally below 20,000 families reached in 1891, negated by an increase again in 1901, by which date 36% of families were still confined to fourth class accommodation. From 1861–81 the number of families in third class accommodation ranged between 16,000 and 17,000 each census year, increases in the second class category were minimal and the numbers in first class accommodation decreased. The slum housing problem of one-roomed dwelling could not in any sense be considered a fringe issue for the municipality.

In the 1870s three distinct types of problem housing were identified: the tenement house, third class houses, and cellar dwellings. In certain streets, all three types could be found: the one-family residence converted to multiple occupancy fronting the building line; cellar kitchens with a separate entrance below ground; and third class cabin housing filling the long garden to the rear. While socially and geographically proximate, different remedies were required in each situation.

[3] Ibid., pp. 51–53.
[4] Jordan, 'Dwellings of the Poor' (1857), p. 12.

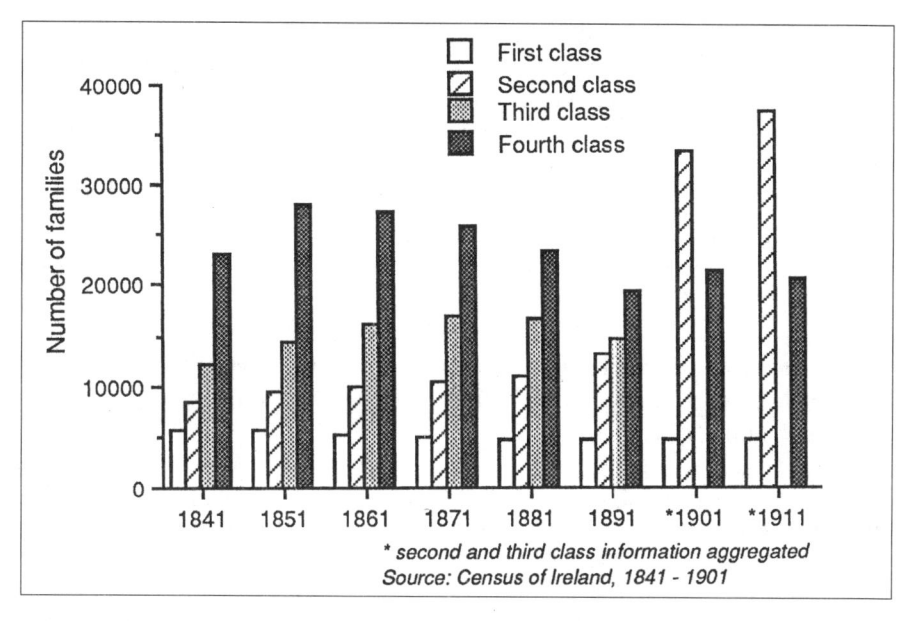

Table 4.1 House accommodation of families, Dublin city 1841–1911.

The Tenement House

The tenement house was to dominate the slum debate in Dublin well into the mid-twentieth century. In 1879 a Royal Commission appointed to enquire into the Sewerage and Drainage of Dublin concluded its critical report by affirming:

> that the tenement houses of Dublin appear to be the prime source and cause of the excessively high death rate; that they are not properly classified, registered, and regulated; that they are dilapidated, dirty, ill-ventilated, much overcrowded, and that disease, a craving for stimulants and its consequences – drunkenness and extreme poverty – are thereby fostered, and that until the condition of these houses shall have been improved the general health of the city will continue to be injuriously affected.[5]

From at least 1805, when Whitelaw's study was published, to the Civic Survey of 1925, in each of the published reports of the Public Health Committee of Dublin Corporation, and in other papers such as the *Dublin Builder* and the *Journal of the Dublin Statistical Society*, the reform of the tenement housing system was presented as fundamental to improving the health and morals of the poorer citizens of Dublin. At the Housing Inquiry of 1913 one witness testified that some of the tenements then occupied were well over a hundred years old, and that the system itself was well established by 1840.[6] During the famine it

---

[5] Report of Royal Commission 1879, quoted in Charles Eason, 'The Tenement Houses of Dublin: Their Condition and Regulation', *Stat. Soc. Inq. Soc. Ire. Jn.* 10, 79, (1899), p. 383 (hereafter 'Tenement Houses').

[6] *Report of the Departmental Committee Appointed by the Local Government Board for Ireland to Inquire into the Housing Conditions of the Working Classes in the City of Dublin*, (hereafter *Dublin Housing Report 1914*), (Dublin, 1914), p. 3.

was claimed the number had leaped from 1,682 to 5,995 houses, and by 1879 the number totalled 9,760.[7] The steady out-migration of the wealthiest to the suburbs and townships (see Figure 1.1) ensured a ready supply of houses to be subdivided, such as in the aptly-named Fade Street (Plate 4.1), where fanlights, door surrounds and fenestration testify to high-class origins.

In 1894 Charles Cameron, medical officer, stated the situation very directly:

> The death-rate of Dublin is, unfortunately, high; a fact which I attribute chiefly, if not wholly, to the comparative poverty of the population. One third of the people of Dublin live in single room tenements, in which they eat, drink, cook, sleep, and often carry on their work for a living.[8]

The structural arrangements of the tenement houses prevented the provision of separate sanitary accommodation for each family, and turned these houses into sanitary nightmares:

> There is no direct means of removing the refuse from the several floors, the common stair soon therefore becomes fouled; while the height of the houses – seldom less than three, and generally four storeys high – in no slight degree operates against cleanliness. Many of these houses possess unoccupied cellars, the atmosphere of which cannot fail to injuriously affect the health of the occupants of the upper rooms.[9]

In Dublin, 'as in London and elsewhere, sanitary accommodation used in common by several families will seldom be properly kept', particularly when anyone could come in off the street and use it.[10] Two outdoor closets and a single stand pipe in a yard were the only conveniences available to the 70 persons who shared a house in Newmarket Street, in 1913 (Plate 4.2). The Corporation placed a target of 20 persons per sanitary convenience, a figure which they found repeatedly greatly exceeded throughout the city. The utter lack of privacy in overcrowded conditions, 'the constantly open doors and the want of lighting in the hall, passages, and landings at night', were considered to be the cause of much immorality, so that one witness to the 1913 Housing Inquiry claimed that the children 'acquire a precocious knowledge of evil from early childhood'.[11]

The biggest difficulty in their regulation was to be the legal aspect, as 'there are sometimes five owners interested in one tenement house'.[12] 'The existing dilapidation of many city houses is due to the defective title of the owners or representatives of the interests on which the duty of repair should properly fall'.[13] Those who endured the privations were those 'without political or municipal

---

[7] *Dublin Housing Report, 1914*, p. 6.
[8] 'Report on Public Health,' *RPDCD*, no. 136 (1894), p. 27.
[9] 'Statement Read Before the Royal Commission at the Close of the Inquiry, on 16 October 1979 by the Secretary of the Public Health Committee,' *RPDCD*, vol. 3, appendix V, (1879), pp. 789–790.
[10] 'Public Health Committee,' *RPDCD*, vol. 3, no. 136 (1894), p. 89.
[11] *Dublin Housing Report 1914*, p. 5.
[12] Ibid., p. 3.
[13] F.R. Falkiner, 'Report on the Homes of the Poor' in *Stat. Soc. Inq. Soc. Ire. Jn.*, 8, 59 (1882), p. 267, (hereafter 'Homes of the Poor').

Plate 4.1 Fade Street c.1879, copy of photo by Millard and Robinson, Irish Architectural Archive.

influence, being mainly non-rate payers', and hence unable to determine the course of decisions made in their regard.[14]

So too the destructiveness of tenants was held accountable for the poor accommodation in some houses, landlords complaining of 'the impracticability of effecting the requisite sanitary reforms owing to the habits of the inmates and the certain destruction which awaited improved appliances'. Further complaints were 'that the more worthless tenants frequently, on falling into arrear, willfully dilapidate or permit dilapidation whilst under notice of eviction, whilst they cannot be dispossessed even by summary order in less than an average of six weeks, and the consequent loss falls, in the shape of increased rent, on the more well-conducted tenants'.[15]

The tenement system was at the heart of the social relations between the poorest persons, and influenced the dealings of the better-off in their regard. The information networks concerning availability of employment, food and other necessities, better or cheaper accommodation, medical assistance, schooling opportunities, religious services, poor relief, and the myriad of other areas of

[14] Ibid., p. 263.
[15] Ibid., p. 269.

Plate 4.2 Newmarket Street, 2 closets for 70 people, 1913, RSAI 85

human importance, were all linked up through this housing system. With such a large number of persons confined to a single dwelling the importance of the street as social space becomes more understandable, and the relief networks: informal, (relatives and friends), official (poor law), and the multiplicity of church charities, operating within the city can be discussed (Chapters 6, 7). The tenement system, where generally each family occupied only one room, and rent was paid on a weekly basis without any long term security of tenure, facilitated mobility, especially if the move was only to another house in the same street or district.[16]

Infill Housing

Along with the tenement housing, attention was continually drawn to the large number of poor cottages or barely converted stable dwellings which had sprung up throughout the city, particularly as infill developments on small sites, and in the gardens, back yards and rear stable lanes of the larger houses, usually in a court or lane configuration which utilised the existing plot to best advantage.[17]

---

[16] Jacinta Prunty, 'Mobility among Women in Nineteenth Century Dublin' in David Siddle (ed.), *Migration, Mobility and Modernisation in Europe* (Liverpool, 1997).

[17] Niall McCullough, *Dublin: An Urban History* (Dublin; 1989), p. 91.

Some could be 'more aptly described as shelters', a number of them were erected in narrow areas 'almost surrounded by high buildings or walls, with alleys or passages, which in some cases are scarcely more than nine or ten feet wide, as a means of approach'. Separate closet accommodation was non-existent, but there was usually a closet and a single tap 'somewhere in the vicinity, common to the occupants of the cottages or anyone who likes to use them'. Along with the 'drawbacks of tenement houses' these cottages suffered the added disadvantage 'of being in some cases surrounded by high walls and buildings which shut out light and air'.[18] The oft-repeated complaint against the rows of 'small cabins built in the gardens and constituting very unhealthy dwellings' is exemplified in the case of Brady's Cottages (Plate 4.3), where the yard space of 16 Francis Street is completely colonised and entrance is secured through an archway passage.[19]

Courtenay Cottages, along Ballybough Road, valued between 15s and £1 10s, were 'damp, wretched hovels, utterly unfit for human habitation, and yet have high rents paid for them'.[20] The colonisation of stable lanes by the poorest was typically associated with the reduction of first class dwellings to tenement status, 'different classes of persons now occupy the houses, and the people in the front houses no longer keep vehicles'.[21] Typical was Henrietta Place, behind the mansions of Henrietta Street (Plate 4.4), where barely-converted outhouses were used as dwellings, their former status still unmistakable in the early twentieth century.

Cellar Dwellings

Cellar dwellings were regarded as the worst possible type of slum accommodation. Willis highlighted the situation of innumerable servants during the cholera outbreak of 1833 'labouring under disease, sleeping in *turn-up beds*, (sic) in the vitiated atmosphere of these kitchens, or sleeping in small rooms adjoining, having no light or air except from the kitchen; the ventilation and light of which were dependent on the gratings in the flagway of the street above'.[22] Yet among those who presumably could exercise more choice over their bedrooms than the house servants, cellars were repeatedly taken: 'cellars at all times bring better rents than single rooms, and many of them are crowded with lodging beds'.[23] On the basis that English law forbade the incarceration of any prisoner, even if condemned to die, in a dungeon or underground room, Willis (1845) called for the outlawing of all underground storeys as sleeping apartments.[24] Jordan recounted the uncivilized situation which still prevailed in 1857 'in the most miserable and most unwhole-

---

[18] *Dublin Housing Report 1914*, p. 6.
[19] *Third Report of H.M. Commissioners for Inquiring into the Housing of the Working Classes.* (hereafter *Housing Inquiry 1885*) Minutes of Evidence &c., Ireland, 1885, c–4547–I, qs. 22,085–6.
[20] General Valuation of Ireland, Dublin, 1854, Mountjoy Ward; *RPDCD*, vol. 3, (1879), p. 988.
[21] *Housing Inquiry 1885*, qs. 22,087.
[22] Willis, *Social and Sanitary Conditions* (1845), pp. 54–55.
[23] Ibid., p. 33.
[24] Ibid., pp. 49, 54–55.

Plate 4.3 Brady's Cottages, 16 Francis Street, 1913, RSAI 18

Plate 4.4 Henrietta Buildings, Henrietta Place, 1913, RSAI 62

some parts of the metropolis' where cellar dwellings, many of which 'can only be entered by a visitor who is a stranger to them, by descending backwards, as a wild animal descends from the top of a tree', were still occupied. While as many as 2,205 cellars had been officially shut up since 1841, some of these were still in use.[25] Moves to rectify the situation could not keep pace with pressure for accommodation from the mid-century flood of refugees from famine and fever.

In 1873, despite the recent closure of 110 cellar dwellings, 57 were still known to be occupied, and could not be touched as 'not coming within the provisions of the "Public Health Act, 1848" sec. 67'.[26] The Public Health Act (Ireland) 1878 prohibited the occupation as a dwelling of any cellar built or rebuilt after the passing of the Act, or not occupied as a dwelling at the time of the Act, and laid down conditions governing the continued occupation of older cellars; non-compliance with the law could lead to a fine and, after two convictions, compulsory closure.[27] By 1885 Dr Cameron was complaining that some of those successfully closed had become receptacles for every type of filth, and if anything were more

---

[25] Jordan, 'Dwellings of the Poor' (1857), p. 17.
[26] John Norwood, 'On the Working of the Sanitary Laws in Dublin, with Suggestions for their Amendment', *Stat. Soc. Inq. Soc. Ire. Jn.*, 6, 43, (1873), p. 235.
[27] *Housing Inquiry 1885*, CC–4547–I, qs 21,784–21,789.

dangerous than when used for shelter.[28] The 1913 housing inquiry reported that at least 1,560 cellar dwellings were occupied.[29]

Slum Clearance Legislation, 1866–1883

The enabling legislation for slum clearance and the construction of housing for the 'working classes' was as unwieldy in its own way as the early public health legislation. The Labouring Classes Lodging Houses and Dwellings Act (Ireland) 1866, was copied from the second of Lord Shaftesbury's acts of 1851, and operated to a minimal extent in Cavan, New Ross, Callan and Waterford, and in Dublin through the Dublin Artisans' Dwellings Company (DADC); the Artizans' and Labourers' Dwellings Act 1868, commonly known as Torrens Act, with its amending legislation of 1879 and 1882,[30] was extended to Ireland, but was described as 'an absolute dead letter'. The Cross Act (1875), as amended in the Labourers' (Ireland) Act 1883, was utilised in Cork, Belfast and Dublin.[31]

Under the Artizans' Dwellings Act 1875 all urban sanitary districts in Ireland, with a population over 12,000 and authorised by the Local Government Board for Ireland, could apply to the Commissioners of Public Works in Ireland for loans to put the act of 1875 into practice, i.e., to undertake slum clearance.[32] The duty of Dublin Corporation, as the sanitary authority for the city, was confined to the acquisition of the property, the removal of the buildings, and the laying out, forming, paving, and sewering of the streets within the area. The powers of the Corporation were therefore limited to facilitating the erection of working class dwellings; only with the consent of the Local Government Board could it undertake its own building schemes, and even then the Artizans Dwellings Act required that it dispose of them within three years after their erection.

Dr Mapother's Report, 1876

With the passing of the 1875 Artizans' Dwellings Act (the Cross Act), Dublin Corporation appeared poised to make at least some small inroad into the problem of slum housing. The Corporation's energetic and able consulting sanitary officer, Dr Edward Mapother, was immediately commissioned to prepare a report identifying some of the very worst areas which might be cleared and redeveloped under the new legislation (Figure 4.1). Anxious to minimise the disruption to poor families which larger scale clearance would involve, Mapother also knew there would be little support among the councillors if substantial finances were involved, so that his 'unhealthy areas' may be regarded as a modest selection

[28] Ibid., qs. 22,058.
[29] *Dublin Housing Report 1914*, p. 4.
[30] Artizans' and Labourers' Dwellings Act 1868, commonly known as Torrens Act, 31 & 32 Victoria c. 64; amending acts of 1879 (42 & 43 Victoria c.64) and of 1882 (45 & 46 Victoria c. 54 part II)
[31] *Housing Inquiry 1885* C–4547–I, qs 21,815–21,908.
[32] Ibid.

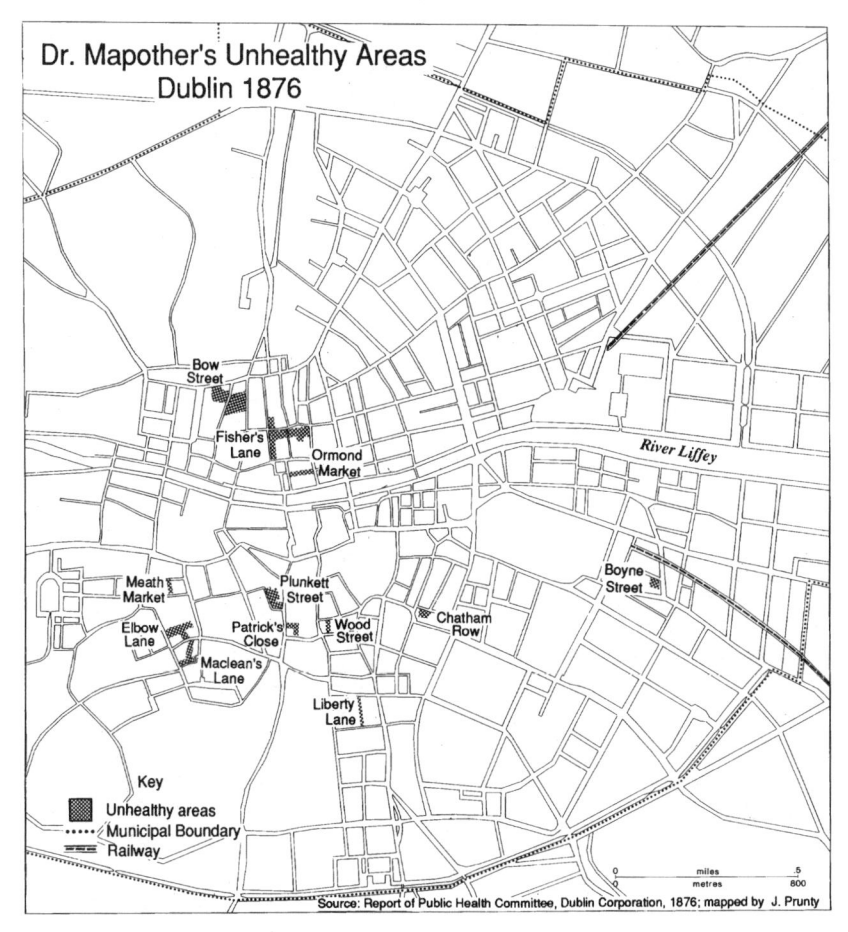

Figure 4.1 Dr Mapother's unhealthy areas, Dublin 1876.

from among the very worst blackspots in the city.[33] Seven of the twelve areas were in the old Liberties: Meath Market, McClean's Lane, Elbow Lane, Plunkett Street, Patrick's Close, Wood Street, and Liberty Lane; also on the south side there was Chatham Row, and the Boyne Street area east of Trinity College. On the north side Bow Street, Fisher's Lane and the Ormond Market, three distinct though nearby areas, were chosen.

The characteristics shared by each of these 'unhealthy areas' illustrate the inclusive understanding of well-being promoted by the emerging public health movement: all the houses were 'unfit for human habitation and incapable of repair' due to 'dilapidation, closeness of the passages preventing ventilation and lighting, want of decent sanitary accommodation, and the difficulty of affording it

[33] 'Report of the Medical Officer of Health, Dr. Charles Cameron', *RPDCD*, vol. 1, (1876), p. 106.

owing to absence of yards and soakage of the earth with animal refuse from ash-pits, slaughter-houses, etc.'. The resulting conditions included a high death rate, especially among infants; a high incidence of zymotic diseases, lung disease and rheumatism; and 'a low tone of general health, filthy habits, intemperance, and debased morals'.[34] The new developments would therefore raise the standard of morals, as well as of physical comfort and cleanliness.

In the Ormond Market area (Figure 4.2) the medical officer proposed:

to open a new street, from Arran Street East, into Charles Street, by removing the houses 59 and 60 East Arran Street, on either side of O'Brien's Court, and continuing the opening through the centre of Ormond Market, and removing two houses in Charles Street. From the structural condition of the circular centre of the market, and the stalls, and houses &c. bounded round it, on the north by Royal Row, on the south by Narrow Row, on the west by Beef Row, and on the east by Dawson Row, and the decayed and rotten state of the buildings, I think that, to carry out this improvement, the entire block would have to be taken down.[35]

This was the general pattern proposed in each of the twelve areas: to widen through-ways to permit the free circulation of air, rather than attempt large scale clearance and rehousing. The contemporary medical obsession with miasmic theory, i.e., the spread of disease by obnoxious but invisible gases, led to the emphasis on broad macadamized streets and open spaces. To the north of Ormond Market, Fisher's Lane and Greek Street were 'so narrow as to obstruct the free passage of air and sunlight, and the roadways remain damp and filthy. Zymotic diseases are frequent from such conditions'. Parke Neville, city engineer, supported the clearance of all twelve areas, with further recommendations such as the removal of an entire block from Fisher's Lane to Greek Street; 'if this was done, a fine open space or lung would be created in the centre of a miserable district, and in this block artisans' dwellings could be erected, with ample courts in centre and fine wide, airy streets all round', while several other blocks 'would also, if enlarged and more square, make capital sites'.[36]

The social geography of the Ormond Market/Pill Lane area was another 'good' reason for its early identification as a black spot requiring 'cleansing'. In the 1836 Poor Inquiry, Pill Lane 'and its immediate neighbourhood' was described not alone as 'the residence of all the fish hawkers, and of a dense population of other extremely poor persons', but the location of between 35 to 40 houses licensed for the retail of spirituous liquors, all 'within a circle of 300 yards radius'.[37] A touching if somewhat melodramatic picture of slum life here is presented by a visiting Biblewoman in 1877:

Have you ever passed through any of the narrow streets in the neighbourhood of the Law Courts? If so, you have doubtless remarked upon the dismal, dirty aspect of the houses, and had you entered you would have found that each room was the abode of a whole family. The

[34] Spencer Harty, 'Some Considerations on the Working of the Artizans' and Labourers' Dwellings Acts, as illustrated in the case of the Coombe Area, Dublin' in *Stat. Soc. Inq. Soc. Ire. Jn.*, 8, 62, (1884), p. 508, (hereafter 'The Coombe Area').
[35] Cameron, *Report* (1876), p. 115.
[36] Ibid.
[37] *Poor Inquiry (Ireland)* appendix (C)., part II, 'Report on the City of Dublin', p. 113.

highest ambition, as far as this world goes, of these much-to-be-respected poor seems to be embraced in that negative happiness to 'get along' – not to perish – to open eyes, however wearily, on a new morning, to satisfy with something, no matter what, a craving appetite, to close eyes at night under some shadow or shade.[38]

Although Mapother had chosen a very modest number of sites, the Corporation had to decide on the 'relative badness' of many unquestionably bad districts. Of the first twelve areas recommended (Figure 4.1), 'official representation' was made to the Local Government Board as to eight of them, and the Corporation drew up schemes for two: the Coombe and Boyne Street.[39] A 'provisional order' permitting schemes in these two areas was issued and confirmed by parliament in 1877, at an estimated cost of £20,000. However, the £20,000 borrowed from the Commissioners of Public Works in Ireland was found to be sufficient for purchasing and clearing the Coombe property alone, and the Boyne Street plans were shelved; the Coombe scheme required an additional £4,000 for constructing new streets, sewering and lighting, and providing a water supply, so that clearance of any of the other 'black spots' clearance of any of the identified by Mapother (in Figure 4.1) was postponed indefinitely.[40]

The partial solution proposed for Ormond Market in 1876 was not acted on, and as conditions continued to deteriorate, and minimal standards of housing and sanitation rose, wholesale clearance came to be the only possibility. The Ormond Market area was not tackled until 1917, when an entirely new street alignment (planned 1914) was imposed on the area, and a mixture of 126 modest residences, including two-roomed flats, and three and four-roomed houses, were erected (Figure 4.3), retaining as a focus the original central granite-paved portion of the old market, along with several local street names.[41]

In the face of this massive housing problem, many years in the making, the Corporation's strategy, formally adopted in 1879, was to pursue the slow, legalistic, piecemeal process of closing condemned tenement houses throughout the city. Efforts to persuade the city's employers to involve themselves in providing better accommodation for their workers had been made, but to little avail. A report in 1857 overstated the achievements, in an effort to encourage such developments:

Many of the extensive employers in the city have taken the greater part of a street into their own hands, and have made improvements on it, for their workpeople, or have actually built cottages expressly for their use. This course has been adopted by Messrs. Pim at Harold's Cross; the proprietors of the Great Southern and Western Railway; Messrs. Jameson and Co., North Anne Street; Messrs. Jameson, Bow Street; &c., &c.[42]

Very few further company projects were undertaken.[43]

---

[38] *Annual Report of the Dublin Bible Woman Mission in connection with the Church of Ireland* (Dublin, 1877), p. 16.
[39] *Housing Inquiry 1885*, CC–4547–I, qs 21,861–21,876.
[40] Ibid., qs 21,861–21,870.
[41] 'Report of the Housing Committee', *RPDCD*, no. 83, (1914), p. 819.
[42] Jordan, 'Dwelling of the Poor' (1857), p. 17.
[43] See Charles Cameron and Edward Mapother, 'Report on the Means for the Prevention of Disease in Dublin', *RPDCD*, vol. 1, (1879), pp. 344–345 for later calls on the city's employers to build for their workers.

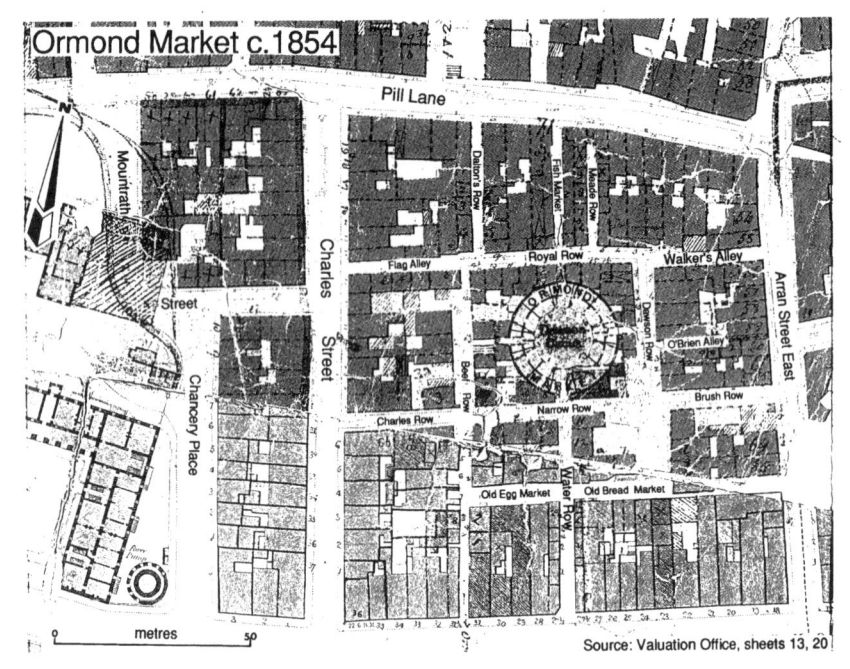

Figure 4.2 Ormond Market c.1854

Dublin Artisans' Dwellings Company, 1876–1887
The Coombe Scheme

The Coombe scheme, was begun under the Artizans' and Labourers' Dwellings Improvement Acts, 1875 (the Cross Act) and 1877.[44] The Artisans' Committee of Dublin Corporation had recommended the renting of the Coombe area to the Dublin Artisans' Dwellings Company (DADC) on the basis that its objects were akin to those held by the Corporation, and that 'a uniformity of design and character in the description and style of dwellings would be maintained'.[45] The DADC was an offshoot of the Dublin Sanitary Association, a voluntary movement of influential citizens concerned to improve health and general living conditions in the city; the DADC company has been described as 'a relatively energetic and efficient company, run by Protestant businessmen and paying modest dividends usually not exceeding four per cent to its shareholders'. Major investors included the Guinness family and Lady Meath.[46]

The area outlined in 1876 by the medical officer of health (Figure 4.1), was extended considerably 'for purposes of widening roadways and for ventilation,

[44] Artizans' and Labourers' Dwellings Improvement Acts, 38 & 39 Vic. c.36 (1875), and 40 & 41 Vic. c.122, Local (1877).
[45] 'Report of the Artizans' Dwellings Committee, Plunket-Street Area Scheme,' *RPDCD*, vol 1, no. 52, (1884), p. 364.
[46] F.H.A. Aalen, *The Iveagh Trust: The First Hundred Years, 1890–1900* (Dublin, 1990), p. 8.

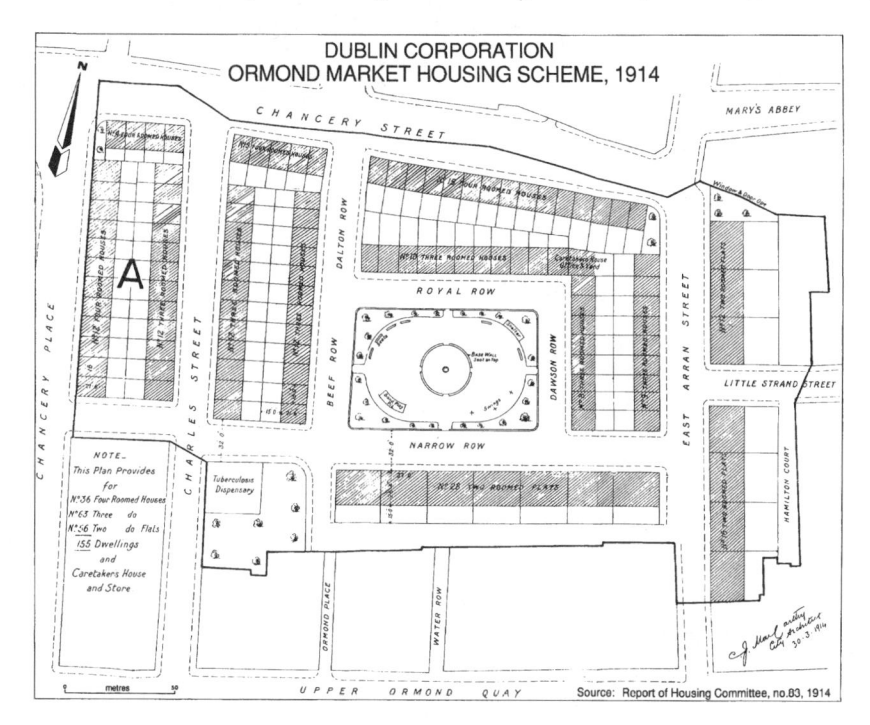

Figure 4.3 Dublin Corporation Ormond Market housing scheme, 1914.

and also included houses and yards which were in an equally insanitary state as the portion the subject of Dr Mapother's report'.[47] The network of alleys and back courts which was to be cleared is illustrated in Figure 4.4, ground plan of 'Area No. 1, Coombe', 1877. The city engineer, Parke Neville, seconded the recommendation for total clearance, with the addition of one extra house, no. 3 Pimlico, to widen the approach to the west. The presence of 'good main sewers' in Pimlico, Meath Street, the Coombe and Great and Little Elbow Lane was in its favour, although to date the link between local domestic arrangements and these sewers was tenuous.

The case for total demolition and rebuilding was earnestly pressed by Dr Grimshaw at the public enquiry held in April 1877. As a physician at Cork Street Fever Hospital he had 'pointed out, on maps of the Coombe district, places marked as indicating houses where fever prevailed, and others in which cholera had prevailed'.[48] Some houses with from 35–40 residents, had 'but one necessary accommodation for the entire, and that in the most disgraceful and neglected condition; the yards were also filthy, reeking with most offensive matter'.[49]

[47] Harty, 'The Coombe Area' (1884), p. 508.
[48] Ibid., p. 510.
[49] Ibid., p. 513.

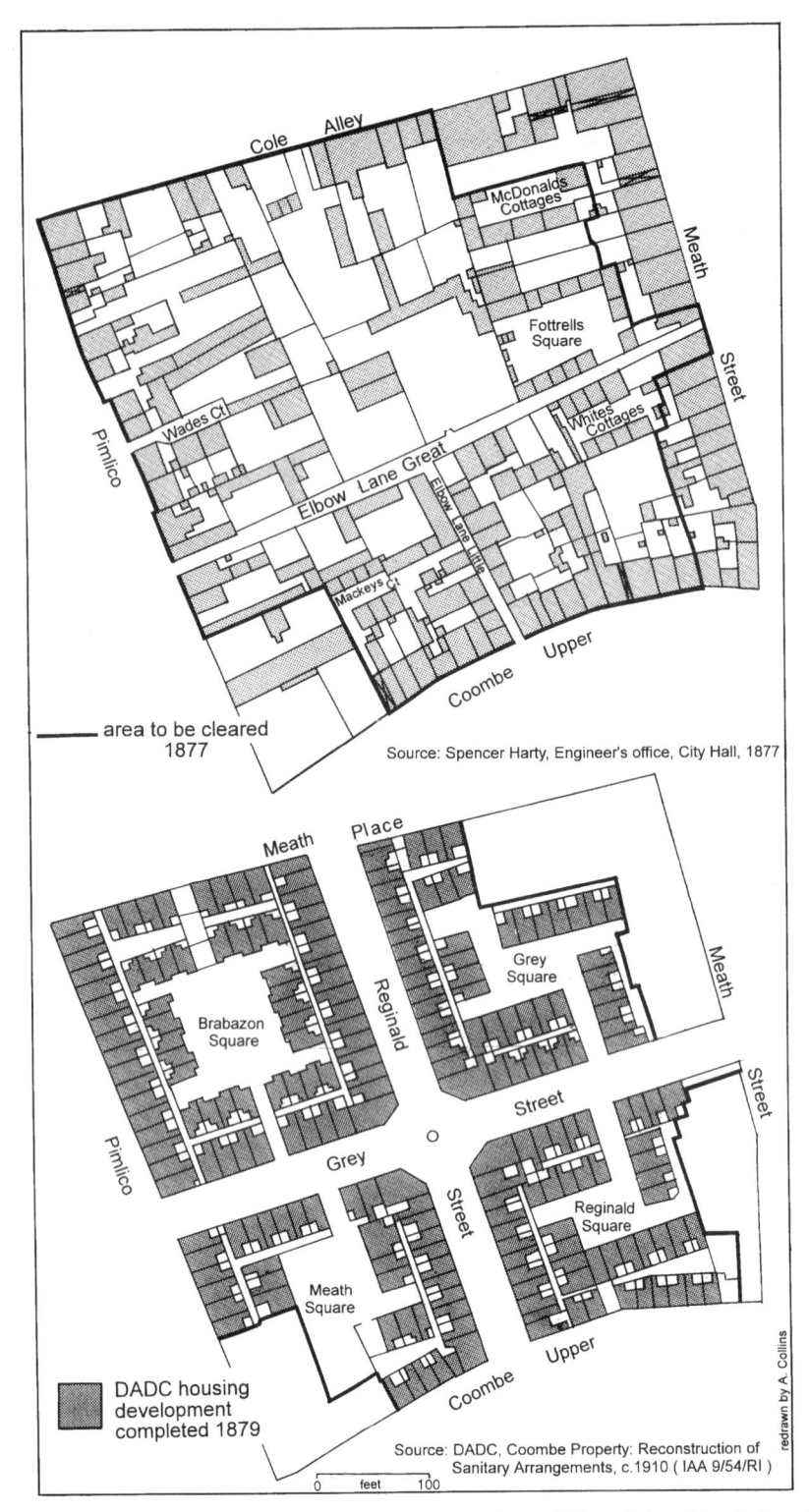

Figure 4.4(a) The Dublin Improvement Scheme, 1877 Ground Plan of Area No. 1, Coombe.
Figure 4.4(b) Coombe Scheme, Dublin Artisans' Dwellings Company, 1879.

The houses of the Coombe area, with leases dating back to 1691, came under the jurisdiction of the Corporation and were liable for municipal rates only from 1840, being formerly part of the Liberty of the Earl of Meath. In the early nineteenth century it was the home of manufacturers of cotton, linen, and starch, and many tradesmen (see Figure 2.2, Rocque 1756), but by 1878, when the land was purchased, there was not a single merchant, manufacturer or trader in the entire area. Their successors were a motley set, some 'in the dog fancying line', others made their living by selling pigs and manufacturing manure, 'while others were engaged in more degraded occupations'.[50] The overall picture is one of near destitution, with persons exploiting every possibility of making a living and at the time of the Corporation purchase determined to maximise on the opportunity of compensatory payments. The site was 'in a very poor locality surrounded by some of the worst habitations, some of which were in a tottering condition and inhabited by very poor persons'. There were 110 dwellings, and about 300 separate tenancies, a population of 984 persons giving a density of about 246 persons per acre. The new scheme resulted in an increase in the local population, consisting of 210 houses, accommodating 1,100 persons, at about 275 per acre.[51] The accommodation of more persons than had been displaced was due only to the large number of premises which were derelict by the time of the redevelopment.

Table 4.2 is an illustration of the rateable value of some Coombe houses, showing the number of weekly tenancies, and the average amount of rent paid in each house. Where families took in 'lodgers', a widespread Dublin practice, the rent burden on families would be reduced somewhat. The weekly rent per family varied generally between 1s 6d to 2s 9d, far below the lowest rates of 3s 6d which were to be levied by the DADC for the smallest cottages, rising to 7s per week for the four-roomed two storey houses, in the new scheme.[52]

The cost to the Corporation of acquiring this site, relative to later suburban schemes, was enormous. The area was first valued at £11,134, but soon increased to £14,421[53], a figure which resulted in much public disquiet, particularly with regard to nine cases in which the jury recommended increases of nearly £120 *per cent*. One woman who paid no rent (she had a squatter's title) was awarded £600 by the jury. A dairy owner and green grocer were awarded a total of £479 by the arbitrator which was increased to £1,350 by the jury, including compensation for trade disturbance; both business people promptly reopened in superior premises nearby. However it was accepted that 'the Corporation paid dearly for the property, but not more than all public bodies have to pay whenever property is required to be purchased for public purposes, so that individuals do not always suffer by measures necessary for the benefit of the public'.[54] The sacredness of

[50] Ibid., p. 513.
[51] Ibid., pp. 510–514.
[52] Ibid., p. 514.
[53] *RPDCD*, vol. 3, (1879) p. 792.
[54] Harty, 'The Coombe Area'; see also W.N. Osborough, *Law and the Emergence of Modern Dublin* (Dublin, 1996), p. 87.

Tenement Houses—Their Rateable Value and the Rents Yielded by Them.

The following Returns have been prepared with a view to illustrate the observations as to the Rateable Value and Letting of Tenement Houses:—

Coombe Area.

Tenement Houses to be taken under the Artisans' Dwellings Act.

STREET	Rateable Value	Weekly Tenancies			Mr. Fitzgerald's Valuation of Tenants' Interest	Arbitrators' Award
		No.	Weekly Amount of Rent	Annual Amount of Rent		
No.	£ s.		s. d.	£ s. d.	£ s. d.	£ s. d.
54 Upper Coombe	6 0	6	8 10	22 19 4	...	...
59 ,,	6 0	6	11 4	29 9 4	10 19 11	22 10 8
63 ,,	7 0	6	10 4	26 17 4	6 14 4	12 2 8
64 ,,	6 0	6	8 7	22 6 4	5 11 7	11 3 8
3 Pimlico	5 0	5	8 0	20 16 0	5 4 0	11 13 0
5 ,,	4 0	4	11 10	30 15 4	since	settled
7 ,,	6 0	4	8 10	22 19 4	5 14 10	11 9 8
9 ,,	2 0	1	3 0	7 16 0	1 19 0	3 19 0
20 Cole-alley	5 0	6	8 3	21 9 0	5 7 3	10 5 10
23 ,,	5 0	1	8 0	20 16 0	5 4 0	10 8 0
29 ,,	10 0	12	21 10	56 15 4	14 3 10	26 4 4
30 ,,	5 0	5	7 5	19 5 8	5 19 5	13 1 10
31 ,,	4 10	4	7 4	19 1 4	4 15 4	9 10 8
32 ,,	4 10	4	7 4	19 1 4	4 15 4	9 10 8
Selection of other Tenement Houses.						
31 Arran-st., East	9 0	3	18 6	48 2 0	...	...
2 Bedford-row	...	3	15 0	39 0 0	...	...
10 ,,	...	5	14 10	38 11 4	...	...
26 Bishop-street	10 0	4	17 4	45 1 4	...	...
2 Bride-street	10 0	5	17 1	44 8 4	...	...
35 Church-street	£5 to £12	5	19 6	50 14 0	...	...
37 ,,	...	5	15 0	39 0 0	...	...
54 ,,	9 0	6	15 4	39 17 4	...	...
149 ,,	9 0	7	16 2	42 0 8	...	...
160 ,,	11 0	4	18 4	47 13 4	...	...
14 King-st., South	10 0	3	16 6	42 18 0	...	...
15 ,,	9 0	4	23 0	59 16 0	...	...
16 ,,	10 0	4	16 3	42 5 0	...	...
4 Meath-street	9 0	8	21 0	54 12 0	...	...
50 ,,	8 0	3	14 6	37 14 0	...	...
24 Kevin-street	4 10	4	14 6	37 14 0	...	...
47 Meath-street	15 0	6	21 0	54 12 0	...	...

Report of the Housing Committee, *RPDCD*, 3, 1879, appendix C

Table 4.2 Tenement houses: rateable values and rents, 1879.

private property, even if tumbledown and seriously endangering the health of occupants and neighbours, had to be respected.

The Corporation merely acquired and cleared the four acre site, at a total cost of £24,367; it then leased it to the Dublin Artisans' Dwellings Company, on very favourable terms: for 10,000 years, at a peppercorn rent for the first two years, and afterwards at £200 per annum. The company was bound to erect 199 houses, containing accommodation 'for at least 984 persons of the artizan or working classes', the houses to be 'well and substantially built and ventilated, and furnished with water supply, proper drainage, and sanitary appliances and apparatus, to the satisfaction of the Corporation or their architect'.[55] The DADC expended £27,600 in buildings. The foundation stone was laid 20 December 1880, and 120 houses of four different classes were erected: one-storey cottages, containing one living-room and one or two bedrooms; and two-storey houses, containing one or two living rooms and two bedrooms. There were also four houses of three stories, used as shops.

The sanitary arrangements were advertised as perfect in every way, where 'each tenant has the satisfaction of having his (*sic*) house and yard reserved to himself and his family' (Figure 4.4). Even the smallest cottages had their own scullery, coal-house, privy, and yard. The cleansing passages at the rere were all kept strictly private, 'even from the tenants, and are in no case open to the public'.[56] These passages allowed each house to be provided with its own water supply, and also allowed sewers to be run into each yard, so that 'no sewers or drains pass under the houses'. The yards were surfaced in concrete, so that 'no foul matter can percolate into the earth'. The sanitary arrangements adopted by the DADC were similar in important respects to best practice in Britain in the 1870s (see Figures 3.1, 3.2). The houses themselves were substantially constructed, the smallest cottages built of Portland cement concrete, the larger houses with front and end walls of redbrick and other walls of concrete. Cubic air-space ranged from a combined bedroom/living room capacity of 2,743 feet for the small two-roomed cottages, to a combined bedroom/living room capacity of 5,310 feet for the four roomed houses. Exterior walls were eight inches thick, the interior walls six inches thick, and the houses were acclaimed as 'all very dry, give great satisfaction to the tenants, are eagerly sought after, and are never untenanted'. The height of the houses being limited to two storeys, (excluding the four shops of three storeys) 'the whole area has the advantage of the sun and air, and the classes of dwellings contrast advantageously with the huge and cheerless barracks to be seen in other places'.[57]

Artisans' schemes such as those pioneered by the DADC made a huge impact on the local urban morphology as well as the social makeup. A comparison of the

---

[55] Appendix to evidence of Mr Beveridge, 'Paper showing the terms upon which the Corporation of Dublin let the Coombe area on lease to the Dublin Artizans' Dwellings Company', *Housing Inquiry 1885*, appendix B (1), p. 107.
[56] Harty, 'The Coombe Area' (1884), p. 517.
[57] Ibid., p. 514.

situation before and after (Figure 4.4) illustrates the very regular layout of the Coombe scheme: four small squares, contained within the lines of the two major streets, Gray Street and Reginald Street, each street forty feet wide from house to house, the streets intersecting at right angles. Both Pimlico and the Coombe itself were widened by ten feet.[58] DADC housing estates were to be characterised by two house types: single storey concrete cottages and two-storey redbrick houses, as in this Coombe scheme. Long repetitive lines of parallel streets, conforming to by-law widths, as laid down under the Public Health (Ireland) Act 1878, which were to characterise several later DADC schemes (such as Oxmantown)[59] are mercifully absent in the Coombe, where a small and compact site facilitated a more pleasing if regular layout.

The effort to provide for the poorest was regarded as a non-starter; in the case of the Coombe scheme the only hope allowed for was that this new colony with its 'increased health and strength and a very much improved tone of morals' should also 'act indirectly on the conduct of the inhabitants of other houses in the streets adjoining'. It was vaguely claimed that the scheme had given the former inhabitants 'the chance of improved dwellings in other places in the city' by taking up the dwellings vacated by the new DADC tenants, and that 'a sort of levelling-up process has been quietly going on'.[60] Although objections were made to the financing of the scheme, there was widespread satisfaction that nothing but good could result from the clearance of such a notorious slum of its 'pest houses, fever and cholera spots, filthy yards, etc.'[61] 'The bulk of the classes rooted out of a condemned area' through moving into dwellings 'somewhat better than they formerly inhabited' were afforded the chance of 'better health and strength for the breadwinner and the family' resulting in a lowering of the death rate and a decrease in pauperism and crime.[62] And the condition of those fortunate enough to occupy these bright new dwellings, built to the highest sanitary standards, was of course presented as idyllic.

Plunket Street Scheme

The Municipal Council adopted a resolution on 3 December 1879 directing the Artizans' Dwellings Committee to carry into execution the Plunket Street Area Scheme, another of the 'black spots' identified by Dr Mapother in 1876 (Figure 4.1), and previously noted by Whitelaw (1805, Chapter 2). As with the Coombe scheme the origins of the project were directly health-related: a month previously the consulting sanitary officer had formally submitted that the greater number of the houses within the area delimited were unfit for human habitation and diseases of 'a low type' had prevailed within the area over a long period, which

[58] Ibid., p. 517.
[59] Aalen, *The Iveagh Trust* (1990), p. 8.
[60] Harty, 'The Coombe Area' (1884), pp. 514–516.
[61] Ibid., p. 515.
[62] Ibid., p. 514.

were attributable to the 'bad condition and narrowness of the streets, courts and houses, to the want of air and proper sanitary conveniences'. Some at least of the houses had no sanitary accommodation whatsoever. There was no way of remedying these defects other than by 'an improvement scheme for the rearrangement of the streets and courts within the entire area'.[63]

Despite the unanimity on the need to tackle this particular slum with its 'fever nests and rack-rented population' the promoters of the new development faced a succession of obstacles. The original estimate for the purchase of the three acre site was £12,470; the provisional order to enable the Corporation to carry out the scheme was issued and confirmed by parliament in 1880 and a loan of £15,000 from the Commissioners of Public Works in Ireland was secured but by 1882 it was found that the purchase money alone of the interests affected by the scheme was £19,115.[64] Application was made to the Local Government Board to sanction an extension of their borrowing powers by another £12,000; while permission was granted in November 1882, the loan could not be made available (under regulations enforced by the Commissioners of Public Works) until after April 1883.[65] For some time the committee was not able 'owing to the want of funds, to push forward the scheme as vigorously as they desired', and the local parish priest, Fr James Daniel, who had assisted Mr Gray in clearing the locality six years earlier, complained that the foundation stone had still not been laid, 'the people have suffered enormously up there in business, and it has given great dissatisfaction'.[66] The final cost of clearing the site and making roads, sewers and footpaths was £27,000, well over twice the original estimate.[67] It was also 'greatly delayed' by 'the difficulty which several of the owners and lessees had in rendering a satisfactory title to their respective holdings'.[68] By 1887 it was largely completed.

The first six-inch edition (1837) of the Ordnance Survey (Figure 4.5) illustrates the 'narrow and crowded lanes' their 'defective air-space, absence of yards and therefore of suitable sanitary accommodation' that made the application of the Artizans' and Labourers' Dwellings Improvement Act to this area 'imperatively necessary'.[69] This area was even more densely populated than the Coombe, as was noted as early as 1805 by Whitelaw: 'From a careful survey, twice taken, of Plunket-street, it appeared that thirty-two contiguous houses contained 917 souls, which gives an average of 28.7 to a house'.[70] By 1879 there were 1,619

---

[63] 'Report of the Artizans' Dwellings Committee', *RPDCD*, vol. 1, no. 52, (1884), p. 361; Harty, 'The Coombe Area' (1884), p. 522.
[64] *Housing Inquiry 1885*, C-4547-I, qs. 21,873-21,876.
[65] 'Report of the Artizans' Dwellings Committee', *RPDCD*, vol. 1, no. 52, (1884), p. 363; also *Housing Inquiry 1885*, C-4547-I, qs. 21,874. Harty (1884), p. 522.
[66] Evidence of Rev James Daniel, *Housing Inquiry 1885*, qs 22,494.
[67] Ibid., qs. 21,917.
[68] 'Report of the Artizans' Dwellings Committee, Plunket-Street Area Scheme', *RPDCD*, vol 1, no. 52, (1884), p. 363.
[69] *RPDCD*, vol. 3, (1879), pp. 616-617.
[70] Whitelaw, *Survey* (1805), p. 51.

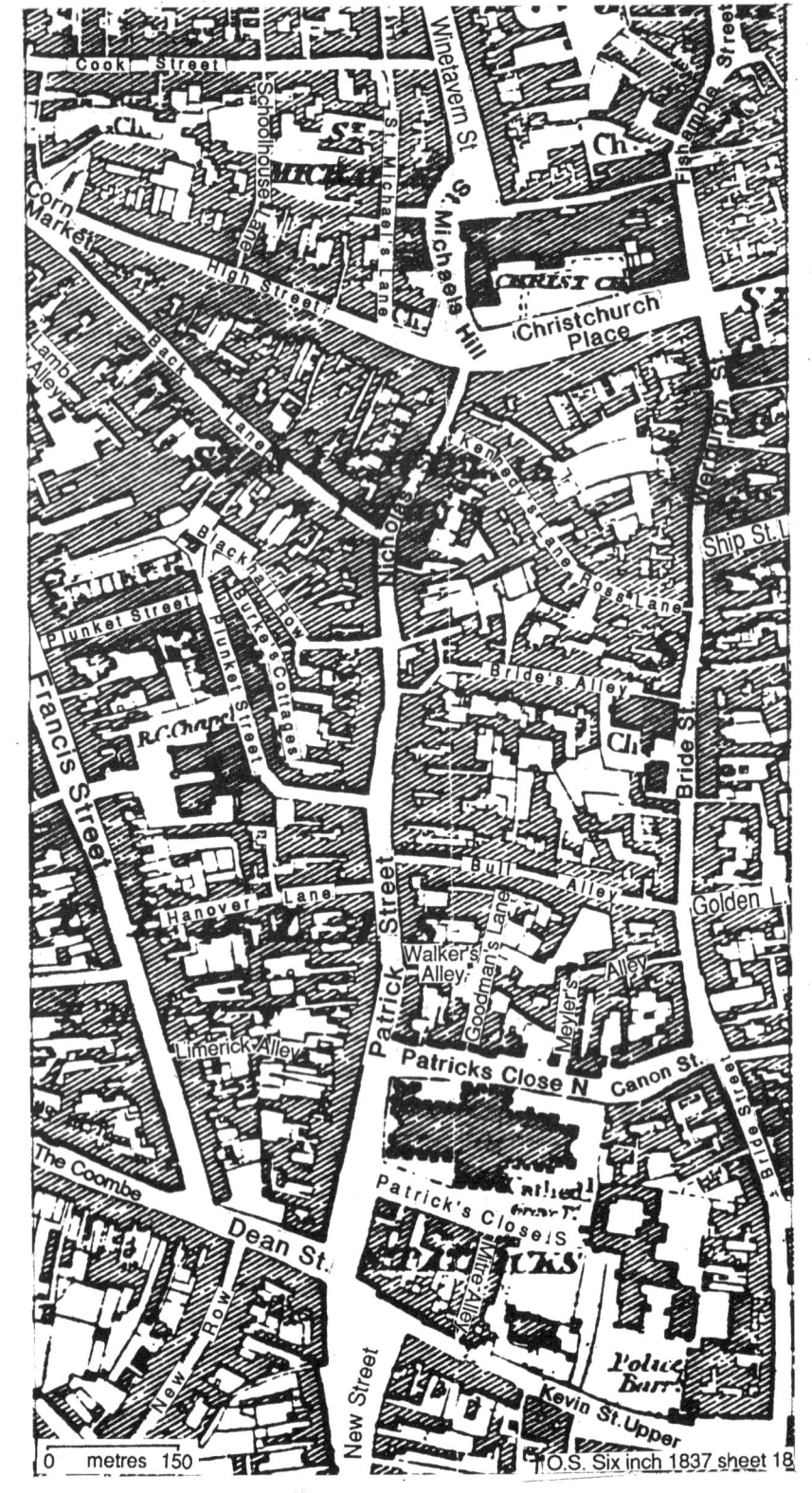

Figure 4.5 Plunket Street and Patrick Street, 1837.

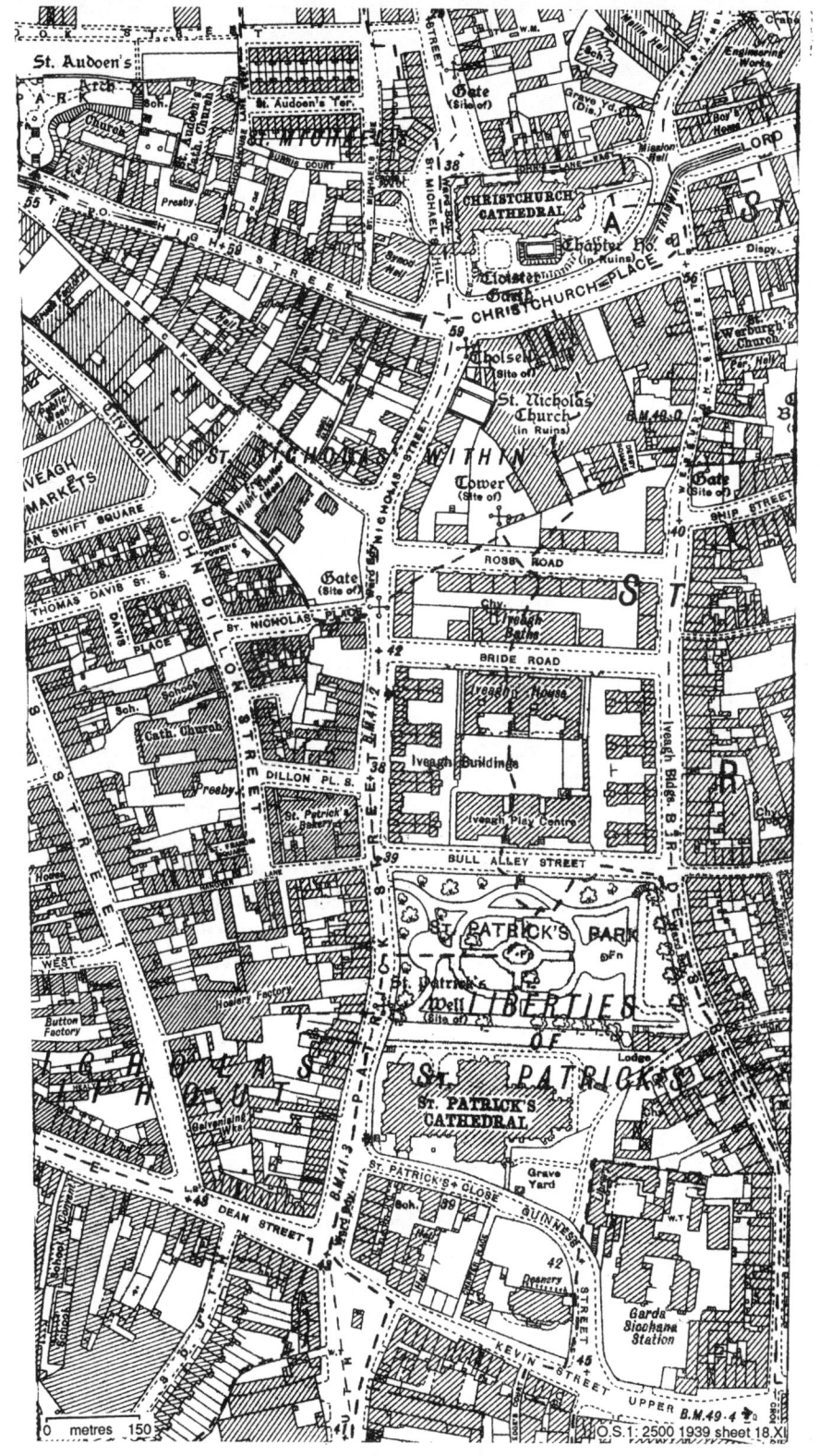

Figure 4.6 Dublin Artisans' Dwellings Company scheme Plunket Street (Thomas Davis Street) and Iveagh Trust buildings, Patrick Street, 1939.

persons living in the area, occupying 161 dwelling-houses, of which 28 had been 'compulsorily depopulated', and not one of which could be regarded as 'substantial' and healthy.[71] The population, with the exception of some butchers, was entirely of the 'humblest class, for whom, as in the Coombe scheme, only the vaguest hopes for their betterment were held:

There are no manufactories or industries within it, but in its immediate vicinity there are several which afford a considerable amount of employment, and as the dwellings of the artisans and labouring classes in the neighbourhood are of a wretched description, there would be a ready demand for suitable accommodation by an industrious class when erected on this site, and a great social and sanitary improvement would thereby be effected.[72]

The rehousing clauses of the Act made the developers' task particularly difficult here. It was feared that 'the same number as those displaced could not be accommodated without building those immense large houses which are both unsightly and unhealthy in any area, as they prevent the free access of sunlight and air, and are very much disliked by the working classes in Dublin'.[73] Some of those displaced had lost their business premises, and the legislation under which the site was cleared precluded any commercial development, despite evidence that 'the provision of a number of shops and stalls to accommodate the numerous traders who were displaced by the removal of the buildings in Blackhall Market [off Blackhall Row, Figure 4.5] is greatly needed'. This was doubly to be regretted, as the Corporation was thus deprived of 'a considerable return' which might be had 'if the Corporation were allowed to put the site to the most advantageous purpose'.[74]

The Plunket street scheme was confined to a more irregular and broken site than that made available in the earlier Coombe venture. A comparison of the situation in 1837 (Figure 4.5) with a modern map (Figure 4.6, 1939) shows how this site was handled: two storey (and a few one storey) houses faced wide, 'healthful' thoroughfares, such as John Dillon Street, Dean Swift Square and Thomas Davis Street, while one-storey cottages faced on to small but open areas, such as Power's Square, Dillon Place, and Francis Square. The scheme was bounded in part by the medieval city wall (Figure 4.6, Power's Square), and surrounded by very mixed landuses, including a bakery, dairy yards and workshops and the tenement houses of Francis Street and Patrick Street.

The dwellings proposed for the Plunket Street site were to model the best sanitary practices, an advance even on the Coombe scheme, as the building conditions spelt out: the whole area of each dwelling and its entire yard space was to be 'covered with asphalte or concrete impervious to water', efficient damp coursing was to be strategically located, 'every room shall have a fire place and a chimney flue', each ground floor was to be between six and nine inches above the level of the adjoining footway or open space, and 'each dwelling shall be pro-

[71] see also *Housing Inquiry 1885* qs. 21,915.
[72] *RPDCD*, vol. 3, (1879), pp. 616–617.
[73] Harty, 'The Coombe Area' (1884), p. 521.
[74] 'Report of the Artizans' Dwellings Committee, Plunket-Street Area Scheme', *RPDCD*, vol 1, no. 52, (1884), p. 364.

vided with a separate water closet, which shall not be entered directly from any habitable room, and that the passage or area from which such water closet is entered shall at all times be in direct communication with the external air'. In matters concerning sewers, water pipes, ventilation, and the removal of ashes, all was to be done in accord with the by-laws and to the satisfaction of the Public Health Committee, and no dwelling was to be used 'as an inn, ale or beer house, victualing house, licensed refreshment house', or for the sale of intoxicating liquor, nor 'for the purpose of any trade or business or otherwise than as a private dwelling house'.[75] Each tenant was to have a key to their house, and so could prevent the 'intrusion of vagrants or strangers who might desire to use the sanitary accommodation of houses to which they have no claim'.[76]

The first residents of the Coombe scheme represented 49 different occupations: among 210 households 61 families, were headed by labourers, 14 were headed by widows, 8 by carpenters, 7 each by pensioners, brick-layers, tailors, 6 by cutters, 5 each by porters, coopers, 4 each by vanmen, bakers, compositors, brush makers, book binders, bootmakers, bricklayers and soldiers, while the remainder were divided among policemen, cab owners, clerks, engine drivers, plasterers, shoemakers, skinners, travellers, and others. What united this diverse grouping was full-time, reliable employment, allowing each family to faithfully meet a rent of from 3s 6d to 7s each week, for in this scheme it was boasted that 'the bad debts are practically nil'.[77]

The social distance between the residents of the two new schemes and those of the surrounding slums was emphasised; in the Coombe 'the houses also show the improved tone in the people, cleanliness and neatness, windows decorated with flowers, books, neat blinds are everywhere to be seen'. Such efforts were encouraged by the benevolence of Lord and Lady Brabazon 'who give substantial prizes for the best kept houses and best window gardening'.[78] Being of such 'an improved class' than the persons displaced, the benefits to traders in the area were also held to be considerable, while the contributions to the municipal and poor law rates had increased tenfold, from a miserly average of £63 per annum collected on the former property, to a total of £611 from the new housing.[79]

Lessons were learned from the Coombe scheme and conditions of sale for the Plunket Street site were more restricted. Here the Corporation specified the rents that could be charged, i.e.,: ranging from 2s 6d to 6s per week, 'in order that the cottages might be let at such a rent as the people could afford to pay', a curb on strictly commercial considerations which would have allowed the DADC to charge more, and a recognition that the covenant in the Coombe lease to house persons of the 'artizans' and working classes' needed to be spelled out. It can be

[75] 'Report of the Artizans' Dwellings Committee, Plunket-Street Area Scheme', *RPDCD*, vol 1, no. 52, (1884), pp. 365, 366.
[76] *Housing Inquiry 1885*, qs. 22,067.
[77] Harty, 'The Coombe Area' (1884), p. 514.
[78] Ibid., p. 517.
[79] Ibid., p. 515.

interpreted as another small step in the move on the Corporation's part towards more active regulation of the housing market, at least as it affected the poorer sectors of society.[80] There was also a greater proportion of larger two-storeyed houses in the Plunket Street scheme than in the Coombe, a recognition that very small houses did not meet the needs of the average Dublin family.[81]

The cost of clearing 'purlieus' by the compulsory purchase of wretched old houses made city centre schemes prohibitively expensive; one authority claimed that all the premises acquired for the Coombe and Plunket Street schemes were unlikely to realise £20,000 if voluntarily disposed of; the Corporation paid almost £52,000.[82] Building for the very poorest could never be recouped in rents, so that without assistance from central government it was regarded as impossible, although in 1899 it was noted that the London County Council had adopted the principle of providing dwellings at a loss to the rate payers, in a special case.[83] The Coombe and Plunket Street schemes were so expensive that further developments were to be very slow, and cheaper suburban schemes increasingly favoured.

Lack of progress in the clearing of the 'condemned areas' identified in 1876 was noted in the Public Health Committee's report for 1879, but even those first small-scale efforts had exposed the very heart of the Dublin slum problem. The residents of the worst slum areas, the citizens most in need of improved accommodation, and least able to procure it by their own unaided efforts, were entirely by-passed by the new developments. In fact, some feared that the DADC schemes by providing for 'a select number of families of a more thrifty section than the working class' in the process were leaving 'a residuum' who are 'by picking out the better people among them even in a more squalid condition on the average than before'.[84] The model lodging-houses and artisans' dwellings recently erected in Dublin brought no advantage to the poorest, the very persons whose condition 'furnishes employment for the sanitary police'; 'it is they who overcrowd rooms, who have insufficient sanitary accommodation, who live in the most dilapidated houses, in the narrowest and most crowded courts and lanes, in old stables and in outhouses, more or less ruinous'. It was on behalf of the hundreds of families paying an average of 1s 6d per week rent that Dr Cameron campaigned, 'not one in fifty of whom can afford to pay the rents demanded for apartments in the industrial tenements dwellings'. One proposal, untried, was to erect quadrangular blocks of cottages, each of which could be let for from 1s 6d to 2s 6d per week, 'the quadrangular form would admit of the cottages being economically provided with water and gaslight'. 'Until such accommodation as this is provided for the poorest class of the population, it will be very difficult to

---

[80] *Housing Inquiry 1885* qs 21,919; 22,025.
[81] Ibid., qs 21,919; Plunket Street requirements: 73 two storeyed cottages, 44 one storeyed cottages, 24 tenements for 24 families.
[82] Charles Cameron, 'The Homes of the Working Classes in Dublin', Appendix A(3), *Housing Inquiry 1885*, pp. 102–103.
[83] Eason, 'Tenement Houses' (1899), p. 398.
[84] Evidence of Mr Frederic William Pim (DSA), *Housing Inquiry 1885*, qs. 22,638.

enforce a proper sanitary state of things among them. So soon as they are forced to leave one place, they go into another equally unfit to live in'.[85]

The practice of taking in lodgers was so long established in Dublin that even the DADC management complained it was 'one of the greatest evils that we have to contend with, and an evil that we cannot satisfactorily deal with'. It extended to the houses of 5s and upwards per week as much as the poorer houses, with examples of lodgers being 'lent by one charitable tenant to another to tide over a temporary difficulty'.[86]

The artisans' schemes in the Coombe and Plunket Street were among the earliest undertaken by the DADC, which was to continue its philanthropic mission of providing modest housing, at a minimal return to its shareholders, at a number of well-scattered locations throughout the city (see Chapter 5, Figure 5.3). By the Civic Survey of 1925 the DADC had provided 3,415 houses, on both cleared and 'virgin' sites.[87]

Condemnation of Insanitary Dwellings, 1879–1882

In 1879 the Corporation was, for the first time, provided with the necessary funds, through the Improvement Rate, to begin a more effective process of sanitary reform under the able leadership of Dr Charles Cameron. The new campaign also corresponds with the first accurate mortality statistics for the city (Chapter 3), so that the improvement in public health can be tracked. The formulation of this plan of campaign was heavily influenced by the expensive Coombe experience; it was clear that the Corporation could not afford to follow the route of wholesale slum clearance for quite some time, but the crisis demanded effective action now. In the face of a task of impossible proportions, the Public Health Committee formally determined in September 1879 that 'it would be better to prune out here and there throughout the city houses in narrow alleyways and courts than to clear out a whole district'. Once demolished, 'only such new houses could be erected in their stead as would have sufficient yard accommodation'. The committee judged there were about 20 courts in Dublin which should be razed, adding that 'some of them are in the best quarters of the city'.[88] The slum geography was more accurately known in 1882 when Cameron directed a 'sanitary survey' of all the inhabited houses in Dublin, resulting in the discovery that 30% of the city's housing stock was occupied by 59% of the city's families, at the rate of 1.5 rooms per family.[89]

[85] 'Report of the Public Health Committee', *RPDCD*, vol. 3, no. 170, (1879), pp. 153, 155.
[86] Evidence of Mr Edward Spencer, (DADC), *Housing Inquiry 1885*, qs. 22,830–22,833.
[87] *The Dublin Civic Survey Report* (Liverpool, 1925).
[88] 'Report of the Public Health Committee, Breviate for September 1879, Clearing Infected Districts', *RPDCD*, 1879, p. 931.
[89] 'Report of the Public Health Committee', *RPDCD*, vol. 3, no. 93, (1888), p. 778. This report includes a summary of the achievements of this committee from 1879–1888; see also Charles Cameron, 'The Homes of the Working Classes in Dublin', appendix A(3), *Housing Inquiry 1885*, pp. 102–103, (hereafter 'Homes of the Working Classes').

136 *Dublin Slums*

A veritable crusade was launched by Dr Cameron and his newly-enlarged staff, with houses which were 'very lofty' and 'unprovided with yards', as well as houses in narrow courts and yards, the first to be targeted.[90] Despite substantial and time consuming difficulties, the sanitary staff had considerable initial success. The total number of houses closed and detenanted as unfit for human habitation from the 31 August 1879 to 31 December 1882 was 1,345, with 389 cellars and 'several hundreds of rooms' also closed. By 1886 a further 721 houses had been closed.[91] The 1883 report of the Public Health Committee lists a total of 841 addresses of premises recently detenanted, which may be regarded as a good

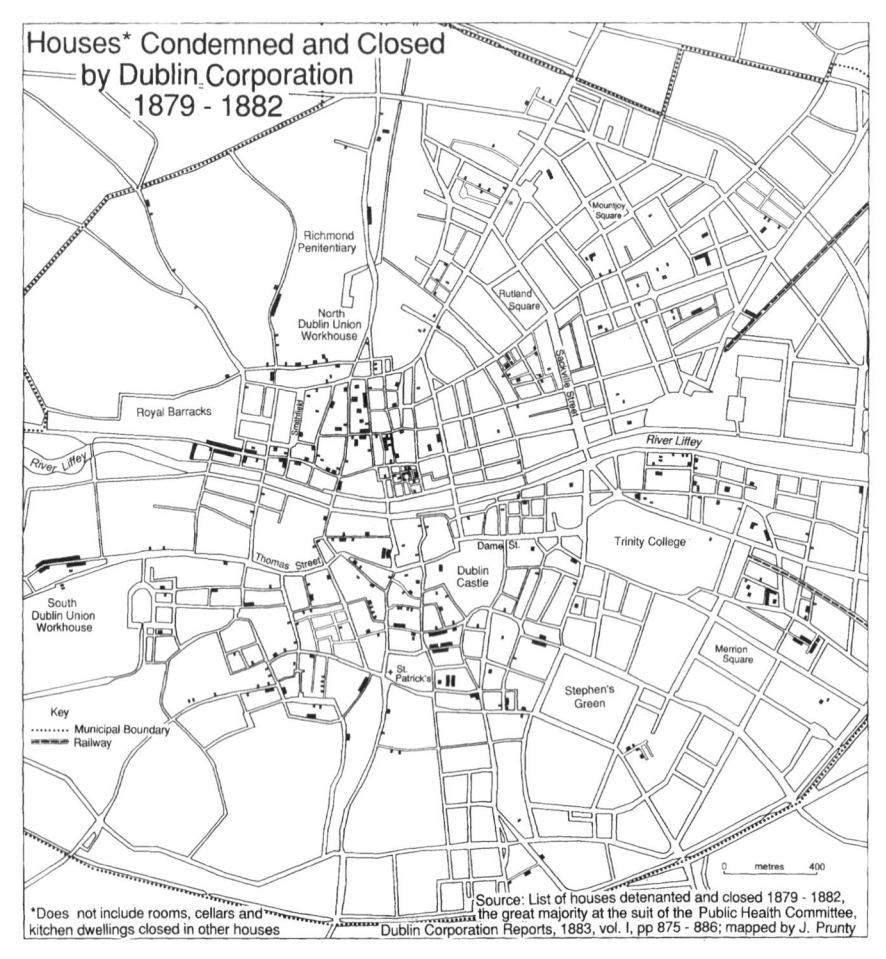

Figure 4.7 Houses condemned and closed by Dublin Corporation 1879–1882.

[90] Ibid.
[91] 'Report of the Public Health Committee', *RPDCD*, vol. 3, no. 93, (1888), p. 778.

sample of the total number condemned and successfully closed.[92] As these were undoubtedly very poor residences, their distribution (Figure 4.7) is a fair guide to the geography of poverty in Dublin 1879–1882. However, it must be kept in mind that they are only a fraction of the number which occupied the attentions of the sanitary staff, for this does not include the greater number which were 'subjected to notices to have nuisances and defects in them abated and remedied,'[93] nor those individual rooms and cellar dwellings which were closed.

North of the Liffey, there were concentrations around Ormond Market, and in the general vicinity of Church Street: North Brunswick Street, Beresford Street, Bow Street, Stirrup Lane, Carter's Lane, and courts behind these streets: Angle Court, Eliza Court, and Deignam's Court. The alleys and lanes close to Henry Street/Moore Street created another black spot, as was the case in the Mecklenburgh/Purdon Street area. Further north, several ruinous cottages in Phibsborough were detenanted, including Pinchgut Lane and Weaver's Alley.

To the south of the river the old Liberties area was the most prominent, but there are also important concentrations between this area and Stephen's Green, including Wood Street, Arthur's Lane, Mercer Street, Chancery Lane, and Bishop Street. From Dame Street to the quays, and to the rear of Trinity College, were found dwellings unfit for human habitation. Some front street dwellings such as Fade Street (see Plate 4.1) were cleared, but rear dwellings which were very effectively hidden such as Brady's Cottages (see Plate 4.3) were especially targeted.

A block of houses extending from St Michael's Hill to St Michael's Lane and adjoining the Synod Hall of Christchurch Cathedral was cleared despite strenuous objections. Dr Mapother regarded them as typical of the closures being effected, in this instance incapable of conversion to healthy dwellings because of their three-storey and quadrangular form: the central yard was only a few square feet in extent and housed the toilet provision for 150 persons, the 'oozings from the filthy so-called ashpit permeated through the foundations of the houses, and ascended through their walls, rendering them damp and noisome'. The stairs were dark and the doors of the rooms opened out onto 'dimly lit and ill-ventilated lobbies'.[94] As there was no proper way of ventilating the building, condemnation was inevitable.

The most striking feature of the closures was the widespread dispersal of such dwellings; apart from the well-known high status residential squares and the central business district (Figure 2.9), there was scarcely a part of Dublin which did not contain at least some substandard dwellings. As this map (Figure 4.7)

---

[92] This address list is made up of 545 'Ruinous, Deserted and Uninhabitable Houses in Dublin, 1882', the 'great majority of which have been closed at the suit of the Public Health Committee' and a further list in the same report 'List of Houses Unfit for Human Habitation, Detenanted and Closed during the Year 1882'. 'Annual Report on Public Health', *RPDCD*, vol. 1, (1883), pp. 873–886.

[93] 'Report of the Public Health Committee', *RPDCD*, vol. 3, no. 136, (1894), p. 85.

[94] Cameron, 'Homes of the Working Classes' (1885), p. 102.

illustrates only those dwellings which the sanitary officers *succeeded* in closing over a four year period, (1879–1882), the geographical extent of the problem was evidently huge. Cameron's statement at the Housing Inquiry of 1885 was clearly well founded:

In British cities we usually find good, bad and indifferent quarters, but always distinct, whilst in Dublin there is really no district which is not permeated with purlieus. Some of the poorest and most decayed streets exist in actual contact with the most fashionable squares and streets. A wretchedly poor population, occupying decayed houses, inhabit the space between St Stephen's Green and Fitzwilliam Square. The stables, in lanes lying in the rear of Merrion Square, have been in great part converted into dwelling-houses. The neighbourhood of Upper and Lower Mount Street teems with a poverty stricken population. Unlike most other great cities, the worst part of Dublin lies to the west. Here there is not a single large street in which tenement houses do not form the major portion of the buildings.[95]

The problems met with by the officers were immense, as rack-renting was a most lucrative and widespread occupation. Members of a Royal Commission in 1880 personally visited a selection of tenement houses, and reported in 'very strong language' on what they found. In one case the rent of a dilapidated house was £10 a year, but the middleman succeeded in extracting £240 from the tenants. Five individuals owned between them 1,100 houses; the gross rents of these houses totalled £5,500 a year, resulting in an income of over £1,100 per 'house farmers' per year.[96] No. 36 Upper Mercer Street, rateable value £18, was home to eleven families, totalling 37 individuals, yielding an annual rent of over £74.[97] These 'house jobbers', who lived 'by screwing the largest amount of rent they can out of the tenants'[98] were a powerful lobby, and as a number of Corporation members were also tenement landlords the sanitary officials were limited in what they could effect.[99] Confusion surrounding title to land and buildings, where there were sometimes six owners to a house,[100] was a further complication which profited the landlord and middleman. So too concern over the lack of alternative accommodation for those evicted could interfere with the processing of orders condemning a house, as in the case of derelict houses 'the magistrates do not feel themselves warranted in giving orders to turn out tenants from such houses when the landlord has failed to evict them and/or there is no owner found'.[101]

The city engineer, Parke Neville, drew attention to the fate of many of the houses which had been detenanted and closed up by the medical sanitary officer's orders, many of which were 'quickly broken into by the roughs and wreckers, who gut them'. Where houses were taken down by the owners as ruinous, or, in

[95] Ibid., p. 103.
[96] *Housing Inquiry 1885*, q 21,908.
[97] Cameron, 'Homes of the Working Classes', (1885), p. 103.
[98] *Housing Inquiry 1885*, q. 22,324.
[99] F.H.A. Aalen, 'The Working Class Housing Movement in Dublin 1850–1920', in Michael J. Bannon (ed.) *The Emergence of Irish Planning 1880–1920* (Dublin, 1985), pp. 91–92.
[100] *Housing Inquiry 1885*, q. 22,109.
[101] John Norwood, 'On the Working of the Sanitary Laws in Dublin, with Suggestions for their Amendment', *Stat. Soc. Inq. Soc. Ire. Jn.* 6, 43, (1873), p. 235.

their default, by men employed by the city engineer, there was little prospect of new buildings, and the sites were left as wasteland. In practice the distribution of houses closed under orders prefigured the distribution of long-derelict sites (see Figures 5.2, 5.7). And 'the moment *they are sought for to effect any public improvement*, the most fabulous valuations would be put on them by professional valuators' (*sic*), the exorbitant claims to be 'supported by the verdict of juries, which is simply robbery on the rate-payers, and must stop many useful schemes for the opening up and clearing away of the rotten, overcrowded and fever-stricken districts in different parts of the city'.[102]

The number of house closures effected by the sanitary officials was repeatedly upheld as a sign of the Corporation's determination to ameliorate the slum situation. At the Royal Commission in 1880, 2,300 houses were reported as unfit for human habitation; at the 1885 Housing Inquiry, it was claimed that 1,875 of these had been detenanted and closed.[103] However, no mention was made of the number of other houses which had deteriorated in the meantime and were now seriously substandard. The policy also directly fostered dereliction, for example in Wood Street and Boyne Street, where it was claimed no rebuilding was possible because of short or uncertain leases, and speculation over the Corporation's future plans for the area.[104]

The condemnation and successful closure of individual tenement houses was not the end of the story, for the houses could be reoccupied once the sanitary staff were satisfied with the improvements effected. Only about one third of those detenanted were closed permanently, according to the Corporation,[105] and in evidence before the Housing Inquiry of 1885 the chairman of the Dublin Sanitary Association agreed that a large number of houses were surreptitiously reopened without any regard whatsoever for the Corporation's sanitary regulations.[106] Thomas Grimshaw, Registrar General, could positively list instances, such as Meath Market off Meath Street, where ten of the twelve houses 'completely closed up' as unfit in every way were fully occupied.[107]

One further stumbling block to the closure of unhealthy dwellings was the unsatisfactory definition of 'overcrowding'. Under the Public Health Act of 1878 (largely the English act of 1874) local authorities were enabled to enforce their own by-laws to regulate overcrowding. Dublin Corporation had adopted a widely-used standard of 300 cubic feet of space per person, a measure which was applicable to the terraces and courts of very small houses produced in British industrial cities, but irrelevant in the context of Dublin, where lofty ceilings in even the worst tenement houses ensured that on paper at least each occupant

---

[102] 'Report of Parke Neville, City Engineer, for the Years 1882 and 1883', *RPDCD*, vol. 2, no. 108 (1884), p. 477.
[103] Evidence of Dr MacCabe, *Housing Inquiry 1885*, qs. 21,906–7.
[104] Evidence of Edward Spencer (DADC), *Housing Inquiry 1885*, qs. 22,902–22, 935.
[105] 'Report of the Public Health Committee', *RPDCD*, vol. 3, no. 93, (1888), p. 778.
[106] Evidence of Mr. F.W.Pim, *Housing Inquiry 1885*, qs 22,642–22,648.
[107] Evidence of Thomas Grimshaw, *Housing Inquiry 1885*, qs. 23,105–23,108.

enjoyed plenty of air. In Dublin, where 12 families were found occupying 12 rooms, but each person had more than 300 cubic feet of air, they could not be moved.[108] And these were the very circumstances where disease was most rapidly communicated. The move to abandon the 300 cubic feet benchmark was very slow, as it was one of the few measures of 'slumness' that allowed comparison across the board; gradually the separation of the sexes became more significant.

Public Health Report, 1883

The 'Return of Sanitary Operations Carried Out in the Year 1883' (see Chapter 3, Table 3.4) provides an overview of the public health measures directed by Charles Cameron in his role as chief medical officer of health. The principal endeavours were in the areas of inspecting and cleansing sewers, privies, water closets, dwellings, and yards, with some construction of sanitary conveniences. Inspections were also undertaken of bakeries, slaughter houses and dairy yards, while the disinfection of clothing and bedding and the serving of notices and summonses for sanitary offences were also key areas. The committee also made public the names of the owners who were fined for the insanitary state of their dwellings, those from whom fines were recovered (131 cases), those who had the fines remitted (12), and those who had failed to pay up and for whom either a warrant of distress was issued (15), or an order committing them to prison had been made (30). One owner, Daniel Connell of Price's Court, was already in prison for defying the magistrate's orders and refusing to pay the fine. The fines in question ranged largely from 5s to £1, although in a few cases went as high as £6 and £7; the publication of lists of offenders was part of the effort to sway public opinion to regard sanitary crimes as despicable, a shift that would take many decades to achieve.

Block Dwellings and Tenement Refurbishment

While the market for low-rent city housing was dominated by one-family houses converted, however unsatisfactorily, to tenement use, and the DADC and similar private companies were building small new houses for a more secure artisan class, there were also attempts to ameliorate the slum situation by building block dwellings. Such complexes accommodated more persons per acre cleared, and were thus essential if the requirement to rehouse the number displaced in densely-packed slums was to be fulfilled. Despite such an obvious point in their favour, there was much public disquiet attached to the issue. Witnesses to the 1885 inquiry maintained that 'the small houses are preferable, the people themselves prefer them, they give them a sort of homeliness',[109] while residents from the DADC blocks in Buckingham Street and Dominick Street reportedly disliked them greatly, 'they did not like to be with so many people', abandoning

---

[108] Evidence of Dr Cameron, *Housing Inquiry 1885*, qs. 22,170–22,173.
[109] Evidence of Rev James Daniel, *Housing Inquiry 1885*, qs. 22,490.

them for small houses whenever possible.[110] However, several flat complexes were built before the end of the nineteenth century; by far the largest and most successful scheme was the Bull Alley project undertaken by the philanthropic Iveagh Trust, (from 1889). The Corporation also built blocks at Barrack Street (later Benburb Street) and Bride Street (Figure 4.6). Small scale blocks were erected on Aston Quay (Crampton Buildings), Echlin Street, Dominick Street, and Stafford Street (see Chapter 5).[111]

The very practical approach of remodelling tenement dwellings and then closely supervising the residents, as pioneered by Octavia Hill in London, was tried in Dublin by ladies connected with Alexandra College, where 'the ladies will take a practical interest in the work by collecting the rents and looking after the houses, and much good will result from the knowledge which will be thereby gained of the conditions of life among the poor'.[112] However it was a very limited scheme, having no more than five tenement houses in Summerhill and Grenville Street in 1908, housing 200 people at rents ranging from 1s to 3s 6d per week.[113] Other examples of praiseworthy refurbishment were found in Stafford Street, where Mr Majoribanks, who owned nearly all of one side of the street, where the houses 'never intended for tenement dwellings had been remodelled 'into something approaching decent tenement dwellings'.[114]

Guinness/Iveagh Trust Scheme

The Guinness family played a leading role in providing low-rent but good quality housing, as chronicled by F.H.A. Aalen. The first Guinness initiative dates from 1872 when the Belle Vue buildings beside the St James's Gate brewery were erected to house their own labourers, followed by further tied housing in Rialto in 1882. These two brewery schemes accommodated a total of 180 families by 1885: 6 were three-bedroomed 'cottage class', the others were described as 'separate dwellings', each with its own hall door and key, water supply, water closet, scullery, sharing only a common staircase, variously described as 'exceptionally strongly built' and what some would even consider 'unnecessarily good'. The high standard of this early 'model housing' was claimed to have brought immediate benefits to the health of the occupants, with rickets, so common among those in 'wretched hovels' in the nearby slums, virtually unknown among these children. However, access was so limited – to Guinness employees, and serving only 14% of the 1,600 labouring men (as distinct from clerks) which the company employed[115] – that its benefits were strictly confined. Major investment

---

[110] Evidence of Mr Edward McMahon (Drumcondra), *Housing Inquiry 1885*, qs. 24,619–24,620.
[111] Niall McCullough, *Dublin: An Urban History* (Dublin, 1989), p. 94.
[112] Eason, 'Tenement Houses' (1899), p. 397.
[113] For this and other minor schemes see Aalen, (1985), pp. 159–161.
[114] Evidence of Mr J.E. Kenny (NDU) *Housing Inquiry 1885*, qs. 23,187.
[115] Evidence of Sir Edward Cecil Guinness, *Housing Inquiry 1885*, qs 22,965–22,047.

in the DADC (from its inauguration in 1876) extended the family's role in ameliorating poor housing conditions, but it was through the Guinness Trust (1890) funding for 'the amelioration of the condition of the poorer of the working classes' in London and Dublin that the family made the greatest impact on slum geography.[116]

A comparison of Figures 4.5 and 4.6 illustrates the scale of the Trust's accomplishments, in the case of the Bull Alley estate: in 1899 Lord Iveagh obtained powers under the Dublin Improvement (Bull Alley Area) Act to acquire and clear the area between Bride Road and Bull Alley, and erect new buildings on it, entirely at his own expense. Control and management of the buildings was by 1903 invested in what was renamed the Iveagh Trust. An area of notoriously poor and densely packed housing, along narrow alleys and closed courts, the intermixing of slaughter houses (see Figure 3.3) and other 'obnoxious' land uses did little to improve the ambience. A branch of the River Poddle ran underground through part of the site, complicating the engineering task in a most expensive manner, while the scheme also required the obliteration of an early ecclesiastical site, the church and yard of St Bride's. Wholesale but phased slum clearance led to a fundamental remodelling of the area: St Patrick's Park (1897), providing a gracious and civilised setting for the national cathedral of the Church of Ireland, and the Bull Alley buildings, incorporating family dwellings and ground floor shops in eight T-shaped blocks each of five storeys, and a lodging house for men facing Bride Road (1905). To complete the complex the Iveagh Baths (1906) including male and female baths as well as a swimming pool was erected by the Trust on Corporation land facing the men's hostel, while a very large two-storied play centre (1915) with a splendid baroque façade faced onto the park. Within the scheme high standards of construction and sanitary services were matched by close supervision of the tenantry, facilitated by perimeter gates controlling access, and its overall self-contained design. The range of accommodation varied, from single-room tenements (144 square feet), at rents of 2s 6d per week, to three-roomed self-contained tenements (i.e., with own laundry and toilet facilities) at 5s 9d per week.[117] Associated with the Bull Alley scheme was the Iveagh Market in Francis Street (1906, Figure 4.6), for the sale of vegetables, fish and second-hand clothes, with an adjoining disinfecting chamber for old clothes; this was to accommodate the dealers who were dispossessed by the Patrick Street clearance. To the north of Bride Road, the Corporation erected its own less ornate flat blocks, continuing the line of five-storey red-brick dwellings as far as the ruined Church of St Nicholas.

---

[116] Aalen, *The Iveagh Trust* (1990), p. 14; see also Richard Dennis, 'The geography of Victorian values: philanthropic housing in London, 1840–1900', *Journal of Historical Geography*, 15 (1) 1989, pp. 40–54.

[117] Ibid., p. 39.

The Legislative Problem Restated: F.R. Falkiner, 1881

F.R. Falkiner, QC, presented a critique of the current legislation governing the homes of the poor to the Social Science Congress, in Dublin, October 1881.[118] His claim that the state of the dwellings of the poor is now 'fully recognized as one of the most potent causes of all that is deplorable in the sanitary and social conditions of this city' points to an inexorable shift in public opinion in favour of further state interference in domestic circumstances. The Royal Commission on the Sewerage and Drainage of Dublin, which sat in the Autumn of 1879, and presented its report the following June, had dispelled whatever fond notions still persisted about the slum housing question 'settling itself' with the aid of occasional inspection and fines. 'All that preliminary inquiry can do has been done effectually, and what is now needed is the application of practical and speedy remedies'. The time for action had arrived, but the plan of campaign required 'the diffusion of a forceful and benevolent public opinion', the assistance of government, and the 'effectual and persistent action of the municipal authority' on behalf of those who being 'without political or municipal influence, being mainly non-ratepayers, and without votes either for Parliament or for the municipal council' could not lobby on their own behalf. 'Their cause must necessarily depend on its own intrinsic merits'.[119]

While wholesale slum clearance had been tried, and the painstaking closure of individual insanitary rooms, cellars and dwelling houses was continuing apace, there were other possibilities which the Corporation was very loathe to explore. Provisions in the Artizans' and Labourers' Dwellings Acts 1875–1879 allowed the Corporation to 'adapt existing buildings and enlarge, repair, and improve them, and fit them with all requisite furniture, fittings and conveniences'; the Corporation could then retain management and control, and 'may with the consent of the Treasury sell any lands vested in them and apply the proceeds to the purpose of the Act'. As the Corporation was already in possession of considerable house property, and there were many other houses 'now defective but which by a judicious expenditure could be made reasonably sufficient' it was considered that such a 'wise application of civic property' would be 'much more economical and efficient towards the object in hand than the acquisition of large areas under the Acts of 1875–1879'. However, there was little fear of the Corporation rashly taking on the role of landlord. The Public Health (Ireland) Act 1878, by which government loans could be made available to the Corporation, at 3½% interest and repayable after fifty years, in combination with the Artisans' Dwellings Acts 'recognize the principle of contributing civic property and state assistance to the supply of homes for the working classes, and of placing these directly under the control of the Corporation, both as to property and maintenance'. At the same time, 'the co-operation of private companies and private persons is invited and encouraged'. However, as legislation stood in 1881 the

---
[118] Falkiner, 'Homes of the Poor' (1882), pp. 263–271.
[119] Ibid., p. 263.

Corporation could establish a supply of model dwellings, but could not allow them to be managed by any body other than itself. It was a no-win situation. Everyone agreed that houses which in separate ownership could not be improved, when successfully grouped together, 'their adjoining open spaces consolidated and made available for the sanitary and convenient requirements of all' and under effective supervision could be made most acceptable; however, private commercial companies, working even for moderate profits, could not afford the initial investment, and the Corporation did not see its remit extending to the long-term management of such ventures.[120]

Royal Commission on Housing in Britain and Ireland, 1884–1885

The 1885 Royal Commission for Inquiring into the Housing of the Working Classes covered urban centres throughout the British Isles, making it an invaluable source for assessing the position of Dublin relative to standards and practices elsewhere. It also led directly and most usefully to the Housing of the Working Classes Act, 1890. While much of the voluminous evidence submitted to the Commissioners on the slum evil was by then common knowledge, through the surveys and reports of the Corporation's public health committee, and papers published by various proponents of the new social sciences, several important shifts can be noted: that the most supportive legislation will do little to reform the housing situation where the political will to effect real change is absent or insufficient; that state powers of compulsory purchase, and new sources of finance were essential.[121] To the forefront came the question of the separation of the sexes, from which perspective the prevalence of one-room occupation became a matter of increasing scandal. The range of 'expert witnesses' was impressive, including sanitary and medical officers, engineers, clergymen, and local councillors; no women were called, an indicator of how the 'solution' of the housing question was regarded as the preserve of public and professional men, although there was ample evidence to show that women made up by far the greater percentage of slum dwellers. Generally regarded as expert in the field of home management and family care, middle class women might be expected to have something of value to contribute to the debate, but were still largely limited to the field of philanthropy (Chapter 7). While outstanding advances on behalf of the poor, and on behalf of poor Dublin women especially, had been made by able and committed middle-class women over the preceding decades, such as Anne Jellicoe (1823–1880), Margaret Aylward (1810–1889, see Chapters 7, 8) and Dr Louis Cassidy (St Ultan's Hospital), such achievements were mostly in the fields of education, employment and health.[122] Women were in general still

---

[120] Falkiner, 'Homes of the Poor' (1882), p. 264; see also *Daily Nation*, 3–5 September 1898.
[121] Evidence of Mr Edward McMahon (Drumcondra), *Housing Inquiry 1885*, qs. 24,594– 24,663.
[122] see Anne V. O'Connor, 'Anne Jellicoe', in Mary Cullen and Maria Luddy (eds.), *Women, Power and Consciousness in Nineteenth Century Ireland*, Dublin: Attic Press, 1995, pp. 125–161; also Jacinta Prunty, 'Margaret Louisa Aylward', in Cullen and Luddy (1995) pp. 55–88

excluded from the closed circle of engineers, medical officers and local government officials which 'controlled' discussion, and hence the 'resolution', of the Dublin slum story. Propertied women were not eligible for election as poor law guardians until 1896.[123] The Alexandra Housing Guild, which developed among students of the pioneering ladies' college founded by Anne Jellicoe, is exceptional, while lady sanitary officers were still to be appointed (Chapter 5). At the housing inquiry of 1885 none of the persons most affected, the occupants of these slum dwellings, men or women, were invited to make submissions, the experts relying on their own assessment of what was best for them.

Extensive public health and housing legislation was already in place by 1885, and the principal concern among the commissioners was why so little effective use had been made of these provisions to date. The catalogue of powers was impressive: under the Public Health Act 1878 the Corporation could widen and improve streets and make new streets; make and enforce by-laws with respect to the structure and materials of new buildings, their sites, foundations, ventilation and drainage; it could prohibit the letting or occupying of cellars as dwellings, and regulate both 'common lodging houses' and houses let in lodgings. The Corporation could deal with 'nuisances' under the definition of 'any house or part of a house so overcrowded as to be dangerous or injurious to the health of the inhabitants, whether or not members of the same family', and had powers to effect closure, along with a multitude of other provisions.[124]

The Corporation's efforts to date were heavily criticised. In the twelve 'black spots' identified in 1876 (excepting the Coombe, Figures 4.1, 4.4), things were considerably worse, not least because 'the rate of decay is greater than any amelioration in the sanitary fittings'.[125] The new houses which had been built 'do not do more than tend to keep down the evil'.[126] Repairs undertaken at the Corporation's insistence were derisively described as 'partially repaired, that is they were touched up',[127] and the direction of all energies 'rather to sanitary improvements than to structural alterations' was condemned out of hand.[128] The method by which the Corporation 'registered' lodging houses was ridiculed; what it had was simply a list, where 'a house is on the register simply from its existence', without any regard for how suitable or otherwise it might be for the number accommodated therein.[129]

Under the heading of minimal structural alterations, criticism was heaped on the total lack of efforts to enforce the separation of the sexes.[130] Where one room

[123] *Report of the Commission on the Relief of the Sick and Destitute Poor, including the Insane Poor* (Dublin: 1928), p. 5.
[124] Falkiner, 'Homes of the Poor' (1882), pp. 265–266.
[125] Evidence of Edward Spencer (DADC), *Housing Inquiry 1885*, qs. 22,84–22,8422,847.
[126] Evidence of Thomas Grimshaw (registar general), *Housing Inquiry 1885*, qs. 23,175.
[127] Ibid., qs. 23,105–23,107.
[128] Evidence of Edward Spencer (DADC), *Housing Inquiry 1885*, qs. 22,858–22,964; Thomas Grimshaw (registrar general) qs 23,174.
[129] Evidence of Edward Spencer (DADC), *Housing Inquiry 1885*, qs. 22,858–22,964
[130] Ibid., Thomas Grimshaw (registrar general) qs 23,174.

was occupied by a family, grown-up children slept along with younger siblings and their parents, a state of affairs it was maintained was fraught with all kinds of dangers. The question did not arise in the single-roomed houses of rural Ireland, especially the poorest West: 'very few of the grown-up members of the families live in the houses, it is only small children. Emigration has dealt with it'.[131] Raising the standards of sexual morality was regarded as part of the total 'civilising' process which the slum-dwellers were to undergo, with one witness maintaining that there are 'two ends to the civilisation process: one by the sanitary process, providing means for the separation of the sexes, and the other by teaching these people how they should live. It is impossible that they should live properly and improve their condition unless structural alterations are provided'. He maintained they should be 'compelled to occupy separate rooms, or failing that, that partitions be erected'.[132] One of the queries put by the Gentlemen's Society of St Vincent de Paul, a Catholic relief agency, was 'are the sexes separated at night?' so that it became 'almost a *sine qua non* of their getting relief, even in the poorest families'.[133]

The limited franchise in Dublin city also came up for question; the voting qualification required the occupation of premises valued £10 or over, with three years' continuous residence in the city. About 5,000 were on the register of voters, out of a population of 250,000[134] so that it was obvious that the overwhelming majority of the city's population 'are rated for the expenses of local government, but they have no voice in the election of the corporate body who spend these rates'. The question of 'no taxation without representation' was raised, and the general domination of municipal bodies by vested interests led to the claim that 'some of those people who are interested in bad property find seats on the Corporations'.[135] Mr Kenny, visiting medical officer of the North Dublin Union, placed the Dublin slum problem within the context of the 'general condition of the people of Ireland', i.e., extreme depression and poverty. He viewed the causes as socio-political, where under the pressure of precarious employment and insecurity of tenure, and the lack of popular representation at a local level 'the human frame becomes exceedingly susceptible to disease'.[136]

Evidence given before the commission relating to the way in which slum clearance was undertaken in South Great Georges Street to facilitate the erection of the South City Markets (Chapter 3), betrays the dismissive way in which residents of condemned property were treated. In his evidence, Alderman Valentine Dillon, solicitor to the company which was formed 'to erect a public market and widen streets in connection with it', stated that 'taking an average of 6 families

[131] *Housing Inquiry 1885*, q. 22,900.
[132] Ibid., q. 22, 893.
[133] Evidence of Fr Robert Conlan (administrator, St Mary's parish), *Housing Inquiry 1885*, qs. 23,293.
[134] *Housing Inquiry 1885*, qs 21,942–21,947.
[135] Ibid., qs 22,016.
[136] Evidence of Mr J.E. Kenny (NDU), *Housing Inquiry 1885*, qs 23,180–23,236.

per house, a low figure, there were 714 families or 3,570 persons removed'.[137] When pressed as to where they had gone on their eviction, he stated he was 'glad enough to get rid of them, and did not follow them very closely, I mean those tenement holders. They went to all parts of the city'. Although the special act of parliament under which the clearance was undertaken required that the developers should rehouse the tenants, 'no application was made by any of them' and they were paid compensation based on the rates previously paid. 'They signed agreements, we paid the money, and they went away'.[138]

The Geography of Tenement Housing: Transformation 1850–1900

The continuing pressure for city accommodation among the poorest, the exertions of the Corporation's sanitary staff in closing many substandard dwellings, and the supply of one-family homes provided by the exodus of the better-off to choice suburban locations, were all factors in the changing geography of tenement housing. In Figures 4.8 and 4.9 houses which were entered as 'tenements' in the commercial street directories (Thom's, Shaw's) have been calculated as a percentage of all premises in each street or lane. Streets where tenements made up over two-thirds (black line) or over one third (dotted line) have thus been identified for 1850 and for 1900. This methodology (first used in a Dublin study by John Martin, 1973),[139] is subject to all the limitations inherent in commercial street directory information. Tenement status is likely to be masked where a business occupies the ground floor, most blatantly along old commercial routes such as along Thomas Street, Patrick Street or Bride Street (south city), or along Church Street or Dorset Street (north city). A small street such as Hanover Lane, with most of its occupiers grandly titled 'clothes broker' (1850), or nearby Dean Street with provision dealers, victuallers and dairies (1900), therefore does not appear as a tenement street although most probably both were in multiple occupancy. Other limitations include the likelihood that later directory editions either ignored certain back courts and alleys, or incorporated back-yard premises in the 'front street' listing, without the original court name. The methodology employed also brings its limitations. Some very long streets, which had a large number of tenement houses, but still too few to reach the 33% or 66% limits will not feature as prominently as their absolute numbers might warrant, while conversely streets with small numbers of total houses may reach the 33% or 66% limits very easily. Kevin Street Lower, despite having 34 premises in tenements, has such a large number of buildings in total that it does not features as strongly in the 1900 map as might be expected. Where a street was not fully built up in 1850, comparison with the case in 1900 might be misleading, for example, in the case of Commons Street (North Wall to Sheriff Street), there is no real 'improve-

---

[137] Evidence of Alderman Valentine Dillon, *Housing Inquiry 1885*, qs. 23,048–23,083.
[138] Ibid.
[139] John Martin 'Aspects of the Social Geography of Dublin City in the Mid Nineteenth Century', unpublished MA thesis in Geography (UCD, 1973), figure 3.2.

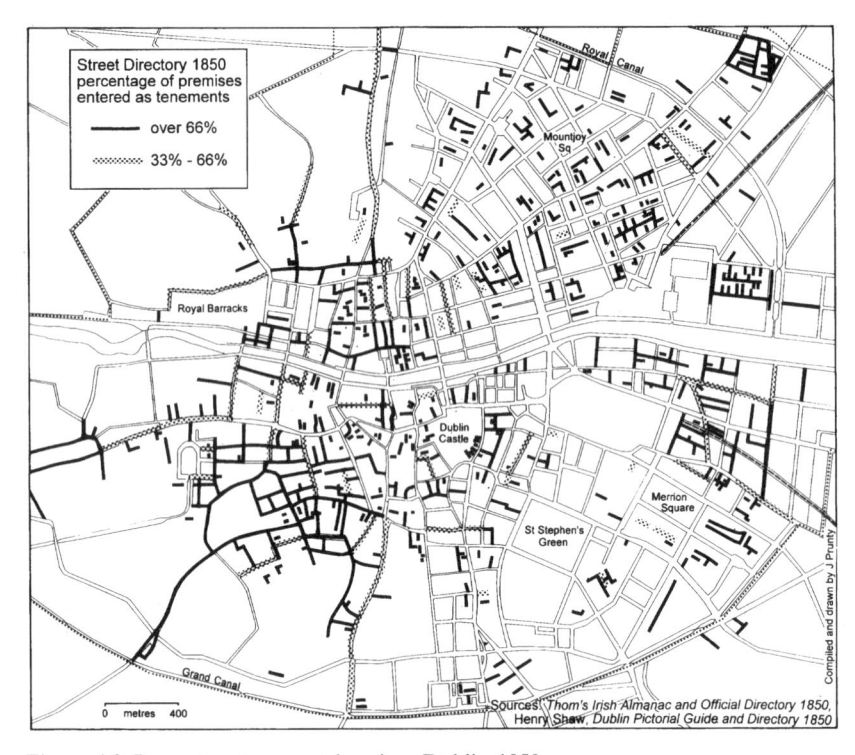

Figure 4.8 Percentage tenement housing, Dublin 1850

ment' in status between 1850–1900, as the absolute number of tenements in 1900 is higher (12) than the number of tenements in 1850 (6) when the street was still unfinished; however, it is the proportion of tenements relative to other premises that is mapped. Despite these and other reservations, Figures 4.8 and 4.9 provide a useful broad-brush picture of the changing geography of tenement housing in the city for 1850–1900.

The shift from back court and alleyway housing into front street tenements is the most striking transformation city-wide over the period 1850–1900. This move may be at least partly accounted for by selective house condemnations and closures, effected since 1879 (see Figure 4.7), which focused most especially on the back courts and alleyways most flagrantly in breach of sanitary by-laws. Some poor housing had also been sacrificed to slum clearance schemes by 1900, as in the Coombe (Figure 4.4), Plunket Street and Bull Alley (Figures 4.5, 4.6).

The pattern of tenement streets which emerges in 1900 (Figure 4.9) is a simplification of the pattern already in place in 1850 (Figure 4.8), which itself is a close reflection of the distribution of low-valued residences at the time (1854, see Figure 2.6, 2.9). The same areas emerge as solidly tenement districts. In the south-western industrial sector, and stretching to the rear of the south quays, streets such as Cork Street, Marrowbone Lane, Island Street, the Coombe,

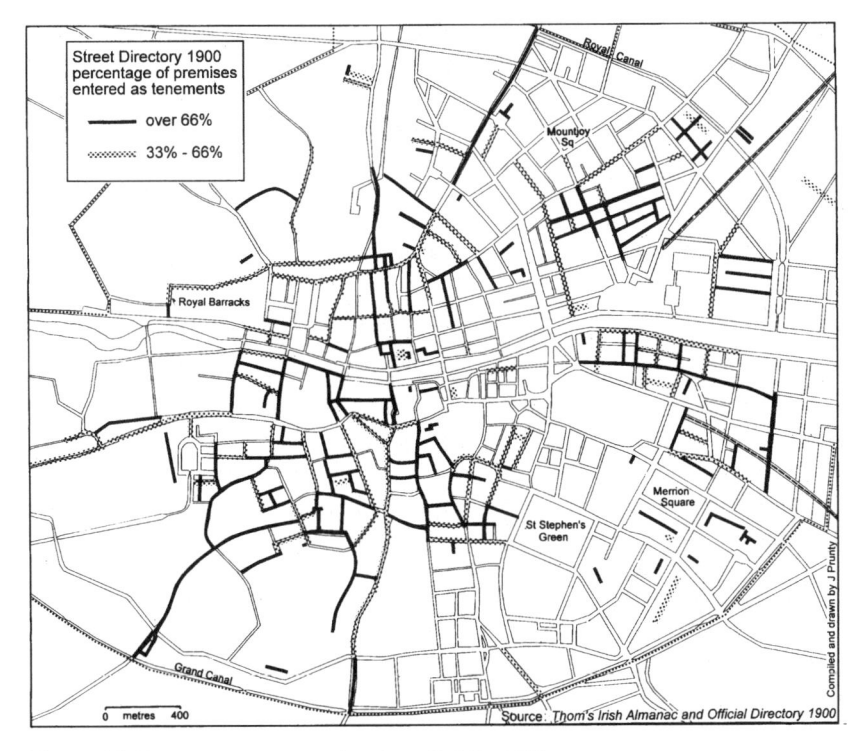

Figure 4.9 Percentage tenement housing, Dublin 1900

Newmarket, and Fishamble Street are almost entirely devoted to tenement occupation from at least 1850 (Figure 4.8), providing a framework around which the tenement geography of the surrounding districts might be very firmly based. Other south side areas which can be identified as long-standing slums are the courts to the rear of the south-east Georgian squares, and the docklands/railway sector to the north and east of Trinity College.

On the north side the abandonment of back lanes and alleys (1850) for the front streets (1900) is even more marked, largely because of the higher status once enjoyed by many of the streets in the north eastern Gardiner district (see Chapter 8, Figure 8.1). The north city slum geography by 1900 is firmly centred on selected aristocratic streets such as Henrietta Street and Gardiner Street, the old markets and barracks areas, the Mecklenburgh/Montgomery Street red light district, and the Sheriff Street docklands (Chapter 8).

The disappearance or apparent 'upgrading' of several major streets with high percentage of premises entered as tenements in 1850 (Figure 4.8), but missing or with a smaller percentage of tenement dwellings in the 1900 map (Figure 4.9), is almost universally due to the expansion of commercial, industrial, institutional and transport-associated landuses. Rare indeed is there any real rise in residential status, excepting a small number of new housing schemes. Thus to the rear of

Trinity College, Boyne Street South no longer features as a tenement street in 1900 because of the expansion of Kinahan's 'limited rectifying distillery', and the Brown and Nolan paper company. Nearby South Gloucester Street also 'improves', but only because Tedcastles coal stores, stables and a mineral water manufactory have edged some of the tenements out, and further east the Bell timber yard and another Tedcastles yard have similarly replaced most of the tenements in Lime Street. In the north docklands Guild Street, with 26 tenement houses in 1850, finds itself practically removed from the tenement list by 1900 because of the expansion of stores and cattle sheds serving three different modes of transport: the City of Dublin Steam Packet Company, the Midland Great Western Railway, and the canal company. Near Ballybough Bridge, heading north east, the tenements of Poplar Row yield to the Dublin and Wicklow Manure Company Ltd. On the edge of the north western institutional sector, Brunswick Street North features less strongly as a tenement street in 1900 (Figure 4.9) only because both the Richmond hospital and the Christian Brothers schools have expanded to take up several more plots, while Stanhope Street in the same district has its tenement dwellings replaced by St Mary's Industrial School. Returning to the south city, Dolphin's Barn Lane also 'improves', but only because of the location of a laundry, national school and coal merchants. In Mill Street the extension of Keeffe's chemical manure manufacturers (later to be popularly known as 'Keeffe's the Knackers') along with dairy yards and stables does little to improve the immediate environs of the five remaining tenement dwellings.

Tenements lost to commercial expansion can be identified in Earl Place (formerly Nelson's Lane) on Sackville Street, taken over by Clerys store; in South Great George's Street and Fade Street where the south city markets were erected; Dame Court and Dame Lane lost to a printing works and goods storage respectively; and Exchequer Street, where the Central Hotel replaces several tenements.

Both north and south the brewing and distilling industries eliminate numerous tenement dwellings in their hunger for more land: Guinness's expansion includes sites in James' Street, Grand Canal Street, Crane Street, Rainsford Street and Robert Street, accounting for much of the simplification of the tenement map between 1850–1900 in the vicinity of the Grand Canal basin, while Power's distillery replicated the pattern in Thomas Street, eliminating tenements in John's Lane West, and Mullinahack Lane, for the purposes of stores and bonded warehouses. The erection of the Augustinian priory and chapel in John Street West (beside Power's distillery) also contributed to the elimination of tenement dwellings in this district. The Dublin Distiller's Company expanded its operations closer to the Liffey, around Island and Watling streets, but did not sacrifice as many dwellings in the process, so that these areas continue to be densely populated literally encircled by distillery buildings. On the north side the expansion of malthouses, spirit stores and yards the property of Jameson, Pim and company, 'ale and beer brewers', eliminates tenements in Cuckoo Lane and May Lane, while also taking over a large section of Beresford Street, again simplifying the pattern apparent in 1850 (Figure 4.8).

The Housing Problem Restated: Tenement Dwellings and the Role of the State

In the final two decades of the nineteenth century several crucial shifts in the housing debate can be identified, which were to have enormous consequences. The feeling was decidedly against the one-roomed tenement system in itself, regardless of what improvements might be effected in the room itself and its immediate environs; where people 'cook and work in and make workshops and living rooms of their bedrooms', it is 'opposed to every sentiment of decency, besides being unhealthy. They are all breathing the same air, and a great many people have lungs more or less tainted, and no matter what the size of the room is it must be bad'.[140] Along with a determination to end single-room family occupancy was the proclamation that the eighteenth century housing fabric of the Dublin tenements was, on the whole, beyond rescue, the great majority constructed of 'slight brick walls, slender wooden beams, and thin planks'; as for the seventeenth century houses, these had, with rare exceptions, completely decayed away, the 'walls are honey-combed, their woodwork rotted, their roofs are masses of small and cracked slates, with innumerable patches upon them; their yards are generally unpaved, their underground stories, formerly cleanly and well-kept kitchens – consequently converted into tenements, are now noisome, dark spaces, mostly shut up, in order to prevent them from becoming the asylums of homeless wanderers'.[141] The days of patching up and limewashing alone were numbered.

There was also an increasingly powerful lobby, headed by Charles Cameron, in favour of the Corporation itself undertaking to house the poorest:

There is no other way in which persons of the lower stratum of the population can be properly housed. Those persons who give the sanitarian the greatest amount of trouble, in whose houses I may say the fires of infectious diseases are kept smouldering, cannot pay rents which would enable ordinary landlords who merely look to the houses as a means of making an income, to keep those houses in a proper sanitary condition. Those persons pay 1s 6d or 1s per week. No ordinary landlord can supply a house with a water closet and with proper yards and accommodation of that kind at a rent of 1s or 1s 6d per week.[142]

In response to a claim that subsidising healthy housing for the poor would 'pauperise' this class, Cameron retorted that state subsidy was already found in innumerable sectors, such as the support given to the Queen's Colleges so that a university graduate in effect paid perhaps one quarter of the real cost of an education which fitted him 'for a remunerative profession'.[143] Considering that the state was already providing near-free elementary education to the poor, and medical dispensary aid to all who could not afford to pay, the provision of public housing was simply a logical extension, and could be defended even more than the provision of poor relief, already granted since 1838.[144] On the basis of self-

[140] Evidence of Dr Cameron, *Housing Inquiry 1885*, qs 22,237–22,241.
[141] Cameron, 'Homes of the Working Classes' (1885), p. 102.
[142] Evidence of Dr Cameron, *Housing Inquiry 1885*, qs 22,254–22,256.
[143] Ibid., qs 22,298–22,301.
[144] Ibid.

defence alone such a new departure could be justified: a 'man going about with insufficient clothing would probably only injure himself, whereas if his house is in a filthy condition it may injure me, and as a means of protection I get his house put into a proper sanitary state'.[145]

Along with the question of providing public housing went increasing concern with classifying those for whom the state could or should provide, at tax-payer's expense. Cameron maintained that only that 'stratum' which could not rise above rents of 1s or 1s 6d per week should be considered, 'well-paid artizans and clerk and persons of that kind I would leave to the ordinary landlords or the Artizans' Dwellings Company'.[146] Spencer similarly recommended that the Corporation focus on 'the poorer labourers and hawkers and seamstresses and those in casual employment', distinguishing them from the 'improving and carefully selected labourers' who could be accommodated in DADC houses.[147] The agenda was set for the next century.

---

[145] Ibid.
[146] Ibid., qs 22,254–22,256.
[147] Evidence of Mr Edward Spencer (DADC) *Housing Inquiry 1885*, qs 22,825–22, 829.

≈ 5 ≈

HEALTH AND HOUSING:
POLICY SHIFTS, 1900–1925

The evil of tenements has been much debated in Dublin, but speakers on the slum evil are inclined to devote nine-tenths of their words to the horrors, and only one-tenth to constructive suggestions.[1]

INTRODUCTION

In the first two decades of the twentieth century the tone of the debate was one of outrage: not just that slum living conditions should still be the lot of a huge percentage of the city's population, but that such sidestepping and hesitancy should characterise the activities of the elected authorities responsible for the public well-being. And there was one particular yardstick which was used to measure the condition of the Dublin poor against that of urban dwellers elsewhere in the British Isles: the rate of mortality (see Tables 3.1–3.3). In 1899 it reached the outrageous figure of 31.9 per 1,000 for the total Dublin registration area, 33.6 for the city; London recorded 19.7, Edinburgh 19.6, and Glasgow 21.6 deaths per 1,000.[2] In 1905 the lowest death rate yet recorded for Dublin was achieved, at 21.2 per 1,000, (22.3 per 1,000 city districts); however, it still compared unfavourably with London, at 15.6 per 1,000, Glasgow at 17.0 per 1,000, Edinburgh at 16.1 per 1,000, and all the other large towns in the United Kingdom. From Table 5.1 (1906) it is clear that the Dublin death rate was closer to that recorded for cities such as Prague, Budapest and Moscow rather than its nearer British and continental neighbours.[3] Despite fifty years of campaigning against infectious diseases, there were still epidemic outbreaks of measles (1899) and smallpox (1903) which caused the Dublin death rate to shoot up, infant

---

[1] *The Dublin Civic Survey Report*, prepared by Horace T. O'Rourke and the Dublin Civic Survey Committee for the Civics Institute of Ireland, vol. II (Liverpool, 1925), vol. II, p. 61, (hereafter *Dublin Civic Survey*).
[2] *Yearly Summary of the Weekly Returns of Births and Deaths in Dublin (including its suburban districts) and in Twenty Two of the Principal Urban Districts in Ireland*, 1899.
[3] *Yearly Summary of the Weekly Returns of Births and Deaths in the Dublin Registration Area, and in Twenty One of the Principal Urban Districts in Ireland*, 1905.

Dublin Slums

Cities	Population (enumerated or estimated)	Date of Return — Week ending	Births	Deaths Exclusive of Stillborn	Annual Death-Rate per 1,000 living	Small-pox.	Measles.	Scarlet Fever.	Diphtheria.	Whooping-cough.	Fever.	Diarrhoeal Diseases
Dublin	378,994	May 26	195	173	25.4	.	56	13	4	101	.	417
Belfast	366,220	" 26	273	151	20.1	.	.	.	1	8	.	5
London	4,721,217	" 26	2,518	1,156	12.8	.	41	15	13	32	8	10
Edinburgh	341,035	" 26	154	111	17.0	.	2	4	.	2	.	3
Glasgow	835,625	" 26	450	304	19.0	.	9	.	1	8	.	7
Calcutta	910,117	April 7	.	909	55.7	137	5	.	.	4	118‡	101*
Bombay	776,006	" 24	396	2,150	144.1	18	66	.	.	1	133‡	177*
Madras	509,346	" 6	318	487	49.7	46	23	?	?	?	91	91*
Paris	2,750,000	—	.	.	.	.	.	.	.	.	.	.
Brussels (with 8 Faubourgs)	612,401	" 5	221	176	14.9	.	2	1	2†	4	2	3
Antwerp	304,975	" 5	139	84	14.4	.	9	.	.	.	.	5
Amsterdam	560,249	" 5	289	154	14.3	.	6	1	1†	.	.	10
Copenhagen	425,000	" 5	211	130	16.0	.	3	.	.	6	.	5
Stockholm	324,488	April 28	140	82	13.1	.	.	.	.	2	.	4
Christiania	222,373	May 12	136	57	13.3	.	.	.	4†	.	.	2
St. Petersburg	1,424,700	" 5	754	824	30.0	5	34	22	16	14	18	97
Moscow	1,092,360	April 7	.	596	28.4	4	4	8	7†	4	6	64
Berlin	2,053,181	" 21	909	648	16.5	.	15	9	3†	8	1	45
Hamburg	803,050	" 28	.	236	15.3	.	2	.	3†	1	.	23
Breslau	475,217	May 12	.	190	20.8	.	.	1	1†	2	2	16
Munich	540,000	" 12	.	202	19.5	.	5	.	1†	.	.	22
Vienna (with suburbs)	1,937,869	" 12	950	829	22.2	.	34	14	7†	3	1	51
Buda-Pesth	859,134	" 12	430	385	23.4	.	8	4	4†	2	2	18
Prague and Faubourgs	460,849	" 5	202	201	22.7	.	4	1	.	2	.	18
Trieste	196,637	April 28	110	117	31.0	.	1	.	.	1	.	6
Rome	526,170	Mar. 17	246	203	20.1	.	7	.	1	.	1	10
Venice	171,709	—	.	.	.	.	.	.	.	.	.	.
New York	4,152,860	April 28	1,936	1,523	19.1	1	39	13	40†	5	9	42
Philadelphia	1,469,126	" 21	.	568	20.1	.	6	2	5†	6	20	16
Boston	595,380	" 28	.	225	19.7	.	2	1	5	3	.	2

* *Including 43 deaths from cholera in Calcutta, 40 in Bombay, and one in Madras.*
† *Including deaths from croup.*
‡ *Exclusive of 301 deaths from plague in Calcutta, and 1084 in Bombay.*

Source: *Official Weekly Returns of Births and Deaths in the Dublin Registration Area and in Twenty-one of the principal urban districts in Ireland* (Dublin: Thom's, HMSO, 1907) table x p. 342.

Table 5.1 Births and Deaths, and Rate of Mortality in London, Edinburgh, Glasgow, Dublin and Certain Indian and Foreign Cities, 1906.

mortality was unacceptably high for a 'civilised' country, and phthisis or pulmonary tuberculosis raged unchecked throughout the city slums. Statisticians, medical officers of health and sanitary officials were called to account for this continuing scandal, and the pleas of some that the state of Dublin should be measured by reference to conditions fifty years previously were curtly dismissed; every other place had made massive advances, why not Dublin too?

The series of health and housing reports which punctuated the period 1900–1920 make depressing reading, as the slum evils are ever more exactly recorded and analysed, while improvement proceeds at a snail's pace. While each report lamented the lack of real progress since the previous data-collection venture, there were several significant developments, which can be overlooked if results in terms of mortality rates, or numbers housed or rehoused, are the only figures examined. The period 1900–1920 was marked by both the steady extension of statutory control into areas which would have been unthinkable fifty years earlier, such as the feeding of infants and regulation of young street traders, and the implementation of more traditional public health policies, such as the mobilising of forces to protect the city from smallpox in 1903. Efforts to bring down the appalling death rate became more focused: among infants, the children of the poorest in the first year of life; and among adults, the vast numbers wasted by TB. The employment of women as sanitary officers and their consultation in matters of housing also marks a significant advance. The number of housing schemes drawn up between 1900 and the outbreak of war in 1914 testify to commendable efforts on the part of the Corporation's architects and housing committee. Throughout the period the questions of health and housing become ever more intertwined, so that by 1925 the Civic Survey speaks of the city's health in terms of 'its disease and tenement cancer'.[4]

Public Health Crises
Report on the Recent High Death Rate of Dublin, Charles Cameron, 1900

A sharp rise in the death rate for Dublin in 1899 (see Chapter 3, Table 3.3) led the Local Government Board to request a report on the probable causes from the superintendent medical officer of health, Sir Charles Cameron. Cameron in turn solicited the considered opinions, orally and in writing, from the sixteen district medical officers, which combined with his own extensive experience led him to report that the excessive death rate was due to a combination of causes. While deaths from measles had assumed 'large and alarming proportions' in the fourth quarter of the year, and had extended to the suburbs, the epidemic did not totally account for the excessively high death rate. Increases in diarrhoeal diseases and in whooping cough were also factors, but did not decimate large numbers. Cameron held that the real cause was an outbreak of epidemic influenza, which

---

[4] *Dublin Civic Survey* (1925), p. 150.

developed into bronchitis, pneumonia and other maladies, so that deaths ascribed to various diseases were indirectly due to influenza.

The catalogue of reasons given for this excessive death rate was a repetition of all that was already too well known: the undue proportion of very poor persons among Dublin's population; insanitary housing conditions and excessive population density in certain localities; the prevalence of slaughter houses and dairy yards; the want of sufficient accommodation for fever cases, and for convalescents from infectious diseases; the storage of sewage in the main sewers and the want of the daily removal of filth from the yards of the tenement houses.

From August 1879 to January 1900 the Corporation had closed by magistrates' orders over 3,000 unsanitary houses, about half of which it was claimed had totally disappeared. But twenty years of this policy, without a corresponding provision of new housing for those evicted, had exacerbated overcrowding; there was little room for further closures. It had proven unsatisfactory in many respects, and the fines imposed difficult to collect. In the report for 1900 a total of 1,164 insanitary premises, where the owners were fined, and from whom the fines were recovered, are listed street by street. 712 persons or 61% paid a penalty of one shilling, a further 213 persons paid between 2s and 5s, and 109 owners paid 10s. In all, 80% of the offenders were fined 5s or less, and only 40 owners, or about 3% of all those from whom fines were recovered, were fined between £2 and £5. The complexity of ownership is also evident from the Corporation listing: while a large proportion of all the fines levied covered several adjoining premises or courts, some premises had several owners, who were fined individually. Matthew O'Neill, for example, was fined 1s for foul premises in three adjoining houses in Moss Street and a further three in Poolbeg Street; four different persons were each fined 1s for the state of Maher's Court, a penalty that was imposed and recovered four times in 1900. From the number of times several addresses reappear again and again it is clear that the fines were an insufficient deterrent; once extracted, conditions reverted to their previous state, and the cumbersome machinery lurched slowly into action once more.

Cameron completed his 1900 report with the observation that 'Dublin is, in truth, a poor city, and no street or square in it is distant 500 yards from a purlieu'.[5] He advocated that certain areas 'should be completely cleansed of their wretched houses and healthy dwellings erected upon the cleared sites'; the areas which had repeatedly required the attention of his sanitary officers were self-selected for such redevelopment.

Report on the Sanitary Circumstances and Administration of the City of Dublin, with Reference to the High Death Rate, Edgar Flinn, (Dublin 1906)

Surgeon-Colonel Edgar Flinn presented a damning review of the principal conclusions and recommendations of two previous Commissions of Inquiry into

---

[5] Charles Cameron, *Report of Public Health Committee for 1899* (Dublin, 1900), p. 7.

the high Dublin death rate, the 1879/1880 'Royal Commission appointed to Inquire into the System of Sewerage and Drainage in the City of Dublin . . .' and the 1900 Local Government Inquiry. The recommendations of the Royal Commission followed on fifteen days of public sittings when the most authoritative persons gave evidence, not to speak of innumerable other meetings and consultations; the 1880 report made no discernible difference to the state of the Dublin slums. Twenty years later, when the Local Government Board began its public sittings, it faced substantially the same body of evidence, and its conclusions, practically repeated but in a more concise form, what had been previously recommended. And six and a half years on, with an appallingly high death rate, the talk of the United Kingdom, Edgar Flinn revealed that the bulk of the considered recommendations of the 1900 Commission had been similarly consigned to the shelf.

The scandalous death rate in Dublin city and suburban districts relative to rates prevailing in Belfast and the major cities of Britain, as well as rates 'in certain Indian and Foreign Cities', are illustrated in Table 5.1. By 1906 Dublin was clearly lagging far behind most British, European and American cities, and showed no sign of making up the deficit. Within the city of Dublin the variations between registration districts were so severe that certain districts reached rates that might bear comparison with cities such as Cairo, Moscow or Madras. Flinn depicted the two most notorious areas on a map he had drawn up to show the boundaries of the dispensary districts and which accompanies this 1906 report (Figure 5.1). Number 2 district, north city, comprising North Anne Street, Beresford Street, part of Church Street and Coleraine Street, and 'innumerable courts and lanes', had returned a death rate of 33.3 per 1,000 for 1900. The local tenement houses 'are of a wretched type, and as a rule overcrowded and inhabited by a very poor class, who are unclean and untidy in their habits'; the entire district was 'the home of great poverty, and has always been a fertile ground for propagating and fostering infectious diseases'. Smallpox, for example, reached epidemic proportions in the district in 1903, but was largely confined to Church Street and North Anne Street.[6]

South city number 1 district, including Thomas Street, the Coombe, Francis Street and Meath Street, was also mapped by Flinn as an 'area of poverty'. Here death rates from all causes averaged 30.3 per 1,000 in the preceding decade, peaking at 38 per 1,000 in 1899. It had the highest phthisis rate in the city, its population (as in the north city) heavily reliant on outdoor poor relief, and 'it comprises some typical slum localities'.[7]

Flinn's main purpose was to draw attention to 'some of the most important questions that manifestly require vigorous and sustained efforts on the part of the

---

[6] Edgar Flinn, *Report on the Sanitary Circumstances and Administration of the City of Dublin, with Reference to the High Death Rate* (Dublin 1906), p. 19, (hereafter *Report on High Death Rate*).
[7] Ibid., p. 20.
[8] Ibid., p. 56.

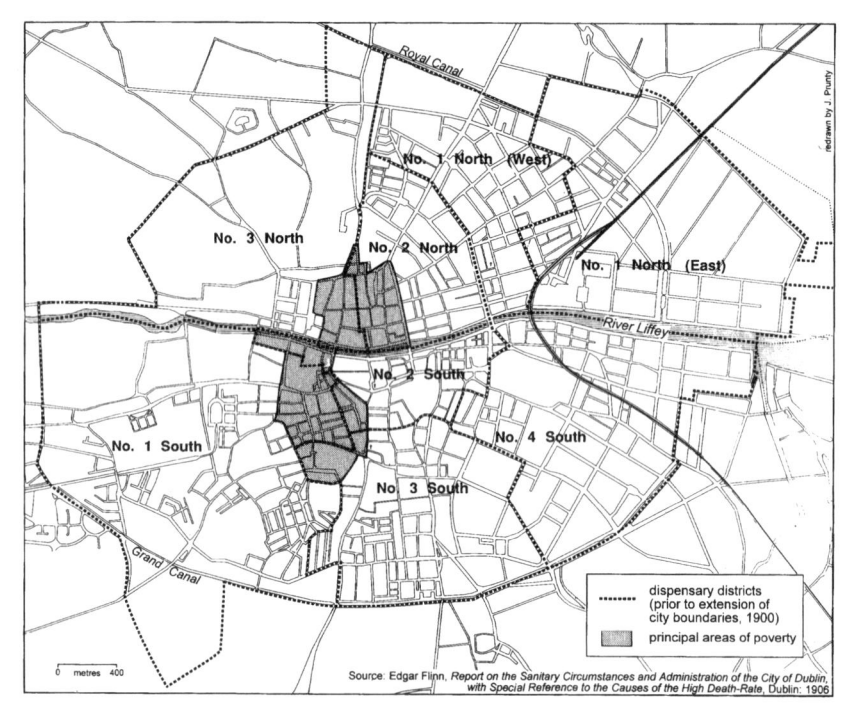

Figure 5.1 Dublin city dispensary districts (prior to the 1900 extension of the city boundaries) and principal areas of poverty, Edgar Flinn, 1906.

Sanitary Authority' if any progress was to be made.[8] His recommendations are a reiteration of the areas most critically in need of attention, and were intended in turn as a standard against which advances could be measured.

In view of the 'stubborn fact' that such a large proportion of the city's population still lived in single rooms, under unhealthy conditions, Dublin required 'exceptional treatment in the question of domestic scavenging and cleansing', when compared with measures judged as adequate elsewhere. 'Vitally important and from a health point of view absolutely necessary' was the supply of water to each floor, and separate sanitary accommodation for at least every two families. 'A daily system of filth removal from the back-yards and precincts of the tenement houses' was also imperative. To prevent overcrowding it was recommended that 'some system of registration should be adopted whereby the number of rooms in each tenement house, and the measurements and cubic capacity of each room could be ascertained, and a register kept recording these details'. The schemes for housing the working classes already undertaken were welcomed, but there was still scope for further efforts in this direction to relieve congestion; in view of the recent (1900) extension of the city boundary he proposed building in the 'added areas' which were not so thickly populated. From Table 5.2 (1896–1911) it is clear that tubercular disease, especially pulmonary phthisis, followed by pneumonia and 'diarrhoeal diseases' (including enteritis) demanded 'a vigorous crusade' if the death rate was to be brought down; compulsory notification of TB was a prerequisite, as was the education of the poorer classes 'as to the infectious and deadly nature of this disease and the measures necessary to prevent its spread'. The planned 'Joint Sanatorium for Consumptives' was supported as 'a most desirable project'.[9]

'Vigorous action' was also promoted relative to the large number of laneways and areas scheduled as 'not in charge of the Corporation', and strict enforcement of regulations governing dairy yards and cow-sheds. It was also desirable to gain some control over the milk supplies arriving in the city, and to improve the system of meat inspection. The persistence of large numbers of private slaughter houses 'in the most unsuitable and thickly populated districts, and in many instances quite close to dwelling houses' was unacceptable; requests to erect an abattoir on the south of the city had been dismissed, and the existing abattoir was underused (see Figure 3.5).[10]

Lady Sanitary Officers and the Care of Infants

The first four lady sanitary sub-officers were appointed in 1899, as a result of a competitive examination at which Miss F. O'Sullivan achieved the first place, and three other women were numbered among the eight highest achievers. Dr Cameron had lobbied strenuously for several years to have women appointed to his staff; he considered they would 'prove most useful, especially in persuading the women of the tenement houses to keep themselves, their dwellings, clothes, bedding, and children in a cleanly condition'. Women could speak with greater freedom on these matters, and encourage mothers to teach their children 'the elementary principles of decency and cleanliness'. Lady sanitary officers had already been appointed in London and various English towns, sanctioned by the Local Government Board. The first four Dublin appointees were noteworthy for their zeal and effectiveness, and 'the success attending their efforts warrant the Public Health Committee in the step they have taken'.[11]

The question of whether women 'in the lower class of life' ought to be encouraged to breast feed or bottle feed was a long-standing element in the debate on infant deaths. Contradictory professional advice was offered to the North Dublin Union guardians in 1879. One medical officer claimed that the poor women employed as wet nurses by the Union were themselves too undernourished 'to enable them to do justice to their own child, not taking into consideration the nurse one'; a colleague insisted that even partial wet nursing was still preferable to the alternative nourishment on offer, 'second-class quality

---

[9] Ibid., p. 56.
[10] Ibid., p. 57.
[11] Charles Cameron, 'Report of Public Health Committee for 1899', *RPDCD*, vol. 3 (1900), pp. 972–973; also Report for 1900, *RPDCD*, vol. 3 (1901), p. 406.
[12] Minute Book, North Dublin Union, letters from Dr Gibbs, Dr Maguire, both dated 12 August 1879.

160 *Dublin Slums*

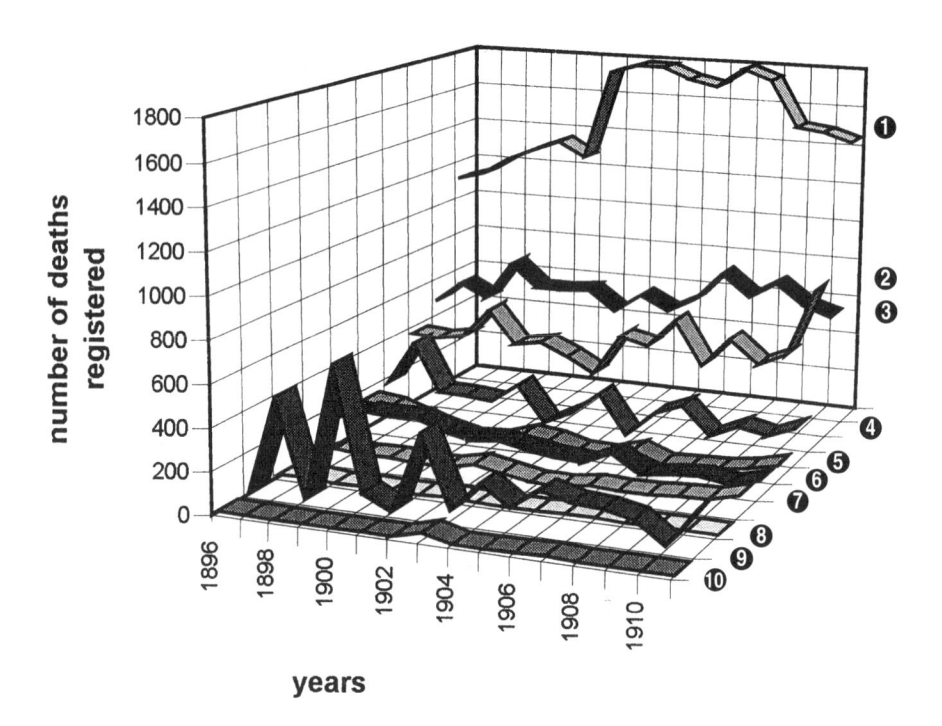

selected 'general' deseases
1 tuberculous disease, including phthisis
2 diarrhoeal diseases
3 pneumonia
4 whooping cough
5 scarlet fever
6 enteric fever
7 diphtheria
8 typhus fever
9 measles
10 small pox

Source: *Summary of the Weekly Returns of Births and Deaths in the Dublin Registration District, 1906 & 1912*

Table 5.2 Deaths from TB and other 'general' diseases, Dublin 1896–1911.

soft bread, soaked in boiling water, and a little well-diluted milk poured over it'.[12] This dilemma was among the first considered by the new lady sanitary officers in conjunction with Dr Cameron. As so few women were employed in industrial work, most of the poorest city infants were breast-fed, a practice which should at least ensure their adequate feeding during the first weeks of life. In practice the contrary was disturbingly the case. While acknowledging the desirability of rearing a child on its mother's milk, rather than on artificial substitutes, Cameron expressed the doubt 'whether or not the addition of a woman's earnings to the income of her family may not enable her children to enjoy a higher standard of comfort than that of the children of unemployed women'.[13] In brief, the child of a working mother, though bottle-fed, was better nourished and likely to thrive better than the breast-fed child of the 'underfed idle mother'.[14]

The Early Notification of Births Act came into operation in Dublin on 1 November 1910, part of the effort to bring down the appalling death rate through targeting the parents of new-born infants. Infant mortality among the labouring classes – 'day labourers, porters, hawkers' – who made up a third of the city's population, was about five times greater than that among the higher classes; if the deaths among this group could be lessened Dublin's vital statistics would receive a welcome and significant boost. And in this particular instance, the causes of the high death rate were widely known, 'at least to those who are interested in the subject': bad management, unsuitable food, insufficiency of nourishment, neglect of medical advice in illness, exposure to cold and damp, want of cleanliness, irregularity and (occasionally) overfeeding. The act allowed for the mother and child to be visited shortly after birth, and so instruction on the proper feeding, cleansing and clothing of the infant could be given. Reports by the six lady sanitary sub-officers, to whom the implementation of the act was entrusted, provide another perspective on the domestic conditions and child-rearing practices in the poorest homes in Dublin.

During the first few months of the implementation of the act, the efforts of the lady officers revolved around the proper feeding, cleansing and clothing of the child. Where bottle-fed the officers insisted on the 'Rotunda-shaped' bottle being used, as less likely to choke the infant. Efforts to do away with dirty 'soothers' were in vain, 'it seems to have a terrible hold on the mothers, particularly dealers and women who are away from their babies for some hours in the day'.[15] The officers urged 'the thorough cleansing of the whole of the baby each day – not, as is sometimes usual, to wipe the face and hands with a cloth that is not in itself clean' and pressed for frequent changing of the clothing – 'often the clothes are not taken off for days at time'. Dr Cameron had prepared a 'card of instruction' titled 'The Feeding of Children' which was well received; officer Elizabeth Byrne reported that among the homes she visited 'the card is hung up

---

[13] Charles Cameron, *Report of Public Health Committee for 1909* (Dublin, 1910), p. 52.
[14] Ibid., p. 89
[15] Charles Cameron, *Report of Public Health Committee for 1910* (Dublin, 1911), p. 138.
[16] Ibid., p. 136.

and referred to by the mothers, as they often say, 'They go by the card'.[16]

The biggest problem was widespread malnourishment of the mothers, both when pregnant and nursing; Miss Smith cited one typical case where the father, a labourer, was out of work for sixteen months, the room was practically empty save for an iron bedstead with a piece of sacking over the iron lathes, and another piece over the woman for covering; milk was procured for the mother for a few days by the attending doctor, 'but after that she got nothing further, except what the other tenants could spare her from their scanty supplies'. While the baby was healthy at birth, he had deteriorated rapidly, and was now very bad with bronchitis.[17] Mrs Emily Brady regularly 'met with pregnant mothers not having anything to eat for as long a period as four days, in other cases only dry bread and black tea'. Mrs Maria Ryan found in the intense poverty of the women the 'great cause and delicacy of children'; 'to try to earn a small pittance to pay for the scanty food, and also the rent' mothers had to leave their children, for several hours each day; inevitably the infants suffer 'from want of mother's care and improper feeding'.[18]

Miss Elizabeth Byrne reported that her efforts were resented by some nurses, who considered her visits 'an intrusion on their rights'; among the mothers some 'are only too anxious to do what is right for their infants and are very grateful for advice. Others are still neglectful and dirty generally'. Mrs Mary Lucas reported that while 'a few women of dirty habits have improved on advice' it was 'very difficult to persuade the majority that by instilling habits of cleanliness into their children they not only improve their health, but save time, trouble and expense'. 'Younger women are very grateful for any information and advice we give them, and always ask that we come see them again'.[19]

The daily contact with the mothers in their own very poor surroundings led to several simple but significant improvements. The lady officers promoted the use of 'a safe and comfortable cot' for the infants to end the very undesirable practice of keeping them in their parents' bed; Margaret Ryan urged the construction of cheap cots in the labour yards, 'to which we could direct and insist on the same being purchased' as so many could not obtain 'even the banana or orange boxes so much in use'. Firescreens were also badly needed, but proved beyond the resources of the tenants.[20] The lady officers called for 'more assistance in providing the necessaries, viz., food for the mothers and clothes for the infants', which would render the working of the Early Notification of Births Act 'more effective'.[21] A woman doctor, Louis Cassidy, FRS, 36 St Stephen's Green established a society 'interested in the welfare of the young', which held its meetings in the Public Health Committee's Rooms, and had 'a semi-official

---

[17] Ibid., p. 134.
[18] Ibid., p. 139.
[19] Ibid., pp. 136, 134.
[20] Ibid., pp. 138, 140.
[21] Ibid., p. 137.
[22] Charles Cameron, *Municipal Health Administration in Dublin* (Dublin, 1914), p. 47.

connection with the Public Health Department'. These ladies assisted poor mothers by contributions of milk, coal, clothing, and 'in other ways'.[22]

TB Crusade

Efforts to bring down the death rate in Dublin were effectively sabotaged by the high incidence of phthisis or 'wasting disease', more accurately termed pulmonary tuberculosis. Improved water supply and sewer provision, the extension of scavenging, the inspection and closure of grossly substandard accommodation, had all played a vital role in reducing the numbers dying from typhoid, typhus, cholera, smallpox, and the other zymotic diseases (Table 5.2; see also Table 3.3). Infant life expectancy was fair, relative to comparable British cities. But there was no shifting the stubborn TB rate which in Ireland was responsible for fully half of the deaths between the ages of 15 and 35, its most frequent victims 'the wage earner, the man who has incurred the responsibilities of life' and the young mother 'on whose care the welfare of young children depends'.[23] The maximum number of deaths was around the age of 25, and women were more likely to die than men, 'thus showing that those who live most at home are those who suffer the most from bad housing, unsanitary surroundings, and want of fresh air'.[24]

The TB crusade was a high-profile international movement, with congresses held in centres such as London (1901), Paris (1905), Washington (1908), and Rome (1911) at which delegates from most western countries presented statistical material, progress reports, lectures and exhibitions proclaiming the latest advances. The Dublin Tuberculosis Exhibition was part of the International Exhibition in Ballsbridge in 1907, and received widespread publicity. In 1908 Dublin hosted a meeting of the British Association for the Advancement of Science, at which the Anti-Tuberculosis Campaign in Ireland was reviewed. Efforts to launch a structured attack on pulmonary tuberculosis in Dublin were initiated by the National Association for the Prevention of Tuberculosis, founded 1901, but it was the Women's National Health Association of Ireland, 1907, under the auspices of the Countess of Aberdeen which with its novel methods and positive approach was to dominate the crusade against the 'white peril'.

By 1900 it was no longer necessary to argue whether or not there should be municipal control of public health; prevailing wisdom was that 'it is only by such authority that large questions of public health can be at all satisfactorily dealt with'. While private enterprise and philanthropic associations were all very

---

[23] Edward P. Culverwell, *Consumption: Its History and How to Prevent its Spread* (Dublin, 1904), pp. 15–16 [reprinted from the *Dublin Journal of Medical Science*, August 1903], (hereafter *Consumption: Its History*).

[24] Countess of Aberdeen, *Report of the Work of the Women's National Health Association of Ireland as it bears on Tuberculosis*, submitted to Tuberculosis International Congress, Washington, 1908 (Dublin, 1908), p. 15, (hereafter *Work of the WNHAI*).

[25] T. Percy C. Kirkpatrick, *The Control of Consumption by the Public Health Authority* (Dublin, 1903), p. 9 [reprinted from the *Dublin Journal of Medical Science*, January 1903], (hereafter *The Control of Consumption*).

laudable, there was little hope of 'permanent advance' without the solid backing of 'those who alone can make compulsory and universal the adoption of those preventive measures on which such advance will depend'.[25] The principal body therefore to deal with TB in Dublin could only be the Public Health Committee of the Corporation.

The first essential in such a public health matter 'is that the responsible authority should be in a position to know where the cases of that disease exist'; death statistics were of little assistance in preventing its spread.[26] Compulsory notification began in New York in 1897, and medical authorities such as Dr Kirkpatrick warned that 'in the face of the results obtained elsewhere' in the war against TB, 'the guardians of our public health incur a grave responsibility if they delay much longer its commencement'.[27] However, the issue of compulsory notification, the only route which had proven satisfactory in any city to date, was hotly disputed; despite its obvious advantages, the fear among patients of being penalised by loss of liberty or of economic opportunity, the breach of 'that most sacred trust' between doctor and patient, and the reluctance to incur any new expenses on the part of the Corporation all delayed its adoption.[28]

The core message of the TB crusade was threefold: the disease is contagious rather than hereditary; simple methods of prevention can be successful; and a cure is possible, if caught in time. It was difficult to convince the public that it had nothing to do with blood links where one family member after another succumbed to it in turn. The fatalism which surrounded the disease, especially amongst the poorest who had every reason to be despondent, was the most serious obstacle to its eradication. 'Experts may know how thousands may be saved', but the target group, those residing in the tenements, was unlikely to adopt 'any precautions much in advance of what the public opinion of their neighbours approves or demands'.[28] Unless there was a fundamental transformation of *popular* belief and practice there would be no success.

Disinfection created a taboo around a house; in Dublin wherever a certificate of death from consumption reached the Registrar-General, disinfection of the dwelling was offered, free of charge, to the residents of the house concerned. In three out of every four cases the offer was refused, the residents preferring to 'keep the thing quiet and run all risks'. 'They will attend wakes, sleep, dwell or visit, in places teeming with infection, without a moment's misgiving, but as soon as ever the officer has been brought to disinfect a house or room, they shun it as if he had brought the plague instead of banishing it'.[29]

The disease could be controlled only if its means of spreading was understood by the public at large. According to one expert, Koch, the source of contagion was the 'tuberculous dust which comes from the sputum left about by careless consumptives, or to the fine tuberculous spray which they emit when coughing'.

[26] Ibid.
[27] Ibid., pp. 10–11.
[28] Culverwell, *Consumption: Its History* (1904), p. 16.
[29] Ibid., p. 17.

Infection, or reinfection, could be prevented by always coughing into 'something which caught the germs given off' and if all the infected materials were 'burned or disinfected before it dried and got scattered about'. Keeping ill persons with the healthy in the close confinement of a tenement room ensured its rapid spread. Another dangerous practice was the purchase, at second hand, of 'the furniture of a consumptive who has never known, or cared to take any precautions', which amounted to a traffic in 'deadly poisons', while those moving into lodgings recently vacated similarly faced huge risks; the only control was compulsory disinfection.[30]

The treatment of the disease among the multitude infected was the most formidable aspect of the problem. One observer noted that 'every bed in all the Dublin hospitals could be filled with consumptive patients without exhausting the supply of such patients in the city', a claim which did not at all overstate the situation.[31] There was simply no possibility of providing isolation hospital treatment for all those infected, regardless of the medical benefits involved. As matters stood, the policy was to refuse consumptive patients admission to the general hospitals of the city; however, when they presented 'with haemorrhage or some other complication' they could not be excluded, so that such patients were found in every general ward in the city, 'side by side with patients who are, perhaps, in a condition which renders them peculiarly liable to infection'.[32]

The strength of the Women's National Health Association TB crusade lay in its appeal to both men and women across all divisions of class and creed. It was founded on the basis that 'in matters concerning public health and the health of the homes, the active sympathy and co-operation of the women of the country must be enlisted if any permanent good is to be effected'. In the spreading of its 'gospel of hope' its aim was to try and make every woman feel that by responding to the appeals concerning fresh air, cleanliness, nutrition and childcare 'that she is doing a great work, not only for her home, but for her country', sure in the knowledge that 'the Irish people – men, women and children – ever respond to the call of patriotism'.[33] From an organisational point of view, it harnessed the energies of educated and well-to-do women as cookery instructors, demonstrators, lecturers, school and home visitors, and through ready co-operation with local doctors and clergy, landlords and employers, ensured it was welcomed. Exhibitions and lectures were organised for Dublin and throughout the country, books and leaflets were published, a journal *Sláinte* (Health) was launched, and a pasteurized milk dairy opened in Dublin.[34] By establishing a local committee of the association, which got to work immediately for some tangible and practical

---

[30] Ibid., pp. 9–10.
[31] Kirkpatrick, *The Control of Consumption* (1903), p. 13.
[32] Ibid., p. 14.
[33] Countess of Aberdeen, *Work of WMHAI* (1908), pp. 13–14.
[34] Charles Cameron, *Report of Public Health Committee for 1908* (Dublin, 1909), pp. 44–45; *Report for 1909* (Dublin, 1910), p. 71.
[35] Countess of Aberdeen, *Work of WNHAI* (1908), p. 13.

end, however modest, 'to make use of the enthusiasm which has been aroused' by the itinerant exhibition and associated lectures, the message gradually penetrated home.[35]

The designation of tuberculosis of the lung as a compulsorily notifiable disease within the county borough of Dublin from 1 October 1909 was directly attributable to the lobbying of the Countess of Aberdeen's organisation, and intense international pressure. It put in place the foundation on which the structure of the TB crusade could be built. All 'medical men' (*sic*) were obliged to report to the medical officer of health all persons suffering from the contagious form of TB and liable to communicate it to others, 'where the person suffering habitually sleeps or works in the same room as any other person or persons not so suffering; or is employed or engaged in handling, preparing, or distributing milk, meat or any other article of human food intended for sale to the public'.[36] The public health committee was to pay a fee of 2*s* 6*d* for each notification, including those made through the dispensary medical officer; those made through the medical officer of a public hospital, infirmary or workhouse resulted in a fee of 1*s* per case.[37] Completed notification forms were to be submitted by the doctors within seven days of first becoming aware of the case.

Once those infected had been identified, their separation from those still well was to follow: the founding principle of the fever hospitals exactly one hundred years earlier, and now advocated as the only way forward for the control of TB. A 'Sanatorium for Consumptives' was established in 1907, under the control of a new joint hospital board, which included representatives from the Dublin Corporation area as well as the adjoining rural districts, with provision for the urban districts of Rathmines, Pembroke, Kingstown and Blackrock to join if they wished.[38] Under the Tuberculosis Prevention Act (Ireland) 1908,[39] the board was enabled to levy a rate of twopence in the pound, with the permission of the Local Government Board, to raise funds; its first expenditure was the purchase of almost 300 acres of south-facing land on the western side of the Dublin mountains, with an excellent spring water supply, on which to erect a fully-equipped sanatorium, with accommodation for fifty patients.[40] By 1914 this Crooksling sanatorium catered for 'early consumptives' while advanced cases were consigned to the Pigeon House Road sanatorium (Ringsend).[41] Other provisions of the 1908 Act included the appointment of a bacteriologist to examine milk, the distribution of leaflets, drugs and 'appliances' to check the spread of the disease, and payment of compensation not exceeding £10 to the owner of a diseased animal condemned as unfit for human food. Disinfection of infected

[36] Charles Cameron, *Report of Public Health Committee for 1909* (Dublin, 1910), p. 65.
[37] Ibid., p. 64
[38] Charles Cameron, *Report of Public Health Committee for 1908* (Dublin, 1909), p. 45.
[39] 8 Edward VII, c.56.
[40] Charles Cameron, *Report of Public Health Committee for 1908* (Dublin, 1909), p. 46.
[41] Charles Cameron, *Municipal Health Administration in Dublin* (Dublin 1914), p. 50.
[42] Charles Cameron, *Report of Public Health Committee for 1908* (Dublin, 1909), pp. 46–47.

premises was allowed under the Act, but as it was not mandatory on the local authorities this provision fell short of what medical officers such as Cameron advocated.[42] The death rate from pulmonary consumption fell dramatically from 1907 to 1911 (Table 5.2); Cameron attributed this largely to the crusade organised by the Women's National Health Association, whose local branches 'worked hard in the domain of preventive medicine'.[43]

Scavenging Revisited

While concern with infant deaths and TB dominated the public health debate during the first decade of the new century, earlier concerns with scavenging continued. A 'feeble attempt' to tackle the problem of streets, lanes and courts 'not in charge of the Corporation', and 'in so filthy a state as to be injurious to the public health' had been made in 1891. The public health report for 1905 included 43 pages describing the objectionable condition of these streets, lanes, alleys, courts and passages; by 1910 there had been no improvement, despite continual harassment of the sanitary staff by irate rate-payers who presumed the Corporation had some authority in the matter. There were by then 900 such filthy streets, lanes, courts, passages and open yards, which if placed one after the other would extend to a distance of 30 miles; the dwellings abutting onto these lanes, &c were occupied by about 12,000 persons. 'The winds distribute the filthy dust from them through the general atmosphere. Hundreds of children play in those filthy places and inhale the impure air, caused by decomposing animal and vegetable matter'.[44] It was time to tackle the issue more courageously. The Public Health Acts Amendment Act 1890 allowed the urban authority to undertake the cleansing of such areas, and then recover the costs from the owners; while this act had become a 'dead letter' the time was now ripe to utilise it.

By 1925 the widespread and long-standing lack of co-operation with the sanitary authorities was again condemned. While the 'privy system' had given way, thankfully, to water closets, removing at least one aspect of the scavenging challenge, the Civic Survey claimed that tenement owners still 'thwart the Sanitary Inspectors as far as possible'. By 1924 more than 15,000 notices to abate nuisances were given annually, 'and about 1,000 summonses to the Police Court have to be issued annually to enforce the observance of the notices'. A staff of twenty-eight hard-pressed sanitary sub-officers were engaged in thankless 'inspectorial work'; enforcing regulations relating to abuse of streets and lanes was immensely difficult, while tenants could not be held responsible 'for certain insanitary conditions created by themselves in their dwellings', such as the destruction of newly-fitted toilets.[45] The battle was all uphill.

---

[43] Charles Cameron, *Report of Public Health Committee for 1908* (Dublin, 1909), pp. 44–45; *Report for 1909* (Dublin, 1910), p. 71.

[44] Charles Cameron, *Report of Public Health Committee for 1908* (Dublin, 1909), pp. 44–45; *Report for 1909* (Dublin, 1910), pp. 96–98.

[45] *Dublin Civic Survey* (1925), p. 49.

TB and the Move towards Public Housing

In my opinion if you separate the poverty problem from the housing one, the matter is plain sailing. It is, however, in my judgement absolutely impossible to keep the two problems separate.[46]

The battle against TB, and the other public health matters still to be effectively tackled such as domestic scavenging, became increasingly identified with the question of providing housing at public expense for the poorest. Some authorities 'continually alleged' that the poor housing was 'a serious factor' in the excessive mortality from TB, a claim that could not be discounted.[47] It was held that the life of the TB germ when expelled from the body 'is long in unsanitary, and short in sanitary, surroundings' while 'the resistance to infection of a person living under conditions generally healthful is far greater than that of a person living in unsanitary surroundings'.[48] Others argued from the opposite direction, that until steps were taken to prevent the spread of consumption the 'great improvements currently being effected in the surroundings and housing of the working classes' would make no difference to the high level of mortality from TB.[49] Dr Cameron, so long committed to publicising health and sanitation scandals, took an equally public part in the debate concerning housing. In fact, his role might be understood as grinding down the opposition, quarter by quarter and year by year, as he relentlessly exposed the situation of the poorest of the citizens, and the insufficiency of the best efforts to date.

In his report for 1909 he called for the 'considerable extension of the provision of healthy dwellings' but aimed at the very poorest, and 'the housing of consumptives still at work and those unfit to labour'. More important was his advocacy yet again of the principle of housing built entirely at state cost:

The poor get gratuitous medical advice, old age pensions, free reading rooms, and practically free elementary education; it is only going a step farther when they are provided with healthy dwellings at the same rent as the unhealthy ones.[50]

A precedent had already been set by the construction of 'healthy dwellings' for rural labourers 'at some cost to the rural sanitary authorities.' It was only logical to ask 'why not extend the same advantages to the urban labourer?' If anything, the urban poor were in a worse situation, densely packed into 'purlieus' where 'the sun's direct rays are almost or entirely unseen'.[51]

[46] City treasurer of Dublin, in a report to the municipal council in 1914, quoted in *Dublin Civic Survey* 1925, p. 57.
[47] Charles Cameron, *Report of Public Health Committee for 1909* (Dublin, 1910), p. 93.
[48] Culverwell, *Consumption: Its History* (1904), p. 13.
[49] Kirkpatrick, *The Control of Consumption* (1903), p. 17.
[50] Charles Cameron, *Report of Public Health Committee for 1909* (Dublin, 1910), p. 92.
[51] Ibid.

While accepting that the Corporation could not carry out extensive building schemes in the city without incurring a loss, he maintained that there were still in Dublin 'some large spaces upon which dwellings could be erected without being handicapped by the cost of insanitary area clearance schemes' and that legislation could be enacted to allow 'many hundreds of ruinous buildings, and practically derelict spaces' throughout the city to be acquired cheaply for new construction.[52] He felt sure that the rate-payers, or at least most of them, would contribute willingly to an additional 'housing improvement rate' to provide healthy dwellings for the working classes, suggesting a rate of sixpence in the pound, which would raise £22,800, which in turn would pay interest and sinking fund on a loan of £540,000 for 60 years.[53]

Housing of the Working Classes: Mansion House Conference, 1903

A joint conference in the Mansion House in September 1903, 'voluntarily formed' by Dublin Corporation, chaired by the Lord Mayor, Timothy Harrington, and attended by the Members of Parliament for the city and county of Dublin, and representatives of the Dublin Trades Council marks a critical shift in popular and official thinking. A series of house collapses had alarmed the public and sidestepping was not to be tolerated for much longer.[54] This conference was presented with tables projecting the numbers which could be housed if city areas officially declared 'unhealthy' were to be cleared and rebuilt upon (1,665 families); the number of derelict houses and sites (532), and the total numbers in 'defective houses' (3,645 families).[55] A breakdown of the numbers and rent levels of all existing Corporation, philanthropic and company dwellings provided to date was included (accommodating 5,394 families), and reference made to other statistical sources, for those still not convinced that an impasse had been reached. Very different practices were clearly now called for: 'It would be a fatal mistake to continue to put a premium on bad sanitation and improper housing by purchasing up, at a ruinous rate, insanitary areas and rebuilding them'.[56] A most attractive new route was proposed, to build 'on the outskirts, cottages or self-contained buildings, and to procure cheap means of transit to and from the city for workers, which the Committee believes will not be difficult to arrange with the Tramway Company and Railway Companies'.[57] To facilitate such a shift, the committee called for the extension to Ireland of the provisions of section I of the

[52] Charles Cameron, *Report of Public Health Committee for 1909* (Dublin, 1910), pp. 91, 93.
[53] Ibid., p. 93.
[54] *Irish Times*, 10 November 1902.
[55] T.C. Harrington, 'Report of the Conference between the Parliamentary Representatives of the County and City of Dublin, the Corporation of Dublin, and the Dublin Trades Council on the Subject of the Housing of the Working Classes', *RPDCD*, vol III, no. 176, (1903), pp. 383–396, (hereafter 'Report of Conference').
[56] Ibid., p. 395.
[57] Ibid.

Housing of the Working Classes Act, 1900 (applicable only to Great Britain to date), which provided for the taking of lands or houses outside the district of a local authority. If this was supplemented by permission being given to local authorities to use for housing purposes lands owned by them in 'outside districts' for housing schemes, the Corporation would be able to overcome the disappointment of the limited extension of the city boundary (1900), and be provided with – literally – boundless opportunity.[58] Meanwhile, back in the city centre, several amendments to current legislation (most of which were already in force in Britain) would streamline the process of slum clearance and rebuilding, such as tighter provisions governing condemnation of slum property and compensation to owners, extension of schemes to include neighbouring lands, the possibility of including shops and recreation grounds within schemes, longer periods before central government loans need be repaid, and up to ten years tax relief for individual entrepreneurs who would undertake to build dwellings for the working classes, subject to Corporation approval concerning construction, condition and rent.[59] The articulation of the 'suburban solution' to the city's slum problems marks an important watershed. From the first years of the new century hopes are clearly vested in not too far away fields and villages.

Local Government Board Inquiry into Dublin Housing Conditions, 1913/1914

The 1913/14 Local Government Board report[60] provides an overview of the total housing situation by that date: derelict sites, dangerous buildings, and insanitary areas are illustrated in Figure 5.2, and artisans' dwellings already erected, either by the Corporation or by private companies, and areas for which Corporation schemes are in preparation, are depicted in Figure 5.3; both maps are based on the original complex coloured map accompanying this report, and on the Corporation's own architect's plans, as appended to the Housing Committee report for 1914. Table 5.5 summarises the housing schemes in which Dublin Corporation was involved from 1889, and was appended to the Local Government report of 1914. A further appendix to the 1914 report is a collection of fifty-five black and white photographs of decayed housing, popularly known as the 'Darkest Dublin' collection (Royal Society of Antiquaries of Ireland), some of which have already been introduced, and which describe the housing standards more

[58] Ibid., p. 393.
[59] Ibid., pp. 393–395.
[60] *Report of the Departmental Committee appointed by the Local Government Board for Ireland to Inquire into the Housing Conditions of the Working Classes in the City of Dublin* (Dublin, 1914), (hereafter *Dublin Housing Report, 1914*).
[61] The original map may be found in the City Archive, with the printed report; the full set of negatives is stored in the Royal Society of Antiquaries of Ireland, 63 Merrion Square. Some negatives from this collection, (filed under streeet names), and from the Dublin Corporation Dangerous Buildings file (unsorted), are stored in the Irish Architectural Archive, 73 Merrion Square, Dublin.

effectively than any statistical tables (see Plates 2.5, 4.2–4.4, also Chapter 8).[61]

By 1914 there was widespread dereliction, along with dangerous and insanitary buildings, throughout the city. The alphabetical street lists appended to each annual public health report, and that produced specially for the 1913/1914 Inquiry, allow individual site histories to be constructed. North of the Liffey concentrations are found in the old markets area from the Royal Barracks to the rear of Capel Street; the markets behind Moore Street, and the workshops and dwellings of Upper Abbey Street and Strand Street; and the Gloucester Street/ Mecklenburgh Street district, behind the Phibsborough Road, and the North Strand. Dominick Street Upper is particularly distinguished for the number of condemned buildings and derelict sites. South of the Liffey concentrations are found in the heart of the medieval city and its Liberties, from the shadow of Dublin Castle, facing Ship Street Barracks, along Cook Street and Back Lane, following through to the long-established assortment of industries and dense housing which characterised the south western sector, increasingly dominated by Guinness's brewery. Other concentrations, in what is by now a well-rehearsed litany, included Temple Bar, the Cuffe Street/Mercer Street district, the south dockland around Townsend Street and to Grand Canal Street, and courts to the rear of the south eastern high-status district.

Figure 5.2 records only derelict sites and housing condemned on structural or 'sanitary' grounds; it does not provide an overview of the tenement situation. By then, despite the huge numbers of houses closed (as evidenced by the widespread dereliction), the problem had worsened, so that 'the general density per tenement house, and the proportion of tenement houses which, though occupied, are stated to be unfit for human habitation', was 'substantially greater' than in 1880, and the 'complete breaking up of the tenement system as it exists' was advocated.[62] Reports that one house was found 'to be occupied by 98 persons, another by 74, and a third by 73', are all reminiscent of slum surveys taken over a century earlier.[63]

The classification system in use by the Corporation's sanitary staff by 1913 lists all tenement houses according to their structural condition (Table 5.3). This however is not the full story, as many of the city's small houses were equally bad, and also merit either substantial renovation (second class) or absolute clearance (third class).[64] In an effort to place the Dublin housing crisis in a larger contemporary context, comparisons were drawn between the tenement situation in Dublin and that in the principal cities of the United Kingdom (Table 5.4). Of the 25,822 Dublin families living in tenement houses in 1913, 20,108 lived in one room. There were 1,560 cellar dwellings occupied. From the 1911 census returns, 22.9% of the city's population lived in one-room tenements, considerably higher than the corresponding figure for any of the large towns in the United Kingdom,

---

[62] *Dublin Housing Report, 1914*, p. 6.
[63] Ibid., p. 4.
[64] Ibid., p. 6.
[65] Ibid., p. 4.

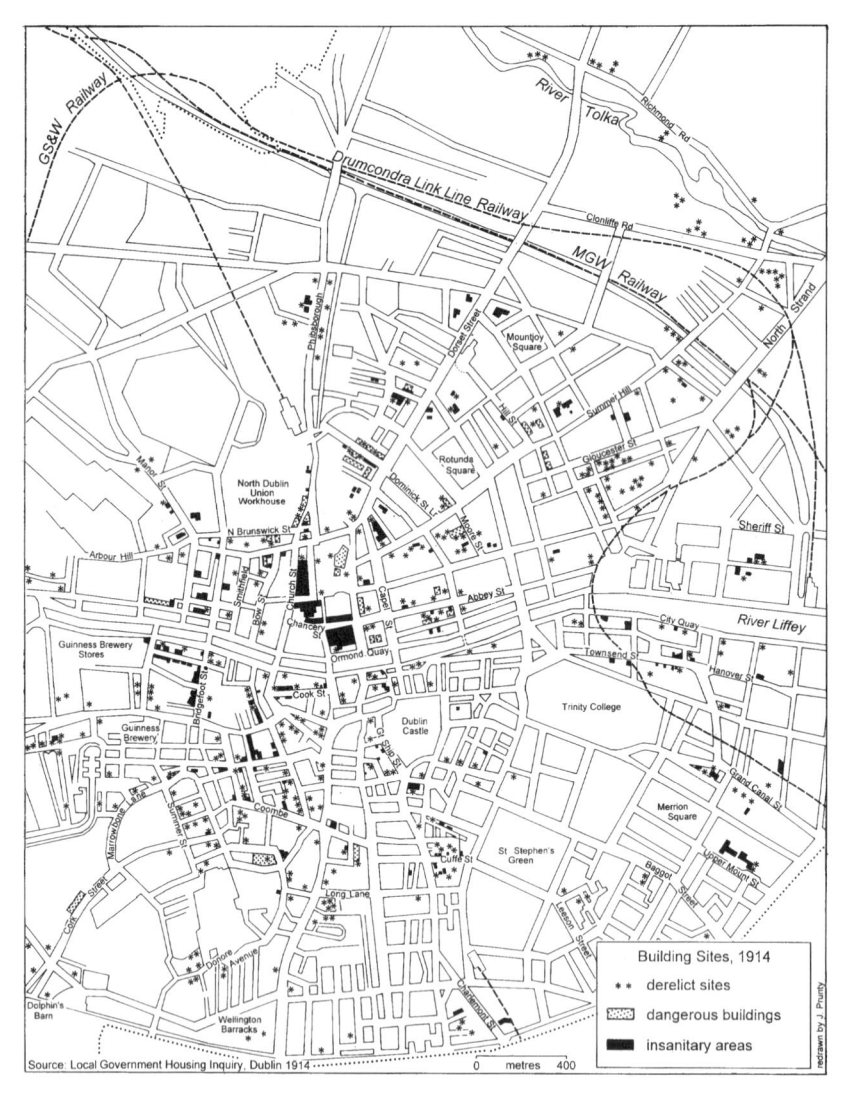

Figure 5.2 Derelict sites, dangerous buildings, and insanitary areas, Dublin 1914

the closest in this respect being Finsbury with 14.8% and Glasgow with 13.2%.[65] With the greatest number of one roomed tenements in the United Kingdom (Table 5.4), the highest occupancy rates per room, and the highest proportion of total population thus accommodated, whatever way one approached the matter the answer was plain: Dublin had the worst housed urban citizenry in the British Isles in 1914.

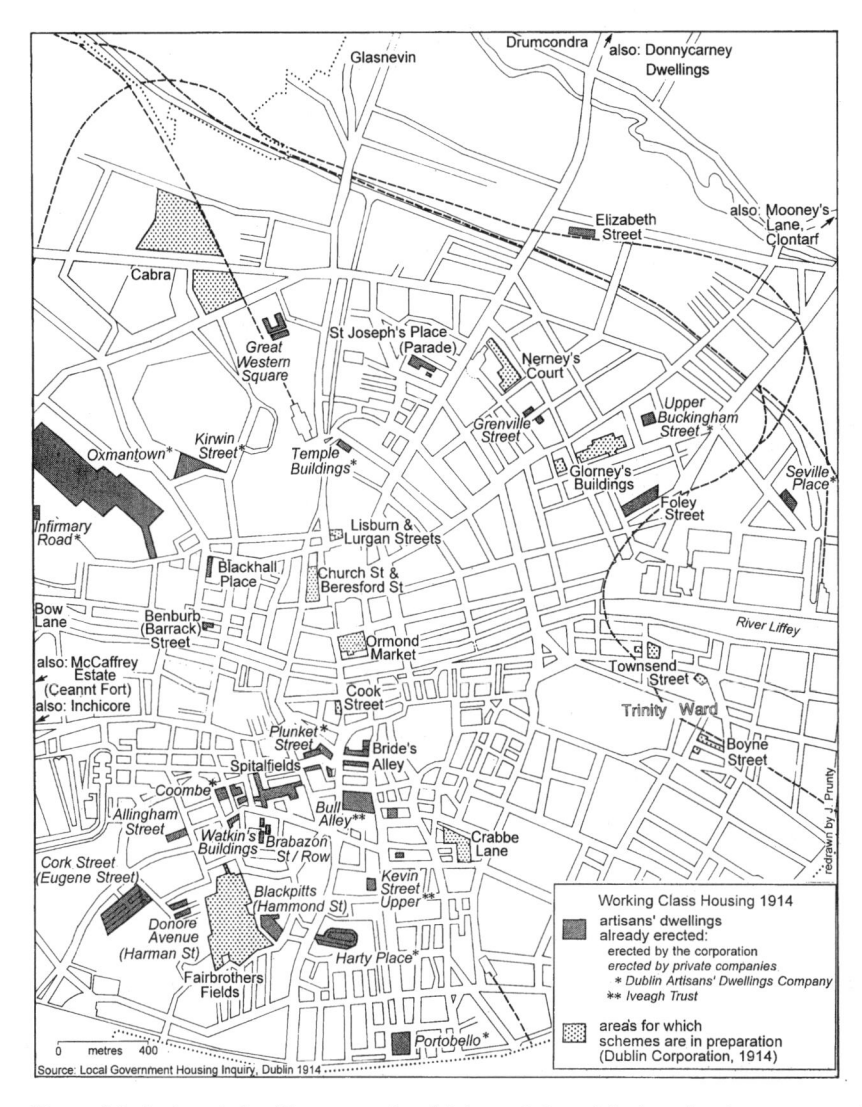

Figure 5.3 Artisans' dwellings completed/planned (municipal and private companies), Dublin 1914

Artisans' Housing Schemes to 1914

Figure 5.3 (and Table 5.5) provides a summary of houses constructed and immediate plans at an important juncture in the Dublin slum story: with the outbreak of world war I, followed by a violent independence struggle and a brief but vicious civil war, the resolution of the Dublin slum crisis was to be placed on hold for several years. The Corporation contribution up to 1914, aside from co-

Returns by Dublin Corporation Sanitary Staff, 1913

First Class: *Houses which appear to be structurally sound; they may not be in good repair, but are capable of being put into good repair.*

1,516 tenements, occupied by 8,295 families, 27,052 persons

Second Class: *Houses which are so decayed or so badly constructed as to be on or fast approaching the border-line of being unfit for human habitation.*

2,288 tenements, occupied by 10,696 families, by 37,552 persons

Third Class: *Houses unfit for human habitation and incapable of being rendered fit for human habitation.*

1,518 tenements, occupied by 6,831 families, by 22,701 persons

Source: *Report on Dublin Housing, 1914*, appendix

Table 5.3 Returns by Dublin Corporation Sanitary Staff, 1913.

Number of tenements of one room, of two rooms, of three rooms, of four rooms per 1,000 total tenements in principal cities of the United Kingdom.

Number of rooms per tenement	Dublin	Edinburgh	Glasgow	London	Liverpool	Manchester	Birmingham	Belfast
1	339	94	200	134	54	18	10	6
2	210	316	462	190	74	35	21	41
3	105	219	189	213	132	97	305	50
4	104	144	66	159	185	406	165	239

Source: *Report on Dublin Housing, 1914* p. 3

Table 5.4 Number of tenements of one room, of two rooms, of three rooms, of four rooms per 1,000 total tenements in principal cities of the United Kingdom.

operation with the DADC and other private companies, and some experimentation with suburban sites, had been notably modest; however, several schemes were at an advanced planning stage. On the northside small city housing schemes had been completed by 1914 in St Joseph's Place (off Nelson Street), Elizabeth Street (Clonliffe) and Blackhall Place (flats and houses), while block dwellings were erected by the Corporation both in Benburb Street (1887) and Foley Street (1905). The controversy surrounding the Foley Street dwellings exemplifies the no-win situation the Corporation faced: 460 small flats were constructed especially for the very poorest, following on three years planning. The Corporation's

Health and Housing: Policy Shifts, 1900–1925

Report on Public Housing Provision 1886–1913.

SCHEME	When Scheme Completed	Number of persons rehoused	Cost per person rehoused £ s d	Cost per family rehoused £ s d	No. of Persons housed to the Acre rehoused	Calculations on which No. of persons to a family are based
Benburb Street	1887	619	45 2 1	193 17 0	1,238	4.3
Bow Lane	1889	370	27 18 1	120 1 2	254	4.3
St. Joseph's Place	1896	344	76 4 4	327 14 8	160	4.3
Blackhall Place	1895	366	37 8 0	160 16 6	418	4.3
Bride's Alley	1911	748	133 6 1	573 2 3	250	4.3
Elizabeth Street (Drumcondra)	1904	60	41 8 9	177 11 8	283	4.3
Mooney's Lane (Clontarf)	1905	245	38 2 11	163 19 4	178	4.3
Inchicore Dwellings	1912	1,100	32 5 3	161 6 3	138	5
Townsend Street	1907	86	48 19 6	210 11 11	491	4.3
Coombe Area	1886	916	60 2 7	258 11 6	305	4.3
Plunket Street Area	1889	542	84 5 7	362 10 8	181	4.3
Cook Street	1913	225	42 17 9	214 8 11	180	5
Foley Street	1905	1,978	32 3 3	138 5 6	989	4.3
Donnycarney Dwellings	1893	40	33 0 0	165 0 0	80	5
Lisburn and Lurgan Streets	**	240	40 0 0	200 0 0	320	5
Trinity Ward Area	**	380	39 15 0	198 15 3	380	5
Beresford & Church Streets	**	905	47 16 11	239 4 6	239	5
Ormond Market	**	500	68 1 2	340 6 0	125	5
Glorney's Buildings	**	1,160	34 11 5	172 16 11	211	5
Spitalfields Area	**	680	40 19 1	204 15 7	247	5
Fairbrothers Fields	**	3,470	48 3 1	240 15 6	158	5
McCaffrey Estate	**	1,170	49 1 2	245 6 0	195	5

** = Not yet carried out.

Source: *Report on Dublin Housing, 1914*, Appendix VIII.

Table 5.5 Corporation of Dublin: summarised history of each housing scheme, presented to the Local Government Housing Inquiry, 1913.

focus on the most needy class of tenant, for whom the DADC houses were well beyond reach, was always controversial as the Foley Street venture was a massive loss maker, while the style of dwellings, monotonous barracks housing occupied by the one class with no 'improving' tenants to lift the complex socially, was condemned for creating a new ghetto.[66] There were Corporation schemes planned for five major slum sites on the north side (see Chapter 8), and in Cabra, a large greenfield site.

On the south side, more Corporation plans than completed schemes were in evidence in 1914: Bride's Alley and Spitalfields were the municipality's principal city-centre achievements, while further to the west there are Corporation schemes in Ceannt Fort and Inchicore. The small scale units collectively known as 'Trinity Ward scheme' are entered as 'at planning' although building commenced on the Townsend Street section in 1907. Other planned schemes include Cook Street and Crabbe Lane (slum clearance) and the large open site of Fairbrothers Fields.

The DADC and Iveagh Trust were by far the major players in numbers housed by the 'private' sector, although the role the Corporation played in procuring and servicing several of the most significant DADC sites, and the dovetailing of Corporation (Bride's Alley) and Iveagh Trust (Bull Alley) schemes must be noted. The DADC ventures in the Coombe (226 houses) and Plunket Street (137 houses) were model schemes on central slum sites cleared at the ratepayers' expense (see Figures 4.4, 4.5, 4.6), but most of the DADC land was acquired in a less costly manner, on the edge of the built-up area, as in Seville Place and Cork Street. The DADC scheme at Portobello (154 houses) was on the site of the Portobello canal harbour, filled in to create a compact 'virgin site' for building.

The advantages to be gained from economies of scale were exploited in the fullest manner in the DADC Oxmantown (Arbour Hill/Aughrim Street) scheme with 1,265 dwellings, further augmented by the nearby Infirmary Road complex (186 houses). The Oxmantown site was part of a large estate, leased in the reign of Charles II but reverting to Corporation ownership in 1884, which provided the municipality with an ideal opportunity to experiment itself with the erection of 'dwellings for the poor under the act of 1866'. Two sites were allocated, and plans to house a total of approximately 800 persons, mostly in one-roomed tenements at the low rent of 1s 9d per week, were advanced.[67] 'Men's lodgings' were also proposed, at 4d per night (72 persons). Even allowing for some larger family dwellings and four shops, it is clear that the Corporation was moving towards restricting its housing role to providing for that 'underpaid class of the population, such as labourers',[68] for whom privately-built houses were beyond reach. The DADC, although a philanthropic venture, was still committed to providing its investors with an annual 4% return.[69] Only the state could carry loss-makers on

[66] *RPDCD*, vol III, no. 183 (1902) p. 250.
[67] *RPDCD*, no. 136 (1884).
[68] Evidence of Dr Cameron, *Third Report of HM Commissioners for Inquiring into the Housing of the Working Classes, Minutes of Evidence & c., Ireland, 1885*, qs. 22,458.
[69] Ibid., Evidence of Mr Beveridge, qs. 22,426–22,440.

the scale the problem required.

The balance between private and municipal housing provided from the 1870s, and the relative significance of the DADC and Iveagh Trust in the private sector, may be deduced from the Civic Survey summary: by 1925 a total of 6,488 dwellings had been erected by housing associations, company and private schemes, of which over half (3,415) were provided by the DADC, and a further 1,224 erected by the Guinness (Iveagh) Trust. Of the remaining 1,800 units, credit has to be spread widely: a number of smaller artisans' dwellings companies, including the Industrial Tenement Company, the City and Suburban Workmen's Dwellings Company, St Barnabas Public Utility Society, the Association for the Housing of the Very Poor; associations which supervised small numbers of remodelled tenement houses, including the Alexandra Guild and the Social Service Tenement Company; railway and tramway companies which built cottages for their own employees (such as Great Western Square), and a small number of other private employers and landlords. Against this must be set the Corporation's contribution of approximately 580 houses and 1,150 flats (over half of which were in the Bride's Alley and Foley Street schemes). Providing a total of 1,730 family dwellings, this was one quarter the number of units provided by the private and philanthropic ventures combined. While the value of each scheme, private or municipal, in its local context, is not to be discounted, they did little to alter the overall picture of Dublin as a slum city.

Report on Dublin Housing, P.C. Cowan, Local Government Board, 1918

The outbreak of World War I brought a sudden halt to housing initiatives, along with excessively high building costs. The rebellion of 1916, 'with its terrible results in loss of life, vast material waste, the re-birth of dying antagonisms, and the setting back of the clock in many most vital movements for the welfare of Ireland might possibly have been prevented if the people in Dublin had been better house'.[70] However, in an effort to regain some of the lost momentum and to build on the 1914 housing report, P.C. Cowan, chief engineering inspector, was appointed in July 1917 by the Local Government Board to take the needs for improved housing, as set out in the report of 1914, and to produce 'a memorandum giving some general ideas as to how a complete scheme for housing the working people in Dublin, who are said to be living in insanitary dwellings, could be carried out in sections for different parts of the city, which could be taken up in rotation or according to need'.[71] For the first time therefore an overall vision had to be formulated, but one wherein the various elements could be put into effect in a staggered way, as there was clearly no prospect of immediately implementing any grand plans on a universal scale.

The task was twofold: to provide for 14,000 'new, self-contained houses of sufficient size to prevent overcrowding and to permit the separation of the sexes,

[70] P.C. Cowan, *Report on Dublin Housing* (Dublin, 1918), p. 31.
[71] Ibid., pp. 8, 3.

with scullery and water closet accommodation for the sole use of each family'; and to remodel 3,803 first and second class tenement houses to provide suitably for 13,000 families in units of one to four rooms. Allowing for the four year elapse since these figures were produced, during which 3,989 families had been forced from their homes through the closure of tenement houses, other property had fallen into dilapidation, and few new houses had been erected, Cowan calculated that an additional 2,500 new houses would be required. In summary, the task ahead was to provide improved housing for at least 41% of the city's population, 135,700 persons or 29,500 families.[72] It was a colossal task, 'immensely greater proportionately' than the task proposed in England and Wales of building 300,000 houses as soon as the war ended.

While it was recommended that the acquisition and development of the sites be entrusted to the Corporation, Cowan was adamant that this authority was totally unsuited to the building and management of such a vast number of houses, a project which 'affects so vitally interests outside the narrow limits of the city'.[73] As matters stood, the Corporation had already built and was landlord of 1,880 houses; to increase their tenant books by perhaps 29,500 was inconceivable, not least because the members 'would be subject to special forms of pressure from tenants' with regard to rents, maintenance and repairs.[74] It was regarded as essential that the houses should be built, managed and sold, 'as soon and as far as possible', under the Small Dwellings Acquisition Act or otherwise, 'by some special authority not likely to be coerced by ill-informed and hasty public opinion'.[75] The power base and unwieldy size of the Corporation led to its unsuitability: the Corporation officials were portrayed as 'nominees of a multitude of needy people', each councillor with a 'direct interest in lavish and unproductive expenditure' and 'no personal interest in efficiency or economy'; a situation 'which practically disenfranchises all who are steadied by the responsibilities and duties of property or of great business concerns' and thus cannot secure good results.[76] There were eighty members of the Corporation, 'and with such a number to share responsibility, it lies lightly on most of the members' while the good work done at committee stage was 'sometimes undone by a decision of the larger and less well-informed body'.[77]

Cowan advocated 'an authority with a constitution, aims, abilities and endowments similar to those of the Congested Districts Board or the Development Commissioners' with 'prompt and drastic' legal powers.[78] He insisted that 'minor amendments of existing statutes' or 'additional statutory provisions on accustomed

---

[72] Averaging 4.6 per family; Cowan, *Report on Dublin Housing* (1918), p. 12.
[73] Ibid., p. 12.
[74] Ibid., p. 16.
[75] Ibid., p. 13.
[76] Ibid., p. 13.
[77] Ibid., p. 14.
[78] Ibid., p. 31.
[79] Ibid., pp. 7, 4.

lines' were to no avail; drastic recommendations requiring the 'abandonment of many old attitudes of mind' were now imperative.[79] The route to a bright and brave new future had been laid by 'experienced pioneers' whose 'breadth of view and invincible energy and faith' had overcome apparently insurmountable difficulties to lead to 'a safe and spacious place in the sun for those whom they guided'.[80] A phrase borrowed from Octavia Hill encompasses the core of this report: 'there are two great wants in the life of the poor of our large cities which ought to be realised more than they are – *the want of space and the want of beauty*'.[81]

By drawing a circle three miles radius from the General Post Office in O'Connell Street, Cowan illustrated the central tenet of his radical plan: how 'unnatural and unsuitable' was the existing city area for the resolution of the Dublin housing question, when viewed alongside the immense amount of cheap land within reasonable reach of the city. What mattered now was to make a start; blocks of 400 houses at Marino, Drumcondra, Cabra and Crumlin (Figure 5.3) were advocated, 'and the early extension of the city tramways arranged to serve the latter two areas conveniently'.[82] He upheld that at least 12,000 out of the total of 16,500 new houses could, and should, be secured in approximately equal proportions in these districts.[83]

This vision clearly drew heavily on the 'garden city' ideals of Ebenezer Howard, already being energetically debated internationally, and in Ireland under the auspices of the Housing and Town Planning Association of Ireland (HTPAI), founded in Dublin 1911, with Lady Aberdeen as its president, and with both lay and professional members dedicated to housing improvement and town planning advancement.[84] Cowan considered that housing a large number of workers along tram lines would put the city and country in close contact, leading to a situation where 'some members of the new households would turn outwards to the farms and others to the city industries', and with the expected rise in pay levels for agricultural work 'it would be a fairly even choice which way the young man would turn especially as in his leisure hours he would have all the advantages of the city within easy reach'.[85] Cheap and rapid transit was the key to the success of these schemes, with the proposal that either free or low cost passes on the tramways might be attached for a number of years to each new house in certain zones.[86]

This expansive approach to slum clearance was based on economic as well as health and moral grounds: housing improvements 'if carried out in a proper manner' were expected to 'so improve the conditions of life and the mental and

---

[80] Ibid., p. 4.
[81] Ibid.
[82] Ibid., p. 19.
[83] Ibid., p. 10.
[84] Michael Bannon, 'The Genesis of Modern Irish Planning', *The Emergence of Irish Planning 1880–1920* (Dublin, 1985), pp. 189–261.
[85] Cowan, *Report on Dublin Housing* (1918), p. 20.
[86] Ibid., p. 21.
[87] Ibid., pp. 9, 7.
[88] Ibid., p. 7.

physical efficiency of at least 30,000 wage earners that an increase in their useful output of work of at least one-fifth may be expected'.[87] The day to be striven towards was when 'healthy houses and healthy economic conditions may be found together'.[88]

Building vast numbers of new working class houses on cleared inner city sites was dismissed on grounds of 'dignity and beauty'; such additions would make Dublin 'a mean city, with its heart buried by what might not very unfairly be called extensions of the North and South Dublin Workhouses'. It was claimed it would 'ruin the city socially, commercially and industrially' and extinguish any hopes of restoring 'healthy economic conditions' to the metropolis. Block dwellings were likened to warehouses, imprisoning housewives, children, sick and the elderly within their narrow confines. 'They have no open space they can call their own, and none that can easily and safely be reached by them'.[89] The only future for the derelict sites in the central area was that 'wise restraint on the early utilisation of cleared spaces in the old city' might allow plots of sufficient size to be assembled which could be devoted to 'new industries for which electricity will be the motive power'.[90] There was also a vague aspiration towards ameliorating the worst effects of high density, 'to humanise and civilise much that cannot be rebuilt but which can be vastly improved by the provision of open spaces, treated in a variety of ways'.[91]

Cowan was less than enthusiastic for the other part of his task, namely the remodelling of 13,000 tenement houses to accommodate 44% of those needing improved dwellings. He doubted whether the quota of satisfactory houses in existing tenement buildings could be met in the first place, and despatched the topic in one brief paragraph, acknowledging the need for improved access to the remodelled houses, the construction of 'sanitary towers' to provide separate sanitary conveniences for each family, and for the 'clearing and proper utilisation of considerable areas lying behind and around the reconstructed tenement buildings'.[92] The only attractive feature mentioned was the large size of many rooms in tenement houses, while their proximity to places of employment, the central reason for their continued attractiveness to thousands of dwellers, was played down.

The 1918 report illustrates a remarkable turnabout in the debate on the slums; practically every previous survey and report acknowledged that at the root of the Dublin slum problem was the poverty of the residents, which was based on insufficient and precarious employment. Without an adequate and reliable income, appalling living conditions could never be erased. Cowan turned this argument on its head, claiming that there was little chance of improvement in the 'terribly depressed conditions of labour' until 'a greater efficiency' on the part of the Dublin worker was secured, and to this end 'no remedial policy is more promising than that of improved housing'. The Dublin docker, 'with no comfort

[89] Ibid., p. 17.
[90] Ibid., p. 19.
[91] Ibid., p. 12.
[92] Ibid., pp. 28–29.

or occupation at home' spent his time between 'alternate periods of miserable idleness at the street corners', and 'exhausting strenuous labour when a ship comes in'. The lot of the Belgian dockers in happier days was held up for emulation: when not busy at the quays they could be found tending their garden allotments some miles away, 'and when the ship came in, travelled to the quays by steam tramway in response to a telephone message sent to the village hall'.[93] An idyllic combination of rural and urban occupations, promoting physical, moral and social well-being, made possible by modern technology.

The economic argument against 'piling houses on top of one another on small confined areas' in 'these days of cheap and rapid transit' was overpowering.[94] The cost of site acquisition in ten slum areas, totalling 15 acres, from 1886–1912 in the city, (excluding Bride's Alley where site costs were excessively high, Table 5.5) averaged £5,059 per acre; when the costs of clearing and preparing the sites was added, the total cost before building worked out at £6,720 per acre, and this before a single brick was laid. While the most recent site acquisitions, in Church Street and Ormond Market, averaged £4,794 per acre after preparation, (1913–1914)[95] such costs were still far in excess of what was demanded on the outskirts of the city. 12½ acres in Inchicore, within the city boundary, was purchased in 1903 for £320 per acre.[96]

The McCaffrey Estate, at Mount Brown and the Fairbrothers' Fields/Weavers' Square scheme, south of Chamber Street, both at an advanced stage of preparation, were applauded as a great improvement on earlier schemes, and 'suitable intermediates in nature and standard' between the most recently completed schemes in Ormond Market (see Figure 4.3) and Church Street (see Figure 8.9), where the houses were too small, and 'the more nearly ideal schemes' proposed for Marino, Cabra and Crumlin.[97] In the case of Fairbrothers' Fields, various revisions of the ground plan point to important shifts in the official understanding of acceptable house size and density: the 1914 draft was designed to house 800 families mostly in three-roomed houses but including 212 two-roomed flats, set in two-story blocks.[98] By 1918 plans for the same site envisaged a total of 370 families accommodated; this time the smallest house size was three-roomed (157), while of the four-roomed houses (128) a quarter were to have parlours. There were also to be 85 five-roomed houses.[99] The 1918 plan was further amended before construction began, so that the final number of families accommodated was closer to 300. However, all such improvements in housing standards were expensive, and the Corporation's own by-laws regulating street widths and surfacing added to the expense of its own schemes, increasing the

[93] Ibid., p. 9.
[94] Ibid., p. 17.
[95] Ibid., p. 49.
[96] Ibid., p. 10.
[97] Ibid., p. 3.
[98] 'Report of Housing Committee', *RPDCD* no. 16, 1914.
[99] Cowan, *Report on Dublin Housing* (1918), appendix.

tax-payers' bill for questionable advantage. The requirement that all new streets must have footpaths of six feet wide with a concreted surface, chisel-dressed granite curbing, and a paved channel three feet wide on each side, applied to all new housing and, it was claimed, was 'quite unnecessary for streets of a residential character' and not required of large schemes in England or Scotland.[100] Development costs including streets, paths, sewers, and gas and water mains were running at £23,010 or £1,046 per acre, in the case of the Fairbrothers' Fields scheme; a reduction in the widths of the channel pavement and sizes of the sewers proposed by the city engineer was not allowable under the by-laws currently in force.[101]

The debate over the number of bedrooms and other rooms per house illustrates the tensions around what should be regarded as acceptable minimum standards. The advice of Lord Leverhulme, the English industrialist responsible for the model factory and garden village in Port Sunlight, was sought; the half dozen two-bedroomed houses he had built in the first phase of Port Sunlight had proven 'for all practical purposes, useless' and he held that three bedroomed houses were the minimum acceptable, as families who had no children or where the children were still infants, were enabled to take lodgers, 'a convenience for the district as unmarried women and men can in this way be provided for'.[102] Despite the more straitened situation of Dublin the minimum advisable was a three-bedroomed house, whereby 'separate sleeping accommodation for parents, girls and boys', might be secured, albeit in a limited way.[103] Following on the Port Sunlight example, Cowan urged that lodgers be permitted, to facilitate single men and women in a way that also allows the host family to add to its comforts in an 'unobjectionable way'.[104]

It was considered most important that pride in the home should be fostered as much as possible, and Cowan recommends that at least 40% of the houses with three or four bedrooms should have parlours. 'It would be a most grievous and irretrievable error to base the standard for new houses on the present homes, habits, and incomes of the poorer classes in Dublin. In many cases they require only the opportunity to respond to better environment, and it should be remembered that the standard of housing has risen steadily for many years, and that the homes erected may have to serve at least two generations'.[105] The new housing would be the means of 'socialising' the poor, and breaking down the bad habits formed in the city tenements, for 'even if it had to be admitted that the older members of the slum population are not readily responsive to new influences, a drastic change is imperatively demanded for the sake of the children – the coming

[100] Ibid., p. 11.
[101] Ibid., p. 11.
[102] Ibid., p. 22.
[103] Ibid., p. 22.
[104] Ibid., p. 23.
[105] Ibid., p. 24.
[106] Ibid., p. 25.

generation. The desire of working class parents to give their children a better chance than they had in their childhood is widely and deeply felt, and most young men are anxious to take their wives to bright and hopeful homes'.[106]

Civics Institute of Ireland, 1914–1925
Dublin of the Future: the New Town Plan, 1916/1922

While state-sponsored housing reports (1914, 1918) quantified (again) the extent of the city slum problem and developed the suburban option, there were significant developments in the new field of town planning, which were to have enormous repercussions for the resolution of Dublin's slum problem. The period 1900–1930s was quite literally packed with promising ideas, public lectures and exhibitions, robust debate, and vibrant new pressure groups, such as the House and Town Planning Association of Ireland (HTPAI) and the Dublin Citizens' Association.[107] The discussion must also be set against a background of economic malaise and labour unrest, the loss of life and massive destruction wrought in the city centre by the Easter Rising of 1916 and its suppression, followed by the war of independence and civil war. There was also the impact of world war II, in which many thousands of Irish men fought; their mobilisation and demobbing impacted on the demand and supply of low-rent housing, while war time exigencies greatly disrupted building supplies. In the midst of this turmoil, there was the first formal application of 'town planning principles' to the resolution of the slum crisis: *Dublin of the Future: The New Town Plan*, (1914, published 1922) and the *Civic Survey* (1922, published 1925), which taken together, 'represent the first concerted attempt to provide a framework for comprehensive planning'.[108]

The Civics Institute of Ireland launched an open international competition in 1914 for the production of a plan for 'Greater Dublin', following similar initiatives throughout Britain and on the continent.[109] First prize was awarded in 1916 to a Liverpool team (Patrick Abercrombie, Sydney Kelly and Arthur Kelly) but publication of their *Dublin of the Future: A New Town Plan* was delayed until 1922, when the 'new epoch' ushered in by independence made it 'a most opportune time to arouse the interest of the Citizens' (*sic*).[110] The plan was essentially rational, aiming to replace the present 'planless and haphazard growth, squalor and extravagance' with a 'well reasoned scheme, outlining an economic system of scientific, artistic and hygienic municipal reconstruction and development, providing specially for the conservation of citizen life and natural resources, and

---

[107] Bannon, 'The Genesis of Modern Irish Planning' (1985), pp. 189–261.
[108] Arnold Horner, 'The Dublin Region, 1880–1982: An Overview of its Development and Planning' in Bannon, Michael J. (ed.), *The Emergence of Irish Planning* (Dublin, 1985), p. 46.
[109] Patrick Abercrombie, Sydney Kelly, Arthur Kelly, *Dublin of the Future, the New Town Plan*, volume I, Civics Institute of Ireland: Liverpool University Press/Hodder & Stoughton, London, 1922; see also Bannon (1985), pp. 189–195.
[110] *Dublin of the Future* (1922), Foreword, p. v.
[111] Ibid.

Plate 5.1 'The last hour of the Night', by Harry Clarke, *Dublin of the Future: The New Town Plan*, Abercrombie, Kelly & Kelly, Liverpool, 1922

the total abolition of slum conditions'.[111] The grim frontispiece produced by Harry Clarke titled 'the last hour of the Night' (Plate 5.1) illustrates at least part of the context within which this study was published: flames engulf three major civic buildings (the General Post Office, Custom House, Four Courts), and a single aristocratic Georgian residence, now a crowded slum, totters in the midst of dereliction, the street acting as both living room and playground.

Dublin of the Future was a bold discussion paper, structured around three core urban concerns: communications and industries, housing, and metropolitan improvements. Under housing, the question of density is explored in detail, distinguishing 'intra urban' from 'extra urban' areas. Obliged by the rules of the competition to consider ameliorative measures in the city slums, Abercrombie and partners preface a scanty treatment with the hope that derelict and vacant plots (as in Figure 5.2), along with existing first class tenement dwellings, might be trusted to 'commercial absorption' as the 'wave of prosperity rises high' in the 'reorganised and enlightened Dublin' under the new conditions of independence.[112] Centrally situated, they should ideally be left to 'business and semi-business purposes', rebuilt or remodelled as the market demands.[113] Unable to

[112] Ibid., pp. 22, 24.
[113] Ibid., p. 24.

avoid the issue of remodelling insanitary but 'first class' tenement houses, Abercrombie and partners suggest 'knocking three of the old houses into one, and retaining the central staircase and converting the two side staircases into sanitary blocks', all the time reminding the public that such a course 'must only be looked upon as a palliative for the time being'. Second and third class tenement dwellings should be demolished forthwith. Similarly pressurised by the conditions of the competition to deal with infill housing on cleared slum sites a 'composite tenement housing scheme', including residences, open space and children's play areas, is offered for Townsend Street, accommodating 3,698 persons reliant on dockland employment.[114] Commitment to the inner city is completed by a vague suggestion that a site beside the Royal Barracks might also be developed.[115]

Figure 5.4, reproduced from the 1922 report, depicts graphically where the existing city slums, packed with women, men and children, fit into the *Dublin of the Future* schema. Rational traffic flow overlies all other considerations, in a great Haussman-style remodelling. The 're-arrangement and refocussing of communications' to the west of O'Connell Street (Sackville Street) was to be based on radial roads feeding directly into 'transit hubs' both north (Upper Ormond Quay) and south (Wood Quay) of the river (Figure 5.4). As a countermagnet to the well-established south side, with its 'legislature and seats of learning', the North Bank (*sic*), the old markets area, 'is to develop as the prosperous business and commercial town',[116] its status enhanced by the erection of a new Roman Catholic cathedral on the Loftus Lane site at the end of a (widened) Capel Street, and a new complex of 'cultural buildings' at the north end of O'Connell Street. Slum dwellings were but slight impediments to such noble metropolitan ends; indeed, the appalling neglect of over a century was to the advantage of such schemes, as many of the improvements are to be carried out 'in areas already requiring demolition: either poor-class Tenements or Derelict Sites' (*sic*).[117] The case of Upper and Lower Dominick Street, 'tenement ridden, but wide and spacious',[118] exemplifies the approach. While its complement of slum housing is notorious, the street, 'perhaps more seriously diseased than its buildings', has to date merely impeded traffic flow because it is so poorly integrated into the overall network; it is proposed to continue the street line to the south, slicing at right angles through Coles Lane (see Figure 8.10), Liffey Street Upper and Lower, across a new bridge (on the site of the pedestrian Ha'penny Bridge), driving an entirely new route through Temple Bar, crossing Dame Street and meeting up with a greatly widened South William Street. The medieval city, west of the castle, is to be remodelled beyond recognition.

[114] Ibid., pp. 24–25, plate xxiv.
[115] Ibid., pp. 24–25.
[116] Ibid., p. 4.
[117] Ibid., plate xxix.
[118] Ibid., p. 4.
[119] Ibid., p. 26.

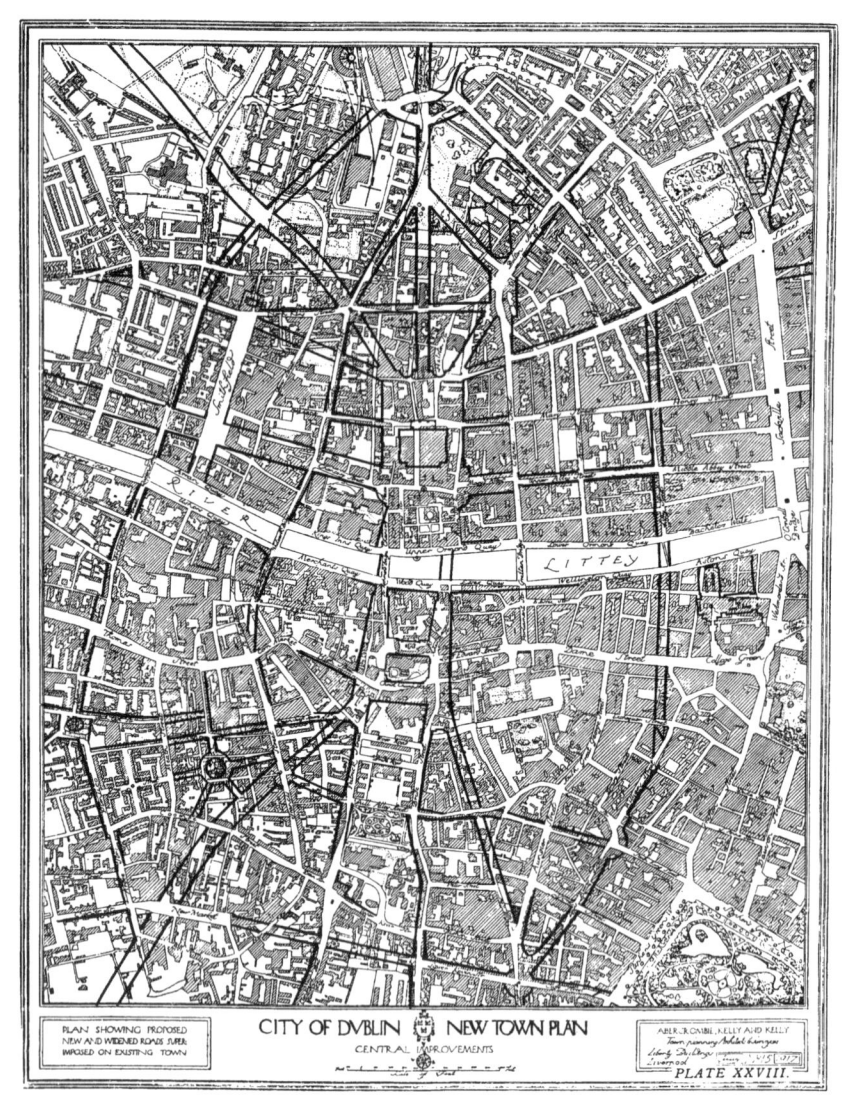

Figure 5.4 City of Dublin: New Town Plan, Central Improvements, *Dublin of the Future: The New Town Plan*, Abercrombie, Kelly and Kelly (Liverpool, 1922).

Meanwhile, the future for over 60,000 of the Dublin poor was to be found in three new 'extra urban' districts: Crumlin, Cabra and Drumcondra, which linked by high-speed trams, operating on dedicated trackways, would bring workmen (*sic*) to their employment in 10 or 12 minutes.[119]

Powered by such an all-embracing vision, Abercrombie argued passionately

[120] Ibid., p. x.

for the creation of a city development plan, for which this and other competition entries could be 'quarried' for ideas.[120] The scattered improvements in housing to date, whatever their laudable intentions, had too often 'blocked anticipated improvements', while other housing schemes and buildings in planning threatened to be similarly obstructive in the absence of an overall 'official scheme of City planning'.[121] 'Piecemeal tinkering' with single aspects of urban life, such as housing, 'neglecting the interrelated problems of work, transport and recreation', would do more harm than good, as would 'the equally dangerous sort of tinkering', which planned for every aspect of civic life within a confined area, but 'without the possibility of relating it to the whole city and its surrounding region'.[122]

The Dublin Civic Survey Report, 1925

The landmark survey prepared by the Civics Institute of Ireland and published in 1925 provides as 'impartially and comprehensively' as possible, a picture of the 'fundamental facts concerning the City and Environs of Dublin' as the city sought to cope with the destruction wrought by several years of rebellion and civil war, and takes on the role of capital city of an independent Irish state. The survey was intended as a compendium of information on all aspects of the city's life, and as the prelude to the formulation of a comprehensive town plan. The town plan competition launched by the Civics Institute in 1914 was to 'elicit plans and reports of a preliminary and suggestive character' of value towards 'the guidance of the city in its various directions', giving due credit for 'suggestions of interest' as well as for 'solutions of value'.[123] The competition process itself, and the winning entry (Abercrombie, Kelly, Kelly) had highlighted the urgent need for a civic survey as a sound basis for future planning, based firmly on the Geddesian paradigm 'survey to analysis to plan'.[124] The driving force behind the survey was Horace T. O'Rourke, 'the keen and earnest City Architect of Dublin'.[125]

It was hoped such a blueprint for the city would control physical development and discourage haphazard extension, and help prevent 'cheap and partial improvements that neglect inter-related problems affecting the whole of Dublin and its environs'.[126] The preparation of this monumental survey, requiring widespread co-operation, would also educate the citizens to their responsibilities, as part of the 'great awakening' which the city needed if it was to take its place among world capitals. The tone of the report is forthright, and there is little energy wasted in apportioning blame; the emphasis is on the collection and analysis of this immense body of information for the purposes of fashioning a

---

[121] Ibid., p. ix.
[122] Ibid., p. x.
[123] Ibid., p. 49.
[124] Michael Bannon et al, *Planning: The Irish Experience 1920–1988* (Dublin, 1989), p. 21.
[125] Lord and Lady Aberdeen, *We Twa*, vol. II (London, 1925), p. 191, quoted in Bannon et al (1989), p. 22.
[126] *Dublin Civic Survey* (1925), p. xix.
[127] Ibid., p. xviii.

new city, and fashioning it now. The Civics Institute motto illustrates its purpose well: 'resurgam' with a phoenix rising from the ashes, set against the city background.[127] It is within this context that the most succinct and damning account of the slum situation to date was presented.

The restoration of capital city status to Dublin in 1922 brought huge changes in the political and economic agenda. Most noticeable is the surge of pride and hope in Dublin, 'a city of magnificent possibilities, not even inferior to Paris, placed astride a fine river, geographically well situated, and generally of great beauty and interest' which only needed wise planning to bring it 'into line with all the requirements of a modern community'.[128] However, top of the programme had to be the situation where 'a high proportion of the population of Dublin starts life without hope of having what makes life worth living – a decent home' and 'children in many thousands are born into an environment which gives no fighting chance of life'.[129] Slum housing was presented as a core political, economic and social issue, as well as a matter of justice in the new Ireland. There could be no equivocation:

Housing in Dublin today is more than a 'question,' and more than a 'problem' it is a tragedy! Its condition causes either a rapid or a slow death – rapid when the houses fall upon the tenants, as has happened already – slow when they remain standing dens of insanitation.[130]

And there was no point imagining that this housing scandal would be rectified 'by a brief and intense application of collective activity'; to rehouse all those urgently in need, as well as providing for the upcoming generation, requires 'nothing short of perpetual construction at the required rate'.[131]

Patrick Abercrombie, professor of town planning at the University of Liverpool (and winner, with his partners, of the earlier competition), directed the preparation of a series of coloured thematic maps, which dealt with density of population, traffic and transport facilities, recreational facilities, public housing and the quality of housing; Figures 5.5 and 5.6 are extracts from the hygiene map, while Figure 5.7 is an extract from the central city housing map.

Correlations between housing density and mortality rates are explored in a systematic manner in the hygiene map. Density of population per acre was calculated on a ward-by-ward basis, and the death rate for each ward appended. The 'hygienic density' was taken as 50 persons to the acre. The suburban areas were predictably all well below this figure, ranging from Rathmines (24.2 persons to the acre), down to Blackrock (9.2 persons per acre). In the city the benchmark figure of 50 was exceeded in most of the central area, but by large margins in Wood Quay ward on the south side (at 138.3 persons per acre) and on the north side in Mountjoy (117.6), Rotunda (113.6) and Inns Quay (103.1) wards. Relative density in these four most congested wards was depicted by means of shading, as

[128] Ibid., p. 5.
[129] Ibid., p. 58.
[130] Ibid., p. 58.
[131] Ibid., p. 73.

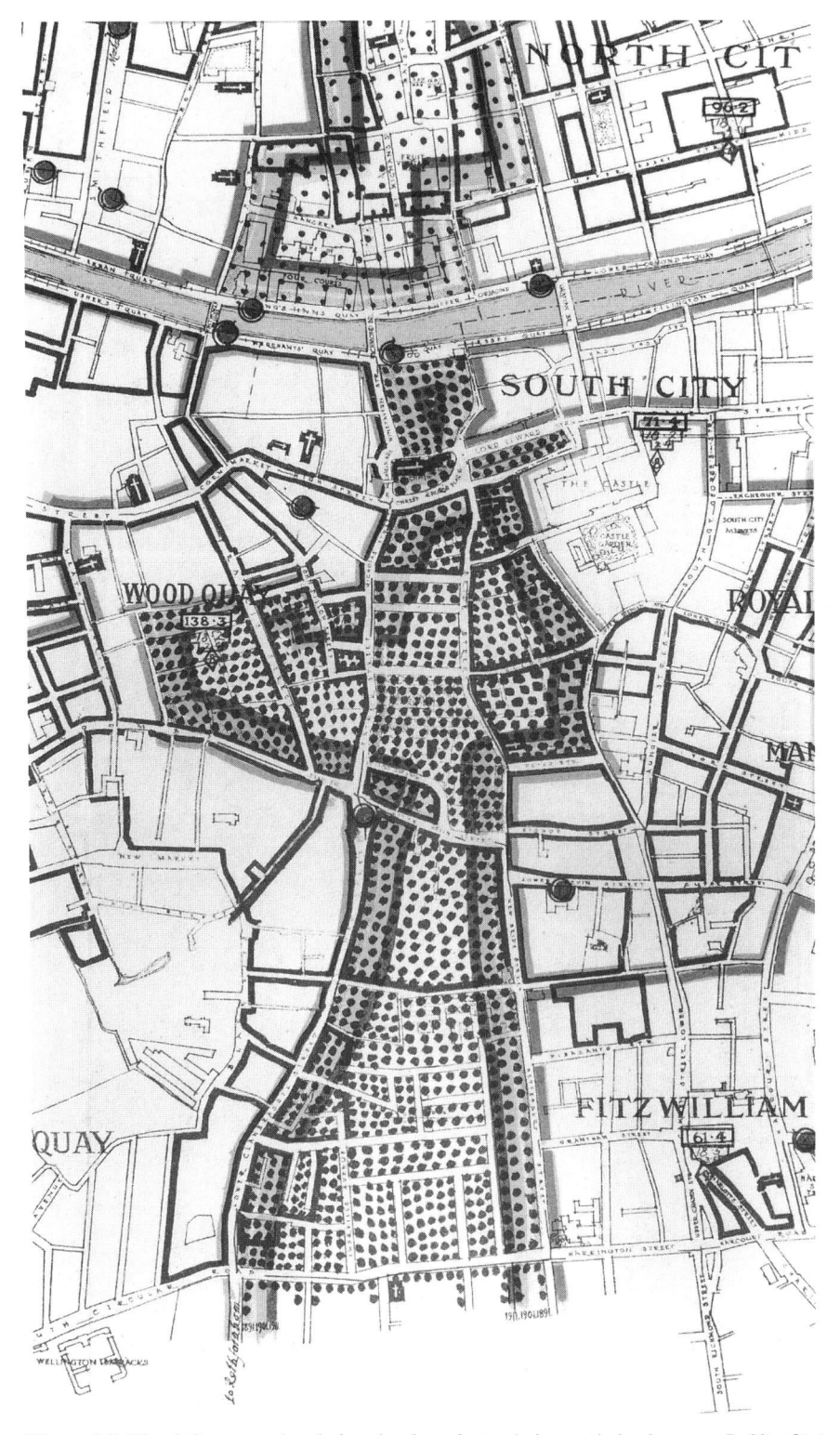

Figure 5.5 Wood Quay ward: relative density of population and death rates, *Dublin Civic Survey*, hygiene map, 1925

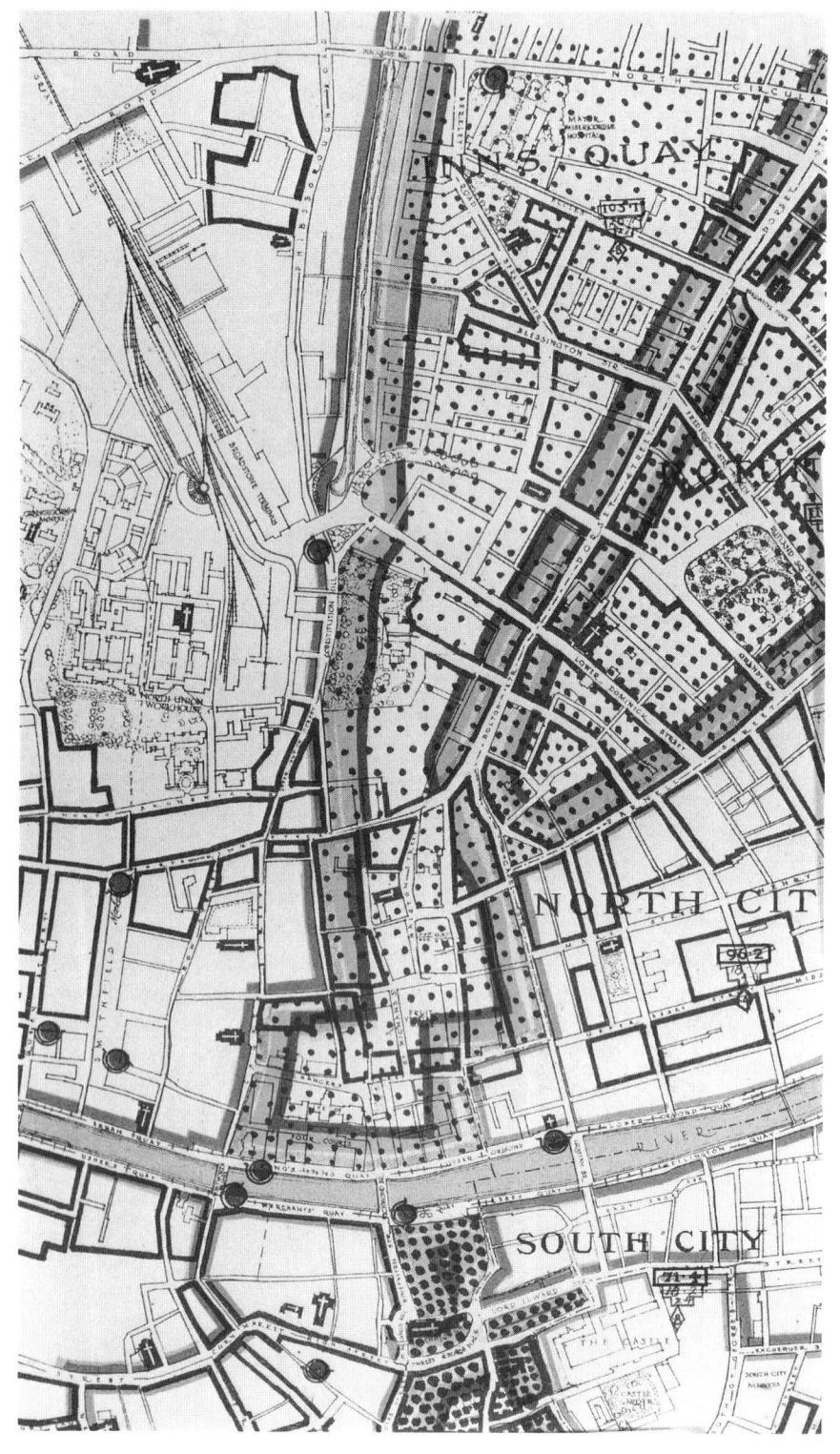

Figure 5.6 Inns Quay ward: relative density of population and death rates, *Dublin Civic Survey*, hygiene map, 1925

in Figure 5.5 (Wood Quay) and Figure 5.6 (Inns Quay with part of Rotunda). Parts of other wards which were also classed as notably 'unhealthy' were outlined in black, as in the areas adjoining Wood Quay ward to the east and west (Figure 5.5) which had little to be proud of in terms of housing standards. It was clear that 'the majority, if not all cases, of serious disease, come from the slums and tenement dwellings – want of sunshine, air and necessary sleeping space undoubtedly predispose to disease',[132] with 'ignorance, poverty and congestion'[133] the cause of the high infant mortality.

In the housing map vast tracts of the city centre are condemned as 'decayed housing areas' by 1925 (Figure 5.7); third class tenements (those 'unfit for human habitation and incapable of being rendered fit without rebuilding') make up the entire housing stock in certain districts. There were also at least 251 families living in houses condemned as dangerous to public safety.[134] Alongside these, existing housing schemes for the working classes, by both municipal and private bodies, were included.

Figure 5.7 indicates the major concentration of decayed housing south of the Liffey, but this extends to the west to include Cork Street and Usher's Island, and to the east the infamous south docks concentration around Townsend Street/Boyne Street, and the slum courts near Merrion Square. The south side catalogue of streets which are almost exclusively occupied by tenements is lengthy, but noteworthy among them are York Street, French Street (Mercer Street Upper), Cuffe Street, Clarendon Street, Bride Street, Clanbrassil Street, Francis Street, Coombe, Meath Street, South Earl Street, Cork Street and Chamber Street, Bridgefoot Street, Cook Street, and along Usher's Quay and Usher's Island. The most conspicuous blank areas on the south side are the Bull Alley Iveagh Trust scheme, and the Coombe, and Plunket Street schemes (Chapter 4), which appear as very small oases in a desert of decay.

On the north side (Figure 5.7) extensive areas of decayed housing stretch along Blackhall Place to North Brunswick Street, to the huge expanse of the former Gardiner estate (Chapter 8). The entire area between Mayor Street and Sheriff Street in the north docks is now decayed. The huge number of northside streets with large concentrations of 'tenements condemned as dangerous' include Gloucester Street, Railway Street (Mecklenburgh Street), Marlborough Street, Gardiner Street Lower, Paradise Row, Denmark Street, Blessington Street, Dorset Street, and very numerously in Dominick Street and Henrietta Street. The bright spots in the northside map are around the former notorious Ormond Market area, and Church Street, now cleared and resettled (see Figures 4.3, 8.9; Plate 8.7)

It was very clear to the authors that the continued migration of 'almost every citizen of substance' to the suburbs, and the consequent subdivision of one-

---

[132] *Dublin Civic Survey* (1925), p. 49.
[133] Ibid., p. 44.
[134] Ibid., p. 60.
[135] Ibid., pp. 62, 60.

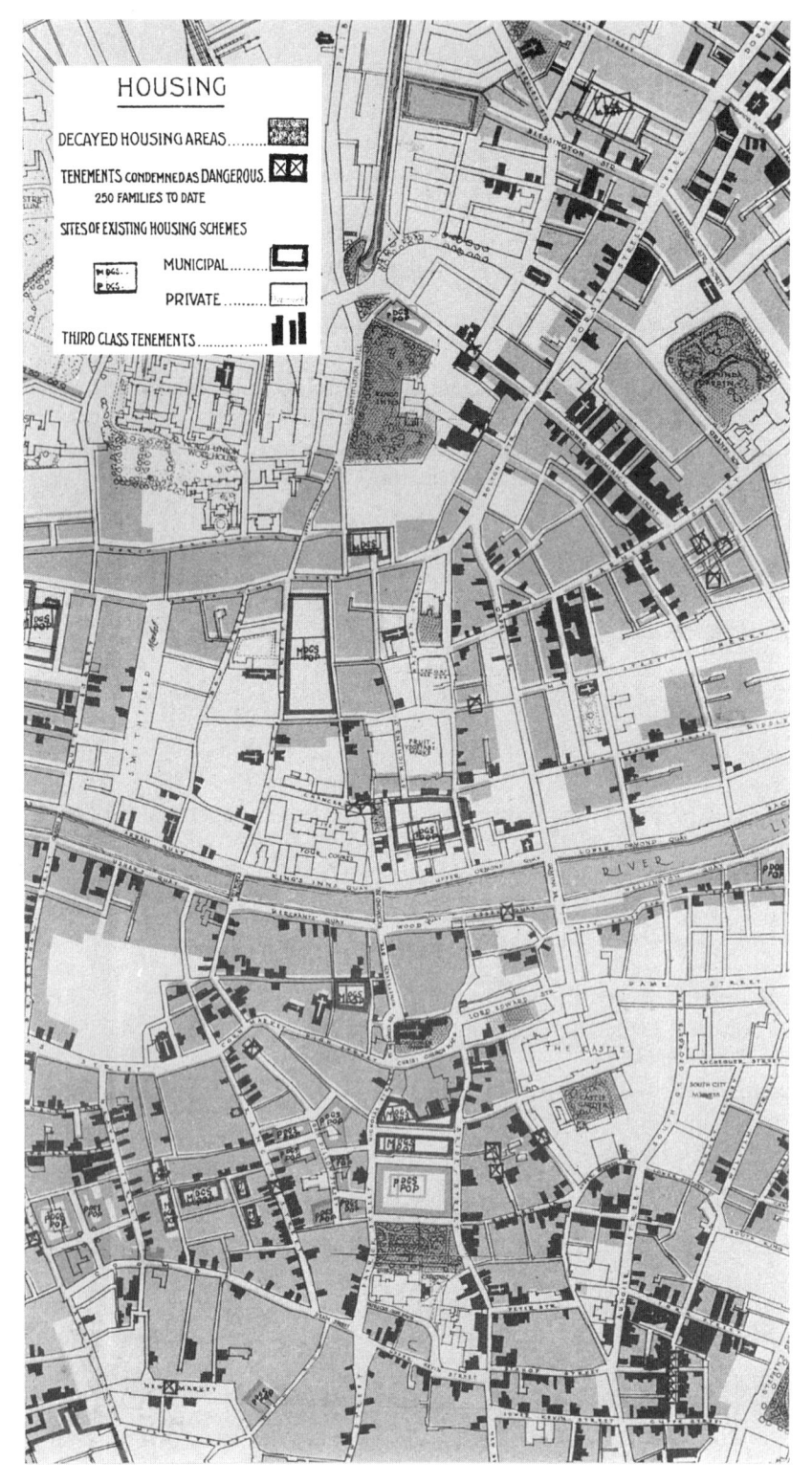

Figure 5.7 Central city, showing decayed housing areas (shaded), third class tenements (black), and tenements condemned as dangerous (X), *Dublin Civic Survey*, housing map, 1925

family homes was ever more trenchantly 'the dominant factor in the whole problem as things are, and as they may continue to be'.[135]

The dilemma of whether to rehouse in the city, through remodelling of tenement houses and building on cleared sites, or a brave new start on the outskirts, widely debated since the 1903 Mansion House conference at least, was squarely faced by the Civics Institute. By 1925 expectations as to what comprised 'minimal tenement provision' had risen to at least two rooms, with 'sufficient cooking and individual sanitary accommodation'. To rely on refurbishment, which may first appear a cheap and reasonable option, to provide for a significant fraction of all who required rehousing, or to build on vacant city sites, could be eliminated on grounds of cost alone. To ensure even a modest rental, new flat blocks would need to be four or five stories, the very type of dwelling which was 'not suitable for the better class workman'.[136] Having established to their own satisfaction the links between high density and high mortality, and having argued the pressing need for more open spaces, O'Rourke, Abercrombie and their colleagues could now hardly advocate building on city sites.[137]

In its place there was the suburban option, a possibility which 'has changed the subject of housing from a hopeless study into a wonderful science. It is comparable to the glowing dawn after a threatening twilight – a step towards the social millenium'.[138] Dublin seemed ideally suited to exploit this 'new' town planning trend, as its current 'physical state readily lends itself to a limitless development for suburban housing for all classes'.[139] Striking contrasts were drawn between life in the city, and the suburban dream. The 'inevitable surroundings' of even good city dwellings were 'the public-house and the street corner, and the paved thoroughfare as a playground for the children'. The 'traditional, but regrettable, attachment to congested surroundings' of city slum dwellers was a minor irritant, which would not be allowed stand in the way of progress.[140] In the suburbs truly civilised living was possible: 'where the father has a little plot for gardening, the mother a space for drying clothes, and the children in the garden are immune from traffic dangers'. The inexorable conclusion is that 'the first environment is a slum, the second a home'.[141]

The key to opening up the suburbs for mass housing was a total remodelling in the transportation network, with an improved 'circular non-stop tramway system' and the extension of the new motor 'bus services, rather than the terminus system already in existence.[142] Some suburban sites, accessible by public transport, were already in the ownership of the Corporation and plans were well advanced, such as in Marino (see Figure 8.12). Glasnevin, including Violet Hill,

[136] Ibid., p. 69.
[137] Ibid., p. 61.
[138] Ibid., p. 58.
[139] Ibid., p. 59.
[140] Ibid., p. 58.
[141] Ibid., p. 69.
[142] Ibid., p. 59.

was a particularly hopeful district, with ambitious plans (later drastically revised) for mass state housing. Within the city there had been few new initiatives since the 1914 Housing Inquiry, so that Figure 5.3 (with most of the schemes in planning completed by 1925) continues to be a fair reflection of progress. Commitments had already been made to certain city-centre schemes, and in any case the total abandonment of city sites was unlikely to prove politically possible, so that 'a combination of the central, on a limited scale, and the suburban methods, with the ultimate hope of eliminating the former' was proposed.[143]

In the ideal world dreamt of by the authors of the Civic Survey 'towns will cease to be places of residence at all, and will be merely used as convenient centres for work and business', but in the meantime something had to be done to 'mitigate their disadvantages'.[144] Investment in small open spaces and playgrounds was upheld for the same good reason proffered for investment in improved housing: to promote 'actual physical efficiency' by providing 'the prime necessities of healthy life – fresh air and sunshine'.[145] The most densely populated parts of the city had very few public gardens or play areas; the widespread dereliction presented in Figure 5.2 was viewed as providing innumerable opportunities for small, immediately accessible and well-tended open spaces, opening up 'lungs' in the midst of congestion, at least pending the final extinction of city dwelling.

Conclusion

The most striking difference exists between the 1876 identification of 'black spots' and 'fever nests' by Dr Mapother, on behalf of the Corporation (Chapter 4, Figure 4.1), and the visionary city-region plan of Abercrombie, Kelly and Kelly (published 1922). The garden suburbs and town planning movements transformed the context within which the city's slum problem was to be addressed, while the more direct correlation of public health with housing (not just sanitary) conditions allowed new understandings on the social responsibilities of the state to take firmer root. The lowering of TB rates required close interference in domestic matters, backed by legislation which would have been unthinkable a few decades earlier. Within a British Isles context the Dublin slum problem was a well-documented scandal; the 1925 Civic Survey is the strongest indictment of previous half-hearted efforts, while articulating one of the major challenges facing the new state. The attraction of the suburban idyll is understandable. But the hardest questions, those relating to grossly inadequate and insecure incomes, at the heart of the grinding slum problem, have not been fairly posed. And Dublin dockers and street dealers, charwomen and beggars, porters and carmen are unlikely to find the answers waiting for them in the wilds of Cabra or Glasnevin.

[143] Ibid., p. 59.
[144] Ibid., p. 16.
[145] Ibid.

6

IDLE VAGRANTS AND STURDY BEGGARS: THE STATE'S RESPONSE

Paupers are entitled to relief in the event they become destitute, without regard to circumstance of previous residence or to the length of time they may be resident. By 10 Vic: Cap 31 guardians are required to give relief to all persons in and out of the Workhouse without reference to time or residence. Time and residence have application to localizing the charge, either general as to the union at large, or particular as to a certain electoral division.[1]

INTRODUCTION

The environmental issues of slum housing and infectious disease were closely related to the question of poor relief. As practically every interested party concurred, the scandalous health and living conditions were only the external evidence of grossly insufficient and precarious income. Where the family income was barely sufficient to meet the urgent needs of food and rent – clothing was well down the list – there was no margin for 'putting by' for the inevitable period of slack work, or for sickness, injury, old age or confinement. It was the irregularity and insufficiency of income which led to the pitiable situation whereby poverty and disease were found 'mutual cause and effect' and those attending the city dispensary 'though they procure medicine, cannot perhaps procure food; though they get our advice, cannot perhaps follow it'.[2] So too lack of regular and sufficient income excluded those who were worst housed from gaining direct advantage from the slum clearance and new housing projects of the later nineteenth century.

Urban slums were depicted as 'nests of fever and contagion', the arrival and departure of 'carriers' of deadly disease both intensifying local distress and ensuring its spread, threatening even the well-to-do. The progress of the 1818–19 cholera epidemic throughout Ireland was unequivocally linked to the movements of 'strolling beggars and labourers traversing the country in quest of employment',[3] while the influx of famine refugees into the slums of British cities

---

[1] Minutes of the North Dublin Union, 5 January 1848 (hereafter NDU Minutes).
[2] T.C. Speer, 'Medical Report containing an Inquiry into the Causes and Character of the Diseases of the Lower Orders in Dublin', *Dublin Hospital Reports*, vol. lll (1822), pp. 167–8, (hereafter 'Diseases of the Lower Orders').
[3] *First Report from the Select Committee on the State of Disease, and Condition of the Labouring Poor, in Ireland, 1819*, appendix p. 80.

during and following the holocaust of 1845–49 created great concern. High levels of mobility were regarded as morally as well as medically reprehensible, with vagrants and vagabonds equated with parasites living off 'respectable' society, while mendicancy was a disease which 'infested' the streets.

Some parties equated beggars with stealing, and other parties vehemently maintained that 'they are beggars, and nothing but beggars', guilty of no other crime.[4] Even among those who maintained the beggar's innocence, there was an underlying presumption that such a lifestyle was only part of a downward spiral, with 'Theft and Robbery, the finale Resources of an unsuccessful Beggar' (sic).[5] No hope at all was held out for the beggar's offspring unless removed from that circle, with claims that very few beggars were the children of beggars, 'for of the children of beggars the girls mostly turn out prostitutes, and the boys robbers'.[6] The use of children in begging was despaired of, with claims by one authority that 'the mendicant tribe' was the most profligate of all, maximising the number of their offspring purposely as they 'estimate their riches by their children, as affording pretexts for their trade, and claims for charity'.[7]

While important distinctions were made between vagrants and mendicants, and between those who followed such lifestyles as a 'professional' occupation and those for whom it was a temporary response to a period of acute distress, it was the visibility of such persons that led to public concern. Their 'loathsome appearance' and importunate alms-seeking, as they harassed the well-to-do, often under the slim pretext of selling some trifle or offering some menial service, made them difficult to ignore. They were also perceived by some observers as a threat to civil order through the pressure of their numbers.[8]

The records of the early nineteenth-century poverty debate in Ireland also reflect the huge gulf between officialdom and the local situation, where two utterly different perspectives were held. A 'Protestant approach to labour' founded on an ideology of hard labour and the economic needs of society has been argued by Max Weber (1930)[9], and certainly English Protestant moralists were obsessed with the deleterious effects of alms-giving on the recipient, on the economy, and on society. Among the Irish Catholic population however, the majority of whom were barely subsisting in the period 1815–1845, a very different value system dominated. Charity was recognised as a duty to the donor and all beggars regarded as deserving of help, 'the Popish peasant is taught that poverty confers a degree of merit both upon him who suffers under it and upon the person who

---

[4] 'On the state of Vagrancy and Mendicity, and the Laws relating thereto', *Poor Inquiry (Ireland)* 1836, appendix (c), part II, p. 140a*, (hereafter 'State of Vagrancy').
[5] Proceedings of the Corporation instituted for the relief of the poor and for punishing Vagabonds and Sturdy Beggars in the County of the City of Dublin, (hereafter House of Industry Proceedings), 9 March 1773; 30 April 1773.
[6] 'State of Vagrancy', *Poor Inquiry (Ireland) 1836*, p. 41a*.
[7] Speer, *Diseases of the Lower Orders* (1822), p. 193.
[8] Ibid., p. 168.
[9] Max Weber, *The Protestant Ethic and the Spirit of Capitalism* (London, 1930).

relieves him'.[10] The calls of religion and common humanity were fulfilled by a generous sharing, and coldly weighing the consequences of one's charity was thus unthinkable. The sociological reasons for such an attitude have been argued by T.P. O'Neill (1973) who claims that where land was often held in rundale, in joint tenancies or in minute holdings, 'self sufficiency' was unheard of, with activities such as booleying and harvesting made possible only through co-operation. The very thin line between 'getting by' and disaster was too well known for many to exclude the beggar from their table, and for large numbers begging was simply part of the yearly cycle without which they would have starved.[11]

The early nineteenth-century British Isles response to the issues of vagrancy, mendicancy and the destitute poor involved a thrust towards a comprehensive policy of confinement and punishment to suppress itinerant wandering for which no justification other than wanderlust could be offered, and a search for controlling mechanisms by which charitable and public assistance could be limited to the 'deserving' and 'helpless' poor. It was part of an urgent international debate, with the merits of poor law systems in Edinburgh, Bath, Hamburg, Munich, Amsterdam, Paris, New York and elsewhere scrutinised and compared with the system proposed for or prevailing in Dublin.[12] As the principal gateway to Britain, and the first port of call for many entering or returning to the country, with a large and highly visible destitute population, and a small but well-travelled upper class, Dublin was thoroughly integrated into the mainstream debate on the formulation of poor relief policy. The ceaseless influx of destitute poor compounded its notorious health and housing situation throughout the century, ensuring that the question of poor relief was always a matter of grave importance, with claims into the twentieth century that Dublin operated as 'the rest house or alms house to which people broken in health, character or fortune come from all over Ireland, to shelter or hide themselves or to take advantage of its numerous hospitals and almost innumerable over-lapping charities'.[13] From 1877 the General Register Office included in its annual summary for Dublin both the overall death rate and a second 'truer' figure excluding the deaths of all persons 'admitted into public institutions from localities outside the Dublin Registration

[10] John Graham, 'An Historical Poem on the State of Ireland' (1820), quoted in T.P. O'Neill, 'The Catholic Church and Relief of the Poor 1815–45', *Archivium Hibernicum, Irish Historical Records*, 31 (1973), p. 133.

[11] Ibid., pp. 132–134.

[12] *Observations on the House of Industry, Dublin and on the Plans of the Association for Suppressing Mendicity in that City* (Dublin, 1818), p. 15 (hereafter *Observations on the House of Industry*); *Report of a Committee Appointed by the Society for the Prevention of Pauperism in the City of New York on the Expediency of Erecting an Institution for the Reformation of Juvenile Delinquents* (New York, 1823); *Arguments in Proof of the Necessity and Practicability of Suppressing Street Begging in the City of Dublin; illustrated by some Important Facts respecting other Institutions which have been Established in Other Places for the Purpose* (Dublin, 1817).

[13] P.C. Cowan, *Report on Dublin Housing* (Dublin, 1918), p. 14.

District'.[14] While such action was taken to try and put the bravest light on appalling mortality figures, it is also indicative of the general hostility with which the city rate-payers regarded the influx of sick and destitute rural poor, a flow they could do little to stem. Once presenting themselves as fit subjects for the workhouse or hospital, place of birth or proof of settlement was not an issue.[15] The flow of sick and poor to Dublin was just part of the general migration to the largest urban centre in nineteenth century Ireland. As is evident from census returns (Figure 6.1) a large proportion of the Dublin population was born elsewhere: in 1881 at least 38% of the inhabitants of the city and country returned birthplaces other than Dublin, with the neighbouring counties especially providing large numbers of female domestic staff and Britain contributing male military and administrative personnel. Tackling the flow of destitute poor and the increase in pauperism was a daunting if not impossible task. The Civic Survey (1925) brings together the questions of statutory poor relief, health and housing conditions in its note that over 39% of the city's population were paupers: 5,338 workhouse inmates (James' Street), and 121,135 on outdoor relief, out of an estimated total population (1922) of 327,000, 'and most hospitals filled with cases from the slums and tenement dwellings'.[16] Such a situation, over a century in the making, was unsustainable on economic grounds alone.

The kind of questions which dominated the public health and housing debate were reformulated in the parallel discussion on the suppression of vagrancy and mendicancy and the relief of the destitute. One current of opinion insisted that it was the 'more than culpable negligence of the upper classes to the primary wants of the poor' that had led to the massively expensive work houses and fever hospitals, maintaining that 'there are few of their inmates who cannot trace much of their present destitution to the widowhood, orphanage and debility produced by diseases having their origin in the unhealthy conditions of their habitations'.[17] Pleas for reform in one area were thus argued on the basis of the benefits which would extend to other areas, such as the claim that 'improved dwellings mean less illness, and consequently less pauperism'.[18]

As with health and housing, the poor relief debate was initiated by private individuals, very often the same medical experts, clergymen and philanthropists who wrote with such perception from the 1790s into the 1840s on the condition of the poor. The creation of suitable administrative machinery was central to the question of policing and relieving the poor, with the parish structure which had

---

[14] *Yearly Summary of the Weekly Returns of Births and Deaths in Dublin, including the suburban districts of Rathmines, Donnybrook, Blackrock, and Kingstown, and in the towns of Belfast, Cork, Limerick, Londonderry, Waterford, Galway and Sligo* (1877), p. iii.
[15] see NDU Minutes, 5 January 1848.
[16] *The Dublin Civic Survey Report*, prepared by Horace T. O'Rourke and the Dublin Civic Survey Committee for the Civics Institute of Ireland vol. II, (Liverpool, 1925).
[17] Thomas Willis, *Facts connected with the Social and Sanitary Condition of the Working Classes in the City of Dublin* (Dublin, 1845), p. 53.
[18] Charles Cameron, *Report of Public Health Committee for 1909* (Dublin, 1910), p. 93.

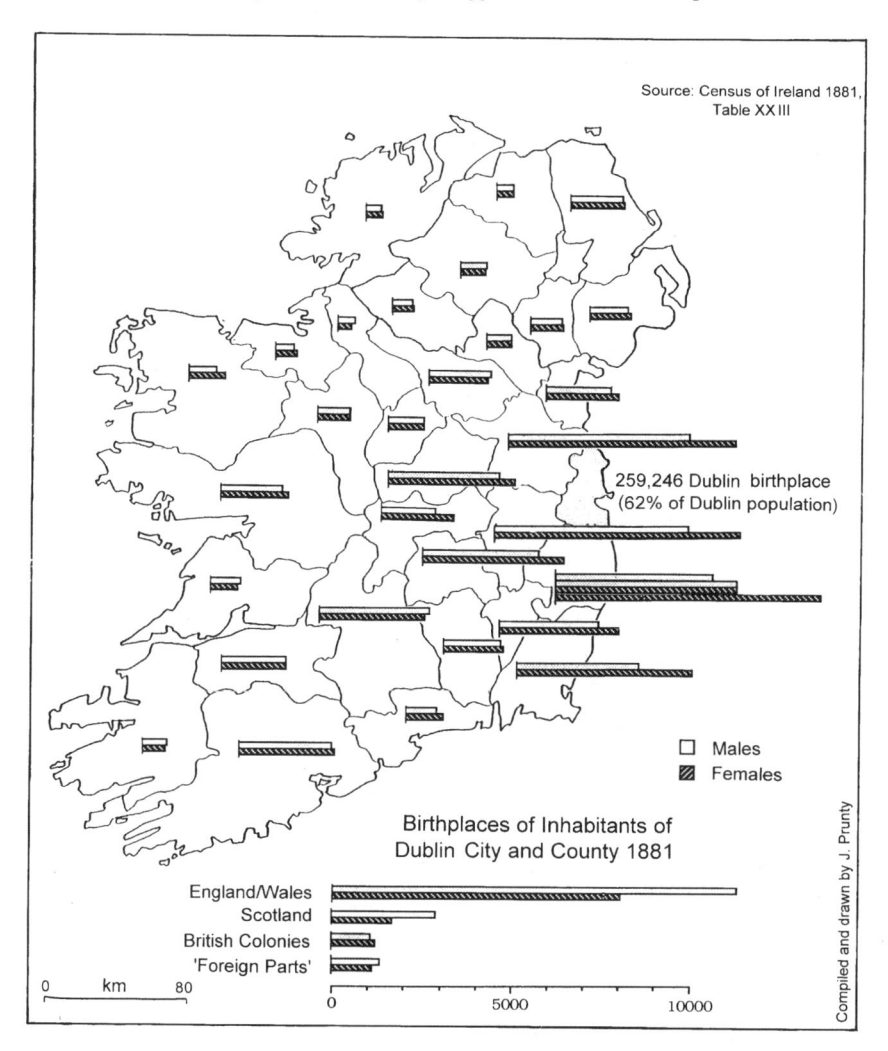

Figure 6.1 Places of birth, Dublin 1881.

proved so inadequate in dealing with the sanitary problems of the early nineteenth century urban slums, similarly ineffectual in the face of large-scale and intense distress. The state's initial response was to minimise rather than extend expensive interference, in keeping with the political philosophy of *laissez faire*, hopeful that voluntary action would at least control if not resolve the situation. The extension of the English Poor Law Amendment Act (1834) to Ireland in 1838 brought enormous changes to the country at literally one stroke: the creation of a class of citizen entirely new to Ireland, the 'pauper'; a totally new layer of local civil administration in the form of the poor law guardians; a new centralised authority, the Poor Law Commissioners, which was to lead to the

Local Government Board for Ireland (1872); a new tax on property, raised and spent locally, and an important new geographical unit, the poor law union, divided into electoral divisions based on property values, and later the basis of dispensary districts. Although founded for the express purpose of raising and administering statutory poor relief, the powers and duties of poor law boards were to quickly expand into the areas of sanitation and health services. Beyond the jurisdiction of town authorities the boards of guardians were responsible for implementing the nuisance removal acts (1848, 1855, 1860), the vagrant act (1847) and the common lodging houses acts (1851, 1853, 1860), while they also operated as burial boards (1856), and sewer authorities (1865). Under the public health acts of 1874 and 1878 the poor law guardians became the rural sanitary authority, while they were also enabled to undertake labourers' dwellings improvement schemes under legislation passed 1883–1896.[19] While many of the supplementary powers of the local poor law boards lay unused, at least initially, the boards (under central government pressure) were to become the prime movers in the battle against rural slum conditions from the 1880s through to independence. In the case of Dublin city, the Corporation was the local sanitary and public health authority. However, the boards of guardians of the North Dublin and South Dublin unions were responsible for the statutory relief of the Dublin poor including the municipal area, funded by taxes on property raised throughout their districts (both rural and urban portions), and for sanitary and public health matters in the areas beyond the municipal boundary. No other single nineteenth century legislative provision can compare in terms of mass impact and long term change with the arrival of the Poor Law to Ireland.

As with statistics dealing with the housing and mortality situation, the collection of reliable data on those seeking relief, and their classification according to need, was vital but highly contentious. Determining the number of infant deaths per 1,000 births which could be regarded as acceptable, or the minimum cubic feet of air per person necessary to good health, however, was simple in comparison with separating the mendicants from the vagrants, the 'deserving' from the 'undeserving'. The task is further complicated when account is taken of the very different perspectives held by those providing the information, and those recording, collating, and analysing the data. There were also substantial shifts in what was regarded as 'acceptable' standards of discipline, nutrition and clothing over the period, where for example, compulsion and physical restraint fell out of fashion, making comparisons over time a contentious matter. The greater sophistication of data collection and analysis was also part of the move 'from charity to social work', with increasing professionalism among those working in the city slums and in poor relief institutions, and the evolution of a body of theory and of literature to support those undertaking reforms.

The role of the state *vis-à-vis* private charities, always an area of some tension, was of enormous consequence in nineteenth century Ireland. Not alone were

---

[19] Virginia Crossman, *Local Government in Nineteenth Century Ireland* (Belfast, 1994), pp. 48–52.

proponents of *laissez faire* political philosophy drawn up against those urging more active state interference, but the debate was permeated at every level by political and religious considerations, which became especially highly-charged from the 1850s (Chapter 7). One of the first initiatives of Saorstát Éireann was an inquiry into the relief of the sick and destitute poor (1928), which explored the role of the poor law in relation to charitable societies, recognising the 'considerable extent' to which such operations 'relieve the rate-payer and tax-payer of financial burdens they could not otherwise escape' and hoping that relations between both state and charities would be that of 'cordial co-operation in achieving a common end'.[20]

Beggars and Vagrants, Dublin City 1800–1838

In the period 1800–1838 the questions of vagrancy, mendicancy and relief of the destitute poor in Dublin became urgent at times of rebellion and whenever infectious disease reached epidemic proportions. However, because of the proximity of the city slums to the wealthy residential districts and the commercial heart of the city (see Figure 2.9), the scandal of the famished and desperate readily spilled over to the very hall-doors and shop-fronts of respectable society, even at times of apparent 'normality'. The long-established tradition among the country poor of resorting to Dublin led to the oft-repeated complaint from the civic authorities that 'this city is become the common receptacle of objects disfigured and frightful, as well as pretending to be miserable, from all parts of the kingdom'.[21] Visitors testified from a different perspective, such as John Gamble (1820) who considered Dublin an 'inexpressibly graceful' city, a copy of London, but 'more beautiful, in truth, in miniature than the gigantic original'; he regarded the large numbers supported by alms as a testimony to the charity of the citizens of Dublin, adding that in London, 'there is much, much suffering, much sorrow, much want in every quarter, in every lane, and in every street – but there are *few* beggars – if there were many they would *starve*' [*sic*].[22] Whatever about 'the maimed, the halt and the blind', the deaf and dumb, the sick and the imbecile, for whom special provision could reasonably be promoted as their total numbers would necessarily be small, it was the apparently limitless army of destitute but able-bodied poor which frightened the rate-payers and civil authorities of Dublin.

At the opening of the nineteenth century there was already a workhouse in the city, established by an act of the Irish Parliament in 1703, maintained by a tax on sedan chairs and on city houses, and the first state provision for the poor in the country.[23] It was located at St James' Gate in the south-western quarter,

---

[20] *Report of the Commission on the Relief of the Sick and Destitute Poor, including the Insane Poor* (Dublin, 1928), p. 84, (hereafter *Poor Relief Commission*).
[21] Lord Mayor, October 1766, Gilbert, *Calendar of Ancient Records of Dublin*, xi, pp. 523–5
[22] John Gamble, *Sketches of History, Politics and Manners in Dublin and the North of Ireland in 1810* (London, 1826), pp. 22, 90.
[23] Joseph Robins, *The Lost Children, A Study of Charity Children in Ireland 1700–1900*, (Dublin, 1980), p. 8.

and from 1838 was to become part of the South Dublin Union workhouse complex (see Figure 2.7). Although initially intended to relieve the destitute of all classes within the city and to punish vagabonds, it gradually became a national repository for unwanted children, known as the Foundling Hospital.[24]

In 1772 'The Corporation Instituted for the Relief of the Poor and for Punishing Vagabonds and Sturdy Beggars in the County of the City of Dublin' commenced its mission of withdrawing from the streets 'objects offensive to the Sight'.[25] In the first stage of the campaign the parishes were required to draw up 'lists of Helpless Poor' who were then granted badges and licenses entitling them to beg; the citizens would thus be 'secured from the Cheats of the Imposter, who stands detected by the want of those credentials'.[26] It was also intended as a means of ascertaining 'the number and wants of the real Poor', as a 'well-grounded estimate' was essential before embarking on building premises for their 'reception and labour'.[27] The system of badging proved unworkable from the outset, not least because of the lack of backing at the parochial level, with many more claiming to be eligible than the parishes had recommended, and after one year's trial it was decided to resort to an 'indoor' system, 'where the helpless might be maintained at less cost, and the idle trained to Industry'.[28] A 'House of Industry' was opened in November 1773 on the northern edge of the built-up area, in Channel Row (North Brunswick Street), the first of several institutional buildings for the poor, which were to act as a barrier to upper class residential development in this sector (see Plate 2.3). While initially reliant on private subscription including charity sermons, in 1776 it received its first parliamentary grant of £3,000. In 1813, with 2,511 paupers on the premises, the grant was over £52,000; over the ten years ending January 1816 the annual parliamentary grant averaged £41,150.[29]

From the outset the House of Industry advertised itself as a 'humane and National institution' as so many of the city's poor originated elsewhere.[30] However, it regarded its responsibility to clear the streets as limited to a radius of two miles from Dublin Castle, a circuit which was later 'stretched to the confines of the county' becoming impossible to police.[31] Its all-inclusive character was also fostered by the neglect of other urban districts (excepting only Cork and Waterford and Limerick) to build 'houses of industry' to confine their local beggars, while occasional forays against all 'foreign beggars' in towns such as Belfast further swelled the Dublin numbers and were greatly begrudged.[32] A

[24] Ibid.
[25] House of Industry Proceedings, 9 March 1773; 30 April 1773.
[26] Ibid., 30 March 1773; 30 April 1773.
[27] Ibid., 30 April 1773.
[28] Ibid., volume I, 1772–75 *passim*; *Observations on the House of Industry* (1818), p. 1.
[29] Ibid., pp. 6, 15.
[30] House of Industry Proceedings, 30 April 1773.
[31] Ibid., 23 April 1821.
[32] *Observations on the House of Industry*, (1818) p. 6.

'great measure' of the 10,329 paupers who 'forced their way' into the institution in 1815 were described as 'adventurers from the kingdom at large'.[33] The national character of the institution is further revealed in the anxiety among the administrators to remove from the Dublin district those who had completed an involuntary three-month confinement in the mendicant cells. Those who wished to return to their former residence, 'whether in England or the country parts of Ireland' were to be speeded on their way, 'the passage of the former shall be paid for and from one shilling to half-a-crown shall be given as a *viaticum* to the latter' while a loaf was also to be given to each, 'provided their conduct has entitled them to such indulgence'.[34]

In the year 1800 as fever raged the situation in the House of Industry was near crisis. The dietary was made more repulsive 'to repel *those capable of labour* who in that year of scarcity were pressing to be inmates' (*sic*); the riots which broke out over the 'lowness of the diet' required 'the interference of the military . . . to inforce subordination'.[35] Continued efforts were made to ensure the unattractiveness of the relief on offer, with strict orders that 'no part of the funds of the Institution to be applied to the Clothing of the Healthy Poor, excepting disgraceful dresses for the Idle and Slothful, and premium dresses as rewards for the Diligent and Industrious'.[36] Strict discipline was enforced both within and without; twelve 'Outside Beadles' were employed 'to attend the Cart for taking up Beggars' as well as the 'Carriage' for conveying patients to Hardwicke Fever Hospital at least three times a week and to keep order at the meals, while the head beadle was 'to inflict or see inflicted such punishments on the idle and refractory' as may be ordered by the authorities.[37] It is clear that the 'indiscriminate admission' of all in need, along with the involuntary admission of beggars, collected three times each week from the streets by the team of beadles and carted back to the institution, resulted in anarchy, and following overcrowding crises in 1815 and 1816 the governing body of the institution determined to wash its hands of the troublesome classes. The annual report for 1818 reports approvingly that the 'aged and infirm now fill the places formerly preoccupied by the vagrant and healthy' and consequently the institution is now enjoying 'more health, cleanliness, sobriety and order'.[38]

In the period 1820–38 the character of the House of Industry became more and more removed from its founding inspiration as a place of incarceration for mendicants and more and more taken over by the care of the aged and the development of the hospitals associated with it. In 1820 the powers of the governor

---

[33] Ibid., (1818) p. 24.
[34] *General Rules, By-Laws and Regulations for the House of Industry with the Duties of the Officers &c. Confirmed by the Board* (Dublin, 1813), p. 9, (hereafter *House of Industry, General Rules*).
[35] *Observations on the House of Industry* (1818), p. 3.
[36] *House of Industry, General Rules* (1813), p. 4.
[37] Ibid., pp. 7, 23.
[38] *Observations on the House of Industry* (1818), p. 6.

were enlarged, and efforts to re-establish the House of Industry as a place of committal for 'sturdy beggars' were made. The police were given orders to 'arrest and transmit such cases of mendicancy as may appear most flagrant' and 24 cells were prepared for their reception, the lower tier for men and the upper tier for women. Here the windows were boarded up, the bedsteads replaced with straw beds, means of restraint introduced, and a punitive regime of 'hard labour, seclusion and moderate food' put in place.[39] But this had little impact on the overall functioning of the House of Industry, by that time providing asylum for 1,300 men and women classed as 'aged and infirm', or 'incurable lunatics' and 'idiots'. There were also 360 poor girls in the adjoining Bedford Asylum (1806), a penitentiary for boys at Smithfield (closed 1821) and three progressive hospitals 'under the government and deemed to be appendages of the House of Industry': the Hardwicke Fever hospital (1803), Richmond Surgical Hospital (1811), and the Whitworth Medical Hospital (1817), each named after the Lord Lieutenant in office at the time of its foundation. It was also closely involved in the neighbouring state-funded Richmond Lunatic Asylum (1814), to which it sent those of its own 'lunatics' for whom a cure was hoped, receiving in return those whom the asylum deemed to be incurable.[40] At committee level the demands of the Lord Lieutenant to receive 150 'sturdy beggars' were discussed and costed but there was no real desire to involve the institution once more in such a thankless task, while to admit more of the 'indigent poor who are daily crowding about the gate' would require a decrease in patient numbers, which was not an option.[41]

The minute books of the mid 1830s make it clear that the administrators, a governor assisted by a committee of seven 'visitors', had withdrawn from any active involvement, with board meetings repeatedly abandoned as no-one bar the register (a paid official) attended; the governor, in receipt of an annual salary of £400, confined his concern to securing his own domestic comfort, such as railing off a small garden for his family's use and replacing the household privy with a new water-closet.[42] The register settled the accounts by the expedient of calling to the private residences of two 'visitors' to secure their signatures on the cheques. Far from being in the front line of the battle against mendicancy, the House of Industry merely provided token resistance to justify its receipt of parliamentary funds. In 1833 it was maintained that there were no more than 24 cells, although an average of 80 beggars per week were committed.[43] The chief constable claimed that the system in operation was an utter failure, as committal to the House of Industry did not operate in any sense as a deterrent; 'they go there quite cheerfully, knowing they will not be long confined. I have known persons break lamps, and valuable panes of glass in a shop windows, on purpose

---

[39] House of Industry Proceedings, 30 October 1820.
[40] Ibid., 29 September, 3 October, 12 October 1820.
[41] Ibid., 19, 30 October, 27 November 1820; 22 January, 23 April 1821.
[42] Ibid., 5 May 1834.
[43] Francis White, *Report and Observations on the State of the Poor of Dublin* (Dublin, 1833), p. 22, (hereafter *Report on the State of the Poor*).

to be sent to gaol, and do the same again the very night they are set at liberty'.[44] George Nicholls, one of the architects of the English workhouse system, dismissed the appellation 'houses of industry' as nonsense, 'there being little work done in any of them, and in some none at all'. In practice they are 'places for the reception and maintenance of a certain number of poor persons, generally aged or infirm, and idiots, and lunatics'.[45]

The Association for the Suppression of Mendicity in Dublin, 1817

Despite abdicating its responsibilities towards the 'sturdy beggars' in favour of treating the sick poor, the House of Industry remained the official state-sponsored instrument in the struggle against mendicancy up until the Poor Law (Ireland) Act, 1838. The overcrowding crisis of 1815–16 which marked the end of compulsory committal on a large scale to the House of Industry, was however followed in 1817 by a series of public meetings to create 'The Association for the Suppression of Mendicity in Dublin'. Claiming that not alone had 'the evil of mendicity' increased to an alarming extent due to the ending of the Napoleonic wars and the disbanding of large portions of the army and navy, followed by 'two years of almost unparalleled scarcity', but that mendicity now possessed 'a character, form and virulence which appeared to place it beyond the reach of cure'.[46] The city, it was claimed, 'presented a spectacle at once afflicting and disgusting to the feelings of its inhabitants', with 'crowds of unfortunate and clamorous beggars' frequently carrying about 'in their persons and garments the seeds of contagious disease'.[47] Unable to force the House of Industry to exercise its powers of 'coercing the sturdy beggar', this association of citizens embarked upon a major house-to-house 'voluntary' collection to fund its campaign, which resulted in a disappointing £1,600. The committee then resorted to 'the ingenious expedient' of parading the mendicants through Dublin, described by one of the organisers as 'a quiet and well-ordered procession through the streets' through which they might 'appeal in person to the hearts and understanding of their more fortunate fellow-creatures'; a contemporary observer reported on how the procession halted in front of the houses of such as refused to subscribe, 'and set up a shout of execration' by which means the rich were frightened into liberality.[48] £9,507 was collected, sufficient to clear the streets of beggars for one

---

[44] 'State of Vagrancy', *Poor Inquiry (Ireland) 1836*, p. 41a*.
[45] George Nicholls, *First Report, Poor Laws (Ireland), 1836* in *Three Reports by George Nicholls Esq. to HM Principal Secretary of State for the Home Department* (London, 1838), p. 14, (hereafter *First Report*).
[46] *Report of the Association for the Suppression of Mendicity in Dublin for the Year 1818* (hereafter *Mendicity Report*), p. 1.
[47] Ibid., p. 2.
[48] Ibid., pp. 10–11; John Douglas, *Observations on the Necessity of a Legal Provision for the Irish Poor, as the Means of Improving the Condition of the Irish People and Protecting the British Landlord, Farmer and Labourer* (London, 1828), p. 24.

year, through actively encouraging one half to leave the city, and providing the remainder with work.[49]

The Mendicity Association made a very simple two-way division: those who were unable to work at any employment due to infancy, age or infirmity, and all other mendicants whose 'rooted habits of idleness, vagrancy and vice' could only be reformed by hard labour.[50] However, there were many constraints governing the kinds of work provided: it could not interfere with 'the ordinary channels of industry', the return had to be far below the usual rates of wages so that any alternative to Mendicity employment would be preferred, and it had to be adequately supervised to ensure no slacking.[51] A complex parish-based system was envisaged, governed by district committees; each parish was divided into 'walks' to be covered by one 'visitor' whose duty was to ascertain the truth of individual testimonies, which were then brought before the 'subcommittee of investigation'. The 'subcommittee of employment' provided the raw materials for work and inspected progress, the 'subcommittee of supply' distributed tickets with the rations specified, while health, education and finance were also in the care of subcommittees, so that any poor person applying to her local Mendicity Association was faced with an immense amount of interviewing and form-filling before reaching the ticket-distribution stage, which was also subjected to further checks and counter-checks before any relief was in hand.[52] This bureaucratic obstacle-course was eased somewhat by reducing the number of parish committees from ten to four, and the development of a central repository in Hawkins Street, although each local committee was also expected to have its own stores.

The first intention was that the labour executed in return for food would be carried out by the poor in their own homes, with one daily inspection of the work in hand to ensure no abuses of the system. However, aside from the administrative difficulties attached to such a system, there was also a decided movement towards institutionalising relief. Case histories of poor relief structures in both Britain and continental Europe, notably Belgium, France and Prussia were cited in the move towards eliminating mendicancy by more thorough control.[53] It was a lot easier to work at 'reclaiming' and 'reforming' the mendicant poor when gathered in a controlled environment, than when allowed free movement through the slums. The first step in breaking such habits was to remove them from the spot of temptation, a dangerous reminder of a 'former easy mode of life', while street life by definition was 'not calculated to effect any moral change'.[54]

[49] Ibid., p. 24.
[50] *Mendicity Report* (1818), p. 5.
[51] *Second Report of the Association for the Suppression of Mendicity in Dublin*, 1819 (hereafter *Second Mendicity Report*) p. 23.
[52] *Mendicity Report* (1818), p. 27.
[53] George Nicholls, *Second Report, Poor Laws (Ireland), 1837* in *Three Reports by George Nicholls Esq. to MH Principal Secretary of State for the Home Department* (London, 1838), pp. 73–74, (hereafter *Second Report*).
[54] *Second Mendicity Report* (1819), p. 5.

The vast majority of Mendicity Association clients were women, and the enterprise favoured for them was spinning yarn, with almost 300 thus occupied in 1819, most of them on the premises at Hawkins Street. Others were employed as cartwomen, soup carriers and scourers, while pulverizing oyster shells for manure was regarded with great favour by the administrators as it required continuous effort but no outlay in machinery. In comparison, sweeping 'the more obscure parts of the city' had mixed success, as whenever supervision slackened the women threw the broom aside, 'the old trade of begging resorted to', and the whole purpose of the exercise was undermined.[55] So too knitting had its drawbacks, as it required some ability if the raw materials were not to be wasted, and 'for females more capable of exertion' was regarded as too soft an occupation.[56] Picking oakum was simpler to oversee, as there was no way in which the raw material (old rope) could be devalued by the paupers, and no tools of any sort were required. Plaiting straw, knitting hearth rugs and making a coarse blanket from cows' hair were also tried, with an occasional effort at more skilled occupations such as lacemaking. Along with monotonous and tiring work, stringent efforts were made to ensure that the standard of food was such that none but the starving would apply. Carts were sent round to the houses of the well-to-do to collect the leftovers, the meat and bones were 'separated as carefully as possible from everything improper, and boiled down with potatoes and other vegetables; the whole was then thoroughly mixed and properly seasoned', and commended not alone for its cheapness but as the very type of food mendicants were accustomed to prepare for themselves.[57] That those who resorted to the Mendicity were in absolute need was unquestionable: one witness Joseph Gabbet, magistrate, spoke of the 'severe labour which they there voluntarily undergo, and the confinement for the whole day to which they submit, for the sake of a miserable allowance and a wretched mess of pottage', proof that they are not 'criminal vagrants'.[58]

Some provision for the poor 'in a settled form' was regarded as the only means 'to prevent them from sallying out, rabid with hunger and infected with contagious disease, produced by poverty, to satisfy their cravings by main force'. Previous to the establishment of the Poor Law in Ireland (1838), parishes were authorised to appoint officers of health, who were 'empowered and required to apprehend all idle poor persons, men, women or children, and all persons who may be found begging or seeking relief, or strolling or wandering as vagabonds' and to see to their removal 'in such manner and to such place as the nature of the case may require'; however, by failing to provide a place to which these persons could be removed, the act was to little effect.[59]

[55] Ibid., p. 5.
[56] *Mendicity Report* (1818), p. 11.
[57] *Second Mendicity Report* (1819), p. 9.
[58] 'State of Vagrancy', *Poor Inquiry (Ireland) 1836*, p. 40a*.
[59] *First Report of Commissioners for Inquiring into the Condition of the Poorer Classes in Ireland*, 1834, Appendix (C), parts l and ll.

The Mendicity Association catered for almost 3,000 clients in its first year of operations (1817–18); in the week ending 31 December 1819 it had 697 clients, of whom 635 were women. It also catered for children, 'born as it were without the pale of society, cradled in misery and nurtured in vice'; in 1819 it had 177 girls on its books, most taught to spin and make nets, 70 to plait straw and read; efforts were made to obliterate 'the traces of the Beggar's Child' from their very appearance.[60] The 'incalculable advantages' which it was claimed to confer on the city were expressed in terms of disease and contagion, reflecting the language used in contemporary slum surveys (Chapter 2): 'To remove the lowest orders, their rags and wretchedness from the other and less forlorn classes, is cutting off the foulest part of a sore, and thus promoting the healing up of the less diseased part'.[61]

The Mendicity was criticised by George Nicholls, for of the 2,047 persons who were inmates on his visit in 1836, 'the far larger portion were seated in idleness. Some of the women and girls were occupied in spinning and knitting, and some in stone-breaking; this last seemed a favourite occupation'. Among the few male inmates a small number were occupied in grinding horse-corn and breaking limestone into gravel; female earnings were capped at 1s 8d per week, male earnings at 2s 6d. While none of the inmates were compelled to work, those who did were charged 1d per day for their subsistence, a further disincentive to exertion, especially considering the back-breaking nature of the work required largely of women.[62]

A perceptive French visitor to Ireland, Alexis de Tocqueville, visited what he termed the Dublin Poor-house in July 1835, but appears to refer to the Mendicity Institute:

A vast edifice sustained annually by voluntary gifts. 1,800 to 2,000 paupers are received there during the day; they receive food, lodging, and when they are capable of it, work. They go to sleep where they can. *The sight inside.* The most hideous and disgusting aspect of destitution. A very long room full of women and children whose infirmities or age prevent them from working. On the floor the paupers are lying down pell-mell like pigs in the mud of their sty. One has difficulty not to step on a half-naked body.

In the left wing, a smaller room full of old or crippled men. They are seated on wooden benches, all turned in the same direction, crowded together as in the pit of a theatre. They do not talk at all, they do not move, they look at nothing, they do not appear to be thinking. They neither expect, fear, nor hope for anything from life. I am mistaken, they are waiting for dinner, which is due in three hours. It is the only pleasure that is left to them, after which they will have nothing more than to die.

Further on are those who are able to work. They are seated on the damp earth. They have small mallets in their hands and are breaking stones. At the end of the day they receive a penny (two sous in France). They are the lucky ones. On leaving there we came upon a small covered wheelbarrow pushed by two paupers. This wheelbarrow goes to the door of the houses of the rich; into it is thrown the remains of the meals, and this debris is brought to the poor-house to make the soup.[63]

[60] Second Mendicity Report (1819), pp. 4, 10, 32.
[61] Speer, *Diseases of the Lower Orders* (1822), pp. 199–200.
[62] Nicholls, *First Report* (1836), p. 14.
[63] Emmet Larkin (ed. and translator), *Alexis de Tocqueville's Journey in Ireland, July–August 1835* (Dublin, 1990), pp. 24–25.

Up to the opening of the union workhouses the vast majority of those relieved by the Mendicity continued to be women: in 1834, the total adult inmates numbered 1,536, 87% of whom were female, and of those relieved outside the institution, 92% were female. While continuing in its founding principle of providing immediate relief to the destitute, once the poor law (1838) structures were in place, the scale of the Mendicity's operations decreased. There was also a significant shift in the composition of its clientele, with only one-third female by 1876, evidence that the workhouse was the preferred destination of women in need, while charitable asylums and refuges run (largely) by church activists (Chapter 7) extended the range of alternatives.

The Parochial System and the Relief of the Poor

At the beginning of the nineteenth century the vestries of the Established Church parishes in the city exercised a diversity of functions, including the care of deserted children, the relief of paupers, firefighting, and the protection of public health; one commentator aptly described them as 'miniature Municipalities'.[64] The inadequacy of the scavenging and associated sanitary matters when the responsibility of the parish, has been amply demonstrated (Chapter 2); matters of poor relief were similarly mismanaged, with Whitelaw (1805) complaining that the spread of wealth throughout the city was so uneven that the antiquated system 'at present universally adopted, of each parish providing for its own poor only, is founded in absurdity itself'.[65]

The arrival of Asiatic cholera in March 1832 exposed the utter uselessness of this parochial system for dealing with either sanitary or relief issues, on anything like the scale which was required. The Mansion House Committee, which had been formed to deal with the exceptional distress, commissioned its honorary secretary, Francis White, to report not alone on the condition of the poor, but on 'the failure of all efforts of the humane and charitable to procure by subscription anything like adequate means for their relief'.[66] Under an act of 1832, intended to lessen the prevailing distress, funds could be advanced by the government to the parish officers of health 'to enable them to distribute nourishment, clothing and other necessaries within their respective parishes';[67] this was of little use as 'the amount so issued must be repaid by parochial assessment', and 'it unfortunately happens that the parishes where the greatest mass of misery exist are precisely those least able to repay anything by parochial assessment'.[68]

When the virulence of the cholera had abated, White undertook a further inspection of the homes of the poor, to see what improvements could be noted.

[64] Charles A. Cameron, *Municipal Public Health Administration in Dublin* (Dublin, 1914), p. 17.
[65] See footnote 1, Chapter 2, Whitelaw, *Survey* (1805), pp. 41–42.
[66] Francis White, *Report and Observations on the State of the Poor of Dublin* (Dublin, 1833), p. 5, (hereafter *Report on the State of the Poor*).
[67] 2 William IV c.9.
[68] White, *Report on the State of the Poor* (1833), p. 28.

However, in the 'haunts of wretchedness in the several parishes' he could find no perceptible change, 'on the contrary they are, with a progressive pace, sinking deeper into misery', 'their clothing appears not improved, and their habitations seem as crowded as ever, with the calamitous addition of about 1,000 orphans thrown completely destitute by the ravages of contagion'.[69] The major city charities were commended for their noble intentions and strenuous efforts, but the facts were plain: 'voluntary contributions have all failed to meet anything like the objects they had in view or set out to relieve, a result which however deeply to be deplored, requires but little penetration must be the inevitable consequence of a system by which the humane and benevolent are called upon exclusively to support the poor, whilst the hard-hearted and uncharitable refuse to bear any portion of the general burden'.[70] The 'stream of charity must dry up', as manufacturing and trade declined and the 'resources of our more respectable classes are dwindling'.[71]

White let the statistics speak for themselves: in 1814 'to relieve a temporary and comparatively trifling distress, occasioned by a heavy fall of snow', £10,000 was subscribed; in 1816–1817, 'for the relief of the poor in a time of scarcity' nearly £19,000 was raised. In 1831, 'even for the purpose of averting the progress of a terrific plague', scarcely any funds were subscribed in the parishes, parochial assessment was totally inadequate, and 'subsequently, when the city was suffering under that dreadful scourge, notwithstanding all the influence of the Mansion House Committee, the amount subscribed but little exceeded £2,000 out of a city valued at £700,000'. And among the city's estimated 250,000 residents fewer than 200 contributed.[72] That the burden of relieving the city's innumerable poor should be more fairly spread was obvious. But what portion of the burden should be carried, by whom, and how?

Report on Vagrancy and Mendicity in the City of Dublin, 1834

The appointment of commissioners under the chairmanship of Richard Whately, Protestant Archbishop of Dublin 'to inquire into the condition of the poorer classes of Your Majesty's subjects in Ireland' and into the various institutions established by law for their relief, and to make recommendations for what further ameliorative measures 'appear to be requisite'[73] resulted in three very lengthy reports covering all aspects of the poverty situation in Ireland. In the case of Dublin there was a specific report on vagrancy in the city, and an 'Investigation into the Operations and Efficiency of the Principal Charitable Institutions within the city, and their effects upon those who give, and those who receive, relief', on the eve of the Poor Law. Several important features emerge.

[69] Ibid., pp. 30, 21.
[70] Ibid., p. 232.
[71] Ibid., p. 30.
[72] Ibid., p. 5.
[73] *Third Report of the Commissioners for Inquiring into the Condition of the Poorer Classes in Ireland*, 1836 (hereafter *Third Report, Poor Inquiry*), p. 3.

It was a field of human endeavour dominated by women: nine out of every ten beggars it was claimed were female, from the 'young widow or the deserted wife, with two or three helpless children' who 'professes her willingness to seek, but her want of success in her endeavours to obtain work', to the huckster who 'urges on your attention the claims of a sick husband or children', to the 'aged female' who seeks relief as 'unable any longer to maintain herself'.[74] Predominant among them, according to one witness, were elderly 'widows whose husbands had been weavers, or in different branches of trade connected with weaving'.[75]

It was repeatedly claimed that Dublin, with its 'superior wealth and population' acted as a magnet to the mendicant classes from all over the country. The attractions of 'a richer harvest . . . augmented by the donations of casual visitors' along with the 'numerous charities' and the 'known benevolence of its inhabitants' served to 'lure' the destitute. The great dearth of alternatives, especially in the period preceding the Poor Law, left many with little option but to head for the capital; it was obvious even to those most critical of the Dublin beggars that 'there is no other place where the needy, or the famishing, will be sustained' so that 'nearly the whole tide of wretchedness and want must of necessity pour in upon Dublin'. And there was nothing to prevent this influx. Once arrived, 'and actually or apparently in a state of destitution, they of course meet with relief in some way'.[76]

In the face of this threat, shopkeepers and wealthy residents in 'almost all the principal thoroughfares' resorted to combining in 'great numbers of small bodies' to employ 'street-inspectors' whose brief was 'to keep the streets clear as far as they can, and more particularly to prevent persons from being annoyed at shop doors'. However, as they had no legal standing whatsoever, their powers were only 'as long as the beggars are in ignorance that these persons are thus but as other frequenters of the street'.[77]

While the most vociferous objections were made to beggars 'infesting' the 'more public and more fashionable streets' it was in the quarters 'frequented by the humbler classes alone' that beggars were most active. Here they 'collect the alms of those little removed above them in the scale of human wretchedness'.[78] All the evidence collected in preparation for the extension of the English New Poor Law to Ireland clearly demonstrated that the pressure of supporting the beggars fell heaviest upon the middle and lower classes. The rich could avoid direct contact; their charity was 'mostly diffused through the medium of public institutions'.[79] Shopkeepers however 'could neither close their doors nor turn their backs upon the wretched objects who were constantly applying to them for aid'[80] while at the entrances to the Catholic chapels 'poor persons who are not worth more

---

[74] 'State of Vagrancy', *Poor Inquiry (Ireland) 1836*, p. 27a*.
[75] Ibid., p. 43a*.
[76] Nicholls, *Second Report* (1837), p. 89.
[77] 'State of Vagrancy', *Poor Inquiry (Ireland) 1836*, pp. 24a* and 29a*.
[78] Ibid., p. 27a*, 43a*.
[79] Ibid., p. 29a*.
[80] Nicholls, *First Report* (1836), p. 17.

than 2*d* in the world will give a halfpenny to a beggar,'[81] the recipient always 'ready to invoke the blessings of the Almighty on the charitable and humane'.[82]

That large numbers of persons, mostly women, made a very precarious living by soliciting alms in the streets of Dublin in the early nineteenth century is an incontrovertible fact. What was widely disputed were their exact numbers and origins, their reasons for begging, and the extent to which this activity supplemented other income. And if the matter was to be tackled effectively and the 'scourge' removed, these facts had to be ascertained. The most useful source of information, the women themselves, was ignored in official reports such as the Poor Commission's *Report on Vagrancy and Mendicity in the City of Dublin*, 1834. To quantify the problem, and draw up a classification system, it was first necessary to clarify what was understood by the term 'beggar'. One witness, chief constable Farrell, considered there were four classes of mendicants: about 100 persons (exclusive of their children) 'who beg from real necessity', whose 'very manner of begging, look and dress bespeak them at once to be objects of real charity' so that he cannot, himself, 'restrain from giving them alms in the streets'; then there were about 500 (including children) 'regular beggars in Dublin' and another 500 'who reside in the extremities of the city, and go out to beg in the neighbouring villages', followed by '100 strangers passing through'. His estimate was greatly below that of his colleague, Constable Goodisson, who ventured the figure of 8,000 'including men, women, their children, and orphans'.[83] One of the magistrates, Joseph Gabbet, refused to speculate on the number of vagrants, 'the same individuals being apprehended and committed over and over again'.[84] In the north city parish of St Michan's alone, it was claimed that at least 18,000 of the 23,918 local population could now be classed as reliant on begging.[85]

George Nicholls arrived at a figure of 5,646 destitute poor (Table 6.1), which led him to claim that the extent of destitution in the city could not be higher than 2% of the population, a figure which must be dismissed as derisory when placed alongside those offered by local experts. The dispute arises in the matter of definition: 'the extraordinary miscalculations' which proceed 'from the very general error of confounding cases of actual destitution requiring relief with cases of distress arising from improvidence, inertness, and lowliness, which public interference never fails to increase'.[86] Among tradesmen, the Lord Mayor's meeting claimed that there were 3,500 requiring relief, and only 500 could get it; this was dismissed as one of those 'emergencies of a commercial community, which are not within the scope of a permanent provision for destitution, and only require a provident use of earnings by families exposed to them'.[87] The

[81] 'State of Vagrancy', *Poor Inquiry (Ireland) 1836*, (c) II p. 41a*.
[82] Ibid., p. 29a*.
[83] Ibid., p. 24a*.
[84] Ibid., p. 39a*.
[85] Nicholls, *Second Report* (1837), p. 147.
[86] Ibid.
[87] Ibid., p. 144.

Idle Vagrants and Sturdy Beggars: The State's Response

An Estimate of the Extent of Destitution in Dublin, 1837, by George Nicholls

House of Industry	991
Mendicity	2,800
Street mendicants	960
local charities	895
total number of destitute poor in Dublin, through the year:	5,646

Other estimates of the total number of destitute poor in Dublin requiring relief, Evidence before Poor Inquiry, 1836

Rev Shore (St Michan's Parish):	40,000–50,000 *totally destitute*
Mr Charles Sharpe (Roomkeepers):	12,000–15,000 *in actual want*
	70,000–80,000 *in need of alms, have not the means of supporting themselves*
Mr Howell (Mendicity):	7,000 *aged impotent poor, wholly unable to earn*
	30,000–35,000 *destitute poor*

Estimate range: 5,600–80,000

Sources: George Nicholls, *Poor Laws Ireland, Three Reports*, London, 1838, appendix to Second Report, table 5, p. 141; *Poor Inquiry (Ireland)*, 1836, appendix (C), part II, pp. 101–119

Table 6.1 Estimated numbers requiring poor relief, Dublin 1836–1837.

extent of begging in the street was but one witness to poverty; of more significance was the number who refrained from the 'shame of begging', 'of the destitute poor very few are regular beggars; they will undergo the greatest misery before they will beg'.[88]

Act for the Effectual Relief of the Destitute Poor in Ireland, 1838

The commissioners appointed 'to inquire into the condition of the poorer classes in Ireland' (1836), in effect to consider the applicability of the new English poor law to Ireland, made a very strong and lengthy case opposing its adoption.[89] The new English workhouse system was designed to replace the discredited Elizabethan poor law (43rd Elizabeth), which had never operated in Ireland, and under which 'partial relief' or outdoor assistance was extended to destitute persons through the parish structure. The system introduced in 1834, was firmly based on the conviction that among the able-bodied seeking relief in England, the 'pauperism of the greater number' 'originated in indolence, improvidence, or vice, and might have been averted by ordinary care and

---
[88] 'State of Vagrancy', *Poor Inquiry (Ireland) 1836*, (c) II p. 41a*.
[89] *Third Report, Poor Inquiry* (1836), p. 5.

industry'.[90] Following from this premise, the only way to ensure that help was strictly limited to the 'deserving poor' was to confine relief within a 'well-regulated workhouse', the regime of which would be sufficiently repugnant to dissuade the idle and fraudulent from applying. Dividing the 'deserving' from the 'non-deserving' poor was thus made eminently simple: 'If the claimant does not comply with the terms on which relief is given to the destitute, he gets nothing; and if he does comply, the compliance proves the truth of the claim, namely, his destitution'.[91] Its simplicity was matched by its economy, according to its creators, as the support of the poor under such a system, uniformly applied, would be much cheaper, 'than when living at large by mendicity or depradation'.[92]

Such a system, designed for a rapidly-industrialising country with an ever-increasing range of occupations and demand for labour, was regarded by the Irish commissioners as utterly unsuited to a 'backward' society which was vastly over-supplied with agricultural labourers. Plainly stated, the difficulty in Ireland 'is not to make the able-bodied look for employment, but to find it profitably for the many who seek it'.[93] It was impossible to separate the destitute from the struggling poor, where so many 'are insufficiently provided at any time with the commonest necessaries of life' and 'in permanent want'.[94] Moralising about improvidence and fraud merely deflected attention from the challenge to provide the people with what was most eagerly and desperately sought, not pauper-relief but work.[95]

While the commissioners produced an overwhelming mass of data 'which proves to painful certainty' that 'there is in all parts of Ireland much and deep-seated distress',[96] to which a workhouse-based poor law was utterly inappropriate, the alternatives they proffered were politically unthinkable. The principal solution envisaged was a massive and integrated rural development programme. The formal constitution of a 'Board of Improvement', supported by the rates, and with powers to compel landlords to contribute as necessary, was proposed, to initiate and oversee such matters as drainage schemes, structural improvements to waterways and harbours, 'good cottier industry', the rehousing of families whose cabins 'may appear unwholesome, or calculated to generate or continue disease',[97] the establishment of model agricultural schools in each district, and improving the conditions under which tenants held land. Such a radical and all-inclusive approach was deemed to be the best route to benefit the single largest class of able-bodied poor, the agricultural labourers. The 'business of agriculture'

---

[90] *Report from His Majesty's Commissioners for Inquiring into the Administration and Practical Operation of the Poor Laws*, 21 Feb 1834, p. 148.
[91] Ibid.
[92] Ibid.
[93] *Third Report, Poor Inquiry* (1836) p. 5.
[94] Ibid., p. 3.
[95] Ibid., pp. 8–9.
[96] Ibid., p. 3.
[97] Ibid., p. 21.

was recognised as 'the only pursuit for which the body of the people of Ireland are qualified by habit' but which would, if fostered, stimulate demand for commodities produced by other sectors and hence increase the overall levels of enterprise and wealth.[98] Free passage to non-convict colonies where the poor 'may have the means of living by their industry' was also urged, not as the ideal solution but 'for the present as an auxiliary essential to a commencing course of amelioration'.[99] The numbers for whom asylum or workhouse relief might be provided was thus drastically reduced to those with special needs, *viz.*, lunatics, epileptics, the deaf and dumb and blind, cripples, 'and all who labour under permanent bodily infirmities', while 'penitentiaries' were proposed for 'the idle who would rather beg than labour', and who were not considered suitable for transportation.[100] While opposing the workhouse principle upon which the English new poor law was established, the Irish commissioners side-stepped the vexatious question of outdoor relief to the able-bodied poor by effectively reducing it to the payment of wages to persons employed on public works.

Despite the considerable attention the Poor Inquiry Commissioners (Ireland) had devoted to Dublin city in their data collection, the question of the urban poor was ignored in their final recommendations. Such poverty, it appears, was considered a spill-over from rural distress, so by targeting rural slums, city problems would right themselves. In any case, the commissioners' radical proposals were swept aside through the hasty appointment of a new one-man commission, in the person of George Nicholls, one of the three poor law commissioners in England and a whole-hearted advocate of the new system. He found, predictably, that the workhouse system, having been 'successfully applied to dispauperize England'[101] could not fail to remedy the ills of the neighbouring island. In his opinion, the 'almost universal prevalence of mendicancy' in Ireland was due to indiscriminate alms-giving, and had led to 'the same reckless disregard of the future – the same idle and disorderly conduct – the same proneness to outrage, and resistance to lawful authority' which pauper relief under the old parish system had led to in England.[102] The mendicant problem compounded with providing for the lunatic and idiotic poor, deserted and orphaned children, the aged, sick, crippled, deaf and dumb, and the fearsome mass of 'able-bodied poor' were to be addressed in a decisive and comprehensive way in the form of the Poor Law (Ireland) Act, 1838.

Based on the assumption that what most needed to be remedied among the 'mendicant class' was not their misery but 'the falsehood, the trickery, and fraud, which become a part of their profession, and spread by their example' the poor law undertook to remove the 'excuse' of needing to beg to subsist.[103] The

[98] Ibid., p. 17.
[99] Ibid.
[100] Ibid., p. 25.
[101] Nicholls, *First Report* (1836), p. 27.
[102] Ibid., pp. 8, 11.
[103] Ibid., p. 8.

function of the poor law was to encourage self-exertion by forcing 'free' labour onto a competitive market, and this required, paradoxically, a dramatic extension of the powers of the central state. On the one hand the reformers constructed a world of autonomous individuals contracting freely in an open labour market; on the other hand they envisioned a landscape of moral discipline and government, 'the Janus face of modern liberalism'.[104] Not alone did the system provide the means of relief for the destitute, but firstly provided 'through the Union authorities, and the operation of the workhouse, the means of testing the existence of such destitution in every instance'.[105] The 'workhouse test' would ensure that only 'the absolutely and unavoidably necessitous' would be provided for, and 'the simulators of that necessity would be subjected to restraint, and be compelled to labour'; as this would be totally 'at variance with their indolent and vagrant habits' the 'undeserving' would be denied relief and could be treated under a different heading.[106] The greatest possible success was predicted for the system in Ireland, based on Nicholl's judgement that the Irish are 'naturally or by habit, a migratory people, fond of change, full of hope, eager for experiment' and 'would wander the world over in search of employment' rather than suffer workhouse confinement.[107] Perhaps the greatest disincentive to resort thither was the rule that 'a family must be taken as a whole, and so admitted, or excluded', i.e., for one member to be relieved the entire family had to be admitted.[108] The quarter-acre clause, denying relief (indoor or outdoor) to any who occupied land above this minimal level, also dissuaded persons most effectively.

Funding for this massive undertaking was through a general assessment upon property, which would spread the 'burthen of relief' more equally, for it was claimed that the 'higher classes generally, and the absentee proprietors entirely', avoided their fair share of the burden,[109] while 'individuals all but destitute themselves' are 'brought down to the lowest level of independent subsistence' by the strain of providing alms.[110] The new administrative divisions within which these rates were to be collected were to be 'compact and convenient units', precisely defined, an amalgamation of townlands (where such were defined) or of parishes but dispensing freely with parish boundaries wherever necessary.[111] The Union with its guardians, paid officers and standardised buildings all funded by compulsory rates swept away the antiquated and erratic poor rating undertaken by the vestries, based on irregular and sometimes uncertain parish borders.[112]

---

[104] Felix Driver, *Power and Pauperism: The Workhouse System, 1834–1884* (Cambridge, 1993), p. 19.
[105] Nicholls, *Second Report* (1837), p. 93.
[106] Ibid., p. 90.
[107] Nicholls, *First Report* (1836), p. 24.
[108] Ibid., p. 38.
[109] Ibid., p. 14.
[110] Nicholls, *Second Report* (1837), p. 69.
[111] Nicholls, *First Report* (1836), p. 34.
[112] Ibid.

The system was designed as a model of tight central control, whereby 'the ordering and directing' of all relief in Ireland was initially in the hands of the English poor law commission, to 'ensure the total freedom from all local, partial or party influences' and 'the certainty of the same application of the same law, and the consequent equality of England and Ireland in this respect'.[113] The arrogant decision to appoint English commissioners (until 1847) to control the spending of Irish funds was to place an impossible strain on relations between local boards of guardians and central authority from the outset, with the guardians of the North Dublin Union (1844) formally protesting against 'an unlimited power of taxation being invested in any commission, the expenditure of such funds being uncontrolled by those from whom they are to be levied, and equally arbitrary and unaccounted for'.[114] The election of local guardians was controlled by property interests: owners and occupiers of property valued over £5 to under £50 were entitled to a single vote, those valued at £50 to under £100 to two votes, to the upper limit of five votes allowed to those whose holdings exceeded £200 value so that 'the cumulative votes of the owners and larger occupiers would serve to counterbalance the number of small rate-payers, and secure the return of competent individuals'.[115] Women were disqualified as guardians until 1896, when on reaching the property qualification they were eligible for election, whether married or single.[116]

The system of relief which was implemented in Ireland was supposedly an extension of the system already in place in England;[117] however much its originators dreamt of a 'unity of principle' and of action leading to an 'identity of result', the reality was very different.[118] It was claimed in 1837 that the outdoor assistance offered in England was 'only tolerated' as 'an evil unavoidable for a time', and to be eliminated as speedily as possible; in Ireland as there was no comparable tradition of statutory poor relief such 'experimentation' was to be avoided from the outset through a prohibition written into the legislation.[119] The maintenance of 'different and opposing principles' in the two countries was a major grievance on the Irish side.[120] On 1 January 1861, 908,186 persons in England were in receipt of relief, 86% of them outside the workhouse; among the 50,683 persons in receipt of relief in Ireland only 6% received it outside the workhouse.[121] Outdoor relief was granted in England to widows; women whose

---

[113] Nicholls, *First Report* (1836), pp. 36, 59, 61; *Second Report* (1837), p. 107.
[114] NDU Minutes, 2 October 1844.
[115] Nicholls, *First Report* (1836), p. 41.
[116] *Poor Relief Commission* (1928) part I, p. 5.
[117] Nicholls, *First Report*, (1836), pp. 25, 35.
[118] Ibid., pp. 60–61.
[119] Ibid., pp. 36–38; see also W. Neilson Hancock, 'The difference between the English and Irish Poor Law, as to the treatment of women and unemployed workmen', *Soc. Stat. Inq. Soc. Ire. Jn.* vol. 3, part XXI (1862), pp. 217–235.
[120] Ibid., pp. 217–235.
[121] Ibid., p. 224.

husbands were soldiers, sailors or marines; women whose husbands were imprisoned, sick or out of employment; and all of their children, as well as to the 'frail and unfortunate' unmarried mothers and their children.[122] Infirm men and women, and their dependents were similarly relieved outside the workhouse. The English practice 'discriminating nicely between the case of women and men, the infirm and the able-bodied, leaving children with their mothers and their infirm relations' was in stark contrast to the Irish situation where 'the one iron rule' was applied to practically all, and the workhouse test 'which was intended as a severe check on idle good-for-nothing-men, is applied to infirm age, helpless youth and unprotected women'.[123]

The moralising tone which accompanied the introduction of the poor law to Ireland betrays the immense gulf between the legislators and administrators of the new law, and those for whom the law was intended to bring relief. The distance was gender-based as well as cultural, social and economic: while all the witnesses to the Poor Inquiry (1836) stated plainly that the vast majority of mendicants were women, and this point could not be missed by anyone passing even briefly through Dublin, all discussion of the proposed legislation centred on the 'able-bodied male'. In practice even the crudest calculations reveal that there were always at least twice as many able-bodied females as there were able-bodied men in the Irish workhouses, and in some years the women outnumbered the men at more than three to one.[124] Despite the admission that destitution was indeed on a large scale in Ireland, poverty was still regarded as a residual rather than a structural problem, and from this line of argument it followed that the able-bodied could, through the exercise of foresight and prudence, provide for occasional periods of unemployment. Those responsible for the extension of the act to Ireland, and for the first phase of its implementation passed harsh judgement on the Irish peasantry the act was intended to help, condemning their 'desultory and idle habits', and insisting that 'if they felt a wish to better their condition, or to appear better, they might do so; but they seem to have no such ambition'.[125]

The North and South Dublin Union Workhouses

The Foundling Hospital, on the south-western limits of the municipal boundary, and the House of Industry on the north side provided the nuclei for each of the poor law workhouses required for the north and south Dublin unions respectively. Workhouses in Balrothery, Dunshaughlin, Celbridge, Naas and Rathdown provided for the adjoining unions. The north Dublin union

---

[122] Ibid., pp. 228–231.
[123] Ibid., p. 229.
[124] Helen Burke, *The People and the Poor Law in Nineteenth Century Ireland* (Dublin, 1987) p. 163.
[125] Nicholls, *First Report* (1836), p. 11.

consisted of six wards, with a population of 97,065 and rateable property valued at £265,586; the wards making up the south Dublin union had a total population of 135,661 and property valued at £402,516.[126]

The status of the district in which the South Dublin Union (SDU) workhouse was located is well indicated by the local streetnames: on its eastern side Pigtown Lane, along the west wall Cut-Throat Lane, and almost facing the entrance Murdering Lane (Figure 6.2).[127] The City Basin acted as a buffer between the city proper and this choice location, so that applicants were steered along James's Street or via Bow Bridge and Murdering Lane, before reaching the forbidding walls of the SDU. As the Foundling Hospital building was incorporated into the SDU complex, the ground floor plan of this workhouse was not as symmetrical as the standardised cruciform plans drawn up by George Wilkinson (1838) for Irish workhouses on 'greenfield' sites.[128] However, in its interior arrangements it was utterly in accord with the forbidding spirit of the workhouse scheme. The first principle, that the workhouses had to have the 'means of accommodating a much greater number than it is computed may be driven there for succour, otherwise the poor-law cannot efficiently be worked as an instrument for raising up the condition of the poorer classes'[129] was fulfilled, in that there was ample room for expansion. While the poor law was intended as the means of 'retaining at or near their source those numerous streams of vagrancy that now flow with an unrestricted current into the capital as the general reservoir'[130] the scale of provision in Dublin had still to be very substantial, as there was the added fear that the Dublin workhouses would be exploited by migrating labourers who would 'leave their wives and families at the place of embarkation'.[131]

The workhouse regime of strict classification, 'labour, discipline, and confinement' is seen in the SDU plan with its series of enclosed yards and barrack blocks, dividing the 'male side' from the 'female side', a strict division of the sexes which extended to all classes of inmates, as children were removed from the adults, the sick from the lunatic, the able-bodied from the infirm, with the burial ground along the back wall of the complex the only stage at which rigid classification was abandoned. The mill capstan in the female yard and the wash-houses and laundry yard underlined the philosophy that the able-bodied poor should pay dearly for their poverty. Seven distinct classes were provided for in 1842,[132] and later subdivisions created more classes such as the sick

---

[126] Nicholls, *First Report* (1836), p. 11.
[127] NDU Minutes, 14 April 1847.
[128] In 1876 the 'very objectionable names' of Murdering Lane and Cut-throat Lane were changed to Mountbrown Lane and Mountbrown Place respectively; *RPDCD* vol. 2 no. 101 (1876).
[129] Nicholls, *Second Report* (1837), p. 147.
[130] Ibid., p. 89.
[131] Ibid., p. 90.
[132] 1842, Commissoners' Workhouse Rules: aged and infirm men/women; able-bodied men/women over fifteen years of age; boys/girls between seven and fifteen years; children under seven years.

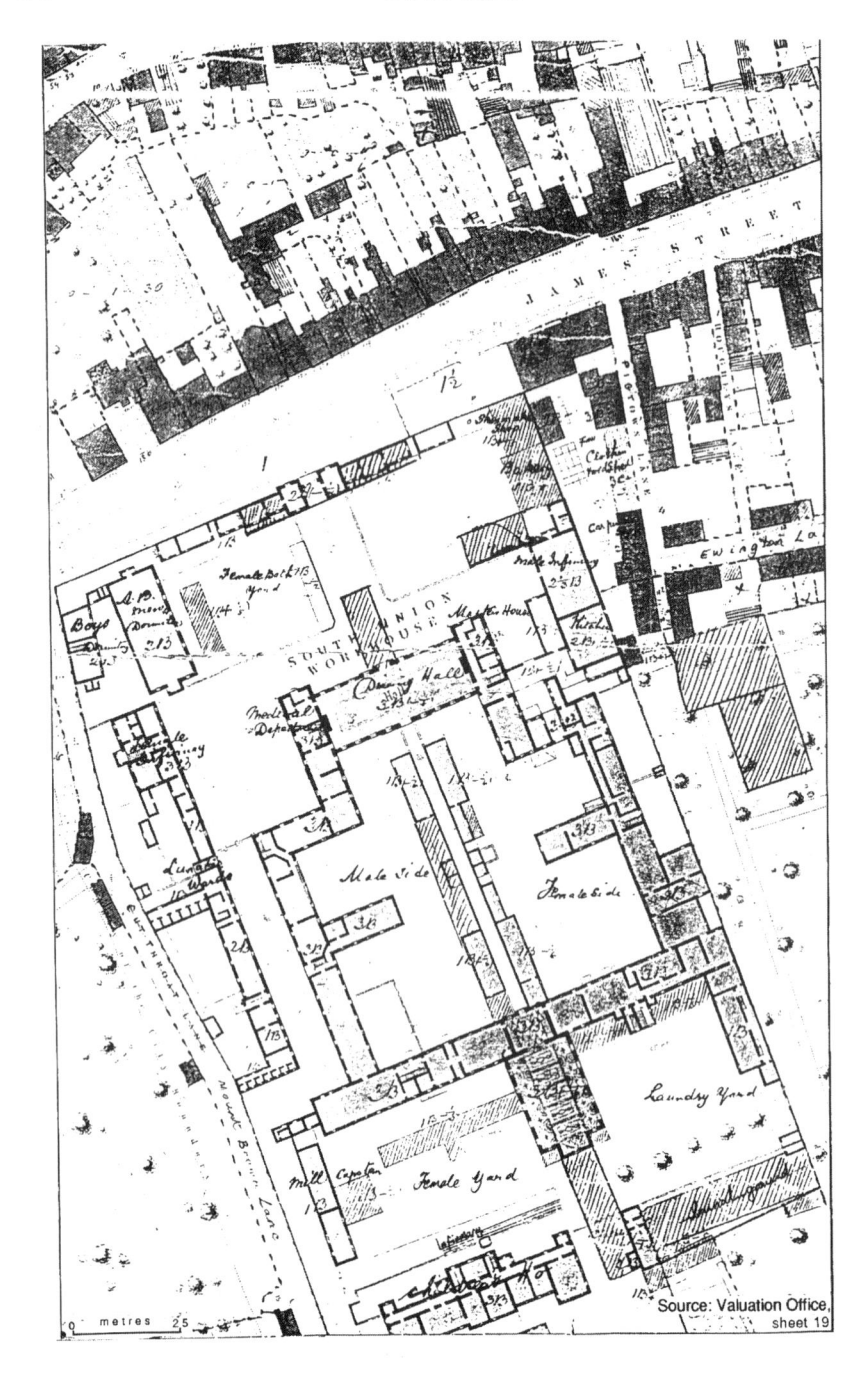

Figure 6.2 South Dublin Union workhouse, c.1854

and fever, lying-in women, vagrants, and the chronically insane.[133] In each case classification was translated into spatial segregation, on the basis that barriers were needed to prevent contagion both physical and moral, creating what Felix Driver has termed 'the moral geometry of workhouse design'.[134] In these circumstances, the prostitute was viewed as the most tainted, the orphan child the most vulnerable. The admissions ward, fronting James' Street, was a distinct structure and designed to keep the latest arrivals separate from the main building until they had been deloused and clothed in the workhouse dress; it also operated as the casuals' or night lodgers' ward. The master's house was in the central building, from where his considerable 'general superintendence and moral influence' could be felt in all parts of the complex, and most especially among those dealing with supplies going into the kitchens.[135] Together with the matron he was to ensure that 'industry, order, punctuality and strict cleanliness are to be maintained'.[136] The central dining hall initially served also as chapel, and when partitioned, as day room for able-bodied men and women. The north-east corner was occupied by a shoemaker's shop and bakery, while a tan yard wedged between the eastern wall and Pigtown Lane was colonised by the institution to accommodate a carpenter's shop and clothes shed, ensuring that such workshop functions were kept apart from the monotonous living quarters. The regular layout made extending the complex through additional wings or extra stories a simple matter. The physical structure and daily routine, cut off from the rhythms of ordinary life, was designed to impress on the inmates the virtues of 'independent' labour, and ensure that none but the utterly destitute would apply, and 'if driven thither by their necessities, they will quit it again as speedily as possible, and strive (generally with increased energy and consequent success) to obtain their subsistence by their own efforts'.[137]

The appropriation of the upper house or main building of the House of Industry for the North Dublin Union (NDU) workhouse in 1838 was entirely understandable. Not alone was the House of Industry already an institution for the poor supported by public monies, but its immense size and physical layout, whereby blocks of buildings were arranged around separate yards, made it ideal for the purposes of the poor law commissioners (Figure 6.3). A rough sketch of the House of Industry in the minute book for November 1820 indicates the divisions already in place. Men were divided from women and classified under three headings: lunatics and idiots, adults, and the aged and infirm. A curious note is that elderly men were to get single beds, presumably a special comfort in their old age, but there is no mention of what other groups enjoyed this indulgence! The girls were in a separate building, the Bedford Asylum, while

---

[133] Driver, *Power and Pauperism* (1993), p. 64.
[134] Ibid., p. 65.
[135] NDU Minutes, 4 June 1845.
[136] Ibid.
[137] Nicholls, *First Report* 1836, p. 23.

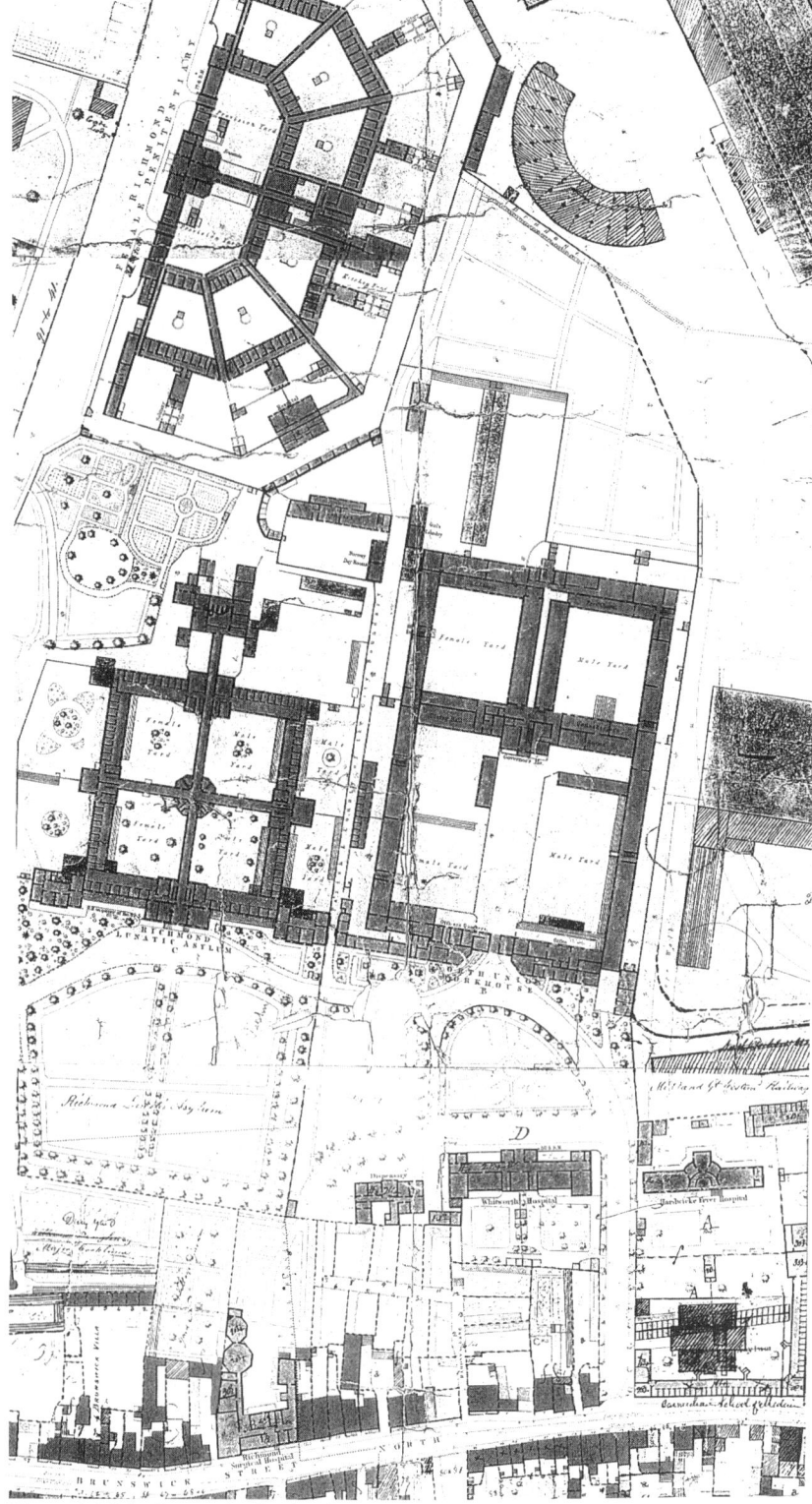

Figure 6.3 North west institutional sector, Dublin c.1870.

Smithfield Penitentiary was for boys only. The premises was handed over to the North Dublin Union in 1838 and those resident at the time relocated: the 'lunatics' to a house in Islandbridge which was reserved to their use until the last inmate died in 1861 (see Figure 2.7), while room was made for other paupers in the hospitals and ancillary buildings, where they continued to be supported by an annual parliamentary grant.[138]

Case Study: The North Dublin Union Board of Guardians

The voluminous records of the North Dublin Union (NDU) provide insights into the day to day workhouse experience, at least from the perspective of the administrators and governing body. They are also invaluable for data on the progress and impact of the great famine of the 1840s on Dublin city, as the workhouses were in the front line of relief efforts. The minute books of the weekly NDU guardians' meetings provide valuable information on matters of discipline, diet, supplies, employment and policy, as well as relations with outside bodies, most importantly the poor law commissioners, but also Dublin Corporation and neighbouring poor law unions.

The bulk of matters discussed by the board were of an irksome but unspectacular nature: the case of Pat Whelan who forced open the gate at Church Street and 'absconded with house clothes, leaving his wife in the House, who is too ill to be taken out',[139] or the problem of thwarting 'those persons who attend for the sole purpose of stealing and not of visiting their friends or relations in this workhouse'.[140] Bitter disputes around the religious denomination under which individual children should be registered recur, reflecting the sectarianism which surrounded the issue of childcare, especially of deserted and orphan children, in the wider society (see Chapter 7).[141] In the NDU the school teachers and chaplains were the principal combatants, with the chaplains pushing to ensure that children of 'their' denomination might be spared exposure to religious instruction by teachers of the 'other' denomination, inundating the board with claims and counterclaims about the 'unwarrantable interference' of the other chaplain with a member of their flock.[142] Requests from paupers to change their religion were met with particular suspicion by the board.[143]

The detailed regulations under which the workhouse operated did not, in practice, cover all eventualities, and much time was spent in debating how

---

[138] Eoin O'Brien, 'Of Vagabonds, Sturdy Beggars and Strolling Women, the House of Industry in the Georgian and Victorian Eras', in Eoin O'Brien, Lorna Browne, Kevin O'Malley (eds.), *The House of Industry Hospitals 1772–1987, The Richmond, Whitworth and Hardwicke (St Laurence's Hospital), a Closing Memoir* (Dublin, 1988), pp. 1–61.
[139] NDU Minutes, 19 May 1855.
[140] Ibid., 5 September 1849.
[141] Ibid., 24 December 1845.
[142] Ibid., 4 March 1846.
[143] For example, NDU Minutes, 6 August 1845; May 1855.

regulations might be applied in individual cases, such as the vexed question of how to manage those persons who discharged themselves but returned the same day, or those who left on a daily pass but returned a little late, upsetting the calculations of the clerk producing the weekly returns.[144] The maintenance of discipline and the safety of the inmates was a major concern, with numerous reports of violence by teachers against children presented to the board, at least some of which resulted in the serious maiming of pauper children.[145] A child James McGovern suffered critical spinal injuries in 1878 as a result of an assault by an assistant schoolmaster, who had a record of abuse.[146] Violent disputes among inmates erupted periodically, such as one woman striking another with a quart tin, but were dealt with speedily and the matter passed on to the 'station house' if considered sufficiently serious.[147] The resolution of one such dispute was typical: 'ordered that the girl Laura Lloyd be transferred from the school to the Woman's yard for beating a woman, and that she and her mother be employed in breaking stones'.[148] The retribution for 'willfully breaking matron's windows with stones', a favoured sport among teenage boys, was 12 or 24 lashes; after one such entry it is noted that the 'boy Brown' did so 'for the purpose of obtaining his discharge from the House stating that he would prefer being in Harold's Cross Prison'.[149] Despite their large numbers, there was very little possibility of the paupers themselves exerting any real pressure on policy or practice; laundry women who had combined to prevent one of them from answering a summons to attend before the board of guardians were dealt with summarily: 'ordered that all the laundrywomen be discharged from the house, forthwith. On intimation of this order to them they became riotous and disorderly and other women having joined them, they were also ordered to be discharged'.[150]

While daily life was harsh and monotonous, especially for children and their parents, there were very occasional but nonetheless brighter days. Such was the decision in 1845 to take 'good children' twice a week 'to the park after dinner', 'and that cloaks be provided for this purpose to protect the girls from the winter weather', while a visit to the zoological gardens was also arranged.[151] Of more widespread but still passing benefit was the decision 'resolved, 22 September 1855, that the inmates of this House get a substantial dinner of Sunday the 30th *inst* in honour of the great victory obtained by our Army and brave allies in taking Sebastipole'.

The rigidity of the geographical layout (Figures 6.2, 6.3) belies the constant flux within the workhouse, as changing numbers of inmates, and their distri-

[144] Ibid., 20 August 1845.
[145] For example see NDU Minutes, 2 July 1845; 9 June 1847; 13 October 1855.
[146] Ibid., November to December 1878.
[147] Ibid., 29 September 1855.
[148] Ibid., 16 July 1845.
[149] Ibid., 13 August 1845; 22 October 1845.
[150] Ibid., 26 July 1848.
[151] Ibid., 1 October 1845; 11 June 1845.

bution among the various classes, required the re-allocation of wards to ensure supply met the demand.[152] The classification system itself was also subject to revision, with regular subdivision, combination of classes, and reclassification of individuals within the workhouse.[153] Fever outbreaks required a rapid response, with calls during such crises to establish 'a probationary or observation ward', separate to the usual admissions ward 'in which cases of a suspicious nature' should be isolated before being allowed join the main body of residents.[154] While such restructuring is most in evidence during the crisis years of 1845–1849, it is a constant subtext in the workhouse story. Typical was the decision in 1879 to separate the 'unfortunates' (apparently those of a better class) from other female paupers, the 'unfortunates' to be allotted a separate ward, and 'some of the old and infirm paupers' to be placed therein to make up the full complement, 'Ward no. 378 could be allocated without inconvenience'.[155]

The central authority, in practice as well as in law, closely controlled the operations of local boards of guardians. Every action of the NDU board was scrutinised, and even the most minor items referred to the poor law commissioners (from 1872 the Local Government Board for Ireland), for clarification. When Margaret Lee of Bull Lane, aged 26, was brought by the police to the workhouse 'drunk and cut about the head and face', she was admitted; headquarters was contacted to clarify whether the master was obliged to admit persons who were intoxicated, to be informed that under the first article of workhouse rules he had discretion in such cases.[156] The union records were constantly subjected to intense scrutiny, the commissioners commenting (with disfavour) on any departure from the letter or spirit of the law. The decision of the guardians to pay a portion of the funeral expenses of a young schoolmistress who died in the workhouse at the height of the famine fever, only three months after her appointment, was noticed by the commissioners, with disapproval,[157] while any item in the minutes which was not followed up was also cause for reprimand.[158] Financial records were also scrutinised, as might be expected, but with periodic requests to provide particulars in the minutest detail, for specified departments over named periods.[159] The speedy exchange of correspondence between the NDU and central authority (up to 1847 in London) was remarkable, most letters being replied to by return of post, ensuring that any bright ideas at local level were extinguished very rapidly, in time for the next (weekly) board meeting.

---

[152] Ibid., 24 September 1845.
[153] Ibid., 10 December 1845; 12 November 1845.
[154] Ibid., 29 May 1880.
[155] Ibid., 11 October 1879; see also 15 January 1879.
[156] Ibid., 12 May 1855; 19 May 1855.
[157] Ibid., 24 November 1847; 1 December 1847.
[158] Ibid., 8 May 1880.
[159] Ibid., 21 June 1848.

Relationships between the NDU and the SDU were delicately balanced at best. The NDU administration kept a close eye on developments south of the Liffey, where for example the salaries of the master and matron were increased in 1845, with the permission of the commissioners; the NDU in response increased the emolument for their officers, although failing to go one better and secure an increase for their hard-working clerk.[160] More seriously, the NDU guardians and rate-payers felt aggrieved that their union although 'less in extent, in population and value' than the SDU, yet 'has a greater number of poor to support, and a lesser amount of property to contribute to its demands', as a result of factors over which the guardians had no control, such as the misfortune to have the North Wall transit point within its jurisdiction.[161] The NDU watched every move of their counterparts across the Liffey, always suspicious, with good reason, that paupers properly the charge of the SDU were being redirected to the heavily-burdened north western sector (see also Chapter 8).

While the founding principle of the Poor Law (Ireland) Act was plainly to limit statutory poor relief to the controlled environment of the workhouse, the need to provide at least some outdoor relief was to vex local boards from the outset. The NDU board engaged in robust exchanges with the central authority, but to little avail, the one iron rule ruled all. The operation of soup kitchens during the famine was most reluctantly permitted, eventually (see below), as thousands died, but as the situation eased there was a concerted effort by the commissioners to impose strict discipline on local boards and return to the founding spirit. In 1879 the NDU put forward a well-argued plan to provide outdoor relief 'in extreme cases of necessity during the present distress', all cases to be doubly certified (by the NDU medical officer and relieving officer of the local district), and confined 'to classes of people whose homes would be broken up if admitted into the workhouse and who would by temporary relief be enabled to tide over the present distressed period'.[162] The Local Government Board, predictably, forbade such a scheme, on the basis that there was sufficient indoor accommodation still available.[163] Overcrowding was running at about 16% that month, evidently a figure to be discounted.[164] The situation under section I of the Irish Poor Relief Extension Act, was (again) spelled out. Outdoor relief could be given to the following classes only: i) 'such destitute poor persons as are permanently disabled from labour by reason of severe sickness or serious accident and are thereby deprived of the means of earning a subsistence for themselves and their families, whom they are liable by law to maintain', and ii) 'destitute poor widows having two or more legitimate children dependent upon them'.[165] The target group, of able-bodied but destitute

---

[160] Ibid., 4 June 1845.
[161] Ibid., 20 January 1847.
[162] Ibid., 13 December 1879.
[163] Ibid.
[164] For example, total capacity 1,845: total number 2,137 (27 November 1880); 2,158 (4 December 1880); 2,157 (18 December 1880); 2,126 (25 December 1880).
[165] Ibid., 20 December 1879.

families, who by some timely assistance could ride out the current crisis without becoming workhouse inmates, was excluded. In January 1880 the desperate appeal by a deputation on behalf of the 'unemployed labourers of Dublin', requesting outdoor relief, was met with the standard response:

Outdoor relief to healthy able-bodied persons under the 2nd section of the Irish Poor Relief Extension Act may only be authorised when it is shown that there is want of room in the Workhouse, or that the Workhouse by reason of fever or infectious disease is unfit for the reception of poor persons'.[166]

The Local Government Board, following on legal advice, circulated the boards of guardians in 1880 with the good news that the prohibition of outdoor relief in the case of an occupier of land more than a quarter acre could be interpreted as applying only to the occupier himself, and his wife and children could be eligible for relief (indoor or outdoor) under the usual conditions.[167] While any such loophole in the law was to be welcomed, it is unlikely to have had much relevance in the Dublin context, with its burgeoning population of unskilled labour, for whom the question of outdoor relief in place of workhouse incarceration was the critical issue.

Inextricable from the question of poor relief was the question of disease: where contagion was introduced to the house it had ample opportunity to wreak havoc among an underfed and dispirited population. The famine crisis (see below) brought the scourge of fever also, but even outside the crisis years of 1845–1849 epidemic disease was rarely far away (Chapters 2, 3). In 1880 asked to account for an outbreak of fever amongst females over 15 years, the medical officer reported that some 'presented the character of typhoid fever, others that of typhus, and while several were cases of scarlatina'. In this instance it was claimed that paupers had been admitted 'with the disease partially developed or in the stage of incubation', and so had not been detected before infecting dozens of other inmates; its spread and continuance however 'is not unconnected with an overcrowded condition of the wards'.[168] Three weeks later there was a smallpox outbreak, and the guardians were called on to provide shed accommodation 'in some rural portion of the union in the immediate vicinity of the city' where the patients could be isolated.[169]

The North Dublin Union and the Famine, 1845–1849

The workhouse records provide a chilling account of the impact of the great famine of the 1840s on Dublin city, the detailed statistics and minutes of the scheduled meetings of the boards of guardians allowing the progress of the crisis, and the official reaction to it, to be tracked week by week. While the western counties were affected on a vastly larger scale, Dublin as a port city became a

[166] Ibid., 31 January 1880.
[167] Ibid., 7 February 1880.
[168] Ibid., 29 May 1880.
[169] Ibid., 19 June 1880.

refuge for thousands fleeing disaster. On 16 September 1845 the poor law Commissioners 'expressing their regret at the unfavourable state of the potato crop' sent an ominous warning to the unions, recommending the NDU 'to be prepared in due time for any increase in the number of inmates which the present circumstances of the union render probable'.[170] In November 1845, when the loss of the sole food of the vast bulk of the labouring population had spread the spectre of famine widely, the NDU guardians take note of a recommendation from the poor law commissioners, that 'the proposed conversion of potatoes into potato flour, starch and pulp may afford suitable employment to certain classes of the pauper inmates'.[171] The NDU guardians attempted in the early stages of the crisis to rally to the call of the Lord Lieutenant and give a lead locally, declaring it 'our duty to prove that the crop, even in a state of decay, may be made productive and eventually useful for the support of the People, and that therefore it is the duty of the Guardians to exhibit to the public a machinery in active operation for that purpose'.[172] Brave but fruitless efforts to manufacture farina from rotting potatoes gave way rapidly to desperate petitions to Her Majesty 'to compel her ministers to open the ports for the purpose of saving the population from the famine which is now impending over the country'.[173]

Repeated failure of the potato crop led to the introduction of Indian meal into the NDU workhouse diet in August 1846.[174] The scandalous inadequacy of the central government response to the catastrophe led the NDU board to be deeply critical of 'the great delay that has taken place in the employment of the Poor on Public Works' while the board 'still more deplore the Principle of Political Economy adopted and acted upon by them in leaving the supply of food wholly to private enterprise, at a time when the energies of Government should be exercised to the fullest extent in providing a starving population with the means of subsistence at such a rate as would enable them by their earnings to support their families'.[175] At this point (7 October 1846) the NDU indoor population had risen to 1,824, with weekly additions of between 80–113 for the remainder of the month. Equivalent figures for October 1844 were an indoor population of 1,632, with weekly additions of approximately 50 persons. The poor law commissioners noting 'the crowded state of the House' offered the helpful opinion that 'no amount of distress justifies the receiving into such an institution a greater number of inmates than is comfortable with their health'.[176] The pressure on accommodation grew daily, with the sheriff's prison and later part of the Linen Hall pressed into service as auxiliary workhouses.[177] In March 1847 the state of

[170] Ibid., 16 September 1845.
[171] Ibid., 12 November 1845.
[172] Ibid., 26 November 1845.
[173] Ibid., 26 November 1845; 17 December 1845.
[174] Ibid., 26 August 1846.
[175] Ibid., 4 October 1846.
[176] Ibid., 9 December 1846.
[177] Ibid., 20 January 1847; 7 April 1847; 16 February 1848.

the children's health, precarious at the best of times, was especially 'endangered by the overcrowding and poor ventilation'.[178]

By May 1847 the NDU had an epidemic in its workhouse: 30 confirmed cases of 'fever', 8 smallpox, 6 scarlatina, with one of the workhouse doctors warning 'that the increase in fever since this day week is immense, and that is assuming a most serious type, and that the crowded state of the Fever Hospitals outside prevent fever cases being sent to them. That numbers of persons are crowding through the streets, in Fever, from want of room in the hospitals, and that unless immediate accommodation is provided for them there will be a fearful spread of fever'.[179] Overcrowding in the sheriff's prison in particular was at crisis level, and disaster assured if fever should spread to it.[180] It was imperative both to reduce the number of NDU inmates and to separate the sick from those not yet ill, against a backdrop of increasing applications for admission.

From 31 May 1847 to July 1848 a temporary fever hospital was erected for the NDU on the banks of the Royal Canal, near Drumcondra, an ideal site from 'the salubrity of the air', the 'continued current of fresh water' which surrounds and intersects the premises, and excellent drainage. Here on 'elevated foundations of brick and stone' wooden sheds were erected, and a large complex of 27 separate wards and associated offices were served by a staff of 92 persons, mostly nurses, laundry and ward maids. Admission numbers peaked in September 1847, when 1,077 patients were received; the total admitted over a twelve month period was 6,389, of whom only 8% died, 'a percentage generally considered to be a very low mortality in epidemic fever'.[181]

Famine fever was at its height in Dublin from July to December 1847. Under the Temporary Relief Act (passed February 1847), direct distribution of food aid was established, but only temporarily, pending the Poor Law Extension Act which set up a separate poor law commission for Ireland, and among other provisions, allowed in law for the first time for outdoor relief for specified classes 'in periods of unusual distress', under the union structure.[182] From March–April 1847 the workhouse total rapidly approached the 2,900 mark, with 241 new admissions in the week ending 21 April 1847 alone, despite the establishment of temporary soup kitchens. From August 1847 the NDU distributed outdoor relief using both their own depots and the Mendicity Institution. Relieving officers were also appointed for the rural electoral divisions to arrange local food distribution.[183] The largest recorded number reliant on the relief provided by the NDU was in April 1848, when almost 6,500 were in weekly attendance at the soup kitchens, and almost 3,300 were simultaneously relieved in the workhouse. However, the NDU decision to distribute relief to the able-bodied destitute was

---

[178] Ibid., 10 March 1847.
[179] Ibid., 5 May 1847.
[180] Ibid., 5 May 1847.
[181] Ibid., 26 July 1848.
[182] Crossman, *Local Government in Nineteenth Century Ireland* (1994), p. 48.
[183] NDU Minutes, 11 August 1847; 1 September 1847.

roundly condemned by the commissioners, who were 'not satisfied with the evidence that such necessity exists as contemplated by the Act of Parliament' ordering the NDU to reserve outdoor relief to the infirm only, and so allow another 400 able-bodied persons to be admitted to the workhouse, with the warning that 'it is desirable to consider the position of rate-payers to prevent the ruinous increase of rate by endeavouring to place the able-bodied on their own industrial fortunes'.[184] What was particularly galling was that the guardians had already authorised the master to offer one shilling and sixpence to any poor person in the 'infirm class' who could be persuaded to quit the workhouse, and had tight controls on readmission.[185] By February 1848 the commissioners were requiring lists of all individuals in receipt of outdoor relief from the NDU, and returning them to the guardians with certain names struck out.[186] By April 1848 they were also forwarding demands for the repayment of loans advanced under the Temporary Relief Act for the purposes of outdoor relief, although the NDU complained that the money had been released 'with an intimation that repayment would not, for a time, be required', and that it could not be raised for the moment 'while business of every kind is standing still'.[187] The NDU guardians were certainly in a no-win situation. The financial burden was increasingly heavy and would have to be met in full, if the rate-payers did not revolt first. They could not simply eject those whom they were bound by law, and by common humanity, to support. And those attending the food depots were clearly starving, whether able-bodied or disabled, married or widowed.

The outdoor relief project, so well intentioned, brought other serious problems. The diet of India meal stirabout was blamed by the medical officer for the prevalence of dysentery complicated with fever, 'exceedingly prevalent among families receiving outdoor relief, and unless the principal cause be removed the consequences will be serious'.[188] To alleviate the situation rice was to be used with the Indian meal,[189] though still a very poor substitute for the nourishing potato. The return to 'normality', the subsistence living which was a feature of the Dublin slums, was delayed by continued outbreaks of fever. On 30 May 1849 the NDU board heard of several cholera cases among the paupers, and within a fortnight over 200 cases of 'malignant cholera' had been treated, with two nurses dead, two more under treatment, and both doctors suffering from 'premonitory symptoms'.[190] Although the fever outbreak was brought under control quickly, the fall in the numbers of those reliant on statutory relief was very slow; by September 1849 there were 603 persons in receipt of outdoor relief, but the workhouse total was 2,034.

[184] Ibid., 11 August 1847; 18 August 1847.
[185] Ibid., 16 June 1847; 11 August 1847.
[186] Ibid., 16 February 1848.
[187] Ibid., 12 April 1848.
[188] Ibid., 15 September 1847.
[189] Ibid., 22 September 1847.
[190] Ibid., 13 June 1849.

While eligibility for outdoor poor relief was to continue as a contentious issue, the Poor Relief (Ireland) Act of 1847, which governed its disbursement, had at least made an important dent in the iron structure of the poor law. Subsequent developments, such as the boarding-out of workhouse children, the development of dispensary and hospital services, and the support of the handicapped and mentally ill in specialised institutions, all to be funded through rates levied on the property of the union, have been thoroughly explored by Helen Burke (1987). The famine experience, which tested the newly-established system beyond its limits, was to ensure that the workhouse would be associated in the popular mind with the darkest period of Irish history to date.

North Dublin Union: Rural Sanitary Authority

While much of the recorded NDU activity relates to workhouse and (intermittent) outdoor relief, with the immense machinery that such duties required, it did not neglect its role as a rural sanitary authority under the Public Health (Ireland) Act 1878.[191] The NDU was responsible for sanitary affairs north of the Liffey, as far as the adjoining unions of Balrothery, Dunshaughlin and Celbridge, but excluding the municipal area (within the Royal Canal), which was the charge of the Corporation. The sanitary and public health work of the NDU parallels that of the Corporation, with many of the residents of the NDU district as loath to co-operate as was the case among owners and occupiers of city slum property. There was also the very urgent need for information on the geography of 'fever nests', so that persons admitted to the workhouse from houses or districts in which fever had raged, might be kept apart from the main body of the house, at least for a brief period. Scattered references to individual houses or lands which were known to be infected indicate that occasional efforts at least were made to this end.[192]

Among numerous examples of the slum challenge on the urban fringe, the saga of Blackhorse Lane, continuing the line of Aughrim Street to the north west, exemplifies the difficulties faced by the local authority in meeting their new statutory responsibilities. Here the NDU in 1879, following numerous complaints, served notice on Patrick Cody for failing to abate a nuisance; but the inspecting officer 'would respectfully beg to suggest the advisability of appointing a man to scavenge and sweep Blackhorse Lane and clean the privies and ashpits therof', as 'the local laundry overflow of suds and other filthy matter is continually accumulating there' and the local occupiers 'have no conception of sanitary arrangements or any idea of cleanliness'.[193] But the problem was larger than merely appointing a local man to clean up the place once a week, and harassing the residents (both of

---

[191] 41&42 Vic c.52 sec. 6.
[192] For example, see yard at rear of 5 North James Street, house 21 North Anne Street, and lands in Glasnevin, Clontarf West, infected with pleuropneumonia, NDU Minutes 19 October, 1878.
[193] NDU Minutes, 15 February 1879.

which were tried). There were no sewers, consequently 'the night soil, suds and foul water are either accumulated around the drains, or thrown into the water channel or on the road surface'.[194] Few of the miserable cabins which lined the road had privies, 'and where two or three do exist, they are placed over the running stream where the soil not only pollutes the water which the people use a little further down, but is exposed to public view in the most objectionable manner'.[195] Clearly major structural work was called for, covering over the drain in the side of the public road, and 'perfecting the same with proper drainage tiles, seven manholes &c., and enclosing and otherwise improving the public watering place known as 'The Poor Man's Well',' at a cost first estimated at £70, but finally rising to £200.[196] Two months later the engineer proudly boasted that the open water course along this lane had been covered in 'and a very grand sewer constructed along its course, with all necessary provisions for sanitary purposes, and the roadway is also rendered quite safe' providing 'a grand and sufficient channel' for the drainage of the locality.[197] But even with that infrastructure in place the NDU, at its weekly meetings held primarily to deal with poor relief, continued to be persecuted with complaints that newly-erected cabins were without privy accommodation or ashpits. One particular owner, Mrs Margaret Kennedy, tested the limits of the sanitary officer's endurance, with repeated appearances before the magistrate and the Northern Police Court for failing to comply with orders to provide toilet facilities of any sort to cottages she had erected.[198] Under duress she provided one set of cottages with what was dismissed as 'actually a receptacle for filth'.[199] Although fined on numerous occasions, she persevered in defiance of magistrate's orders, and the catalogue of complaints continued, even after fine new sewers were in place and a local man in receipt of 15s per week for (desultory) sweeping.[200]

Comparable situations were to be met with throughout the North Dublin Union, with tension particularly evident between residents of the 'respectable' classes, the rate-payers occupying new houses on the fringe of the city, and the unfortunate and very poor population clustered in cabin dwellings without proper sanitation. Places such as Howth, Baldoyle, Philipsburgh Avenue, and Yellow Lane, Drumcondra[201] feature regularly. While the troubles of the NDU are a repetition of all that the Corporation's public health and housing committees simultaneously faced within the canals, the task of providing expensive

[194] Ibid., 1 March 1879.
[195] Ibid., 1 March 1879.
[196] Ibid., 8 March 1879; 10 January 1880.
[197] Ibid., 24 May 1879.
[198] Ibid., 23 August 1879; 10 January 1880.
[199] Ibid., 4 October 1879.
[200] Ibid., 8 March 1879; 6 September 1879; 4 October 1879; 17 January 1880; 24 April 1880; 1 May 1880; 8 May 1880.
[201] Ibid., 8 May 1880; 1 February 1879; 14 June 1879; 21 June 1879; 21 February 1880; 13 March 1880.

sewage and water facilities over a large area for (relatively) small populations was particularly daunting, with the guardians all the time strictly accountable to their rate-payers, not to speak of the ever-vigilant Local Government Board.

Conclusion

The evolution of poor law policy from the forced and intermittent incarceration of 'idle vagrants and sturdy beggars' in the early nineteenth century to the situation where the destitute were entitled to relief as a right, even if to qualify one had to submit to voluntary incarceration in a workhouse, was part of the move towards central government involvement in many spheres of social life. Poor relief is closely allied to the questions of vagrancy and disease, which in turn were part of the wider economic questions of access to paid employment and housing. Proposals in 1907 titled 'Some remedies for overcrowded city districts' exemplify how each of these threads was tied up in the tangled web of the Dublin slum story. The overcrowding of tenement housing 'causes the general physical deterioration, apathy and indolence that result in demoralisation'. The slum environment affected the character ('especially when, as in average cases, hereditarily weak and plastic') no less than physical health, nurturing the 'lowest strata of society', 'the totally submerged and homeless', the 'vagrants and non-workers', and dragging down the 'deserving classes' whose misfortune it was to share the same 'insanitary rookeries'. Slum reform therefore would require the eradication of 'slum habits', preparing slum dwellers for better housing by closely supervising current household practices. And an amended poor law would be part of this reform, allowing the state the possibility 'of giving truer aid to those who are the flotsam of humanity' rather than 'allowing their continuance in the freedom which for them under existing conditions means degradation and ignorance'. Outdoor reflief was proposed, but only on condition 'of certain standards of order' that 'relief should aid industry, instead of increasing pauperism'.[202]

In the case of statutory poor relief, despite important extensions in the areas of specialised care and medical services, from 1838–1921 the principal features of the Poor Law remained unchanged. 'In 1921 there were still Unions, Workhouses, and Boards of Guardians', and 'the discretion of the guardians was exercisable only within a narrow administrative field, and that under strict and minute control there was little room for initiative or independence of action'. Relief to the able-bodied, men and women, was still confined to the workhouse, 'which in many instances pressed heavily on deserving poor'.[203] Along with health and housing reform, the reform of poor relief structures was to be firmly on the agenda for Saorstát Éireann. In the case of the vast majority of Dublin's population, it was a matter of the greatest urgency.

---

[202] Miss Roney, 'Some remedies for overcrowded city districts', *Journal of the Statistical Society of Ireland*, 87 (1907), pp. 52–61.
[203] *Poor Relief Commission* (1928), pp. 6–8.

7

CHURCH CHARITIES RESPOND: WOMEN AND CHILDREN, 1850-1900

A glorious work lies before them [the Soeurs de Charité*], they will see poverty, rags, misery, wretchedness, such as I do believe they never saw before.*
MARGARET AYLWARD TO PÈRE ETIENNE, 1856[1]

INTRODUCTION

Concern with morality and religious practice was part of the slum story in the nineteenth century. In the case of Dublin city, condemnation of appalling sanitary conditions, overcrowding and excessive mortality was often accompanied by generalised references to the real or presumed immorality and ignorance festering therein. Many of the appeals for reform of living conditions were based on the Christian imperative to 'succour your perishing brethren', while in the suppression of rampant beggary the discipline of religion was considered an essential tool. The city clergy, by virtue of their office, had immediate familiarity with the poorest; as instigators of surveys, such as Reverend Whitelaw (1805) and as witnesses to state and other inquiries, they had first-hand knowledge of the condition of the poorest members of their flock, and contributed to publicising and relieving both physical and spiritual distress. Religious orders which pioneered education on Irish lines for the very poorest, such as Blessed Edmund Rice (Christian Brothers, Presentation Brothers), and Margaret Aylward (St Brigid's Schools of the Holy Faith), saw that 'the only hope of improving the lot of the poor was through education', 'making good Catholics, self-supporting men and women', out of slum children for whom the road to the workhouse, reformatory or jail otherwise beckoned.[2] Similarly the Protestant ragged schools would 'elevate into decency' children of an 'abject and demoralised condition'.[3] Only the uplift provided by education would break the cycle of destitution and despair that characterised life in the city slums.

[1] Margaret Aylward to Père Etienne, 8 October 1856, GA: MA/CH/02 no. 46a.
[2] Edmund Rice, quoted in Desmond Rushe, *Edmund Rice, The Man and His Times* (Dublin, 1981), p. 36; *Thirty First Annual Report of St Brigid's Orphanage*, 1888, p. 18 (hereafter *SBO Annual Reports*).
[3] *The British Metropolis in 1851: a Classified Guide to London* (London, 1851), p. 260.

The Established Church parish structure was the principal but most ineffective vehicle for sanitary, public health, poor relief, foundling and education matters in the first quarter of the nineteenth century. The major churches, Protestant and Roman Catholic, also controlled a large portion of all funds collected for charitable purposes among the poor. However, the demographic situation within which church charities operated must first be noted. The earliest reliable data on religious affiliation dates from the 1861 census, and divides the total population within the municipal area into approximately 19% Established Church, 3% Presbyterian and Methodist, 77% Roman Catholic, and 'all others' at less than 1%. As Figure 7.1 illustrates for civil parishes,[4] the demographic reality was that the numbers of Catholics overwhelmed all other denominations in all the older and more congested parts of the city: south of the Liffey, St Catherine 90%, St Audeon 89%, St Michael 93%, St John 86%, St Nicholas Within 89%, St Nicholas Without 90%, St Luke 88%. On the north side the oldest parish, St Michan's, has a similar over-representation of Catholics, at 93%. These statistics help explain the hostility of Catholic clergy towards Protestant mission agents who undertook to visit the poor in their homes; by definition, general visitation of 'the poor' meant visitation of the Catholic poor. The Protestant poor, whose exigencies could certainly match those of their Catholic neighbours, were so much fewer in number that well-to-do Protestants expressed alarm that their poorer co-religionists would be overwhelmed in a papist flood if relief efforts were not directed specifically towards them.

Despite its small numbers the Protestant, i.e., Established Church was notable by mid century for the number and range of its charity institutions, while the Quaker community contributed out of all proportion to its small population.[5] However, the Roman Catholic charity network at the beginning of the century was grossly underdeveloped by any standards. The granting of Catholic emancipation in 1829 was but a small step along the road towards full religious, political, social and economic equality, and the development of a comprehensive range of Catholic charitable institutions cannot be disentangled from this historical context. The Penal Laws prevented the open endowment of Roman Catholic charities, describing all such uses as 'superstitious and void', while the 9Geo.2,c.3, which required all charitable endowments in lands to be constituted by deed, and enrolled in chancery, could not be fulfilled by Catholics 'because enrolment of the deed of foundation involved some amount of publicity given to it; and a founder who disclosed or made public a Roman Catholic charitable use, exposed it to the risk of being defeated or set aside'. 'Partial relief' was granted in 1832

---

[4] The census returns detail only those parts of each parish within the municipal boundary; the non-city parts are included under the appropriate barony or 'town' (e.g., Harold's Cross Town, Ballsbridge Town). The city parishes which extend significantly beyond the municipal boundary, and the population of each extra area are: St George 1,177; St James 1,743; St Peter, 587.

[5] See Maria Luddy, *Women and Philanthropy in Nineteenth Century Ireland* (Cambridge, 1995).

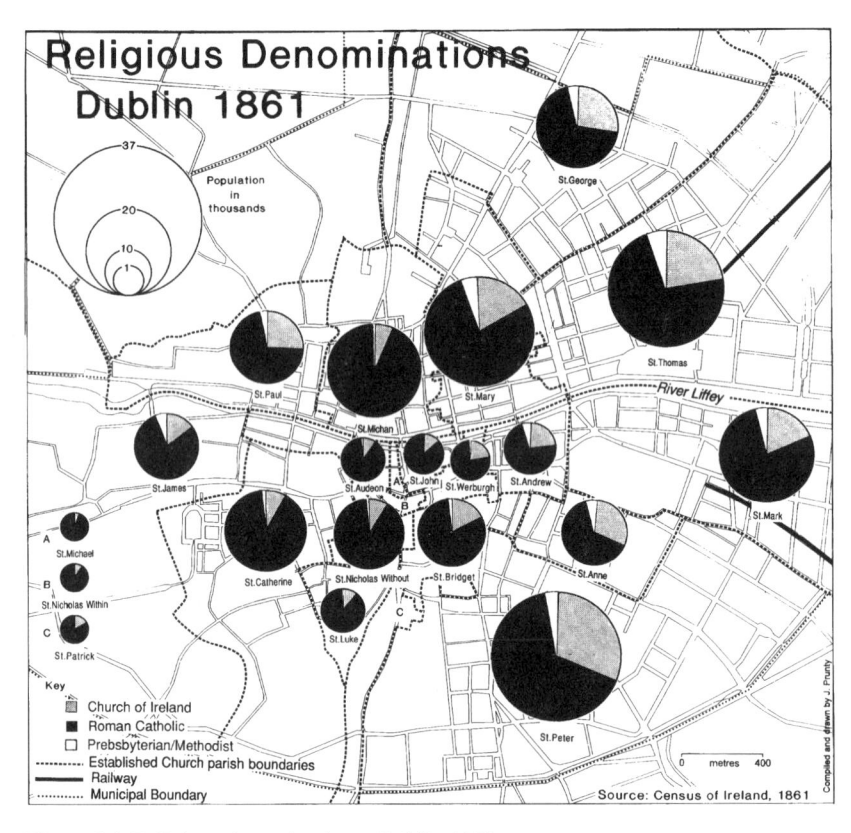

Figure 7.1 Religious denominations, Dublin 1861

with the 2&3 Will.4.c.115 enabling Roman Catholics 'to give lands for the building of churches and chapels, for schools, and for the maintenance of bishops or secular priests, without the fear of seeing those gifts defeated by the courts'.[6] It was only however in 1860 that the question of defective title was legally settled to the satisfaction of Catholic interests, and that year some 400 Roman Catholic charities were enrolled, including it appears 'the greater part of the Roman Catholic charities then in existence under foundations of an earlier date'.[7] The Catholic network therefore, despite the vast majority of Catholics country-wide and in Dublin city, was still considerably behind the organisation and funding levels of the Protestant churches at midcentury. The second half of the nineteenth century was to see an upsurge in Roman Catholic charities, and their re-organisation on a scale and with a professionalism previously unknown. The premier Catholic relief agency was to be the St Vincent de Paul Society, while on

[6] *Report from the Select Committee on Conventual and Monastic Institutions*, 23 June 1871, p.v. DDA: Cullen, 328/4 file 1, laity, Jan–June 1871.
[7] *Ibid.*

the Protestant side the Association for the Relief of Distressed Protestants fulfilled a similar function.

The most visible expression of this new assertiveness is in the re-organisation of the Catholic parish network, and the extraordinary surge in church building (Figure 7.2). Emmet Larkin writes of the energy, ingenuity, perseverance and confidence that were displayed in fund-raising throughout Ireland, from local bazaars and sodalities to sending priest–collectors to canvass the far flung Irish missionary empire.[8] Under Dr Murray's episcopate (1809–52) 97 churches were built in the diocese of Dublin[9]; under Dr Cullen this investment continued apace. New parishes were formed from the 1850s to provide for expanding areas, such as the division of the parish of Francis Street in 1865 to create Harrington Street parish, and the separation of the northern part of St Michan's to create the parish of Berkeley Road in 1870 (Figure 7.2). Beyond the city boundary new parishes were created in an effort to keep pace with suburban expansion. Within the municipal area the commandeering of strategic sites by both parochial and order churches contrasts greatly with the former back street locations of chapels in penal days, while the scale and grandeur of the new churches, and the large-scale rebuilding and refurbishment of existing chapels, speaks of wealth, respectability and confidence.[10] The church building and boundary revisions begun under Cullen were continued by his successors, Edward McCabe (archbishop 1879–1885, cardinal from 1882), and William Walsh (archbishop 1885–1921).

The freedom to operate boldly and publicly, as exemplified in the wave of church building, was matched by investment in Catholic educational and charitable projects on a large scale. But there was another, sharper, spur, namely the activities of evangelical missionaries in the city. The direct relationship of these missions to the slum areas is exemplified in the account of the planning which preceded the foundation of the Dublin Visiting Branch of the Irish Church Missions:

> [Fanny Bellingham] took a map of the city of Dublin, and with the help of the late Arthur Guinness, Esq., divided the poor parts into districts for the labourers, and the richer parts into districts in which ladies might gather the funds necessary for the maintenance of these men, thus binding together poor and rich, and seeking to draw out the sympathies of the upper classes for the ignorant and degraded people inhabiting these lanes and courts into which they themselves dare not enter.[11]

From the outset therefore, the Irish Church Missions (ICM) sought to establish itself in the poorest parts of the city, with those on whom the double calamity of destitution and allegiance to Rome weighed most heavily.

---

[8] Patrick Corish, *The Irish Catholic Experience: A Historical Survey* (Dublin, 1985), p. 168.
[9] Emmet Larkin, *The Historical Dimensions of Irish Catholicism* (Washington, 1984), p. 27.
[10] See also Conchubhair O'Fearghail, 'The Evolution of Catholic Parishes in Dublin City from the Sixteenth to the Nineteenth Century' in F.H.A. Aalen and Kevin Whelan (eds.), *Dublin City and County: From Prehistory to Present* (Dublin, 1992), pp. 229–250; Peter Costello, *Dublin Churches* (Dublin, 1989).
[11] *'Them Also', the Story of the Dublin Mission* (London, 1866), p. 4, (hereafter *Them Also*).

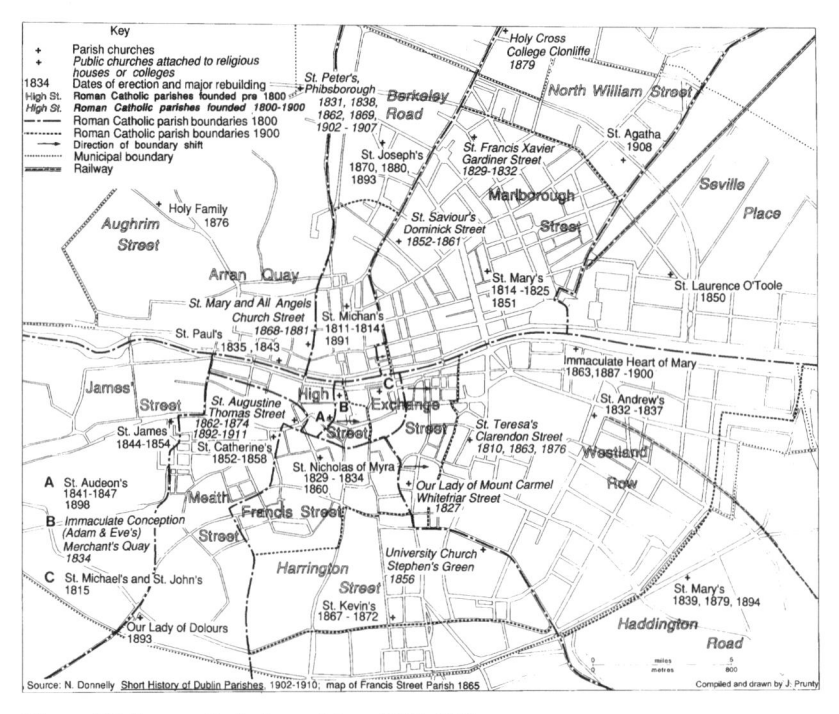

Figure 7.2 Roman Catholic parishes, 1800–1900.

The denominational struggle between Catholic and Protestant charities, in the battle for souls and bodies, is a constant theme, occasionally erupting into full scale and very public warfare. In terms of popular teaching the sides were irreconcilable, as each was convinced that adherents of the other denomination were surely condemned to eternal damnation. The pro-active approach of evangelical groups such as the Dublin Visiting Branch of the Irish Church Missions was guaranteed to cause offence, as their scripture readers were trained 'to go in and out amongst the people, inviting them to schools, classes and services', organised by the ICM, acting as 'the connecting link between the teachers and the taught'.[12] Visitation was regarded as essential, for

Ignorant Roman Catholics will not go to the well of life for themselves; we must bring them little tastes of its refreshing waters, and then they will go to the sermons and classes to get more.[13]

It was the concentration on the poorest, particularly children, that most enraged Catholic opinion:

It is the poor and the helpless and the innocent that are attacked by the enemies of their faith. It is base, it is cowardly. Why doesn't Dr Whately or Mr McCarthy go to some of our Catholic judges or to some of our Catholic nobility and ask them for their children? But they

[12] Ibid., p. 271.
[13] Ibid., p. 75.

go or send their agents to the poor widow who has pawned her last article of dress and while the hunger cry of her infant is rending her heart they say 'we will take your children, and educate them and raise them in the world, and we will procure a situation for yourself and to prepare you for it we will send you to the Providence Home'.[14]

The only solution was plainly the provision by the Catholic community of free schooling with associated food, clothing, and family relief in the poorest areas, which the ICM's activities clearly located, and the provision of substantially more residential or foster care places for the many children in need of such services, either temporarily or permanently.

However, despite important denominational and class differences, there was more to unite than separate church charities and missions on both sides. Both Catholic and Protestant organisations acted out of a genuine conviction that the welfare of their clients had spiritual and material dimensions, and both sides could be very imaginative in their approach. All sides were united in opposition to the demoralisation of the workhouse, and aimed to make their clients self-supporting, claiming to afford relief 'as may tend not to encourage a system of beggary and dependence, but to lift out of poverty and raise to self-supporting and honest industry', well removed from 'the union'.[15]

The multiplicity of church charities in Dublin, and the high standards of record-keeping in many instances, provide an invaluable and little-used source of information on daily life in the slums. The wide range of data represented, including relief registers, journals, accounts, published reports, and letters on divers matters to a multitude of persons and institutions, serve to confirm, contradict and enlarge on the information provided by the statutory organisations. Most importantly, they allow names and individual case histories to be attached to particular addresses, and so contribute to 'peopling the past', as advocated by Richard Lawton.[16] Charity records, with their strong emphasis on the minutiae of day-to-day living, also serve as important reminders that there were many other aspects to life in the city slums aside from the well-documented areas of sanitary provision, public health and housing. In this welcome shift from the slum dwelling to the occupants, glimpses of the school experience, daily diet, and employment opportunities are provided. Family structure, residential mobility, neighbourhood links, and information flows are also important aspects of the social geography of poverty. Dublin had the most sophisticated charity network in the country, by virtue of its size and poverty, and the activities of individuals who made Dublin the chief field of their endeavours; even allowing for losses over time, Dublin is particularly rich in such sources.

---

[14] *SBO Sixth Annual Report*, 1862, p. 19.
[15] *Thirtieth Annual Report of the Association for the Relief of Distressed Protestants*, 1867, p. 1 (hereafter *ARDP Reports*).
[16] Richard Lawton, 'Peopling the past', *Transactions of the Institute of British Geographers*, New Series, 12, 3 (1987), p. 263; see also Stephen J. Page, 'A new source for the historian of urban poverty: a note on the use of charity records in Leicester 1904–1929', *Urban History Yearbook* (Leicester, 1987), pp. 51–60.

The dominance of women in the creation of charity records ensures that a female perspective is included, a matter of importance considering that the professional fields of medicine, ordained ministry and public service, from which most of the early slum surveyors were drawn, were (largely) male preserves in the nineteenth century. Women dominate the slum story from the charity perspective: as church workers, bible readers, home visitors, jubilee nurses, women religious, Ladies of Charity, or simply good neighbours or employers, women both visited and relieved poverty on a far greater scale than their male counterparts.[17] Indeed, upon closer examination several of the bodies which at first glance appear to be exclusively male, had very active women members, such as the Mendicity Association, in which the ladies of 'College Green district' organised a penny a week subscription towards purchasing a wheel for each woman in need, and recruited women to superintend girls' needlework.[18] Wealthy women were crucial to fundraising, not alone for what they themselves contributed, but through their social connections 'they can claim the bounty of the prosperous and the rich'.[19] Charity work provided well-to-do women with a wide range of possibilities, within which they could contribute very usefully, and respectably, to society. Most congregations of nuns operating in Dublin were heavily involved in at least some work among the poor, and provided opportunities for women to devote themselves wholly to the service of God and neighbour in the face of very apparent need; in the Dublin diocese the number of nuns was approximately 575 in 1850; by 1883 the number had risen to at least 1,793. By 1900 there were above 1,825 nuns, divided between c.97 convents, serving practically every part of the diocese.[20] And among those enduring the poorest circumstances and in need of such support, the over-representation of women was a well-established fact.

The scale and complexity of church charity operations in nineteenth century Dublin are such that tight boundaries must be set to this study. Two major areas of concern have been selected. As childcare is an issue central to all slum discussion, not least with infant mortality rates repeatedly used as an index of 'slumness', this study focuses on the 'boarding out' of destitute children, and the introduction of 'ragged' schools. Case study material is drawn from the Holy Faith achive, the religious congregation founded by Margaret Aylward with Fr. John Gowan CM and which continued the boarding-out orphanage and poor school network which she initiated. The slum question must also be considered from a gender perspective, as the imbalance between the sexes is so evident on the ground; this study then examines the issue of shelter for women most desperately in need, those who relied on the magdalen asylums,

---

[17] See also F.K. Prochaska, *Women and Philanthropy in Nineteenth Century England* (Oxford, 1980).
[18] *Second Report of the Association for the Suppression of Mendicity in Dublin*, 1819, pp. 4, 12.
[19] *A Brief Record of the Female Orphan House, North Circular Road, Dublin 1790–1892, compiled by NEMO* (Dublin 1893), p. 9.
[20] *Irish Ecclesiastical Register and Guidebook*, 1851, 1884 and 1901 editions.

discharged prisoners refuges, or night shelters. The date 1850 marks a new departure in charity organisation in Dublin, with the reform of the Corporation finally relieving each Catholic household from the obligation to contribute to the vestry cess (EC),[21] while the poor law union had (since 1838) taken over statutory charge of deserted children, and so provides a good starting point.

Childcare
Boarding Out of Destitute Children

The 'boarding-out' system of rearing young deserted children in families, under the Dublin Foundling Hospital (1703–1838), had been greatly discredited. Repeated parliamentary investigations in the eighteenth and early nineteenth century exposed scandalous neglect and mortality among the infants, the destitution of the foster-mothers and the irregularity of their payment, the disinterest of the governors, and a failure to keep correct records so that thousands of children were quite simply unaccounted for.[22] With the passing of the Poor Law (Ireland) Act in 1838 responsibility for deserted and destitute children became the charge of the union, which in its turn attempted to have children under two years of age nursed by country mothers, but was initially very reluctant to allow older children this advantage.

The relative merits and demerits of boarding out charity children was a major topic of public debate throughout the British Isles, one which involved financial considerations as well as human welfare, as the level of poor law rates and the disbursement of these funds interested every rate-payer to some extent.[23] The health and mortality of young children within the workhouses was repeatedly exposed as scandalous. The workhouse system, however distasteful to adults, was entirely unsuited to the needs of children, separated from their mothers and fathers.[24] In 1847 there were complaints in the North Dublin Union (NDU) about the 'neglected persons of the boys', not a matter of surprise considering that one woman had the sole charge of 300 boys.[25] In 1849 an NDU medical officer, Dr Monahan, reported that 'the majority of the children in the class 2–7 years are tainted with scrofula' and suggests that they should be removed to the 'sheds' (formerly the temporary fever hospital) on the banks of the Royal Canal,

---

[21] *SBO Thirteenth Annual Report*, 1869, p. 3.

[22] Including the years 1730, 1737, 1743, 1758, 1760, 1791, 1826, see J. Robins, *The Lost Children: A Study of Charity Children in Ireland 1700–1900* (Dublin, 1980; 1987 reprint), chapter ll '*The Foundling Hospitals*' pp. 10–59.

[23] For a comparison of the various boarding out systems in England, Scotland and Ireland, see Isabella Todd, 'Boarding out of Pauper Children,' *Stat. Soc. Inq. Soc. Ire. Jn.* 7, 54, 1876, pp. 293–299; also *Report from the Select Committee on Poor Law Relief, (England)*, 1988 (363) xv pp viii–ix; Minutes of Evidence pp. 14–17.

[24] See for example the case of women nursing children not their own, Minutes of North Dublin Union, 24 September 1845 (hereafter NDU Minutes).

[25] Ibid., 3 November 1847.

where 'their liability to disease would be lessened and their health greatly improved'.[26] At a meeting of the guardians of the NDU in 1857 a resolution was passed requesting the police commissioners, who were seeking admission for a number of foundlings in their care, 'to have the children kept for the present, as it would be nearly certain death to receive them into this house'.[27]

Although the indoor system was clearly not working, there was the serious question as to whether a sufficient number of good homes could be found for all those whom it was permissible (from 1862), to board out: orphan and deserted children, up to the age of eight years, for whom the union had sole guardianship. While complaints about the lot of 'indoor' union children continue, the introduction of 'boarding out' also led to regular complaints to the guardians about the neglect of individual NDU children at nurse. However too often more energy was directed to clearing the good name of the person accused than in ensuring that the children were properly cared for. The supervision of such children was assigned to the relieving officer of the district, who was responsible for handing over the child to the foster family after he or she had been vaccinated, to visit the child at least once a month and to report on its health, cleanliness and treatment, and should the child die, he was to see to the burial.[28] In 1878 complaints were made to the NDU guardians about the residence of a nurse in Finglas which however the relieving officer declared to be 'as clean and healthy as any of the union nurses and more so than many of them'.[29] Mr Dennis, of Ballygall House, inspected and 'in his opinion the nurse children in her charge are fairly treated, they look healthy, and appear to be cleanly kept'. He considered the nurse's residence 'not unhealthy'[30], to which the exasperated doctor who had requested the inquiry replied 'all I have to say is, God help the children at nurse, under the workhouse system'.[31] The national school teacher in Chapelizod complained that the Browne children at nurse locally did not get sufficient food, 'they are always picking up the bits of bread that the children throw away and seem to have little more to exist on'.[32] The lot of the union foundling or orphan was unenviable either inside or outside the workhouse.

Boarding-out was operated from an earlier date, and apparently with more success, by charities of different denominations. The Protestant Orphan Society operated from offices at 16/17 Upper Sackville Street, from where the children were 'placed in country parishes, in the county of Wicklow with Protestant nurses of good character and in comfortable circumstances, who are subject to the superintendence of the respective parochial clergymen and the inspection of the

[26] Ibid., 21 March 1849.
[27] W. Neilson Hancock, 'The Mortality of Children in Workhouses in Ireland', *Stat. Soc. Inq. Soc. Ire. Jn.* 3, 21, 1862, p. 197.
[28] Robins, *The Lost Children* (1987), p. 275.
[29] NDU Minutes, 23 November 1878.
[30] Ibid., 7 December 1878.
[31] Ibid., 30 November 1878.
[32] Ibid., 11 January 1879.

Committee. Great care is taken that they should be resident within a convenient distance of some scriptural school and the parish church'.[33] As the Protestant Orphan Society could only take children both of whose parents were Protestant it was not involved in controversy; the Protestant Orphan Union however, located in the same building, was constituted for the express purpose of caring for orphans of mixed marriages, and inevitably became enmeshed in disputes. The out-door system of childcare was operated by both orphanages, which along with the benefits of health and family ties, allowed greater numbers to be cared for than in a single building. On the Catholic side several small orphan societies boarded out their very small numbers, such as in the vicinity of Clondalkin; the only large Catholic orphanage operating the same system was St Brigid's (founded 1856).

St Brigid's Outdoor Orphanage for Girls and Boys

The system of 'family rearing' developed by Margaret Aylward with Fr. John Gowan CM was comprehensive and closely regulated, and within a few years on a scale far larger than that of any of the other orphan societies based in Dublin then using this system. In operation from 1857, St Brigid's campaigned relentlessly for the boarding-out of all workhouse children, and was credited with the adopion of this principle by the Poor Law Unions (for some children at least) from 1862.[34] Its first group of 37 infants were in fact workhouse foundlings who had been nursed by poor Catholic women in Wicklow, and were on the point of being returned to the North Dublin Union (where, by law, they would be registered as Protestants) as the nurses would no longer be paid for their maintenance, when Margaret Aylward and the parish priest of Francis Street, Fr. Edward McCabe, intervened. The nurses were persuaded to return home with their charges, on the understanding that the newly-formed St Brigid's would pay them every half year:

> These *enfants trouvés*, the poor deserted tho' innocent children, were accepted by St Brigid's, as no other Catholic institution in the city existed which could admit them.[35]

The admission of foundlings was always characteristic of the institution, although the number was small relative to the overall figures. The abandonment of infants was a feature of Dublin poverty in the 1850s, the situation facing young unmarried mothers being especially pitiable. Margaret Aylward estimated in 1858 that approximately 100 children were exposed in the city annually.[36] The case of the five week old infant surnamed Vincent is typical, and illustrates the urgent need that existed for child care and parental support:

---

[33] *Protestant Orphan Society, Thirty Fifth Annual Report, for the Year ending 31 December, 1863* (Dublin, 1864), p. 20.
[34] See *SBO Seventh Annual Report*, 1863; Fanny Taylor, *Irish Homes and Irish Hearts* (London, 1867), p. 56.
[35] St. Brigid's Orphanage Register, vol. 1, pp. 3, 5, 7 (hereafter SBO Register).
[36] *SBO Second Annual Report*, 1858, p. 17.

Mother's name Byrne – this child was left in a wad of straw in the middle of the road – child was born in the Coombe Lying-In Hospital. Mother was found and prosecuted – refused to take the child, said she could not support it – appeared almost dying.[37]

The vision of the city slums as nests of infamy and disease, popularised by the melodramatic accounts of journeys to the 'nether world', was presented very effectively by the promoters of St Brigid's Orphanage for fundraising purposes. These particular children, many of whom on admission were 'weak, pale, emaciated, diseased, full of sores' having spent their infancy 'in the courts and back lanes of the city, at the rears of which quantities of organic matter are allowed to accumulate, and putrefy, and infect the atmosphere'[38] needed 'healthy' locations, a requirement which was understood in both medical and moral terms:

> The children are reared at a distance from large towns, in isolated country places, where there is the least amount of vice, and the least amount of danger of contamination. The children are located likewise in small groups, four being the largest number in any one house, and this only in three or four cases, where usually the nurses have no children of their own, and where they have proved themselves capable of taking great care of them.[39]

> In case of epidemic, either physical or moral, their isolation in very small bodies is a happy security.[40]

The home addresses of the children admitted from Dublin are widely dispersed, with every slum area of the city (as illustrated in Chapters 2–4) represented. Such phrases as 'mother in great poverty,' 'wretchedly poor', 'in great distress', 'starving' 'very badly off and bad health' and occasionally 'all fearfully wild and neglected' punctuate the register entries, confirming the orphanage's policy of accepting only those destitute Catholic children, the poorest of the poor, for whom provision cannot otherwise be made, without danger to their faith.

Although the vast majority of the children were resident in Dublin city directly prior to admission (for example, 78% of all those entered 1868–1875 gave addresses from within the municipal boundary), the orphanage's managers were quick to emphasise that

> Though found in Dublin, they are from all parts of Ireland. Their poor parents, unable to live at home, or, perhaps, uprooted from that home of their childhood and their affections, drag their weary bones to Dublin, die and leave us their Orphans.[41]

The geographical spread of the foster homes can be illustrated by mapping the home addresses of all the foster mothers who had care of children during a

---

[37] SBO Register no. 104 (27 November 1858); other examples of children deserted by parents are nos. 912 (5 November 1870); 922 (16 March 1871); 955 (12 September 1871). It was customary in St Brigid's to give a foundling the surname Vincent after St Vincent de Paul; it was a marked improvement on naming children after the street or church door at which they were found, a widespread practice at the time.
[38] *SBO Sixth Annual Report*, 1862, p. 11.
[39] *SBO Sixteenth Annual Report*, 1873, p. 10.
[40] *SBO Second Annual Report*, 1858, p. 14.
[41] *SBO Fifth Annual Report*, 1861, p. 13.

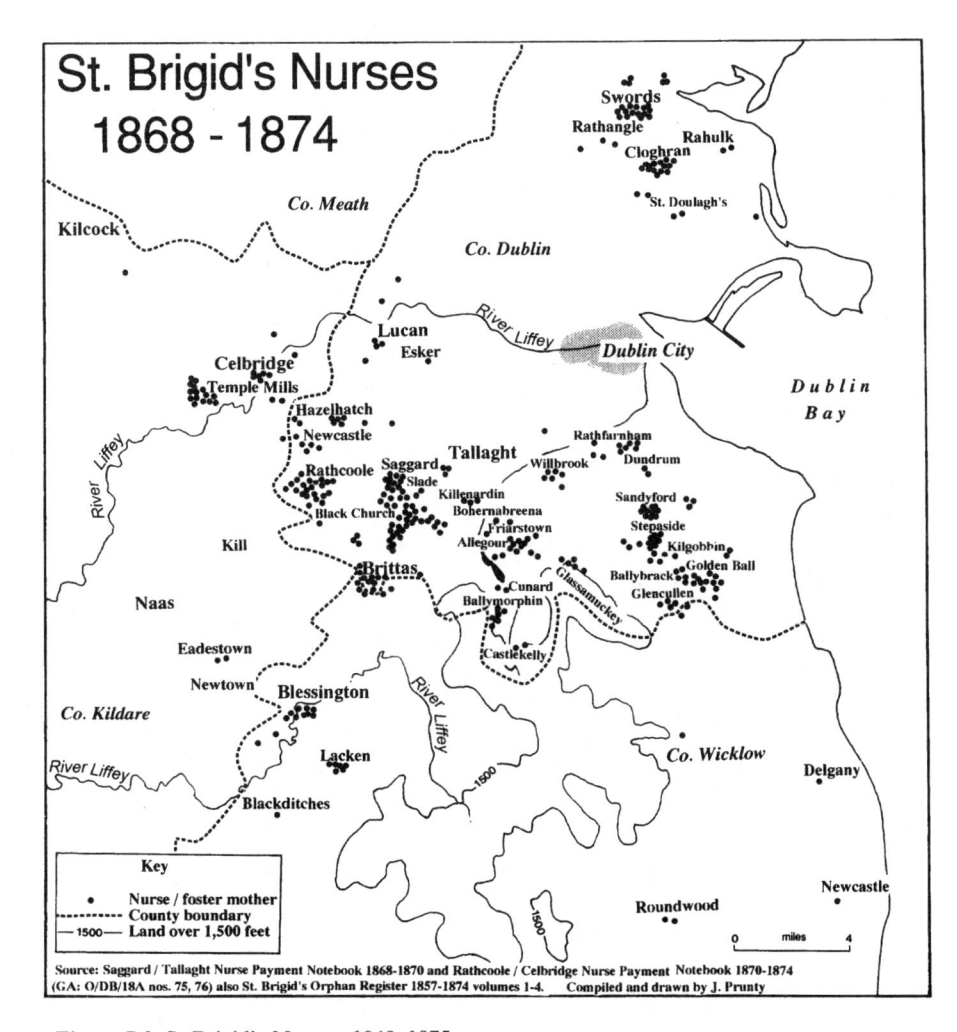

Church Charities Respond: Women and Children, 1850–1900

Figure 7.3 St Brigid's Nurses, 1868–1875

sample period 1868–74, when the orphanage accepted between 64 and 100 new children annually, and had an average of 292 in its care at any one point. The geographical pattern (Figure 7.3) was very well defined: two distinct settlements in north county Dublin, focusing on Swords and Cloghran; similar colonies to the west, on the county border with Kildare, in Celbridge, Hazlehatch, Newcastle and Rathcoole, continuing to the border with County Wicklow at Brittas, and from the foothills of the Dublin mountains towards the higher land of Wicklow. Saggard was the focus of one of the largest groupings, stretching southwards, while the valley of Glenasmole, south of Tallaght, was another important concentration of St Brigid's nurse children. This was a particularly remote area, quite self-contained both physically and socially in the nineteenth century, and worlds removed from the city slums. William Nolan's geographical study of this valley reveals close-knit kinship groups, the careful control of subdivision so that individual tenancies were viable, and the labour intensive reclamation of marginal land throughout the nineteenth century,[42] all factors which influenced the readiness of the families to take in nurse children and the willingness of the orphanage to entrust them to their care.

The grouping of these Dublin children facilitated supervision, characterised by twice-annual inspections and lightning 'unannounced visits that the lady visitor might see everything in their real, everyday state'[43] for 'then there can be no making up'.[44] This system had also the advantage of rearing boys and girls together, 'a happiness nearly impossible to us in any other arrangement'.[45] The primary requirement was good 'nurses' or foster mothers, recommended in writing by the local clergy (or by another nurse), and willing to 'act towards St Brigid's children as if they were her own and be a true mother to them'.[46] 'They are all small farmers, except one, all in possession of more or less land, with a greater or less stock of cows'.[47] The earliest register entries detail the family and economic circumstances of each nurse.[48]

The rural rearing provided by St Brigid's was the antithesis of the Dublin slum experience and associated workhouse relief. The institution constantly and very publicly compared its system with that of the poor law, stating for example that the mortality rate among children under 7 years of age in the workhouse was 60%, while St Brigid's, which accepted ill and invalid children and never operated a health test, could boast a rate of under 12%. The children who

---

[42] William Nolan, 'Society and Settlement in the Valley of Glenasmole,' in F.H.A. Aalen and Kevin Whelan, (eds.), *Dublin City and County: From Prehistory to Present* (Dublin, 1992), pp. 181–228.
[43] *SBO First Annual Report*, 1857, p. 5.
[44] *SBO Twenty Seventh Annual Report*, 1884, p. 5.
[45] Ibid., p. 14.
[46] *Instructions to the Nurses, St. Brigid's Orphanage*, (Dublin, 1858, reprinted 1899) p. 4.
[47] *SBO Second Annual Report*, 1858, p. 11.
[48] For example, SBO Register entry no. 104, 27 November 1858: Nurse Mrs. Anne McEvoy sister to Mrs Carroll, Ballintubber, 4 cows – 4 acres & 1/2 inside land, 3 young cattle, ass. 5 boys & a girl. – Kylebeg – Blessington. Recomd. by Mrs. McCreedy.

survived to seven years of age in the workhouse then risked 'scrofula, ophthalmia and pulmonary complaints' and were 'spiritless, dwarfed and prematurely old'. St Brigid's children, on the contrary, were 'playing and bounding in the green fields, the limbs lithe, the chest expanded and the rose in the cheek'.[49] At a safe remove from the dangers to health and morals which the city slums represented, St Brigid's child 'will grow up a branch of a fruitful tree', with 'a home and a hearth and a bit of land that he calls his own', among the 'religious, warm-hearted simple, brave unselfish peasantry of Ireland'.[50] St Brigid's Orphanage demonstrated in practice how 'boarding out' of charity children could be carried out successfully, when closely supervised, to the advantage of all parties concerned: children, foster families, rate-payers and subscribers. It provided an alternative model of childcare for destitute slum children rather than playing a role in the reform of slum life *per se*; that task was taken up by its associated poor or 'ragged' schools, St Brigid's schools of the Holy Faith.

Ragged Schools

The location of 'ragged schools' is yet another guide to the geography of poverty in Dublin, especially for the period 1850–1890s. By definition slum schools, the term was already in popular use in London, where several such foundations were made:[51]

> intended to elevate into decency those children whose abject and demoralised condition debars them from all other means of instruction and improvement.[52]

In the early 1850s the 'Ragged School, Shoe Black, Broomer and Messenger Society' advertised its ambition 'to afford general instruction, and industrial education as far as possible, to the children of the lowest ranks in Dublin' through its Protestant schools in Lurgan Street (north city) and Mill Street (south city).[53] The Catholic Ragged Schools similarly hoped 'to afford a literary, moral and industrial education to the children of the really destitute'.[54]

Protestant Ragged Schools and Homes: Irish Church Missions

On the Protestant side, the Irish Church Missions (ICM) was by far the most significant group involved in this type of education, with charge of at least seven such institutions in the 1850s and 1860s, (see Table 7.1, Figure 7.4). Most but not all originated with Sunday School movements. An evangelical missionary

---

[49] *SBO Seventh Annual Report*, 1863, pp. 6–7.
[50] *SBO Second Annual Report*, 1858, p. 13.
[51] In Field Lane, corner of West Street, Victoria Street and Holborn Hill; and Westminster Ragged Dormitory, New Pye Street, Westminster.
[52] *The British Metropolis in 1851: a Classified Guide to London* (London, 1851), p. 260.
[53] *First Annual Report of the Ragged School, Shoe Black, Broomer and Messenger Society*, 1852.
[54] *Second Annual Report of the Catholic Ragged Schools*, May 1853, p. 18.

IRISH CHURCH MISSIONS SCHOOLS AND HOMES, DUBLIN 1849–1900

1850 Inquiring Class, and Sunday School, St Michan's School Room, Bow Street (ends in 1855)

no date, but pre 1854, Mountjoy School, Inquiring Class

1852 Mission House, 27 Townsend Street, Sunday Ragged Schools
Mount Brown Sunday School
Ragged Day School for Boys, 27 / 53 Townsend Street (then to 167 Townsend Street)
Ragged Day School for Girls and infants, temporarily in stables rere of Mission House, Townsend Street
Ragged Boys' School, Grand Canal Street (corner of Grattan Street); also (later) Girls' and Infants' Day School, and sewing class for women, night school for boys

1853 Mission House licensed for Public Service
Boys' Ragged Schools, firstly in Weavers' Hall, removes to Skinner's Alley, the Coombe 1857
Ragged Schools, Lurgan Street (near Linenhall Barracks)
Girls' and Infants' Ragged Schools, firstly in Weavers' Hall, in 1854 removed to temporary accommodation in New Row
Girls' and Infants' Ragged School, 19 Luke Street
Training School for Female Teachers, 18 Luke Street

1856 Oriel Street, St Thomas's parish
Irishtown Sunday Schools (closed 1857)

1857 Coombe Schools – new school house
Ragged Sunday School, Fishamble Street

1858 Boys' Dormitory, 52 Townsend Street

1859 Birds' Nest, 12 York Road, Kingstown (new building 1861); branch home called 'Nead le Farraige' at Spiddal

1861 Grand Canal Street Boys' Dormitory

1861 Luke Street Girls' Dormitory

1868 Boys' Home, Coombe

1870 second Girls' Home in Luke Street

1872 Elliott Home for Waifs and Strays, 167/168/169 Townsend Street (later to Bray, and then to Charlemont Street)

1883 Home for Big Lads, 168 Townsend Street

1888 "Helping Hand" Home, 18 Hawkins Street

Compiled by J. Prunty from the Minute Books of the Irish Church Missions; annual published reports of the Dublin Visiting Mission, and the ICM-sponsored Smyly schools and homes; *"Them Also," the Story of the Dublin Mission*, (London, 1866); Alexander Dallas, *The Story of the Irish Church Missions, continued to the Year 1869* (London, 1875)

Table 7.1 Irish Church Missions Schools and Homes, Dublin 1849–1900.

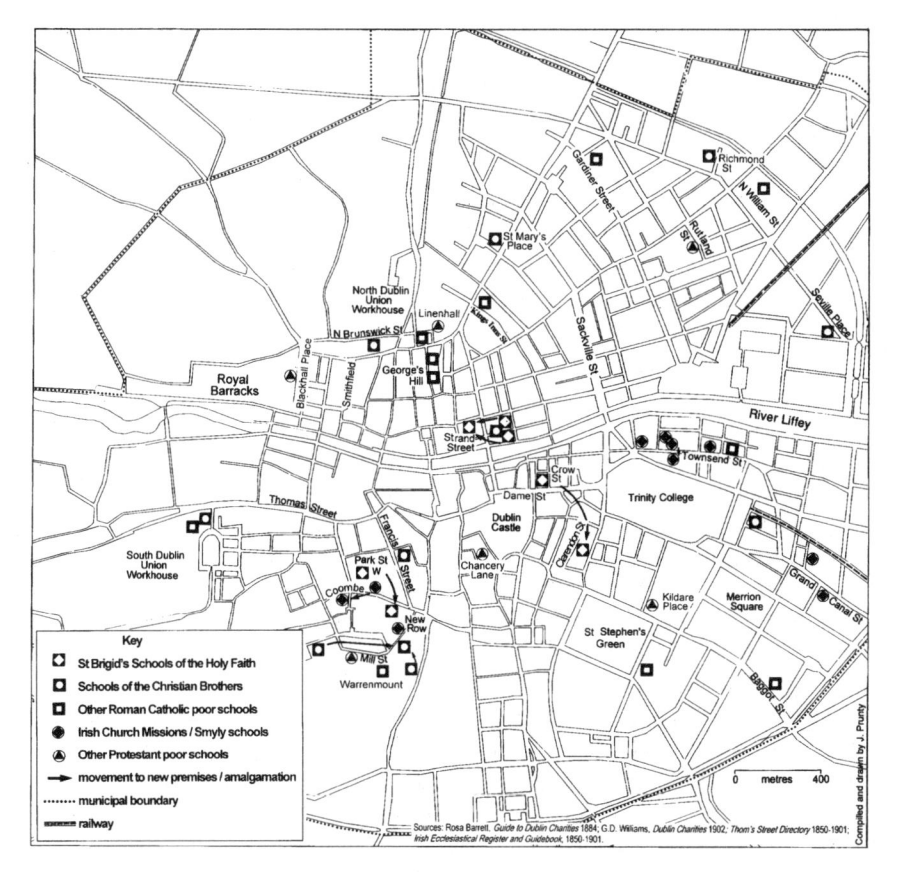

Figure 7.4 Selected Ragged/Poor Schools, Dublin 1850–1900.

movement committed to the conversion of Irish 'papists', the ICM is popularly associated with its most successful mission in Connemara.[55] However, its minutes clearly state the pre-eminence of Dublin in its all-Ireland ambitions:

> The most important missionary station of the Society is Dublin. Here are our Training establishments, our model schools, our largest material to work upon, and our most important machinery. I need say nothing to convince the committee that the Dublin mission with all its accompaniments must beyond doubt be maintained.[56]

Dublin was a locality 'most likely to attract and sustain the interest of all parties', 'offering such promise to missionary labours'.[57] A tenement house in Townsend Street (no. 27) in the very poor south dock area, was refurbished as headquarters, and the text 'Search the Scriptures' boldly stretched across the

---

[55] See Desmond Bowen, *Souperism: Myth or Reality, a Study in Souperism* (Cork, 1970); also Pascal Majerus, *The Second Reformation in West Galway: Alexander R. Dallas and the Society for the Irish Church Missions to the Roman Catholics, 1849–1859*; unpublished M.A. history thesis (UCD, 1990).

[56] Minutes of the Irish Church Missions, 'Report of Honorary Secretary', 9 June 1859, (hereafter ICM Minutes).

[57] ICM Minutes, 25 Nov. 1858, no. 2959.

facade. Here 'the wildest, and the lowest and the poorest were invited to come in'.[58] The plan of the new mission church (1853) is indicative of the climate of hostility within which the ICM operated, and of their express mission to the poorest: it had two entrances, the main entrance through the Mission House, and another at the back, through Rath Row, for 'the Nicodemuses who came in secret, the poor persecuted ones who wished to be hidden, and the shivering naked poor ones, who clustered round the stove warming their poor bodies, and perchance catching the good news of a home prepared in heaven even for them'.[59] Illustrations from Alexander Dallas' *A Mission Tourbook in Ireland* . . . (1862), (Plates 7.1, 7.2) further emphasise these aspects, as the curious creep into the night school from the semi-darkness, and in the tenement dwelling a barefoot woman and children listen to the scriptures being expounded by the agent, while even the reluctant man of the house is seen listening in despite himself.

The targeting of slum areas by the ICM provoked intense criticism, largely because of the material aid which the schools and homes provided. It was a complex matter. 'Supplying the bodily wants and raising into a state of civilisation the poor wanderers' was a prerequisite for successful schooling of any denomination; as the ICM stated plainly, 'without such means, teaching and schools would be of little avail'.[60] As a mission society schools were a legitimate activity, but the ICM was not a relief agency. By arranging in Dublin that the ICM would take charge of the 'education department', and the material needs would be the responsibility of a zealous and very able friend Mrs Ellen Smyly, and her committee, Dallas circumvented this obstacle in a most effective manner.[61] In the case of the Birds' Nest Home, Kingstown, for example, the teachers were paid by the society, but 'private charity' maintained the children.[62]

The support of several influential individuals and organisations including Archbishop Whately, the Protestant archbishop of Dublin, contributed to the strong financial position of the ICM in Dublin.[63] Its most ardent supporter was the aforementioned Mrs Ellen Smyly, 8 Merrion Square. A close friend of Dallas she began her first bible school in an old unused forge in Harmony Row, near Grand Canal Street about 1850. In conjunction with Dallas she started day schools first, as listed in Table 7.1: in Townsend Street, Grand Canal Street, the Coombe, Lurgan Street and 19 Luke Street, followed by residential homes in the same areas. Although each school had its own committee and published its own report, the same members sat on several committees; only the slightest efforts were made to keep the material and spiritual sides of the enterprises

[58] *Them Also* (1866), p. 17.
[59] *Them Also* (1866), pp. 14, 21.
[60] *Them Also* (1866), p. 272.
[61] *The Early History of Mrs. Smyly's Homes and Schools*, speech by Miss Vivienne Smyly (granddaughter) given 29 May 1976.
[62] Alexander Dallas, *The Story of the Irish Church Missions, continued to 1869* (London, 1875), p. 208, (hereafter *ICM Story*).
[63] Dallas, *ICM Story* (1875), pp. 122, 208, 239.

Church Charities Respond: Women and Children, 1850–1900 251

THE NIGHT SCHOOL

THE SCRIPTURE READER

From Alexander Dallas, *A Mission Tourbook in Ireland showing how to visit the Missions in Dublin, Connemara etc.*, 1862.

Plate 7.1 *The Night School*, ICM 1862
Plate 7.2 *The Scripture Reader*, ICM 1862

separate so that from the outset they became totally entwined.[64] Their overlapping structure explains why criticisms that were directed against the ICM schools were regularly extended to include Lurgan Street, Mill Street and other Protestant poor schools (Figure 7.4).[65]

Residential homes were an important part of the ICM/Smyly network. Chancery Lane, in the heart of the Liberties, was in operation before 1850, and was supported but not controlled by the ICM, being granted permission in 1870 to build a refuge for boys on property belonging to the ICM in the Coombe.[66] It was however for 'boys who had gained admittance by their good character' and did not reach the many 'poor wandering Arabs' who attended the ragged schools by day and in the evenings 'pressed around the stove and begged to be allowed to sleep on the floor near it'. In 1858 no. 52 Townsend Street was purchased, hop sacks were filled with straw for beds, blankets purchased, and forty boys took up residence.[67] More suitable premises were built onto Grand Canal Street school in 1861, where the boys were already attending night classes.[68] Immediately on the opening of the ICM Ragged Boys' Home in Townsend Street, a Catholic dormitory was opened in number 80. Despite the publicity which surrounded its foundation, and the active encouragement of Cardinal Wiseman, the Catholic institution was a spectacular failure and closed within a few months. A 'great bazaar' in the Rotunda to supply the funds was an embarrassing and very public disaster, raising only £3, a circumstance that the ICM ensured was well known.[69]

The ICM opened a ragged school in Fishamble Street in 1857, 'a very poor part of the town and, and the very place for missionary work'.[70] This moved to temporary accommodation in Wicklow Street and then to neighbouring Werburgh Street in 1863, at which stage a fundraising drive was led by Miss Whately of 5 Elgin Road, with a committee of wealthy women, to establish a proper schoolhouse, which would accommodate Sunday, night and evening classes, and a daily school 'much needed to reclaim the swarming multitudes around us'.[71] The fundraisers claimed attendance of over 800 would result if they had but space enough, regretting that so many of 'these poor, ragged people, anxious as they are to learn the gospel' are being constantly turned away.[72]

---

[64] Ibid., 23 March 1871 no. 4890; 25 Jan. 1872 no. 4982.
[65] *Them Also* (1866), p. 42–43; *Second Annual Report of the Catholic Ragged Schools*, May 1853, p. 11.
[66] ICM Minutes, 24 Nov. 1870, no. 4846.
[67] *Them Also* (1866), op.cit., p. 86–89.
[68] Ibid., p. 126.
[69] Ibid., pp. 78, 89.
[70] Ibid., p. 72.
[71] Appeal for building a schoolhouse for a ragged school already existing in one of the worst parts of Dublin, 1863, DDA: 320/2 no. 70.
[72] Ibid.

Roman Catholic Ragged Schools

The first lay Catholic Ragged Schools (1851), established by 'a number of good men, chiefly of the Confraternities'[73] served two areas: North Anne Street/Halston Street/Church Street on the north side, and to the south in Chamber Street and Blackpitts 'the poorest part of the most impoverished district of our city' (Figure 7.4).[74] The object was 'to afford a literary, moral and industrial education to the children of the really destitute'.[75] A firm distinction was drawn between the 'children of those who are usually denominated the poorer or lower class' and for whom parochial, national, Christian Brothers and convent schools provide, and those even lower in the social scale:

that class of children, who, some through the indolence or vice of their parents, others through real destitution, are thrown out on our streets to beg their food – perhaps to procure it by even more disreputable means – or, who, in order to sustain a miserable existence, are compelled to attend at those schools opened for their perversion by the enemies of our holy faith.[76]

The emphasis therefore was on providing for those children 'of want and destitution', exposed to the triple evils of ignorance, vice and irreligion, liable to get 'so inured to crime, so hardened in infamy, as to become pests to society, a disgrace and reproach to their country', finally forming 'that class from which our prisons and convict ships have ever received most of their denizens'.[77] Attendance at the competing Protestant ragged schools, it was claimed was only likely to compound their troubles, exposing them 'to the heretical doctrines of a creed which teaches them to revile all that we hold sacred'.[78]

The title 'ragged school' was in use by the Catholic committee for a very brief period, 'adopted by us more as a matter of expediency than choice, suggesting itself as it did in the condition of the children for whose benefit they are intended', and as early as their second report in 1853 some subscribers complain of the title as derogatory. On taking charge of the Catholic Ragged School at West Park Street, the Coombe in 1865, Margaret Aylward's first move was to rename them after St Brigid: 'She could never be induced to adopt the name ragged. She said that Irish children, though poor, have a certain hereditary nobility of mind that resents degradation'.[79]

The frequent amalgamations and relocations of the Catholic ragged schools, as well as the changes of name, and the different types of instruction provided, (with Sunday Schools, daily schools and night classes), make this aspect of the slum geography as difficult to disentangle as was the case with the Protestant schools (Figure 7.4). Blackpitts and Chamber Street Sunday schools were

---

[73] *SBO Thirty Fourth Annual Report*, 1891, p. 10.
[74] *Second Annual Report of the Catholic Ragged Schools*, May 1853, p. 12.
[75] Ibid., p. 18.
[76] Ibid., p. 6.
[77] Ibid., p. 18.
[78] Ibid., p. 6.
[79] *SBO Thirty Fourth Annual Report*, 1891, p. 10.

amalgamated a year after their foundation (1851), and became part of a large daily and Sunday school, in New Row; the Sunday school in Church Street operated for one year only, and the children attending it were redistributed mainly to North Anne Street and Halston Street, while both Sunday school and daily schools were opened in Westland Row in 1853.

One of the most significant contributors to the Roman Catholic ragged or poor school network, Margaret Aylward, at the suggestion of her close friend and collaborator Fr John Gowan CM determined on establishing 'small *poor* schools (about 50 children in each, boys up to a certain age and girls) thro' the city – where there are no schools', or where only children who could not afford the school penny per week would be taken, 'the more abandoned more destitute children we would take'.[80] The geographical spread of St Brigid's schools can be understood in relation to the avowed intention 'to carry the schooling into the poor localities, to the doors of the room-keepers and inhabitants of cellars'[81] and 'to withdraw the children of the neighbourhood from Protestant and proselytising schools'.[82] The earliest south city foundations were in Crow Street (1861), part of the Temple Bar district, in a house provided free by the Oblate fathers, followed by West Park Street, the Coombe (1865), and Clarendon Street, a street of doubtful status near St Stephen's Green where five tenement houses were thrown down and new schools and a convent built in 1870.[83] On the north side in the old Markets area, in 'the centre of a dense and poor population'[84] schools were opened in a warehouse in 14 Great Strand Street (1863) and in a tenement house in 65 Jervis Street (1870), both of which removed to fine purpose-built schoolrooms in Little Strand Street in 1888. The Holy Faith poor school geography, in several instances, also reflected that of the Christian Brothers who had already established Catholic poor schools for boys, and maintained themselves independent of the National Board (excepting a brief experimental period in the 1840s). The Rice foundations in Waterford, Aylward's home city, had provided the inspiration for the project, while the Christian Brothers gave practical and moral support to the Aylward venture from the outset. In the case of Strand Street and the Coombe, pre-existing Christian Brothers' schools provided for the local boys, while St Brigid's provided for the infants and girls of the same families.

The principal difference between the national school system, and these 'ragged' or 'poor' schools, as far as the families involved were concerned, was the provision of food each day and the occasional distribution of clothing. However, the distinction was not so straightforward, as a number of convent national schools, such as in George's Hill (Presentation convent) and King's Inns Street (Mercy convent), were heavily involved in providing their pupils with

[80] Margaret Aylward to Dr. Kirby, 29 November 1860, GA: Mc/K/12 no. 26b.
[81] *SBO Ninth Annual Report*, 1865, p. 14.
[82] *SBO Seventh Annual Report*, 1863, p. 15.
[83] *SBO Fifteenth Annual Report*, 1872, p. 13.
[84] *SBO Thirty Third Annual Report*, 1889, p. 12.

food and clothing despite the disapproval of the Commissioners of National Education. Such flaunting of strict regulations precipitated a special investigation in 1864, into whether such schools used relief as an inducement to non-Catholic children to attend.[85] While the convent schools mentioned were entirely cleared of any underhand motives, their attendance being exclusively Catholic ('but it is also unmixed in all the large ordinary schools north of the Liffey within the city'[86]), the investigation is indicative of the climate within which the national schools operated; to ensure a free hand in relief as well as in religious matters the ragged schools' purpose was best served by operating outside the state sector.

The Coombe: Ragged Schools in Competition

Sectarian competition between schools established avowedly to serve the very poorest children of the city slums is well illustrated in the case of the Coombe, the curved street in the heart of the south-western industrial sector known as the Liberties that featured without fail in every city slum inquiry and report since 1797 (see Chapter 2, Figures 2.1, 2.7). The Irish Church Missions identified the district as ideal mission territory:

> The quarter of Dublin called "the Liberties" was the stronghold of Papal darkness and intolerance. The appearance of the streets, once the abodes of splendour and opulence, now of squalor and wretchedness, indicated the fact; the same houses only sheltering now the famishing victims of ignorance and vice. In the very centre of this misery were erected, by the benevolence of Christian friends in Dublin, the Coombe Ragged Schools, which stand in strange contrast with the filthy mansions around them, a beacon in the darkness and a protest against the system which perpetuated it.[87]

The Weavers' Hall, facing the main thoroughfare of the Coombe, was used temporarily as a Protestant schoolhouse (c.1853). 'The dense mass of Roman Catholics who inhabit the narrow lanes and courts of that low district' provided ample numbers from the outset.[88] Over 100 children were taught upstairs, one visitor recording that 'few amongst them had washed face and hands; scarce one had on a single garment in a whole condition; some were shirtless, some coatless, and some everything-less save filthy rags'.[89] In 1854 the Weavers' Hall numbers were so large that the girls and infants were removed to a tumbledown house in New Row, but the boys' day school, Sunday schools and Thursday evening 'controversial classes' for both adults and children, continued to be held in the hall.[90]

Battle between the local Catholic clergy and their supporters, and the equally zealous and well-supported managers of the ICM school, was inevitable,

---

[85] *Special Report on Convent National Schools in Ireland, 1864*, (405) XLVI.63.
[86] *Ibid.*, pp. 73, 77.
[87] *ICM Story* (1875), p. 178.
[88] Ibid., p. 179.
[89] *Them Also* (1866), p. 23.
[90] Ibid., p. 31.

especially considering that the vast majority of the local population was Roman Catholic (as was the case in every city slum area, see Figure 7.1). The Protestant missionaries described their new school in the Coombe in military terms as a brave attempt to enter the 'stronghold of Popery' and 'take their citadel by storm'.[91] The Dublin Mission 'had taken open standing-ground, and had plainly sounded out the cry, "Come out of her, my people"'.[92] The Roman Catholic reply, as led by St Brigid's orphanage and poor schools, was to call on its adherents to 'take again the road of our forefathers, a road of trials, tears, fines, imprisonments, and blood, and we will try to fight out the fight they fought for the Faith which is found in the one Holy Catholic and Roman Church'.[93]

There can be no doubting the intense hostility which surrounded the Coombe schools. Sporadic outbreaks of violence in the early 1850s, with readers occasionally 'pelted with mud and stones' were superseded by more intense and disciplined efforts to oust them.[94] Public scrutiny was led by Margaret Aylward, who although heavily involved in home visitation of the 'sick poor' of the north city parishes of St Mary's and St Michan's (Chapter 8), made time to research the city-wide activities of the ICM in a professional manner. Published reports by Margaret Aylward for the 1850s describe the scenes encountered whenever they penetrated the mission schools, and the interviews later held with the women, where 'we found their dread of the poor house so great, that for the morsel of dry bread doled out to them in the Sunday school, they pledged their immortal souls'.[95] In the Coombe the observers she placed to keep watch over the ICM school reported that poor women came to give them their name, address and religion, 'in the hope that they could get them employment'.[96]

Street violence erupted periodically, the blame on each occasion very firmly laid at the feet of the opposition. The placing of Catholic 'observers' outside the school premises was guaranteed to increase tension, with the ICM agents complaining that 'these Ladies are about to persecute our people, they are organising a persecution against the Protestants'.[97] There are reports of children being dragged away by the school mistresses to prevent them being interviewed by the Ladies of Charity, of the Catholic ladies distributing crucifixes among the children, and the Protestant missionaries removing these 'idols' from them, of crowds of Dublin men, women, and children assembling to join in the excitement, urging on the disputing parties with cries of 'more power to you!'[98] Nothing daunted, the ladies persevered. 'The disagreeable labour of watching these

---

[91] Ibid., p. 58.
[92] Ibid., p. 41.
[93] *SBO Third Annual Report*, 1859, p. 22.
[94] *ICM Story* (1875), p. 178.
[95] *First Annual Report of the Ladies of Charity of St. Vincent de Paul*, (Metropolitan Branch) Dublin, 1852, p. 23, (hereafter Ladies of Charity).
[96] *Ladies of Charity, Fifth Report*, 1856, p. 9.
[97] Ibid.
[98] *Ladies of Charity, First Report*, 1852, p. 22.

schools, of pursuing the poor children through the windings of the wretched lanes and courts, of breaking through the excuses, equivocations, and lies of the infatuated parents, was cheerfully endured by them'.[99] On several occasions the police were called and names taken, an incident in the Coombe in 1856 receiving special note. The policeman who had been summoned was pressurised by the Protestant superintendent to 'make a clean job of it, man, and take them to the station-house', while crowds of bystanders gathered protesting 'shame on you, to speak so to ladies!' and calling out derisively (concerning Margaret Aylward) 'who charges her and with what?'

> The crowd poured out benedictions, a body guard surrounded them, declaring they would protect them while the sky was over them. They expressed a wish for a car; a boy flew, apparently with winged feet, to get one for them, and still the poor Souper appeared not satisfied, and at the car, he stood waving his hand after those who entered it.[100]

This Coombe incident only served to spur the ladies on to greater efforts, even more members volunteering to watch the Irish Church Mission school in Townsend Street the following Sunday.[101] The ICM was no less discouraged, and redoubled its commitment to the Coombe.

On 11 February 1857 fine new ICM premises were opened, 'The gospel standard was anew unfurled, and an invitation sounded out to the lowest and most degraded of God's human creation to flock around it'.[102] The *Daily Express* described each group of children in turn: the ragged infants were held together by the 'stout check bib' provided by the institution; some of the boys wore 'discarded military coats, faded in colour and not strikingly accurate as to fit', but most 'had nothing to cover them from the wintry blast but ragged shirts, black as the earth, that was, doubtless, the accustomed bed of their wretched wearers'. 'Features prematurely old' characterised them, and 'some were so charred, and more than usually discoloured, as to betray a nightly acquaintance with the limekiln or the coke-oven'.[103] To secure more pupils to fill these new schoolrooms the agents 'determined to go to more distant streets, getting the children from these first, and gradually approach the school'. This plan 'succeeded very well; the children from a distance were not suspected'.[104]

Six weeks after the opening of the new school-house the expected hostilities recommenced, with the ICM claiming that some of the children were waylaid and forcibly carried off to the Catholic Ragged School in West Park Street; a few weeks later 'the female teachers were rolled in the mud and their bonnets torn from their heads', obliged to take a cab to and from the school for safety.[105] On 13 May of that eventful year, 1857, a 'very trifling occurrence' ignited 'the

---

[99] *Ladies of Charity, Fifth Report*, 1856, p. 9.
[100] Ibid., pp. 10–11.
[101] Ibid., p. 11.
[102] *Them Also* (1866), p. 55.
[103] *Daily Express*, 12 February 1857, quoted in *Them Also* (1866), p. 57.
[104] *Them Also* (1866), p. 60.
[105] Ibid., p. 62.

smouldering ashes of discord', a mob was gathered 'from every lane and by-way in the Liberty', joined with the congregation leaving Francis Street Chapel, and attacked the Mission Schools, the Weavers' Hall, and Luke's Schools with stones and brickbats. The police arrived to face a mob of three thousand:

Prisoners were made and rescued; the police were driven back; and the mob, encouraged by their temporary triumph, redoubled their exertions, threatened "death to the soupers", and loaded them with maledictions.[106]

The rabble regrouped several times, but most of the damage was inflicted upon the rioters themselves, 'who fell upon one another, and hundreds were beaten and bruised in this fearful affray'.[107] The resident ICM agent, Mr. Holden, was, providentially, the only Protestant injured; for the rest of his life the absence of two front teeth served 'as a token of the danger and deliverance' of that memorable night.[108]

By 1866 such open violence had ended, but the hostility and suspicion which surrounded the Coombe Ragged Schools was to continue. The ICM, criticising in particular the charities with which Margaret Aylward was associated, acidly noted the shift in tactics adopted by their Catholic competitors:

Bazaars, and feasts, and flattery, are henceforth to take the place of mobs, and missiles, and massacres, and we are to be let alone. This is a decided improvement in the system of Rome, and we thank God for it.[109]

The battle for the souls of the Dublin poor was inextricably bound up with a real concern for their daily efforts to make ends meet, and gave a sharp focus to interest in the city slums from the late 1840s.

St Brigid's Schools, West Park Street, the Coombe
Distribution of Relief

Efforts were made in the mid 1850s to place the struggling Catholic ragged school in West Park Street, the Coombe, on a firmer footing by transferring its management to a religious community, the *Soeurs de Charité*. This was a French congregation founded by St Vincent de Paul for the service of the very poorest (and known in Ireland as the Daughters of Charity), which Margaret Aylward considered ideal to take on the long-term management of the charities she had founded, in collaboration with a committed lay membership. In October 1856 she decided to try and expand their proposed role in Dublin, and suggested to the newly-appointed parish priest of Francis Street, Fr Edward McCabe, that

---

[106] Ibid., p. 63.
[107] *ICM Story* (1875), p. 179.
[108] *Them Also* (1866), p. 64.
[109] The two associations of 'our blessed Lady of *charity*', here criticised are the Ladies' Association of Charity of St Vincent de Paul, Marlborough Street (Chapter 8), and the Queen of Charity House, Jervis Street, taken over by Holy Faith Sisters in 1870. *Them Also* (1866), pp. 97–98.

the *Soeurs* might also take charge of the ragged school in his parish. The Vincentian superior was assured that 'a glorious work lies before them, they will see poverty, rags, misery, wretchedness, such as I do believe they never saw before' in a part of the city where proselytism 'raged'.[110] While the Daughters of Charity, through Margaret's active diplomacy, did come to Dublin, and began an 'indoor' orphanage and later school in North William Street (near the North Strand), they did not take up the invitation to manage her charities or the West Park Street schools; the charge of the ragged schools was taken on by Margaret Aylward and her own fledgling religious congregation, the Sisters of the Holy Faith, from October 1865.

Journals dating from their relaunching as St Brigid's Catholic Schools of the Holy Faith in 1865 (first entries by Cecilia Donovan) have survived for this 'ragged' school, providing insights into the role such institutions played among those living locally, in what have been so thoroughly documented as appalling slum conditions. St Brigid's mission as a school which welcomes the very poorest (while not excluding others) cannot be distanced from its role as a relief agency, at least up to 1927 when it went under the national board of education. Its managers found themselves 'obliged' to provide daily breakfast, and clothing as required, or the school could not operate at all.[111] While defending themselves against counter-charges of proselytism, they also had to educate public opinion in support of investing in the very poorest, popularly regarded as wild and unteachable; in West Park Street 'though very poor, they are good children, quick, intelligent, and easily trained in virtue. It would be a pity to abandon such children'.[112]

The type and quantity of relief provided can be judged from the journals, although some of the entries are very brief, e.g.: '60 articles of clothing distributed on the day of the holidays, 22 December 1865'. The number of articles of clothing at any one 'distribution' in the boys' school ranged from 40 to 148, and an almost identical quantity was provided in the girls' school. 'Distributions' were usually held twice yearly, at midsummer and Christmas, occasions which also served as concert days and prize giving, so that a typical entry for the boys' school reads:

22 December 1875. Premiums were distributed consisting of: 50 shirts, 39 pairs of trousers, 20 coats, 2 prayer book, 2 pair of beads, 3 medallions, and 1 statue.

In the girls' schools a similar situation existed; on the 13 April 1881 'the following articles of clothing were distributed to the poor children by Mrs Teeling: 28 dresses, 43 bibs, 38 chemises'. The clothing situation depended on what was donated or could be spared from the 'breakfast fund'; it was always therefore quite precarious, and on several occasions a particular appeal was made, as in 1880 when the managers report: 'We have continued to give the food, and

---

[110] Margaret Aylward to Père Etienne, 8 October 1856, GA: MA/CH/02 no. 46a.
[111] *SBO Sixteenth Annual Report*, 1873, pp. 11–14.
[112] Ibid.

even increased the quantity latterly, but the state of our funds for the last nine months did not permit us to give any clothing'.[113]

A greater number of families benefited by food relief than were clothed. Cecilia Donovan recounts that on arrival to open up the sisters would often meet 'a row of little boys standing by the wall in their caps to keep the feet warm while waiting at the school door',[114] the first of the breakfast queue. About 200 children were provided with breakfast in school and sent home with a loaf of bread, a very real incentive to scholarly exertion; there were also periodic distributions of food to these families, and a relief order at Christmas could be relied upon. The donors are credited with sponsoring such distributions where applicable. A typical Christmas entry reads:

1884, On Christmas Eve tea and sugar were given to the poor children, 2oz of tea and ½lb of sugar with two loaves to each family; if only one child, one loaf was given. 400 packages of tea and 200 of sugar were ordered at Mr Burk's and Mr Flanagan's. This tea and sugar were ordered and paid for by the superior.

The quantities and proportions varied, some years 3oz tea and 1lb sugar being available, and 'an order for 2 stones of coal' to the 'most deserving families'. The number of families receiving the Christmas relief rose inexorably throughout the period, to the number of 2,205 persons recorded for Christmas Eve 1903, and '521 articles of clothing given away'. The staples of tea, sugar, bread, coal and clothing rarely change, even in the festive season; an entry for 1897 reads 'On Friday 240 families received bread, tea and sugar for Christmas dinner'. In 1909 meat, blankets and money were added to the relief list; by then the tea and sugar were provided by means of an 'order' to Mrs McCaffrey, 7 New Market Street, and 'tickets for 2 tons of coal from the Mansion House' were distributed.

The reliance of many of the children on the school food, as advertised in the annual reports,[115] cannot be doubted as it apparently had to continue even when there was a break from classes: 'The day the retreat commenced August 10 1896 the poor children who get breakfast every day at the school received one loaf each and a 3oz package of tea with 1lb of sugar instead of coming to the school for breakfast for the week'.

Assessment of St Brigid's Schools, The Coombe

One of the founding principles of St Brigid's schools was to 'try to fit the children for their position in society' by teaching the poor children 'reading, writing, and some ciphering, and the girls as much sewing as will enable them to mend and make for an humble family'.[116] While no extravagant hopes were entertained for the pupils, tremendous pride was taken in their achievements.

---

[113] *SBO Twenty Third Annual Report*, 1880, p. 9.
[114] Sr. Cecilia Donovan, *ms* History West Park Street Schools, 1915, GA: Hc/S/21 no. 18.
[115] *SBO Twenty Third Annual Report*, 1880, p. 9.
[116] *SBO Fifth Annual Report*, 1861, p. 12.

The educational standard in the boys' poor school compares favourably with that in the adjoining private school which boasted that 'as a rule the boys are in fifth standard of the Christian Brothers reading book before leaving the Holy Faith School to continue their studies elsewhere'.[117] An examination of 138 poor boys of all ages in St Brigid's on 3 December 1889 reveals that there were 16 boys or 12% on the fifth reading book, and altogether 31% of the poor boys were on either the fourth or fifth reading book.[118] While St Brigid's boys undoubtedly had a shorter school career, many attained a high standard in that time.

The journal for the boys' school records the careers of many past-pupils, and in several instances the contacts exploited to secure these positions. Thus Michael Noon became manager of a factory in Waterford 1876; 'Patrick Connor got a situation in the Post Office through the interest of Fr Roache CM. James Griffin was taken into Duffy's Essex Quay, through Fr Hickey and got the trade of book binding. John Conroy is a coach painter, 1886'. In 1890 six boys who were taken on by the 'National Press Office' are named, also boys who got jobs as messengers, porters, carpenters, or 'are in the employment of Messrs Brown and Nolan'. Other employers are Guinnesses, the Clarence Hotel, the Post Office and the GPO, while there are several entries which simply give the name of the employer such as 'Mr Kavanagh's' or the place of employment such as 'Chatham Street'. Several boys got work in England, and others are 'doing business at home'. In 1900 a former pupil, now manager in the Dublin Printing Company, 'takes on a boy to keep accounts'. There is special mention made of Patrick Madden, who started school in 1872, and stayed 'five or six years before going for a sailor'. Having met with an accident which 'disqualified him for the duties of a sailor' he resumed his studies and became a school master: 'He is now teaching Indians on the mountains of California and is in the receipt of £216 a year. His letters to his mother in the parish of St. Nicholas breathe much filial piety'.

The opening of a boys' industrial class 26 August 1901, when '18 boys commenced with mufflers', followed by the presentation of a new sewing machine by the superior the following year, may have enhanced their employment prospects, but by then the journal has largely ceased to record notes on past pupils. While the careers of only a fraction of the vast numbers of boys who passed through the schools are known, and the girls' journal keeps no such record at all, it appears that the claims made in the annual reports were not without foundation:

Many of the poor children are now in good situations and profitable employment, having lifted themselves out of poverty by means of the solid literary education they received in the Schools of the Holy Faith. What is still better, many of them made their widowed mothers comfortable, while some others are known to have rescued their parents from habits of dissipation and sin, by persuading them to go to confession and practise their religion.[119]

---

[117] Donovan, *ms* History West Park Street (1915).
[118] West Park Street Journal, 3 December 1889, examination by Fr. Hickey.
[119] *SBO Thirty First Annual Report*, 1888 p. 16.

Another effect, claimed to be huge but impossible to quantify, was the success in keeping families together during times of hardship. During Richard Peel's absence in America his five children were maintained at home: 'gave them everything the school could afford otherwise they must have gone to the workhouse'; similarly a homeless woman Mrs Byrne had the rent paid for her and her children kept in school. The precariousness of daily life in the city slums meant that school food was too often a significant support; by ensuring that children did not abandon home out of sheer hunger, St Brigid's claimed to have successfully kept families together: 'It is a blessed thing to keep the family together while the children are young. God has built civil order upon the family, and if it be well ordered, society will be healthy and prosperous'.[120]

Ragged Schools as Civilising Influences

The civilizing effects of education on the 'street arabs' is emphasised by all school promoters, the denominational affiliation of the managers determining to which church their reformation and reclamation can be credited. Graduates of the Boys' Home, 52 Townsend Street, now working at trades throughout the city, were described as 'a noble set of youths, rescued from vice and degradation, and from Romish delusion, and all manifesting with Irish warmth their love and gratitude' to their sponsors, Mr Dallas and Mrs Smyly.[121] Under scriptural training 'the children are divested of their natural ferocity, and wild wandering habits', their 'quickness, seriousness, and steadiness' cannot fail to impress.[122] The ICM credited their Coombe schools with exercising a 'holier, gentler influence' and 'transforming lawless ruffians into loyal quiet citizens'.[123]

St Brigid's in the Coombe likewise prided itself on the fact that 'these wild children become, after three or four years, quite tractable, so much so, that the Sisters prefer the labour of teaching them to that of any other children'.[124] On returning from a visit, Archbishop Walsh declared himself 'delighted with all I saw today. Everyone who was at the schools was talking of the graceful bearing of the children' and that the work 'plainly is bringing a great blessing on that poor neighbourhood'.[125] Keeping children out of prison, and so saving society that expense, was publicised as another cause for pride. Of the 3,000 children who passed through the school over a period of 20 years, six who had spent only brief periods as pupils 'were brought before the magistrate and punished'; 'of those who had been under the discipline of the school three years or more, none are known to have become criminals'.[126] The institution was therefore advertised

---

[120] Ibid., p. 21.
[121] Dallas, *ICM Story* (1875), p. 297.
[122] *Them Also* (1866), p. 97.
[123] Dallas, *ICM Story* (1875), p. 179.
[124] *SBO Thirty First Annual Report*, 1888, p. 20.
[125] Willam J. Walsh to Fr. John Gowan, 4 March 1890, GA: JG/ML/07 no. 18.
[126] *SBO Thirty Fourth Annual Report*, 1891, p. 15 .

as promoting social order, keeping the very poor from 'gnawing in their despair the very bonds of society'.[127]

In the case of St Brigid's, it was claimed the secret to success was grounded in the interaction between very poor and slightly better-off children, transforming 'wild and apparently untamable children into steady and self-respecting boys and girls', as they gradually learn to behave 'as their betters do' in terms of obedience, self-discipline and courtesy. Allied with this was the thorough integration of religion into the school day and beyond, ensuring that 'the Sacrifice, the Sacraments, the Liturgy and the pious practices of the Catholic Church are active agents in the education of these children'.[128]

Women and Destitution

The near and absolute destitution which was the lot of many women in Dublin throughout the nineteenth century has been well documented.[129] This appalling situation, at the core of the slum problem, was directly related to an oversupplied pool of unskilled casual labour, and the paucity of female employment opportunities:

Dublin is almost unpossessed of manufactories affording employment for females, an unusually large proportion of whom, therefore, live in involuntary indolence; as a necessary result, the earnings of a family are mainly confined to those of the adult males, and are, therefore limited.[130]

It is against this backdrop of very limited opportunity that the questions of prostitution, crime, and vagrancy among women must be viewed, and the role of the charitable asylums examined.

Asylums for 'Penitent Magdalens'

The rescue and reform of prostitutes was seen as a major work of mercy by both Protestant and Roman Catholic church activists in nineteenth century Dublin. The extent and nature of prostitution was the subject of various official inquiries, but the government did not concern itself with the social causes of the practice, nor its effects on the women involved. Such was the taboo surrounding venereal disease that the North Dublin Union workhouse, though the last refuge of the broken and desperate, as well as of those temporarily in need, ordered in 1847 that any woman found to be with VD be discharged at once, an exclusion which extended to no other class or disability, even cases of the most contagious disease.[131] Legislation such as the Contagious Diseases Acts (1864, 1866, 1869)

---

[127] *SBO Fifth Annual Report*, 1861, p. 11.
[128] *SBO Thirty First Annual Report*, 1888, p. 16.
[129] See especially Chapter 2.
[130] 'Statement Read Before the Royal Commission at the Close of the Inquiry, on 16 October 1879 by the Secretary of the Public Health Committee', *RPDCD*, vol. 3 (1879) appendix V, p. 788.
[131] NDU Minutes, 10 March 1847.

was not intended to put down prostitution, 'but to make the women who practise it less diseased, or as little diseased as may be, and therefore to make prostitution less injurious to mankind', it was 'for the sake of the sailors and soldiers that this was done, and not for the women'.[132]

It was volunteer women, in connection with the churches, who were first to respond to this particular area of need, modelling their response on Christ's dealings with Mary Magdalen: 'Divine encouragement is given to undertake the rescue of so degraded a class'.[133] Variously described as 'the outcast women of society', 'fallen but penitent', and 'magdalens', the perception was that women who attempted to make their living in this way were 'seduced', and became so degraded that they 'fell' further into degradation, sin and shame. Their rescue was therefore moral and spiritual, as well as economic, so that Church involvement was a pre-requisite. Committees of 'Ladies' whose aim was to support 'those who may desire to abandon the thorny road of sin and enter on the way of life and peace',[134] undertook this branch of philanthropic activity with great energy, as it required their domestic as well as organisational and fundraising skills. It was also a charitable area which plainly excluded men, who would be exposed to the charge of soliciting.

The ladies' committees which responded to this social evil were not noted for incisive criticism of the factors propelling women into this, and their various attempts at control and rehabilitation had mixed results.[135] The few economically viable means of making a livelihood for women in Dublin outside domestic service, which Maria Luddy's studies of nineteenth century prostitution exposes,[136] resulted in substantial numbers of women choosing this hazardous career. There was a small percentage of women engaged in prostitution who could not be regarded as poor, such as certain of the Mecklenburgh Street ladies who it was claimed 'have carriages to drive about, and horses to ride; ladies dressed in the pink of fashion'.[137] These however attended private practitioners when diseased, and so do not appear in the records of the Westmoreland Lock Hospital (for the treatment of sexually transmitted diseases); and do not solicit in the streets and so avoid the attentions of the police.[138] The fact that some few could make a good living does not invalidate the general correlation of poverty with prostitution. Luddy's study of the police records reveal the vast majority of

---

[132] *House of Commons Select Committee on the Administration, Operation and Effects of the Contagious Diseases Acts of 1866–1869*; HC 1881 (351) viii Qs 6591 (hereafter *Select Committee* 1881).
[133] *Dublin by Lamplight, Thirteenth Annual Report*, for 1867, p. 6.
[134] Ibid., p. 3.
[135] Luddy, *Women and Philanthropy* (1995), pp. 97–148.
[136] Ibid., pp. 131–133; Maria Luddy, 'Prostitution and Rescue Work in Nineteenth Century Ireland', in Maria Luddy and Cliona Murphy, (eds.) *Women Surviving: Studies in Irish Women's History in the Nineteenth and Twentieth Centuries* (Dublin, 1990), pp. 51–84.
[137] *Select Committee* 1881, Qs 6574.
[138] Ibid.

'common prostitutes' to be typically poor, illiterate, between twenty and thirty years of age, and with a previous police record.[139]

The problem of prostitution in Dublin was also directly related to the huge numbers of soldiers garrisoned in the city. The extent of venereal disease among British troops was the subject of several official enquiries, and the force behind the passing of the Contagious Diseases Acts of 1864–69, which in effect subjected women who were on the street to arbitrary and compulsory medical examination, and if found to be infected, confinement in a Lock Hospital for up to nine months, and registration as a prostitute.[140] In 1881 a House of Commons Select Committee on the administration, operation and effects of these acts heard evidence from medical officers, senior army personnel, clergymen and others (all male) on the nature and extent of the problem in each place where British troops were stationed.[141] On the evidence presented before that inquiry, Dublin's problems were enormous. A colonel commanding the 80th Regiment testified that in the first ten months of his regiment's arrival in Dublin 166 men with primary syphilis, and 118 men with gonorrhoea, were admitted to hospital; in all 'considerably over 43% of the unmarried portion of my regiment have been incapacitated from duty'.[142] Mr Rawton Macnamara, senior surgeon of the Westmoreland Lock hospital, was 'not in the least surprised' to hear these figures, and assured the Committee that the same thing applies to every other regiment in the Dublin garrison, quoting recent four-year returns of the army medical officer to substantiate these claims.[143] Practically all admitted to the Lock Hospital were in a 'very advanced' and 'actively contagious' stage of disease, according to Macnamara, the practice being 'that as long as they possibly can keep out of the hospital they do, and they are only driven in by very severe and urgent symptoms'. Once getting some relief, but still not cured, the majority of patients discharge themselves, 'I knowing thoroughly that she is going back to her trade and thoroughly aware that she is capable of diseasing anybody that comes into contact with her'.[144]

Police records for Dublin 1870 reveal a total of 11,526 arrests for prostitution and of alleged prostitutes, (i.e., women who were known to be prostitutes but were charged with other crimes), while the number of brothels known to the police averaged 96 per year in the 1870s.[145] Mr Macnamara of the Lock Hospital claimed in 1881 that there were more prostitutes in Dublin than ever before, and more diseased, and that there were as many as 'some thousand or fifteen hundred' well-known prostitutes using Grafton Street for soliciting, in much the same fashion as London's Haymarket.[146]

[139] Luddy, 'Prostitution and Rescue Work' (1990), p. 57.
[140] Luddy, *Women and Philanthropy* (1995), p. 137.
[141] *Select Committee* 1881 (351) viii Qs 6431–6606.
[142] Ibid., 6449, 6450.
[143] Ibid., Qs 6576–6578.
[144] Ibid., Qs 6449–6463.
[145] Luddy, 'Prostitution and Rescue Work' (1990), p. 57.
[146] *Select Committee* 1881, (351) viii, Qs 6474, 6475, 6529.

The geography of prostitution in Dublin varied; according as one brothel area was suppressed another emerged: 'you move them from one site to another, you do not put them down at all'.[147] Whitelaw in his slum survey published 1805 (Chapter 2) claimed that 'it was perhaps not generally known that not one house of ill-fame exists in the Liberty'. This he attributed not to its superior virtue but, regrettably, to its poverty as from among the 'nocturnal street walkers that infest the more opulent parts of the city, a large proportion issues from the Liberty'.[148] In 1881 a resident of St Stephen's Green claimed that almost all the houses of ill fame were concentrated in nearby French Street (renamed Mercer Street Upper) and Clarendon Street, but:

We did not like to have such people near us and we were anxious to close it. Clarendon Street is the locale of a very beautiful chapel, and the priests did not like to have them there. The result was that police were put at the doors and took down the names of every one who came; these were what we call the upper class, if there can be such a thing, of prostitutes, and the police took down the names of all gentlemen going to enter, and that at once drove them out of that and then they went to the banks of the canal. But they were removed from there, and the result is that they are scattered in different outlying parts, Mecklenburgh Street.[149]

While such 'purges' remodelled the local geography of prostitution, at least temporarily, the long-time association of prostitution with the military ensured that Barrack (later Benburb) Street, in the shadow of the Royal (Collins) Barracks, would continue to be notorious for such activity (see Figure 2.3, Plate 2.4).[150] In an examination of Lock hospital and police records c. 1857–68, Luddy noted the recurrence of three north city streets in the addresses of those hospitalised or arrested: the traditional market areas of Mary's Lane (to the rear of the Four Courts) and Moore Street (to the west of Sackville Street), and also Purdon Street, part of the Mecklenburgh/Montgomery district to the north east of the Custom House (see Chapter 8). The 'cleansing' of this latter and most extensive brothel area, and the care of those formerly working as prostitutes, would have to await the zeal and good organisation of the Legion of Mary in the 1920s. Intervention to stem the flow of women into prostitution was advocated by activists such as Margaret Aylward, who opened poor schools and associated convents in Clarendon Street (south city) and 65 Jervis Street (north city) in 1870, with the one intention, that the sisters will live locally,

in the midst of the poor, looking after their children, watching the little girls, many of whom go to trades or into workshops at twelve years of age: these they will try to teach at night-schools and Sunday schools, binding them together in associations sanctioned by the Church, and as far as possible preserve them from evil during the dangerous period of their growing into womanhood.[151]

---

[147] Ibid., Qs 6473.
[148] Whitelaw (1805), p. 64 (see Chapter II, footnote 1).
[149] *Select Committee* 1881, (351) viii, Qs 6472.
[150] *North City Survey* 1918, p. 104.
[151] *SBO Fifteenth Annual Report*, 1872, p. 14.

The location of penitent asylums in 1850–1900, mapped in Figure 7.5, follows two distinct patterns: foundations near or in the areas most frequented by prostitutes, in fairly well-defined parts of the city slums, and those founded at a definite remove, giving the 'poor girls an opportunity of repairing the past by a virtuous and penitential life',[152] well distanced from their former haunts. There were also three other principal requirements: a sufficiently large premises or one which could be extended to accommodate the women; adequate room to take in laundry work and sewing, the staple income of all these asylums; and, in the case of the Protestant asylums, space for the erection of a chapel which will provide comfortable accommodation for the public, 'claiming assistance to maintain its services for the inmates of the institution'.[153]

The earliest city penitent asylum was founded in 1765 by Lady Arbella Denny, at 8 Leeson Street, a very respectable new residential street, but strategically located near the notorious St Stephen's Green; similarly Baggot Street Upper was a suitable location for another Protestant asylum in 1835, complete with episcopal chapel where 'one third of the sittings are free'.[154] The earliest asylum serving the poor women of the Liberties was the Protestant Brown Street asylum (1830). Changes of premises, amalgamations and closures complicate the distribution; an asylum in Chancery Lane moved to James's Street and by 1850 (Figure 7.5) had relocated to Marlborough Street,[155] while an early asylum in 91 Townsend Street near the quays, by 1837 had removed to Donnybrook. No. 21 Townsend Street was also the location of the Lock Hospital.

On the north side in 1850 in the most notorious 'red light' district of the city are three Catholic-managed asylums: 104 Gloucester Street (1822), 76 Lower Mecklenburgh Street (1833), and Marlborough Street (1826). This north city network was extended by the addition of two Protestant asylums: the 'Dublin Midnight Mission and Female Refuge', 31 Marlboro Street (1862), and the 'Rescue Mission Home', 33 Gardiner Street Lower (1875), while the 'Dublin by Lamplight' institution in Ballsbridge (1854), opened an office in 30 Great Charles Street. Together with the asylum in 28 Dominick Street, and that for former prisoners in 10 Henrietta Street, these serve as a good indicator of the continuing serious extent of prostitution, and the steady decline in status in what was formerly a desirable residential district (see Chapter 8).

In terms of scale all the city centre asylums were relatively small, from about twelve residents in the Rescue Mission Home, 33 Gardiner Street, to forty in Baggot Street. The penitent asylums located outside the city centre were of greater importance numerically: the *Olivemount Institution of the Good Samaritan*, Dundrum, founded 1843 and catering for both discharged female prisoners and women formerly of the street, had 140 inmates in 1845, but by 1851 the number

---

[152] St. Patrick's Refuge, Crofton Road, Kingstown, 1798; G.D. Williams, *Dublin Charities* (Dublin, 1902).
[153] Dublin Female Penitentiary, Berkeley Place, North Circular Road, *Thom's* 1884.
[154] Asylum for Penitent Females, Upper Baggot Street, 1835, *Thom's* 1852.
[155] *Catholic Registry* 1851, p. 348.

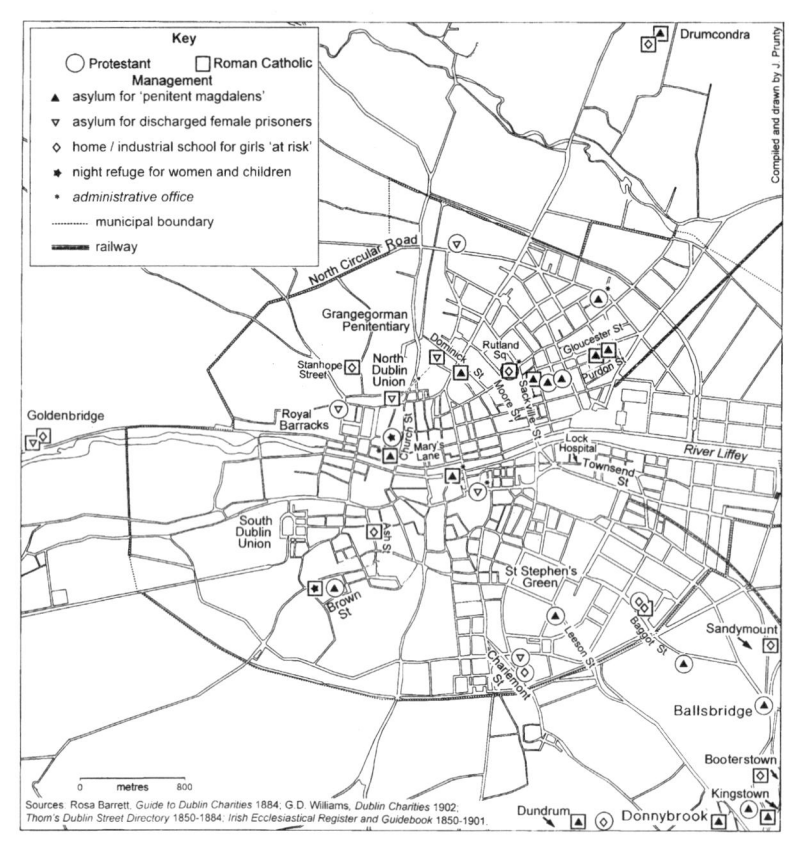

Figure 7.5 Asylums for women, Dublin 1851–1883

recorded was 80, and it closed around 1857.[156] The 'General Magdalen Asylum', first located at 91 Townsend Street, moved to Donnybrook where it could accommodate 50 inmates in 1850, and 120 by 1883.[157] Similarly St Mary's Asylum, Drumcondra Road (1833) had forty inmates in 1851, but by 1883 could accommodate 160 penitents, which increased again to 210 by 1900.[158] On the Protestant side, the 'Dublin by Lamplight' institution in Ballsbridge could accommodate 72 penitents at the end of the century.[159]

Penitent asylums outside the city centre, both Catholic and Protestant, maintained links with potential clients and subscribers by keeping offices down town; these dealt with applications for admission, but also served as laundry depots and depositories, where the handiwork of the penitents was displayed and sold. Olivemount, during its brief existence, had a central office at 15 Arran Quay, not far from Barrack Street; St Mary's, Drumcondra Road, had a similar office at 23 Essex Quay, and the Dublin by Lamplight institution in Ballsbridge kept contact with the core area near Mountjoy Square through its office at 30 Great Charles Street.

[156] *Catholic Registry*, 1851, p. 348; Luddy, *Women and Philanthropy* (1995), p. 169.
[157] Rosa Barrett, *Guide to Dublin Charities* (Dublin, 1884).
[158] *Thom's* 1852 and 1884; Williams, *Dublin Charities* (1902).
[159] Ibid.

Church Charities Respond: Women and Children, 1850–1900

The development of suburban asylums in more commodious custom-built premises can be largely ascribed to the involvement of women religious in the 'reformation' of the 'outcasts' and the widespread relocation of institutions to healthier suburban sites.[160] The handing over of lay Catholic charities to the care of religious was a recurrent theme in Dublin from the mid-nineteenth century on.[161] The transformation of the lay charitable community established by Margaret Aylward and her co-workers (running St Brigid's orphanage and poor schools) into a religious order is a variation on the very same theme. In the case of the Catholic 'magdalen' asylums there was a steady drive to place them under religious management. The Sisters of Charity took charge of the asylum at 91 Townsend Street in 1832, its exact location recorded in the court name Asylum Yard; the enterprise was relocated to Donnybrook in 1837, 'in the premises lately occupied by the Castle School, and hence has many obvious advantages for washing, and making up family and fine linens'.[162] The pattern is repeated, with the Mercy sisters taking charge of St Patrick's Refuge, Kingstown, and for a period the asylum in 104 Lower Gloucester Street. Gloucester Street in 1877 is entrusted to the sisters of Our Lady of Charity of Refuge, who also ran the largest magdalen asylum of all, in High Park Drumcondra. In 1873 the Good Shepherd sisters who ran magdalen asylums in Belfast, Cork, New Ross, Waterford, and Limerick, sought to open an asylum in Dublin and suggested taking over the lay Catholic asylum in 76 Mecklenburgh Street; however this asylum was absorbed by that of Gloucester Street, and cames under the charge of the High Park sisters.[163]

Close examination of the Gloucester Street register titled 'Entrance of the Penitents and their Leaving' for the period 1887–1897 provides valuable glimpses into the role such asylums played in supporting women in need. While the age on admission ranged from 14 years to 58 years almost half were in the 21–29 years bracket, 25 years being the overall average. Most striking is the enormous turnover of residents; admittance was freely given, and the vast bulk of residents left after short stays varying from a few days to several months. Of 511 admissions between 17 February 1887–26 December 1897, at least half left the house of their own accord, another c.40 women took temporary refuge in the house *en route* to or from hospital, and about the same number were 'sent away' or 'sent out' of the house, with 'expelled for disorder' or 'disobedience' entered after the names of three women. 30 women were sent to 'situations' from the house, of whom 3 left for America and 4 to Australia ('doing well'), a brave new start in a

---

[160] For example, see the relocation of the Molyneux blind asylum, 1860, DDA: 333/5 no. 177.
[161] Among many examples could be noted the Sisters of Charity taking charge of the Widows' House, Belvidere Place (*Catholic Registry* 1900); the Christian Brothers taking charge of the orphanage of St Vincent de Paul, 1877, the Holy Faith Sisters take over of the Queen of Charity, 65 Jervis Street (1870), and the Daughters of Charity of St Vincent de Paul taking charge of the Sacred Heart Home, Drumcondra Road.
[162] *Thom's* 1852.
[163] Sr. Mary of the Immaculate Conception, Good Shepherd Convent, Limerick, to Cardinal Cullen, 13 February 1872, DDA: 335/1 file lll, nuns, no. 6.

very different world. While the asylum regime may appear unattractive a century later, the fact that at least 10% of those who entered Gloucester Street during the period 1887–1897 entered a second or third time testifies to positive experiences (at least relative to the workhouse alternative) and the genuinely open admissions policy. While place of origin is not always noted, it is also clear that this asylum caters for more than the Dublin district. At least 46% of entrants give a non-Dublin city address, widely dispersed throughout Ireland (211 women) Britain (13 women), and the British Empire (2 from India, 1 from Canada). Within Dublin the few detailed addresses refer, not surprisingly, to Cumberland Street, Purdon Street and Brewery Yard (see Chapter 8, Figure 8.5).

Asylums for Discharged Female Prisoners

The asylums for discharged female prisoners have much in common with those for 'magdalens' (Figure 7.5). As female prisoners were almost exclusively of the destitute class, these asylums are also part of the network of relief and support services for the poorest women. Begun by Committees of Ladies 'whose exertions are directed to the religious and moral improvement of the women, and their advancement in habits of order and industry'[164] there was perhaps an added emphasis given to having them 'disciplined, if possible, and made industrious'[165] with the Harcourt Road asylum welcoming only those who 'on being discharged from prison, may appear desirous of reforming, and are willing to put up with hard fare, continued labour, and strict discipline'.[166] Interdenominational competition was also an element in their foundation, one Catholic charity claiming that Protestant societies enticed Catholic discharged prisoners through the use of bribes, held out both inside and outside the prison gates.[167]

The siting of several asylums in the north western institutional sector (see Figure 6.3) is not surprising. The Prison Gate Mission in Blackhall Place was designed, as its name suggests, to meet women on the morning of their discharge and 'to try to reclaim them from their evil companions' and provide a means of honest livelihood.[168] Similarly the nearby refuge in 63a North King Street (later relocated to 10 Henrietta Street) and run by the Daughters of Charity was 'to help Roman Catholic discharged prisoners who are just *commencing* a life of crime, to leave their evil ways'. As in the case of the magdalen asylums, there was also the attraction of building at a remove from the city's temptations, such as the Dublin Female Penitentiary on the North Circular Road, where in 1813 a 'large commodious house was erected for the penitents, in an extremely healthy situation on the North Circular Road, near Eccles Street, behind which is a

---

[164] Dublin Female Penitentiary, Berkeley Place, North Circular Road, *Thom's* 1852.
[165] Prison Gate Mission, 22 Blackhall Place, Barrett (1884).
[166] Shelter for Females Discharged from Prison, 4 Harcourt Road, *Thom's* 1852.
[167] *Third Annual Report of the Discharged Female Roman Catholic Prisoners' Aid Society*, 1884.
[168] Prison Gate Mission, 22 Blackhall Place, Barrett (1884).

spacious chapel'[169] and sufficient room to allow the inmates engage in the standard asylum occupations of washing, bleaching, mangling and needlework.

St Vincent's Convict Refuge, Goldenbridge, run by the Mercy sisters in co-operation with the prison board, was an 'intermediate prison' for women in their last year of sentence in Mountjoy prison who have made themselves 'eligible by works and by conduct'. Places were highly sought after among the prisoners, so that the superioress requested in 1863 that the adjoining girls' industrial school be phased out to allow them accept the greater number without overcrowding the premises, 'as we have observed for the last few years that the women are seldom so good or so happy when the number exceeds fifty, nor do they have the *home* feeling they always have when there are not too many here, and besides we find it difficult to instruct and know them *individually* as we do now'.[170] This institution offered a scheme of assisted emigration to America, a similar package being available to Canada through the North King Street (Henrietta Street) asylum, both religious communities using their convent networks abroad to provide the emigrants with a place of residence on arrival and recommended situations.[171] The Protestant Prisoners' Aid Society operated an employment office in 7 Dame Street, a respectable city centre location.

Night Asylums for Homeless Women and Children

The concerns that led to the provision of 'magdalen' and discharged prisoner asylums for women led also to the opening of night shelters for women and children (Figure 7.5). The first was the Bow Street Asylum, 1838, which also accepted men, suitably located in the heart of the Markets district on the north side of the Liffey. The accommodation was basic: 'Neither food nor beds are provided, only benches; a wooden ledge serves as a pillow for the sleepers on the floor'. Under Protestant management, the bible was read aloud each evening, 'but none are obliged to be present'.[172] Handbills seeking subscriptions to fund a similar facility in the Liberties were distributed in 1861, urging the compassionate public to consider the hundreds who spend the nights 'forlorn and deserted by all' in open hallways, under archways, and in 'the roofless garret, the foul and fetid cellar, the filthy and crowded lodging'. Dr Spratt, the Carmelite clergyman who led the campaign, urged the vulnerability of destitute young women above all, those who are refused permission to shelter in the police stations 'because there was no charge against them' and 'unable to bear up against the cold and hunger, succumb and lose their virtue'. Its promoters were confident of the immense good a well-regulated refuge would effect:

---

[169] G.N. Wright, *An Historical Guide to the City of Dublin* (London, 1825; facsimile reprint Dublin, 1980), p. 121.
[170] Sr. Mary Magdalen Kirwan to Dr. Cullen, 26 February 1863, DDA: 340/9 no. 26.
[171] *Third Annual Report of the Discharged Female Roman Catholic Prisoners' Aid Society*, 1884.
[172] Night Asylum for the Houseless Poor, 8 Bow Street, 1838, Barrett (1884), *op.cit.*

wherein the comfort of a clean bed of straw would be afforded to all poor females and children who would present themselves before a certain hour at night, with a ticket from a clergyman or respectable householder; and where night prayers would be a preliminary to their retirement to rest; and their departure in the morning not only be preceded by morning prayer and meditation, but, if funds would allow, some refreshment, a portion of bread with milk, cocoa, or soup be also afforded.[173]

This asylum was located in Brickfield Lane, in a disused auxiliary workhouse of the South Dublin Union between Cork Street and Brown Street, a three storey building which had been built in 1815 by Thomas Pleasants as a 'tenter house' for the poor weavers of the Liberties to dry their cloth (marked H, Figure 2.7).[174] The accommodation was initially quite spartan, but by 1884 it was reported that 'there are large rooms with clean and comfortable beds and a lavatory' and it could accommodate 200 persons. Major rebuilding at a cost of £3,000 made this building 'more habitable for the homeless poor' though as may be expected funds were solicited to defray the expense. Again, in what appears to be the only way of securing an income sufficient to maintain such institutions and at the same time usefully employ the women, the asylum sought to open a laundry to provide work for the girls without homes who were allowed to stay all day.[175] By 1871, eleven years after its foundation, Canon Farrell the parish priest of St Catherine's Meath Street, in which parish the shelter was located, had secured the services of the Mercy sisters to manage it.[176]

Conclusion

The response of the churches to the Dublin slum reality is an area which still has to be fully explored, but what is certain is that charities played an important role in the alleviation of daily hardships, when set against the backdrop of the limited and generally disagreeable state (poor law) provision. Church charity workers were involved in a wide variety of relief areas, including schools and orphanages, asylums, refuges and homes, and family relief. Such initiatives laid the foundation for many social services, with church activists also contributing directly to the improvement of the state's response through active involvement in the boarding-out debate, workhouse visitation and employment in workhouse infirmaries. Where a large majority of the citizens lived at or near the poverty level, familiarity with charity personnel and with networks of information mattered. It could on occasion make all the difference between 'getting by' and personal disaster.

---

[173] Fundraising circular, John Spratt, DDA: 335/5 no.163, 1860.
[174] Wright, *Historical Guide* (1825), pp. 187–188.
[175] St Joseph's Night Refuge for Homeless Women and Children, Brickfield Lane, Cork Street, Barrett (1884), see also DDA: 328/7 file V, nuns, no 109, 16–20 December 1871, concerning efforts to secure the services of sisters, for what is called St Joseph's Asylum, 'which alone can secure its permanent well-being'.
[176] Sr. M.E. Forde, Baggot Street, to Cardinal Cullen, 6 September 1871, DDA: 328/7 file v, nuns, no. 76.

The intensity and viciousness of the very public 'battle for bodies and souls' which raged between the Protestant missionary movement and Catholic organisations in nineteenth century Dublin cannot be overstated. It was an ever present factor in the organisation of poor relief, and while it may be unpalatable to face in this more ecumenical age, it did contribute positively in providing a real spur for advances in the care of the poor:

> Perhaps the chief good that resulted indirectly from Proselytism is the increased attention that is paid to the poor, the zeal that seeks them in their wretched abodes, brings them to school and instructs them, the sympathy that has been created among wealthy Catholics, by which large sums of money and other advantages have been secured for the amelioration of the lot of the poor. Perhaps the best indirect result of the Proselytism will be the many Catholic institutions founded to counteract it, for these will flourish and confer blessings upon the poor when the names of Whately, Dallas and Co. shall have been forgotten.[177]

The ICM concurred in this general analysis, noting, from its own experience:

> It is a very strange fact, and one unknown to those who have had no mission experience, that as long as the poor are left in ignorance no effort is made to help them, but as soon as the rays of truth begin to dawn upon them, the alarm is taken. They will be "*lost to the Church*", is the cry, and they must be rescued by *any* means.[178]

The Dublin slums provided boundless scope for Christian endeavour, under every party banner.

---

[177] *SBO Twentieth Eight Annual Report*, 1885, p. 5.
[178] *Them Also* (1866), p. 89.

∼ 8 ∼

A CLASSIC SLUM: DUBLIN NORTH CITY

The foregoing survey of the decline in character of nearly every old street on the north side of the city illuminates with inexorable logic the process which has brought about the present deplorable conditions under which the poorer classes are housed.

NORTH CITY SURVEY, 1918

INTRODUCTION

At the beginning of the 1800s the Gardiner estate, dominating the north city RC parishes of St Michan's and St Mary's (Figure 8.1) included some of the most desirable and exclusive places to live, with handsome townhouses set in regular terraces fronting wide thoroughfares and gracious parks. The resident families included nobles and professional persons, bishops and peers. A visitor in 1826 marvelled at the 'wide and commodious' streets, 'the houses uniform, lofty and elegant', with Sackville Street 'a noble avenue, a hundred and twenty feet wide, terminated by the Rotunda and public gardens'.[1] By 1925 the Civic Survey recorded row after row of condemned dwellings, third class tenements and expanses of dereliction. Chronic overcrowding, filth, and high mortality were widespread. Pulmonary tuberculosis consigned large numbers to an early grave. On the eastern flank of this once-select sector prospered an infamous brothel district, the 'nighttown' of Joyce's *Ulysses*.[2] The scale of problems was the despair of sanitary officers and charity workers alike.

The rapid loss of status which characterised the Gardiner estate during the nineteenth century is perhaps the most spectacular element in the Dublin slum story. However, the downgrading of aristocratic residences to tenement occupation was only one of many strands. This case study focuses on the geographic area delimited by the Roman Catholic parishes of St Mary's and St Michan's, and examines how the various strands intersect at a local level: the exposure of slum conditions through personal surveys, official inquiries, valuation and housing records, and lists of those reliant on charitable relief especially as served by

[1] John Gamble, *Sketches of History, Politics and Manners in Dublin and the North of Ireland in 1810* (London, 1826), p. 22.
[2] James Joyce, *Ulysses*, Bodley Head ed. (1937), pp. 410–574.

A Classic Slum: Dublin North City 275

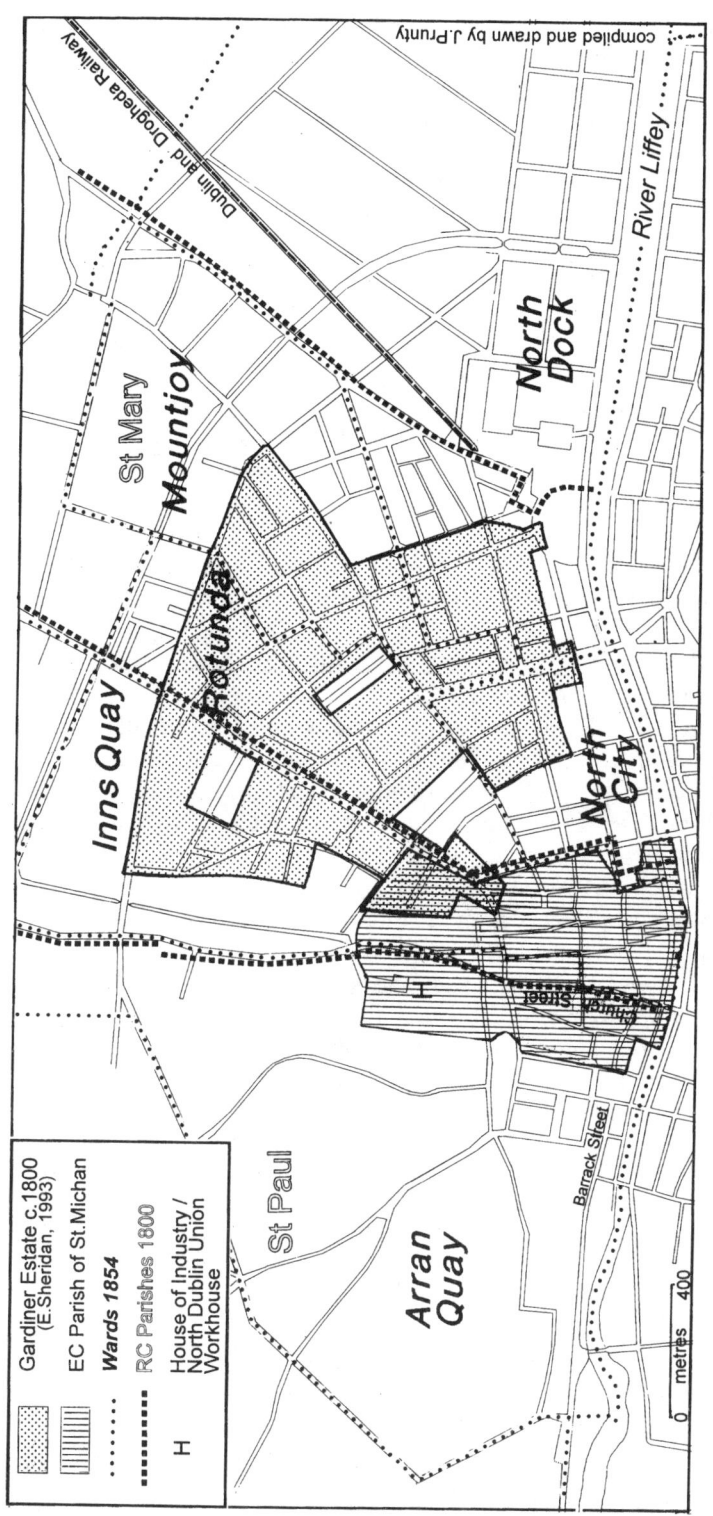

Figure 8.1 Case study area, Dublin north city

Margaret Aylward and her Ladies' Association of Charity (1850s). The diversity of sources possible in such a study is reflected in the range of geographical divisions utilised in data collection: the private estate (including amalgamations and extensions), the parish (both Established Church and Roman Catholic compilations), and the municipal ward (1840 and 1850 divisions, Dublin city), as illustrated in Figure 8.1. Other useful divisions are the dispensary districts (see Figure 5.1), while the North Dublin poor law union (1838) covers both urban and rural areas north of the Liffey to the county boundary.

The Gardiner Estate

The extensive area north of the Liffey that was to be known as the Gardiner estate (Figure 8.1) was assembled as a result of land acquisitions initiated by a young banker Luke Gardiner I in 1714.[3] The first project was the creation of a prime aristocratic quarter, Henrietta Street, a series of twelve individual mansions which included his own residence, and set the tone for what was to follow. Gradually streets and squares were opened up to the east, along the line of the old north road (Dorset Street–Drumcondra Road), and south toward the Liffey, in the form of Sackville Mall (1749–1751). Under Luke Gardiner ll who inherited the property in 1769, the eastward expansion continued apace, so that by his untimely death in 1798 urban development had extended to include three sides of Mountjoy Square, set in a healthy elevation, and the lower part of Summer Hill (Figure 8.2). The fortunes of the estate were to diminish rapidly under his successors, and there was little further development excepting the completion of certain projects such as Mountjoy Square and the erection of a new parish church, St George's (Established Church, 1802–1813). In 1846 the residue of the Gardiner estate was sold in the Encumbered Estates Court for the sum of £120,000 to Charles Spencer Cooper of Sandringham, second husband of the deceased Countess of Blessington, Harriet Gardiner.[4] It was sold on piecemeal to individual bidders, as recorded in newspaper advertisements over the following months.[5] The loss of sole ownership marked the end of unified central management, and of any overall vision for the future shape of the estate.

Of significance for the subsequent degeneration of the Gardiner area into slums was the undeveloped eastern frontier: although the estate extended to the Circular Road, there was little development beyond the (unfinished) Mountjoy Square by 1811, while the demand for high class housing was in sharp decline before plans for Gloucester Place and Upper Gloucester Street, drawn up in

---

[3] See National Council for Educational Awards, *Gardiner's Dublin: A History and Topography of Mountjoy Square and Environs* (Dublin, 1991), pp. 23–29; Niall McCullough, *Dublin: An Urban History* (Dublin, 1989), pp. 62–69.

[4] NCEA, *Gardiner's Dublin* (1991), p. 29.

[5] *Dublin Evening Mail*, 14 August, 2 & 7 December 1846, as quoted in John H. Martin, 'Aspects of the Social Geography of Dublin City in the Mid Nineteenth Century' (unpublished MA thesis in Geography, UCD (1973), p. 67.

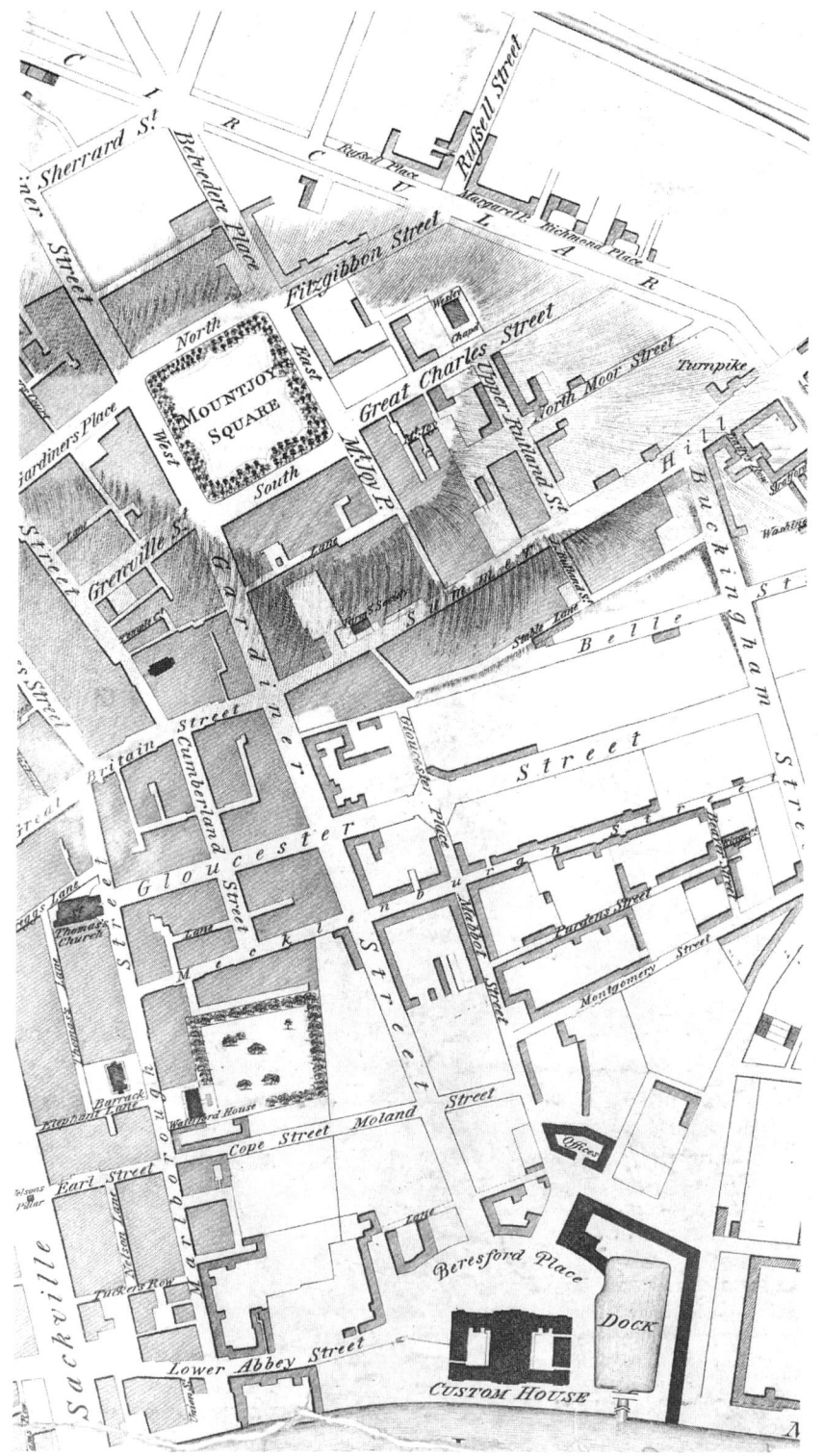

Figure 8.2 Gardiner Street – Mountjoy Square, *City of Dublin surveyed by M. Thomas Campell, under the directions of Major Taylor, 1811*

1791, had been fully implemented (Figure 8.2).[6] The area south of Summer Hill and east of Gloucester Place/Mabbot Street was part of the Aldborough estate in the eighteenth century, and thus beyond the Gardiner ambit at the time of peak development. The morphology of the Gardiner developments and the local topography were also to influence subsequent slum creation. The stable lanes and associated mews buildings which were built to serve the fine front-street houses (Plates 8.1, 8.2) succumbed easily to low-status residential use. Similarly, as the higher land rising in a ridge along Summer Hill (Figure 8.2) had been laid out in long narrow plots along fine broad thoroughfares, in so doing it had enclosed irregular shaped hollows which were to be rapidly colonised by lowly dwellings. The creation of Mountjoy Square was made possible only by centring on a limited area of elevated land, and avoiding several small quarries nearby such as that to the rear of Upper Rutland Street (Figure 8.2). Topography, opportunity, vision and market demand all combined to create a very mixed geography on this north eastern fringe of the built-up area.

Parishes of St Mary's and St Michan's: RC and EC Divisions

Successive changes in the parish boundaries of this north-city area are a good indicator of its changing fortunes. Until 1697 the parish of St Michan's was the only Protestant (Established Church) city parish north of the Liffey, but the expansion of urban settlement eastwards under Humphrey Jervis and his collaborators necessitated the creation of two new parishes: to the east, St Mary's, and to the west, St Paul's, with St Michan's retaining the central portion (see Chapter 7, Figure 7.1).[7] A similar division was followed in 1707 by the Roman Catholic authorities (see Figure 7.2). The Roman Catholic parish of St Mary's became the mensal parish (the parish retained by the archbishop) for the diocese of Dublin in 1797, taking over from St Nicholas Without, Francis Street, a clear indicator of the changing fortunes of these areas.[8] While St Nicholas Without, in the medieval core, lost its wealthy parishioners to the expanding suburbs, and was burdened with debt, the north city estate of Gardiner was one of the most attractive areas for those prosperous persons seeking to reside in wide, well-ventilated streets, and a suitably prestigious district for a new Roman Catholic cathedral, a project that could hardly find support in the most impoverished part of the city.[9]

---

[6] 'Part of Gardiner Street and Part of Gloucester Street Dublin laid out in lots for building', Thomas Sherrard 1791, in McCullough, *Dublin: An Urban History* (1989), p. 66.

[7] 'The History of the Roman Catholic Church and Parish of St. Michan, Dublin', reprinted from *The Irish Builder* (Dublin, 1892), pp. 3–4.

[8] Conchubhair O'Fearghail, 'The Evolution of Catholic Parishes in Dublin City from the Sixteenth to the Nineteenth Centuries' in F.H.A. Aalen and Kevin Whelan, eds., *Dublin, City and County: from Prehistory to Present* (Dublin, 1992), pp. 230–231.

[9] Ibid., p. 231.

The Roman Catholic parishes of St Mary's and St Michan's covered the greater part of the north city in 1850: from Capel Street in the west to the Custom House and the North Strand in the east, and north of the Liffey to just beyond the Circular Road (Figures 8.1, 8.3). The Established Church or civil parish was initially the basis for the organisation of 'official' poor relief (to 1838) and public health (to 1849), and was important as a census division; it is the unit utilised in early slum surveys and inquiries. While its importance as a civil administrative division diminished with the establishment of new city wards in 1840 (revised in 1850), it continued to be central to charity structures as organised by the Established Church/Church of Ireland. The Roman Catholic parish emerged strongly from the mid nineteenth century as the organisational basis for charity and school provision; as the denomination to which the vast majority of the poor belonged, it was an administrative unit of very immediate significance.

The Ladies' Association of Charity of St Vincent de Paul

The first Dublin city branch of the association (founded in France, 1617) was established by Margaret Aylward in 1851 in what was known as the pro-cathedral parish (St Mary's) and was also to visit in the adjoining parish of St Michan's (Figure 8.1, 8.3).[10] The mission of the Ladies of Charity was intended to be all-encompassing, combining the relief of distress with catechesis, instruction in parenting and household management:

> The Members deem it a duty, on their Visitation, besides bringing to each family the relief-order allotted to them for that day, at the Council Meeting held every Tuesday, to read for the Sick, to instruct them, to pray with them, to induce all to frequent the sacraments, to hear Mass on Sundays and Holidays, to urge upon the parents the necessity of making their children attend catechism, to inquire whether they frequent Catholic schools, and to insist, as far as they can, upon cleanliness, order, industry and regularity being perceptible in their homes.[11]

A church charity of real significance locally, it distributed considerable amounts of relief in very many forms, and it had a network, after five years of existence, of 148 lady visitors.[12] While the area covered is extensive, its policy and practice generated records rich in detail at the household level, the type of information which is the most difficult to locate. As a source for studying the social geography of the north city, its records are invaluable: its relief books record name, address, circumstances making relief necessary, by whom recommended, and type of relief given, in an almost unbroken sequence from 1851–1927.[13] Records for the subscribers and donors of clothing are regrettably less complete over

---

[10] *First Annual Report of the Ladies' Association of Charity of St Vincent de Paul, Metropolitan Branch*, 1852, p. 7 (hereafter referred to as *Ladies of Charity, Reports*).
[11] *Ladies of Charity, Third Report*, 1854, pp. 7–8.
[12] *Ladies of Charity, Fifth Report*, 1856, p. 4; not all of the active members registered were, however, available for visitation.
[13] GA: A/LO/36 no. 3: 'List of Clothes Given to the Poor by the Charitable Association of St. Vincent de Paul', dates from 1851–1927; A/LO/36 nos. 4, 7: *Relief to the Amount of . . . *. dates 1877–1911; GA: A/LO/36 no. 3: Clothing records December 1851–April 1856 are

Plate 8.1 Gardiner Street Middle 1980, Geoffrey White, Irish Architectural Archive

Plate 8.2 Gardiner Street Lower 1950s, T. Affleck Greaves, Irish Architectural Archive

time, but still invaluable for the early years of the association.[14] An important supplement to the above are the eleven published reports, from 1852–1862, when the Ladies' Association became separate from St Brigid's Orphanage, an 'accessary work' of the association which was to develop independently (see Chapter 7). There are also sundry letters relating to the affairs of the Association, mainly to do with its active role in bringing the *Soeurs de Charité* to Dublin in 1856.[15] The possibility of mapping the homes of both those who subscribed to a parochial charity, and those who were relieved by it over the same period, is most useful for the reconstruction of the social geography on the parish level, while the nature of the records, which cover much more than merely money contributions, give some insight into the interaction between the poorer and the better-off at the local scale. The commentary and analysis which accompanied the public launch of the early annual reports are also valuable contributions to the ongoing exposure of slum realities in the district. The interest of the association in the mundane business of daily life, including the details of diet, clothing, rent, sickness, job opportunities and the practice (or neglect) of religion all provide a welcome counterbalance to source materials focused on the built fabric alone. Since much of the contemporary information on Dublin poverty focuses on the more localised 'slum' district of the Liberties, the southside medieval core, northside information is doubly valuable.

North City Sectarian Competition

Charitable relief operations, while played out against a geography of need, were also heavily influenced by the operations of competing religious denominations (Chapter 7). The north city parishes of St Michan's and St Mary's feature prominently in such struggles: it was in the north city slums that the Irish Church Missions first got a Dublin foothold, and from which a citywide 'fact finding tour' and subsequent attack was launched against them by Catholic activists. Bow Street, to the west of Church Street, was the location of Fanny

quite complete; there is a less complete list to 1861; then an undated list. 'Calico and Flannel' lists, with few addresses, exist for 1868–1878; and practically complete clothing lists for November 1909–September 1927; GA: A/LO/36 no. 7: 'Relief to the Amount of...' from October 1877–December 1894 c. 4,000 entries; continued in GA A/LO/36 no. 4: from January 1895–February 1901 c. 1,725 entries; from January 1901–October 1911 several thousand entries. Lists names, very many addresses, type of relief given (eg: tea, sugar, bread), also amount of relief in money, by whom recommended, (generally a clergyman), and reasons for needing relief (eg: 'extreme poverty', 'weakness', 'decline').

[14] GA: A/LO/36 no. 3, 'List of the Ladies who have Charitably Sent in Clothes to the Association for the Use of the Poor', which dates only from July 1851–November 1856, with one further 1872 *Petticoat/Chemise List*; GA A/LO/36 no. 4, 'Members making yearly, half yearly and quarterly payments', also 'donations', 1851–52; for other years see annual reports for persons donating 10s and upwards; in these however, few addresses are included.

[15] See *Ladies of Charity First Report*, 1852, p. 4; also communication between Margaret Aylward and Père Etienne, Philip Dowley, and John Gowan, all Vincentian priests. 15 January 1851–16 March 1857, GA: MA/CH/02 nos. 40–50, 56.

Bellingham's first 'controversial classes', to teach 'the truths of the gospel, not in the way they are taught to Protestants, but as opposed to the errors believed by Roman Catholics, so that in receiving the one they *must* of *necessity* give up the other' (*sic*).[16] Rev. C.F. McCarthy, minister of St Michan's, was the first Dublin agent of the Irish Church Missions, and responsible for training the agents in Townsend Street. His eloquence as a preacher, and skill in conducting 'controversy', drew large crowds so that by the end of 1851 the Dublin Mission claimed that upwards of seven hundred persons were attending their Tuesday Evening 'Inquiring Class' in St Michan's school room.[17]

The metropolitan branch of the Ladies' Association of Charity, although not founded as a foil to the evangelical missionary movement, very rapidly became aware of the activities of its agents. Following on a number of 'fact finding excursions', open warfare was declared. The ladies 'did what they could to warn and protect the poor'[18] from Protestant institutions which the parents repeatedly claimed had assured them that 'the children's religion was not meddled with'[19] and that 'there is nothing else to keep them out of the poor-house'.[20] A scene from one 'ruined tenement' as painted in the annual report for 1854 encapsulates the struggle exactly:

In the floor was a large aperture, another in the ceiling, and the wall itself gave a welcome to the wind and cold as they chose to enter. When the Bible-readers were engaged with some of the miserable occupiers below stairs, they could be heard distinctly above; and when the Ladies read or prayed with the sick woman, there were, unknown to them, attentive listeners on high.[21]

The Downward Slide: Survey Evidence
1800–1850

Slum survey evidence for the north city from 1800–1850 focuses on the Church Street and Barrack Street districts, to the west of the Gardiner estate (Figure 8.1; see also Chapter 2, Figure 2.3, Plates 2.3, 2.4). The social fortunes of these areas were heavily influenced by the complex of institutional buildings covering a vast expanse of the north city as far as the Circular Road. The Royal Barracks dominated the only access route to the west, Barrack Street (see Figure 2.3); north of King Street was the House of Industry and the associated Hardwicke Fever Hospital, which from 1838 formed the nucleus of the North Dublin Union Workhouse complex (see Figure 6.3). To complete the sector there was an imposing

---

[16] *'Them Also:' The Story of the Dublin Mission* (London, 1866), p. 3 (hereafter *Them Also*).
[17] Ibid., p. 11; his removal to the Townsend Street Mission House, 1855, may be one of the reasons for the loss of ground in the parish (*op.cit.*, p. 32); the activities of Margaret Aylward and the Ladies of Charity was certainly another factor, as was the conduct of parish missions by Catholic priests.
[18] *Ladies of Charity, Sixth Report*, 1857, p. 12.
[19] *Ladies of Charity, First Report*, 1852, p. 21.
[20] Ibid., p. 23 also *Fourth Report*, 1855, p. 8.
[21] *Ladies of Charity, Third Report*, 1854, p. 12.

Female Penitentiary, three refuges for discharged female prisoners, a selection of lunatic asylums, and two further hospitals, the Richmond and the Whitworth.

The area also traditionally had important market functions: potatoes, vegetables and roots, poultry, eggs, fish and butter, and 'an extensive meat market' were all recorded by 1836. Such markets were an obvious disincentive to better class residential development, while attracting 'individuals who endeavour to obtain a scanty subsistence by vending the products of these several markets throughout the city at large'.[22] The combination of markets, barracks, asylums, and above all the propinquity of the House of Industry (later union workhouse) and the fever hospital, placed serious limits on its social ambitions.

The survey evidence points to contemporary concerns: the role of the local topography (especially drainage) in spreading disease, poor sanitation, high infant mortality, endemic poverty, and the mobility of the pauper class who especially as refugees from famine, fever and misfortune, carried contagion very personally into this district.

In the 1817/1818 survey undertaken by Dr Cheyne of the Hardwicke Fever Hospital, the focus was on the two streets which supplied the hospital with the greatest number of fever patients during the recent epidemic: lowlying Barrack Street, with its prostitutes, lodging houses, drinking dens and slaughter houses (see Chapter 2), and densely crowded Church Street, where 'a few respectable shopkeepers excepted, the entire street is inhabited by persons of the lowest order'.[23] The vulnerability to fever of the population in the immediate locality, whether newly arrived or already settled, was obvious: the preceding season had been one of 'unparalleled distress', leaving the people 'scantily fed and clothed' and labouring under 'great depression of mind'. When compounded by sustained contact or 'close approximation' to persons affected with fever, the resulting virulence of the epidemic was entirely to be expected.[24] The 'neglect of cleanliness and the density of the population' were also relevant factors, with the early removal of the sick and the cleansing and whitewashing of their rooms proving 'very remarkable in checking the progress of the disease'. Unfortunately such action was the exception rather than the rule over many months, with the stream of country persons in the last stages of fever staying overnight before admission to the house of industry or fever hospitals ensuring that the disease obtained 'so firm a footing' locally.[25]

The huge percentage of the local population which subsisted on general alms, or on the relief provided by the House of Industry or by various charities, was noted with amazement by Cheyne for 1817. He quoted from the medical officers

---

[22] 'Report upon the Principal Charitable Institutions of Dublin', *Poor Inquiry (Ireland) 1836*, appendix (c), part II, p. 15 (hereafter Charities Report).

[23] J. Cheyne, *Medical Report of the Hardwicke Fever Hospital for the year ending on the 31st March 1818 including a brief account of an epidemic fever in Dublin* (Dublin, 1818), p. 48 (hereafter Hardwicke Fever Hospital).

[24] Ibid., p. 4.

[25] Ibid., p.49.

who had carried out the door-to-door survey and found among the 1,318 persons resident in Barrack Street at least 332 adults with no source of employment, 'the greater number of whom are in a state of extreme indigence'.[26] This aspect of the slum question was explored more fully by a survey of all persons requiring relief in St Michan's parish also for 1817, undertaken by an expert team comprised of clergy 'of both denominations', the Strangers' Friend Society, and the Roomkeepers' Society. As reported by the house of industry, this inquiry decided that of the 22,000 population, at least 10,799 were in need of relief. This group was further subdivided on a gender basis: male artisans and labourers, dependent on the building trade (997) or on 'other useful arts' (230), and 'females capable of earning' (2,242), while the largest group was dependants of both sexes, incapable of labouring from infancy, old age, or bodily infirmity (7,351 persons).[27] Among adults capable of working but unemployed, the huge excess of women over men is a finding in line with contemporary accounts.

The 1836 Poor Inquiry also made special note of the Barrack Street/Church Street district, quoting a police magistrate who swore on oath that the Arran Quay or Barrack division, with 545 licensed houses, 'contains considerably more impoverished and pauperized inhabitants, and more vicious and depraved characters, than any other two divisions in the city'.[28] Barrack Street was singled out as 'the most disreputable street in Dublin', containing 98 houses 'of the most heterogeneous description', of which 19 were licensed to sell spirits, 'besides many more in its immediate vicinity'.[29] Reverend Shore, curate of the parish of St Michan's (Established Church division, Figure 8.1) and also honorary secretary to the Roomkeepers' Society, estimated a total population figure of 25,000 persons, of whom at least 10,000 were so destitute that 'they know not in the morning how they will obtain support in the day'. While concerned with the situation of the poor in the city as a whole, Shore noted that the downturn in glove-making had impinged badly on his parish, while the general lack of female employment was the most critical aspect. Women were limited to 'selling fish, fruit, vegetables &c. in the street, washing rooms, and a very few employed by the pin and comb manufacturers'; for children there was no work 'except what is disgraceful and ruinous to them'. The initiative shown by 'schools, penitentiaries and asylums' by taking in needlework and washing had 'thrown a vast number of poor women out of the means of support'.[30] It is no accident that Barrack Street becomes the scene of the earliest direct Corporation intervention in the housing market, with the erection of block dwellings in 1887.

The 1836 Poor Inquiry also provides evidence that the tenement system was well established in the older areas north of the Liffey by then, Shore lamenting

---

[26] Ibid., p. 47.
[27] *Observations on the House of Industry, Dublin and on the Plans of the Association for Suppressing Mendicity in that City*, (Dublin, 1818), p. 24.
[28] Charities Report, *Poor Inquiry* (1836), p. 113.
[29] Ibid.
[30] Ibid., p. 2, also supplement.

that many houses once held by 'respectable' people, 'are now in a wretched condition, being let in rooms; at least three-fourths may now be called poor'. Density was very high, with 'on average two or three families in each room, a family being generally composed of four or five individuals'. He himself had counted 36 persons in one room about 32 feet by 13 feet. The lodging houses, the lowest class of dwelling excepting only the street itself, had 'generally no bedding, but a handful of straw and the clothes worn by day; very badly ventilated and mostly in wretched repair', with the sewers 'ill supplied, and in a most dreadful state for want of cleanliness'.[31]

The Willis survey of 1845 on the question of infant mortality among the working classes within and without the North Dublin Union workhouse led to a consideration of the causes for that excessive mortality and how it might be decreased; the survey was extended to the working classes as a whole, 'which inquiry necessarily embraced their social condition'.[32] Under that heading, Willis's survey, as outlined in the preface, brought together all angles of the slum question: public health, housing, subsistence and poor relief. Well aware that his statements were 'of such a startling nature as to appear incredible to those whose attention has never been directed to such matters' he emphasised the authenticity of every claim, hoping only to 'concentrate public opinion' on the condition of the labouring classes, that their situation might be ameliorated. He was crystal clear about the means required: 'providing for them residences fit for human beings', and establishing 'a large and constant supply of pure water'; with that in place the next essential was to inculcate 'the absolute necessity of cleanliness, general and personal'. Slum reform was much more than purely environmental upgrading, Willis then endeavouring to 'stimulate them to habits of social decency – by teaching them to husband their little means, and to rely solely on themselves in sickness and in health'. Thus well and cleanly lodged, with habits of thrift and hardy independence instilled, they will come 'to shun the public hospital, not only as a physical but a moral pest-house, and to look on the workhouse as the refuge of the most worthless'.[33]

In his introduction to the sanitary state of the parish of St Michan's (EC), Willis regarded its geology and relief most favourably: much of the parish had a 'dry gravel bottom, with a gradual ascent from the river to every part', the streets were well laid out originally, 'with proper inclinations for the discharge of surface water', and each with a 'good fall' with nothing to obstruct the natural drainage. But from there on the picture disimproved, as there were few private or branch drains to join up with the single sewer which runs through the centre of the parish, 'a large proportion of the houses have *not* necessaries' (*sic*), and those that have are rarely connected to the sewer 'but must be emptied by carrying out

---

[31] Ibid., supplement.
[32] Thomas Willis, *Facts Connected with the Social and Sanitary Condition of the Working Classes in the City of Dublin* (Dublin, 1845), p. 58 (hereafter *Social and Sanitary Condition*).
[33] Ibid., pp. iii–iv.

through the house'.³⁴ Rere yards 'are so many depots of putrid animal and vegetable matter', so that where a yard 'necessary' was included it simply added to the hazards.³⁵ Public 'necessaries', 'urinaries' or water closets of any sort were practically unknown, and not one house in ten of those let in weekly tenancies was connected with a water main. The intermittent supply from public fountains was the best that could be had, the people congregating with 'the kettle and broken jar', struggling to secure a small refill. Willis was amazed at the innumerable uses to which every tumbler of water was put, his inquiry as to why the filthy stuff was still in the room invariably meeting with the reply that 'it was *yet* wanted'. Thus it might first be used to wash the man's shirt, then 'some little white linen', then to wash coarser things, and eventually as a 'noisome semi-fluid poison' was used to mop out the room or stairs.³⁶

Every criterion which might be employed in defining a place as a slum was found here to a notorious degree: St Michan's (EC) was the most overcrowded parish in Dublin, at 16.51 persons per house, according to the census of 1841, and easily surpassing the most congested district in London, which returned a figure of 10.94 persons per house. Most families in St Michan's endured fourth class accommodation, the local gentry were all gone, and the housing market was in the hands of 'house-jobbers' with no interest in the houses save their weekly rents. 'Pipe water, lime-washing, dust-bin, privy' were all wonders unknown in the entire district, and 'the stench and disgusting filth of these places are inconceivable, unless to those whose harrowing duty obliges them to witness such scenes of wretchedness'. It was not infrequent to see more than twelve persons crowded into a space not fifteen feet square, so that Willis could state incontrovertibly 'that every cause that can contribute to generate contagion exists here in full vigour, and that disease in every aggravated form, with all its train of desolating misery, is rarely absent'.³⁷

The mass influx of famine refugees placed huge strains on an already vulnerable locality. Under immense pressure of numbers due to the ravages of famine in April 1847, the Board of Guardians of the NDU workhouse formally stated its objection to the manner in which the South Dublin Union workhouse in James' Street was avoiding a fair share of the increased numbers seeking relief, despite having more highly-valued property to draw upon.³⁸ The numerous 'bona fida residents' of the surrounding very poor district were not the main problem, but the streams which constantly augmented their numbers. At the North Docks, steamers offload 'the sick and disabled sent from England and Scotland', the 'destitute persons broken down in constitution', sent home when of no further use, to burden the north city ratepayers. Nearby Bow Street asylum for the 'houseless poor' (see Figure 7.5), the only such asylum in the city to date,

[34] Ibid., p. 42.
[35] Ibid., p. 45.
[36] Ibid., p. 43.
[37] Ibid., p. 45.
[38] Minutes of the North Dublin Union, 14 April 1847.

attracted the 'distressed and starving population of country districts, flying from their wretched and famine stricken homes', who found a place to hide 'until hunger drives them to seek the shelter of the poor-house'. The asylum also acted as a magnet to 'wretched people from all parts of the city', who were driven to 'congregate here, and centralize in this locality a frightful mass of destitution':

> all flocking to the metropolis in vain hope of relief, impressed with the belief that where the seat of Government is, the noble and the wealthy will be found, but alas, on their arrival sad disappointment is their lot, they find nothing but distress and destitution and see around them, as it were, a making of their wants in the deserted mansions of the noble and untenanted dwellings of the once opulent Merchants, and then in the bitterness of despair hide themselves in this [Bow Street] asylum until hunger drives them to seek the shelter of the poor-house.[39]

The reforms urged by Willis for the parish of St Michan's were what was generally recognised as necessary – indeed, in some instances were already legislated for – but requiring a degree of interference with private property as yet unthinkable.[40] He recommended officers of health 'or something of a medical police' who would have power to compel owners of all tenement property to have their premises thoroughly lime washed twice yearly, or oftener in the case of contagious epidemics. The yards were to be paved, 'with a sufficient fall to privy pit', pigs, asses and poultry to be banned, dogs taxed, sleeping in cellars to be outlawed, and all such regulations imposed 'under a penalty recoverable in the most summary manner'.[41] The introduction and enforcement of such measures in this most neglected district was to take several decades more.

The Downward Slide: Survey Evidence 1850–1900

The downward slide of the oldest part of the north city, the parish of St Michan's (Figure 8.1), was well underway as early as the first quarter of the nineteenth century; indeed several streets and lanes had very little distance to fall before the term 'slum' could be fairly applied. However, moving eastwards from Church Street (Figure 8.1), beyond the areas developed by the Jervis and Moore families (c.1660–1750), the decay of the Gardiner estate into slums was of a very different character and magnitude.

The downward slide of the Gardiner estate was underway before the dissolution of central administration in 1846, with the loss of wealthy residents to the suburbs. However, the most dramatic evidence of the deterioration in status in the following decades is the rapid increase in the proportion of aristocratic one-family residences classified as 'tenements'. The commercial street directories allow this transformation to be mapped on a yearly basis, house-by-house. When other social indicators are also mapped, such as the residences of those contri-

---

[39] Ibid.
[40] 47 George III, c. 109, sec 103, imposed a penalty of £20 on the occupier, or next landlord, or landlords, for deficiencies in the matter of yards and privies.
[41] Willis, *Social and Sanitary Condition* (1845), p. 49.

buting to and relieved by the Ladies of Charity of St Vincent de Paul, and the rateable value of residences as recorded in the General Valuation (Dublin City 1854), the complex geography and nature of the north city slum crisis becomes clear. The limitations of commercial directory information alone are overcome at least in part by employing complementary but independently-generated sources.

Tenement Dwellings 1850

When all dwellings entered as 'tenements' in either *Thom's* or *Shaw's* 1850 street directories are mapped as Figure 8.3 a very definite geography of poverty emerges.[42] Moving eastwards from the very poor southern part of St Michan's parish, tenement dwellings dominated the Church Street/Beresford Street area north of the Four Courts, and the lowlying Ormond Market district and adjoining Little Strand Street to the rear of Upper Ormond Quay (see also Figure 4.2). Extending north of Pill Lane and the Ormond Market, tenements dominated Fisher's Lane and Bull Lane, whose names clearly betray their role in the local economy. East of Capel Street, a wide boulevard laid out in the 1670s as the principal commercial axis of the expanding north side, tenement use again dominated both streets and lanes: along Jervis Street and Stafford Street, to the rear of Lower Ormond Quay in Great Strand Street, and in the markets zone between Great Britain Street and Henry Street. In what may be termed the Gardiner sphere of influence (Figure 8.1), tenements dominated the alleys and courts behind Dorset Street and Gardiner Street, in the fringe areas bounded by Gloucester Street Lower and Montgomery Street, and close to the Royal Canal. Beyond the Gardiner estate, at the north eastern limit of the municipal boundary, the Ballybough/North Strand area, comprising Taaffe's Village and Spring Gardens, was very poor. Courtenay Cottages, valued between £1.5.0 and £2.0.0 in Griffith's (1854), were described in 1879 as 'damp wretched hovels, utterly unfit for human habitation and yet have high rents paid for them'.[43]

The Ladies' Association of Charity of St Vincent de Paul: Recipients of Sick Poor Relief (1851–1856) and Subscribers/Contributors (1851–53)

Figure 8.4 maps the distribution of house addresses on the 'sick poor roll' of the metropolitan branch of the Ladies' Association of Charity of St Vincent de Paul for the period 1851–56. In many instances more than one family was relieved in each house, so that the total number of persons assisted was considerably larger than is evident from the map. Practically all the individuals and families assisted

---

[42] The data on tenements is almost identical in both; however, Shaw's enters 'vacant' for several of the premises returned by Thom's as tenements, and Thom's also includes several minor courts which are not entered in Shaw's. Henry Shaw, *New City Pictorial Directory 1850 to which is added a Retrospective Review of the Past Year* (Dublin, 1850); facsimile reprint published as *The Dublin Pictorial Guide and Directory of 1850* (Belfast, 1988); *Thom's Almanac and Official Street Directory* (Dublin, 1850).
[43] Report of the Public Health Committee, *RPDC*, vol. 3, (1879), p. 988.

were entered repeatedly on the roll, some as many as twelve times, and over periods ranging from a few weeks to the full six years covered by this sample survey. The distribution of persons relieved by the Ladies' Association may be contrasted with the addresses of the subscribers to the charity, (active and honorary members) 1851–52, and those who donated clothing, bedding and other necessities for the period 1851–56.

It is immediately obvious that the charity kept very strictly to the RC parish boundaries of Church Street/Phibsborough to the west and Amiens Street/North Strand to the east. Families in Willis Court, Maher's Court, and Catherine's Lane on the west side of Church Street were assisted, and in Phibsborough, just outside the boundary with St Paul's parish, while only one person, a Mary Byrne of Oriel Place, was included in the adjoining Seville Place parish. The Mayor Street and Sheriff Street district was composed almost entirely of poorer dwellings (see Figure 2.6), exclusion of this district makes it very clear that the parochial limits were closely monitored. The exclusion of the North Strand/Ballybough district, also undoubtedly very poor, reinforces impressions gathered from elsewhere that this area was never considered to be within the sphere of city life, compared with equally distant areas such as Phibsborough which at least merit occasional mention in city discussion.

Within the parish limits a very distinctive geography of poverty emerges, strongly reinforcing that already established by mapping the distribution of tenement dwellings (Figure 8.3). The pattern most often repeated (Figure 8.4) is the concentration of the poor in the numerous back lanes and courts behind the main streets, very effectively hidden from view by archways or reached only through first entering the front house. From the foundation of the metropolitan branch the numerous lanes and courts behind the highly desirable residences of Gardiner Street were on the visiting lists of the ladies. They also gave particular attention to the area between Montgomery Street and Gloucester Street Lower, adjacent to Gardiner Street Lower. Off Dorset Street, one of the oldest major thoroughfares in the city, there are numerous lanes and courts where many poor households were visited. The offices of the charity were located at 20 Lower Dorset Street from 1851–54; in 1855 they moved a short distance around the corner to 6 Middle Gardiner Street, while Margaret Aylward, founder of this branch, had her own lodgings at 14 Middle Gardiner Street during this period.[44] The courts and alleys off both Dorset Street and Gardiner Street received more attention perhaps than the many equally poor areas at a greater remove from the administrative headquarters.

Between Great Britain Street and Henry Street a number of addresses appear in the relief rolls. The pattern in the southern part of St Michan's parish,

[44] Margaret Aylward was living in 6 Berkeley Street in 1857; in 1858 she moved to 42 Eccles Street (renumbered 46 in 1869), which was rented as an administrative headquarters for St Brigid's Orphanage, and also became the home of the group of lay women who devoted themselves to the charities; this group was formed into a religious congregation, the Sisters of the Holy Faith, and approved in 1867.

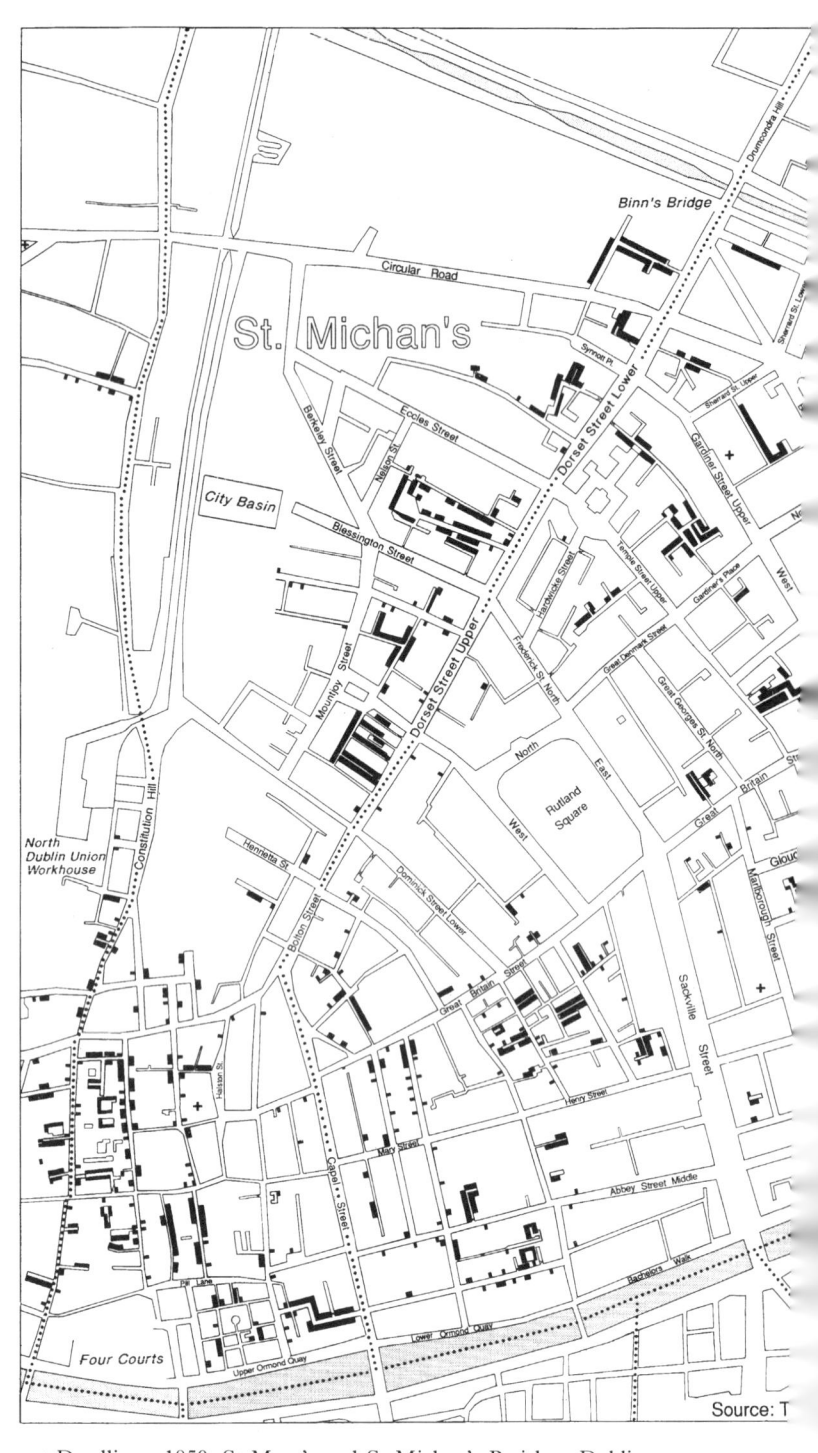

Figure 8.3 Tenement Dwellings, 1850, St Mary's and St Michan's Parishes, Dublin

Tenement Dwellings 1850
St. Mary's and St. Michan's Parishes

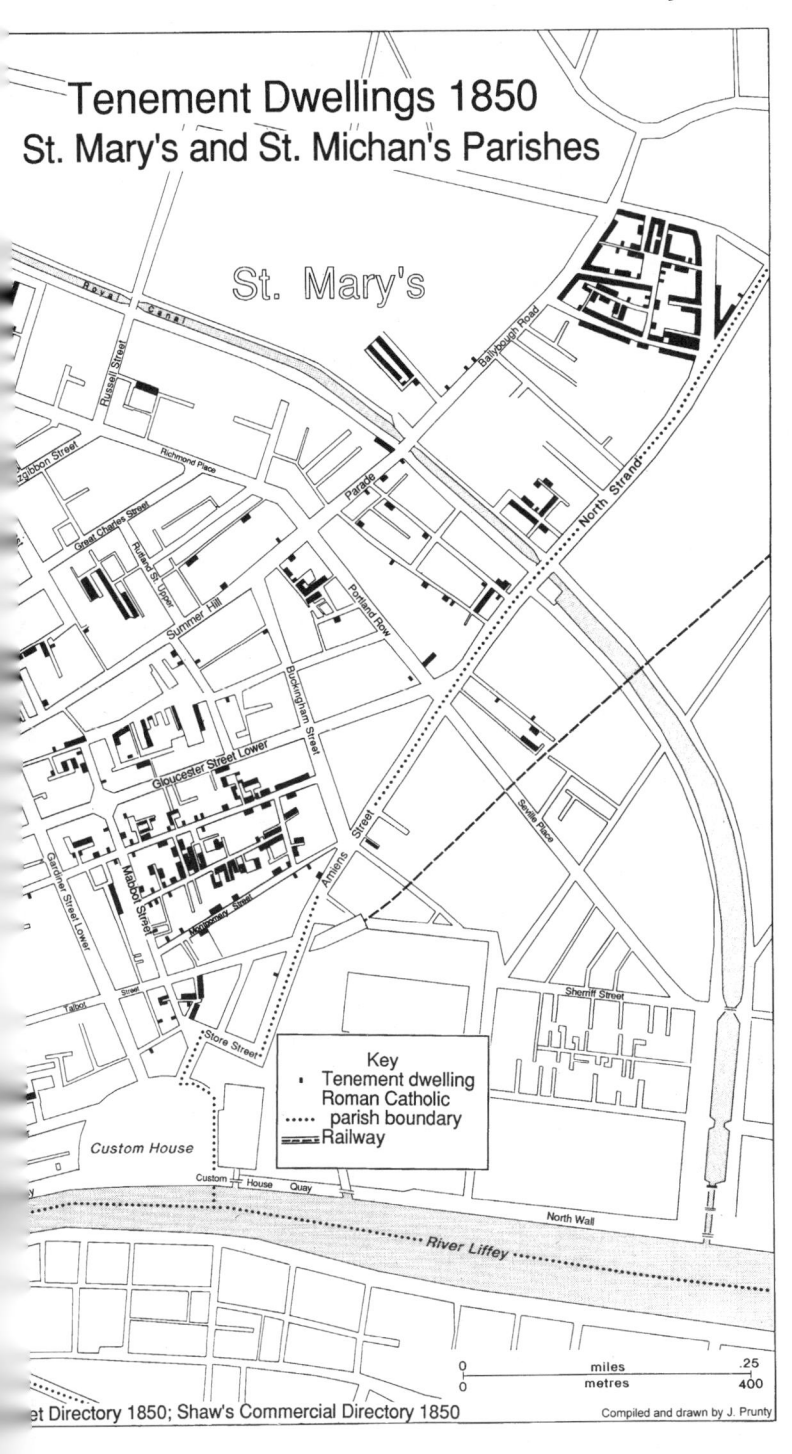

Key
- Tenement dwelling Roman Catholic
- ····· parish boundary
- ▬▬▬ Railway

Custom House

River Liffey

North Wall

0 — .25 miles
0 — 400 metres

...et Directory 1850; Shaw's Commercial Directory 1850

Compiled and drawn by J. Prunty

between the Linen Hall and Upper Ormond Quay was more dispersed, with persons visited in several of the narrow streets, lanes, and courts.

Attempting to correlate the names of persons residing in these courts and alleys and relieved by the charity, using the names and addresses in the 'official' (Griffith's valuation) and commercial (street directory) sources, is an excellent illustration of the invisibility of the poorest. In no instance whatsoever does the name of the listed occupier correspond with the name and address entered on the relief roll, even though the charity generally noted very full addresses, such as '6 Britain Court'. The street directories deal summarily with the poorest courts and alleys, such as 'Temple Court 1–13 tenements'. Griffith's valuation combined with the five foot Ordnance Survey maps are excellent for locating the premises of least value but, as this study has proven, are of little assistance in identifying the poorer residents of tenement dwellings. The detail available in the relief records becomes increasingly more valuable.

Alongside the geography of poverty in these adjoining parishes is the geography of wealth. When the home addresses of the charitable persons of some affluence and status who formed or supported the Ladies' Association (Figure 8.4), are placed alongside the addresses of those whom they visited and relieved, a striking picture of two very different worlds in close proximity is revealed. These people are very visible, their residences fronting major thoroughfares, wide streets and exclusive squares. The street directories include their names and very often their occupations, so that the charity entry such as donated 'assorted coloured bedgowns' or annual subscription of '4s4d paid in full' can be filled out with family occupation, and occupations of neighbours. While confirming residency with *Shaw's* and *Thom's* street directories (1850, 1851), with the more reliable information on tenancy available in Griffith's (1854, see Figure 8.5), it was noted that a large section of the membership was drawn from women holding property in their own right, who might be considered 'women of substance' or of independent means, not surprising in a charity run by well-to-do women. An occupation is given only if the woman has a trade, such as milliner, so that it is impossible to determine the exact family circumstances of persons such as 'Mrs Jane O'Hagan, 69 Blessington Street'. However, taking into account the rateable value of the premises, and the occupations of immediate neighbours, along with the evidence from the relief records, a fairly accurate assessment of the women members' economic and social status can be made.

The separateness of the social spheres which the lady visitors and recipients of relief occupied was part of the association's understanding of its role, and the commitment of 'ladies' of some social standing an aspect of the charity that was constantly advertised. As the members visited 'the courts and alleys where the poor are to be found', it was felt that 'the consideration of persons above them in life, coming to them by the impulse of spontaneous charity, gave a special efficacy to the efforts of the Members in ministering to their wants and necessities'.[45] These ladies

---

[45] *Ladies of Charity, First Report*, 1852, p. 9.

assiduous in their domestic duties in the morning and perhaps mingling in the course of the day in innocent amusement and recreation, and in society more congenial to their rank, will be seen going into these obscure alleys without a witness but God, and there finding their way into the abodes of the Sick, the unhappy and the miserable, and silently relieving them.[46]

The benefits of such works which 'bring into contact different grades of society' was stressed, where 'the rich and the poor see each other, commune with each other, and edify one another', the rich privileged to witness 'the great virtues of many of the poor', and the poor in many instances so grateful, and offering 'such heartfelt prayers for their benefactors, that it is a real happiness to serve them'.[47] Geographically, the distances were minimal, but socially the gulf was immense.

Griffith's Valuation 1854: Mountjoy Square/Gloucester Street

The General Valuation of Ireland (Griffith's Valuation) for Dublin City, 1854, provides further evidence for the geographical proximity of the poor and the wealthy. Figure 8.5 is a detailed mapping of house valuation in a sample area, the Mountjoy Square/Gloucester Street district. In the 1790s, when the Gardiner estate was the main centre of development in Dublin, Gardiner Street linked up the newest aristocratic quarter, Mountjoy Square, with the city's finest public building, the Custom House.[48] In Plates 8.1–8.2 the architectural correctness of the Georgian terraces, the high standard to which each house was completed, and the broad streets which these terraces lined are in evidence. The row of very fine houses, with values ranging from £30 to £95 (Figure 8.5), was broken only for a short stretch near the junction with Great Britain Street/Summerhill. Mountjoy Square was the preserve of the wealthiest, its houses still three bay, an essential feature of the aristocratic districts, although even within the square there were gradations between the east and north, where values reached £110 and £100 respectively, and the south and west, where values reached £85 and £80. The roads radiating from Mountjoy Square extended this exclusive zone, most notably along Gardiner's Place and Great Denmark Street to join up with Rutland (Parnell) Square (see Figure 8.4), an earlier and less regular development but with more magnificent houses, where values in 1854 ranged between £60 and £250. Parts of Summer Hill shared the same high status origins, but otherwise such development stopped well short of Aldborough House (1794), which played little part in aristocratic urban development and by the time of the Crimean war had fallen to the ignominy of being occupied as a barracks.

The poorest housing, valued at less than £5, was to be found concentrated in the back yards and alley ways, often in courtyard formation, and filling up

---

[46] *Ladies of Charity, Third Report*, 1854, p. 4.
[47] *Ladies of Charity, Eighth Report*, 1859, pp. 5–6.
[48] Louis M. Cullen, 'The Growth of Dublin 1600–1900: Character and Heritage', in F.H.A. Aalen and Kevin Whelan, (eds.), *Dublin, City and County: from Prehistory to Present* (Dublin, 1992), p. 258.

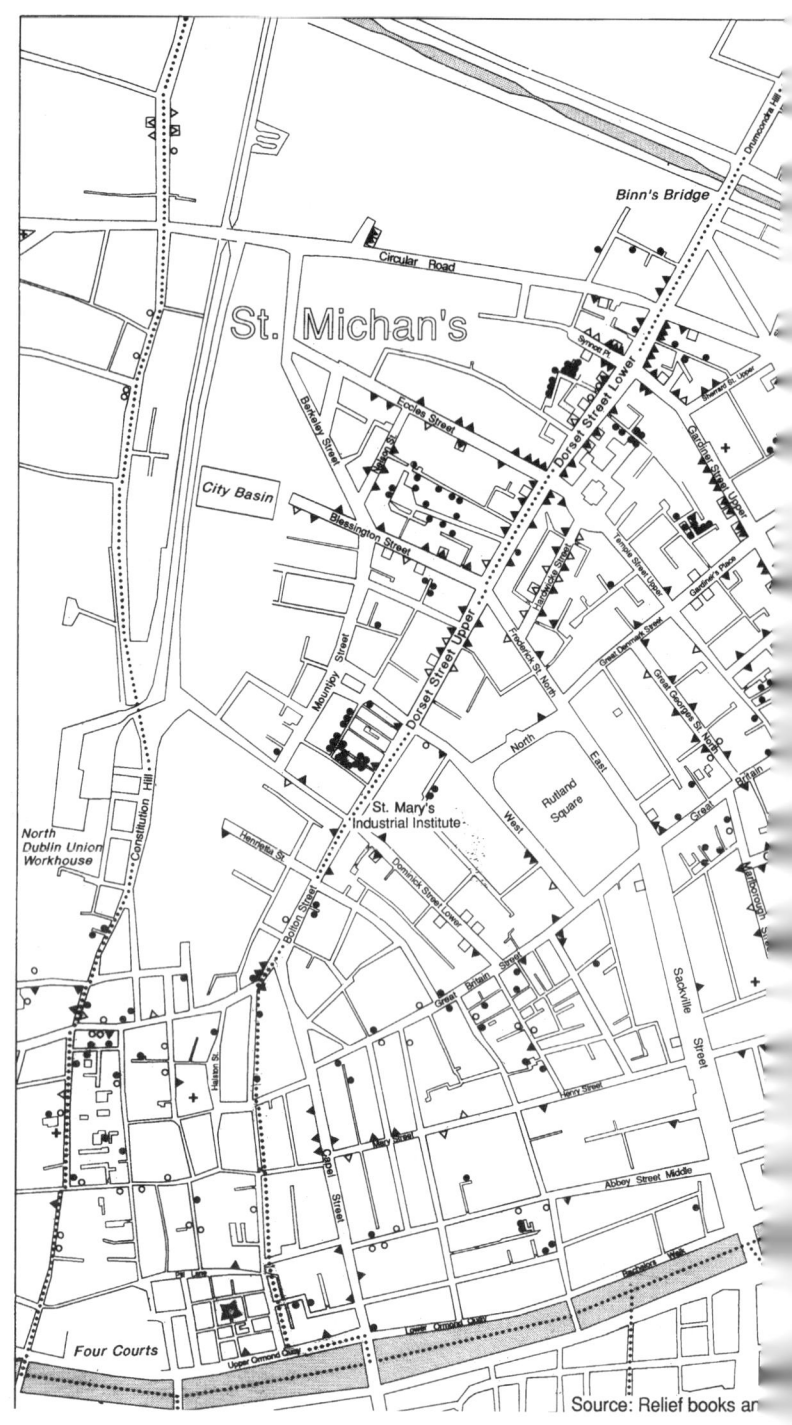

Figure 8.4 Ladies' Association of Charity 1851–1856, St Mary's and St Michan's Parishes, Dublin

A Classic Slum: Dublin North City

Ladies' Association of Charity
1851 - 1856
St. Mary's and St. Michan's Parishes

Key

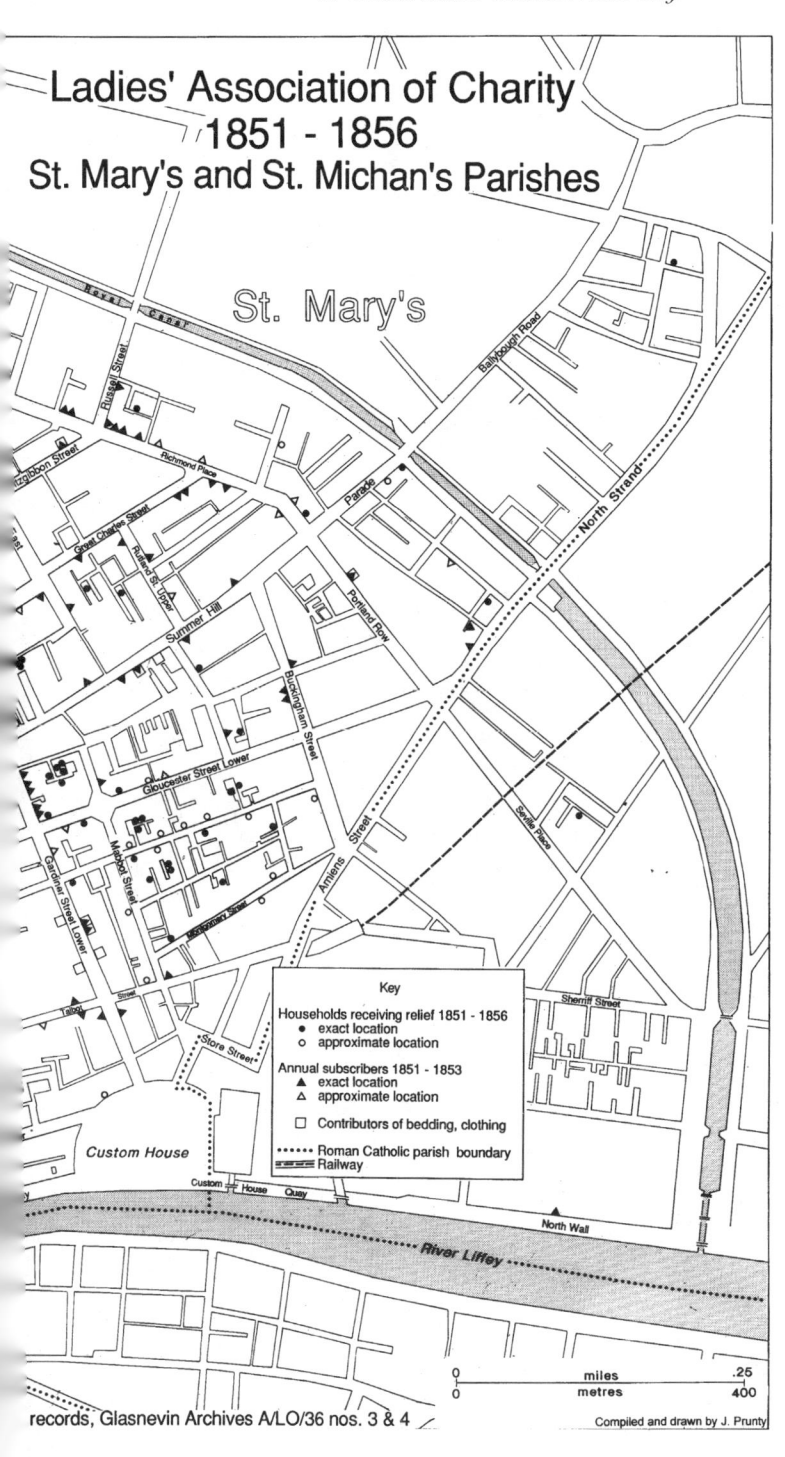

Households receiving relief 1851 - 1856
● exact location
○ approximate location

Annual subscribers 1851 - 1853
▲ exact location
△ approximate location

☐ Contributors of bedding, clothing
••••• Roman Catholic parish boundary
━━━ Railway

records, Glasnevin Archives A/LO/36 nos. 3 & 4

Compiled and drawn by J. Prunty

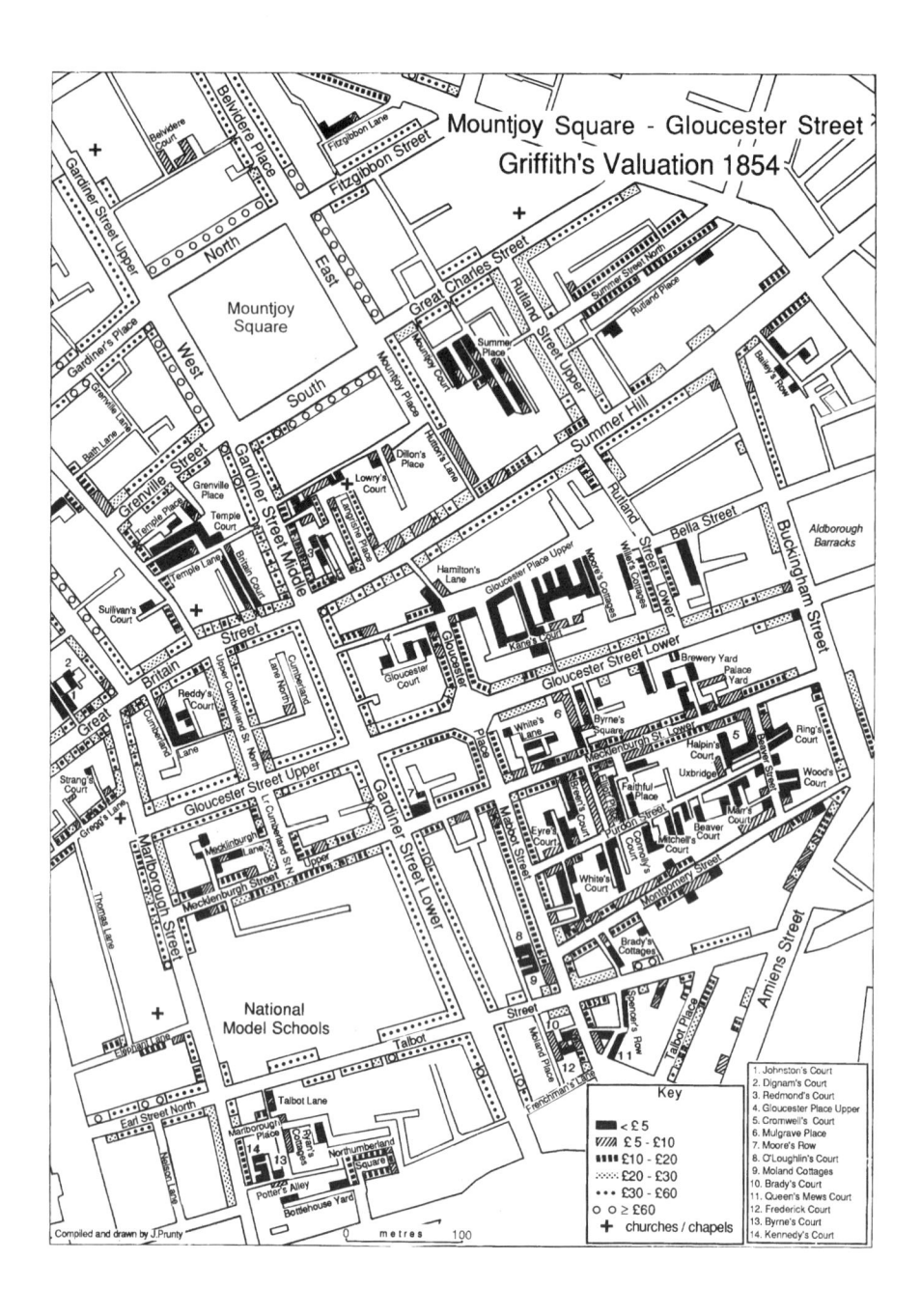

Figure 8.5 Gloucester Street – Mountjoy Square, Griffith's Valuation, 1854

irregular spaces. Lowry's Court (Figure 8.5) to the rere of Mountjoy Square consisted of three houses 'built upon a space not large enough for one', and with some rooms not more than 8 feet by 8 feet; 'a dirty petit graces the entrance to the court'.[49] Along the back lanes competition between stables/carriage houses and inexpensive dwellings most often resulted in the accommodation of both. While some of the stable lanes belonging to the best houses, such as Mountjoy Square, Great Charles Street and Summerhill (numbers 26 to 60), preserved their non-residential character, most had one side reserved as stable lanes and the other filled in with cheap housing. Mecklinburgh Lane[50] for example provided the stables for Gloucester Street Upper on the north side, while the south side had four tenement dwellings. The stable lanes of Great Charles Street and Rutland Street Upper accommodated, besides the equipage of the wealthy, a dense network of poor dwellings: Summer Place, Mountjoy Court, and Rutland Place.

The pattern of poor dwellings was more confused between Summerhill and Gloucester Street Lower, where the uneven topography (Figure 8.2) led to an irregular network of cottages set in rows and around small courts: Kane's Court, Willet's Cottages, Moore's Cottages, Hamilton's Lane. From a comparison of maps from 1811 (Figure 8.2) and 1854 (Figure 8.5) it is clear that much open ground had been filled in before the mid nineteenth century in a scheme that was far removed from the grand plans of the Gardiners. Similarly the wedge from Mecklenburgh Street Lower almost to Store Street was still open ground in the early nineteenth century (Figure 8.2); by 1854 this accommodated courts named Breen's, Ayre's, Carroll's, White's, Faithful Place, Elliott Place and Brady's Cottages. Here however the main arteries: Mecklenburgh Street Lower, Purdon Street, and Montgomery Street, were only barely more valuable than the poorer dwellings they shielded from view. The Ordnance Survey name book (1837) draws the contrast neatly. Mountjoy Square North: 'Street wide and clean, macademized footways, gravelled and flagged, lighted with gas. Houses very good, 5 stories high with spacious reres and stabling. Inhabitants, private families, gentlemen of the Medical and Legal Profession'. Nearby Purdon (or Purden) street is the location of 'Institution for worm complaints for the poor. Street narrow and dirty paved, middle footways lighted (*sic*). Houses of various qualities with dirty reres. Inhabitants Provision dealers, Huxters, a great number of destitute Poor, dissolute and depraved characters in both sex, laborers'. This is the heart of the 'Monto', the redlight district which repeatedly featured in references to the geography of prostitution (Chapter 7).[51]

The street nomenclature (Figures 8.5) is a clear guide in these north city areas to the two very different geographies in evidence. Among the best streets are found names relating to the lord lieutenants and their families, thus Rutland,

---

[49] Report of the Public Health Committee, *RPDC*, vol. 3 (1879) p. 942.
[50] Both spellings, Mecklenburgh and Mecklinburgh, are variously used in Dublin Corporation reports, and in the annotated maps of the Valuation Office.
[51] 'Name Book, Dublin City: Notes concerning the City of Dublin complied during the progress of the Ordnance Survey in 1837'; John Finegan, *The Story of Monto: An Account of Dublin's Red Light District* (Dublin, 1978).

Granby, Cavendish, Dorset, Sackville, Hardwicke, Buckingham and Henrietta. The Gardiner family as the most important property dynasty in the area is commemorated in the name Gardiner and in other family titles: Mountjoy, Blessingon, Florinda and Montgomery. The Beresford, Dominick, and Eccles families, all property magnates, are similarly immortalised, while Mecklenburgh, Gloucester, and Cumberland are all connected with the monarch who was reigning at the time of their development. The first Duke of Marlborough, Lord Chancellor Fitzgibbon and Viscount Amiens are eighteenth century public figures whose memories are also perpetuated in north city street names.

The back streets and poor courts share a different nomenclature altogether. Here we have mostly plain local names, rather than grand English titles: McCann's Cottages, Kelly's Row, Smith's Court, Graham's Court, Brady's Row, Rorke's Cottages, Walsh's Row, Murphy's Cottages, Connolly's Court, Byrne's Square, Dillon's Place. Examination of the valuation record and street directories reveals that the vast majority are simply the name of the immediate landlord and enjoyed a certain fluidity, as the change of lessee could bring a change of name. Thus Kane's Cottages of 1854 are clearly renamed Murphy's Cottages; Ward's Cottages, 47 Church Street, (Plate 8.4) were formerly known as Delany's Court, and previous to that as Price's Yard. The court behind 18 Church Street was first known as Humphrey's Court, before being known as Dunn's Court, and by 1854 Dignam's Court. Current or former land uses are often recalled in the nomenclature of the poorer streets: Brewery Yard and Queen's Mews Cottages. Some of the more exotic court names, with historic or at least folklore associations, are Cromwell's Court and Palace Yard.

Anne Mosher and Deryck Holdsworth's study of the alley lexicon in late-nineteenth and early-twentieth century Pennsylvania led them to conclude that such changes reflect the informality of alley worlds as well as the rapidity with which the local meaning and social characteristics of alleys could change.[52] In the Dublin context the relatively frequent naming and renaming of courts and lanes points to a similar situation, especially when linked in with a high level of residential mobility.

Slum Realities: Records of the Ladies' Association of Charity

The archive of the Ladies of Charity of St Vincent de Paul provides graphic descriptions of the family circumstances and daily struggles of the residents of the tenement and cottage dwellings illustrated in Figures 8.3–8.5. Anxious to attract both active members and financial support, the annual reports gave a selection of 'such cases as seem best to illustrate the every-day nature of our charity'.[53] The stories are invariably told with much drama, in the popular

---

[52] Anne E. Mosher and Deryck W. Holdsworth, 'The Meaning of Alley Housing in Industrial Towns: Examples from Late-Nineteenth and Early-Twentieth Century Pennsylvania' *Journal of Historical Geography*, 18, 2 (1992), pp. 174–189.
[53] *Ladies of Charity, Fifth Report*, 1856, p. 7.

journalistic style favoured by the authors of such slum classics as *The Bitter Cry of Outcast London* (1883),[54] the ladies with difficulty picking their way up a 'crumbling staircase' in semi-darkness, to the 'roof of a tottering house', entering the semi-darkness of some 'dreary garret' with 'frameless windows, and large apertures in the boards' where little 'pale, half-clad children' with 'wasted forms' are shivering at a few 'dying sparks'. The sick person lies almost naked on a handful of straw, not having tasted food for several days:[55]

> The father and mother were seated near a few embers; another child, now struck by sickness, lay on a little straw in a corner; no earthly comfort was there; the entire comfort consisted of two stools! No chair, nothing that could convenience them.[56]

In 'one of the narrow lanes of St Michan's parish', they sought a poor woman, to whom they brought relief:

> On a damp, earthen floor a few particles of straw were strown to serve as a bed for this poor widow: her tattered garments and the squalid appearance of her son, a lad earning three or four shillings a week, almost the sole support of his mother and little sister, sufficiently indicated the poverty of the whole.[57]

The challenge of such situations was faced courageously by the Ladies' association, under Aylward's inspired leadership; the relief books tell exactly what was given to each family, while the annual reports provide the context in which the particular type of relief was decided upon. The two largest items of expenditure were 'just those most wanted – bread and fuel'. The greatest care was taken 'to unite economy with real relief, and discrimination with kindliness'. 'We observe economy, but we are not its slaves'.[58] The emphasis was on the intervention of 'timely aid and encouragement', to try and prevent utter destitution, though it is clear that many of those relieved were already in a state of great want. Table 8.1 lists the items distributed in the first year of operation; later reports included cabbages and flour as major expenses, and small quantities of coffee, porter and wine, fish, and soap. Other additions were 'golden ointment for the eyes, medicine &c', 'to the Mendicity for warm baths', 'car-hire for poor to hospital'; 'passage of poor woman to England' or 'to the country to a situation', and 'towards procuring a mangle for a poor family'. Cod-liver oil was found to be of 'incalculable benefit to the Poor in cases of Scrofula and affections of the lungs'.[59]

---

[54] Andrew Mearns, *The Bitter Cry of Outcast London* (London, 1883); see also Alan Mayne, 'Representing the Slum', *Urban History Yearbook* (Leicester, 1990), pp. 66–84.
[55] *Ladies of Charity, Third Report*, 1854, p. 9; *Fourth Report*, 1855, p. 7; *Fifth Report*, 1856, p. 5; *Seventh Report*, 1858, p. 6.
[56] *Ladies of Charity, First Report*, 1852, p. 10.
[57] *Ladies of Charity, Fourth Report*, 1855, p. 10.
[58] *Ladies of Charity, Seventh Report*, 1858, pp. 5–8.
[59] *Ladies of Charity, Fourth Report*, 1855, p. 6.

Sick Relief in Kind:	£101.19.9
	lbs oz
bread	8228 0
meal	2279 0
meat	180 4
sugar	598 8
tea	82 5
butter	69 5½
rice	3 8
milk	121 pints
cocoa	2 lbs.
candles	3
eggs	452
porter	5 pints
straw	10½ cwt.
coal	96 bags 6¼ stones
clothes:	£1.5.8½
cod-liver oil:	4s 6d
Sick Relief in Money:	£27.0.1½

Source: *First Annual Report*, 1852, p. 27

Table 8.1 *Relief distributed by the Ladies' Association of Charity of St Vincent de Paul, Metropolitan Branch, Dublin, 1851.*

Most of the recipients of relief, whether of clothing, food or other items, were women, even where it is clear that they are collecting on behalf of husbands or grown sons. Only occasionally is a man listed, such as John Maher, 136 Britain Street, who received a pair of boots in May 1852, and boots, vest and a necktie the following month.

'Donations of old clothing, carpeting, sheets, rugs, blankets, shoes etc.' were repeatedly requested.[60] The items of clothing most often distributed may be listed as follows: bedgowns, flannel petticoats, calico chemises, shawls, vests, night shifts, drawers, stockings, night wrappers, bonnets, frocks, gowns, shirts, coats, jackets, trousers and, less often, shoes and boots. The provision of warm underclothing was the most important area of clothing relief, along with bedding: sheets, carpet for covering, or simply 'bedcovering', or 'bedstuff', blankets, quilts, bedticker, pillow, were all distributed between 1851–56. 'The poor man's bed (straw), which alas! is often a great boon, has been given to every one that asked

---

[60] See final page of each of the *Annual Reports of the Ladies of Charity*.

it'.[61] Sheets were 'lent'; presumably the Ladies of Charity took the same precaution against the pawning of bedclothes as did the Association for the Relief of Distressed Protestants, which had its blankets branded and all pawnbrokers warned against accepting them in trust, as they were the property of the ARDP.[62]

It is impossible to track the movements of persons who change residence during the period, as some individuals and families were certainly very mobile. There were Mahers receiving relief in 136 Britain Street, (John, Mrs, 1852), Coffey's Court, Greggg's Lane (John, Mrs, children; 1853); 34 Mountjoy Street, (Mrs, Mrs Maher's son, 1853–55), and Green Street (Daniel, 1856). Other names which reappear at several addresses are Rock, Sands, Redmond, Scully, and the more numerous Byrnes, Murphys, Callaghans, Dunnes, and O'Neill's.

Money relief, recorded from 1877, but in operation previous to that, was given in association with 'tea, sugar, bread'. The sums were small but not insignificant: 2/6, was above the average rent demanded for a one room tenement. Some persons were visited and relieved on a daily basis, 'others two, three, or five times a week, according to their wants and necessities'.[63] The release of clothes from pawn to enable a daughter who had been in service, 'with good discharges, but no clothes now to make 'an appearance" was typical, 'to a widow to assist her in business', to place an orphan in Josephian Orphan House', recover tools, 'purchase working implements for labourers', or apprentice a 'poor lame girl to the boot-closing trade'.[64] Where the breadwinner had employment to return to, or where some work could be procured for him/her, there was a some possibility of effecting a lasting improvement in family circumstances; one man was enabled to recover his tools, and 'put a little clothes upon himself . . . so, he is at his work again, and thus the whole family are raised up. They are not yet, indeed, out of poverty, but they are content'. The 'sick poor' funds could only be used for such needy persons; however the council 'as well as many individual members, had recourse to other charitable persons, in favour of the more distressed' and also operated a small 'destitute poor fund', amounting to £13.4.6 in 1855.[65]

One other aspect of the association's relief efforts was the 'volunteer services' given by individual members in a wide range of capacities: teaching the 'ignorant', sending children to school, procuring employment and places for the destitute, 'bringing absentees to their duty' and preparing adults for the sacraments at twice weekly classes in the Church of St Francis Xavier, Upper Gardiner Street.[66]

Likewise some members undertook the instruction of the First Communion children in the parish schools of St Michan's.[67] Determined to thwart the efforts

---

[61] *Ladies of Charity, Sixth Report*, 1857, p. 5.
[62] ARDP Annual Report for 1876, quoted in Kenneth Milne, *A History of the Association for the Relief of Distressed Protestants* (Dublin, 1989), p. 10.
[63] *Ladies of Charity, Third Report*, 1854, p. 7.
[64] *Ladies of Charity, Fourth Report*, 1855, pp. 11, 20; *Fifth Report*, 1856, p. 6; *Eighth Report*, 1859, p. 6.
[65] *Ladies of Charity, Fifth Report*, 1856, pp. 6, 8.
[66] *Ladies of Charity, Sixth Report*, 1857, p. 9; *Second Report*, 1853, p. 13.
[67] *Ladies of Charity, First Report*, 1852, p. 20.

of Protestant mission agents, they penetrated the Sunday schools where 'crowds of unhappy Catholics, men, and women, were to be found, lured by the offer of a small cut of bread, and then obliged in return to listen to blasphemous language, and a sermon from a minister'.[68] As the neglect of religion was seen as 'the very cancer of society, the feeder of the poor house, the prison and the hospital', catechesis was regarded as an important contribution to the alleviation of poverty.[69] And in the climate of suspicion and sectarianism which prevailed, each denomination saw salvation solely on its own terms.

Poverty Structures

Embedded in lengthy descriptive passages on the state of the poor of this district are significant insights into the structures behind the poverty situation. The want of employment, especially among women, was presented as the over-riding cause of destitution. The almost immediate consequence of sickness was inability to labour, and where it involved the bread winner, the impact on a poor family could be disastrous. A long and detailed report on poverty in this parish was prepared by a curate, Fr. O' Neill, with whom Margaret Aylward worked closely,[70] and focused especially on work opportunities, or the lack of them.[71] Such was the desperation of women seeking work that 'while men have been paid from nine to twelve shillings per week wages, I have frequently known able-bodied women to be most happy to be engaged at *manual labour* at *three pence per day!*', i.e., at about one-eighth of the male wage:

In consequence of this exclusive dependence on the father's labour, as well as because of the low rate of wages, the dearness of provisions and the consequent impossibility of saving, it is manifest that the stoppage of the *father's* wages through illness or other causes must always produce *immediate* and *absolute* want to all families so dependent on him. And it may be added that the illness of *any member* of a family so situated, as it always must bring additional expenses, has always the effect of inflicting great privations on those whose scanty means were already overtaxed.[72]

Among women of that class, domestic service, often residential, was the most usual option, with charring, washing and dealing of various sorts the other principle avenues of support. One young woman left widowed was distraught: 'the Poor-house stared her in the face; few saw any prospect of support for her, for she knew not how to sew or wash'.[73]

The division between the utterly destitute and the labouring poor, a recurring concern in slum surveys, was perilously thin. The availability of employment, generally unskilled, manual work, and the health and strength of the men, and

---

[68] *Ladies of Charity, Fifth Report*, 1856, p. 9.
[69] *Ladies of Charity, Seventh Report*, 1858, p. 9.
[70] For example Margaret Aylward to Fr. O'Neill, 29 October 1857, GA: PC/C/11 no. 3.
[71] Fr. P. O'Neill to Dr. Cullen, 2 May 1861, DDA: file 1 secular clergy, 340/1 no. 70.
[72] Ibid.
[73] *Ladies of Charity, Fourth Report*, 1855, p. 5.

indeed women, that they might procure such employment, was the major factor in determining which side of the division one fell. Important too was the sense of responsibility, when earning, in providing for dependants. Reporting on the 26 families now on the 'Sick Poor Roll' in 1861 the Association simply stated: 'They are poor now for they are sick and they cannot work'.[74] The most prevalent kind of sickness recorded among those visited was pulmonary complaints: consumption, cold, bronchitis and 'chest disease', while the general terms 'weakness', 'decline', 'debility' and 'delicacy' were also apparently related to the prevalence of TB.

The failure of persons who had migrated to Dublin in search of work to realise their hopes was another recurrent theme, and now, thrown among strangers, they were particularly vulnerable. One aged widow in Greek Street 'was not so fluent in English as in her native Irish'; this family 'came from the country; they were one among the many who have been swept away out of their little holdings into the back lanes of the city'. On the death of that woman her distraught daughter 'in the howl peculiar to the country, was giving immoderate vent to her grief'. Her keening was hushed by the visitor, who led the prayers for the dead.[75]

A severe winter could plunge a family into real distress. In June 1853 the Association reported how 'the dearness of provisions, the severity of the past winter, and, consequently, the many and pressing necessities of the poor sufferers, rendered an additional amount of aid imperative on us'.[76] Again in the winter of 1854–55 the sufferings of the poor were 'almost unparalleled during the protracted season of frost and snow' and 'three sets of visitors were obliged for a long period to go almost daily amongst them, to alleviate in some degree their wants by a little timely relief'. Watching by the death bed of one poor man, a lady visitor tried to comfort the wife. 'The *starvation* of the winter, she said, bursting into tears, it was that came against him, he wasn't used to it'.[77] The year ending June 1859 was, on the contrary, 'a remarkably good year for the poor. They have been, for the most part profitably employed, and on this account have suffered less from sickness'.[78]

The first refuge of the poorest in times of crisis was among their own relations and neighbours. There are graphic illustrations of the care of the poor for one another, particularly of women taking care of children alongside their own. One dying widow lay on 'a hard palliass' with the ticken removed to serve as a cover; this wretched straw bed was obliged to accommodate, 'beside the dying woman, her two children and her sister's two children'.[79] In another instance one very poor widow and her children, living in appalling accommodation were visited one Sunday, where they were about to enjoy the very occasional treat of sheep's head broth, when they recalled another family 'who will, I fear, be found

[74] *Ladies of Charity, Tenth Report*, 1861, p. 6.
[75] *Ladies of Charity, First Report*, 1852, p. 16.
[76] *Ladies of Charity, Second Report*, 1853, pp. 3–4.
[77] *Ladies of Charity, Fourth Report*, 1855, pp. 4, 12.
[78] *Ladies of Charity, Eighth Report*, 1859, p. 7.
[79] *Ladies of Charity, Second Report*, 1853, p. 11.

dead in their room of starvation', and were sent a share in the precious broth; "'They have not eaten a bit", she said, "today (it was then late). *I sent them something yesterday*". That poor starved creature sharing with her poorer neighbour!'[80]

Lady visitors of other denominations similarly record how among 'those doleful, dilapidated houses to which we should never dream of applying the words "Home Sweet Home" the visitor was repeatedly 'touched by the tenderness and beauty of the family affections frequently displayed by those struggling most bitterly with want'.[81] The relief provided by charities such as the Ladies' Association must always be regarded as supplementary to the mass of assistance, largely unrecorded, which was provided by the poor themselves.

Annual Subscribers and Other Contributors to the Ladies' Association of Charity, 1851–53

The distribution pattern of persons subscribing to the charity 1851–52 (Figure 8.4) is well-defined and contrasts sharply in every respect with the poor they served. This was very definitely the geography of north city Catholic wealth, both professional and business. All of Gardiner Street was represented, with the west side of Mountjoy Square completing the unbroken line from Dorset Street Lower to Talbot Street. The lady manager, Margaret Aylward, took lodgings at 14 Middle Gardiner Street, almost exactly midway along this primary axis. Adjacent high status streets which also provided members, both active and honorary, were Mountjoy Square South, Great George's Street North, Hardwicke Street, Blessington Street and Eccles Street. The better-off commercial streets were well represented: Capel Street, Mary Street, Earl Street and Talbot Street. The Jesuit community in Gardiner Street Upper also played a role in influencing this pattern, particularly John Curtis SJ, who presided at the first meeting in the church of St Francis Xavier, and at whose suggestion the Association moved its annual meetings from Gardiner Street church to the parish church in Marlborough Street, in June 1855, to emphasise its character as a *parochial* charity and widen its appeal.[82]

The subscribers can be divided into three social groups, each with a locally well-defined geography. The primary group consisted of the wives and daughters of solicitors, barristers and doctors. Another group can be found among merchant families, and a third among those involved in the grocery and provision trade.

Practically all the subscribers mapped for Blessington Street, Buckingham Street Upper, Gloucester Street Upper, Grenville Street, North Frederick Street, Hardwicke Street, Belvidere Place and Mountjoy Square were from legal families. Typical was Mrs Henry Dillon, a solicitor's wife, 28 Mountjoy Square,

---

[80] *Ladies of Charity, Fourth Report*, 1855, pp. 10–11.
[81] *Annual Report of the Dublin Bible Woman Mission in connection with the Church of Ireland*, 1877, p. 16.
[82] *Ladies of Charity, Fourth Report*, 1855, pp. 7, 12.

or neighbours Mrs Coffey, 54 and Mrs Fotrell no. 57 Dominick Street who both contributed substantial amounts of clothing to the association. Apart from these two major groups, one schoolteacher, Miss Wilhelmina Killeen, 13 Upper Gardiner Street, and one wine merchant's daughter, Miss Kelly, 89 Lower Gardiner Street, can be identified. Among the subscribers from Gardiner Street there were twelve unmarried and seventeen married ladies whose surnames were not those of the listed occupier; some at least of these are, like Miss Margaret Aylward in 14 Middle Gardiner Street, a highly respectable class of lodger.

Eccles Street was an important source of support, although the professions of most of these families, excepting Mrs Mackey, from no. 9, a solicitor's wife, was covered by the comprehensive term 'Esq.'. Eccles Street could be considered a stronghold of Catholic influence in the diocese, indeed in the country, for in 1854 it contained the residences of several prominent Catholic ecclesiastics: Archbishop Cullen resided at no. 55, Dr Murray his secretary, at 42. In 1855 Margaret Aylward determined on nos. 18 and 19, 'two fine houses, quite detached from those in the neighbourhood, with a good sized garden' and very fine rooms as the residence for the *Soeurs de Charité* whom she wished to make a foundation in Dublin (see Chapter 7). Eccles Street she considered most suitable as it is 'a highly respectable and healthy street' with the houses in question, priced at £3,500, strategically situated directly opposite Cullen's residence, where the sisters were sure to be brought to the notice of 'the large number of Ecclesiastics who are daily calling on him [Cullen] from all parts of the country'. While such contacts would further their prospects for foundations outside Dublin, situated in such a high class area 'they would be in the way of getting good subjects with fortunes', boosting their membership for the worthy undertakings ahead.[83]

The wealthy areas which were not represented among the subscribers to the Ladies of Charity can be partly accounted for by the distribution of wealthy Protestants. The charity was avowedly, even aggressively Roman Catholic; however, the disjunction between denominational charities was not so simple, with a subscriber such as Benjamin Lee Guinness heading the Ladies of Charity subscription lists in the 1850s, while simultaneously very actively supporting the Irish Church Missions. The most highly valued properties in Rutland Square and along the north and east of Mountjoy Square were occupied by Protestants,[84] while Henrietta Street, with its eighteenth century Georgian mansions too large for single families, was by mid century being used as legal offices and chambers. Only one house was represented here, Miss Kate Corry and Miss Farrelly, 11 Henietta Street, presumably in lodgings in a house advertised as the offices of solicitors and proctors.

The wives and daughters of wine merchants form the second social grouping. Mrs Denman, 49 Middle Abbey Street; Mrs Dunne, 39 Arran Quay; and Miss

---

[83] Margaret Aylward to Père Etienne, 19 August 1855, GA: MA/CH//02 no. 56a.
[84] Evidence for this is from the subscription lists of the Smyly schools.

Nagle, 12 Earl Street, all belong to wine merchant families, serving the large market for their produce provided by the near presence of so many wealthy households. The most important of all Margaret Aylward's co-workers was Miss Ada Allingham, of a wealthy and very generous wine merchant family in Capel Street; she was to join the Ladies' Association in 1860, and through her loyalty and commitment ensured the continuation of the charity and associated ventures into the 1890s and beyond.

The third group consisted of manufacturing and business families. Typical was Mrs Whitty, of 33 Bolton Street; her husband Moses had a soap and candle manufactory here, while the family also owned the premises numbered 33–35, taking in lodgers and keeping a provision shop. Other ladies from Bolton Street were Mrs and Miss Keon, no. 61, from a pawnbroking family, and Mrs McCourt, no. 60, corn factor and seed merchant. Continuing along this major artery into Dorset Street the wives and daughters of provision merchants feature prominently. Miss Mary Barlow runs her own grocery store at 133 Upper Dorset Street, while other subscribers' occupations that can be identified along this street are apothecary (Miss Murphy, no. 79) and cabinet maker and upholsterer (Mrs Hickey, no. 97).[85]

This pattern extends along Great Britain Street where there was a selection of business families who were generous subscribers: Mrs Frew, no. 98, and Miss Mary Catherine Harte, no. 118, both grocers; Mrs. John Hughes, no. 115, husband a wax and tallow chandler, and Mrs. Eleanor Wyer, 117 Great Britain Street a linen draper, whose family also occupied the adjoining property.

While the front street/back court dichotomy between rich and poor was the most recurrent spatial pattern in mid-nineteenth century Dublin, exceptions to this rule abound, and the mapping of both recipients from and subscribers to the one charity highlight this anomaly. Coles Lane, for example (see Figure 8.10), is written off in *Shaw's Directory* of 1850 as 33 tenements. However, Mr. James Farrell occupied no. 32, valued at £32, a substantially more valuable property than most others along the lane, and so was unlikely to have missed the 4s 4d he paid to the association.

The requisite annual subscription of 4s 4d, though doubtless beyond the means of the majority of the Catholic parishioners in this very extensive area, nevertheless spread the subscription net quite widely. There were a number of contributors who could not be described as wealthy, but who equalled and indeed exceeded the generosity of those better off than them. Where a servant contributed a note is taken, thus Grace Kearns, a servant employed by Nicholas O'Gorman, QC, in 45 Blessington Street, is credited with paying the annual subscription in one instalment, while another subscriber was Thomas Green, a

---

[85] Upper Dorset Street, grocers or victuallers: Mrs. Duffey no. 20; Mrs. Kirwan no. 28; the Misses Byrne no. 36; Mrs O' Callaghan no. 37; Mrs. Byrne, no. 70; Mrs. Marks, no. 71; Mrs McCann, no. 100; Mary Barlow, no. 133 bakers: Mrs Brennan no. 22; Mrs Delaney no. 57.

gardener in lodgings at 18 Bolton Street. James Byrne, a boot and shoemaker, 2 Clarence Street, occupying a house valued at £3 appears to be in the most modest of circumstances, yet paid his subscription along with the well-to-do.

It is not possible to distinguish the active or visiting lady members from those who merely contributed financially, using the subscription lists alone. However, by also mapping all who donated clothing, bedding etc. from 1851–56, and identifying those who served on the committee from 1851–1862, a core group of particularly active and generous ladies can be identified. Geographically these ladies are concentrated between Eccles Street, Blessington Street, Dorset Street Lower, Gardiner Street, North Great Georges Street, Dominick Street Lower, and Summerhill. The southern part of the parish of St Michan's provides practically no such ladies, excepting Miss Coyne of 141 Capel Street, a Catholic publishing house. It can be clearly seen therefore that the charity was largely controlled by the wives and daughters of legal and medical practitioners, and those of high status business or merchant backgrounds.

Individual members who can be identified are Mrs Agnes Scully, 9 Fitzgibbon Street, who was responsible for securing huge amounts of clothing for the poor. Other generous members were Miss Corbally, 2 Cowley Place; Mrs Whelan, 33 Summer Hill; Mrs Hussey, Eccles Street and Mrs Jane O' Hagan, 69 Blessington Street. Mrs Frances Murray, treasurer, was 'a native of France but she had, long ago, taken Ireland for better for worse, and she was faithful to her plighted troth to the end'. This lady gave considerably of her own means; 'besides, her interest, her time, and her information, were at the service of those who had recovered from sickness, to procure situations for them',[86] and her death in 1861, at a crucial point in the fortunes of the association, was a serious blow. Other very active members were Mrs Margaret Mara, Lower Gardiner Street, and Mrs McDermott, 39 Upper Sackville Street.[87]

The Changing Geography of Poverty: St Mary's and St Michan's Parishes, 1895–1900
Tenement Dwellings, 1900

Over an interval of forty years substantial changes occurred in the geography of poverty in these two north city parishes. Mapping all dwellings listed as tenements in Thom's street directory of 1900 (Figure 8.6) reveals a two-pronged movement: the clearance or abandonment of the back courts and alleys for a share in a house facing a main street, and the almost complete colonisation of certain streets by tenements. The Church Street/Beresford Street area is the most striking example of this abandonment of the rear courts. The Summerhill-Montgomery Street sector illustrates both aspects: the downgrading of residences

---

[86] *Ladies of Charity, Tenth Report*, 1861, p. 9.
[87] see 'List of Ladies who have charitably sent in Clothes to the Association for the use of the Poor', 1851–1856, GA A/LO/36 no. 3; also annual reports 1852–62.

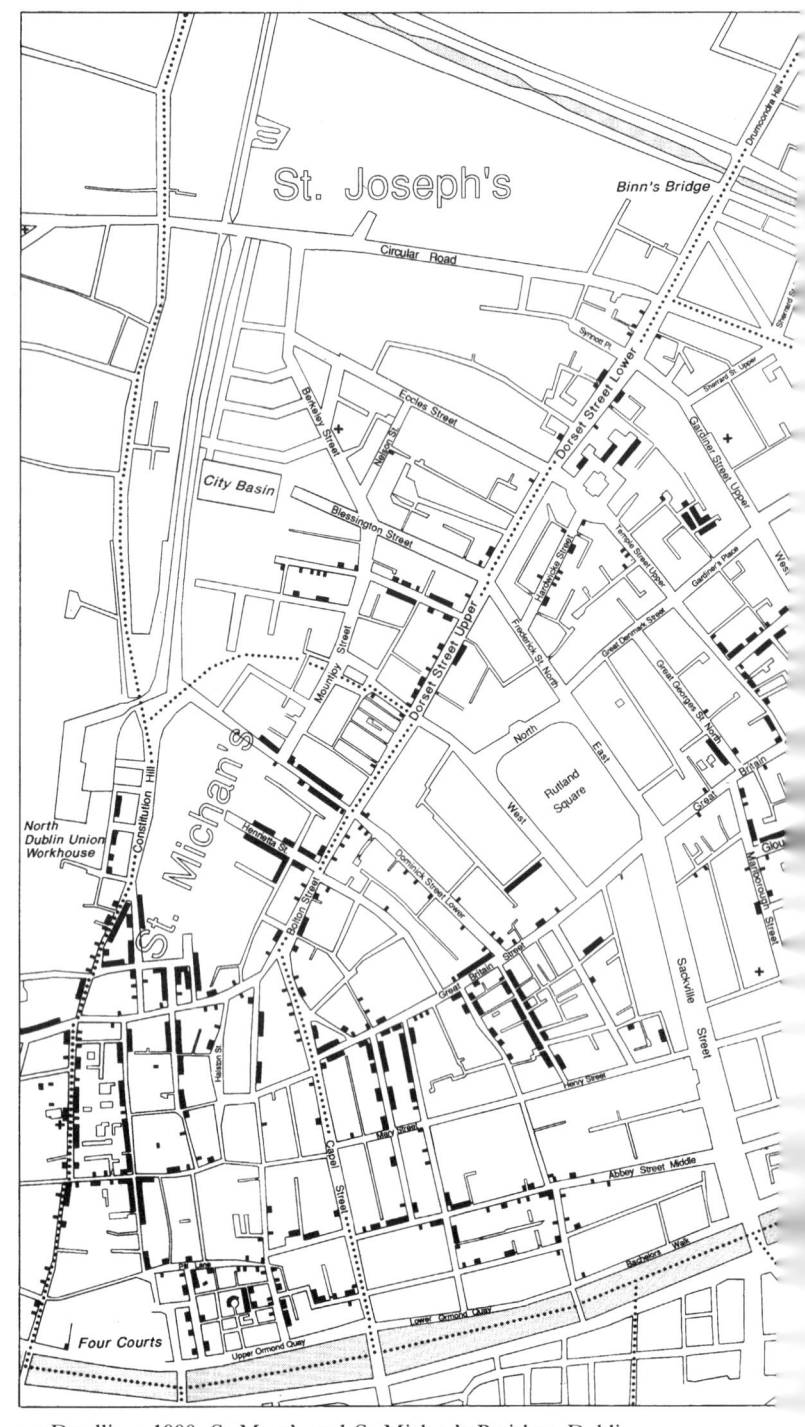

Figure 8.6 Tenement Dwellings 1900, St Mary's and St Michan's Parishes, Dublin

A Classic Slum: Dublin North City 309

Tenement Dwellings 1900
St. Mary's and St. Michan's Parishes

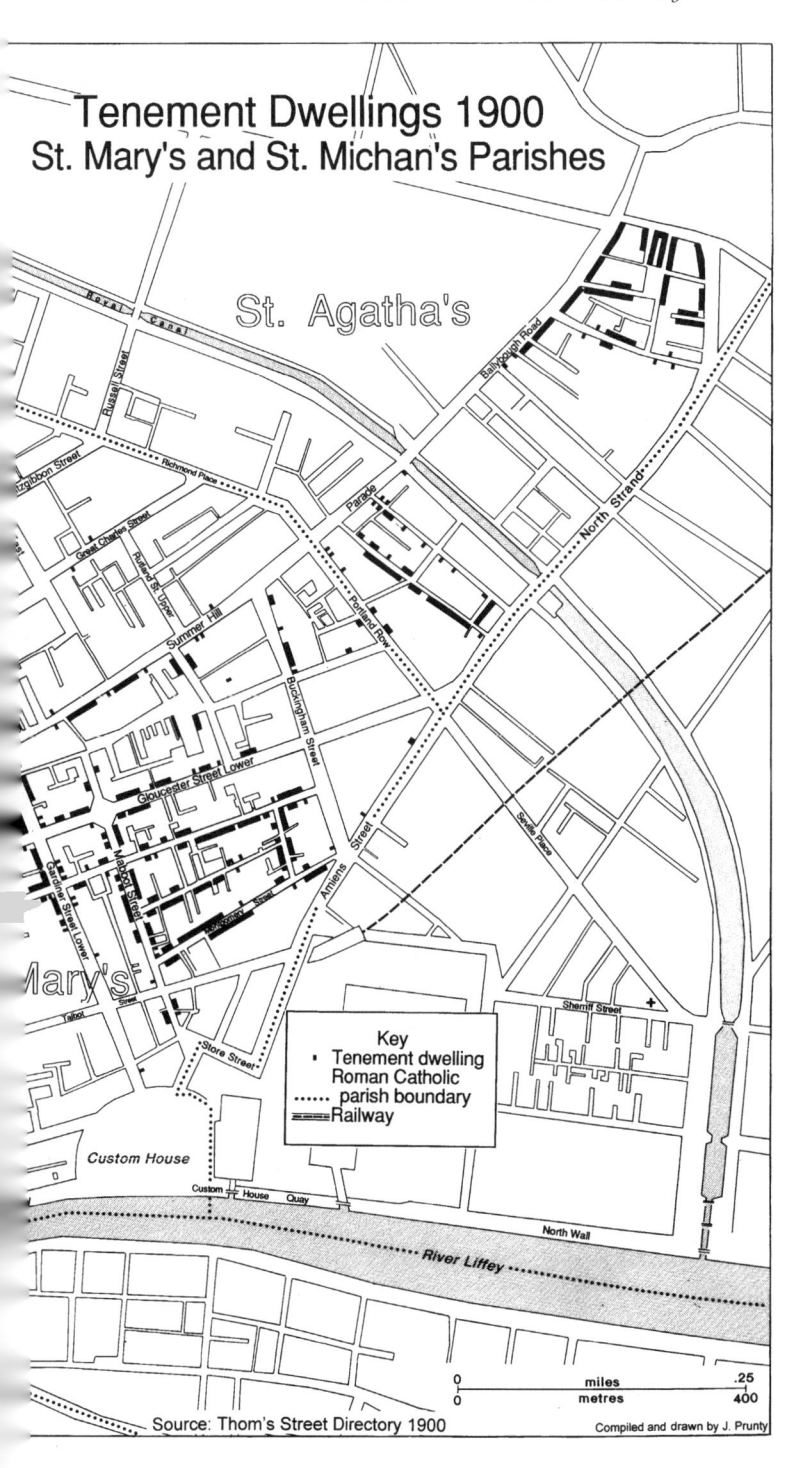

Key
· Tenement dwelling
····· Roman Catholic parish boundary
═══ Railway

Source: Thom's Street Directory 1900

Compiled and drawn by J. Prunty

which were very highly valued in 1854 (Figure 8.5) including Upper Gloucester Street, Upper Cumberland Street North, Gardiner Street Lower, and the southern side of Summerhill, with the abandonment of many of the inner network of poor courts and alleys: White's Lane, Byrne's Square, Cromwell's, Ring's, Wood's, Connolly's, and Carroll's courts have all disappeared, contributing to the widespread dereliction exposed by the 1913/1914 housing inquiry (see Figure 5.2). Far from being hidden (Figure 8.3) it was now claimed that 'as a rule the tenement houses face a thoroughfare of the city, though some are to be found in courts and alleys'.[88] The movement towards this situation is well illustrated by the rows of tenement dwellings lining Church Street, Bolton Street, Dorset Street, Great Britain Street, Summerhill and Gardiner Street Lower. The 1898 *Daily Nation* exposure of the 'slum evils' of the North City called on the 'burgesses' of 'the various important localities' such as Rutland and Mountjoy square to demand 'an end to the continuous menace to health which now exists practically within sight of their windows' from stinking slums such as those in Frederick Lane, Gardiner's Lane and Grenville Street.[89] In 1913 it was claimed that while tenement houses were to be found all over the city, and quite close to the most fashionable parts, some streets 'may be said to be entirely devoted to them'; north side streets of note were Railway Street [Mecklenburgh Street], Corporation Street [Purdon Street], Cumberland Street, portion of Gardiner Street, Dominick Street, 'and many others'.[90] In the case of Gloucester Street Lower, it was only the extension of the magdalen asylum and laundry buildings along much of the south side that prevented it featuring more prominently in the tenement geography.

Recipients of 'Sick Poor' Relief, 1895–1900

Changes in the geography of relief between the 1850s (Figure 8.4) and the period 1895–1900 (Figure 8.7) reflect the changes already evident from a comparison of tenement maps for 1850 (Figure 8.3) and 1900 (Figure 8.6). There are two major movements: poor persons in receipt of the Association's help are now more evident along the main roads rather than in the alleys and courts to the rear, and streets which were formerly the residence of subscribers to the charity have now been taken over by those in need of the charity's help.

The downgrading of formerly fashionable streets to the tenement system is particularly striking where the very houses of lady volunteers have bowed to the inevitable: thus 14 Grenville Street, in 1850 the home of Miss Dignam whose father was a barrister, is by February 1896 the home of Mary Anne McGrath, in receipt of two bags of coal from the association. Similarly 115 Gardiner Street

---

[88] *Report of the Departmental Committee Appointed by the Local Government Board for Ireland to Inquire into the Housing Conditions of the Working Classes in the City of Dublin* (Dublin, 1914), p. 3 (hereafter referred to as *Housing Report* 1914).
[89] *Daily Nation*, 5 September 1898.
[90] *Housing Report* 1914, p. 3.

Lower is in 1850 the home of Miss Fallon, (occupier Patrick Lawless, Esq.); by December 1895 a Mrs McDonnell who 'has sick children' is resident there and is in receipt of 6/6 relief and Christmas dinner.[91] Brian Murnane's analysis of the household census data for 1901 provides a good indication of the numbers of persons per house. 14 Middle Gardiner Street, where Margaret Aylward took very respectable lodgings in 1851, by 1901 returned a total of 73 residents, under 18 separate heads of household. Occupations for the men in this house included labourer, brass moulder, carpenter and chimney cleaner; for the women book-folder, flower dealer, and dress mantle maker.[92] Summerhill, Grenville Street, Gloucester Street Upper, Middle and Lower Gardiner Street, Upper Cumberland Street, Dominick Street and Dorset Street, all formerly respectable addresses for the professional and business classes that made up the membership of the Ladies of Charity, have now succumbed to being colonised by the poorest in need of their ministrations.

The movement outwards from the rear lanes and alleys was partially due to the closure of premises as unfit for human habitation, as mapped in Figure 4.7. However, this movement outwards did not mean the total abandonment of the inner courts and alleys, as illustrated by the persistence of addresses such as Dispensary Lane, Windsor, Graham's, Britain, and Mountjoy courts, Moore's Cottages, and Dillon Place, which continued to be visited by the ladies.

The southern portion of the parish of St Michan's, undoubtedly still an area of great need, is no longer on the visiting books of the ladies. This may be accounted for by the establishment of a local branch of the men's St Vincent de Paul Society in 1859, as an account book in the sacristy testifies, although unfortunately this book does not include addresses either of recipients of relief or of members of this society.

No membership roll of the Ladies' Association survives for the later part of the nineteenth century, so that the home addresses of the charitable lay women now running the association cannot be determined. However, as the meetings are now held in 46 Eccles Street (headquarters of St Brigid's Orphanage), it appears that the Eccles Street/Upper Gardiner Street area continues to be an important centre.

Housing Inquiry, 1885

Evidence given to the Housing Inquiry of 1885 highlights some of the key concerns surrounding the downward slide into tenements so evident throughout the north city and explored in Figures 8.3–8.4 (1850s) and Figures 8.6–8.7 (1895–1900).

---

[91] Relief list, GA: AL/LC/36 no. 4.
[92] Brian Murnane, 'The Recreation of the Urban Historical Landscape; Mountjoy Ward Dublin circa 1901' in William J. Smyth and Kevin Whelan, (eds.), *Common Ground: Essays on the Historical Geography of Ireland* (Cork 1988), pp. 202–203.

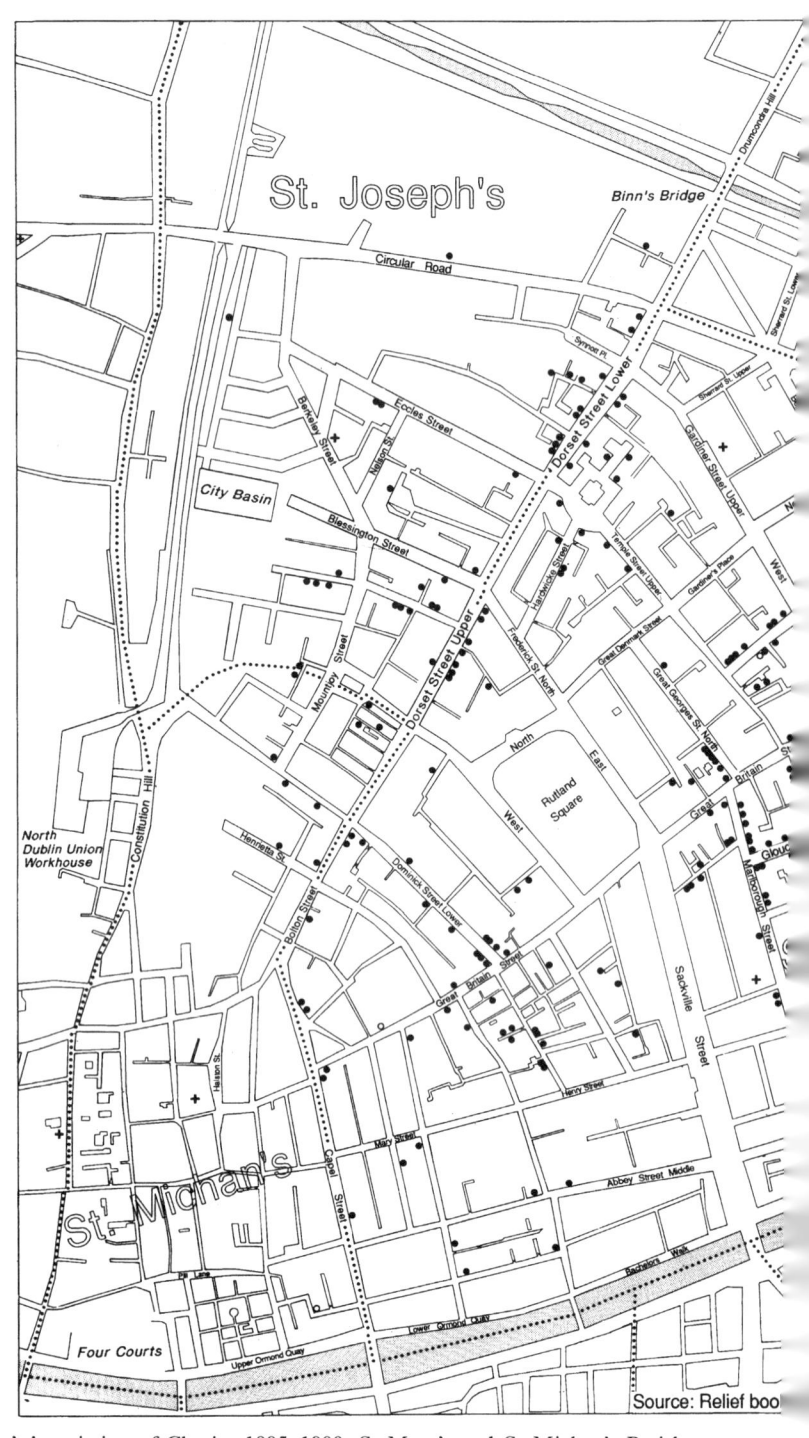

Figure 8.7 Ladies' Association of Charity 1895–1900, St Mary's and St Michan's Parishes,

A Classic Slum: Dublin North City

Ladies' Association of Charity 1895 - 1900
St. Mary's and St. Michan's Parishes

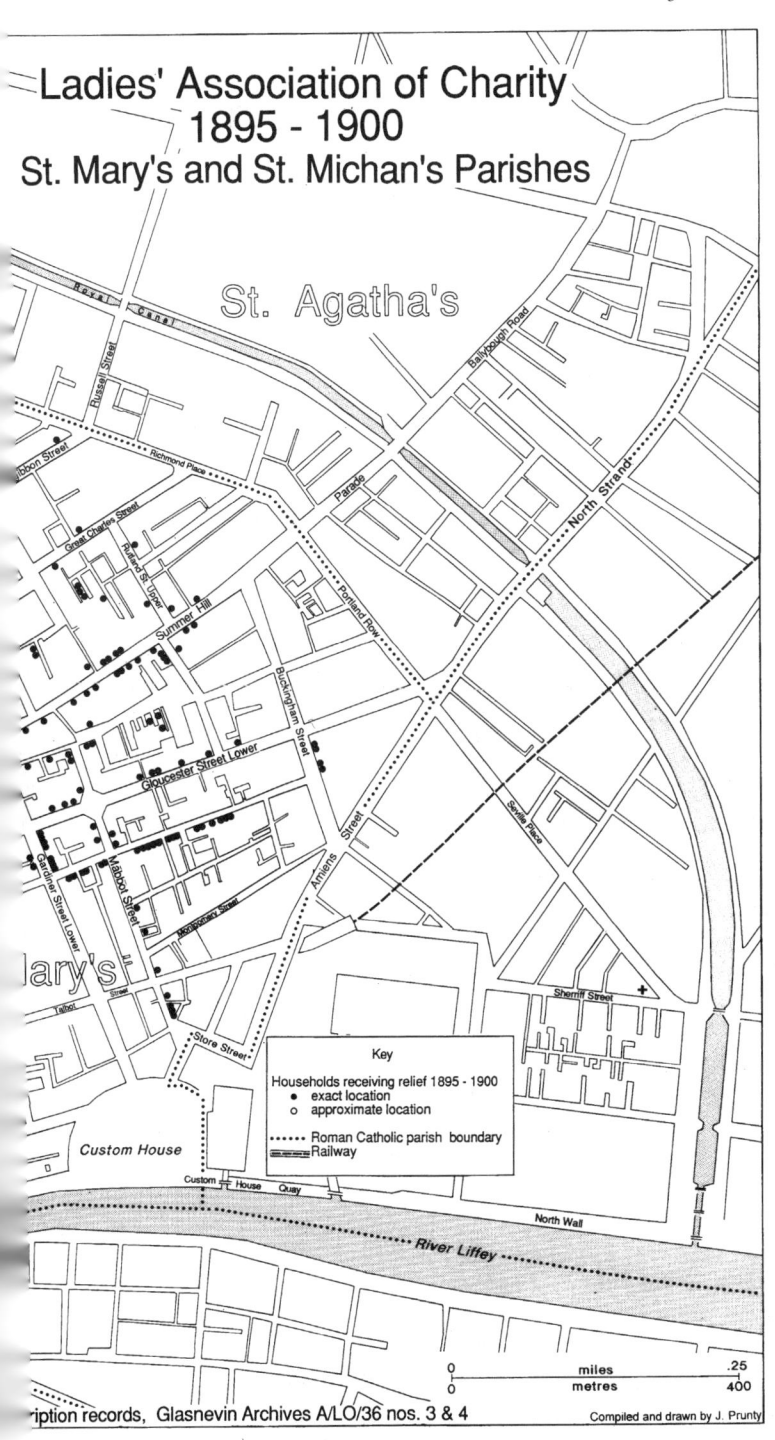

Key

Households receiving relief 1895 - 1900
- • exact location
- ○ approximate location
- ····· Roman Catholic parish boundary
- ══ Railway

0 .25 miles
0 400 metres

iption records, Glasnevin Archives A/LO/36 nos. 3 & 4   Compiled and drawn by J. Prunty

House valuation, the basis on which municipal and poor law rates were levied, was a particular source of discontent. Failure to have a thorough revaluation was condemned, the 'annual revision' in place being completely inadequate as it referred only to minor alterations such as extensions to a house, or changes in the name of the occupiers. Thus the 1854 valuation (Figure 8.5) was left intact in most instances, oblivious both to the increasing attractiveness of some districts and the downgrading of others.[93] Houses in the 'decaying part of the city' were so highly over-rated that the 'letting value and actual valuation are much the same'; such nonsense pertained in Gardiner Street, for example, where 'the houses are valued at a rate that no one would now give for them; and the result is that they are rapidly becoming tenement houses'.[94]

Rev. Robert Conlan, a Catholic clergyman from St Mary's parish, in his evidence to the housing inquiry on the downgrading of houses in the area, considered that fashion 'has a good deal to do with it.' The old houses 'have not modern appliances, particularly the under storey', and their mode of construction, most notably the 'extraordinary way of plunging one storey in the ground', militated against refurbishment. Less technically, he also noted the disincentive of high city taxation, 'and as the people can get fresh air, and everything outside in the suburbs, with lower taxes, they go there'.[95]

Distinctions in status between dwellings in adjoining streets are evident from Griffith's valuation (Figure 8.5), and from the relative proportion of residences classed as tenements in various streets (Figures 8.3, 8.6); Rev. Conlan provided detail on the very real gradations within the large tenement houses themselves. Rents varied from the kitchens to the garrets:

The people in the front kitchen will pay 2s per week; the people in the back kitchen will pay 1s 6d per week; in the front parlour they will pay 3s 6d per week; in the back parlour about the same; in the front drawing room about 3s 6d., and in the back drawing room about 3s. Then upstairs the rents will be 2s 6d., and in the garrets above they will be about 2s 6d to 2s.[96]

One worrying aspect of the spread of an unregulated tenement system was the takeover of houses 'for improper purposes', most notably in the parish of St Mary's. This was a most difficult problem to address, according to Rev. Conlan: those living by prostitution 'settle in a tenement house greatly to the trouble of the poor and honest people above and below them' and 'the good people above and below them do not exactly like going to call in the authorities to get these improper characters turned out'. Even when steps were taken to have such persons evicted, 'those that will visit the place will not always be able to know

---

[93] *Third Report of H.M. Commissioners for Inquiry into the Housing of the Working Classes, (Ireland, 1885),* c–4547–I, qs. 23,237–23,300, evidence of Mr William Scott (Valuation Office) *Housing Inquiry, 1885,* qs 22,653–22,788, (hereafter *Housing Inquiry, 1885*).
[94] Ibid., evidence of Dr Cameron, qs 22,323–22,334.
[95] Ibid., evidence of Rev. Robert Conlan (administrator St Mary's parish) qs. 23,237–23,300.
[96] Ibid., q. 23,250.

the character of the inmates, because when they go round the rooms they are very sanctimonious, and you would not know that there was anything the matter'.[97] The Dublin Metropolitan Police, 'a highly respectable body and greatly respected', were dismissed as useless in policing such slum matters, with their standing as a centralised force alienating them from the citizens they were supposedly serving, 'if they were under the Municipality they would be regarded as our police, at present they are regarded as masters'.[98]

Halting the spread of the tenement system was regarded as containing both moral and social evils, and protecting the rights of the respectable rate-paying citizen. A committee was formed, of which Rev. Conlan was an active member, and a campaign started to prevent any further streets being added to the tenement list. There was no room for compromise with individual premises: only by maintaining entire streets tenement-free could property values be protected, 'because when they start in a street the whole street will directly run into tenement houses'.[99] Success was to be very limited.

Efforts were made by the residents of Upper Mecklenburgh Street in 1886, describing themselves as 'members of the respectable working classes', to dissociate themselves from the lower part of the street where 'many of the houses are used for improper purposes and inhabited by persons of the worst character' so that 'for a long time past that name [Mecklenburgh] has been a notorious one'.[100] The residents succeeded in their suit, and the upper part of the street was renamed Tyrone Street (1887). However, this was to little purpose as the lower part then became known as Lower Tyrone Street, so that in 1911 the issue was settled: the upper part became Waterford Street and the notorious lower part Railway Street.[101] It was impossible to insulate any one street from its immediate environs; nearby Mabbot Street was 'notorious' not alone for its heavy concentration of tenement housing by 1900 (Figures 8.6, 8.7), but because 'many of the houses in this street were brothels'.[102]

The 1885 housing inquiry included some novel suggestions for the reform of tenement housing. Dr Cameron advocated a system of 'reparation', where tenement houses which were 'in a really substantial structural condition', could

---

[97] Ibid., q. 23,256.
[98] Ibid., qs. 23,267–23,268.
[99] Ibid., qs. 23,255–23,265.
[100] 'Report of the Paving and Lighting Committee', *RPDCD*, vol. 1, no. 75 (1886).
[101] Other name changes which should be noted are: Montgomery Street renamed Foley Street (1930); Gregg's Lane renamed Findlater's Place in 1882, and with Gloucester Street Upper, became known as Cathal Brugha Street in 1933; Gloucester Street Lower became Sean McDermott Street 1933; Temple Street Lower became Chatterton Street from Nov. 1885 to March 1886 when it was renamed Hill Street.
[102] *Report of the Housing Committee, being a Survey of the North Side of the City of Dublin, containing historical notes on the City's expansion north of the Liffey, illustrated by maps and other particulars, together with statistical information shewing the evolution of the tenement system and an outline of the housing requirements, RPDCD,* vol. I no. 13 (1918), pp. 81–145 (hereafter *North City Survey*).

be taken on by the Corporation, refurbished, and let directly by the authority, cutting out the middle man who was the real beneficiary of inflated rents. The 'mansions' of Henrietta Street provided a perfect place to experiment: here there were eight or ten houses 'sublet at the present time at rents which are three times greater than the sum which the landlord gets from the middlemen; if they were worked *en bloc* the rents could be reduced probably by at least 50 or 60 per cent'. Dr Cameron was characteristically practical about what would be required to bring these houses up to standard: the roofs and floors repaired, yards improved, sanitary accommodation installed, also dust shoots, and 'systematic cleaning' arranged. He himself was strongly in favour of building an outside stair, for a variety of safety and logistical reasons, but knew that would be flatly rejected by the occupiers, 'because they think it gives the place so much of a public institution or barrack-like appearance. That is a matter of sentiment, and as you know, the people in Dublin are very much moved by sentiment'.[103]

Health and Housing Reform: North City 1900–1925

The exposure of the 'fever nests' of St Michan's and other older parts of the north city which characterised the period 1800–1850 was overtaken during the later part of the century by concern with the inexorable decline of the aristocratic Gardiner sector (Figure 8.1). As was so often the case, concern for the north city slums, whether those of long standing or those in the process of creation, far outpaced action and by 1900 much was known, but relatively little, beyond the most urgent sanitary reforms (see Chapter 3), yet accomplished. Really workable ideas, such as the 'reparation' of individual streets advocated by Dr Cameron in 1885, were not acted on, while decline continued inexorably. An overview of the situation was provided by the comprehensive North City Survey of 1918, to be followed by the city-wide Civics Institute survey of 1925. Before moving again to the larger canvas and expansive plans for the future, this study first focuses on two of the traditional north side slum areas: the oldest north city axis of Church Street, and the Coles Lane markets area.

Church Street

Church Street (Figure 8.8), named from St Michan's church (1095), forms the western boundary of the Catholic parish of St Michan's (see Plate 2.3, Figure 8.1), and is the oldest known north city road. By means of Dublin Bridge (replaced by Whitworth Bridge 1818), it joined Ostmantown, or the village of the Vikings, with the medieval city south of the river Liffey. Church Street has a special significance in the slum story of both nineteenth and early twentieth century Dublin. It features prominently in slum studies of 1818 (Cheyne) and 1836 (Poor Law Inquiry). The housing report of 1885 used Church Street as

---

[103] Evidence of Dr Cameron, *Housing Inquiry, 1885*, qs 22,403–22,409.

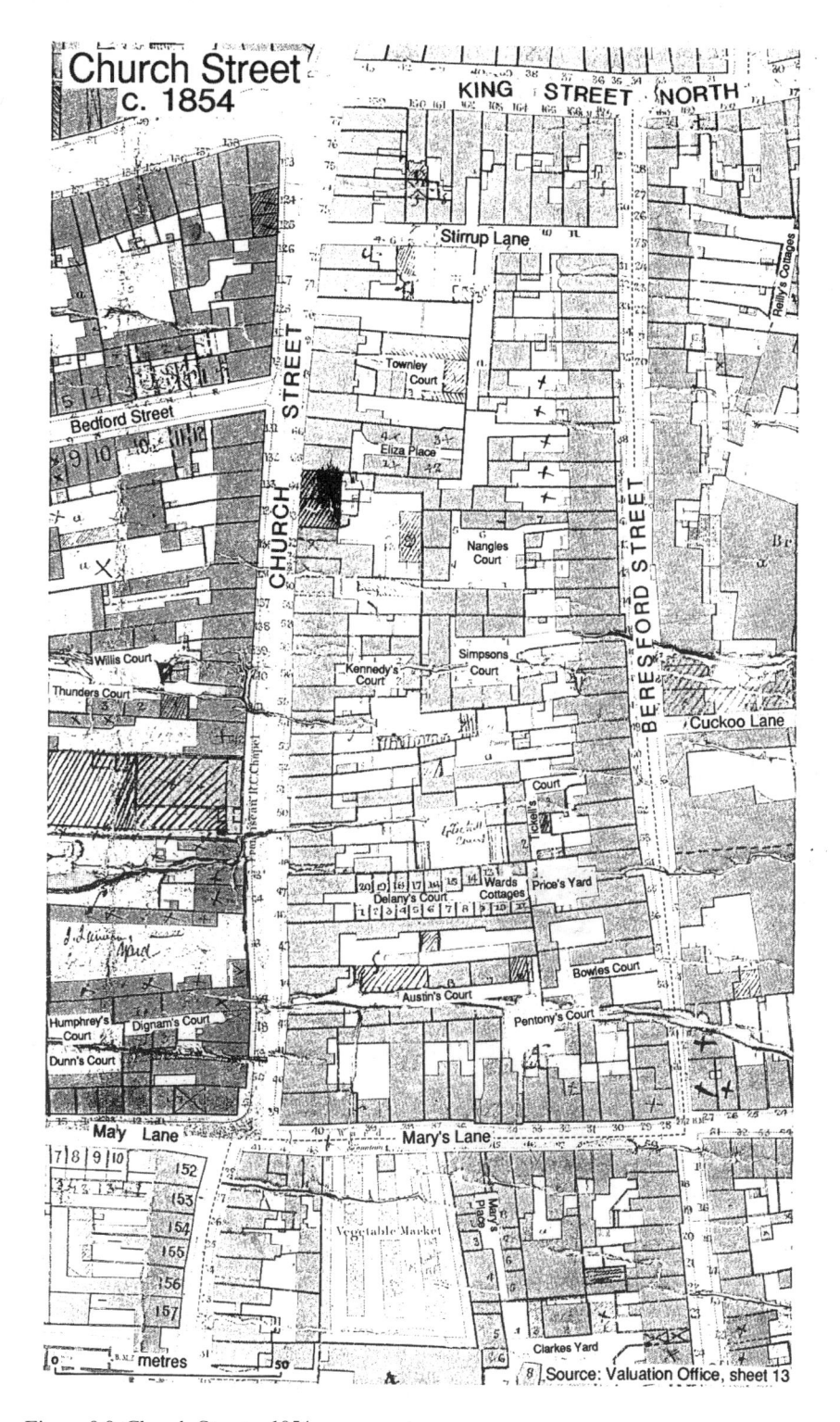

Figure 8.8 Church Street c.1854

one of four case studies to illustrate the rent, valuation and occupancy rates of tenement housing in Dublin.[104] The 1898 *Daily Nation* slum explorations gave special attention to this district. It was the collapse of nos. 66 and 67 Church Street that created the catalyst needed for the housing inquiry of 1913 which, including photographic evidence, revealed very publicly, the massive extent of the housing crisis in Dublin.[105] It was the site of one of the earliest and largest city centre Corporation housing schemes, completed in 1917.

The 1817/1818 survey undertaken by Dr Cheyne of the Hardwicke fever hospital singled out Church Street and Barrack Street for close scrutiny on the basis of their fever numbers. Church Street had recorded 123 cases within three months, not in the least surprising when the density of population, the local morphology and sheer destitution of the residents are considered: the street consisted of 181 houses 'which, with those in the adjoining courts, are much more crowded than the houses of Barrack Street'. In a sample of 71 houses and adjoining courts, 'consisting of 393 apartments', the inspectors found 1,997 persons, an average of five persons per room; among the residents almost one third had no employment.[106] The 1836 Poor Inquiry heard that of the 180 houses in Church Street, 25 were licensed for the retail of spirituous liquors, 'besides at least as many more in its immediate vicinity'.[107] Heavily critical of allowing such a situation to continue unchecked, one witness considered Church Street and environs as 'peculiarly remarkable for the density and poverty of the inhabitants, and also as being the residence of vicious and depraved characters', and consequently 'the more improper and injurious neighbourhood or situation for retail spirit shops and public houses'.[108]

A photograph of 1861, before the Capuchin church was rebuilt (Plate 8.3) reveals a mixed streetscape of two, three and four storey houses. However, behind this facade was a dense network of courts and alleys, several totally enclosed and entered only through the houses fronting Church Street or Beresford Street (Plate 8.4, Figure 8.8). The 1818 report complains that 'foul lanes, courts and yards are interposed between this [Church Street] and the adjoining streets'.[109] Many front street houses included cellars, with no light but from the open door, 'which, in several, is nearly closed by bundles of rags, vegetables and other articles exposed to sale'. In such foul bunkers 'the inhabitants sleep on the floors, which are all earthen, but in general they have bedsteads'. In the back courts matters worsened (Figure 8.8). Most 'are crowded and filthy', such as Nicholsons's court, 'which immediately joins the Root-market' and had

---

[104] *Housing Inquiry 1885*, p. 104.
[105] *Irish Times*, 17 September 1913; *Housing Report 1914*.
[106] J. Cheyne, *Medical Report of the Hardwicke Fever Hospital for the year ending on the 31st March 1818 including a brief account of an epidemic fever in Dublin* (Dublin, 1818), p. 48 (hereafter *Hardwicke Fever Hospital*).
[107] Charities Report, *Poor Inquiry (Ireland) (1836)* p. 113.
[108] Ibid.
[109] Cheyne, *Hardwicke Fever Hospital* (1818), p. 48.

Plate 8.3 Church Street 1861, Irish Architectural Archive
Plate 8.4 Ward's Cottages, Church Street 1913, RSAI 57

been afflicted by fever. Here 151 persons were living in 28 small apartments, of whom 89 were unemployed; 'their state is very miserable, there being only two bedsteads and two blankets in the whole court'.[110] The *Daily Nation* 1898 slum reports reiterate many of the points made sixty years earlier, and heap derision on the ineffectual efforts to date of the Corporation sanitary department.[111] Ward's Cottages (Plate 8.4) is typical of the infilling of plots which characterised this area: a narrow line of twenty whitewashed cottages, with a cobbled laneway and central open drain, the only access through an archway from Church Street. A similar situation is illustrated by the picture of Tickell's Court (Plate 8.5). To the rear of 51 Beresford Street a very narrow lane separates four cottages, which are effectively hidden from view by the narrow archway. The houses in Angle Court, Beresford Street (corrupted from Nangle's Place) are far larger, set around a cobbled yard, and with common access to one pump (Plate 8.6). This photograph, taken in 1913, testifies to the large numbers of tenants such houses continued to accommodate. The etymology of the court names is a good indicator of the separate geography that existed: the major streets are officially named, the courts and alleys by acclamation are called after the immediate landlord or lessee, to whom the tenants pay rent.

The Church Street Corporation housing scheme, in planning from 1913 but executed in amended form in 1917, with some urgency, required the acquisition, complete razing and reordering of the unit bordered by Stirrup Lane, Mary's Lane and Beresford Street (Figures 8.8, 8.9).[112] Here 146 modest self-contained artisans' dwellings, of both one and two storeys, were erected, facing onto wide but short roads, a central square, or the busy Church Street thoroughfare (Plate 8.7). The opportunity afforded for some street widening was welcomed, so that 'what was formerly a narrow, congested street, with dark and unhealthy alleys and passages, is now a fine open thoroughfare, forming a more fitting environment for the imposing edifice erected by the Capuchin Fathers'.[113] The transformation of the situation from 1900, when 73 tenement houses were listed for Church Street, to 1918 when 28 tenement houses were recorded, is largely due to this scheme; however, due attention to other parts of this long and decaying street was to be very much delayed.[114]

Coles Lane, Henry Street

The Coles Lane markets area, between Moore Street and Henry Street, (Figure 8.10), a dense network of narrow lanes and courts, was one of those areas identified by the maps of recipients of relief and of tenement dwellings (Figures 8.3, 8.4 and 8.6, 8.7) as a concentration of poverty in the period 1850–1900. A

[110] Ibid.
[111] *Daily Nation*, 3 September 1898.
[112] see *RPDCD* vol. l, no. 15 (1914) pp. 59–66.
[113] *North City Survey* (1918) p. 99.
[114] Ibid.

A Classic Slum: Dublin North City 321

Plate 8.5 Tickell's Court, 18 Beresford Street 1913, RSAI 58
Plate 8.6 Angle Court, Beresford Street 1913, RSAI 60

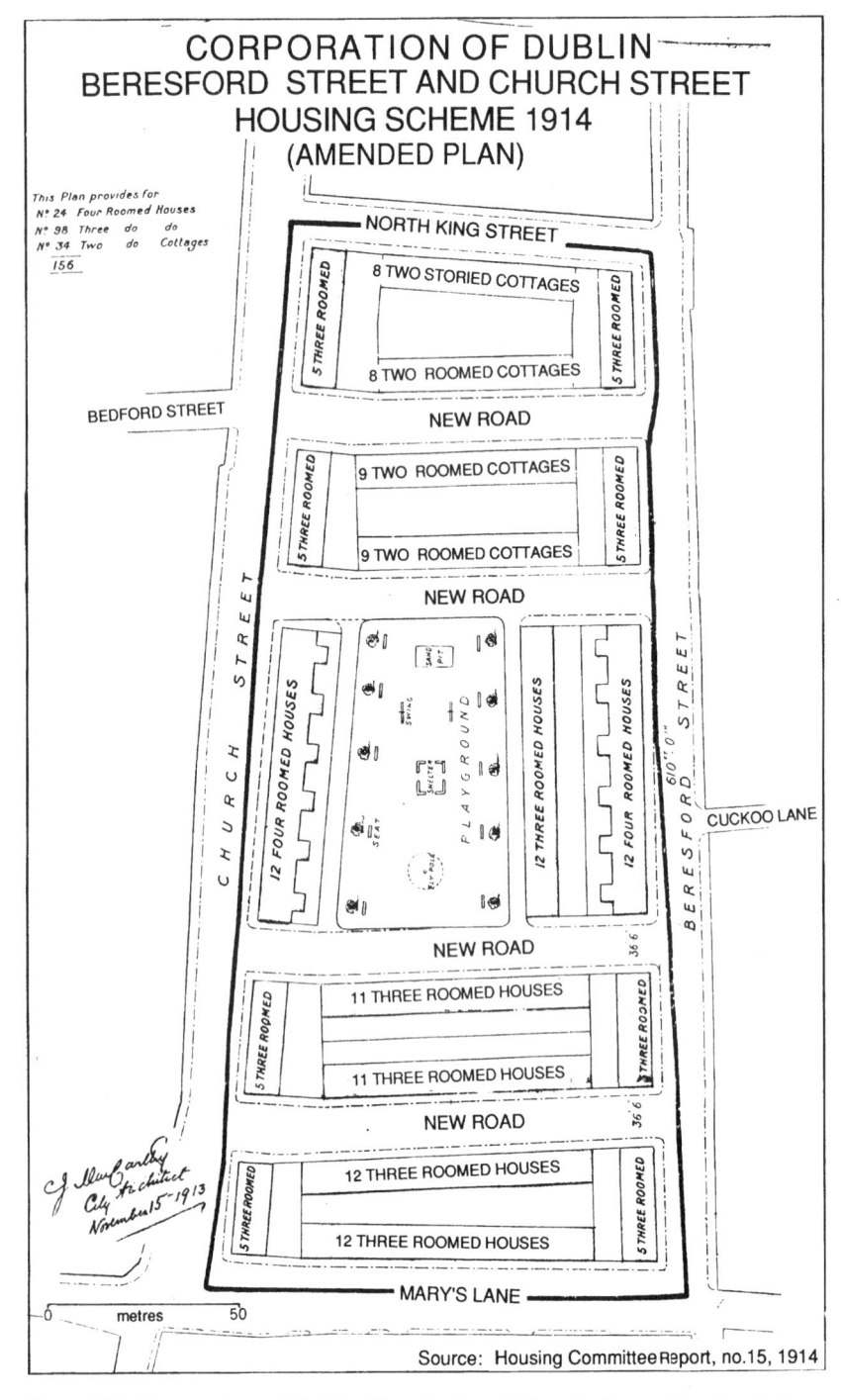

Figure 8.9 Corporation of Dublin Beresford and Church Street Housing Scheme 1914 (Amended Plan)

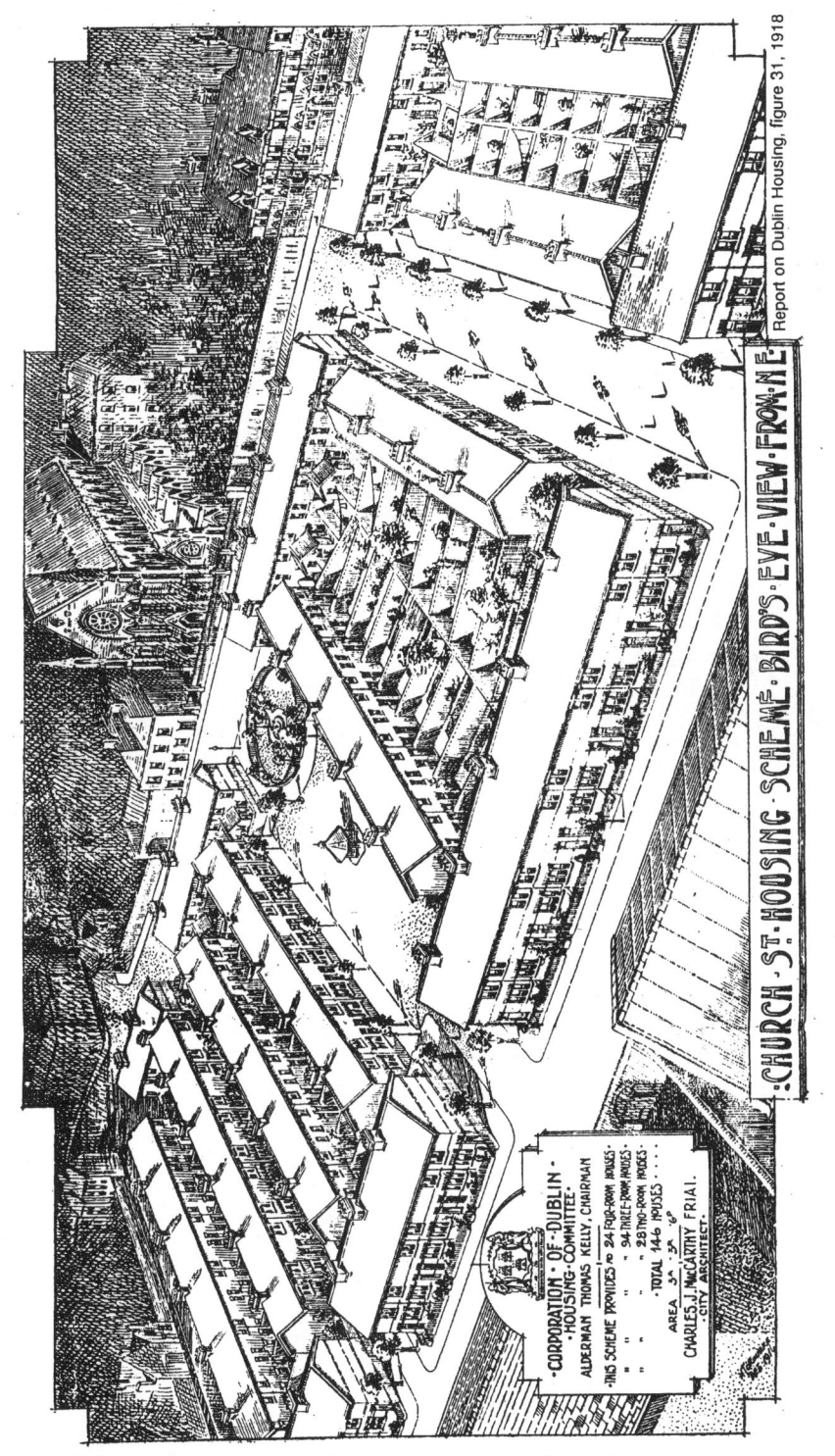

Plate 8.7 Church Street housing scheme: bird's eye view from NE, 1918

Plate 8.8 Riddell's Row, Moore Street, RSAI 86

photograph of Riddell's Row (Plate 8.8, 1913), which links Coles Lane with Moore Street, illustrates both the narrowness of the arteries and one of the most important local functions, the sale of second hand clothing and footwear. Figure 8.11 details its character as recorded in a fire insurance map for 1926 (Goad).

Coles Lane, named from one of the earlier countesses of Drogheda, of the estate was part of the Moore/Drogheda family, who subsequently sold land to the east to the Gardiner family, where under Luke Gardiner I the narrow Drogheda Street was entirely transformed into Sackville Mall. The Moore Street/Coles Lane area received no such attention; failure to regulate plot layout and construction tightly from the outset resulted in a very mixed morphology. While parts of Moore Street and Great Britain Street exhibited uniformity, variety was more typical (Figures 8.10, 8.11). The long garden plots behind the houses facing Great Britain Street, stretching to Riddell's Row (formerly Gregg Street), were ideally suited to infilling, while an undeveloped open area to the rear of the regular Moore Street plots was to become the site of a conglomeration of markets and stalls, including Fountain Row/Market Street, Anglesea Market, Bell's Alley and Moore Place. In 1881 plans were drawn up by the city engineer to raze almost the entire area, excluding only the premises directly facing Great

Britain Street, Moore Street and Henry Street, and erect a covered market in its place. This was to follow the scheme already underway in the South City Markets in George's Street, and in line with the plans for the new vegetable market in Mary's Lane.[115] In the case of Coles Lane such ambitions came to nothing. The 1918 North City Survey records that Coles Lane 'is now and has been for many years occupied by the small shops of second hand furniture and clothes dealers', and notes the steady progress of tenement housing: 4 in 1850, 29 by 1875, 45 by 1900.[116] A large block centred on Coles Lane, but extending from the rear premises of Henry Street to include Upper Liffey Street to the west, is shaded red in this survey, as one of about a dozen 'schemes in contemplation by Housing Committee' (Figure 8.12); the vagueness of this title, coupled with the lack of detailed ground plans, are sufficient to indicate that Coles Lane is still nowhere near the top of the Corporation's slum clearance agenda.

The quality of housing in this densely packed residential and markets area, and the immense difficulties inherent in enforcing regulations, is well illustrated in the report of the Public Health Committee for 1899, in a case brought against Mr Taaffe, of Taaffe's Row (Figure 8.10). Under the Housing of the Working Classes Act 1890 notice was served on this person that his ten houses were altogether unsuitable for human habitation; failure to comply with notices to put matters in order was followed by summons to court. Court evidence, substantiated by a visit to the premises in question by the presiding judge, maintained that the houses were without yards, built back-to-back thus 'excluding all light and ventilation from the rere, and seriously interfering with the circulation of air necessary for health'. The only sanitary provision was four closets 'placed on the opposite side of the street, in which sufficient means are not taken to ensure privacy'. The Corporation required that certain of the houses be removed, allowing yards and closets to be constructed, 'and by the opening of further apertures in the remaining buildings to secure proper ventilation'. Dr Cameron testified that the lower floors were occupied by disused shops by 1898, 'the ascents to the upper stories (*sic*) are made through very narrow and defective stairs', and when these were momentarily lighted up by the opening of the door of one of the wretched apartments within, he had 'ready and conclusive reason to appreciate the want of a proper circulation of fresh air'.[117]

The Corporation regarded their victory in the case taken against Taaffe as a landmark decision; that it took until the end of the century for what were fairly minimum sanitary standards to be enforced is also an indictment of action to date. Much more offensive than Taaffe's row of stinking, tumbledown houses were the local slaughter houses. The extract from the 1926 fire insurance map (Goad plan) reproduced as Figure 8.11 exposes the lack of progress which

---

[115] see 'Map of portion of the City of Dublin prepared for purpose of showing the scheme proposed for Moore Street Market and North City improvements', 'Report of the City Engineer', *RPDCD* vol. 1, no. 26 (1882).

[116] *North City Survey* (1918), p. 99.

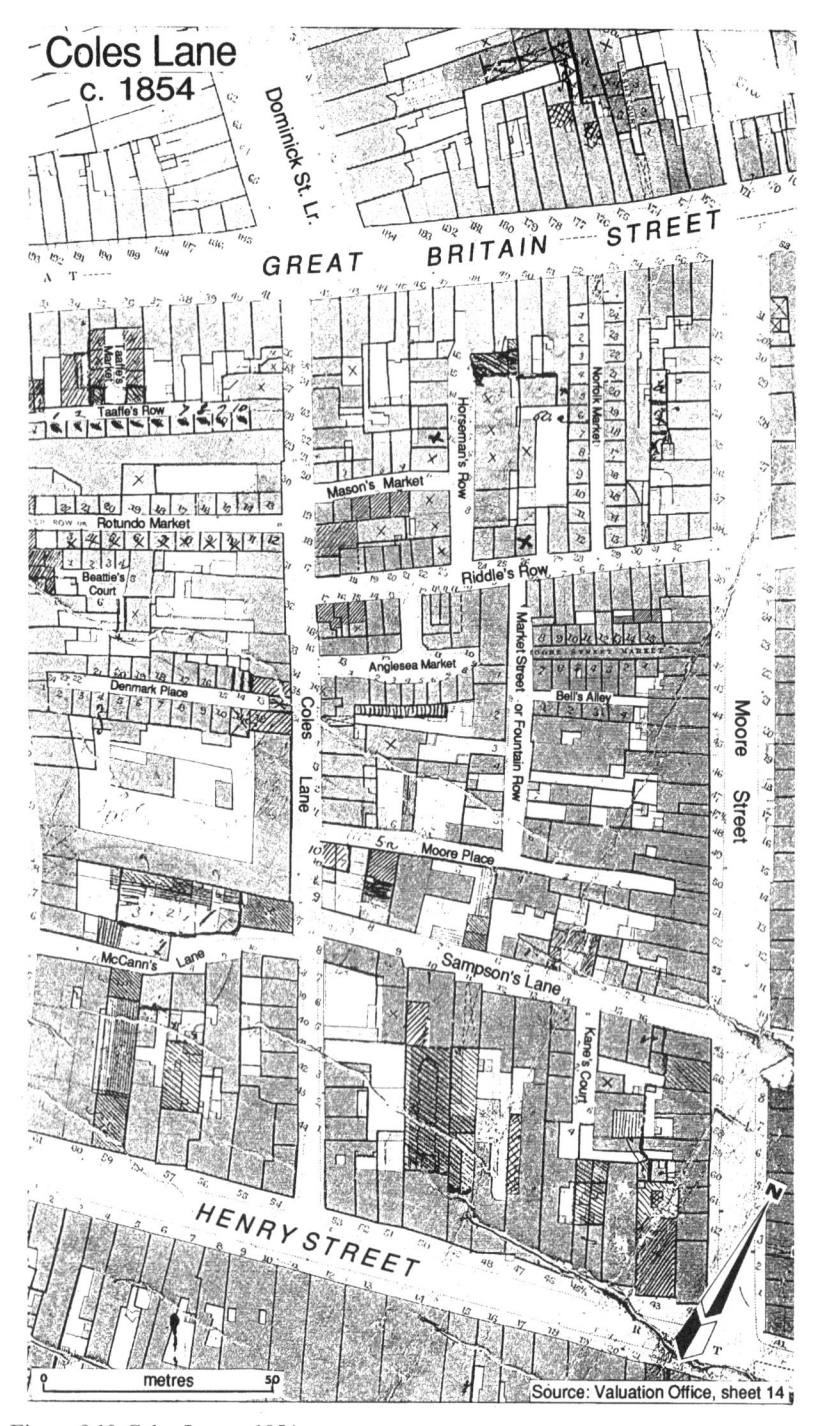

Figure 8.10 Coles Lane c.1854

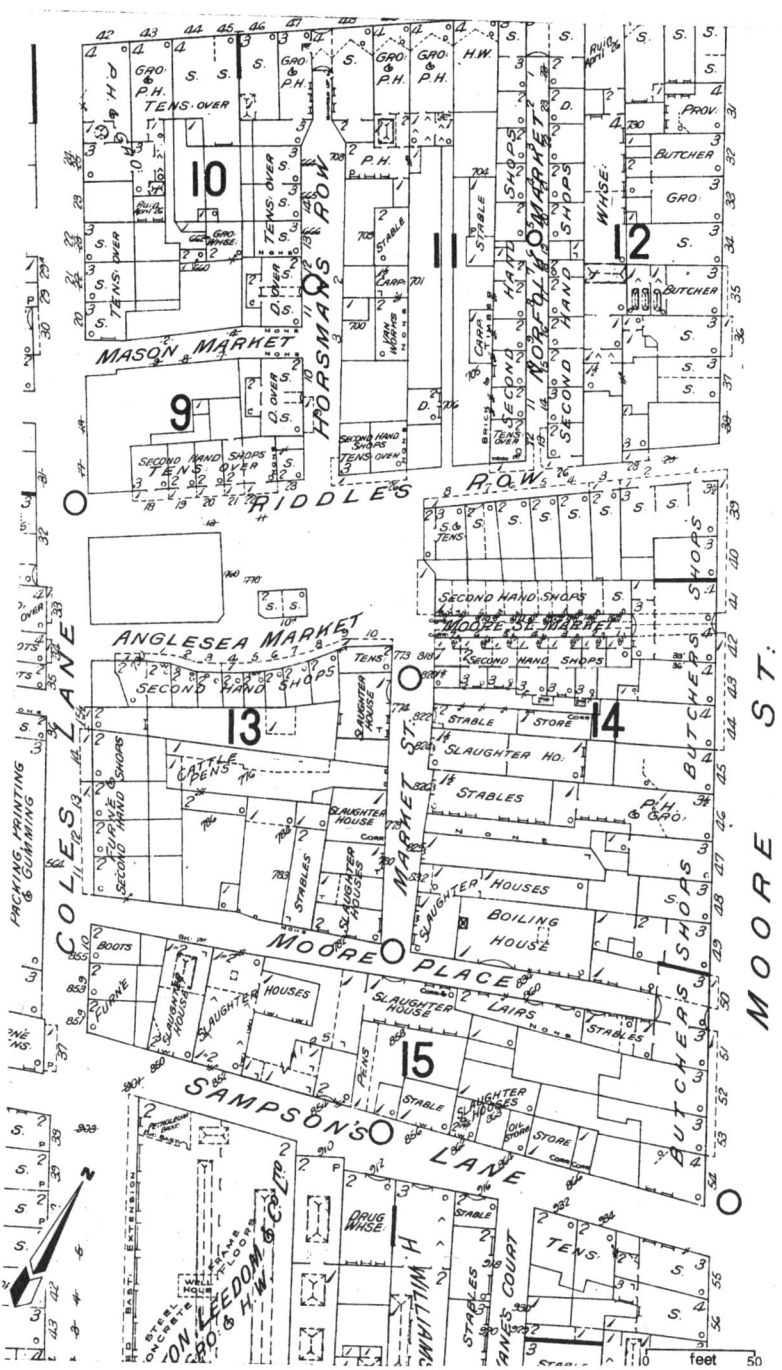

Figure 8.11 Moore Street Market, *Insurance Plan of Dublin*, sheet 3, April 1926, Charles E. Goad

characterised this major sanitary issue. Portion of Coles Lane was destroyed by fire at Easter 1916,[118] but judging from Figure 8.11 this did not have a major impact on its long-established trading and residential mix. Between Moore Street and Coles Lane, dealers in second hand goods jostled for space with the butchers of Moore Street who served their customers meat prepared, quite literally, on the premises. Landuse was dominated by slaughter houses, with associated pens, lairs, 'boiling house' and the butchers' shops already mentioned. In the closest proximity to the slaughtering trade were numerous second hand clothes shops, most with tenements over, as well as grocers (also with residences or tenements over), other tenement dwellings, stables, furniture stores and various warehouses. The sterling efforts of the Corporation to remove slaughtering from the city centre by the 'softly softly' approach of erecting a model abattoir beyond the built-up area (Chapter 3, Figure 3.5) and advertising its advantages, clearly had little impact on the local Coles Lane/ Moore Street situation.

North City Survey, 1918

The survey of the north city commissioned by the Municipal Council in June 1917 in response to a proposal by the housing committee, opens with a virulent attack on the 'ill-considered and ill-informed statements' published in the press by 'irresponsible and inexperienced social reformers', who 'in their desire for public notoriety, have only succeeded in creating a jumble of confused ideas in the public mind with regard to the problem of Dublin housing'. The 1913/1914 departmental committee report (Local Government Board) on Dublin housing had expressed a low opinion of the Corporation's sanitary and housing efforts to date (Chapter 5), and the housing committee was coming under intense pressure from several quarters to act, and be seen to act, more effectively. The destruction wrought by the Easter Rising of 1916, in places such as Coles Lane, Mary's Lane and Ormond Market, added to the sense of urgency.

In defence of the Corporation's record to date, the 1918 survey first traces the morphological development of the north city as depicted on maps (dating from Speed, 1610), followed by a brief description of the commercial and tenement situation of each street, in alphabetical order, as entered in directories for 1850, 1875 and 1900. This is supplemented by the housing committee's own data on numbers of tenement houses for 1917. There is a very plain equation of tenements with slum dwellings; the terms are used interchangeably.

The purpose of the first part of the report was to expose the inexorable nature of the spread of tenement housing throughout the north city, due to the flight of 'every citizen of position or wealth from the circumscribed area' to the suburbs. The process of slum-making was greatly exacerbated by movement in the opposite direction: the provincial labouring classes 'attracted by the prospect of

[117] *Report of Public Health Commitee for 1899*, (Dublin, 1900), pp. 976–977.
[118] *North City Survey* (1918), p. 99.

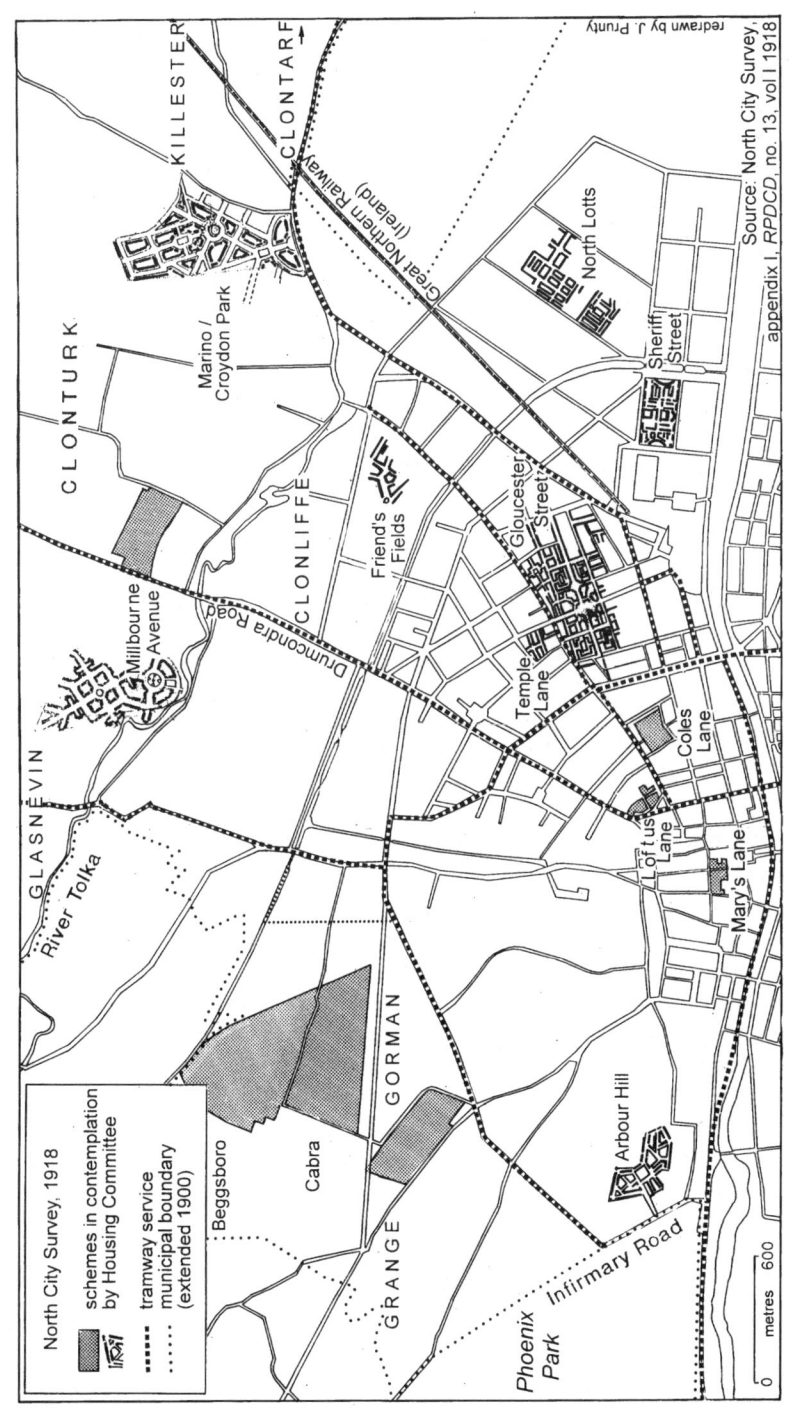

Figure 8.12 North City survey: schemes in contemplation by the housing committee, Dublin Corporation, 1918

wages or by the advantages or enjoyments which a city life can offer', arrived in their hundreds, and once the job which brought such an immigrant to Dublin ended, was 'content to make his abode in a City tenement and wait there for some new occupation to turn up', swelling the ranks of the city's poor. The situation was made most iniquitous by the refusal to expand the city's boundary, 'in accordance with the city's natural expansion', in effect denying the city administration any benefit from rising land values beyond the canals.

However, the principal purpose of the north city survey was to establish, geographically and statistically, the 'present conditions as regards the housing of the working class population of the north city'. Armed with this updated information, and working within the expanded municipal area (1900), this report then proceeds to enumerate the number of new and improved dwellings required, and where and how they might be provided. This discussion brings together contentious elements of the slum reform debate as played out at the local level: the differences in standard between existing tenement houses and the difficulties thus posed for policy formulation; the impossibility of financing all the new housing required in the short term, and the 'necessary' waste of funds on ameliorative action in the interim; and the powers of the local authority *vis-à-vis* private enterprise where housing has been traditionally traded under open market conditions. Sanitary standards are no longer central to the debate; it is taken as granted that scullery and WC for the 'sole use of each family' will be installed, and that dwellings should be 'of sufficient size to prevent overcrowding and to admit of the separation of the sexes'.[119]

The North City survey maps which accompany the written report are graphic illustrations of the energy currently being invested by the housing committee in the slum question, and of the immense possibilities opened up by the extension of the city boundary. Appendix I, 'Schemes in contemplation by the housing committee 1918' including existing tramway service is redrawn as Figure 8.12. Appendix II is a large format colour-coded map showing landuse and housing conditions (public institutions, business premises, tenements, ruins and wasteland, grass lands, cultivated lands, devastated area). It places the north city area within the context of its suburban and rural hinterland for the first time, with promising stretches of farmland and institutional land providing a counterpoint to the tenements, ruins/wasteland and 'devastated areas' of the city centre. Including the lands of Grangegorman to the north west, Glasnevin/ Drumcondra/Clonturk to the north, and Killester and Clontarf to the north east (Figure 8.12), the parameters within which the north city slum problem may now be tackled have changed utterly, at least on paper.

The street-by-street examination of the tenement situation undertaken in Figures 8.3–8.7 (1850–1900) is updated to 1917 in this survey. Tenement status, an index of slum creation, spread rapidly between 1900–1917, most notably in 'fine

[119] Ibid., p. 118.

rows of structurally sound houses' which it would be 'quite unjustifiable to demolish'. Many of the 627 first class tenement houses thus identified in 1917 were among those most highly valued in 1854 (Figure 8.5). Blessington Street, 'almost entirely of a first-class residential character up to the end of the nineteenth century' (Figure 8.6) deteriorated most rapidly, to 28 tenement houses by 1917; similarly Great Charles Street, with two tenement houses in 1900 (Figure 8.6) had increased its total to 28 tenements in 1917. Other new additions to the tenement map are Eccles Street, Fitzgibbon Street, North Great Georges Street, George's Place, Temple Street Upper and Rutland Street Lower. Several streets which had some tenement houses in 1900 are now entirely dominated by such low-status use: Dorset Street (90 houses), Gloucester Street (81 houses), Dominick Street (75 houses), Summer Hill (72 houses), Capel Street (46 houses), Bolton Street (29 houses), Temple Street Upper (21 houses), Portland Row (8 houses). Along most of the streets well on the downward slide by 1900 (Figure 8.6) the proportion of tenement dwellings relative to other uses continued to increase by 1917; the exceptions are those few areas which benefited by redevelopment in the intervening period (see Figure 5.3); a few areas lost to commercial expansion (such as houses to the rear of quayside premises, as in Strand Street); and areas devastated in the 1916 rising, including the aforementioned markets areas of Ormond Circus and Coles Lane. One of the few streets to be upgraded was Manor Street, part of the middle class development in the Circular Road district.

Tenement Houses 1918: Demolition, Improvement or Drift

There were three possible responses to the north city tenement situation: demolition, improvement or drift. Rehabilitation of first class tenement houses was recommended by most of the 1918 housing committee, requiring the division of each house into independent flats, each with its own sanitary and scullery accommodation. This could be achieved by allotting one floor per family, and erecting a small return building to the rear of each flat to house the new facilities. Such refurbishment would provide satisfactory accommodation for 2,192 families (at an average of 3.5 families per house). However, those dispossessed by such refurbishment (1,599 families) along with the 8,503 families currently residing in tenements either unfit for human habitation or fast approaching that state, would remain to be housed. The minimum number of new houses required for the north city alone was calculated roughly at 10,100.

Estimating the cost of acquisition and alteration of existing 'first class tenement houses' was fraught with problems, with the adoption of a round sum of £150 per flat regarded as an entirely arbitrary figure by at least one member of the committee. Councillor W.T. Cosgrave was adamantly opposed to tenement refurbishment on a dozen well-argued grounds, and formally dissented from the final report.[120]

---

[120] *North City Survey* (1918), pp. 122–123.

Schemes in Contemplation by the Housing Committee, 1918

The largest slum clearance and rehousing scheme in contemplation in 1918 was a 32 acre site stretching from Great Britain Street/Summer Hill to Marlborough Street in the west and Montgomery Street to the south (Figures 8.12, 8.6), with Gloucester Street and its diamond as its central axis. There was also a small extension to the north, covering Temple Lane (between Gardiner Street Middle and Temple Street Lower/Hill Street). Detailed building plans for a 5½ acre section (Glorney's Buildings) of this larger site were in place since 1914. Clearance of this smaller site would have dispossessed 589 persons in 1914, a figure which was regarded with equanimity as 'a large section of the area is composed of old stables and stores at the reres of houses in Gloucester Street and Summerhill, and there is also a considerable portion derelict'.[121] Failure to proceed with such small schemes before the outbreak of war left the post-war housing committee with a backlog of redundant plans on their hands, as decay had worsened and spread. The projected level of rents for the Glorney's Buildings schemes, at 4/6 for two roomed, 6/6 three roomed, and 7/– four roomed dwellings,[122] make it immediately evident that they will be beyond the means of the very poorest, such as those on the relief rolls of the Ladies of Charity. Refusal to include a night shelter or a building for the accommodation of working boys, despite representations from the Countess of Aberdeen and others, illustrate the Corporation's extreme reluctance to extend its involvement beyond the provision of residences for those who can guarantee payment.[123]

The other large slum clearance scheme under consideration in 1918 was Sheriff Street/Newfoundland Street in the north docks, to cover 11 acres, and for which detailed plans were also ready. Smaller schemes, covering between 2–3 acres each, and for which plans were not yet so far advanced, covered Mary's Lane (south side), Loftus Lane, and Coles Lane as already discussed. In all, it was estimated that 80 acres could possibly be acquired in the central city area for slum clearance, providing space for 2,000 houses (at 25 houses per acre).

A catalogue of north city 'black spots' which had already been dealt with by direct Corporation involvement (see Figure 5.3, 1914) includes Barrack (Benburb) Street (1887), Blackhall Place and St Joseph's Place (1896), Lurgan Street (1913), Church Street and Ormond Market (1917), Foley (Montgomery) Street (1905), and Elizabeth Street.[124] The major north city contribution by the Dublin Artisans' Dwellings Company was in Oxmantown, with smaller schemes widely dispersed (see Figure 5.3). The stage was set for considerably more direct municipal involvement in the housing question.

The shortfall of 8,100 dwellings was to be met by building on virgin sites, with the proviso that sites would be considered relative to the places of employment of the class of persons housed. The commentary on north city employment, based on

---

[121] 'Report of the Housing Committee', *RPDCD* no. 17, (1914), p. 86.
[122] 'Report of the Housing Committee', *RPDCD* no. 15, (1914), p. 65.
[123] 'Report of the Housing Committee', *RPDCD* no. 23 (1914), p. 161; no. 83 (1914), p. 820.

detailed listing of occupation and wage levels of all heads of tenement households, stresses the importance of heavy industry (shipyards, ironworks), distribution (railway termini, the 'carrying trade'), distilleries, manure works, bakeries, printing works and 'quay labour'. However, in the original listing (appendix F to the survey) the largest numbers are entered under 'labourer' and 'soldier's dependants', while charwoman, seamstress, servant and dealer, all areas dominated by women, are also significant. The North Lotts 'virgin site' (15 acres) was particularly well placed relative to the docks (Figure 8.12). Where sites were further out, the necessity of negotiating cheap tram and rail fares for commuting workers was noted, with extensions to tram lines wherever the number of dwellings would warrant such investment. All schemes 'in contemplation by the Housing Committee' in 1918 were mapped in relation to the tram and rail services then in existence (Figure 8.12). The Marino/Croydon Park scheme (50 acres) was the best served by both tram and rail; the sites to the east (Clonturk lands) and west (Millbourne Avenue) of the Drumcondra Road could be accessed from the tram line along this major artery, while the small Friend's Fields scheme was within reasonable reach of the Summer Hill/Ballybough tram line. The Arbour Hill/Infirmary Road site although not connected to a tramline was near the quayside and Smithfield markets areas, centres of at least casual employment. The most poorly connected area was, understandably, the 96 acre site in Cabra, the extensive tract which held most promise at this point in the Dublin slum story.

Dublin Civic Survey, 1925

The geography of slum clearance and new housing schemes in the north city completed up to independence can be assessed by reference to Figure 5.3, which shows artisans' schemes completed or in planning in 1914, and as there was little house building during world war I and the independence struggle it is still a fair indication of progress up to 1922. A fuller, and more discouraging, picture is provided by the Civic Survey of 1925 (Chapter 5). Figure 8.13, an extract from the hygiene map, shows relative density and death rates in Mountjoy ward in 1925. All units classed as insanitary are outlined in bold, and the areas with the worst hygiene records in the city are indicated by a dot pattern. It is a most depressing scene. Mountjoy ward with a population density of 117.6 persons per acre is followed closely by adjoining Rotunda ward with a density of 113.6 persons; 50 persons to the acre was laid down as the 'hygienic density' for urban living. Practically every unit is heavily outlined, so that it is easier to locate the few non-slum areas. Mountjoy Square is relegated to slum status on three sides; its western side alone has preserved some of its earlier noble standing. Gardiner

---

[124] See *Lurgan Street*: *RPDCD* (1913), I (90), p. 1074, *Irish Builder and Engineer* (1913) LV, p. 617; *Ormond Market*: *RPDCD* (1914), 1 (83), pp. 816–826; *RPDCD* (1915), 1 (74), pp. 686–687; *RPDCD* (1915), 1 (78), pp. 712–713; *Irish Builder & Engineer* (1914), LVI, p. 682; *St. Joseph's Place*: *RPDCD*, 1 (19), (1892), p. 172; *Foley Street*: *RPDCD*, III (183) (1902), p. 250.

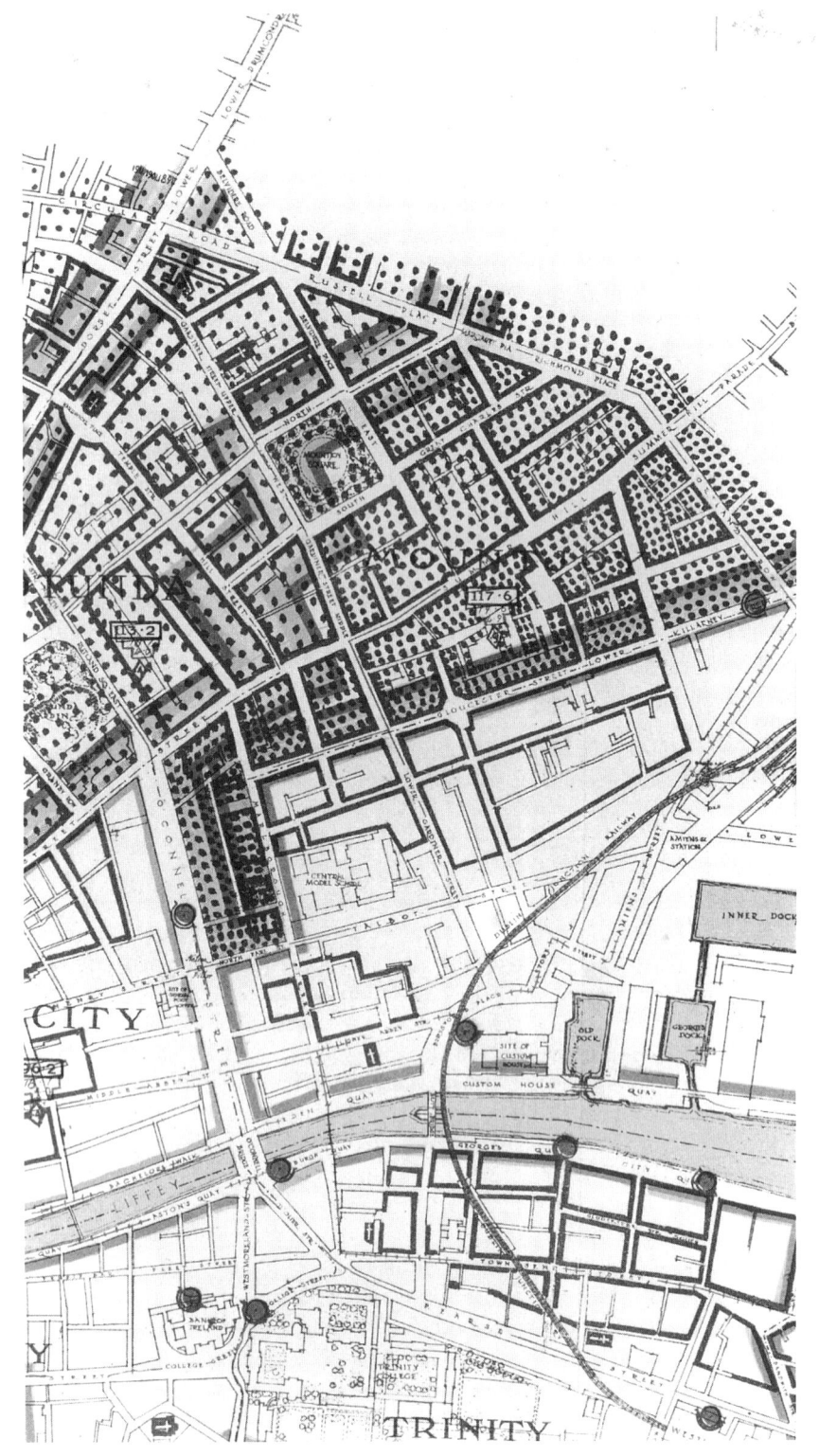

Figure 8.13 Mountjoy ward: relative density of population and death rates, *Dublin Civic Survey*, hygiene map, 1925

A Classic Slum: Dublin North City

Street Upper continued this line to the north, while along Gardiner Place/Great Denmark Street/Gardiner Row a line of high quality residences still resist the slide into tenements, linking up Mountjoy Square with the earlier and larger Gardiner venture of Rutland Square. Apart from such limited stretches of high class housing (compare with Figure 8.5), further commercial development along well-defined spines (Sackville Street, Talbot Street, Abbey Street, the quays), and significant institutional land use such as in Marlborough Street, the entire area is a solid mass of insanitary and condemned housing.

Practically no progress was made between the North City Survey of 1918 (Figure 8.12) and the Civic Survey of 1925 (Figure 8.13); the notes 'site of Custom House', and 'site of general post office' in O'Connell Street (Figure 8.13), are poignant reminders of the devastation so recently visited on the north city, and among the first challenges facing Saorstát Éireann. Corresponding approximately to the area covered by the 1811 extract (Figure 8.2), the 'new' north city slum encompasses both former Gardiner development and later more piecemeal additions to the east (the Gloucester Street district); added to this the continued devastation to the west (see Figures 5.6, 5.7) and the entrenched low-status nature of the Barrack Street and Church Street districts, despite small oases of improved dwellings, and the picture is very bleak. It is as well that the north city has the 'suburban dream' to dream about.

9

CONCLUSION

Few social problems have been subjected to such thorough examination by such a multitude of parties: Royal Commissions, Departmental Committees, Inspectors, Corporation Surveys, Social Service organisations, and philanthropists.[1]

THE SLUM CITY: THOROUGHLY EXPLORED

The Dublin slum situation engaged the professional and humanitarian attentions of a multitude of persons and organisations from the 1800s through to independence: medical doctors and proponents of the new 'sanatory science', clergymen of all denominations, mission agents and charity workers, religious sisters and journalists, police officers and scavenging staff, census enumerators and valuation office staff, Ordnance Survey fieldworkers and statisticians, lady sanitary officers, members of the public health, housing, drainage and markets committees of the Corporation and their associated employees, certain poor law guardians and various commissioners, both self-appointed and those appointed formally to inquire into the condition of the city's poor. Also drawn into commenting sensitively on the situation of the poorest were certain visitors, such as Alexis de Tocqueville and Charles Dickens. The mass of generalised information, case study detail and perceptive commentary both on the underlying causes and means of reform increased relentlessly from 1800, a period incomparably rich in record-making, by municipal, parliamentary, voluntary, commercial and church bodies as well as by private individuals.

While weighed down by the voluminous information thus available, it must be noted that the voices least likely to appear in the records are those of the slum residents themselves. Little survives about local customs, music or dance or any type of amusement excepting tomes of disapproving scrutiny of the liquor and dram shops; references to the Irish language are scant, and separate sub-groupings based on occupation or rural origin are difficult to distinguish in the

---

[1] *Report of Inquiry into the Housing of the Working Classes of the City of Dublin, 1939/43* (Dublin, 1943), p. 15.

written record. The intervention of officialdom in the areas of public health, sanitation, housing and poor relief all ensured that these would be closely documented in a 'professional' way, but to the neglect of many other aspects of life in the city slums. The charity record provides some valuable detail ignored in the 'official' record but in a piecemeal fashion. Oral histories are the obvious means towards rectifying this imbalance, as exemplified by Kevin Kearns; in the case of Dublin city, data collection dates largely from the early 1980s (with the Irish Folklore Council and the Dublin Folklore Project), to be greatly supplemented by Kearns' own research project.[2] However, it is self-evident that the oral historical method is most useful for periods within living memory (in Kearns own work dating largely from the 1920s), so that the difficulty of filling out the nineteenth century persists.

The scale and structure of the slum problem

Although the Dublin slum situation was meticulously exposed with energy and vision, and most observers concluded their inquiries with very practical suggestions for reform, effective action was to be long delayed. That progress was so slow is testimony to the scale and complexity of the problem, and the lack of political will. While the appalling living conditions of the majority of the central city's population (into the 1940s) were well advertised, it was the widespread inability to pay the rents required for better accommodation in the free market that made resolution of the problem on the scale required impossible. The structure of the tenement system where so many, including both politicians and persons little removed socially from their tenants, relied on rents for their livelihood, made slum clearance particularly complicated. Details on living conditions such as straw for bed, a diet largely of tea and bread, the absolute necessity each 'ragged' school faced of supplying their pupils with breakfast and clothing, and the difference a suit of clothes or a small relief order could make to those on the brink of disaster were provided for individual charity cases. When multiplied by the huge numbers we know shared those economic circumstances they provide some sense of the human struggles facing a large proportion of Dublin's citizenry.

While the Dublin slum problem was interlinked in a complex manner, there were several discernible threads to the story: contagious disease, poor sanitation both public and domestic, multiple occupancy and overcrowding of old building fabric, moral and physical 'degradation', vagrancy, begging, homelessness, and the policing, control and relief of the poor by state and charity organisations, all set against a backdrop of (initially) worthless local government and endemic poverty. Only gradually did the slum problem become crystalised as 'the housing question', or more correctly in the Dublin context, the 'tenement question'. Even when housing became the focus, and the suburban dream the stage upon which the next movement will be acted out, the association with contagious disease (especially TB), poor relief (outdoor relief orders, both from the state and from

[2] Kevin C. Kearns, *Dublin Tenement Life: An Oral History* (Dublin, 1994).

charities), and depressing employment prospects continued.

The changing geography of poverty

Poverty in Dublin was geographically widespread and patterned in a complex and dynamic way. On a city-wide basis several key areas recur, whether mapping insanitary areas, condemned housing or infectious disease from the Corporation archive, housing of low quality from Griffith's valuation, tenement dwellings from street directories, or the home addresses of destitute children and the 'sick poor' from charity records. On the south side the Liberties and the Townsend Street docklands district, on the north side the areas centred on Beresford Street, Mecklenburgh Street and the North Strand, and the Sheriff Street docklands area, could all be considered slums. However these areas did not at all contain the city's poor who were found throughout the urban area: wedged in small courts behind commercial streets such as Grafton Street and Dame Street; between St Stephen's Green and St Patrick's Cathedral; across from the stables and carriage houses of the lanes attached to the best Georgian houses in Merrion Square and Mount Street; more publicly in the ever increasing number of tenement houses which lined the poorer streets, but also along major arteries such as Church Street, Bolton Street and Dorset Street. Even the cellars of houses along the quays and in Abbey Street were homes to the poor.

The pattern varied over the time span 1800–1925, acting in two directions: confirming the run-down nature of the slum areas already mentioned so that the poor areas become even less attractive to residents with a possibility of living elsewhere; and spreading into better districts, as the fine houses of the north city Gardiner estate in particular are colonised by the poor. The steady movement from the substandard housing of the back courts and lane ways of this district into single rooms in the substantial dwellings lining streets such as Dominick Street and Gardiner Street Lower is linked both with the exertions of the Corporation's public health officials to close insanitary dwellings and eliminate 'nests of fever', and the steady exodus of the better off to the suburban townships. The reopening of condemned houses both with and without official approval, the infill of building plots to the rear of such dwellings, and the efforts at slum clearance and rebuilding by the Corporation and philanthropic housing companies further complicate the geography of poverty over time. While philanthropic and some Corporation housing gave a small social uplift to discrete areas, as a general rule very rarely do slum areas succeed in being effectively 'upgraded'. The disappearance of slum dwellings from places such as Watling Street and along the north docks is tied in with the land-hunger of commercial concerns such as the Guinness brewery, the railway companies and freight handlers. It is no accident that areas identified with poverty in the 1800s continue to feature in

[3] For example see Kieran McKeown, Grace Fitzgerald and Ann Deehan, *Religious Community and Social Justice: A Franciscan Initiative in the Inner City of Dublin, 1989–1992* (Dublin, 1993).

catalogues of urban deprivation in the 1990s.[3]

The intellectual context

The Dublin poverty debate reflected many contemporary international concerns: the perception of the slums as nests of fever, the equating of moral and medical disease, the struggle between proponents of *laissez faire* and those who advocated state interference for the greater good of society, and the obsession with classification and subdivision for statistical and policy purposes. The language of contagion was used to describe various ills, from the spread of typhoid and venereal disease, to the corrupting of young girls in the workhouse through proximity to those who had 'fallen'. The 'otherness' of the slums was emphasised, as journeys into these districts by middle class ladies such as the Ladies of Charity were likened to exploratory ventures, and in the case of the agents of the Dublin Visiting Mission who undertook to bring the assistance of the wealthier to their poor and benighted brethren in the city slums, without subjecting the wealthy to the disagreeable task of penetrating these dark regions for themselves. The proximity of wealth to abject poverty was a recurring theme in Dublin as in other urban centres from London to New York to Sydney, but the steady reduction of certain parts of the city to single class residential areas, as the wealthy fled the city centre, meant that the Dublin poverty debate always included discussion of the boundary and hence financial constraints of the municipality, as well as the scandal of those with so little of life's necessities living so closely to 'the brightest prosperity'.[4]

Spurred on firstly by the arguments for self-preservation in the face of contagious disease, and later with the insistence that economic consideration justified loss-making state investment in healthy housing for the working classes, the absolutist case against *laissez faire* was at least partially eroded. In the disbursement of public monies, whether collected from voluntary subscribers in the case of charities, or through property taxes in the case of the Poor Law and Corporation funding, or (as was increasingly the case) a combination of both, in the case of undertakings such as church-run industrial schools and hospitals, a certain degree of public accountability was required. Charities published annual reports including statements of philosophy and aims as well as subscription lists, Corporation committees published lengthy minutes of their meetings, and the Poor Law guardians had their every move checked and cross-checked by the Local Government Board. Across the wide range of such activities, the obsession with classification and subdivision, (supposedly) ensuring 'value for money', comes through: dividing the able-bodied workhouse pauper from the lunatic and insane, the 'deserving' poor artisan from the professional beggar, the 'fallen' from the virtuous females, and the multiplication of classes into which deaths might be entered by the Register General's office. Side by side with slum reform is found

---

[4] Thomas Jordan, 'The Present State of the Dwellings of the Poor, chiefly in Dublin', *Journal of the Dublin Statistical Society*, vol. 2 (1857), p. 13.

a concern with the 'lowest strata' of society, those who are by-passed by advances in domestic comfort and cleanliness and by increasing opportunities for education. The Dublin Artisans' Dwellings Company was accused of providing for 'a select number of families of a more thrifty section than the working class' and in the process leaving 'a residuum' who are 'by picking out the better people among them in a more squalid condition on the average than before'.[5] Improvements in the living conditions and life chances of some slum residents must not be taken as indicators of general and widespread advances.

Migration and mobility

Migration is a recurrent feature in the making and remaking of Dublin's slum geography. The continual migration of rural labourers and cottiers to Dublin, often *en route* to Britain, was part of a massive country-wide remaking of the rural economy, and many of Dublin's poverty problems were discussed at the time with regard to rural collapse rather than as an 'urban' problem.[6] Official opposition to mendicancy and vagrancy was unrelenting, with such travellers very understandably blamed for the spread of contagious disease but also for spreading moral turpitude, and general insubordination.[7] The unwillingness of the general public to collaborate in the stamping out of such mischievous predatory movements through their 'indiscriminate alms-giving' and 'what is called charity', was a source of great frustration to the proponents of that model of tight control and confinement, the workhouse.[8] The gulf between the average inhabitant of a slum district and officialdom, especially when as far removed as London, was immense; the poorer Dubliner was too close to forced migration and beggary herself to close her heart and hand to a neighbour, and whatever shame might attach to begging was still less than that of delivering oneself up to the aforementioned 'model' workhouse.

Short distance movements within the city were frequent among the poor, made necessary in some cases by the closing of insanitary housing and by slum clearance, but more usually as a result of the tenement housing market where a single room could be rented on a weekly basis from one of the many 'house jobbers' who controlled access. As furnishings were minimal the move did not require the upheaval house-moving implies today. The steady inflow to Dublin of persons from the country included servant girls and women who on being

---

[5] *Report of the Royal Commission appointed to Inquire into the Housing of the Working Classes* (Cd. 4547), 1884–1885, Evidence of Mr Frederic William Pim, qs. 22,638 (hereafter *Housing Inquiry 1885*).

[6] See W. Neilson Hancock, 'On Laissez Faire and the Economic Resources of Ireland', *Transactions of the Dublin Statistical Society*, vol. 1. (1848), pp. 305–319.

[7] George Nicholls, *First Report, Poor Laws (Ireland) 1836* in *Three Reports by George Nicholls Esq. to HM Principal Secretary of State for the Home Department* (London, 1838), (hereafter *First Report*), p. 49.

[8] Ibid. pp. 49, 59.

widowed or deserted turned their steps to Dublin in search of work. The paucity of employment opportunities elsewhere, especially for women, fostered mobility and in the case of service employment ensured a steady flow of labour between the poorer city areas and the high-class residential suburbs to the south and east especially. The stationing of large numbers of soldiers in Dublin also had an impact on migration flows, as their wives and unmarried partners followed them to their next post abroad or, as is more usually recorded, these women when widowed or deserted returned to Dublin to seek employment and assistance with childcare.

Among both male and female workers the Dublin pattern of commuting from a city tenement to the wealthy townships for work, facilitated by the Dublin and Kingstown railway and the tram companies' early and late workers' connections, was the opposite to that known in most British cities. While elsewhere cheap workers' housing was built on the outskirts, in Dublin private enterprise, most blatantly in the case of the Pembroke township to the south east, had been progressively replacing old and inferior houses with high-value new houses when the leases on the former fell out, thus propelling the poorer classes into rather than out of the city slums.[9] There was little chance of suburban housing of an acceptable standard for the poorest until the state intervened in a definitive manner.

Slum solutions

In the complex Dublin slum story a succession of short-term and piecemeal solutions overlap throughout the period 1800–1925, with some singular efforts at formulating an overall plan of campaign. Although some of the most essential reforms were articulated clearly as early as 1798 (Whitelaw, 1805), it was to take almost a century before basic matters such as street and domestic scavenging, interment, slaughtering, and the sewerage and drainage of the city could be described as safely in hand. From the fever outbreaks of the first decades of the nineteenth century the close connection between domestic and courtyard filth, the inane public health / sanitation structures in place (the parish vestry), and repeated outbreaks of malignant fever were made. The opening of a fever hospital (Cork Street) which would separate the sick person from those of his close circle who were still well was advocated as only part of a more comprehensive (but unsuccessful) plan for the eradication of the source of fever, the local tenement environment. Repeated waves of typhus, relapsing fever, dysentery, smallpox and cholera spread through the poorest and most crowded districts from 1798 to the 1830s, often carried by infected persons fleeing epidemic disease elsewhere, and were tackled on an *ad hoc* basis. The catastrophe of the 1840s famine with the influx of sick and starving persons, the desperate and the destitute, placed enormous strains on the workhouse and fever hospital accommodation which had been provided by then, but they did at least limit the spread of 'famine fever'

---

[9] *Housing Inquiry 1885*, Evidence of Dr Cameron, qs. 22,312 – 22,322.

(especially typhus) through the city. Vaccination had largely eliminated smallpox, an appalling and highly infectious disease (with the vaccination of infants compulsory from 1864), but contagious diseases more directly associated with filth and malnutrition were more difficult to shift. By 1885 it was claimed that the common staircase in tenement houses still hastened the spread of scarlet fever and measles, but that improved sanitary arrangements had by then brought typhoid under control, and ended the 'terrific epidemics' of typhus fever which had decimated Dublin periodically over the preceding centuries.[10]

The crisis management which characterised the early decades of the nineteenth century was only gradually superseded by a more organised, professional approach. The establishment of a statutory poor relief structure under the Poor Law (Ireland) act of 1838, followed by the long-overdue reform of the Corporation in 1850, and the Public Health (Ireland) act 1878 are milestones in the very slow movement towards effective public health and poor relief management. Nevertheless the tedious repetition of the same complaints, the repeated singling out of the same notorious 'black spots' or fever nests characterise the second half of the century. The increasingly expansive and sophisticated data collection structures and the advance in analytical methods serve rather to confirm what is already too well documented than to provide any brave new insights on the crisis.

The reform and enforcement of sanitary legislation and the provision of at least some new dwellings by the municipal authority on a loss-making basis in the last two decades of the nineteenth century were very welcome developments. However, such developments were characteristically piecemeal, without a 'broad based integrating mechanism or plan'.[11] The enthusiastic embracing of 'town planning principles' and 'garden city ideals' especially as articulated by Patrick Geddes, who was heavily involved in the Dublin scene, provided the framework for the first comprehensive town plans for Dublin[12] with the Civic Survey of 1922 (published 1925) providing the fullest compendium of information to date, and an attractive and convincing articulation of the suburban solution to the city's slum problem.

Women and poverty

The resilience and fortitude of women coping with severe poverty in Dublin 1800–1925 has been a recurrent theme. Whether unmarried or widowed, as the wives of soldiers, prisoners, invalids, or where the husbands deserted or migrated for work, large numbers of women in particular were left as the sole providers of

---

[10] Ibid., qs. 22,059 – 22,060.
[11] Michael J. Bannon, 'The Genesis of Modern Irish Planning', *The Emergence of Irish Planning*, vol. 1 (Dublin, 1985), pp. 189–261.
[12] P. Abercrombie, S. Kelly and A. Kelly, *Dublin of the Future: The New Town Plan* (Liverpool, 1922); P. Abercrombie, S. Kelly and M. Robertson, *Dublin Sketch Development Plan* (Dublin, 1941).

childcare in Dublin. In an oversupplied market, wage rates were low and the power to negotiate improvements very limited. That some resorted to prostitution as a realistic option is not at all surprising, and the fact that official coverage of this activity was driven entirely by concern for the health of Her Majesty's forces barracked in Dublin makes it clear whose welfare was of concern.

The paucity of female work opportunities was repeatedly noted by observers, and attempts to improve the situation in Dublin, though brave, were limited.[13] This affected any woman who had to provide for herself and dependants, including women of the middling ranks who were thrown on their own resources. One commentator complained that in Ireland 'sympathetic associations and prejudices regard with greater favour and compassion a starving than a struggling woman; we worship those we martyr, those who decline the privilege we ridicule':

> It is a terrible indictment of our social existence that the resources for gaining a livelihood open to women are so few. At present, the language practically held by modern society to destitute women may be resolved into, marry – stitch – die – or do worse.[14]

The heroic struggles of poorer women to provide for themselves and especially for the children left to their care, and the evidence they have left for the importance of the primary relief network of the family, neighbours, employers and fellow employees, places the efforts of the official and voluntary relief organisations in context. The vast majority of Dublin's poor relied largely on their own exertions and ingenuity to provide, and in times of especial distress the first assistance was sought, and generally provided, from among their own circle, in which women as agents of relief figure most prominently.

The churches and poverty relief

At the outset of the nineteenth century several major Protestant charities, some of which were openly accused of proselytising, were handsomely funded by the state, while the majority religion, the Roman Catholic Church, was forbidden to endow charities; by the end of the century the situation had undergone a transformation, whereby the state was entrusting large amounts of money to Catholic congregations for the care of poor children at risk and other vulnerable groups (by sponsoring their maintenance in 'extern institutions'), and Catholic nuns were state employees in workhouse hospitals. By the time of independence 'the operations of charitable societies cover a very wide field and, to a considerable extent, relieve the ratepayer and taxpayer of financial burdens they could

---

[13] See Jacinta Prunty, 'Margaret Louisa Aylward 1810–1889', pp. 61–66; Mary Cullen, 'Anna Maria Haslam', pp. 168–170; Maria Luddy, 'Isabella M.S. Tod', pp. 200–208; in Mary Cullen and Maria Luddy (eds.) *Women, Consciousness and Power in Nineteenth Century Ireland* (Dublin, 1995).

[14] Edward Gibson, 'Employment of Women in Ireland', *Soc. Stat. Inq. Soc. Ire. Jn.*, vol. 3 (1862), pp. 138–143.

[15] *Report of the Commission on the Relief of the Sick and Destitute Poor*, including the Insane Poor (Dublin, 1928), p. 84.

not otherwise escape', although they were 'mostly urban, and reach the greatest development in Dublin'.[15] For the most part functioning independently of the state, it was hoped that relations between charitable societies and the Poor Law would be characterised by 'cordial co-operation in achieving a common end', the particular contribution of the societies being recognised as their flexibility in responding to individual needs and their nature: 'they are voluntary and actuated by higher motives than the provision of material necessities' alone.[16]

The contribution of both Protestant and Catholic churches to the relief of poverty in nineteenth century Dublin was substantial and enduring. Church charities pioneered social developments of great consequence. Through local visitation and the need for support in terms of members and funds the condition of the poorest was widely publicised by individual clergy and lay groups such as the Ladies of Charity. Alongside the exertions of sanitary officials and medical officers especially, such reports helped to create a climate of public opinion which supported, in due course, reforms in sanitary arrangements, housing and relief structures.

Voluntary church societies provided very necessary social services in advance of the state. In providing, for example, industrial training for girls, education for the deaf and dumb, and the care of 'criminal' children, they opened a wide range of possibilities, and showed, in practice, how such services could be beneficial to society, and operated without exorbitant expense. By providing an alternative to the state workhouse provision, especially before outdoor relief 'on the union' became generally available to at least some classes of paupers, church charities saved large numbers from resorting thither. From the sickness and death rates which the union registers themselves record it is not an exaggeration to state that by providing alternative relief in a more flexible and acceptable manner, such as through school meals or grocery orders, train tickets or the redemption of tools from pawn, church charities saved large numbers from the health risks as well as the ignominy of the workhouse. The state's willingness to support voluntary associations such as societies to help discharged female prisoners which, after all, provided services at minimal cost to the rate-payer, is a confirmation of the regard in which they were held. The 'boarding out' system of childcare developed by Margaret Aylward through St Brigid's Orphanage is a good example of the state following, in time, the lead set by a church charity. It is also an example of a voluntary organisation putting great pressure on the state to provide, but in the meantime co-operating with what was already in place, as in the case of the workhouse children who were fostered with St Brigid's nurses.

The metropolitan branch of the Ladies' Association of Charity of St Vincent de Paul may be regarded as typical of those church charities, both Protestant and Catholic, whose avowedly spiritual aims were very much enfleshed in the material assistance of their poorer brothers and sisters. Undertaking to organise the visitation of the 'sick poor' of an extensive district was a daunting task, and

---

[16] Ibid. pp. 85–87.

the courage it required of women from comfortable backgrounds to venture into the courtyards, attics and hovels of their poor neighbours, risking infectious disease, is not to be underestimated. The means at their disposal were small relative to the extent of poverty, but the difference even modest additions to the family budget meant to a destitute family must not be understated. The flexibility of such associations, in providing a wide range of relief items, made it more likely that what they provided matched what was in fact required by the poor, and the gradual replacement of relief in kind by money made it possible for persons to exercise discretion and spend it according to their own agenda. The continuity of such associations was another important factor; in the case of the Ladies of Charity, families who removed from their visiting district could seek the association's assistance on their return, and those who had come to rely on the weekly visits of the Ladies, socially as well as in some measure economically, were rarely disappointed. The fostering of daughter branches was another important contribution: elsewhere in Dublin city and townships (Arran Quay, Rathmines, Clontarf) and in Cork, 'under the personal care of the Bishop of that diocese'. In January 1857 at a spiritual retreat organised by the metropolitan branch to which 'the different associations of the city and suburbs were invited' more than three hundred ladies attended, from Rathmines, Clontarf, Kingstown, and of course the organising branch. The metropolitan branch was able to look back with satisfaction 'to the help we gave to some of them in their infancy'. Other Dublin branches such as Westland Row (1876) continued to be opened throughout the century.[17]

The social mission of the Catholic Church in nineteenth century Dublin is intimately bound up with the spread of communities of religious women, who provided a huge proportion of the social services for the city's poor by the end of the century. The focus on education for the children of the city slums by both Protestant and Catholic activists was of enormous long-term importance. The very careful records kept by successive Roman Catholic archbishops of prevailing illiteracy rates in the city and county is an indication of the primary position attached to education by the church.[18] By proving, in practice, that the wildest 'street arabs' could be educated, and indeed responded positively to the attention thus bestowed, church activists laid the best possible basis for the long-term 'civilisation' and advancement of the poorest. The gradual uplift which education, it was held, would provide did not in the meantime threaten social stability; if anything it served the conservative agenda of the churches. As the schools themselves were at pains to demonstrate, their purpose went beyond mere bookwork, and included the promotion either directly or indirectly of self-esteem, personal hygiene, temperance, self-control, 'good manners' and deportment, and a generally biddable and co-operative manner which would serve the

---

[17] *Ladies of Charity, First Report*, 1853, p. 6; *Sixth Report* 1857, pp. 6, 12.
[18] Ages and education lists, Dublin city and county 1841–1891, DDA: Laity 340/2 no. 177, 1861.

children well in the limited range of domestic or labouring employment on offer. In the Christian Brothers and Holy Faith poor schools especially, the awakening of national consciousness and a pride in being an Irish Catholic were also regarded as positive outcomes. The contribution of the churches to the provision of social services in Dublin was noted by outside observers, such as one Protestant gentleman who addressed the Dublin Statistical Society in 1898 stating, 'I fear that other denominations, such as my own, fail sometimes to realise all that the Catholic orders have done for Ireland in social problems, in so far as law has left them scope'.[19]

Sectarian competition

The issue of sectarian competition has been a frequent theme and examination of the archival material available on both sides of the denominational divide reveals plainly that it was a very significant factor in the targeting of slum areas for mission activity and associated poor relief in nineteenth century Dublin. It influenced the location of church charities, the ministries they undertook and their methods of operation. It was a significant area of tension in the union workhouse. The records of the Irish Church Missions and associated Smyly schools make clear that both in principle and in practice it was intended to convert the poor of Dublin from the 'popish' faith; the Catholic records are no less definite about their intention to thwart these efforts. The controversial activities of the evangelical missionary societies in the slum areas led to a general increase in the provision by Roman Catholics of social and religious services for the poor of their own denomination, thereby benefiting a large percentage of the city's populace. However, it would be wrong to dwell on that aspect alone for increased Roman Catholic efforts were also related to the improved public standing and wealth of the Church which made the endowment of charities possible in the second half of the nineteenth century. There was a growing number of educated middle class Catholics who had the finances and good will necessary to back charitable projects among their poorer co-religionists. A strong lead had been set by communities of religious men and women, whose self-sacrifice on behalf of the poorest, especially in the cause of education, prompted public support. Outstanding individuals such as Margaret Aylward and Ellen Smyly, operating on either side of the sectarian divide, exploited contacts within Ireland and overseas for the support of their 'ragged' schools and other charities. There was also a broad basis of support among the poorer citizens themselves, whose small contributions were the backbone of many charities, such as the penny contributors throughout the city who subscribed to the breakfast fund of St Brigid's School, West Park Street. Among activists of all churches a genuine social commitment and sympathy for their poorer neighbours could always be found, for whom the denominational aspect of service was relatively secondary.

[19] E. D. Daly, *Soc. Stat. Inq. Soc. Ire. Jn.*, 10, 50 (1898) p. 362.

Slum geography today

Twentieth century Dublin has seen huge advances in statutory provision of housing, health care and social assistance, with indoor sanitation now the norm, greatly improved free medical services, and the right to a minimum income guaranteed at least in principle by the provision of unemployment assistance, social welfare payments, children's allowances and old age pensions. Recent tax-driven urban renewal initiatives have seen some of the former slum areas attracting private sector home-owners for the first time this century, while the remodelling of the city has also included the refurbishment by the Corporation of flat complexes which it built on cleared central-city slum sites dating (largely) from the 1930s on.[20] The standards of housing are perhaps the most visible measure of the progress achieved. The development of antibiotics (including those used to control TB) as well as vaccines against measles, polio and other dangers, along with improved nutrition and sanitation have all greatly enhanced life expectancy, and infant death is now uncommon. Criticism of current services does not negate the huge advances made, particularly since independence in 1921, in the transformation of the 'slum city'. However, the slum days are not entirely over; considerable numbers of Traveller children are still reared in conditions which resemble those condemned as unfit a century ago, a reproach to a wealthy, 'civilised' society. The increasing spatial segregation of the poorest from the wealthiest which characterised the nineteenth century has continued apace, leaving Dublin as one of the most socially divided cities in Europe.[21] The multiple deprivation which characterised slum areas can be found today in certain housing estates on the urban fringe, well beyond the ambit of those with power, influence and money; ironically, it is the 'overspill' of lawlessness threatening the commercial and wealthy residential districts which has focused attention on these areas. Drug abuse, including alcohol addiction, drags many individuals and families to the brink of disaster and even premature death as effectively as did contagious disease in a previous age. Beyond Dublin, the poor environment and restricted life chances which are associated with the nineteenth century urban slum are the lot of too many persons living in the squalid shanty towns of 'third world' cities. The challenge continues.

---

[20] Jacinta Prunty, 'Residential Urban Renewal Schemes, Dublin 1986–1994', *Irish Geography* 28 (2) 1995, pp. 131–149.

[21] See Joe Brady, 'Dublin: Change and Challenge', in Hugh Clout (ed.), *Europe's Cities in the Late Twentieth Century*, Nederlandse Geographische Studies no. 176 (Amsterdam, 1994), pp. 69–84.

APPENDIX

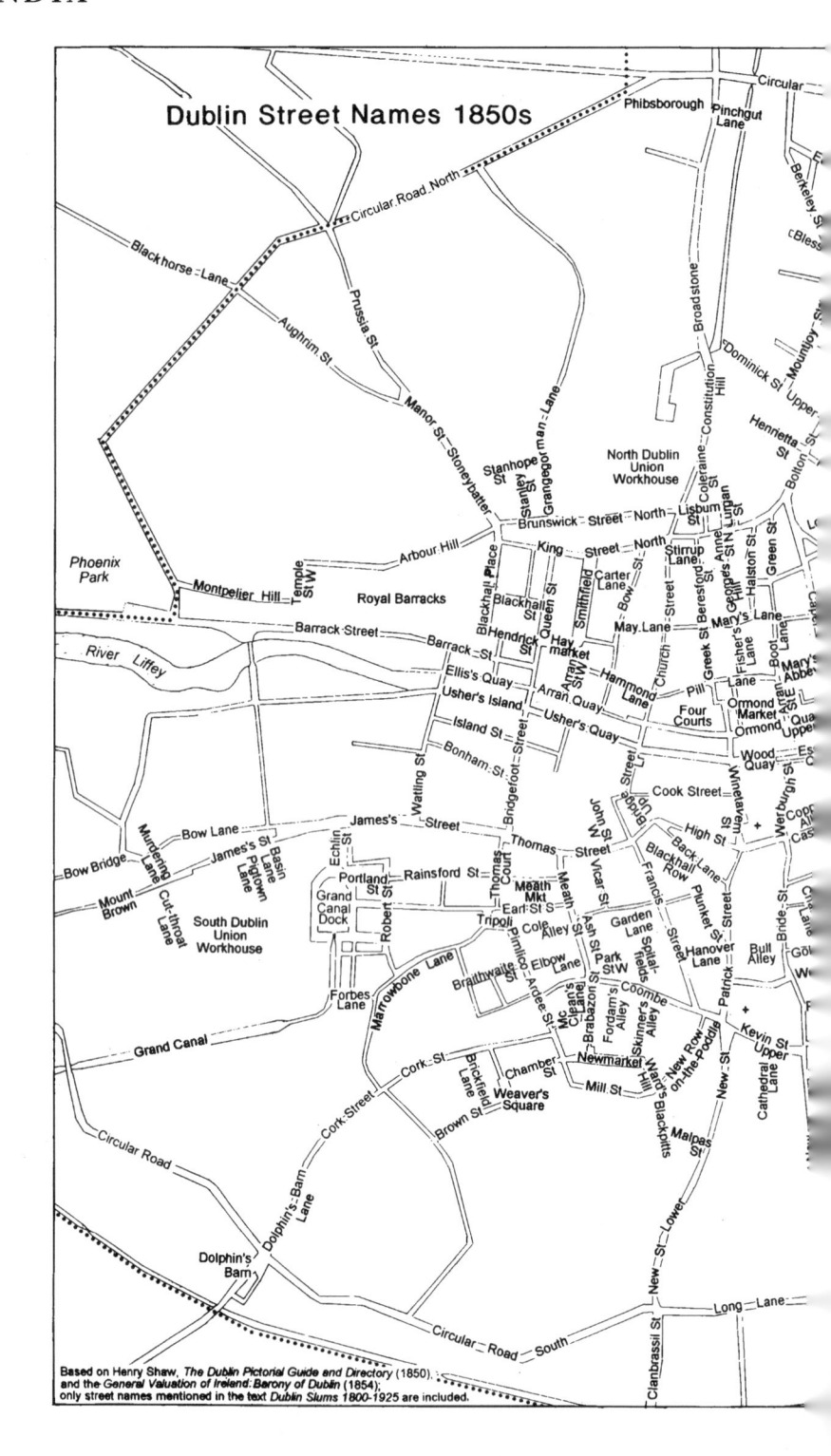

Appendix

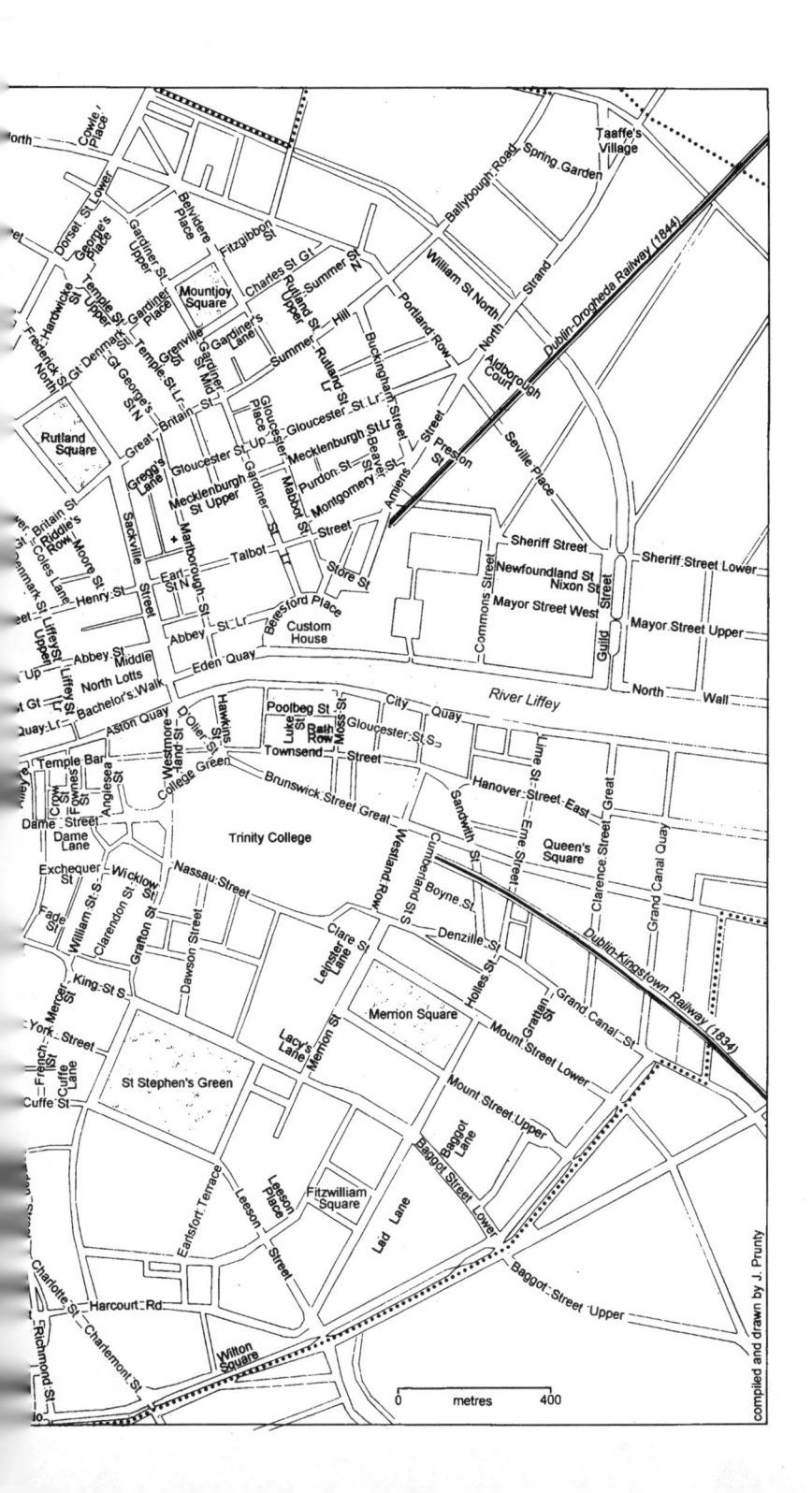

BIBLIOGRAPHY

Aalen, F.H.A., 'Dublin's Physical Growth and Rise to National Pre-eminence,' in MacLaran, A. (ed.) *Dublin in Crisis*, Trinity Papers in Geography 5, Dublin: Department of Geography, Trinity College, pp. 2–16.

Aalen, F.H.A., *The Iveagh Trust: The First Hundred Years, 1890–1990*, Dublin: Iveagh Trust, 1990.

Aalen, F.H.A., 'Public Housing in Ireland, 1880–1921,' Planning Perspectives, 2, 1987, pp. 175–193.

Aalen, F.H.A., 'The working class housing movement in Dublin 1850–1920' in M.J. Bannon (editor) *The Emergence of Irish Planning 1880–1920*, Dublin: Turoe Press, 1985, pp. 101–160.

Aalen, F.H.A., 'Approaches to the working class housing problem in late Victorian Dublin: the Dublin Artisans' Dwellings Company and the Guinness (later Iveagh) Trust,' Mannheimer Geographische Arbeiten 17 Rainer Joha Bender (Ed.) *Neure Forschungen zur Sozialgeographie von Irland*, Mannheim: 1984, pp. 165–184.

Aalen, F.H.A., 'Health and Housing in Dublin c.1850–1921' in Aalen, F.H.A., and Whelan, Kevin, (eds.), *Dublin City and County: From Prehistory to Present*, Dublin: Geography Publications, 1992, pp. 279–304.

Barrett, Rose M., *Guide to Dublin Charities*, vols. 1–3, 1884.

Beames, Thomas, *The Rookeries of London: Past Present and Prospective*, London: Bosworth, 1852.

Badcock, Blair, *Unfairly Structured Cities*, Oxford: Basil Blackwell, 1984.

Booth, Charles, *Life and Labour of the People in London*, 17 volumes, London: Macmillan, 1889 to 1905.

Booth, Charles, *Descriptive Map of London Poverty 1889*, facsimile reproduction, no. 130, London: London Topographical Society, 1984.

Booth, William, *In Darkest England and the Way Out*, London: Salvation Army International H.Q., 1890.

Bowen, Desmond, *Souperism: Myth or Reality, a Study in Souperism*, Cork: Mercier Press, 1970.

Bowen, Desmond, *Paul Cardinal Cullen and the Shaping of Modern Irish Catholicism*, Dublin: Gill and Macmillan, 1983.

Brady, Joseph E., 'Social contrasts in Dublin,' in Horner, Arnold, and Parker, A.J., (eds.), *Geographical Perspectives on the Dublin Region*, Dublin: Geographical Society of Ireland, 1987, pp. 1–15.

Briggs, Asa (ed.) *The Nineteenth Century, The Contradictions of Progress*, New York: Bonanza, 1985.

Burke, Helen, *The People and the Poor Law in 19th Century Ireland*, Dublin: Women's Education Bureau, 1987.

Burke, Nuala, *Dublin 1600–1800: a Study in Urban Morphogeneisis*, unpublished PhD thesis, Dublin: University of Dublin, 1972.

Carter, Harold, and Wheatley, S., 'Residential segregation in nineteenth century cities,' *Area*, 12, 1, 1980, pp. 57–62.
Carter, Harold, *An Introduction to Urban Historical Geography*, London: Edward Arnold, 1983.
Carter, Harold, and Lewis, C. Roy, *An Urban Geography of England and Wales in the Nineteenth Century*, London: Edward Arnold, 1990.
Cherry, Gordon E., *Urban Change and Planning: a History of Urban Development in Britain since 1750*, Henley on Thames, Oxfordshire: G.T. Foulis, 1972.
Cherry, Gordon E., *Cities and Plans: the Shaping of Urban Britain in the Nineteenth and Twentieth Centuries*, London: Edward Arnold, 1988.
Cherry, Gordon E., 'Public policy and the morphology of western cities: the example of Britain in the nineteenth and twentieth centuries' in Lawton, Richard, (ed.), *The Rise and Fall of Great Cities: Aspects of Urbanization in the Western World*. London: Belhaven Press, 1989, pp. 32–44.
Clare, Anne, 'A Series of Sketches: Anne Devlin, Margaret Aylward, Constance Markievicz,' in Purcell, Emer, *A Short History of Winetavern Street and its Environs*, Dublin: ASTI, 1996, pp. 59–61.
Clark, Peter, (ed.), *Country Towns in Pre-Industrial England*, Leicester: Leicester University Press, 1981.
Clear, Caitríona, *Nuns in Nineteenth Century Ireland*, Dublin: Gill and Macmillan, 1987.
Clear, Caitríona, 'The Limits of Female Autonomy: Nuns in Nineteenth-Century Ireland' in Luddy, Maria, and Murphy, Cliona, (eds.), *Women Surviving: Studies in Irish Women's History in the Nineteenth and Twentieth Centuries*. Dublin: Poolbeg, 1990, pp. 15–50.
Clout, Hugh, (ed.), *The Times London History Atlas*, London: Times Books, 1991
Conzen, M.R.G. 'Morphogenesis, morphological regions and secular human agency in the historic townscape, as exemplified by Ludlow,' in Denecke, Dietrich and Shaw, Gareth, (eds.), *Urban Historical Geography: Recent Progress in Britain and Germany*. Cambridge: Cambridge University Press, 1988, pp. 253–272.
Conzen, Michael, P., 'Historical geography: changing spatial structure and social patterning of western cities,' *Progress in Human Geography*, 7, 1, 1983, pp. 88–107.
Coolahan, John, *Irish Education, History and Structure*, Dublin: Institute of Public Administration, 1981.
Corish, Patrick J., *The Irish Catholic Experience: A Historical Survey*, Dublin: Gill & Macmillan, 1985.
Cosgrave, Dillon, *North Dublin City and Environs*, Dublin: M.H. Gill & Sons, 1909.
Cosgrove, Art (ed.) *Dublin through the Ages*, Dublin: College Press, 1988.
Costello, Peter, *Dublin Churches*, Dublin: Gill and Macmillan, 1989.
Craig, Maurice, *Dublin 1660–1860: A Social and Architectural History*, Dublin: Allen Figgis, 1969.
Crossman, Virgina, *Local Government in Nineteenth Century Ireland*, Belfast: Institute of Irish Studies, QUB, 1994.
Cullen, Louis M., 'The growth of Dublin 1600–1900: character and heritage,' in Aalen, F.H.A., and Whelan, Kevin, (eds.), *Dublin City and County: From Prehistory to Present*, Dublin: Geography Publications, 1992, pp. 252–257.
Cullen, Mary, 'Breadwinners and Providers: Women in the Household Economy of Labouring Families 1835–6,' in Luddy, Maria, and Murphy, Cliona, (eds.), *Women Surviving: Studies in Irish Women's History in the Nineteenth and Twentieth Centuries*, Dublin: Poolbeg, 1990, pp. 85–116.
Dallas, Alexander, *The Story of the Irish Church Missions, continued to 1869*, London: Nisbet, 1875.
Daly, Mary E., *A Social and Economic History of Ireland since 1800*, Dublin: Educational Company, 1981.

Daly, Mary E., 'Late nineteenth and early twentieth century Dublin,' in Harkness, David and O'Dowd, Mary (eds.), *The Town in Ireland*, Belfast: Appletree Press, 1981.
Daly, Mary E., 'Housing conditions and the genesis of housing reform in Dublin 1880–1920,' in M.J. Bannon (ed.) *The Emergence of Irish Planning 1880–1920*, Dublin: Turoe Press, 1985, pp. 77–130.
Daly, Mary E., *Dublin, the Deposed Capital: A Social and Economic History*, 1860–1914. Cork: Cork University Press, 1985.
Daly, Mary E., 'Dublin in the nineteenth century Irish economy,' in Butel, P. and Cullen, L.M., *Cities and Merchants: French and Irish Perspectives on Urban Development, 1500–1900*, Proceedings of the Fourth Franco-Irish Seminar of Social and Economic Historians, Dublin: Department of Modern History, TCD, 1986, pp. 53–65.
Daly, Mary E., 'Irish urban history: a survey,' *Urban History Yearbook*, Leicester: Leicester University Press, 1986.
Daunton, M.J., *House and Home in the Victorian City: Working Class Housing 1850–1914*, London: Edward Arnold, 1983.
Dennis, Richard, 'Distance and social interaction in a Victorian city,' *Journal of Historical Geography*, 33, 1977, pp. 237–250.
Dennis, Richard, 'Why study segregation? More thoughts on Victorian cities,' *Area*, 12, 1980, pp. 313–317.
Dennis, Richard, 'Stability and change in urban communities, a geographical perspective,' in Johnson, James H., and Pooley, Colin G., (eds.), *The Structure of Nineteenth Century Cities*, London: Croom Helm, 1982.
Dennis, Richard, *English Industrial Cities of the Nineteenth Century: a Social Geography*, Cambridge: Cambridge University Press, 1984.
Dennis, Richard, 'The geography of Victorian values: philanthropic housing in London, 1840–1900,' *Journal of Historical Geography*, 15, 1, 1989, pp. 40–54.
Dennis, Richard, 'The social geography of towns and cities 1730–1914,' in Dodghson, R.A., and Butlin, R.A., (eds.), *An Historical Geography of England and Wales*, London: Academic Press, 1978; second ed. 1990.
Dennis, Richard and Clout, Hugh, *A Social Geography of England and Wales*, Oxford: Pergamon Press, 1980.
Dodghson, R.A. and Butlin, R.A., (eds.), *An Historical Geography of England and Wales*, London: Academic Press, 1978; second ed. 1990.
Donnelly, Nicholas, *Short History of Dublin Parishes*, 17 parts, 4 volumes, Dublin: Catholic Truth Society, 1909–1920.
Driver, Felix, 'Moral geographies,' *Transactions of the Institute of British Geographers*, 1988.
Driver, Felix, 'The historicity of human geography,' *Progress in Human Geography*, 12, 4, 1988.
Driver, Felix, 'The historical geography of the workhouse system in England and Wales, 1834–1883,' *Journal of Historical Geography*, 15, 3, 1989, pp. 209–286.
Driver, Felix, *Power and Pauperism The Workhouse System, 1834–1884*, Cambridge: Cambridge University Press, 1993.
Dublin Charities, Association of Charities, 1902.
Dyos, H.F. *Exploring the Urban Past – Essays in Urban History*, Cannadine, David, and Reeder, David (eds.) Cambridge: Cambridge University Press, 1982.
Dyos H.J., and Wolff, M., (eds.), *The Victorian City: Images and Realities*, London: Routledge and Kegan Paul, 1973.
Englander, David and O'Day, Rosemary (eds.), *Retrieved Riches: Social Investigation in Britain 1840–1914*, Aldershot, Hants: Scolar Press, 1995.
Fahy, A.M., 'The spatial differentiation of commerical and residential functions in Cork city 1787–1863,' *Irish Geography*, 17, 1984, pp. 14–26.
Finnegan, Frances, *Poverty and Prejudice: a Study of Irish Immigrants in York 1840–1875*,

Cork: Cork University Press, 1982.
Ford, Donal, *Dr. Barnardo*, London: Black, 1958, reprint 1966.
Fraser, Derek, *Power and Authority in the Victorian City*, Oxford: Basil Blackwell, 1979.
Fraser, Derek, (ed.), *The New Poor Law in the Nineteenth Century*, London: Macmillan, 1976.
Gardiner's Dublin: A History and Topography of Mountjoy Square and Environs, Dublin: National Council for Educational Awards, 1991.
Garwood, John, *The Million Peopled City; or One Half of the People of London Made Known to the Other Half*, London: 1853.
Gaskell, Martin S. (ed.), *Slums*, Leicester: Leicester University Press, 1990.
Gauldie, E., *Cruel Habitations,: A History of Working Class Housing 1780–1918*, London: Unwin, 1974
Genevese, E.D., and Hochberg, L., *Geographic Perspectives in History*, Oxford: Basil Blackwell, 1989.
Gibbons, Margaret, *The Life of Margaret Aylward*, London: Sands, 1928.
Gibson, Romuald, *Tomorrow Began Yesterday: Reflections on Margaret Aylward*, Dublin: Holy Faith Sisters, 1982.
Guelke, Leonard, *Historical Understanding in Geography: An Idealist Approach*, Cambridge: Cambridge University Press, 1982
Hall, Arthur, *The British Metropolis in 1851: A Classified Guide to London*, London: Virtue, 1851
Hall, Peter, *Cities of Tomorrow: An Intellectual History of Urban Planning and Design in the Twentieth Century*, Oxford: Basil Blackwell, 1988, 1990 reprint.
Harkness, David and O'Dowd, Mary, (eds.), *The Town in Ireland*, Historical Studies XlII Papers read before the Irish Conference of Historians, Belfast, 1979, Belfast: Appletree Press, 1981.
Harris, Cole, 'The historical mind and the practice of geography,' in Ley, David and Samuels, Marwyn S., *Humanistic Geography: Prospects and Problems*, London: Croom Helm, 1978, pp. 123–137.
Haynes, Barry, (ed.), *Working Class Life in Victorian Leicester: The Joseph Dare Reports*, Leicester: Leicester University Press, 1991.
Hearn, Mona, 'Life for Domestic Servants in Dublin, 1880–1920,' in Luddy, Maria, and Murphy, Cliona, (eds.), *Women Surviving: Studies in Irish Women's History in the Nineteenth and Twentieth Centuries*, Dublin: Poolbeg, 1990, pp. 148–179.
Helferty, Seamus and Refaussé, Raymond, (eds.), *Directory of Irish Archives*, Dublin: Irish Academic Press, 1988.
Hill, Octavia, 'The work of volunteers in the organization of charity,' *Macmillan's Magazine*, 26, 1872, pp. 441–449.
Hill, Octavia, 'A more excellent way of charity,' *Macmillan's Magazine*, 35, 1876, pp. 126–131.
Himmelfarb, Gertrude, *The Idea of Poverty: England in the Early Industrial Age*, London: Faber and Faber, 1984.
Hollingshead, John, *Ragged London in 1861*, London: Smith Elder, 1861; New York: Garland, 1985.
Horner, Arnold, and Parker, A.J., (eds.), *Geographical Perspectives on the Dublin Region*, Dublin: Geographical Society of Ireland, 1987.
Horner, Arnold, 'The Dublin Region, 1880–1982: An Overview on Its Development and Planning,' in Bannon, Michael J. (ed.), *The Emergence of Irish Planning 1880–1920*, Dublin: Turoe Press, 1985.
Johnson, James H. and Pooley, Colin G., (eds.) *The Structure of Nineteenth Century Cities*, London: Croom Helm, 1982.
Johnston, Máirín, *Around the Banks of Pimlico*, Dublin: Attic Press, 1994.
Kay, Jeanne, 'Landscapes of women and men: rethinking the regional historical geography of the United States and Canada,' *Journal of Historical Geography*, 17, 4, 1991.

Kearns, Gerry, 'Zivilis or Hygaeia: urban public health and the epidemiologic transition' in Lawton, Richard, (editor) *The Rise and Fall of Great Cities: Aspects of Urbanization in the Western World.* London: Belhaven Press, 1989, pp. 96–124.
Kearns, Kevin C., *Dublin Tenement Life: An Oral History*, Dublin: Gill and Macmillan, 1994.
Kearns, Kevin C., *Dublin Street Life and Lore: An Oral History*, Dublin: Glendate Press, 1991.
Kearns, Kevin C., *Dublin's Vanishing Craftsmen*, Belfast: Appletree Press, 1986.
Keenan, Desmond J., *The Catholic Church in Nineteenth Century Ireland: A Sociological Study*, Dublin: Gill and Macmillan, 1983.
Lambert, Brooke, 'Charity: its aims and means,' *The Contemporary Review*, 23, 1874.
Larkin, Emmet, *The Historical Dimensions of Irish Catholicism*, New York: Arno Press, 1976 (reprint 1991).
Larkin, Emmet, *The Making of the Roman Catholic Church in Ireland, 1850–1860*, University of North Carolina Press, 1980.
Lawton, Richard and Pooley, Colin G., 'The Urban Dimensions of Nineteenth Century Liverpool,' *Social Geography of Nineteenth Century Merseyside Project: Working Paper 4*, Liverpool: 1975.
Lawton, Richard and Pooley, Colin G., *The Social Geography of Merseyside in the Nineteenth Century*, Liverpool: Merseyside Project, SSRC, 1976.
Lawton, 'Mobility in nineteenth century British cities,' *Geographical Journal*, 145, 1979, pp. 206–224.
Lawton, Richard, 'Peopling the Past,' *Transactions of the Institute of British Geographers*, New Series, 112, 3, 1987, pp. 259–283.
Lawton, Richard and Pooley, Colin G., *Britain 1740–1950: An Historical Geography*, London: Edward Arnold, 1992.
Lee, Joseph, *The Modernisation of Irish Society, 1848–1918*, vol. 10 of the Gill History of Ireland, Dublin: Gill and Macmillan, 1973; reprint 1983.
Lerner, Gerda, *The Majority finds its Past: Placing Women in History*, Oxford: Oxford University Press, 1979.
Lindsay, Deirdre, *Dublin's Oldest Charity: the Sick and Indigent Roomkeepers' Society*, Dublin: Aniversary Press, 1990.
Lowe, Michelle S., and Short, John S., 'Progressive Human Geography,' *Progress in Human Geography*, 14, 1, 1990, pp. 3–8.
Lowenthal D., *The Past is a Foreign Country*, Cambridge: Cambridge University Press, 1985.
Luddy, Maria, 'Women and charitable organisations in nineteenth century Ireland,' in *Women's Studies International Forum*, xi, 4, 1988, pp. 301–5.
Luddy, Maria, 'Prostitution and rescue work in nineteenth century Ireland,' Luddy, Maria, and Murphy, Cliona, (eds.), *Women Surviving: Studies in Irish Women's History in the Nineteenth and Twentieth Centuries.* Dublin: Poolbeg, 1990, pp. 51–84.
Luddy, Maria, 'An agenda for women's history in Ireland, part II 1800–1900,' *Irish Historical Studies*, 28, 109, 1992.
Luddy, Maria, *Women and Philanthropy in Nineteenth-century Ireland*, Cambridge: Cambridge University Press, 1995.
Mackenzie, Suzanne, 'Women's place – women's space,' *Area*, 12, 1, 1980, pp. 47–49.
Majerus, Pascal, *The Second Reformation in West Galway: Alexander R. Dallas and the Society for the Irish Church Missions to the Roman Catholics, 1849–859*, unpublished M.A. history thesis (UCD, 1990).
McCord, Norman, 'The Poor Law and Philanthropy,' in Derek Fraser, (ed.) *The New Poor Law in the Nineteenth Century*, London: Macmillan, 1976.
MacCurtain, Margaret, and O'Corráin, Donncha, *Women in Irish Society: the Historical Dimension*, Dublin: 1978.
Mac Suibhne, Peadar, *Paul Cullen and his Contemporaries 1820–1902*, 5 vols. Naas: Leinster Leader, 1961–77.

Maltby, Arthur and Maltby, Jean, *Ireland in the Nineteenth Century: a Breviate of Official Publications*, Guides to Official Publications, vol. 4, Pergamon Press, 1979.

Martin, John H., *Aspects of the Social Geography of Dublin City in the Mid Nineteenth Century*. Unpublished MA thesis in Geography, UCD, 1973.

Martin, John H. 'The social geography of mid nineteenth century Dublin city,' in Smith, William J. and Whelan, Kevin, (eds.), *Common Ground: Essays on the Historical Geography of Ireland*, Cork: Cork University Press, 1988, pp. 173–188.

Mayne, Alan, 'Representing the slum' in Richard Rodger (ed.), *Urban History Yearbook*, 17, Leicester: Leicester University Press, 1990, pp. 66–84.

Mayne, Alan, 'A barefoot childhood: so what? Imagining slums and reading neighbourhoods,' *Urban History*, 22, 3, 1995, pp. 380–389.

Mayne, Alan, 'A just war, the language of slum representation in twentieth century Australia,' *Journal of Urban History*, 22, 1, 1995, pp. 75–107.

McCready, C.T. *Dublin Street Names, Dated and Explained*, 1892; facsimile ed. Dublin: Carraig Books, 1987.

McCullough, Niall, *Dublin: An Urban History*, Dublin: Anne Street Press, 1989.

McLoughlin, Dympna, 'Workhouses and Irish Female Paupers, 1840–70,' in Luddy, Maria, and Murphy, Cliona, (eds.), *Women Surviving: Studies in Irish Women's History in the Nineteenth and Twentieth Centuries*, Dublin: Poolbeg, 1990, pp. 117–147.

Milne, Kenneth, *Protestant Aid 1836–1986: A History of the Association for the Relief of Distressed Protestants*, Dublin: Protestant Aid, 1989.

Moody, T.W. et. al., *The Church of Ireland 1869–1969*, London: Routledge and Kegan Paul. 1975.

Mosher, Anne E., and Holdsworth, Deryck W., 'The meaning of alley housing in industrial towns: examples from late nineteenth century and early twentieth century Pennsylvania,' *Journal of Historical Geography*, 18, 2, 1992, pp. 174–189.

Murnane, Brian, 'The recreation of the urban historical landscape: Mountjoy Ward, Dublin c1901,' in Smith, William J. and Whelan, Kevin, (eds.), *Common Ground: Essays on the Historical Geography of Ireland*, Cork: Cork University Press, 1988, pp. 189–207.

National Library of Ireland, *Historic Dublin Maps*, compiled by Noel Kissane, Dublin: National Library of Ireland, 1987.

Ní Chearbhaill, Maire, *Margaret Aylward, Foundress of the Sisters of the Holy Faith*, Dublin: Holy Faith Sisters, 1989.

Ní Chumhaill, An tSiúr Aine, *O Gheamhar Go Cruithneacht, Beatha Mhaighréad Aighleart – Margaret Aylward*, Baile Atha Cliath: Foilseacháin Abhair Spioradálta, 1990.

Nolan, William, *Tracing the Past, Sources for Local Studies in the Republic of Ireland*, Dublin: Geography Publications, 1982.

Nolan, William, 'Society and settlement in the valley of Glenasmole, c.1750–c.1900,' in Aalen, F.H.A., and Whelan, Kevin, (eds.), *Dublin City and County: From Prehistory to Present*, Dublin: Geography Publications, 1992, pp. 181–228.

O'Brien, Joseph V., *Dear Dirty Dublin: A City in Distress, 1899–1916*, Berkeley and Los Angeles: University of California Press, 1982.

O'Donnell, E.E., *The Annals of Dublin, Fair City*, Dublin: Wolfhound, 1987.

O'Fearghail, 'The evolution of Catholic parishes in Dublin city from the sixteenth to the nineteenth centuries,' in Aalen, F.H.A., and Whelan, Kevin, (eds.), *Dublin City and County: From Prehistory to Present*, Dublin: Geography Publications, 1992, pp. 229–250.

Offen, Karen; Roach Pierson, Ruth; and Rendall, Jane, (eds.), *Writing Women's History: International Perspectives*, London: Macmillan, 1991.

O'Neill, T.P. 'The Catholic Church and Relief of the Poor 1815–45,' *Archivium Hibernicum, Irish Historical Records*, 31, 1973.

Osborough, W.N., *Law and the Emergence of Modern Dublin*, Dublin: Irish Academic Press, 1996.

Page, Stephen J., 'A new source for the historian of urban poverty: a note on the use of charity records in Leicester 1904–1929,' *Urban History Yearbook*, Leicester, 1987.

Pooley, Colin and Lawton, Richard, 'The social geography of nineteenth century British Cities: a review,' in Denecke, Dietrich and Shaw, Gareth, (eds.), *Urban Historical Geography: Recent Progress in Britain and Germany*, Cambridge: Cambridge University Press, 1988, pp. 159–174.

Pooley, Colin G., 'Working class housing in European cities since 1850,' in Lawton, Richard, (ed.), *The Rise and Fall of Great Cities: Aspects of Urbanization in the Western World*, London: Belhaven Press, 1989, pp. 125–143.

Preston, Margaret H., 'Mothers' Meeting and Lady's Teas: Lay Women and Philanthropy in Dublin 1860–1880,' unpublished M.A. history thesis, UCD, 1991

Preston, Margaret H., 'Lay Women and Philanthropy in Dublin, 1860–1880,' *Eire–Ireland*, Winter 1993, pp. 74–85.

Prochaska, F.K., *Women and Philanthropy in Nineteenth Century England*, Oxford: Clarendon Press, 1980.

Prunty, Jacinta, 'The textile industry in nineteenth century Dublin: its geography, structure and demise' in Diederiks, Herman and Balkenstein, Marjan (eds.), *Occupational Titles and Their Classification: the Case of the Textile Trade in Past Times*, Göttingen: Max-Planck Institut für Geschichte, 1995, pp. 193–216.

Prunty, Jacinta, 'From city slums to city sprawl: Dublin in the nineteenth and twentieth centuries,' in Clarke, Howard (ed.), *Irish Cities*, Thomas Davis Lecture Series, first broadcast April-June 1995, Cork: Mercier Press/Radio Teilifis Eireann, 1995, pp. 109–122.

Prunty, Jacinta, 'Residential urban renewal schemes, Dublin 1986–1994,' *Irish Geography*, 28, 2, 1995, pp. 131–149.

Prunty, Jacinta, 'Margaret Louisa Aylward, 1810–1889' in Luddy, Maria and Cullen, Mary (eds.), *Women, Consciousness and Power in Nineteenth Century Ireland*, Dublin: Attic Press, 1995, pp. 55–88.

Prunty, Jacinta, 'Mobility among women in nineteenth century Dublin', in Siddle, David (ed.), *Migration, Mobility and Modernisation in Europe*, Liverpool: Liverpool University Press, 1997.

Prunty, Jacinta, *The Geography of Poverty Dublin 1850-1900, The Social Mission of the Church with particular reference to Margaret Aylward and Co-workers*, unpublished PhD thesis in Geography (UCD, 1992).

Riis, Jacob, *How the Other Half Lives*, New York: Hill and Wang, 1957 reprint.

Robins, Joseph, *The Lost Children – a Study of Charity Children in Ireland, 1700–1900*, Dublin: Institute of Public Administration, 1987.

Rose, Gillian, and Ogborn, Michael, 'Feminism and Historical Geography,' in *Journal of Historical Geography*, 14, 4, 1988.

Royle, Stephen, 'The socio spatial structure of Belfast in 1837: evidence from the first valuation,' *Irish Geography*, 24, 1 1991, pp. 1–9.

Rose, Michael E., (ed.) *The English Poor Law in its Urban Context 1834–1914*. Leicester: Leicester University Press, 1985.

Rose, Michael E., *The Relief of Poverty 1834–1914*, prepared for Economic History Society, 2nd edition 1986.

Scott, Joan Wallach, 'Gender, a useful category of historical analysis,' *American Historical Review*, 91, 1986, pp. 1053–75.

Scott, Joan Wallach, *Gender, and the Politics of History*, Columbia: Columbia University Press, 1988.

Shaw, Gareth, 'Recent research on the commercial structure of nineteenth century British cities,' in Denecke, Dietrich and Shaw, Gareth, (eds.), *Urban Historical Geography:*

Recent Progress in Britain and Germany, Cambridge: Cambridge University Press, 1988 pp. 236–249.

Shaw, Henry, *New City Pictorial Directory 1850 to which is added a Retrospective Review of the Past Year*, Dublin: 1850; facsimile reprint, Belfast: 1988.

Sheridan, Edel, *Dublin and Berlin: a Comparative Geography of Two Eighteenth Century European Capitals*; unpublished Phd thesis in Geography (UCD, 1993).

Stedman Jones, Gareth, *Outcast London: A Study in the Relationship between Classes in Victorian Society*, Oxford: Oxford University Press, 1971; London: Penguin, 1984.

Tarn, J.N. *Working Class Housing in 19th Century Britain*, Architectural Association paper no. 7, London: Lund Humphries, (n.d.).

Taylor, Fanny, *Irish Homes and Irish Hearts*, London: Longman, Green and Co., 1867.

'*Them Also,' the Story of the Dublin Mission,* 2nd ed., London: Nisbet, 1866.

Tivers, Jacqueline, 'How the other half lives: the geographical study of women,' *Area*, 10, 4, 1978, pp. 302–306.

Torrens, W.H., 'What is to be done with the slums?,' *Macmillan's Magazine*, 39, 234, 1879.

Ward, David, 'The Victorian slum: an enduring myth?,' *Annals of the Association of American Geographers*, 66, 1976, pp. 323–336.

Ward, David, *Poverty, Ethnicity and the American City 1840–1925: Changing conceptions of the slum and the ghetto*, Cambridge Studies in Historical Geography, Cambridge: Cambridge University Press, 1989.

Ward, Margaret, *The Missing Sex: Putting Women into Irish History*, Dublin: Attic Press, 1991.

The Waterloo Directory of Irish Newspapers and Periodicals 1800–1900, phase ll, Waterloo, Ontario: North Waterloo Academic Press, 1986.

Whitehand, Jeremy, 'Recent developments in urban morphology,' in Denecke, Dietrich and Shaw, Gareth, (eds.), *Urban Historical Geography: Recent Progress in Britain and Germany*, Cambridge: Cambridge University Press, 1988, pp. 285–296.

Whitelaw, James '*An Essay on the Population of Dublin, being the Result of an Actual Survey taken in 1798 with Great Care and Precision, to which is added the General Return of the District in 1804, with a Comparative Statement of the Two Surveys, also Several Observatons on the Present State of the Poorer Parts of the City of Dublin, 1805,*' reprinted in *Slum Conditions in London and Dublin*, Farnborough, Hants: Gregg International, 1974.

Williams, G.D., (ed.) *Dublin Charities: A Handbook*, Dublin, 1902.

Wohl, Anthony S. *The Eternal Slum: Housing and Social policy in Victorian London*, London: Edward Arnold, 1977.

Wohl, Anthony S., *Endangered Lives: Public Health in Victorian Britain*, London: Methuen, 1984.

Woodroofe, Kathleen, From *Charity to Social Work in England and the United States*, London: Routledge and Kegan Paul, 1962; 1974 reprint.

Woolf, Stuart, *The Poor in Western Europe in the Eighteenth and Nineteenth Centuries*, London: Methuen, 1986.

Wright, G.N., *An Historical Guide to the City of Dublin*, London: 1825; facsimile ed. Dublin: Irish Academic Press, 1980

Yelling, James A., *Slums and Slum Clearance in Victorian London*, London: Allen and Unwin, 1986.

INDEX

abattoir, 92-93, 98-99, 159, 328
Abbey Street, 43, 45, 171, 294-295, 305, 335, 338
Abercrombie, Patrick, 183-194
Aberdeen, Countess of, 163-167, 179, 332
Aldridge, John, 47-48
Alexandra Housing Guild, 144, 177
Allingham Street, 173
Allingham, Ada, 306
Amiens Street, 52, 289, 296
Anne Street North, 106, 157, 253-254
Annesley Bridge, 86
Antisell, Thomas, 69-70
Arbour Hill, 173, 176, 329, 333
Ardee Street, 21, 58, 59
Arran Quay, 32, 268, 284, 294-295, 305, 345
Arran Quay ward, 46, 275
Arthur's Lane, 137
artisans' dwellings, 98-99, 110, 118-135, 140, 152, 170, 173-177, 318, 320, 322-323, 329, 333, 338
Association for the Relief of Distressed Protestants, 10-11, 237, 301
Aston Quay, 141
asylums, 11-12, 56-58, 204, 240-241, 263-272, 286-287
Aughrim Street, 50, 55, 173, 176
Aungier Street, 106
Aylward, Margaret, 14, 144, 234, 240, 243, 253, 256-259, 266, 269, 279, 344, 346-347; *see also* Ladies of Charity, St Brigid's orphanage, St Brigid's schools
Bachelor's Walk, 43
Back Lane, 49, 171
Baggot Street, 43, 104, 267-268
Ballybough Bridge, 150
Ballybough Road, 52, 115, 288
Barnardo, Thomas, 13
Barrack Street (Benburb Street), 31-33, 45, 141, 173, 266, 282-284, 318, 332
Bass Place, 54
bath houses, 63, 78, 98-99, 142
begging, *see* mendicancy, vagrancy
Belfast, 14, 73-75, 103, 154, 157, 174, 202
Bellingham, Fanny, 281-282
Belvidere Place, 294-296, 304
Benburb Street, 173-175, *see* Barrack Street
Beresford Place, 99
Beresford Street, 137, 150, 157, 173, 175, 288, 298, 307-309, 317-320, 338
Berkeley Street, 45
Birmingham, 3, 86, 88, 174

birthplaces, 198-199
births, registration of, 7, 35, 72-73, 154
Bishop Street, 45, 137
Blackhall Place, 98-99, 173-175, 191, 268, 270, 332
Blackhall Row, 130-132
Blackhorse Lane, 55, 231-232
Blackpitts, 22-23, 173, 253
Blackrock township, 188
Blackrock, 166
Blessington Street, 71, 101, 191, 294-295, 298, 304, 306-307, 331
block dwellings, 131-132, 140-142, 173-176, 180, 193, 284, 316
Bolton Street, 45, 294-295, 306-310, 331, 338
Booth, Charles, 6, 12
Bow Bridge, 50, 219
Bow Lane, 173, 175
Bow Street, 119, 137, 268, 271, 281, 286
Boyne Street, 52, 119, 121, 138, 150, 173, 191
Bradford, 88, 89
Brady, Emily, 162
Braithwaite Street, 24
brewing, 56-57, 59, 150, *see* also Guinness
Brickfield Lane, 56, 272
Bride Road, 131, 142
Bride Street, 45, 106, 130-131, 141, 147, 191
Bride's Alley, 130, 173, 175-177, 181
Bridgefoot Street, 45, 191
Britain Street Great, 106, 288-289, 293-296, 300-301, 306, 308-310, 332
Broadstone, 55
Brown Street North, 32
Brown Street South, 267-268, 272
Brunswick Street Great, 98-99
Brunswick Street North (Channel Row), 137, 150, 191, 202
Buckingham Street, 140, 173, 294-296, 298, 304
Bull Alley, 91-92, 130-131, 148, 173, 176, 191, *see* also Iveagh Trust
Bull Lane, 225, 288
burials, 25, 79, 101
Burke, Helen, 231
Byrne, Elizabeth, 161-162
Cabra, 173, 179, 181, 186, 194, 329, 333
Camden Street, 45, 91-92, 107
Cameron, Charles, 3, 70, 77-78, 80-82, 88, 97, 102-105, 112, 117, 134-136, 138, 140, 151-152, 155-156, 159, 168-169, 315-316

canal companies, 55-57
Capel Street, 98-99, 106, 171, 185-186, 279, 288, 294-295, 304, 306-307, 331
Carman's Hall, 91-93
Carter's Lane, 137
Cassidy, Louis, 144, 162-163
Castle Market, 91
Castle Street, 98-100
cattle market, 98-99
Cavendish Street, 298
Ceannt Fort, *see* McCaffrey estate
cellar dwellings, 37, 79, 103, 110, 115-118, 136, 145, 171, 287, 318, 338
census: Whitelaw 20-22; state 7-8, 19, 41-44, 48, 72, 110-111; special reports on Dublin 40-48, 59-61
central business district, 42-45, 59-61, 137
Chamber Street, 24, 181, 191, 253
Chancery Lane, 56, 137, 249, 252, 267
charity records, 239-240, 259-261, 276, 279-281, 288-289, 292-295, 298-307, 339
Charity, Sisters of, 9
Charlemont Street, 45, 107
Charles Street Great, 267, 296-297, 331
Charlotte Street, 107
Chatham Row, 119
Chatham Street, 91-92, 98
Cheyne, J., 18, 31, 283-284, 316, 318, 320
cholera / choleraic diarrhoea, 18, 36, 38, 65, 67, 70, 74, 76-77, 109, 115, 123, 154, 163, 209, 230, 341
Christ Church Place, 49, 98-100, 130-131
Christian Brothers, 150, 234, 249, 253-254, 261, 346
church building, 10, 237-238
church charities, 9-12, 200-201, 210, 234-273, 337, 339, 343-344
Church Street, 5, 31-33, 48, 54-55, 106, 137, 147, 157, 173, 175, 181, 191, 253-254, 282-284, 287-289, 296, 298, 307-310, 316-320, 332, 338
Circular Road North, 15, 93, 270, 276, 279, 282
City basin, 219
City Health Preservation Committee, 69
City Quay, 52, 103
Civic Survey, *see* Dublin Civic Survey
Clanbrassil Street, 191
Clare Street, 38
Clarence Street, 307
Clarendon Street, 191, 249, 254, 266
classification, of poor, 5, 20-22, 152, 196-197, 200-206, 212-214, 219-221, 224-226, 253, 284, 302-303, 339-340; *see also* house, street classification
Clear, Caitriona, 9
Coleraine Street, 157
Coles Alley, 24, 49, 126
Coles Lane, 48, 54, 91-92, 185-186, 294-295, 306, 320-328, 329, 331-332
College Green, 60
Collins barracks, *see* Royal barracks
Commissioners of Paving and Lighting, *see* Paving Board
Commons Street, 147
Conlan, Robert, 314
contagion, theory of, 26-27, 33, 62, 86, 120, 164, 167-168, 208, 221
Contagious Diseases acts, 263-265
convalescent hospital, 102, 156, 165-166
Cook Street, 49-50, 105-106, 130-131, 171, 173, 175-176, 191
Coombe, 22-23, 49-50, 56-58, 91-92, 106, 126, 130-131, 147-148, 157, 191
Coombe DADC scheme, 98-99, 106, 121-128, 133-135, 173, 175-176, 191
Coombe schools, 5, 11, 58, 234, 248-263, 346
Copper Alley, 100
Corish, Patrick, 9
Cork Hill improvement scheme, 98-100
Cork Street, 24, 26, 50, 148, 173, 176, 191
Cork Street fever hospital, 18-19, 63-64, 91, 341
Cornmarket, 56-57, 106
Corporation Street, *see* Mabbot Street
Cowan, P.C., 3, 177-183
Cowley Place, 307
Crabbe Lane, 173, 176
Crampton buildings, 141
Crane Street, 150
Crow Street, 249, 254,
Crumlin, 173, 179, 181, 186
Cuckoo Lane, 150, 317
Cuffe Street, 171, 191
Cullen, Paul, 9-10, 237, 305
Cumberland Street North, 270, 296, 298, 308-311
Cumberland Street South, 52, 107
Custom House, 184, 196, 334-335
Cut-throat Lane (Mount Brown Lane), 219, 220
Cutpurse Lane, 57
D'Olier Street, 68
dairies / dairy yards, 25, 33, 56-57, 78-79, 91, 94-96, 140, 156, 159
Dallas, Alexander, 247-251, 262, 273
Dame Lane, 150
Dame Street, 43, 68, 97, 137, 185-186, 268, 271
Daniel, James, 129
Daughters of Charity, 234, 258-259, 270, 281, 305
Dawson Street, 43
Dean Street, 130-131, 147
Dean Swift Square, 131-132
death rates, *see* mortality
Denmark Street, 191, 293
denominational divisions, 11, 13-14, 201, 223, 235-239, 255-258, 270, 273, 281-282, 301-302, 305, 346-347
dereliction, 28, 39, 138-139, 171-172, 180, 184-185, 191-192, 194, 332
diarrhoeal diseases, 74, 86, 154-155, 159, *see also* dysentery
Dickens, Charles, 58, 336
diet, 34-35, 39, 162, 207, 223, 228, 230, 239, 281, 300, 337
Dillon Place, 131-132
Dillon, Valentine, 146-147
discharged prisoners' refuges, 270-271, 283
disinfecting depot, 103-104, 142
disinfection, 64, 78-79, 101-103, 140, 142, 164-167, 283, 287
dispensary districts, 157-158
distilling, 56-57, 59, 121, 150

Index

docklands, 49-54, 60-61, 149-150, *see also* Sheriff Street
Dolphin's Barn, 50, 56
Dolphin's Barn Lane, 150
Dominick Street, 42-43, 140-141, 171, 185-186, 191, 267-268, 294-295, 298, 305, 307, 311-313, 331, 338
Donnybrook, 268-269
Donovan, Cecilia, 259-260
Dorset Street, 45, 54, 86, 147, 191, 276, 288-289, 294-295, 298, 304, 306-313, 331, 338
drainage, 4, 86-88, 105, 123, 156, 231-232, 285-286
dram shops, 25, 34, 284, 318
Drew, Thomas, 99-100
Driver, Felix, 221
Drumcondra, 15, 173, 179, 186, 229, 232, 276, 333
Dublin Artisans' Dwellings Company, 98-99, 118, 122-135, 152, 173-177, 332, 340
Dublin Builder, 111
Dublin castle, 49, 171
Dublin Citizens' Association, 183
Dublin Civic Survey 1925, 93, 115, 155, 167, 177, 183, 187-194, 198, 274, 316, 333-335, 342
Dublin Corporation (structures, committees): 14, 16, 68-69, 85, 91, 96,140, 178, *see also* municipal franchise, municipal boundary, tenements
Dublin Housing Inquiry 1913, 77
Dublin Improvement Act, 1849, 16, 68-69, 91, 96, 342
Dublin Metropolitan Police, 69, 77, 85, 96-97, 212, 264, 265, 284, 315
Dublin of the Future (1922), 183-187
Dublin Sanitary Association, 78, 82, 103-106, 122
Dublin Statistical Association, 6, 78, 110-111, 346
Dublin Trades Council, 169-170
dysentery, 27, 64, 74, 80, 341
Earl Place, 150
Earl Street North, 294-295, 304, 306
Earl Street South, 24, 191
Earlsfort Terrace, 43
Early Notification of Births act (1910), 161-162
Easter Rising 1916, 173, 177, 183, 187, 328, 331, 334-335
Eccles Street, 42-43, 294-296, 298, 304-305, 307, 311-313, 331
Echlin Street, 141
Eden Quay, 43
Edinburgh, 73-74, 81, 88, 90, 153-154, 174, 197
Elbow Lane, 24, 119, 123-124
Elizabeth Street, 173-175, 332
Ellis's Quay, 98
emigration, *see* migration/mobility
enteric fever, *see* typhoid
Erne Street, 107
Essex Quay, 268
evangelical missions, 237-239, 247-255, 273, 281-282
Exchequer Street, 150
explorations/ inquiries, of slums, 3, 6-7, 16, 17-61, 62, 109-110, 274, 281-282, 286, 336
Fade Street, 97, 112-113, 137, 150
Fairbrothers' Fields, 5, 173, 175-176, 181-182
Falkiner, F.R., 143-144
famine 1845-1849, 8, 223, 227-231, 225, 227, 286-287, 341-342

fever hospitals, 25-33, 63-64, 101-102, 166, 229, 283, 341
fever nests, 3, 17, 62, 76, 108, 109, 118-120, 128-129, 134, 138, 145, 156, 168, 172, 194, 195, 231, 316, 332, 341-342
Finsbury, 172
Fishamble Street, 45, 49, 100, 106, 130-131, 149, 248, 252
Fisher's Lane, 119-120, 228
Fitzgibbon Street, 294-296, 307, 331
Fitzwilliam Square, 60, 68, 138
Fitzwilliam ward, 189
flats, *see* block dwellings
Flinn, Edgar, 156-159
Foley Street, 173-177, *see* Montgomery Street
Forbes Cottages, 58-59
Fordam's Alley, 22-23, 38-39
Four Courts, 53-54, 184
Francis Square, 131-132
Francis Street, 49, 58, 98-99, 106, 115-116, 130-132, 157, 191, 278
Frederick Lane, 310
Frederick Street North, 294-295, 304
French Street (Mercer Street Upper), 191, 266
Friends Fields, 329, 333
Fumbally's Lane, 56
Gamble, John, 201, 274
Garden Lane, 91-92
garden suburbs, 4, 179-182, 342
Gardiner estate, 52, 191, 267, 274-276, 293-295, 297, 316, 335
Gardiner estate, 60-61, 91, 149, 274-278, 287-288
Gardiner Place, 293, 296-298, 335
Gardiner Row, 335
Gardiner Street, 43, 106, 149, 191, 267-268, 280, 288-289, 293-298, 304-305, 307-313, 314, 333-335, 338
Gardiner's Lane, 310
General Valuation of Ireland, 7-8, 19, 48-61, 219, 288, 292-293, 296-297, 314
geology/topography, 56-57, 105-106, 278, 283, 285-286
George's Hill, 254
George's Place, 331
George's Street Great North, 294-295, 304, 307, 331
George's Street Great South, 45, 97, 150
Glasgow, 12, 73-74, 81, 88, 153-154, 172, 174
Glasnevin, 193-194
Glenasmole, 245-246
Glorney's Buildings, 173, 175, 332
Gloucester Place, 173, 276-278
Gloucester Street (Sean McDermott / Cathal Brugha streets), 42-43, 54, 105-106, 171, 191, 267-269, 276, 288-289, 293-298, 304, 308-313, 329, 331-335
Gloucester Street asylum, 267-270, 310
Gloucester Street South, 150
Goldenbridge, 268, 271
Good Shepherd sisters, 269
Gowan, John, 14, 240, 243
Grafton Street, 43, 338
Grand Canal Street, 107, 150, 171, 248-250, 252
Grand Canal: 48, 56; basin 56, 150, harbour 56-58
Grangegorman Lane, 32, 50, 55, 85
Grattan Street, 107

362   Dublin Slums

Gray Street, 124, 128
Gray, John, 71, 81, 129
Great Western Square, 121, 173, 177
Greek Street, 120, 303
Gregg's Lane (Findlater's Place), 301
Grenville Street, 141, 173, 294-296, 304, 310-311
Griffith's Valuation, *see* General Valuation of Ireland
Grimshaw, Thomas, 77, 123, 139
Guild Street, 150
Guinness family: 101, 122, 305; brewery: 56, 59, 141, 150, 171, 338
Guinness Trust, *see* Iveagh Trust
habits / morals, 29, 34-36, 40, 62, 68, 82, 84, 101, 110-113, 120, 128, 146, 162, 167, 182-183, 196, 215-216, 218, 233, 234, 253, 262-263, 279, 284-285, 318, 345-346
Halston Street, 253-254
Hamilton's court/row, 37
Hanbury Lane, 24
Hanover Lane, 130-131, 147
Hanover Street East, 52
Harcourt Road, 270
Harcourt Terrace, 43
Hardwicke Fever Hospital, 18, 25, 31, 64, 203-204, 282-284
Hardwicke Street, 294-295, 298, 304
Harty Place, 173
Hassett's Gateway, 37
Hawkins Street, 206, 248
Haymarket, 32, 96
Hendrick Street, 32
Henrietta Place, 115-117
Henrietta Street, 42-43, 149, 191, 267-268, 270, 276, 298, 294-295, 305
Henry Street, 45, 137, 288-289
High Street, 56-57, 100, 106, 130-131
Hill Street, 101 *see also* Temple Street Lower
Hill, Octavia, 141, 179
Holy Faith sisters, 259, *see also* Margaret Aylward, Ladies of Charity, St Brigid's Schools, St Brigid's Orphanage
hospitals, 165, *see also* fever hospitals, house of industry
house classification, 4-5, 20-22, 41-44, 48, 72, 110-111, 171-172, 174, 184-185, 191-192, 286
House of Industry (and associated hospitals), 25, 31, 36, 64, 71-72, 94, 202-205, 218, 221-223, 282-284
House of Recovery, Cork Street, 18-19, 63-64, 91, 341
house valuation, *see* General Valuation of Ireland
Housing and Town Planning Association of Ireland, 179-180, 183
housing inquiry 1885, 82, 138, 140, 144-147, 311, 314-316, 318
housing inquiry 1900, 157
housing inquiry 1913/1914, 58, 77, 111-112, 114, 116-118, 170-177, 318-319, 320-321, 324, 328
housing legislation, 83, 118, 143-144, 170, 325
housing report 1918, 177-183
housing standards *see* tenements, artisans's dwellings
housing, *see* tenements, artisans' dwellings
Howard, Ebenezer, 179-180
Inchicore, 173, 175-176, 181

infant feeding, 155, 159-161
infant mortality, 46-47, 65-66, 72, 120, 155, 159-161, 163, 191, 240, 246-247, 285
infectious diseases, notifiable, 16, 46-47, 106-108, 159, 164-166
infill housing, 114-115, 185, 317, 319-321
Infirmary Road, 173, 176
influenza, 74, 76, 155-156
Inns Quay ward, 45-46, 188, 190, 275
inquiries / explorations of slums, 3, 6-7, 16, 17-61, 62, 109-110, 274, 281-282, 286, 336
inspectors of nuisances, 30, 69, 70, 77
international context, 6, 12-14, 153-155, 157, 163, 183, 188, 339, 197, 199, 206, 339
Irish Church Missions, 10, 13, 237-239, 247-252, 255-258, 281-282, 305, 339, 346-347
Island Street, 50, 148, 150
Islandbridge, 56-57, 59, 223
Iveagh Trust, 92, 99, 141-142, 173, 176-177, 191
James's Street, 45, 49, 56, 59, 71, 82, 150, 219-221, 267
Jellicoe, Anne, 144-145
Jervis Street, 106, 249, 254, 266, 288
John Dillon Street, 131-132, *see also* Plunket Street scheme
John's Lane West, 150
Jordan, Thomas, 19, 110, 115, 117
Kearns, Kevin, 337
Kevin Street, 130-131, 147, 173
Kilmainham, 15, 56, 59
King Street North, 32, 37, 45, 106, 268, 270, 317
King Street South, 45, 82
King's Inns Street, 254
Kingstown township, 148, 150, 166
Kirwan Street, 173
Lacy's Lane, 38
Ladies of Charity of St Vincent de Paul, 256-257, 279-281, 288-293, 298-309, 339, 344-345
lady sanitary officers, 155, 159-163
laissez faire, 7-8, 13, 199-201, 228, 339
landlords, 28, 39, 68; *see also* tenements, ownership
Larkin, Emmet, 10, 237
Lawton, Richard, 239
Lee, Joseph, 10
Leeds, 88
Leeson Place, 54
Leeson Street, 42-43, 267-268
Legion of Mary, 266
Leinster Lane, 38
Leverhulme, Lord, 182
Liberties, The, 13, 26-30, 37-38, 43-45, 49, 55-60, 68, 106, 119, 122-135, 137, 171, 255, 266, 338
Liberty Lane, 119
libraries, public, 98-99
lice, *see* typhus
life expectancy, *see* mortality
Liffey Street West, 32
Liffey Street, 185-186
Liffey, river, 69, 82, 86-88, 105-106
Lime Street, 150
Lisburn Street, 173, 175

Index

Liverpool, 81, 88, 174
Local Government Board for Ireland, 6, 77, 93-94, 100, 118, 121, 129, 155, 157, 159, 166, 170-183, 200, 225-227, 328, 339
local taxation, 67-68, 169, 200, 216-217, 226, 241, 286, 314
Lock hospital 264-265, 267-268
lodgers, 135, 182
lodging houses, 134, 142, 145, 176, 285
Loftus Lane, 185-186, 329, 332
London, 6, 12-13, 73-74, 94, 112, 134, 141, 142, 153-154, 159, 163, 174, 201, 247, 286, 339
Lord Edward Street, 98-99
lord lieutenant, 36, 64, 69, 204, 228
Loreto sisters, 9
Lucas, Mary, 162
Luddy, Maria, 264-266
Luke Street, 248, 250
Lurgan Street, 173, 175, 247-248, 250, 252, 332
Mabbot Street (Corporation Street), 278, 315
Macnamara, Rawton, 264-265
magdalen asylums, 263-270
Maguinness' Court, 80-81
main drainage, 80-81, 86-88
Malpas Street, 23, 56
Manchester, 3, 26, 81, 88, 90, 174
Manor Street, 99, 331
Mansion House conference 1903, 169-170
Mansion House relief funds, 36, 64-65, 209-210, 260
Mansion House ward, 46
Manual of Public Health for Ireland, 74, 77
Mapother, Edward, 70, 77-78, 118-121, 128, 137
Marino, 179, 181, 193, 329, 333
markets, 54-55, 63, 78, 85-86, 91, 96-99, 142, 283, 317, 324-325, 333
Marlborough Street, 45, 191, 267-268, 294-296, 304, 332, 334-335
Marrowbone Lane, 50, 56-58, 85, 103-104, 148
Martin, John, 48, 59, 147
Mary Street, 294-295, 304
Mary's Lane, 9, 97, 266, 317, 325, 329, 332
May Lane, 150, 317
Mayne, Alan, 12
Mayor Street, 191, 289
Mayor Street West, 49
McCabe, Edward, 237, 243, 258-259
McCaffrey estate, 5, 173, 175-176
McCarthy, Rev. C.F., 238, 282
McClean's Lane, 119
measles, 74, 76, 153-155, 342
Meath (Brabazon) family, 122, 125, 133
Meath estate *see* Liberties
Meath Market, 119, 139
Meath Street, 123-124, 157, 191
Mecklenburgh Lane, 296-298
Mecklenburgh Street, 54, 105-106, 137, 149, 171, 191, 266-269, 296-298, 310, 315, 338 (Tyrone/ Railway/ Waterford streets)
medical officers of health, 70, 76-77, 92; *see also* Charles Cameron

Meetinghouse Lane, 98-99
mendicancy, 16, 37-38, 195-198, 201-218, 219, 233-234, 340, *see also* vagrancy
Mendicity Association, 5, 38, 205-209, 229, 240
Mercer Street Upper (French Street), 191, 266
Mercer Street, 45, 137-138, 171
Mercer's Hospital, 94-95
Merchants Quay ward, 46
Mercy sisters, 9, 254, 271-272
Merrion Square, 42-43, 54, 60, 104, 138, 191, 250, 338
Merrion Street, 38
miasmic theory of disease, 26-27, 33
migration / mobility, 2, 4, 14, 23, 27, 112, 191, 193, 195-197, 199, 211, 227-228, 244, 270-271, 283, 286-287, 301, 303, 328, 330, 338-339, 340-341; *see also* vagrancy
Mill Street, 22-23, 50, 56-57, 150, 249, 252
Millbourne Avenue, 329
Montgomery Street (Foley Street), 54, 149, 266, 288-289, 296-298, 307-309, 332, 334
Moore Street, 54, 91-92, 137, 171, 266, 320, 324-328
morals / habits, 29, 34-36, 40, 62, 68, 82, 84, 101, 110-113, 120, 128, 146, 162, 167, 182-183, 196, 215-216, 218, 233, 234, 253, 262-263, 279, 284-285, 318, 345-346
Morgan, Francis, 96-97
mortality, rates of, 3, 7, 18, 40, 45-48, 65-66, 71-77, 87, 106, 120, 153-159, 188-191, 197-198, 246-247, 274, 285-286
Moss Street, 156
Mount Brown, 56, 59, 181
Mount Brown Lane (Cut-throat Lane), 219, 220
Mount Street, 104, 138, 338
Mountjoy Court, 296-298
Mountjoy Square, 42-43, 52, 60, 276-278, 293-298, 296-298, 304-305, 308-310, 333-335
Mountjoy Street, 45, 301
Mountjoy ward, 46, 188, 190, 275, 333-334
Mullinahack Lane, 150
municipal boundaries, 14-15, 93, 158, 170, 329-330, 339
municipal franchise, 48, 67-68, 112-113, 143, 146
municipal improvements, 78, 97-103, *see also* drainage, water, scavenging
municipal restructuring, 68-69, 91, 96, 342
municipal wards, 45-46, 48
Murdering Lane, 219, 220
Murnane, Brian, 311
Murray, Dr Daniel, 9, 237, 305
Murray, Frances, 307
Murray, T.A., 25
Nassau Street, 68
Nelson's Lane (Earl Place), 150
Nerney's Court, 173
Neville, Parke, 80-81, 86-88, 120, 123, 138-139
New Row, 22-23, 49, 52, 56-59, 130-131
Newfoundland Street, 332
Newmarket, 22-23, 56-57, 149
Newmarket Street, 112, 114
newspaper reports, 3, 12, 108, 257, 310, 318, 320
Nicholas Street, 130-131, 142
Nicholls, George, 205, 208, 212-213, 215-218

night shelters, 271-272, 332 *see also* asylums, north and south Dublin union
North City Survey 1918, 316, 325, 328-331, 335
North City ward, 46, 189-190, 275
North Dock ward, 46, 275
North Dublin Union rural sanitary authority, 86, 93, 200, 231-233
North Dublin Union workhouse, 18, 48, 55, 59, 65-66, 72, 159-160, 180, 200, 217-218, 221-223, 241-243, 254, 263, 282-283, 286-287
North Lotts, 329, 333
North Strand, 52, 60-61, 105-106, 171, 279, 288-289, 338
North Wall, 92-93, 147, 226
nuns, 9, 234, 240, 254, 258-259, 267-272, 281, 345, 305, *see also* Margaret Aylward
O'Connell Street, *see* Sackville Street
O'Neill, Fr. P., 302
O'Neill, T.P., 197
O'Rourke, Horace T., 187-194
O'Sullivan, Frances, 159
oral history, 337
Ordnance Survey, 19, 48, 129-132, 292, 297, 336
Oriel Place, 289
Ormond Market, 5, 48, 54-55, 91-92, 98-99, 106, 119-122, 137, 173, 175, 181, 191, 288, 331-332
Ormond Quay, 185-186, 288, 292
Ormond Street, 24
orphans, 4, 112, 210, 240-247, 344
Our Lady of Charity of Refuge, sisters of, 267-270
Oxmantown, 32, 128, 173, 176, 316, 332
Paradise Row, 191
parish divisions, 235-237, 275-267, 275-276, 278-279, 289, 316
Park Street West, 106, 249, 254
parks, 63, 101, 142, 194
Parnell Square, *see* Rutland Square
parochial poor relief, *see* poor relief
Patrick Street, 91-92, 96, 130-132, 147
Patrick's Close, 119
pauperism, 198-199, 208, 213-214, 223-224, *see also* poor law, mendicancy
Paving Board, 29-30, 65, 68
Pearse Square, *see* Queen's Square
Pembroke estate / township, 14-15, 87, 91, 94, 166, 341
penitent asylums, 263-270
Phibsborough, 50, 55, 137, 171, 289
philanthropic housing, 110, *see* Iveagh Trust, Dublin Artisans' Dwellings Company
Phoenix Park, 60, 101
phthisis, *see* tuberculosis
Pigtown Lane, 219, 221
Pill Lane, 96-97, 120, 288
Pim, Frederic, 82, 121
Pimlico, 24, 58, 123-124, 126, 128
Pinchgut Lane, 137
Plunket Street, 119, 130, 148
Plunket Street DADC scheme, 98-99, 106, 128-135, 173, 175-176, 191
Poddle, 21-23, 56-57, 142
police, 69, 77, 85, 96-97, 212, 264, 265, 284, 315

political philosophy, 7-8, 13, 199-201, 228, 339
Poolbeg Street, 156
Poole Street, 24, 58
Poor Inquiry (Ireland) 1833/34, 19, 38-40, 120, 241, 283-285, 316
Poor Law (Ireland) act 1838, 199-201, 205, 213-218, 230-231, 243, 342
Poor Law Commissioners for Ireland, 6, 70, 199-200, 225-227, *see also* local government board
poor law unions, *see* North Dublin Union, South Dublin Union
poor relief debate, 13, 16, 196-201, 206-207, 210-211
poor relief: parochial 67-68, 206-207, 209-210, 213, 235-279; charities 11, 239, 280, 281-282, 288-289, 292-295, 298-307; through schools, 250, 254-255, 258-260, 262, 344; statutory, 151, 198, 213-233
Poplar Row, 150
population density, 21-25, 37-38, 57-58, 125, 127, 146-147, 156, 171, 175, 180, 188-191, 193, 283, 286, 318, 333-335
population, 14, 20-22, 146, 154
Port Sunlight, 182
Portland Row, 331
Portobello, 71, 173, 176
Power's Square, 131-132
Power's distillery, 56, 59
Presentation sisters, 9, 254
Price's Court, 140
privies / WCs, 25, 28, 78-82, 87-90, 105, 112, 114, 115, 123, 127, 133, 137, 167, 180, 285-287 *see also* scavenging (domestic)
proselytism, *see* denominational divisions
prostitution, 32-33, 196, 263-270, 274, 283-284, 297, 343
Protestant Orphan Society, 242-243
Protestant Orphan Union, 243
Prussia Street, 50, 55
Public Health Committee (Corporation), 3, 6, 71, 82, 85-86, 93-94, 102, 133, 136-137, 135, 159, 166
public health legislation, 8, 16, 64-65, 69-71, 76-78, 82-84, 91-93, 102, 117-118, 139-140, 143-145, 159, 164, 167, 342
Purdon Street (Corporation Street), 137, 266, 270, 296-298, 310
Queen Street, 32, 45
Queen's Square, 101
ragged schools, 12-13, 58, 240, 247-263, 266, 345-346
railway, 51-55, 177, 329, 338
Railway Street, 191, *see* Mecklenburgh Street
Rainsford Street, 150
rateable valuation, *see* General Valuation of Ireland
rates, *see* local taxation
Rathmines township, 14, 87, 166, 188
Reginald Street, 124, 128
register general, *see* mortality
relapsing fever, 27, 64, 341
rent levels, 23, 39, 125-126, 113-114, 125-126, 133-134, 138, 141-142, 151-152, 176, 314, 316, 332, 337
Rerum Novarum, 9
Rialto, 141
Rice, Edmund Ignatius, 234, 254

Richmond General Penitentiary, 36, 55, 283
Richmond Lunatic Asylum, 55, 204, 283
Richmond Street South, 107
Richmond Surgical Hospital, 204, 283
Riddell's/Riddle's Row, 324-328
Ringsend, 86, 166
road widening, *see* street schemes
Robert Street, 150
Rochdale, 88-90
Rocque, John, 20-21, 23-24, 58
Roe, Henry & Sons, 56, 59
Roomkeepers' Society, 212-213, 284
Rotunda ward, 46, 188, 190, 275, 334
Royal Barracks, 32, 54-55, 91-92, 171, 185, 283, *see also* Barrack Street
Royal Canal, 48; harbour 55, 86, 288
Royal Commission on Housing 1884/1885, 82, 138, 140, 144-147, 311, 314-316, 318
Royal Commission on the Sewerage and Drainage of Dublin 1879/1880, 77, 80, 84, 87, 111, 138-139, 143, 157, 180
Royal Exchange ward, 45-46
rural contrasts / discussion, 3, 62-63, 82, 146, 168, 180-181, 197, 200, 214-215, 244-247, 287, 340
Rutland Place, 296-298
Rutland Square (Parnell Square) 60, 293-298, 305, 308-310
Rutland Street, 277-278, 296-298, 331
Ryan, Margaret, 162
Ryan, Maria, 162
Sackville Street / Mall (O'Connell Street), 43, 54, 60, 71, 185-186, 274, 276, 294-295, 298, 307, 335
sanatoria, 102, 156, 165-166
Sandwith Street, 52
sanitary accommodation, *see* privies
sanitary legislation, *see* public health
sanitary officers, female, 155, 159-163
sanitary staff, 69-71, 76-77, 155, 159-163, 167, *see also* inspectors of nuisances, medical officers
Saorstǎt Eireann, 201, 233, 335
scarlatina, 101, 154, 227, 229, 342
scavenging depots, 56-57, 85-86, 98
scavenging: public streets 29, 63-64, 66-67, 78, 84-86, 158-159, 167, 285; backyards / domestic 25, 28-31, 33, 63-64, 67, 78-82, 156, 158, 285-286, *see also* privies
schools, *see* ragged
Scully, Agnes, 307
Sean McDermott Street, *see* Gloucester Street Lower North
sectarianism, *see* denominational divisions
Seville Place, 106, 173, 176, 289
sewerage, *see* drainage
sexes, separation of, 140, 144-146, 177, 182, 330
sexually transmitted diseases, 263-265, 267-268
Sheriff Street, 49, 51, 98, 105-106, 147, 149, 191, 289, 329, 332-333, 338
Ship Street, 130-131, 171
Shore, Rev., 284
Skinner's Alley, 22, 37
slaughter houses, 25, 29-30, 33, 56-57, 70, 78-79, 85, 91-96, 98-99, 107, 140, 156, 159, 325-328

slum measurement, 4-5, *see also* statistics
slum, concept of, 2-4, 286, 328, 339-340
smallpox, 76, 101, 153-155, 157, 163, 229, 341-342
Smithfield, 32, 45, 96, 223, 333
Smyly, Ellen, 248, 250-252, 262, 346-347
Society for Bettering the Condition of the Poor, 25
socio-economic patterns, 59-61
soldiers, 2, 3, 32-33, 198-199, 265, 341
Solly Flood, Frederick, 38-40
Souers de Charité, 234, 258-259, 270, 281, 305
soup kitchens, 64, 226, 229-230
South City Markets, 97, 146-147, 325
South City ward, 46, 189-190
South Dock ward, 46
South Dublin Union workhouse, 48, 56-57, 180, 198, 200-202, 218-221, 226, 272, 286-287
Speer, T.C., 12-13, 34-36, 62
Spitalfields, 91-93, 173, 175-176
Spratt, John, 271-272
Spring Garden, 51-52, 288
St Audeon's parish, 68
St Augustine Street, 98-99
St Brigid's Orphanage, 243-247, 344
St Brigid's schools: 5, 234, 346; the Coombe, 5, 249, 254-263, 346
St Catherine's parish, 20
St Joseph's Place/Parade, 173, 175
St Mary's parish, 274-335
St Michael's Hill, 130-131, 137
St Michael's Lane, 130-131, 137
St Michan's parish, 65-66, 72, 212, 235-238, 274-335
St Michan's Park, 101
St Stephen's Green, 42-45, 49, 54, 60, 97, 101, 104, 138, 266, 338
St Vincent de Paul Society (men), 146, 236-237, 311
Stafford Street, 106, 141, 288
Stanhope Street, 150
Stanley Street, 85-86
Statistical and Social Inquiry Society for Ireland, 6, 78, 110-111
statistics, science of, 5-7, 63, 71-76, 200, 342
Stirrup Lane, 137, 317
Stoneybatter, 55
Store Street, 296-298
Strand Street, 171, 249, 254, 288, 331
Strangers' Friend Society, 284
street classification, 16, 41-45, 339
street cleansing, *see* scavenging (public)
street directories, 15, 19, 59-61, 147-150, 287-288, 290-292, 306-309, 287, 292, 304-310, 328
street names, 216, 296-298, 315-320, 324
street schemes, 63, 78, 97-100, 120-123, 185-187
subculture, 34-36
suburban solution, 4, 61, 169-170, 173, 176, 179-183, 186, 193-194, 329-333, 335, 337-338, 342
suburbanisation, 14-15, 23, 147, 341
Summer Hill, 141, 276-278, 293, 294-298, 307-313, 331-332, 334-335
Summer Place, 296-298
Summer Street North, 296

Taaffe's Row, 325-326
Taaffe's Village, 52, 288
Talbot Street, 294-296, 304, 335
tanyards, 56, 59, 221
Tara Street, 98-99
Temple Bar, 54, 106, 171, 185-186
Temple Buildings, 173
Temple Lane, 329, 332
Temple Street, 331
tenement dwellings:
  changing geography of, 147-150, 191-192, 290-291, 307-310, 328-331, 338
  collapse, 169, 188, 318
  condemnation / closure, 79, 121, 135-140, 143, 156, 171-172, 191-192, 325-327, 338
  decline into, 19, 171, 274, 282-288, 310-311, 314-316, 338
  demolition, 123, 320, 331
  disinfection, 79, 102-103, 287
  inspection, 3, 40, 48-49, 71, 78-79, 82-84, 315-316, 331
  legal obstacles, 29-31, 69, 78, 83-84, 112-113, 156
  numbers accommodated, 110-112, 118, 135, 169, 171, 177-178, 331
  one-room system, 40, 112, 114, 151, 158, 285, 340
  overcrowding, 20-23, 32, 135, 156-158, 171, 182, 184, 285-286, 318, 320, 333-335, 337
  ownership, 28, 38, 83, 112, 129, 138, 156
  regulation, 59-61, 79, 112-113, 158, 287
  rehabilitation, 140-141, 143, 180, 184-185, 193, 315-316, 331
  tenure, 83, 114, 340, *see also* rent levels
  ventilation, 27, 35-36, 39, 63, 115, 137, 325-327
textiles, 56-59, 125, 211, 272, 191
third class houses, 110, 114-115, *see also* house classification
Thomas Court, 24
Thomas Davis Street, 131-132, *see* Plunket Street scheme
Thomas Street, 45, 56-57, 91-92, 98-99, 106-107, 147, 150, 157
de Tocqueville, Alexis, 208, 336
toilets, *see* privies
topography/ geology, 56-57, 105-106, 278, 283, 285-286
town planning, 183-194, 342
Townsend Street, 11, 49, 54, 80-81, 91-92, 105, 171, 173, 175-176, 185, 191, 248-250, 252, 267, 269, 282, 338
township development, 14-15, 23
trams / transport, 169, 179, 181, 185-188, 193-194, 329, 332-333, 341
Trinity College, 137
Trinity ward, 46, 173, 175-176
Tripoli, 24, 49
tuberculosis (phthisis), 63, 74, 76, 109, 155, 157-159, 163-168, 247, 274
Tuberculosis Prevention Act (1908) 166-167
typhoid, 71, 78, 86, 94, 103-106, 109, 154, 163, 227
typhus fever, 27, 33, 64, 69, 76, 163, 227, 341
Usher's Island, 32, 191
Usher's Quay, 32, 98-99, 191
Usher's Quay ward, 46

vagrancy, 5, 16, 133, 195-213, 283, 340, *see also* mendicancy, migration
valuation, *see* general valuation
Vartry water scheme, 4, 71, 103
vestry, 64-65, 67-68, 198-199, 209-210, 226, 241, 341
voting, *see* municipal franchise
Ward's Hill, 22-23, 49, 52
water supply, 4, 71, 103, 158, 285-286
Watery Lane, 56, 59
Waterford Street, *see* Mecklenburgh Street
Watling Street, 59, 150, 338
Weaver's Alley, 137
Weaver's Square, 24, 58, 181
Weavers' Hall, 23, 57-58, 248-249, 255, 258
weaving, *see* textiles
Weber, Max, 196
Werburgh Street, 130-131, 252
Westland Row, 52-54, 345
Westmoreland Street, 68
Whately, Archbishop, 10, 210, 238, 273
Whately, Miss, 252
White, Francis, 18, 36-39, 209-210
Whitelaw, James, 7, 17-18, 20-25, 49, 91, 111, 129, 209, 234, 266
Whitworth Medical Hospital, 204, 283
whooping cough, 74, 76, 154-155
Wide Streets Commissioners, 68
Wilde, William, 18, 40-48, 59-61, 72-74
Wilkinson, George, 219
William Street South, 45, 185-186
Willis, Thomas, 18-19, 39-40, 64-66, 72, 109-110, 115, 286-287
Wilton Square, 43
Wilton Terrace, 43
Winetavern Street, 100
Wiseman, Cardinal, 252
Women
  and destitution / mendicancy, 37-39, 263-272, 144-145, 207-209, 211-212, 218, 284, 302-303, 343
  charity workers, 12, 144-145, 240, 292-293, 303-304, *see also* Ladies of Charity, St Brigid's schools, St Brigid's orphanage
  employment, 161, 207-208, 263, 272, 284, 302, 333, 340-343
  exclusion of, 144-145, 240
  mothers, 66, 162
  sanitary officers, 145, 155, 159-163
  workhouse guardians, 215
Women's National Health Association for Ireland, 163-167
Wood Quay ward, 45-46, 188-189
Wood Quay, 45, 85, 185-186, 191
Wood Street, 119, 137-138
workhouse, 8, 45, 180, 198, 201-202, 209, 218-219, 239, 285, 340, *see also* North Dublin Union, South Dublin Union, Poor Law (Ireland)
York Street, 21, 42-43, 191
Young, James, 85.